American Wildlife

& Plants

ALEXANDER C. MARTIN
Biologist, Patuxent Research Refuge
U. S. Fish and Wildlife Service

HERBERT S. ZIM
Educational Consultant, U. S. Fish and Wildlife Service
Associate Professor of Education, University of Illinois

ARNOLD L. NELSON
Director, Patuxent Research Refuge
U. S. Fish and Wildlife Service

A GUIDE TO WILDLIFE FOOD HABITS:

the use of trees, shrubs, weeds, and herbs by birds and mammals of the United States. Prepared under the direction of the United States Fish and Wildlife Service, Department of the Interior, at the Patuxent Research Refuge, Laurel, Maryland. Published by agreement with the United States Department of the Interior, Fish and Wildlife Service, Bureau of Sport Fisheries and Wildlife.

DOVER PUBLICATIONS, INC., NEW YORK

Preface

With the aim of making the information in this book available for wide use, we have tried to present it in a form acceptable to diverse groups. It has been planned not only for wildlife technicians, sportsmen, naturalists, bird students, and all others directly interested in wildlife, but also for foresters, landscape gardeners, botanists, and additional groups concerned with the vegetation upon which our country's wildlife depend.

The volume is divided into three main units. Part I is introductory. It aims to provide orientation and interpretation and its final chapter explains the symbols and other devices used in Parts II and III.

Part II treats the wildlife of the country group by group and gives data on their foods (particularly plant parts), ranges, habits, and economics. Since the term "wildlife" as used in this book has the generally accepted connotation of birds and mammals, only a small space at the end of Part II is reserved for the cold-blooded vertebrates (fish, reptiles, and amphibians). Direct use of plants by these latter groups is limited and has received comparatively little study.

Part III turns the focus on plants. It denotes the value of different genera of trees, shrubs, weeds, aquatics, and cultivated crops to various kinds of wildlife in different parts of the country. The final chapter of Part III presents a classified ranking of wildlife plants—tentative ratings which may alter as food-habits information grows.

THE AUTHOR

Acknowledgments

Acknowledging all the contributors to the food-habits information of this book would involve the names of hundreds of individuals from the 1870s down to the present. Except for one serious complication, recognition for each might have been accorded by citing sources of regional or local data presented in Part II. The obstacle to this is the fact that in the great majority of instances, the star-rating tables on food use for a single wildlife species represents a combining of information from several or many sources— commonly a dozen or more. Foremost among these unspecified cooperators are the many who conducted food-habits studies in the former Biological Survey. More recently this fundamental research has been continued in various states under the auspices of the Federal Aid to Wildlife program and the Cooperative Wildlife Research Units. The multitude of contributions, great and small, from this corps of unnamed research workers constitute the foundation upon which this book has been built.

Credit and thanks for technical assistance are due to Chandler S. Robbins (bird ranges), Hartley H. T. Jackson (mammal ranges), Robert T. Mitchell (vertebrate and invertebrate foods of animals), and Samuel F. Hildebrand (fish classification). Helpful criticism and many constructive suggestions were received from Neil W. Hosley, Edwin R. Kalmbach, Olaus J. Murie, Gustav A. Swanson, Ira N. Gabrielson, Clarence Cottam, Charles Sperry, William H. Stickel, Robert E. Stewart, Allen J. Duvall, John W. Aldrich, and Ralph B. Nestler. Most of the animal drawings were prepared by Walter A. Weber and the plant drawings by John W. Brainerd. Diagrams and maps were inked in by Katheryne C. Tabb, and a few illustrations were contributed by Oscar Warbach, Robert W. Hines, and the senior author. For faithful assistance in routine details of compilation, recognition is due to Miriam C. Raines, Robert Lillibridge, John Weigel, Jerome Watts, and Mrs. Gallatin Cobb. Much of the routine work of compilation was made possible by the Civilian Public Service program.

Contents

PART I

INTRODUCTORY CHAPTERS

For more than two centuries, we Americans have been making over the face of the country with ax, plow, bulldozer, and tractor. As the wilderness gave way to farms and factories, deer, bear, wild turkey, and chickadees have had to adapt themselves to altered conditions. And the remarkable thing is that most wildlife species could and did adjust. Now we have the spectacle of birds and mammals of the wilderness period surviving and often thriving in man's industrial and agricultural domain. Migrating waterfowl share the air lanes with stratoliners, meadowlarks flourish in man-made meadows, and phoebes nest on our porches or under our bridges. Some species like the passenger pigeon, elk, bison, beaver, and many kinds of fish have suffered or have been exterminated, but foxes, raccoons, quail, robins, bluebirds, and numerous others are probably more plentiful now than they were in precolonial times.

The secret of success in this shift from primitive to artificial or man-made conditions is largely in the food habits of wildlife. Opening up the formerly unbroken forests has provided a diversity of food plants, both herbaceous and woody, that has compensated—or more than compensated—for man's damage to wildlife. Many species that formerly subsisted on wild native foods now share in the crops of corn, wheat, oats, and accompanying weeds—often without causing economic loss. To our regret, some aggressive species like the coyote, starling, and crow have prospered too well by their association with man.

Research on the food habits of this country's wildlife has been in progress since the latter part of the past century and has resulted in many reports, each dealing

with particular species or groups. In this book, the data resulting from hundreds of these studies have been brought together in comprehensive form. Part I explores briefly the relationship of wildlife to plants, indicates the types and parts of plants used, shows the role of crop plants to wildlife, and presents a summary of research into wildlife food habits. The final chapter (Four) provides an explanatory key to the tabular data which follows in Parts II and III.

CHAPTER ONE

The Plant Roots of Wildlife

ALL ANIMALS OWE their existence to trees, grasses, weeds, farm crops, aquatics, or other forms of vegetation. Animal-eating species are no exception to the rule —their dependence is, at most, a step or two removed. Plants are the immediate or ultimate source of all food and most of the shelter used by wildlife.

There are a number of animals so characteristically associated with a particular plant that common names have been given accordingly, to either the plant or the animal. *Cedar* waxwing, *piñon* jay, *sage* grouse, *rabbit*brush, *buffalo*grass, *deer*vetch, and *duck*weed are a few of these common instances. More often, however, such relationships are not reflected in names. The elf owl of the Southwest depends very considerably for existence upon the larger cacti in which the bird makes its nest. Some warblers such as the bay-breasted, Cape May, and black-poll nest only in the northern conifers. So do kinglets. The ivory-billed and, to an extent, the pileated woodpeckers are confined to mature forests where there is standing dead timber—the species of tree does not seem important. Redwing and yellow-headed blackbirds prefer cattail marshes. Catbirds often live and nest in tangles of wild grape or greenbrier. These examples, however, begin to drift from a direct relationship between particular plant and animal species and break down into the more universal pattern of plant-animal communities.

The close relationship of animals to plants is also indicated in extensive censuses of wildlife populations in different vegetational areas. Western big game (deer, of various kinds, elk, antelope, bear, etc.) average as high as 1.5 individuals per hundred acres in the national forests. In contrast to this, the figure runs down to about 0.1 big-game animal per hundred acres on Indian reservations where commonly there are wide expanses of sparsely vegetated wastelands. Bird populations of 0.5 to 1 bird per acre are typical of the dry western plains, while fields in the East support 1 to 3 birds per acre. In deciduous forests the numbers range upward from 1.5 to 10.5 per acre.

In the three centuries since colonization, drastic changes have been made in our rich plant resources. Devastating inroads into the magnificent virgin stands of forests and destruction of the prairie sod have rendered extensive areas uninhabitable for such native wildlife as the wild turkey, ruffed grouse, heath hen, passenger pigeon, ivory-billed woodpecker, bison, antelope, and moose. The draining of marshes and swamps for agricultural purposes has eliminated vegetation that furnished a favorable habitat for waterfowl, muskrats, and other important wildlife. Silting and roiling of water from farmland erosion has destroyed much of the aquatic plant growth in streams, ponds, and lakes that formerly supported large numbers of fish and waterfowl.

However, the story is not entirely one-sided. Transformation of the former American wilderness into agricultural lands has actually created an increase in

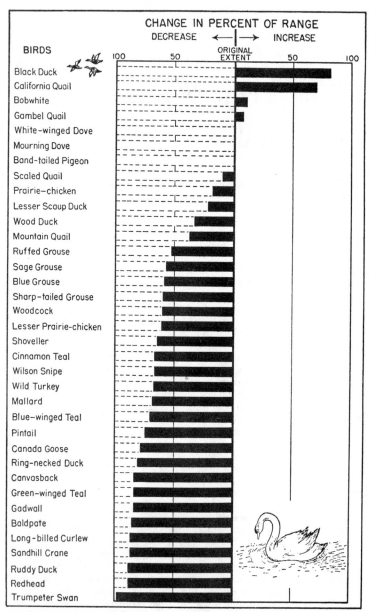

CHANGE IN RANGES OF GAMEBIRDS OR FORMER GAMEBIRDS

4

marginal areas where formerly there were unlimited forests or vast grassy plains. The change has favored wildlife species that thrive in or near border zones. Horned larks have spread eastward till their range now spans the continent. Meadowlarks are now more common than they were in the past. Bobwhite quail have spread northward and so have the opossum and the armadillo. The range of the bobolink has been extended westward, and the cardinal has pushed to the North. The animals benefited by agriculture also include some species that are regarded as pests—the pocket gophers, prairie dogs, coyotes, English sparrow, and crow. All in all, agriculture has increased tremendously the supply of choice plant foods relished by many kinds of wildlife.

In spite of what we have done to our original native flora, we still have rich plant resources. Native plants of one kind or another are present practically everywhere in this country, and to a large extent they make the environment what it is. The plants of New England typify that area, and the same is true of the prairie, the Pacific coast, the Gulf states, and other regions. On a cross-country trip one can readily detect floral transitions in which characteristic plants of one region are replaced by others.

Locally, too, different forms of plant life are adapted to many diverse, circumscribed kinds of habitat. Lichens grow on bare rocks under conditions varying from alpine cold to desert heat. Some algae are found on tree trunks, on wooden fences, or on soil; still others thrive in the hot springs of Yellowstone National Park. Many other kinds of plants grow submerged in water, and some species grow well in relatively sterile beach sand. Trees and woodland herbs are present in regions where moisture is sufficient, while grasses of some kind or other are found almost everywhere—moist or dry, hot or cold. It is this widespread distribution of plants that has made possible the nearly universal occurrence of animal life.

Diversity in form is a factor that has helped to adapt plants to their varied environments. The plant kingdom includes both the largest and the smallest living things. With the exception of the viruses, the smallest living organisms are probably *Coccus* bacteria, tiny spheres about 0.00002 inches in diameter—fifty thousand side by side to the inch. Of the flowering plants, we have both the smallest and largest within the United States. The smallest is a duckweed or "duckmeal" *Wolffia*—a floating spot of green about one twenty-fifth of an inch in diameter. At the other extreme is the General Sherman tree, a big tree (*Sequoia*) growing on the moist slopes of the Sierra Nevadas. Its trunk is 36 feet in diameter and 272 feet high. Its estimated weight is over a thousand tons—at least a dozen times as heavy as the largest whale. All these plants, minute or gigantic, terrestrial or aquatic, evanescent or ageless, have a share in supporting the country's varied wildlife population.

The Plant Groups and Their Importance to Wildlife

The lower plants, from bacteria and algae up through the mosses and ferns, are of only limited direct value to wildlife. This does not mean that they are inconsequential. On the contrary, they are very important. Bacteria are not only significant to wildlife as disease producers, but certain kinds have immeasurable importance to all life in the vital processes of nitrogen fixation and the decomposition of organic materials. They even enter into digestive processes. Without these bacterial contributions there would be neither wildlife nor any other life, as we know it.

Among the algae are many minute forms that constitute a large part of the plankton upon which protozoa, crustaceans, aquatic insects, and other invertebrates subsist. In turn, these small forms of animal life furnish food for many

important kinds of wildlife. Filamentous algae are sometimes consumed by ducks in quantity, and the sea-lettuce of the Atlantic coast is eaten by brant as well as by some other waterfowl. The muskgrasses (*Chara* and *Nitella*), which botanists generally class with the algae, are aquatic plants that are important as duck food.

Only the larger fleshy fungi are of direct value to animals. Apparently wild creatures find mushrooms, puffballs, and morels as palatable as does man. Squirrels, chipmunks, and other rodents, turtles, deer, elk, armadillos, skunks, shrews, moles, and grouse feed on fleshy fungi. But these plants are rarely an important food for our more valuable kinds of wildlife.

Lichens, consisting of an alga and a fungus growing in close partnership, are of limited direct use to our wildlife, being eaten to a small extent by deer, elk, moose, and grouse. In arctic regions, however, they are a main constituent of the tundra flora on which northern browsers rely for much of their food. Fragments of lichens are commonly used in the nests of hummingbirds, the wood pewee, and the blue-gray gnatcatcher. These primitive plants are pioneers in soil making. The organic acids they produce help to decompose the rocks on which some of them grow.

Mosses are almost negligible in their value as food for wildlife, but like lichens and ferns, they help pave the way for the growth of the higher, more useful plants by building up organic material in the soil. The water moss *Fontinalis* is an exception since it is eaten by swans in considerable quantity.

Ferns, being larger plants than mosses, are used as food by most woodland animals that feed on green vegetation. They and their relatives, the clubmosses and horsetails, are eaten by deer, elk, mountain sheep, moose, rabbits, wood rats, wild turkey, and ruffed grouse. The fact that Christmasfern, grapefern, and some of the woodferns remain green after most other vegetation has been frost-killed makes them especially valuable during fall and winter.

The final and highest botanical group—the seed plants—is by far the most important to wildlife. This large group with its two main subdivisions, the conifers and the broad-leaved flowering plants, includes about 25,000 species in the United States. In it are all the common trees, shrubs, vines, weeds, marsh plants, and farm crops. The higher plants are so useful to wildlife in such a variety of ways that an accounting of their value constitutes a major undertaking and is the substance of Part III of this book.

Plants As Wildlife Food and Cover

Food is one of the primary necessities of all life, and for wild animals, cover is not far behind as a vital requirement. Survival in critical periods—during inclement winter weather, during spring and summer rearing of young, or when subjected to attack by enemies—depends largely on these fundamental factors, food and cover. From mouse to moose these factors dominate the welfare of all kinds of wildlife and determine, in large degree, the increase or decline of animal populations.

Not only are many kinds of plants utilized by wildlife, but nearly all parts of

6

plants are eaten by one animal species or another. Fruits, seeds, leaves, twigs, bark, stems, and roots all furnish food to different kinds of animals. Which parts of which plants are used by what animals and to what extent are details indicated in Part III. Some indication of the nutritive value, availability, and fooduse of various plant products is given below:

FLESHY FRUITS. Fruits, rich in carbohydrates and vitamins, are especially important, relished foods. Fleshy fruits are mainly products of woody plants and are generally available in summer and fall. Some persistent ones like holly, grape, snowberry, mountain-ash, manzanita, and persimmon are also available to wildlife in winter. The widely distributed rose family (*Rosaceae*) provides a large proportion of the more important wild fleshy fruits including blackberry, strawberry, raspberry, cherry, rose, serviceberry, hawthorn, apple, and mountain-ash. Additional fleshy fruits of wildlife importance are grape, holly, blueberry, persimmon, sassafras, and blackgum. These are valuable to many kinds of birds and some mammals such as the raccoon, deer, bear, fox, squirrel, skunk, and opossum.

NUTS. Botanically, nuts are fruits with a dry, hard exterior. Animals use these hard-shelled fruits extensively, probably because they are unusually rich in fats and proteins and are available over long periods. Dry fruits from woody plants (maple keys, elm samaras, etc.) as well as the seeds of pines are sometimes classed with nuts under the ambiguous name of mast. Of all the nuts, acorns are the most widely available and most commonly eaten by wildlife. Next in order come pecans, beechnuts, and cultivated walnuts. Hickory nuts, hazelnuts, black walnuts, and butternuts, because of their especially thick, hard shells, are of importance only to squirrels, chipmunks, and their kin.

SEEDS. Like nuts, seeds are concentrated food parcels and are eagerly sought. They constitute the major food of many birds and small mammals, making up practically the entire diet of some common species. New crops of seeds usually mature in summer or fall, but part of the crop may remain available for use later in the season, either on the plants or on the ground. Weeds are generally unwelcome intruders, but because of their abundant seeds, they are more valuable as wildlife foods than most of our more attractive, showy flowered plants. The number of seeds produced on a single annual weed may be enormous. Pigweeds are known to bear as many as 100,000 seeds per plant. The most important weed seeds used as wildlife foods are from common, widespread species—pigweed, ragweed, crabgrass, bristlegrass, goosefoot, doveweeds, filaree, smartweeds, knotweeds, redmaids, tarweeds, dock, and deervetch. The seeds (grains) of wheat, corn, barley, and oats are, of course, especially attractive to wildlife and are used whenever available. Pine seeds and seeds of other conifers also rank high in food use.

VEGETATION. Browsing and grazing mammals, some rodents, and a few gamebirds make the vegetative parts of plants a major part of their diet. Almost

any kind of foliage is taken by hoofed browsers, though eating of tough leaves (such as conifer needles) may sometimes represent necessity rather than choice. In open land, forage grasses and other herbaceous plants become important to antelope, buffalo, rabbits, and other grazers. All aerial parts of grasses and small herbaceous plants are eaten, though the flowering or seed-producing parts are often favored. Clover leaves are a favorite food for several kinds of wildlife; alfalfa is relished too. Browsing on woody plants usually includes the eating of leaves and twigs together, except in winter. The leaves, stems, tubers, and seeds of aquatic plants are consumed by waterfowl, muskrats, beaver, moose, and occasionally by deer. Water plants of outstanding food value are the pondweeds, wildcelery, wildrice, widgeongrass, eelgrass, and naiads.

MISCELLANEOUS PARTS EATEN. Besides twigs taken by browsers, inner bark or wood is important only for a few mammals: the beaver, porcupine, rabbits, and certain mice.

Underground parts of plants—rootstocks, bulbs, tubers, and roots—are eaten by muskrats, gophers, moles, ducks, geese, wild turkeys, and others. Plants with underground food-storage organs include sago pondweed, cattails, arrowheads (duckpotato), chufa, violets, and springbeauty.

Sapsuckers actually take sap and cambium tissue of trees as food, though much of their diet is insects. Other special uses of plant parts include nectar from flowers used by hummingbirds and plant galls taken by the California bushtit and various other birds as well as by the gray squirrel.

Availability of Foods

A prime factor in the use of any kind of food by wildlife is its availability. Unfortunately, there is no such thing as a constantly available food supply for wild creatures, and so birds and mammals live under seasonal threat of starvation, just as man did centuries ago before he became a tool-using animal.

The availability of plant food is limited not only by the ranges and habitats of the plant concerned but also by seasonal factors. In the spring, swollen buds, tree flowers, fresh, tender vegetation, and a few rapidly maturing dry fruits (such as of elms and silver maple) become available. Later in summer many more kinds of seeds mature and fleshy fruits ripen. These supplement the abundant insects which many birds consume. Fall is the season of plenty when plant products abound and when most animals become fat. Seeds, nuts, and fleshy fruits can be obtained without much trouble by animals which eat them.

Winter—especially late winter—is a time of hardship for most wildlife. It is a critical period for food supply. In the temperate regions, especially the north temperate, the whole character of the environment changes. The available supply of both insect and plant food decreases markedly as the weather grows colder and the first frosts arrive. The insect supply suffers most, and wildlife species turn more and more to plant foods. Both plant and insect eaters must search more intensely over wider areas to find food.

During this season of comparative scarcity, plants that provide persistent seeds, fruits, or other edible parts are especially useful for wildlife. Fruits and seeds that fall to the ground are often washed away, buried in the leaves or soil, or covered with snow. Plants that bear their seeds or fruit high enough so they are not covered with snow become unusually valuable sources of food. Among the fruits or seeds that are available over much of the winter are the following:

Bluestemgrass or Broomsedge	Manzanita	Ragweed
Greenbrier	Mountain-ash	Russianthistle
Hackberry	Persimmon	Snowberry
Holly	Pigweed	Sumac
Japanese Honeysuckle	Pine	
Juniper	Poison-ivy	

The availability of plants as winter food is often the crucial factor that determines the wildlife population of a region. Some species of animals may locally increase beyond the permanent, all-year carrying capacity of the land. When the pinch comes, it usually comes in winter. This has been a special problem with deer, elk, and some of our more common gamebirds. Artificial feeding to stave off starvation of an overpopulated winter range is not a satisfactory permanent solution of the problem. Improvement of the range or reduction of the population to the maximum carrying capacity of the environment during winter is a preferable recourse both for wildlife and for the environment.

Vicissitudes of weather frequently influence the continuity of plant food supplies and their use. A blanket of early snow may bury all the seeds and fruits which have fallen to the ground. Sleet often makes both wild and cultivated winter foods unavailable. Weather may be an important factor in an entirely different way by causing variations in crop yield. Heavy spring rains or unseasonable frosts during the period of pollination or fruit-setting may curtail fruit and seed production. Conversely, an early warm spring in the East gives crabgrass a good start and ensures an early supply of seeds for smaller birds.

Thus, the availability of plant food varies from year to year, from season to season, and from day to day. Pines produce bumper crops of seeds some years, and in others the yield is comparatively small. There seems to be a cycle of fruit production in apples, grape, holly, persimmon, and probably in other plants. Larger crops are produced in alternating years, though some fruit may be produced each year. The oaks carry this system further. The white oak group produces its acorns annually, and only occasionally produces a large crop. The black oak group usually takes two years for its acorns to mature, and the crop is comparatively larger. These alternating seed years are important in the wildlife food supply.

Plant succession is also a long-term factor in availability. The plants that first take over an abandoned field are very different from the forest or prairie flora that eventually establishes itself there. Fallow-field annuals that produce large seed crops for songbirds are generally crowded out by perennials within two or three years, and then, in some regions, woody plants take over. Their shade produces an entirely different substory of herbaceous plants. Thus there are slow but continual changes in the plants of an area till a mature or climax stage is reached. Species that are abundant in early stages may be rare or lacking later. These changes all have a bearing on the availability of food and cover plants. They influence the animal populations, both in numbers and kinds.

Food Storage and Food Hunting

Since availability is the key to the wildlife use of plants, it is interesting to note that only a few wildlife species solve this problem by the storage of food.

9

Among birds, there is very little food storage at all, and there is some doubt whether the storage that has been observed actually serves a good purpose. Outstanding as hoarders of food are California and Lewis woodpeckers of the West. They have the unusual habit of making holes in the bark of trees and even in telephone poles and depositing acorns in them. Each acorn is placed singly in a hole, though sometimes dozens are placed near one another. Red-headed woodpeckers and blue jays occasionally store nuts and seeds, but not as a regular habit.

Food storage by mammals is restricted largely to rodents. The storage of nuts by tree squirrels is commonly regarded as an expression of their proverbial thrift. Field studies have questioned the effectiveness of these hidden nuts in providing future food. Often the tidbits are so well hidden that the squirrels do not recover them. Ground rodents, on the other hand, do definitely store food and use it. They spot their burrows with caches of seeds and grasses. The coney makes regular haystacks for its future use. Chipmunks and kangaroo rats store nuts, dry fruits, and seeds. Muskrats put away tubers, and beavers drag logs under water to supply inner bark for winter food, after their ponds freeze.

From the agricultural point of view, it may be something of a blessing that there is so little food storage by our wildlife. If all wildlife stored food to the extent that rodents do, the human species might have a hard time maintaining itself. The grasses cut and stored by field mice and gophers appreciably deplete the amount left for grazing. However, the habit of storage is limited, and wildlife species generally live a hand-to-mouth existence, spending most of their time looking for food.

Even the search for foods is beset by limiting factors. Very few animals wander indefinitely looking for something to eat. In the winter season mockingbirds set up their own private territories and protect their sources of food against encroaching individuals. Some species feed singly and, seasonally, others like elk, bison, wolves, starlings, and blackbirds make the hunt for food a group activity.

In seeking food, the seasonal aspect is a paramount factor. The larger browsing mammals, elk, mule deer, and mountain sheep, will move out of the mountains during the winter to lower levels where plant food is more plentiful. Some birds in the higher mountains similarly move to the valleys during the winter season. Some authorities go so far as to speculate that this type of seasonal movement, in search of food and away from cold, is the basis of bird migration. Whether or not this is so, some migrating species move as flocks in search of food as they travel.

Whitetail deer offer an unusual exception in regard to winter movements. In the North, they return instinctively to the same circumscribed area each winter and, as the snow piles up, remain there feeding on whatever plants are available. They refuse to move out of this area even when starving, though adequate plant food may be available at only a short distance. These places of congregation, known as deer yards, are readily recognized by the way they have been over-browsed by the deer. After use by an excessive concentration of deer, the locality may need many years to regain its normal plant cover.

Food Preferences

When foods are abundant, animals have opportunity to exercise preference among the different kinds available. The best gauge of this preference is the extent to which a plant is used in comparison with its abundance. Wildlife investigators have recently made a practice of measuring both the use and availability of foods and thereby getting data upon which preference can be expressed.

Not much is known about the interpretation of wildlife food preferences. A number of factors may enter into it. One may be palatability—roughly, the taste of the food. It is not surprising that browsers prefer soft, succulent leaves to leathery ones and often pass by plants with bitter or milky juices. Some poisonous plants seem to be avoided instinctively. The nutritional needs of the animal may unconsciously make it select foods to meet its deficiencies.

The following list of Wisconsin white-tailed deer foods illustrates preferences of this animal as judged by field observations and palatability tests:

Preferred Plants[1]

Alternate Dogwood	Hemlock	Red Maple
Wintergreen	Mountain-ash	Black Currant
Yew	Sumac	
Whitecedar	Red-osier Dogwood	

Second Choice

Mountain Maple	White Pine	Leatherwood
Sugar Maple	Cherry	Birch
Honeysuckle	Willow	Holly
Basswood	Bur Oak	Black Ash
Sweetfern	Red Oak	Hazel
Serviceberry	Blueberry	Aspen
Jack Pine	Labrador-tea	

Starvation Foods

Norway Pine	Raspberry	Black Spruce
Balsam	Larch	
Alder	White Spruce	

Nutritional Values of Wildlife Plants

The last war brought us stories of individuals who, when forced down over jungle and desert, survived for long periods on the wild foodstuffs of the region. Both the Army and Navy instructed men on how to live off the country—as wildlife has always done. By their very existence, wildlife species have demonstrated their ability to maintain themselves on native wild resources though they have no reluctance in substituting farm products once they become acquainted with them. When the facts about the nutritional values of wildlife plants are known, it is easy to understand how animals can not only maintain themselves, but also grow fat on a diet of wild foods.

There are many parallels between the nutrition of wildlife and that of humans. We recognize that our own diet must do three things: furnish heat and energy, promote growth and reproduction, and protect against deficiency diseases. So must the diet of wildlife. Wild animals, like ourselves, may suffer from vitamin and mineral deficiencies. Normally, the diet of birds and mammals is balanced in terms of their needs, and the foods preferred and selected are generally those suited to the animal's welfare. The importance of this instinctive ability to select needed nutrients cannot be overestimated. There are times when weather, forest fires, or other limiting factors force animals to subsist on diets unsuited for their optimum health. Growth and vitality are usually affected, and sometimes death results. Comparable to this is the livestock mortality on western ranges when, because of droughts or overgrazing, cattle and sheep eat poisonous weeds that they would ordinarily avoid.

[1] W. S Feeney, *Wis. Wildlife Research-Progress Reports*, Vol. V (1), January, 1946.

The nutritional value of plant food varies in different parts of the same plant and also from plant to plant. Leaves are primarily a carbohydrate food and tend to be richer in vitamin A and calcium than other parts of the plant. They have, however, a high moisture content and so are of relatively low nutritional value. Buds and flowers are similar to leaves nutritionally, though buds contain less water. Roots, rootstocks, bulbs, and corms are packed with carbohydrates and some proteins. Inner bark, in spite of its unsavory appearance to us, is quite nutritious. In carbohydrate content it is at least the equivalent of leaves.

Fleshy fruits are rich in carbohydrates and vitamins. Seeds and nuts are the most concentrated of plant foods. They are the richest sources of fats and proteins and also contain minerals and most of the B complex vitamins. As wildlife foods they have no equal. Add to this the fact that spoilage is low and some seeds and nuts are available throughout the winter, and you can see why they rank as high as they do.

From a nutritional angle, one could list wild plant foods according to their richness in the various nutrients, but this is hardly important since neither

Comparative Composition of Some Wild and Cultivated Plant Products*

(Expressed in percentages)

Wild or cultivated	Plant	Part	Water	Protein	Fat	Sugar and starch	Crude fiber	Minerals
Wild...	Paspalum	Seed	9	8	2	50	26	5
Cult...	Oats	Seed	10	11	5	61	11	2
Wild...	Partridgepea	Seed	9	33	7	40	7	4
Cult...	Soybean	Seed	9	38	17	26	5	5
Wild...	Shelbark hickory	Nut	2	13	73	9	1	2
Cult...	English walnut	Nut	4	18	64	13		
Wild...	Red oak	Acorn	38	4	13	41	2	2
Cult...	Chestnut	Nut	52	3	2	41	1	1
Wild...	Cherry	Fruit	65	2	2	23	7	1
Cult...	Cherry (sweet)	Fruit	84	1	Tr.	15		
Wild...	Hackberry	Fruit	21	6	3	42	6	22
Cult...	Raisins	Fruit	18	3	3	76		
Wild...	Greenbrier	Leaves	55	5	5	27	6	2
Cult...	Spinach	Leaves	92	2	Tr.	3	1	2
Wild...	Alder	Catkins	49	8	7	25	9	2
Cult...	Cauliflower	Fl. head	91	3	Tr.	4	1	1
Wild...	Serviceberry	Buds	51	4	5	26	10	4
Wild...	Yellow birch	Inner bark (air dried)	6	9	3	54	25	3

* Data assembled from various sources.

wildlife nor humans base their diet on a conscious selection of nutrients. Yet, it is worth mentioning that many seeds contain more than 25% protein—compared to eggs with 14%, sirloin steak 19%, and chicken 22%. Such seeds include black locust, lespedeza, sweetclover, partridgepea, pine, jewelweed, etc. Seeds and nuts are rich in fat also. Hazelnuts, hickory nuts, acorns, and seeds of jewelweed, bayberry, pine, and a number of others assay 25% fat or over. American cheese contains 35% fat, pork chops 24%, and veal 16%. Plants in general are good sources of carbohydrates, persimmon fruits yielding as high as 85%.

For an over-all picture of the nutritional values of different wildlife foods, the preceding table will indicate what a quail, opossum, or deer may get from its wild foods in comparison to cultivated ones.

There is a good deal of difference between knowing the composition of wild foods and knowing what the wild animals get out of them. Wildlife nutrition is a new field, and we are just beginning to accumulate the needed data. Recent studies with gamebirds show that young pheasant and bobwhite chicks use 25 to 30% protein in their diet to achieve optimum growth. Bobwhite breeding stock requires the same high level of protein to maintain a maximum reproduction, though adults will live on about half that amount. Vitamin requirements are not well known though recent studies indicate they may be important. Lack of vitamin A, associated with low fat in the winter diet of gamebirds, may reduce chances of survival appreciably. Experiments with bobwhite show a need of about 2,500 international units of vitamin A per pound of feed for optimum winter survival and subsequent reproduction. Pheasant chicks need more vitamin D and riboflavin than chicks of domestic fowl.

Despite the high value of seeds and nuts, plant foods have their nutritional limitations. As compared to animal products, they are generally low in protein and even lower in fats. We know from human nutritional studies that the amino acids in plants are not so diverse or as suitable for our needs as animal proteins. These limitations seem to be recognized by wildlife. Many birds swing to an insect diet in the spring, returning to plant foods gradually as the insect population decreases toward late summer. The young of nearly all smaller land birds are fed largely on an insect diet and do not shift to plant food until they are fairly well grown. In this respect, the diet of juvenile birds may vary greatly from that of adults. A diet rich in protein is needed to promote growth, and an insect bill of fare raises the protein level to meet that critical need.

Water from Plants

Though the role of plants in supplying food for wildlife is of primary importance, their value as a source of water is also significant. Browsers, including rodents and rabbits, usually obtain sufficient water from the leaves they eat. Feeding at night or early morning, most herbivorous mammals take the advantage of the dew that is often present on plants. Fleshy fruits and berries have a high water content also. The fruit of cacti (cactus pears) are especially succulent and may be taken as much for their liquid content as for their seeds. Under semiarid or desert conditions, water obtained from plants takes on an even greater importance than it does in the humid East.

Plants As Cover

Food and shelter are primary necessities of both humans and wildlife. For wildlife the two are more intimately connected. Frequently, the same plants that serve as food also provide cover.

Cover has been defined technically, but in common terms it implies all the forms of environmental protection which help an animal stay alive. Cover usually involves plants, but occasionally it consists of rocks, snow, water, soil, or even a hole in the ground. First of all, cover provides protection from enemies, especially from predators. Conversely, however, cover may also help these predators to stalk their prey. Cover may furnish protection through concealment, and it may give additional safety through impenetrability to enemies. Cover also means protection from weather: protection from cold, rain, snow, wind and especially from the combination of cold and wind. Both mammals and birds also need protection from maximum heat during the summer. Desert life seeks shelter during midday, when the temperature rises so high that neither warm- nor cold-blooded animals can stand it.

Cover needs vary according to the wildlife species and according to daily and seasonal activities. The proximity of cover while wildlife is feeding is especially important, for this is a time when the animal's attention is partly occupied by matters other than safety. Suitable nesting cover is important to birds in spring and summer. Cover requirements for escape, for sleeping, and for protection from inclement weather are likely to differ for different kinds of wildlife. Plants that provide cover for rodents and small ground-feeding birds offer no shelter at all for deer and larger mammals. Furthermore, the value of cover plants depends upon the abundance of vegetation in a particular area; the more barren the region, the greater the cover value of the plants that are present. Fences, stones, stumps, bushes, weeds, grass, and even soil and water offer shelter to some animals. When snow covers the northern landscapes, it both limits and supplements much of the herbaceous cover. Rabbits and ruffed grouse use the white snow blanket as escape or roosting cover. But the snow cover is temporary, even more temporary than much of the vegetation.

Crop plants are a typical temporary cover. Nevertheless, protection does not disappear entirely when crops are harvested. Grain stubble continues to afford concealment to small birds and rodents. So do standing shocks of grain. Hedgerows, woodlots, marshes, and shrub growths provide more enduring cover. Actually the cover supplied by woody plants is gradually modified. As woods develop, the understory changes and a mature stand of timber may only offer cover for birds in its upper branches.

Quality of cover is only a part of the problem. The quantity or areal extent of cover assumes a position of great importance for some species. Thus deer, bear, and wild turkey must have large acreages of good-quality plant cover if they are to survive as wild creatures. This requirement explains why wild turkey restoration is so difficult. Excellent units of turkey range can still be found in eastern United States, but much of this is in blocks too small and too isolated by intervening farmland.

In a deciduous forest, any evergreen trees or shrubs present have extra cover value, especially in winter. Mountainlaurel, rhododendron, pine, and hemlock serve in this important role in northeastern hardwood forests. On the other hand, some pure unbroken coniferous forests may actually have meager wildlife population. The edges of such areas are often productive, but not so the interior. If the cover and shade are such that suitable food plants cannot get a start, few wildlife species will thrive. All cover and no food are certain to send wildlife away. But when good cover exists in proximity to a good feeding area, conditions are ideal. So, openings in forests or forest edges—clearings, thinnings, or even roadway openings—are better for wildlife than an unbroken, dense wilderness of trees.

Most wildlife species use cover of some kind. Some need it for every phase of their existence. Others need it only at specific times. For a few species, space, isolation, and inaccessibility seem to take the place of cover. Thus during daylight hours, the dodging, diving swallows need only space to hunt and feed and at the same time be fairly safe from harm. Gulls and terns and shorebirds use relatively little cover even when nesting. The duck hawk relies on an inaccessible ledge to protect its nest and young. On the other hand, cover of one kind or another is essential for the safety of gallinaceous birds such as pheasant, quail, partridge, grouse, and turkey. Ducks, geese, marshbirds, and muskrats find marsh cover important. Deer, elk, and moose take refuge in forest cover. In general, the wildlife species which lack other means of self-protection compensate by effective use of cover or by ability to move quickly.

Dual-purpose Plants

In restoration programs, dual-purpose plants have a special place. Plants that offer both shelter and food have more than a double advantage. This ideal combination of food and shelter is provided by many plants in varying degrees of adequacy. Holly and some pines are good dual-purpose trees for many birds. Bobwhite quail have found a recently introduced perennial, shrub lespedeza (*Lespedeza bicolor*), an excellent dual-purpose plant. The heavy crop of seeds of this legume is relished by the bobwhites, and the dense growth provides some cover in winter as well as during the growing season. Wildrice and bulrushes are fine food and shelter plants for waterfowl. Sorghum, sunflower, millet, cowpeas, and soybeans that are sometimes planted for gamebirds furnish cover as well as food; but for maximum value for quail, pheasant, and turkey, the food patches are often placed alongside hedgerows or against woodlots so that the birds have accessory cover available when feeding. In the last decade, multiflora rose has come into extensive use as a dual-purpose plant. It furnishes cover and food, and also serves as a living fence.

Another type of dual-purpose plant is set out primarily to control soil erosion and to get denuded land back under plant cover. These plants are selected because of their tolerance to unfavorable conditions, because of their rapid growth, or because of root systems that are effective in anchoring soil. Secondarily they provide food and cover for wildlife. Grasses, lespedezas, and other legumes are planted to hold the soil in open fields. Conservation studies have made it clear that worthless eroded land planted with dual-purpose soil-conservation and wildlife plants may begin to yield a wildlife harvest in just a few years.

HEDGEROWS. Hedgerows are valuable since they serve the dual purpose of providing cover and food for wildlife. A hedgerow forms naturally when native plants are allowed to develop along a fence or field border. This strip is, in effect, an extension of the forest border—a natural wildlife path into the cultivated areas. It provides food as well as escape and nesting cover. The proximity of nesting birds in hedgerows may provide some measure of protection against insect depredations to crops. Many of the hedgerow plants that establish themselves naturally in the East are valuable food producers for wildlife (poison-ivy, wild cherry, persimmon, blackgum, dogwood, honeysuckle, etc.). Farther west, hedgerows are planted for the primary purpose of establishing windbreaks. Typical wildlife of hedgerows includes many kinds of songbirds, several upland game-birds, and various mammals, such as rabbits, opossums, raccoons, foxes, and small rodents.

Common hedgerow plants that become established naturally along eastern fences include the following:

Trees

Wild Cherry	Sassafras	Plum
Dogwood	Sumac	Sweetgum
Blackgum	Elm	Oaks
Persimmon	Hawthorn	Redcedar

Shrubs and Vines

Poison-ivy	Virginia-creeper	Hazelnut
Blackberry	Viburnum	Elderberry
Greenbrier	Chokeberry	Wild Rose
Honeysuckle	Dogwoods	Grape

Herbaceous Plants

Ironweed	Pokeweed	Broomsedge
Goldenrod	Burdock	Purpletop
Wildcarrot	Motherwort	Bluegrass
Asters	Yarrow	Milkweed

AQUATICS. Another special group of plants useful to wildlife because of their combined cover and food potentialities are the aquatic and moist-soil plants that attract ducks and geese to our swamps, marshes, and waterways. Like hedgerows, many of these plants grow naturally and, unless disturbed by drainage, changes in water level, or harmful burning, will maintain permanent cover and a good food supply for marsh wildlife. Plants like sago pondweed, other pondweeds, duck-weeds, and wildcelery are excellent waterfowl foods that also furnish cover for fish. The bulrushes, wildrice, wildmillet, spikerush, and similar erect, densely growing plants provide nesting cover as well as a fall and winter supply of seeds.

Duck hunters have attempted to encourage waterfowl by planting marsh and aquatic species. These efforts have resulted in the establishment of a small industry in which a number of dealers specialize in selling aquatic plants for this purpose. But, because aquatic conditions are so variable, they need close study before the introduction of plants is attempted.

The knowledge of the principles of plant ecology is a prerequisite to sound management of wildlife. In any large-scale, long-term attempt to modify plant life for the benefit of desirable wildlife, we must move within the natural current of the environment and take advantage of the basic laws of plant and animal life.

CHAPTER TWO

Farm Crops and Wildlife

A DESERT, A MARSHY lake, a hardwood forest, or an ocean beach, each has its natural plant communities which provide food and shelter for local animals. The somewhat less natural plant communities of farm croplands also have their associated wildlife. A principal difference between these plant-animal associations is the fact that, on the farm, man teams up with nature in providing food and shelter for wildlife.

Agricultural crops that have the greatest appeal to wildlife are naturally the ones intended for man's own consumption or for his domestic livestock. Among these are corn, wheat, barley, oats, sorghum, rice, alfalfa, soybeans, cowpeas, and various cultivated fruits. Some major crops such as cotton, tobacco, sugar beets, and potatoes do not benefit wildlife much, if at all. Orchards, vineyards, gardens, and ornamentals planted about our homes and along streets are attractive to songbirds and to some mammals. Cultivated cherries or plums have fully as much appeal to wild creatures as do the native uncultivated species of these fruits. It would be strange indeed if figs, mulberries, apricots, walnuts, and similar fruits that we enjoy were not relished by wildlife. As sorghum became a crop of

17

increasing importance in Texas and adjoining states, it was eaten more and more by ducks, especially mallards, till now the damage to this crop is a vexing local problem. Rice is also such a desired food that the crop suffers from the depredations of bobolinks and redwings wintering in the southern rice fields. In California rice-growing areas, damage by ducks and blackbirds frequently becomes serious.

Not only are cultivated crops widely used by wildlife, but the attendant growth of weeds is also an important source of food for ground-feeding birds and rodents. Numerous immigrant weed species valuable to wildlife have become abundant on our farm lands—filaree from the Mediterranean region, Russianthistle, chickweed, goosefoot, some of the pigweeds, and others from various Old World sources. Whether or not the common ragweed, so important to birds, is native, is not quite certain.

Wildlife economics is sometimes subject to wishful thinking and misleading statistics. Numerically correct, but otherwise shortsighted interpretations of food analysis data have led to evaluation of each animal species according to the percentage and type of insects or weed seeds eaten. Not so long ago we had practically all wildlife species pigeonholed as "good, bad, or indifferent," and we figured out almost to a cent their positive or negative value.

It would be fine if the problem were as clean-cut as that. Today we no longer designate wildlife as good or bad with facility and finality. In relationship to man and man's plants and livestock, wildlife species are neither black nor white, but of various shades of gray—and they change in complexion seasonally and locally. Even the species that have the fewest redeeming features in our economy generally have some value. Gulls that are destructive to New England's wild blueberry crop are otherwise valued scavengers and insect eaters. The mallard duck is a favorite to sportsmen, but not to farmers in the Texas Panhandle where, during the winter, it feeds heavily on sorghum. Meadowlarks are beneficial insect eaters, except in early spring when they do extensive damage to sprouting corn in the Carolinas. Robins are popular songbirds except to those of us whose cherry trees have been plundered by them. Snowshoe hares are a favorite game species in the North but are a bane to foresters—especially when the hares are in one of the abundant phases of their periodic cycles. Prairie dogs and pocket gophers, though detrimental to some crops, have partially redeeming features in their role as soil makers—stirring up the soil, letting air and water penetrate more easily, and burying vegetative material. Even the despised starling has the merit of being one of the principal avian enemies of the equally despised Japanese beetle.

Beneficial Activities

There is no denying that certain species of wildlife are beneficial by destroying harmful insects, rodents, or other obnoxious animal life. Some wildlife also feed on weed seeds or on pest plants. However, to evaluate their importance as controlling agents in this direction is another matter. Such an appraisal must consider wildlife apart from the rest of the environmental controls—something which is both difficult and unrealistic. In destroying insects, and this is the phase of wildlife activity that has received the most unstinted praise, birds (and sometimes mammals) act as only one repressive part of the insect's total environment. Climate, disease, parasites, and other factors also help limit the growth of insect populations. If none of these natural controls operate, the diminishing food supply for the insects will itself prove effective. But since that food supply is often a human food supply, we prefer other controls for insects than their ultimate starvation.

Those who stop to consider the complicated interrelations of insects, plants, and wildlife don't expect birds to produce miracles in insect control. Nevertheless in some localities birds have brought insect pests under control very effectively. Definite testimony of this can be given by the celery growers in Florida whose crops are protected every year from serious damage by the celery-leaf tier through the feeding activity of warblers and swallows. The Mormons in Utah will never forget the gulls which in 1848 and again in 1855 came in sufficient numbers to rout insect hordes that were laying waste the land.

Similar principles are involved in the destruction of weed seeds. Seed-eating birds literally eat thousands of tons of seed a year, but weeds produce such an oversupply of seeds that those removed by birds may not be significant. There are many more seeds scattered through the top inch of soil than most people realize. Many seeds are resistant and persistent for years and finally, when conditions become right, they germinate. Birds, in feeding on seeds, may merely thin down the potential surface growth and reduce the stifling competition between seedlings of the same species. In other words, the consumption of weed seeds by birds may actually promote weed growth. Furthermore the theoretical good that may be accomplished in weed destruction by birds is often counterbalanced by their widespread dissemination of seeds from undesirable plants. Again, there is no question that weed seeds are destroyed, but some of the impressive computations on the value of this destruction are misleading.

The food habits of other kinds of wildlife besides insectivorous or seed-eating birds are of some benefit to man. Hawks, owls, foxes, and some other animals feed extensively on rodents, including pest species, and act as one of the natural controls over these animals. Vultures, gulls, magpies, crows, and coyotes serve as professional scavengers and help clean up dead animal litter. All in all, the benefits that accrue to man through the feeding habits of wildlife are probably great. But exact evaluation is difficult and beset with pitfalls. It is quite possible that our agriculture could not exist on its present large scale if it were not deeply involved in the natural plant and animal communities associated with it.

Though we may not be able to point to a single species of insect, weed, or rodent that has been effectively suppressed over an extensive range by wildlife, it cannot be doubted that many kinds of birds exercise a beneficial role in agriculture and forestry—one which justifies their protection. Though no farmer can sit back and let the birds do his pest-ridding job for him, he can, by developing hedgerows or raising other plants that supply food and nesting sites, encourage the avian populations which feed on his enemies. By so doing, he will not free himself of pest problems, but will bring to bear a natural force which helps to mitigate damage.

Much of the dissemination of weed seeds, poison-ivy fruits, seeds of pricklypear cactus, and the like by wildlife may properly be regarded as obnoxious. But there is also a beneficial service accomplished by this biological means of distribution. Interestingly enough it is beneficial alike to the particular plants involved, to the animal disseminators, and also, indirectly, to man. This is well-exemplified in most of our natural hedgerows. Seedlings of wild cherry, persimmon, blackgum, viburnum, grape, sumac, cedar, blackberry, elderberry, greenbrier, hawthorn, and pokeweed growing along fence rows usually start from seeds deposited there by birds or by mammals that have been feeding on these plants. Thus, inadvertently, these wildlife species benefit themselves or their descendants.

The dependence of plants upon animal carriers is rarely as complete as in the case of mistletoe; yet, in many instances, the relationship is probably much more significant to the flora than is generally realized. A wildlife investigator in Virginia has expressed the belief that practically all the redcedar trees growing in the state were planted by birds or mammals. Similarly, the mystifying spread of seeds or other propagules of marsh and aquatic plants to remote isolated lakes in the prairies or deserts seems to be best explained by assuming the agency of birds or other wildlife.

Destructive Activities

Problems of economic damage by wildlife are inevitable. What else can be expected when the plant crops we raise are the equivalent of an inviting banquet table! Under these circumstances we can always expect periodic local damage, though in terms of the nation's crops, wildlife damage is minor compared to destruction from frost, drought, erosion, insects, and plant diseases. But, in particular localities, wildlife depredations may prove disastrous. To prevent this harm or reduce it without resorting to killing is often a difficult problem.

The destruction of farm crops, fruits, or forest growths by wildlife is definitely related to local abundance of wildlife and the pattern of local food supplies. Beyond this, generalizations are of little value. The problem must be studied from the standpoint of each locality. Seasonal factors are involved, and often the same animals that are a nuisance one time of the year may be clearly beneficial in another season. There is always the danger of precipitate and extensive control action before essential facts are available—as when crows shot in a field of young corn were found to have been feeding on destructive insects rather than on the plants. When wildlife damage actually does occur, the results are usually clear and obvious. Anyone can see the evidence. In contrast to this, the benefits contributed are widely diffused, obscure, and not likely to be fully appreciated.

Popular reports of wildlife destruction to crops are often colored by factors which make their accuracy questionable. In 1937, following recurrent complaints of crow damage to crops in Oklahoma, two trained investigators made a careful survey of the situation.[1] They found damage that may have eliminated 1% of the state's corn and sorghum crops. In some areas, damage was clearly higher and an important local problem existed; but the investigators had to add to their con-

[1] Imler and Kalmbach, *U.S. Biol. Survey Wildlife Leaflet*, BS-123, 1939.

Some Wildlife Species That Are Locally Destructive to Crops

FARM CROPS

Bobolink........................ Rice
Crow........................... Corn, sorghum, other crops
Ducks: Mallard and Pintail........ Sorghum, grain crops
  Widgeon....................... Irrigated green crops
Goose, Canada.................. Young plants of grain crops
Meadowlark..................... Young plants of corn, peas, other crops
Pheasant, Ring-necked........... Grain crops, truck crops
Redwing........................ Rice, corn
Sparrow, English................ Grain crops, fruit, young garden plants
Deer........................... Farm, orchard, or garden crops
Ground Squirrels................ Forage and grain
Prairie Dogs.................... Forage and grain
Raccoon........................ Corn, melons

ORCHARDS

Finch, House.................... Buds, ripening fruit
Finch, Purple................... Buds of fruit trees
Jay, Blue....................... Fruit, walnuts, almonds
Robin.......................... Fruit
Sapsucker...................... Shade, orchard, and forest trees
Starling........................ Fruit
Thrasher, Brown................ Fruit, corn
Waxwing....................... Fruit
Gophers........................ Orchard and garden crops
Moles.......................... Orchard and garden crops
Mouse, Meadow................. Apple orchards

GARDENS

Lark, Horned................... Truck-garden plants
Sparrows: Gambel, Golden-crowned,
  Nuttall....................... Young garden plants
Rabbits........................ Garden and orchard crops
Squirrel, Gray.................. Garden crops
Woodchuck..................... Garden crops

FORESTS

Sapsucker...................... Lumber trees
Mouse, White-footed............ Pine seeds
Porcupines..................... Lumber trees
Rabbit, Snowshoe Hare.......... Young forest trees

clusions "that estimates of the percentage of crops lost was about six times, and of financial losses, sixteen times greater in the returns from questionnaires than in the data obtained from field appraisal—appraisal of crop losses by their owners is almost certain to be exaggerated."

It is difficult for the general public to evaluate logically and unemotionally the role of birds and mammals if their feeding activities conflict with man's economics or recreation. Farmers, hunters, fishermen, and others whose particular interests seem to be jeopardized are inclined to condemn these forms of native American wildlife as vermin. Overemphasis of the destructive activities of these species without due regard to their redeeming features often leads to prejudice that is difficult to erase. Biologists who have studied wildlife crop damage have found compensatory aspects in the activities of most of the commonly condemned species.

Control procedures vary with the crop, the wildlife species, and the locality. Fundamentally they are of two types: deterrent and lethal. The first includes automatic noisemakers, flashing lights, the conventional scarecrows, streamers of cloth or wax paper, netting to cover plants, predator-proof enclosures for animal yards, and hanging of dead predators in exposed situations. In some instances it has been found that deterrents are effective at first but gradually lose their value as wildlife species become accustomed to them. Methods must be shifted and revised constantly to be effective. The principal lethal measures are trapping, poisoning, and shooting. Use of these means of control may require permits because of state or Federal wildlife regulations.

One practical solution to crop damage is the employment of good farming practices. Grain left shocked too long in the field is an open invitation to injury from both weather and wildlife. This idea of adjustment in farm practices has been expounded for some time,[1] and it deserves reemphasis. There is no single method of preventing damage by wildlife. The crop, location, season, wildlife species, and economic factors must all be considered. But there is no doubt that those farmers who choose to help themselves can mitigate wildlife damage to their crops by preventive measures and especially by early, safe storage of harvested crops.

[1] E. R. Kalmbach, Protecting Grain Crops from Damage by Wild Fowl, *U.S. Biol. Survey Wildlife Res. Leaflet* BS-13, 1935.

CHAPTER THREE

Wildlife Food-Habits Studies

T HE SCIENTIFIC STUDY of food habits has proved one of the most essential tools in gaining an intelligent understanding of our wildlife. Knowing the foods of birds and mammals, we are in a position to alter their environment—especially the plant environment—so as to influence or control animal populations. Food-habits studies also serve as a final court in deciding whether some species are harmful or beneficial and to what extent. It is only by knowing what a crow, fox, coyote, or English sparrow eats that we can determine its economic relationship to other animals and man. Through wildlife food studies we arrive at reliable conclusions on predator-prey relationships and on competition between species for the same kind of food.

About 65 years of research on the foods of American wildlife has resulted in a mass of information, which, sifted, organized, and interpreted forms the principal contribution of this volume. The aggregate of data is very considerable, and yet, at best, it provides only a fragmentary indication of the foods of our wildlife. The gaps in information are often as conspicuous as the solid framework of knowledge. And even for wildlife species that have been studied intensively, as the bobwhite quail and the white-tailed deer, we have only part of the story of food preference, food requirements, and food availability, plus an incomplete accounting of the items actually eaten. No research is ever complete, but if the present data, such as they are, receive wide and wise use, the benefits to wildlife conservation may be substantial.

The inauguration of Federal wildlife food-habits research in 1885 was by no means the beginning of studies in this field. Observations on the food of animals had been made and recorded for centuries—and probably formed part of the campfire gruntings of prehistoric hunters. Laboratory studies on wildlife foods, however, are comparatively recent. The products of the two methods—field and laboratory—have been fused in this book. Recognition of the supplementary roles of field and laboratory research in food habits is important. Used together they give a more complete and accurate picture and help avoid mistaken conclusions.

Field Studies

Although field studies of food habits antedate laboratory studies, they are by no means outdated. They are still essential and will continue to be as long as wildlife problems are studied. Careful and extensive field observations by qualified investigators can give an adequate picture of the foods eaten by a particular kind of wildlife. In some respects the conclusions may be more satisfactory than the findings from laboratory studies on the same species. It is only from field observations that we can learn certain aspects of the complete story of food use, particularly as to *how*, *where*, and *when* the food is taken and to what extent the sources of supply have been depleted. The importance of this added *how*, *when*, and *where* is particularly evident in economic studies—as, for example, in determining if wildlife species are damaging crops or are merely gleaning waste grain in

stubble. The special value of such field work is emphasized by E. R. Kalmbach.[1] One instance, which treats of depredations by ducks in California, may be quoted:

On the basis of about 150 stomachs of four species of ducks it [laboratory examination] revealed that pintails ate a greater percentage of barley (43 percent) than the other ducks, a fact quite generally recognized by local sportsmen and farmers. It also verified the generally accepted belief that widgeons ate more sprouting alfalfa than any of the other species. It also showed that the little green-winged teal ate less barley (22 percent) than the widgeon (24.5 percent).

What, however, did field studies show? In the first place, they told something of the extent of the devastation wrought. They shed light on the acreage of damaged fields and the fact that, in addition to the immediate injury, the ducks often so puddled and de-aerated the fine silt of the grainfields that an unfavorable soil condition was created that lasted for several seasons. They revealed that the 30 percent of young alfalfa eaten by the widgeon meant, at times, a severe economic loss in uprooted plants. They disclosed the fact that the widgeon, a more abundant and more voracious feeder, far out-stripped the diminutive teal as a destroyer of barley seed, although stomach examination showed only slight disparity between the proportions of barley found in each. And back of all that, they told the vital story that so severe had the damage been in some winters that illegal shooting to protect crops was frequently resorted to; that honest efforts to protect grain were being discredited by abuses on the part of hunters who offered "their services in the cause of crop protection"; that game protective movement in this locality was jeopardized largely because of a lack of understanding of what ducks can

[1] Field Observations in Economic Ornithology, *Wilson Bul.* Vol. 46, pp. 73–90, 1934.

sometimes do. All in all, in the study of this local but vital problem of economic ornithology, field studies played a decidedly important role.

Because the field picture of food habits is so essential, it is unfortunate that it cannot be obtained in a quick, simple way. Observations need to be made over representative parts of the range of the wildlife species and must include seasonal and other varying aspects. Local food supplies need to be appraised quantitatively in order to compare their abundance and availability with the extent of actual use. This method provides an index to food preferences—a significant feature in tabulating food items.

The skill and experience of the observer are as important in field study as in laboratory research. In either realm, carelessness can easily cause serious and embarrassing mistakes. Though there probably is more amateur participation in outdoor observation of birds than in any other amateur scientific field, very little of this popular pursuit is concerned with the rather technical study of food habits. The great majority of the field observations on food use recorded in the Fish and Wildlife Service files were made by professional workers in the course of field duties. These files of field notes accumulated over many years have been of special value as a supplementary source of information.

Field studies on food habits are subject to some uncontrollable limitations in the accuracy of observations. The kinds of insects taken by swallows, warblers, or other insect-eating species cannot be accurately determined by field studies alone. It is frequently impossible to ascertain from observations just what seeds or insects birds are feeding upon. Thus a bird in the hand is often worth more than two in the bush—for purposes of investigation.

An unavoidable limiting factor in field observations is the statistical or quantitative element. The amount of each different kind of food taken is difficult to judge and equally hard to express in meaningful terms. Furthermore, there is the problem of combining this information with data from laboratory analyses. Another handicap of field observations is the difficulty of checking data. Materials from a stomach specimen may be stored away for laboratory reference if, at any time, there is a question about the identity or quantity of the contents. But, the wildlife species observed in the field have moved on and the identical situation cannot be reproduced.

The importance of supplementing field observations by laboratory research is best illustrated by one of the many specific problems that has been faced by the Fish and Wildlife Service. In Louisiana, shortly after the Migratory Bird Treaty Act was passed, local residents claimed that the yellow-crowned night heron was a menace to both the frogging industry and game fishing. In an authorized investigation, 113 stomachs of the yellow-crowned night heron were collected in the section from which the complaint originated. Careful laboratory examination of each stomach was made, and seven, being nearly empty, were excluded from the final computation. All but one of the remaining 106 stomachs contained crayfish (*Cambarus* sp.), which in 99 cases made up the entire contents. Not a single trace of frog or fish was found in any. Professional field observations gave no evidence that the birds were destructive, yet neither conclusive nor convincing proof exonerating them was obtained until laboratory stomach examinations were completed. Incidentally, and probably significantly, it developed that juvenile herons were being eaten by the residents as a choice article of food—a practice that directly threatened the future of the species.

Laboratory Studies

Even as long as a century ago it had become the practice of field naturalists to examine stomach contents of the birds and other animals killed for their collections. Such examinations were cursory. We find Audubon and others recording stomach contents as "wild fruits and grains," "weed seeds," "insect and plant materials." These broad categories denote a limitation of this type of observation and indicate the advantages of the more precise determinations that characterize modern laboratory studies.

Laboratory examination of stomach material is a highly specialized, technical task. Generally the laboratory worker cannot examine the actual plant or other food source on which the bird was feeding but must base his determinations on reference collections and on his fund of knowledge. He must work with seeds that are often broken or worn, fruit pulp, disassociated fragments of insects, and other partly digested animal material. Indeed, the laboratory analyst working on food habits must be a keen detective in order to reconstruct something worth while from the residues at hand.

Professional work on the food habits of wildlife began in 1885. The names Beal, Fisher, Barrows, and Judd of the Department of Agriculture are prominent among the workers in that pioneering period, as was Forbes of the University of Illinois.[1] McAtee, Lantz, Kalmbach, Wetmore, Gabrielson, Sperry, Kellogg, Uhler, Cottam, and numerous others of the Biological Survey staff followed early in the 1900's. Government bulletins reported the findings of these food-habits studies—most of them concerned with the helpful or harmful role of birds and mammals in their immediate relations to the farmer. Subsequently, emphasis was placed on waterfowl, and more recently on upland gamebirds, fur and game mammals, and other species. Within the past decade, state and private investigators on food habits have become very active. Techniques and reference collections have improved constantly, and the work has grown in extent as well as in quality.

The early food-habits studies dealt nearly exclusively with birds. They combined field observations and collecting of study specimens with laboratory analyses or, in some instances, examinations in the field. Gizzard contents were the principal sources of information on food use. Regurgitated pellets of hawks and owls also received attention in early studies aimed at determining the helpful or harmful status of these birds. When in the 1920's and later, upland gamebirds began to receive attention, their well-developed crops containing unworn, undigested food provided a more ideal basis of obtaining food information. In crops, in contrast to gizzards, the contents are more recognizable for identification purposes, and there is the additional advantage of finding the various foods more nearly in the original proportions consumed.

In the late 1930's, studies of bird droppings and mammal scats (droppings) began to become prominent. This medium of food-habits information has received increasing and merited recognition—especially for obtaining information on foods from reduced species of wildlife or during seasons when killing specimens for examination is illegal or otherwise undesirable. Thus, in the case of the wild turkey, crops and gizzards furnish detailed data from the late fall and early winter hunting seasons, but for the rest of the year, droppings constitute the best source of information on the foods of this depleted species. For mammals, in addition to stomach contents and scats, food-use information has been obtained from food caches, den remains, cheek pouches, and similar sources. Use has been made of all these varied media and methods in assembling the food-habits information of this book.

The first stomach listed in the extensive series collected, examined, and stored

[1] For a more complete account of the early studies, see Economic Ornithology, W. L. McAtee, published in the American Ornithologists' Union Memorial Volume, Fifty Years Progress of American Ornithology, 1933.

away in the Fish and Wildlife Service archives was that of a song sparrow, shot in a brackish marsh near Sing Sing, N.Y., at 6 P.M. on the evening of July 3, 1885. It was collected by Dr. C. Hart Merriam, who later became first chief of the Biological Survey. Examination of this particular specimen by Dr. Sylvester Judd occurred later, and the examination card on which the stomach contents were recorded was listed as No. 1 in a series that now exceeds a quarter of a million. Thousands of additional examination cards for mammals, reptiles, and amphibians make this store of food-habits information the most outstanding in the world.

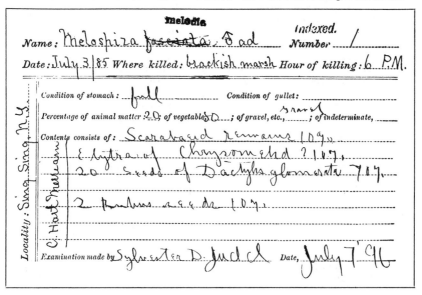

But the files of the Fish and Wildlife Service are by no means the sole source of the data in the following chapters. State conservation departments and fish and game commissions have done a great deal of research on food habits in recent years. This work has usually been financed jointly by Federal and state funds made available through the Pittman-Robertson Act. Substantial contributions have also been made by the Cooperative Wildlife Research Units supported jointly by the Wildlife Management Institute, by the state concerned, and by the Fish and Wildlife Service. The results of many of these state or local studies have been incorporated and summarized in this compilation.

Procedures for collecting study materials and for preserving, analyzing, and recording the food contents of stomachs are discussed in several Fish and Wildlife Service leaflets. Since food-habits studies have served as the foundation of this book's data, summarization of the important principles and practices is appropriate.

THE COLLECTION OF STUDY MATERIAL. This initial phase is all-important since the value of the food-habits study as a whole depends on the adequacy or inadequacy of the collecting. If the materials obtained fail to represent the typical seasonal, regional, or local food use of the animal, there may be little justification for subsequent painstaking, time-consuming steps of analysis and recording.

The extent of collecting and the kind of study units used depend directly on the kind of wildlife, as well as on the time, help, or money available. Whether the units of study consist of crops, stomachs, droppings, caches, cheek pouches, den materials, or only field observations will depend on whether the species concerned is the bobwhite, white-tailed deer, common crow, raccoon, gray fox, kangaroo rat, or some other form of wildlife. Generally all available sources of information are tapped, especially in the case of wary, scarce species, or when closed seasons limit the availability of study materials. Regardless of the units (stomachs, droppings, etc.) chosen for collecting purposes, there is always one paramount requirement: adequacy of the sample collected. The examination of just a few stomachs of a wildlife species in a single season or place provides only a partial and imperfect picture of that species' food habits. A more satisfactory story of food use will require adequate sampling that covers the region in all seasons concerned—an ideal goal that cannot always be attained.

A vital part of the collecting is the keeping of pertinent records. Notes are made relating to the when and where of the capture as well as to anything else (sex, maturity, etc.) that may be useful in giving real meaning to the final result. Consecutive numbers applied in the field to the collected materials and to notebook records help avoid confusion. Usually the stomach, crop, or intestines are removed from the collected specimen and are wrapped in a small square of gauze to which is affixed a waterproof label.

If, as commonly is the case, the specimens are not examined immediately, they must be protected from decomposition or from mold or insect attack. A 5 to 10% solution of commercial formaldehyde or a 70% solution of alcohol is commonly used for preserving. If the materials are largely seeds or plant remains, they may be dried with no preservatives other than an insecticide to deter weevils. Samples of stomach contents from large ruminants such as deer, elk, moose, antelope, and the like are also handled dry, though sometimes if the drying is slow and incomplete, mold develops and spoils the material. A temporary soaking in dilute formaldehyde prevents mold formation.

If study materials are retained for possible future rechecking, they are usually preserved in dry condition.

EXAMINATION OF MATERIALS. Specific examination procedures depend on whether the food contents are to be estimated visually, measured volumetrically, counted as to number of each kind, or simply listed as to presence or absence. Often two of these expressions are used in the same study. Each method has distinct advantages and limitations. Consequently, diverging schools of thought have developed as to the relative merits of the alternatives.

In predator investigations there is widespread agreement that *numbers* of each kind of item consumed are likely to be especially significant—the number of cottontails or bobwhites eaten by a gray fox, the number of chickens eaten by a coyote, or the number of bass present in the gizzard of a great blue heron. These are more meaningful to the researcher than either the volumetric proportion of each item or a simple record of its presence or absence.

In examining the crop contents of upland gamebirds a few investigators restrict their data to occurrence (presence or absence) of each item. Many more prefer to determine the volumetric proportion of each item in the diet—either by visual estimates or by actual measurements. In the analyses of droppings, the occurrence method is the most widely used, though recently there has been an increasing tendency to supplement it with some approximate indication of quantities. In stomach studies of birds, ruminants, and other mammals the volumetric system (involving either the estimating of proportions or their definite measurements) has been dominant, though quite a few students have employed other criteria.

The principal methods used may be illustrated by three ways of recording data from a single ruffed grouse crop in which 31 serviceberry buds constituted 40% of the total contents:

Occurrence method...................... Serviceberry buds
Numbers method........................ 31 Serviceberry buds
Numbers and volumetric combined........ 31 Serviceberry buds: 40%

Partial or complete segregation of food items is a common preliminary operation, regardless of whether the final objective is to determine occurrence, numbers, volume, or estimated percentages. Sieves, forceps, blowers, and other means may be employed to speed up the process. Like materials are gathered together into small piles. Sand and grit, if present, are put to one side. In some mixtures of foods, or residues of mixtures, it is undesirable or impossible to segregate the various component items. In such instances, estimates of the percentage of each constituent are made, with or without measurement of the total volume of the mixture.

Identification, measurement (estimated or precise), and enumeration generally follow segregation. The problem of identifying worn or fragmented remains is a technical task requiring skill and patience. Inaccuracies at this point can readily undo much of the care exercised in collecting and examination. Reference collections are essential for this purpose, but even the best collections are not adequate by themselves. The researcher himself must be thoroughly familiar with the identity of major biological groups which may be represented in the plant and animal food. Otherwise professional assistance is needed.

Food-habits investigators, professional or amateur, from all parts of the country, can and do avail themselves of the privilege of using the highly developed reference collections, the excellent laboratory facilities, and the technical assistance of specialists of the Fish and Wildlife Service at either the Patuxent Research Refuge, Laurel, Md., or at the Wildlife Research Laboratory, Denver, Colo. The extensive reference collections developed over many years include representative

---

COLINUS V. VIRGINIANUS   Sex ♂   No. 247 222
State NORTH CAROLINA   Co.   WAKE   Loc. V E AUSTILL FARM
Date 1-1-44   Hr. 5:00 PM   Collector   WOODARD   Coll. No. 20
Stom. --- cc. Crop 3.9 cc. Anim. TR. % Veg. 100 % Grit TR. cc. ____ %
Examined by   J Weigd + H. Swib   Date APRIL '44

		cc.	%
28	PINUS TAEDA	.8	20
120	DIGITARIA SANGUINALIS	.3	8
15	CHAMAECRISTA NICTITANS	.1	3
25	LESPEDEZA SP.	.1	3
!	GALACTIA SP.	TR.	
43	RHUS COPALLINA	.6	15
	LONICERA JAPONICA (FRUITS & SEEDS)	2.0	51
	DIPLOPODA	TR.	
	ARANEIDA : OXYOPIDAE : OXYOPES SP.	TR.	
	ACRIDIDAE : MELANOPLUS SP. (?)	TP.	
5	FORMICIDAE : LASIUS SP. (FEMALES)	TR.	
	GRIT	TR.	

U. S. GOVERNMENT PRINTING OFFICE   16—15791   3-174 a—(4-40)

series of insects, crustaceans, mollusks, reptiles, amphibians, mammals, birds, and plant materials.

A final phase of each examination is the recording of findings. The items identified and the quantities of each are listed in order on examination cards, each of which is distinguished by its collec or's number for the particular animal examined. Thousands upon thousands of cards like these have been used in preparing the summaries which follow in Parts II and III.

Each food-habits study, large or small, is, in itself, a special problem for which detailed procedures cannot be prescribed. The methods used with antelope are distinct from those employed with the English sparrow, and these in turn differ markedly from techniques suitable for studies on hawks and owls, upland game-birds, or rodents. Furthermore, methods used in different studies on the same wildlife species may need to be adapted to particular objectives or to other factors. Each is, to some degree, a unique problem, though similar guiding principles apply to all.

The fact that digestion alters the proportion of different foods in a stomach makes it necessary to keep constantly in mind that food-habits information is not precise, exact, and final. Instead it gives only an approximate indication of the kind and extent of food use. It is largely for this reason that the extent of use and importance of an item are denoted by stars in this book rather than by percentages.

Information on specific techniques in food-habit studies and more detailed discussions of related problems may be found in the references listed below.

General References: Procedures in Wildlife Food Studies. Alexander C. Martin. *U.S. Dept. Int. Wildlife Leaflet* 325, 1949.

Methods of Estimating the Contents of Bird Stomachs. W. L. McAtee. *Auk*, Vol. 29, pp. 449–464, 1912.

Field and Laboratory Technic in Wildlife Management. Howard M. Wight. University of Michigan Press, Ann Arbor, 1938.

Economic Ornithology and the Correlation of Laboratory and Field Methods. Clarence Cottam. *U.S. Dept. Agr. Wildlife Res. and Mgt. Leaflet* BS-30, 1936.

Field Observations in Economic Ornithology. E. R. Kalmbach. *Wilson Bul.*, Vol. 46, pp. 73–90, 1934.

Economic Ornithology. W. L. McAtee. Published in the American Ornithologists' Union Memorial Volume, Fifty Years Progress of American Ornithology, 1933.

CHAPTER FOUR

Interpreting the Data of This Book

P ARTS II AND III summarize our present knowledge of wildlife food habits on a dual basis: first, by focusing on the animal users (Part II), and then on the plants used (Part III). A compact compilation of information from hundreds of thousands of stomach and crop analyses, from innumerable droppings, and from many field observations in all parts of the country would have been impossible without developing a system of symbols, abbreviations, and other space-saving features. The special arrangements require some explanation. Even the four seasons and the wildlife regions, as used here, need to be defined. Therefore, the following pages are primarily concerned with explaining the presentation of food-habits data in the remainder of the book. The sequence is as follows: first, the problems that relate to both Parts II and III, then those concerned exclusively with animals (Part II), and finally those dealing primarily with plants (Part III).

THE STAR SYSTEM OF RATING. Stars (asterisks) have been used instead of percentage figures to indicate the extent of use of food items. There are two reasons for this. One is the danger of attributing unwarranted finality or accuracy to the food-habits data as expressed in percentages. An approximate, tentative picture of the food habits of an animal or the extent of food use of a plant is all that should be attempted or implied. The other point in favor of rating by stars is the fact that this method is familiar and easy to grasp. Important items stand out and automatically receive attention.

The star rankings are, for the most part, based directly on percentages from food-habits tabulations. The system as used here has the following approximate percentage equivalents:

$$- = \text{Use to an undetermined extent}$$
$$+ = \tfrac{1}{2} \text{ to } 2\% \text{ of diet}$$
$$* = 2 \text{ to } 5\% \text{ of diet}$$
$$** = 5 \text{ to } 10\% \text{ of diet}$$
$$*** = 10 \text{ to } 25\% \text{ of diet}$$
$$**** = 25 \text{ to } 50\% \text{ of diet}$$
$$***** = 50\% \text{ or more of diet}$$

All items preceded by one or more stars are likely to have some importance for the wildlife species concerned. There are few—and only a very few—5-star items. These are so exceptional that they imply a very unique relationship between a wildlife species and a particular plant or plant group. In these few cases the actual percentage base is also given, as a matter of interest.

Food items included in the listings with a plus sign (+) instead of a star make up a small but appreciable part of the food of the bird or mammal in question.

It is more than a trace, in the ordinary sense of the word. A complete listing of *all* foods found in every stomach analysis of important, much-studied wildlife species such as the bobwhite, Gambel quail, mourning dove, English sparrow, ruffed grouse, crow, redwing, horned lark, and others would, in each instance, run into the hundreds if not thousands of different items. Most of these numerous minor food items have little known significance in the animal's diet, and presenting their total array would becloud and complicate a picture which attempts to set forth the typical, more important foods eaten.

REGIONAL UNITS. The boundaries which limit different kinds of wildlife are, to a large degree, vegetational ones. The vegetation in turn is determined by an interplay of temperature, rainfall, soils, and other climatic and physiographic factors. The complex, overlapping plant provinces of the United States have been

defined into 6, 13, 22, or 32 regional units by different investigators. For the purposes of this book—presenting food-habits data for the whole country on a simple, easily used geographic basis—a compromise has been required. Five major regions (see map) involving important transitions in the kinds of food taken by wildlife have been formulated as the principal vegetational and wildlife areas of the country. Obviously these five regions are an oversimplification of the complex vegetative zones of this country. But in considering those plants which form a significant part of the diet of birds and mammals, these areas and their subdivisions are well suited to present purposes. They represent a compromise between a summation lacking any geographic delimitation and one which meets ecological standards. The latter probably could not be used as a basis for presenting a significant picture of the foods of our nation's wildlife without another 65 years of research.

The boundaries of each of the five regions have been determined mainly by the distribution of key plants or types of plants. Within each region, however, the vegetation varies considerably with latitude, altitude, soil, rainfall, and other local conditions. But even these variations conform to a general pattern or vegetational complex that characterizes the region. The boundaries are approximate, and near their limits there may be considerable intermixing with plants from adjoining regions, the extent often varying with physiographic determinants. For example, tongues of eastern woodland extend westward into the Prairies and pockets of upland prairies are found in the midst of the Rocky Mountains.

Range of green-winged teal in U.S.

Various subdivisions of these five primary regions have been used whenever the data were sufficient to justify the breakdowns or when the information represented smaller geographic units much better than the region as a whole. Thus northern or southern segments of regions (northern prairies, southern prairies, etc.) as well as even smaller units like states or parts of states (Ohio, California, coastal North Carolina, etc.) have been used as substitutes for the region as a whole. Another and opposite departure from the five-region standard occurs in the occasional combination of regions, or parts of regions, such as West (three western regions treated as one), Southwest (the southern part of the three western regions), North (the northern part of the entire country), etc. In short the geographic basis for data compilation has been kept flexible in order to make it adaptable to the varied situations encountered.

RANGE MAPS. Depicting the distribution of various kinds of plants and animals is a difficult matter—mainly because information on the territorial limits of wildlife species and of plants is rarely adequate enough for detailed mapping. Sometimes segments of the range of a species are known in detail because of intensive local studies, while the rest of the distribution is clouded by uncertainty. In some animals, migration adds a major complication. Further than this, ranges are not static; those of some plants as well as of many wildlife species have been shrinking while still others have been expanding. Because of inadequacies in detailed range information, small outline maps have been chosen for the present purpose. These range maps convey a quick, over-all picture of the distribution of the animal or plant without attempting to define limits precisely.

The range maps are based largely on *species* in the case of animals and *genera* for plants. This is the same basis on which food-habits data have been compiled and reported—by species (or occasionally by subspecies) of animals and by genera (in the main) of plants. The principal source of animal-range information has been the extensive records that have been accumulating in Federal government files since the Biological Survey's earliest explorations. Information used in preparing plant-range maps has been derived from numerous sources including various floras—both regional and local—check lists, monographs, and from first-hand knowledge obtained in field studies in all parts of the United States.

Crosshatching on range maps for mammals and sedentary birds indicates year-round presence of the species in the area so marked. In the case of migratory birds, seasonal distribution is shown by the direction of the slanting hatched lines. Summer range is denoted by downward (left to right) hatching and winter by upward (left to right) lines. The overlapping of summer and winter ranges results in crosshatching similar to that used for sedentary species.

Plant-range maps, in addition to showing the distribution of the plants—generally by simple hatching—sometimes present further information on abundance of the plants or the extent of their use by wildlife. In general the more close or dense the shading on the map, the more abundant is the genus or species.

33

INTERPRETING THE DATA OF THIS BOOK

In some generic maps, such as for oaks, lupines, and doveweeds, the number of species present in different parts of the country is indicated on a zonal basis. In these zoned maps, adding together the species in each of the zones will not necessarily give the correct total for the genus in its entire range since it commonly happens that certain widespread species are not confined to a single zone. Occasionally, separate "bulls-eyes" on the maps represent isolated occurrences.

SEASONAL UNITS. To indicate seasonal variations in food use, the four common units, winter, spring, summer, and fall, have been adopted. Biologists often employ a six-season system or use an ever greater number of units, but the pattern of four calendar seasons has two important advantages for present purposes: (1) The seasons coincide largely with major changes in wildlife diet, and (2) they have the obvious advantage of familiarity.

Practical use of the four-seasons system is possible only by applying flexibility and judgment. Seasons measured by fixed calendar dates are by no means equivalent in all parts of the country. Spring for Miami, Fla., is not spring for Bangor, Maine. Winter may arrive in parts of Idaho when it is still fall in North Carolina, and winter (as a cold season) may never arrive at all in Southern Arizona, Texas, or Southern California. New plant growth, emergence of insects, and the appearance of flowers and fruit vary with changes in length of day, in rise or fall of average temperature, and with other conditions that depend upon regional climate. Allowance had to be made for this in defining local seasons for wildlife.

Stomach contents collected during the first two or three months of the calendar year in peninsular Florida and in semitropical areas of the Southwest were tabulated with *spring* material. Contents collected early in April in the most northerly states were included with *winter*. These divergences in practice have tended to correlate the corresponding seasons in different regions or subregions without setting up an elaborate system of local wildlife seasons that would have made the compilation of general food-habits information impracticable.

Winter, for most wildlife, is a period of about five months—from November through March—beginning when deciduous woody plants have lost their leaves and continuing till buds swell and the first new vegetation appears. In the semitropical South, this season is, of course, shorter. But in both North and South it is a period of relative food scarcity with the readily available supply of insect and plant foods markedly reduced.

Spring, for much of the country, is confined to the two-month period of April and May, though in Southern California and Florida it arrives while winter is still prevailing over most of the land. The spring season is characterized by new vegetative growth and by the reappearance of numerous insect species. The typical summer period—June, July, and August—brings increased plant and insect food. Quantities of insects abound for fledgling birds as well as for their parents; early fruits and seeds are available; grasses are abundant for grazing animals; and marsh and aquatic plants are in full growth. Fall is a short, closing season—typically, the months of September and October. Insect populations drop off with the first frosts or with cooler weather, and the plant diet of many species increases during this season because of the relative abundance of matured seeds and fruits.

Seasonal indications are given in two places in the tables of data in Part II. The first is in the breakdown of the number of specimens examined. This appears at the head of the table after the name of the region. Thus for the baldpate (page 60) there is the listing: West 104 (73-2-1-28). This concise listing indicates that 73 of the 104 western baldpates studied were obtained in winter, 2 in spring, 1 in summer, and 28 in fall. This sequence of *winter*, *spring*, *summer* and *fall* is used regularly in parentheses to indicate the seasonal breakdown of stomach-analysis data. It immediately makes clear the strength or weakness of the data that follow. Information on most game species, as in the case of the baldpate, is mainly limited to that obtained from individuals bagged during the hunting season.

The table of data for the baldpate in the West, and practically all other tables, also shows another seasonal indication. This is the *season of use*, noted after the name of each plant. Thus, the first part of the baldpate table is as follows:

> *West,* 104 (73-2-1-28)
> *** Pondweed, veg. and sd. *SuFW*
> *** Widgeongrass *SuFW*
> ** Spikerush, veg. and sd. *FW*

The abbreviations, *W* for winter, *Sp* for spring, *Su* for summer, and *F* for fall indicate the season or seasons in which the plant or plant part was used. The table above shows that pondweeds were consumed by the baldpate in summer, fall, and winter. The seasons of use are listed in sequence, following the one in which the plant or plant part first became available for use. In tables where only one season is involved (as indicated in the table heading) seasonal symbols (*W Sp Su F*) are omitted.

COMMON NAMES. The priority given to the use of common names in this book is consistent with our purpose of serving the interests of the layman as well as the technician.

The common names used for plants are usually the ones given in the second edition of Standardized Plant Names.[1] This monumental reference has established the policy of combining the constituent words in many common names and eliminating most of the hyphens that have been used previously. Some of the long, compounded names, such as Russianthistle and the like, are likely to seem objectionable the first time they are met—and possibly even the second or third time.

Deviations from this source of names have been made occasionally. Mountain-ash, for example, has been kept as a hyphenated word. The plant is not a true ash, but when one word is made of the name, the eye is likely to combine *n* and *ash* into *nash*, ending up with a tongue twister. Some names, like sago pondweed and coontail, are in our opinion too well established in the minds of American sportsmen to be supplanted by fennelleaf pondweed and hornwort, the standardized designations. Other exceptions, for these and other reasons, have been made.

Common names of birds are more widely used than their Latin equivalent. The common names used here are based almost entirely on the American Ornithologists' Union Check List.[2] Exception has been made in one particular: the possessive apostrophe and *s* have been deleted from all names. Thus *Gambel's quail* becomes *Gambel quail*, *Audubon's warbler* becomes *Audubon warbler*, etc. This policy, for which there is growing support, prevails generally in the common names of mammals. The Latin binomials listed beneath the birds' common names vary from the Check List whenever it seemed advisable to bring the nomenclature up to date. There is no single recognized standard of nomenclature for mammals but names in this book are based largely on Anthony.[3]

[1] Standardized Plant Names. Harlan P. Kelsey and William A. Dayton. 2d ed. J. Horace McFarland Co., Harrisburg, Pa., 1942.

[2] A.O.U. Check List of North American Birds. 4th ed. American Ornithologists' Union, Lancaster, Pa., 1931.

[3] Field Book of North American Mammals. H. E. Anthony. G. P. Putnam's Sons, New York, 1928.

REFERENCES. Selected bibliographies of a few of the more outstanding works in the field concerned are supplied. The reference listings do not pretend to be complete.

Features of Part II (Animals)

ANIMAL GROUPS. The interest of the reader is likely to center in certain major animal groups that are distinct in habitat or in economic, game, or aesthetic value. Some people are particularly interested in waterfowl, some in large game animals, some in songbirds, some in fish, and others in rodents or other special groups. For this reason all the forms of wildlife dealt with in Part II have been grouped into natural or seminatural assemblages. Within each category, the

BIRD GROUPS

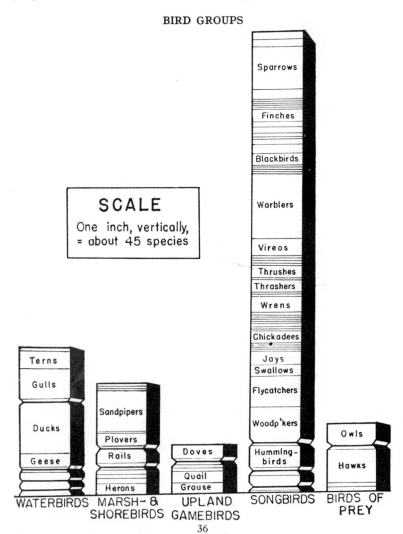

SCALE
One inch, vertically,
= about 45 species

animals are arranged in approximate natural sequence. The major groups themselves are also arranged in approximate natural order, except for the fish, amphibians, and reptiles which are placed at the end of the animal series because of their secondary importance in the book.

The size of the groups and identity of well-known representatives is indicated in the accompanying diagrams, one for birds, one for mammals and the third for amphibians and reptiles. Fish, not diagramed, include 1,700 species and about 100 orders in the United States.

MAMMAL GROUPS

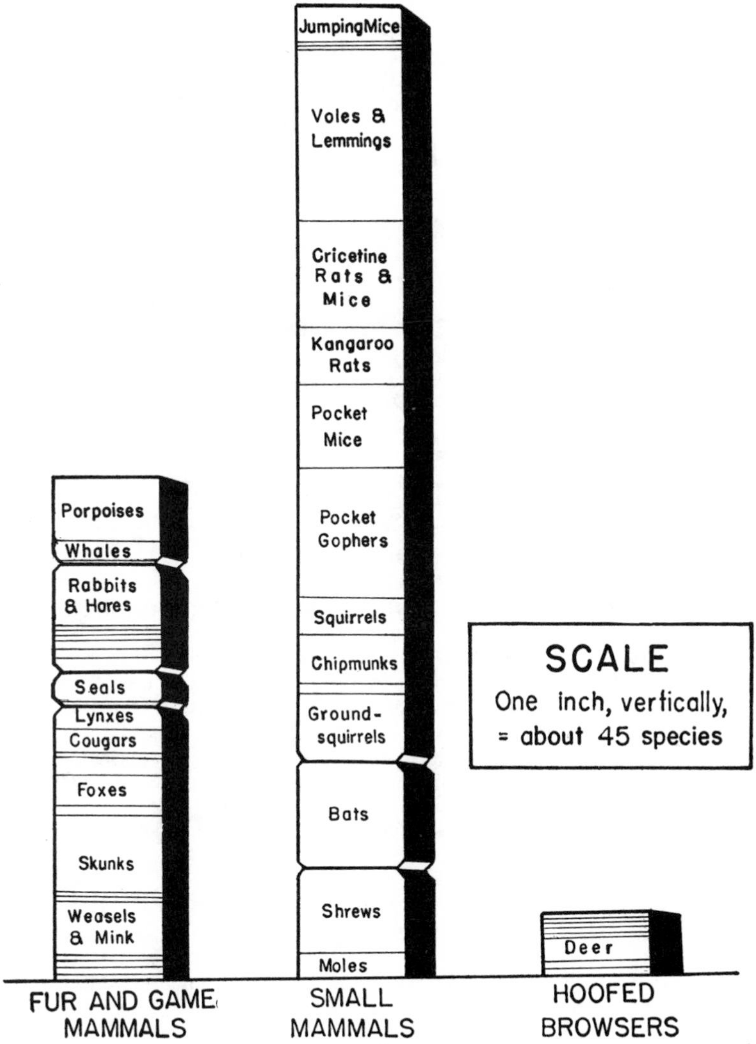

FUR AND GAME MAMMALS	Porpoises, Whales, Rabbits & Hares, Seals, Lynxes, Cougars, Foxes, Skunks, Weasels & Mink
SMALL MAMMALS	JumpingMice, Voles & Lemmings, Cricetine Rats & Mice, Kangaroo Rats, Pocket Mice, Pocket Gophers, Squirrels, Chipmunks, Ground-squirrels, Bats, Shrews, Moles
HOOFED BROWSERS	Deer

SCALE
One inch, vertically,
= about 45 species

37

ORDERS OF AMPHIBIANS AND REPTILES

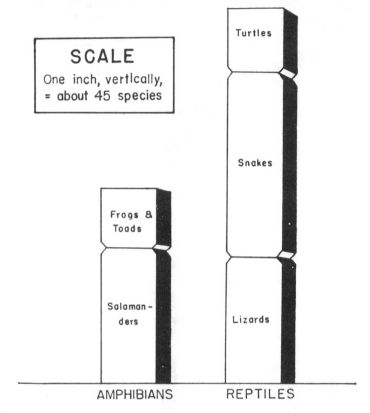

SCALE

One inch, vertically,
= about 45 species

Turtles

Snakes

Frogs &
Toads

Lizards

Salaman-
ders

AMPHIBIANS   REPTILES

NUMBER OF SPECIMENS EXAMINED. A dependable picture of wildlife food habits begins to emerge only when a large number of analyses has been made. The reliability and significance of such data depend in large measure on the breadth of their foundation. For this reason, the number of specimens (stomachs or crops unless specified otherwise) from which data were obtained is listed prominently in the heading of the table for each wildlife species treated. When field observations have played an important part as a source of information, this is noted also. In the case of our well-used example, the baldpate (page 60), the headings for the three regional tables indicate the number of species examined as follows (the figures in parentheses being the seasonal breakdown as explained earlier):

Northeast, 35 (6-12-1-16)
Southeast, 60 (52-8-0-0)
West, 104 (73-2-1-28)

ANIMAL-PLANT FOOD RATIO DIAGRAMS. Where data are sufficient, a ratio-graph has been prepared to show, at a glance, the seasonal changes in the proportions of plant and animal foods eaten. The ratio-graph is divided into the four unequal seasons, described previously. The shaded lower part denotes plant food, while the unshaded upper part represents animal food. Also indicated in the blocks above the season name is the number of specimens on which the seasonal information is based.

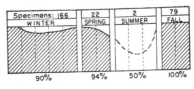

In instances where this number of individual specimens is definitely too low to be reliable, as when it falls below 10 for a season, the curve is denoted by a broken line and the shading is omitted, though the percentage figure is given below. If specimen numbers do not coincide with totals obtainable from accompanying regional data, this may be do to statistical limitations rather than error.

FOOD DATA. With each wildlife species that is not completely herbivorous—and only a small minority are wholly plant eaters—a concise summary of the principal flesh or insect foods is given under the heading Animal Food. Though this listing of animal foods is brief and without quantitative measure, it helps to round out the dietary picture in each instance. In the case of animals that are mainly or completely carnivorous or insectivorous, the dietary account is confined to a summary of principal types of food used.

Unless otherwise stated, seeds or fruits are the plant parts consumed. Ordinarily a plant name in a table implies that the seeds or fruits of that plant are the parts eaten. Exceptions are noted after the plant name, or as in the case of hoofed browsers and some others, the prevailing use of vegetative parts is indicated in comments preceding the tabular data.

Plant names included in the tables as wildlife food are listed in the collective singular (pondweed, oak, bristlegrass, etc.), regardless of whether one or many species are involved.

When more than one regional listing is included for a given animal species, the regional progression is given from East to West and secondarily from North to South.

Data have been assembled largely on species in the case of animals and on genera in plants. For a few animals, in certain regions or localities, food-use data presented in Part III relate to sub-species instead of species.

Features of Part III (Plants)

PLANT GROUPS. The 290 plant genera that have considerable food value to wildlife are organized under four major, somewhat arbitrary groupings in order to serve the practical convenience of individuals with special interests in forestry, farming, horticulture, waterfowl, ecology, or other phases of plant or wildlife management. The four categories are:

Woody Plants (trees, shrubs, and vines)................... Chap. Fourteen
Upland Weeds and Herbs............................... Chap. Fifteen
Marsh and Aquatic Plants............................. Chap. Sixteen
Cultivated Plants (grain crops, orchard trees, ornamentals, etc.). Chap. Seventeen

In addition, Chap. Eighteen gives listings of plant genera arranged according to their value to wildlife.

GENERIC BASIS. Plant data in the tables of food use are set up on a generic basis. But whenever possible, information on the importance of particular species is discussed in the treatment of the genus. The use of a generic foundation is a practical, realistic course. Our present knowledge about the relative wildlife value of various species within a plant genus is generally too meager, except in certain instances, to permit using the species as the primary basis. The identification of plant remains from stomach contents cannot be carried beyond the genus with consistent safety. Some species can be identified positively by their seeds or other plant parts, but many more cannot. Hence the necessity to consolidate data under the genus.

STAR-USER RATING OF PLANTS. Prominently placed in the treatment of each plant is a numerical ratio which gives a rough quantitative index of the value of the plant as a wildlife food. For example, on the first page devoted to oaks (page 308) is the ratio of 263*/96 users. The numerator, 263*, is the aggregate of stars recorded for the use of oaks by 96 kinds of animals in all regions—omitting subregions or states that would duplicate the use of the plant in any given region. In computing these totals a record such as ** Mouse, White-footed, *E*, would add four stars, two for the Northeast and two for the Southeast. Similarly * *W* means addition of three stars, one for each of the three western regions. Since the star aggregations are not of equal prorated value, *i.e.*, * equals 2 to 5%, but **** equals 25 to 50%, the totals do not give an exact mathematical basis, yet they provide a food-use index which, though approximate at best, is useful. The denominator, 96 users in this particular example, indicates the total species of animals that use acorns or other parts of oaks to an appreciable extent (½% or more). These figures make possible a quick, over-all interpretation of the use of the plant. A low numerator (stars) over a large denominator (users) indicates that the plant is used by many wildlife species but only to a limited extent by each. A higher numerator and small denominator characterizes a plant of great importance to a limited segment of our wildlife.

DATA ON PLANTS USED. In the presentations of data denoting the use of particular plants by wildlife (Part III) each heading for a category of animal user (Waterbirds, Hoofed Browsers, etc.) is followed by a parenthetical indication of the part or parts of the plant eaten. Thus under Maples, page 340, is the heading Songbirds (seeds, buds, flowers), making it clear that these are the main parts of maples eaten by songbirds. Exceptions to the use of parts specified are noted after the name of the animal concerned. Thus in the example cited, after yellow-bellied sapsucker (sap) is indicated as the part used by this particular bird.

If a plant or its parts are used to different extents by the same kind of animal in several different regions or subregions, priority is given to the region in which the use is greatest, and this is listed first. Thus, sagebrush (page 367), includes the listing:

*** Deer, Mule, *No.Mt.–Des.;* ** *So.Mt.–Des.;* * *Pac.*

Season of use of plant items is not indicated in these tables, since this information is already listed under the animal users in Part II and is available by cross reference to the particular wildlife species concerned.

Summary of Explanations

A digest of symbols, abbreviations, condensations, and other features of Parts II and III that need explanation is presented below. Whenever possible, examples or illustrative diagrams have been included:

INTERPRETING THE DATA OF THIS BOOK

ABBREVIATIONS

PLANT PARTS[1]

fr. = fruits
lf. = leaves

sd. = seeds
veg. = vegetative parts

REGIONS (in progression from East to West)

NE = Northeast
SE = Southeast
Pr. = Prairies

Mt.–Des. = Mountain-Desert
Pac. = Pacific

SEASONS

W = Winter (Nov. to Mar., typically)
Sp = Spring (April to May, typically)

Su = Summer (June to Aug., typically)
F = Fall (Sept. to Oct., typically)

ANIMAL GROUPS

The nine groups of animals named below are treated consecutively in chapters as indicated. Within the chapters, the species of animals are generally presented in natural family order.

BIRDS

Waterbirds (Chap. Five: ducks, geese, swan, herons, pelicans, etc.)
Marshbirds and Shorebirds (Chap. Six: sandpipers, rails, cranes, gulls, etc.)
Upland Gamebirds (Chap. Seven: quail, grouse, doves, turkeys, etc.)
Songbirds (Chap. Eight: sparrows, thrushes, woodpeckers, jays, blackbirds, etc.)
Birds of Prey (Chap. Nine: hawks, eagles, owls, vultures, etc.)

MAMMALS

Fur and Game Mammals (Chap. Ten: rabbits, foxes, skunks, squirrels, etc.)
Small Mammals (Chap. Eleven: ground squirrels, rats, mice, chipmunks, gophers, etc.)
Hoofed Browsers (Chap. Twelve: deer, elk, antelope, moose, etc.)
Fish, Amphibians, and Reptiles (Chap. Thirteen)

PLANT GROUPS

Woody Plants (Chap. Fourteen: trees, shrubs, and vines)
Upland Weeds and Herbs (Chap. Fifteen: wild herbaceous upland plants)
Marsh and Aquatic Plants (Chap. Sixteen: pondweeds, bulrushes, etc.)
Cultivated Plants (Chap. Seventeen: grain crops, orchard trees, ornamentals, etc.)
(Within each chapter the plants are presented in systematic sequence.)

ANIMAL-PLANT FOOD RATIO DIAGRAMS

These diagrams depict the relative proportion of animal-plant food consumed in different seasons of the year—the shaded portion of the graph representing the plant food. The number of specimens on which the data are based is indicated above each season, and the actual percentage is shown below.

[1] Unless otherwise specified the parts eaten are seeds or fruits.

INTERPRETING THE DATA OF THIS BOOK

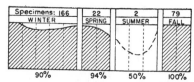

When the number of specimens examined is below 10 as for the summer season in this diagram, the curve is marked by a broken line with the shading below omitted.

Ratio diagram for baldpate

MAPS

BIRD RANGES

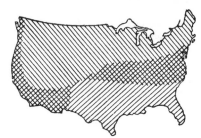

Downward hatching (left to right) = summer range.

Upward hatching (left to right) = winter range.

Crosshatching = (1) overlapping of winter and summer ranges, or (2) permanent range of sedentary species.

Range of robin in U.S.

MAMMAL RANGES

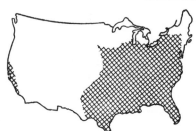

General range of the species is shown by crosshatching.

Range of opossum in U.S.

PLANT RANGES

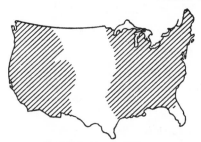

The majority of the plant-range maps are of a comparatively simple type, showing only the limits of distribution of the plant genus or occasionally of species.

Range of alders in U.S.

42

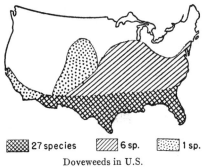

The more complex plant maps denote by comparative closeness of markings (crosshatching, simple hatching, dots, or broken lines) either (1) relative abundance (of species or individuals), or (2) relative extent of use by wildlife.

▓ 27 species ▨ 6 sp. ▨ 1 sp.

Doveweeds in U.S.

THE STAR SYSTEM OF RATING

— = Use of food item to an undetermined extent
+ = ½ to 2% of diet
* = 2 to 5% of diet
** = 5 to 10% of diet
*** = 10 to 25% of diet
**** = 25 to 50% of diet
***** = 50% or more of diet

STAR-USER RATING OF PLANTS

Filaree 84*/50 users

This rating example denotes the aggregate number of stars (84) for filaree based on its use by 50 different kinds of animal users in all regions concerned. For explanation of the method of totaling stars, see Tables of Data for Plants, following.

TABLES OF DATA FOR ANIMALS

Harris Sparrow

Eastern Prairies, 101 (75-21-0-5)
**** Ragweed *FWSp*
** Knotweed *WSp*
** Bristlegrass *FWSp*
** Corn *FWSp*
* Goosefoot *WSp*
* Oats *W*
+ Sunflower, Panicgrass, Timothy, Wheat

The numerals after the heading Eastern Prairies indicate that 101 stomachs of Harris sparrow were examined, 75 collected in winter, 21 in spring, none in summer, and 5 in the fall. The seasons of principal use are indicated after the name of the plants, for example: "Ragweed *FWSp*" means that the seeds of ragweed were eaten in the fall, winter, and spring.

TABLES OF DATA FOR PLANTS

Witch-hazel, 5*/6 users

Upland Gamebirds (seeds)
** Grouse, Ruffed, *Ohio*; * *Pa.*
+ Turkey, Wild, *E*
Fur and Game Mammals (bark, foliage, seeds)
— Beaver, *W.Va.*
+ Rabbit, Mearns Cottontail, *N.Y.*
* Squirrel, Fox, *Ohio*
Hoofed Browers (twigs, foliage)
** Deer, White-tailed, *N.Y.*

The wildlife species are listed alphabetically within the animal categories —using the generic common name (grouse, turkey, etc.) as the key word.

The star-user ratio (explained in the preceding topic) is 5*/6 users even though a total of 6 stars can be counted. Since Ohio and Pennsylvania are both in the Northeast region only one star rating (the largest) is recorded under ruffed grouse. The star rating for the region or subregion of greatest use is listed first, and to give the primary rating special prominence, it is placed in front of the animal's name, as is done with ratings for lesser use. Had the plus sign for wild turkey in the East been a star, the star-user ratio would have been 7*/6 users since one star would have to be added for both the Northeast and for the Southeast.

PART II

ANIMALS AND THEIR FOOD

Part II is concerned primarily with the birds and mammals of our forests and farms, mountains and plains, deserts and lakes. In particular, it deals with their food and feeding.

Presenting this information in a manner that will serve both popular and scientific purposes is a difficult task that has required compromise. For practical considerations, the animals have been grouped into nine major units, each of which is treated as a separate chapter.

The nine categories are as follows:

Within each of the chapters, the presentation of animals follows a natural, family-tree sequence. This has the important advantage of placing related forms of wildlife together. The phoebe and kingbirds are treated with other members of the flycatcher family, while the robin, bluebird, and veery are placed near their natural relatives in the thrush family. An alphabetical arrangement would not do this.

The treatment of species and genera in Part II is selective—if for no other reason than the impracticability of dealing equally with our 1,000 or more species of birds and mammals. Groups that make little or no use of plants for food receive only brief comment. So do those which are rare or have a limited range. Species which use more plant food are treated in greater detail, especially if they are of economic or recreational importance.

Information on the foods of hundreds of species of birds and mammals is an indispensable foundation for intelligent management of our wildlife. The wisdom of our present policies on the crow, robin, marsh hawk, gray fox, and many others depends on clear understanding of the dietary roles of these species. Likewise, success in increasing gamebirds, songbirds, and fur animals has its foundations in knowledge of their choice foods in various seasons of the year.

CHAPTER FIVE

Waterbirds

T HE CATEGORY WATERBIRDS embraces all members of the great natural family of waterfowl (ducks, geese, brant, and swan) plus several additional groups of birds that obtain their food largely from the water. Gulls, terns, and pelicans are included despite the fact that they spend much of their time resting on shore. Also the coot, because of its duck-like habits and habitat, has been brought forward from its marshland relatives, the rails. Shearwaters, petrels, alcids, and other oceanic birds that rarely reach our shores and bays have been excluded. Herons, egrets, and other shallow-water waders are grouped with related long-legged birds in Chap. Six, Marshbirds and Shorebirds. The groups treated in this chapter, in their natural sequence are:

Loons	Water-turkey	Coot
Grebes	Swan	Gulls
Pelicans	Geese	Terns
Cormorants	Ducks (including Mergansers)	Skimmer

The waterfowl segment of the waterbirds, particularly the ducks and geese, is regarded by many Americans as the country's greatest recreational asset. More than two million hunters go afield after these birds each year. Managing and perpetuating this national resource is a task that has been made increasingly difficult by advancing agricultural and industrial invasion of marsh and aquatic habitats as well as by the rise in number of duck hunters.

Waterfowl proper, plus the coot, are mainly plant feeders, but other waterbirds feed largely on animal life. For this reason, the heading Waterfowl is generally used in tables of plant-food data in Part III, as a substitute for the more inclusive heading Waterbirds. Geese, brant, and swan are almost entirely vegetarian, feeding largely on foliage and rootstock. Ducks are mainly omnivorous. The surface-feeding species and a few divers subsist largely on plants, while mergansers and sea ducks depend largely on animal food. The other groups of waterbirds feed mainly on fish, crustaceans, and mollusks.

General References: The Ducks, Geese and Swans of North America. F. H. Kortright. American Wildlife Institute, 1942. 476 pp.

North American Waterfowl. Albert M. Day. Stackpole and Heck, Inc., 1949. 329 pp.

Life Histories of North American Wild Fowl. Arthur Cleveland Bent. *U.S. National Museum Bul.* 126, 1923, 250 pp., and *Bul.* 130, 1925. 376 pp.

Life Histories of North American Diving Birds. Arthur Cleveland Bent. *U.S. National Museum Bul.* 107, 1919. 237 pp.

Loons: *Gaviidae*

LOONS. Three species of loons occur in the United States: the common, the red-throated, and the Pacific. In winter these large, long-necked, pointed-bill divers

are widely distributed along the Atlantic, Gulf, and Pacific coasts. In summer they are largely north of our borders, though a few nest in northern states.

Loons are entirely animal feeders, and the three species are similar in their food habits. Fish are the main food item—most of the kinds eaten being unsuitable for human food. Crabs, mollusks, frogs, and insects are also frequent in the diet.

Grebes: *Columbidae*

GREBES. Five species of grebes, or helldivers, are widely distributed throughout the country on inland lakes and along the coasts. In addition, the Mexican grebe is found in southern Texas.

These wary, diving birds are somewhat similar to loons but are smaller. Stomach analyses indicate that they eat proportionately less fish than loons, filling in the balance of their diet with crayfish, aquatic insects, mollusks, and small crustaceans. The fish consumed are usually small species, and there is very little indication of economic loss. Interesting to note is the fact that all grebes eat their own feathers; masses of feathers are commonly found in their stomachs.

The eared, Holboell, horned, Mexican, and western grebes are similar in their diet which includes the following in approximate order of importance: fish, aquatic insects, mollusks, and small crustaceans. The diet of the small, widespread pied-billed grebe differs in leading off with crustaceans, including crayfish, and then in order come small fish, mollusks, and aquatic insects.

Pelicans: *Pelecanidae*

PELICANS. There are two species of these large-billed fish eaters: the white pelican of the West and the Gulf region, and the brown pelican of warmer areas along all our marine coasts. Viewed resting on land, pelicans seem grotesque and ungainly, but in flight they are very graceful. Groups of them generally travel in single file, flying low over the water with alternating rhythm of a few wing beats followed by a long glide.

Pelicans eat almost nothing but fish. For this reason they have been accused of being harmful to man's interests. At one time the white pelican seemed doomed, mainly because of slaughter due to unwarranted prejudice. A number of careful studies in different areas has disclosed that probably less than 1% of the pelican's food is fish edible to man. More than 90% of the diet of pelicans in the Gulf region consists of menhaden—a noncommercial fish. These facts have made it possible to give the pelican needed protection, but a good deal of unjust prejudice against them still exists.

Reference: Birds in Relation to Fishes. Clarence Cottam and F. M. Uhler. *U.S. Fish and Wildlife Service Leaflet* 272, 1945. 16 pp.

Cormorants: *Phalacrocoracidae*

CORMORANTS. There are five or six species and several subspecies of these dark, long-necked waterbirds in the United States. Cormorants, also called shags, occur on the Great Lakes and in a few other inland localities, but they are found primarily near the coast. One often sees them flying low in single file, a short distance offshore.

All species of cormorants are similar in their diet which consists mostly of fish, with some crustaceans and marine worms. They feed on the surface but dive and swim under water as well. Cormorants have been persecuted by sportsmen and commercial fishermen on the assumption that the birds were serious competitors for desirable fish. Studies made along the coasts of this country and Canada indicate that this prejudice is unfair. In Maine (see reference below), "80% of the food eaten consisted of cunners or sculpins, which are known to be direct enemies of commercial fish."

Reference: Birds in Relation to Fishes. Clarence Cottam and F. M. Uhler. *U.S. Fish and Wildlife Service Leaflet* 272, 1945. 16 pp.

Water-turkey: *Anhingidae*

WATER-TURKEY. The water-turkey, or snakebird, is primarily a tropical species that ranges from the southern parts of the United States to northern Argentina. It ordinarily remains resident in the general vicinity of its nesting area.

The water-turkey is not only like the cormorant in appearance but also in its food habits. Fish are the principal mainstay—chiefly nongame species. Mullets, sunfish, catfish, suckers, and pickerel are among the kinds taken. Other food items include crayfish, crabs, shrimps, aquatic insects, tadpoles, water snakes, and small terrapins.

Swan, Geese, Ducks: *Anatidae*

SWAN. Two species of swan are native to the United States. The whistling swan is widely distributed along both our Atlantic and Pacific coasts in winter, while the nearly extinct trumpeter swan is confined to a few localities in the Northwest. Both of these magnificent waterfowl are making a comeback, though it is improbable that they will ever regain their former abundance.

Not much is known about the foods of swan. It appears that they subsist almost entirely on plants, but insects, crustaceans, and mollusks are also eaten as a minor part of their diet.

WHISTLING SWAN
Cygnus columbianus

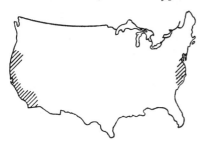

south as North Carolina) and Pacific coasts, but does not get into the Gulf region.

The total population of whistling swan, though considerable, is small compared with other species of waterfowl. Their numbers were once much greater. With protection, this bird is maintaining itself reasonably well, but it has not recovered sufficiently to be placed on the list of game species.

Of the two species of swan native to North America, the whistling swan is the smaller and more abundant. It winters along both our Atlantic (as far south as North Carolina) and Pacific

Animal food: The very small amount of animal items consumed includes larvae of aquatic beetles and of dragonflies.

Plant food: Swan require large quantities of food, and sometimes they are guilty of despoiling the duck food supply in hunting areas. They feed on grasses along margins of ponds and lakes as well as on aquatic plants.

East, 10 (8-2-0-0) and observations
*** Grasses, veg. *Sp*
*** Wildcelery, veg. *W*
*** Pondweed, Sago, veg. and sd. *W*

*** Smartweed, Ladysthumb *Sp*
** Spikerush, Squarestem, veg. and sd. *W*
** Arrowhead, veg. *FW*
* Mermaidweed *W*
+ Muskgrass, Bulrush, Horsetail
West, 5 (4-1-0-0)
**** Grasses, veg. *WSp*
*** Pondweed, Sago, veg. and sd. *W*
*** Horsetail, veg. *Sp*
*** Burreed, veg. and sd. *W*

TRUMPETER SWAN
Cygnus buccinator

The trumpeter swan, largest of all North American waterfowl, is reported to have once been a common bird in the northwestern states. By 1929, however, its numbers had hit a low of about 30 individuals in this country—with another and somewhat larger contingent in western Canada. Since then, with careful management and protection, the population of this magnificent bird has increased about tenfold over the 1929 minimum. The number in Canada is probably near 1,000.

Animal food: The scant firsthand information available shows no use of animal food, though the trumpeter is reported to feed on mollusks, crustaceans, and insects to some extent.

Plant food:
Montana and British Columbia, 6 (1-4-1-0) and observations
***** (60%) Pondweed, Sago, veg. and sd. *SuWSp*
** Waterbuttercup, White, veg. *SpSu*
** Arrowhead, veg. *SuF*
* Bulrush, veg. *Su*
* Moss, Aquatic, veg. *Sp*

GEESE. Six species of geese (including brant) winter in the United States. The majority concentrate in marshes on the Gulf coast or in other warm parts of the country. The six species are the Canada (including several subspecies, which some regard as species), snow, and white-fronted goose, the brant, and the blue and Ross goose. In addition, there are two other species that occasionally enter the northern corners of our country: the emperor goose on the Pacific coast and the barnacle goose on the Atlantic.

While wintering in this country, geese feed almost exclusively on plants, particularly on vegetative parts such as foliage and stems. Little is known about their food habits in summer. The arctic emperor goose is something of an exception. It is reputed to feed largely on shellfish.

CANADA GOOSE
Branta canadensis

The familiar Canada goose, or honker, has been divided into seven races or subspecies, groups which range from birds weighing about nine pounds

in two of the subspecies, down to three or four pounds in two others. The seven subspecies also differ from each other in markings and in geographic distribution.

The common Canada goose is the only subspecies wintering all along our coasts and in the southern half of the country. It nests in our northwestern states, in western Canada, and around Hudson Bay. Most of our food-habits data are from this common subspecies.

The cackling goose, a small race of small-sized individuals, winters exclusively in California valleys. The giant, dark, western Canada subspecies winters along the Pacific coast as far north as Alaska. Another race, the lesser Canada goose, winters along the Pacific and in the Southwest, while the Richardson goose goes way down into Mexico and is seen in this country only when in transit.

Canada geese, all races of them, are choice gamebirds. Hunters gladly spend hours stalking them for a good shot. The successful hunter is well repaid in sport and in several pounds of fine-tasting meat. For him, as well as for those who don't go gunning, the sight of geese, honking high above in flying wedges or in long undulating lines is an incomparable thrill.

Animal food: Ordinarily the winter diet of Canada geese includes little or no animal food.

Plant food: The winter food consists largely of vegetative parts of marsh plants. Rootstocks are especially sought.

Atlantic Coast, 48 (44-0-0-4) plus observations

**** Cordgrass, veg. *FW*
*** Widgeongrass, veg. *W*
*** Spikerush, veg. and sd. *W*
** Sea-lettuce, veg. *W*
+ Naiad, Glasswort, Eelgrass, Bulrush, Saltgrass

Gulf Coast, 10 (10-0-0-0) plus winter observations

*** Cordgrass, veg.
** Saltgrass, veg.
** Glasswort, veg.
** Bulrush, veg. and sd.
* Bermudagrass, veg.
* Naiad, veg.
* Lycium, fr. and veg.

Mt.-Desert (mainly Bear River Refuge, Utah), 183 (92-0-19-72) plus observations

*** Saltgrass, veg. *SuFW*
*** Pondweed, Sago, veg. *SuFW*
*** Glasswort, veg. *FW*
** Wheat, veg. *SuW*
** Bulrush, Alkali, veg. and sd. *FW*
** Widgeongrass, veg. *SuFW*
* Bromegrass, veg. *FW*
* Wildbarley, veg. *FW*
* Rabbitfootgrass, veg. *SuFW*
* Seepweed, veg. *FW*
* Peppergrass, veg. *FW*
+ Golden Dock, Saltbush, Arrowhead, Cattail, Alkaligrass

Pacific, 45 (35-0-1-9) plus observations

**** Pondweed, Sago, veg. *FW*
*** Barley, veg. and sd. *W*
*** Bulrush, Hardstem, veg. and sd. *FW*
** Wheat, veg. and sd. *W*
** Wildbarley, veg. *W*
** Bromegrass, veg. *W*
* Oats, Wild, veg. *W*
+ Tansymustard, Saltbush, Alkaligrass, Saltgrass

BRANT
Branta bernicla

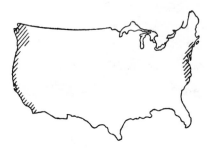

Specimens: 60	33	9	
WINTER	SPRING	SUMMER	FALL
100%	93%	94%	

The brant, or brant goose, is an arctic bird that winters on our Atlantic and Pacific coasts. It resembles its close relative the Canada goose—both belonging to the genus *Branta*. Two subspecies of brant occur in the United States: the common, or American, brant (*B. bernicla hrota*) in the East and the black brant (*B. bernicla nigricans*) in the Pacific region.

The common brant feeds in shallow coastal waters at ebb tide, pulling up rootstocks and leaves of its favorite food, eelgrass. When this marine plant was greatly depleted along the eastern seaboard by disease about 1931, the common brant suffered seriously. It had to turn to second-choice foods such as algae and widgeongrass. Recently, however, the eelgrass beds have made a good comeback, and so has this fine gamebird.

The black brant, like the eastern subspecies, feeds in eelgrass beds at low tide. Disease did not injure the West coast stands of eelgrass; so the black brant prospered while the eastern birds suffered hardships. Its population in California increased from nearly 50,000 in 1931 to much more than twice that number in 1935.

Animal food: Animal foods constitute only a small proportion of the diet, even in spring and summer. Principal animal items eaten are gastropods and bivalves, annelid worms, crustaceans, hydroids, and a few insects.

Plant food: The data on plant foods of the common brant are presented on the basis of two eras: the period before and the period after the eelgrass demise. These show the tremendous dietary change made to survive a natural emergency.

Atlantic Coast (N.C. to Quebec), 102 (60-33-9-0)
Prior to 1932, 29 (27-0-2-0)
***** (88%) Eelgrass, veg. *SuW*
** Widgeongrass, veg. *W*
+ Alga
1932 to 1941, 73 (33-33-7-0)
***** (76%) Alga, mainly Sea-lettuce *SuWSp*
*** Widgeongrass, veg. *W*
** (7%) Eelgrass, veg. *W*
+ Cordgrass
Pacific Coast, 62 (56-4-1-1)
**** Eelgrass, veg. *W*
* Surfgrass, veg. *W*
+ Alga

References: Food Habits and Management of American Sea Brant. Clarence Cottam, John J. Lynch, and Arnold L. Nelson. *Jour. Wildlife Mgt.*, Vol. 8(1), pp. 36–56, 1944.
Fifth Annual Black Brant Census in California. James Moffitt. *Calif. Fish and Game*, Vol. 21(4), pp. 343–350, 1935.

WHITE-FRONTED GOOSE
Anser albifrons

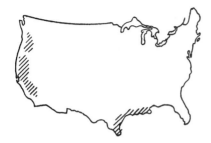

Valley of California. Here the birds feed in grain fields as well as in tule marshes—sometimes becoming pests to the farmers. The tule goose's nesting area, far up in the Arctic, was not discovered until 1941.

Food data on the two forms of the white-fronted goose are scant and are limited to winter feeding in this country.

There are two subspecies of the white-fronted goose—both found in the Far West. Because of dark streaks splotched horizontally across the underparts they are called speckle-bellies by sportsmen.

The regular whitefront (*A. albifrons albifrons*) comes from its nesting areas in the Arctic to wintering grounds on the Pacific coast, Gulf coast, and Mexico. It is more numerous than the similar but larger tule goose or tule whitefront (*A. albifrons gambelli*). The latter has a distinct and very limited wintering range in the Sacramento

Louisiana, winter observations
 ** Panicgrass, veg.
 * Sawgrass, veg.
Oklahoma, fall observations
 ** Wheat, veg. and sd.
California (whitefront), 11 (6-0-0-5)
 *** Rice *FW*
 *** Grasses and Sedges, veg. *FW*
 ** Wildmillet, sd. and veg. *FW*
 * Barley *W*
California (tule whitefront), 27 (25-0-0-2)
 *** Barley *F*
 *** Wheat, veg. *W*
 ** Cattail, rootstock *W*
 ** Bulrush, rootstock *W*

SNOW GOOSE
Chen hyperborea

The snow goose earns its name by being snow-white except for black wing tips, and by nesting in the land of arctic snows. It winters along the coasts of the United States.

Two subspecies of snow geese are recognized: the greater snow goose and

the lesser. One is simply larger than the other. Though regarded as less choice gamebirds than the Canada goose, hunting has helped reduce the population far below its former level. Nevertheless the number of snow geese compares well with the Canada goose, as judged by recent field estimates.

Food information for this species is limited almost entirely to studies on wintering grounds in this country.

East, 9 (6-3-0-0) plus observations
 *** Cordgrass, Saltmarsh, rootstock *Sp*
 * Saltgrass, veg. *W*
 * Horsetail, veg. *W*
 * Wildrice, veg. *Sp*

Gulf Coast, winter observations
** Bulrush, Saltmarsh and Olney, rootstock
** Cattail, rootstock
** Spikerush, Squarestem, veg. and sd.
** Cordgrass, rootstock
* Panicgrass, veg.
* Rice

West (mainly Bear River Refuge, Utah), 3 (2-0-0-1) plus observations
*** Bulrush, rootstock *F*
*** Wheat, veg. *FW*
* Wildbarley, veg. *F*
* Buffalograss, veg. *F*
* Glasswort, veg. *F*
* Horsetail, veg. *F*
* Saltgrass, veg. and sd. *F*

Reference: Family Life of the Snow Goose. John J. Lynch. *Audubon Magazine*, Vol. XLVI (1), 1944. 6 pp.

BLUE GOOSE
Chen caerulescens

Relatively few people have an opportunity to see the blue goose, and for this reason it is often thought to be a rare species. Actually the blue goose population is as great as that of several of our well-known ducks. All the blue geese converge into the very limited wintering area in coastal Louisiana. Hence, only stragglers are likely to be seen elsewhere. The breeding territory of this goose was a mystery until 1929 when J. Dewey Soper discovered part of the nesting grounds far up in the Canadian Arctic—about 3,000 miles from the Louisiana coast.

Data on foods of the blue goose are confined largely to studies made on birds obtained from the Gulf coast.
Animal food: None.
Plant food: Rootstocks and other vegetative parts of marsh plants constitute the principal winter food of this goose.

Gulf Coast, 26 (26-0-0-0) plus winter observations
**** Bulrush, rootstock and sd., mainly Common, Olney, Threesquare, and Saltmarsh
** Cattail, rootstock
** Cordgrass, rootstock
** Saltgrass, rootstock
** Spikerush, Squarestem, veg. and sd.
+ Panicgrass, rootstock
Prairies, 11 (3-3-0-5)
**** Cattail, rootstock *FW*
*** Grasses, veg. *SpW*
** Horsetail, rootstock *W*

Reference: Life History of the Blue Goose. J. Dewey Soper. Boston Society of Natural History, 1943. 97 pp.

ROSS GOOSE
Chen rossii

The Ross goose is the smallest of our geese—a duck-like miniature of the snow goose. It's population is also the lowest. In recent years estimates of the total numbers of birds in the wintering area usually ran into the hundreds or low thousands. Now, and for quite a few years, there has been a completely closed season on the Ross goose, but even with this protection its existence

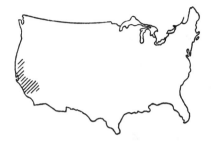

dant and was sought and killed by market hunters.

These geese nest in a remote, restricted area north of the arctic circle. The locality was not discovered till 1940. They winter in the central valleys of California. Only a little has been learned about their winter feeding, but even less is known about the arctic foods they eat during the summer.

seems precarious. It is hard to believe that at one time the species was abun-

California, 6 (6-0-0-0)
***** (83%) Oats, sd. and veg.
* Barley, sd. and veg.

DUCKS. Ducks are classified into five subfamilies. Three of these (the tree ducks, the ruddy duck subfamily, and the mergansers, or fish ducks) are of minor interest. The surface-feeding ducks (*Anatinae*) and the diving ducks (*Aythyinae*) furnish the bulk of our duck population and practically all of our game species. These two major groups (except for some of the seafaring members) are plant feeders in large degree. The ruddy duck also feeds on plant material to a considerable extent.

Among the diving ducks are a number of marine species, known as sea ducks, that eat little or almost no plant food. These include the several species of eider ducks, the harlequin ducks, and the old squaw—all northern birds that winter sparingly along our Atlantic and Pacific seaboards or on the Great Lakes. None are important as game species. The scoters are also sea ducks, but their diet includes slightly larger proportions of plant food. The diet of various sea ducks is largely similar in containing crustaceans (shrimps, amphipods, and hermit crabs) and mollusks as the principal food. These are supplemented by aquatic insects, fish, starfish, worms, sea urchins, and sea anemones. Food-habits studies have indicated that neither the mollusks nor the crustaceans eaten by sea ducks are kinds that have value for man.

The fulvous and the black-bellied tree ducks occur near the southern limits of the United States, from Texas to California. These goose-like ducks are not present in this country in sufficient numbers to be significant as game. Information on their foods is negligible.

The mergansers are represented by three species in this country. The common (American) and red-breasted are similar and closely related, while the hooded merganser is so distinct that it is placed in a separate genus. These diving ducks are primarily fish eaters. Crayfish, shrimps, frogs, insects, and mollusks make up the rest of their diet. Plant food is generally negligible. There can be no doubt that, locally, mergansers—especially the common merganser—cause appreciable destruction of fish. In the main, however, the popular opinion of damage done by these birds represents some exaggeration. A study of 107 stomachs of common mergansers, collected in large part from trout streams, gave evidence that trout and other good pan fish constituted nearly a third of the diet while low-grade and rough fish made more than 40% of the whole. Examination of 130 red-breasted merganser stomachs revealed not a single trout, though about 14% of the food consisted of pan fish. This is explained partly by the fact that, while the common merganser is largely a bird of inland waters, the red-breasted is a marine species during winter. The handsome hooded merganser eats a somewhat smaller proportion of fish than do the other two species.

References: Birds in Relation to Fishes. Clarence Cottam and F. M. Uhler. *U.S. Fish and Wildlife Service Leaflet* 272, 1945. 16 pp.
Food Habits of North American Diving Ducks. Clarence Cottam. *U.S. Dept. Agr. Tech. Bul.* 643, 1939. 140 pp.

COMMON MALLARD
Anas platyrhynchos

Specimens: 1666	26		123
WINTER	SPRING	SUMMER	FALL
91%	82%		93%

The mallard is the most important and most abundant duck in the country. It is widely distributed over much of the Northern Hemisphere.

The typical habitat for this best known of our ducks is inland ponds, shallow lakes, sloughs, and rivers. It is characteristic of mallards occasionally to leave the water and forage on upland areas for food. They not only seek acorns that have dropped to the ground, but they also invade grain fields in some localities. Their damage to grain crops has created a real problem in the Texas Panhandle and some other western areas.

Animal food: As indicated in the food-ratio diagram, the mallard is largely vegetarian. Over half of its limited animal diet consists of aquatic beetles and their larvae, nymphs of dragonflies and damselflies and adults and nymphs of aquatic bugs. Mayflies, stoneflies, and caddisflies also are consumed, usually as larvae.

Plant food: Though the mallard subsists primarily on marsh and aquatic plants, the upland feeding of this species on acorns and farm crops such as corn, sorghum, barley, and wheat is significant, as shown in the tables of data.

Northeast, 165 (98-8-0-59)
    *** Wildrice *FWSp*
    *** Pondweed, sd. and veg. *FW*
    *** Smartweed *FWSp*
     ** Wildcelery, veg. and sd. *SpF*
     ** Wildmillet *FWSp*
      * Naiad, veg. and sd. *FW*
      * Corn *W*
      * Cutgrass, Rice, sd. and corms, *W*
      * Oak *FW*
      + Burreed, Coontail, Arrowhead, Bulrush, Duckweed, Watershield, Buttonbush, Widgeongrass, Muskgrass

Southeast, 266 (266-0-0-0)
     ** Wildmillet *W*
     ** Smartweed *W*
     ** Bulrush *W*
     ** Duckweed, veg. *W*
     ** Spikerush *W*

** Pondweed, sd. and veg. *W*
** Rice *W*
* Naiad, veg. and sd. *W*
* Widgeongrass, sd. and veg. *W*
* Oak *W*
* Arrowhead, tuber *W*
* Coontail, sd. and veg. *W*
* Buttonbush *W*
* Chufa, tuber and sd. *W*
* Baldcypress *W*
+ Wildrice, Corn, Beakrush, Sawgrass, Watershield, Cordgrass, Burreed, Sweetgum, Horned-pondweed
West (excl. Pacific), 68 (30-0-7-31)
*** Pondweed, sd. and veg. *SuFW*
*** Bulrush *SuFW*
** Sorghum *W*
** Horned-pondweed, sd. and veg. *Su*
* Wildmillet *FW*
* Spikerush *SuFW*
* Muskgrass, veg. *FW*

* Corn *FW*
* Sedge *SuF*
* Alga, veg. *SuFW*
+ Coontail, Marsilea, Smartweed, Widgeongrass, Chufa, Burreed, Watermilfoil, Oats
Pacific, 87 (58-0-0-29)
*** Pondweed, sd. and veg. *FW*
*** Bulrush *FW*
** Barley *FW*
* Spikerush *FW*
* Watermilfoil *FW*
* Smartweed *FW*
* Oats *W*
* Marestail, sd. and veg. *FW*
* Cowlily *FW*
* Burreed *FW*
* Waterhemlock *FW*
* Arrowgrass *F*
+ Alfalfa, Eelgrass, Wheat, Sorghum, Cyperus, Widgeongrass

BLACK DUCK
Anas rubripes

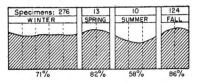

The black duck is a near relative of the common mallard but has a more restricted range. It may be found in creeks, ponds, and coastal marshes from the Gulf coast up into eastern Canada.

The black duck is heavily hunted in a region where some other species have diminished in number; yet it is more than holding its own. The total population of this species compares well with other ducks that have a much larger range.

Animal food: Black ducks subsist on animal food to a much greater extent than mallards. Those feeding in brackish coastal bays use animal foods the most. Half of the animal diet consists of mollusks, particularly univalves. Next in importance are crustaceans and insects—particularly immature stages of aquatic beetles, bugs, and dragonflies. Fishes are consumed to a limited extent.

Plant food:
Northeast, 256 (112-14-4-126)
*** Pondweed, veg. and sd. *SuFSp*
** Wildrice *FWSp*
** Cordgrass *FW*

** Bulrush *FW*
* Smartweed *FW*
* Widgeongrass, veg. and sd. *FW*
* Burreed *SuFW*
* Wildcelery, veg. and sd. *FW*
* Arrowhead *F*
* Eelgrass, veg. and sd. *FW*
* Corn *FW*
* Naiad, veg. and sd. *SpSuF*
* Sedge *SpSuF*
+ Alga, Duckweed, Pickerelweed, Waterhemp, Arrowgrass, Spikerush, Muskgrass

Southeast, 82 (82-0-0-0)
*** Pondweed, veg. and sd.
** Smartweed
** Naiad, veg. and sd.
** Alga, veg.
** Widgeongrass, veg. and sd.
** Spikerush
* Wildrice
* Bulrush
* Cordgrass
+ Holly, Beakrush, Wildcelery, Corn, Saltgrass, Pickerelweed

MOTTLED DUCK
Anas fulvigula

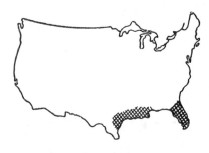

The mottled duck and Florida duck are closely related subspecies. Both are treated here under the heading Mottled Duck. These nonmigratory mallard-like ducks are the only ones remaining regularly in the Gulf coast marshes after spring migration. For this reason they are often called summer ducks.

Of the two subspecies, the one more commonly known as the mottled duck (*A. fulvigula maculosa*) has the wider distribution, ranging from Louisiana to Texas in the coastal sections. Its population is small but appears to be maintaining itself. The other subspecies, *A. fulvigula fulvigula*, is generally called the Florida duck. It is lighter colored and is limited in range to the peninsular part of Florida. Its population is also small but reasonably constant.

Animal food: The mottled duck (using the name in the inclusive sense) consumes a higher proportion of animal food than any other nondiving duck. Five-eighths of the animal diet consists of mollusks, particularly snails. Insects, chiefly dragonfly nymphs, water bugs, caddisfly larvae, water beetles, and horsefly larvae, are next in importance. Crustaceans and fishes make up the balance.

Plant food: The plant food consists primarily of seeds.

Gulf Coast, 57 (29-2-23-3)
**** Bulrush *SuFW*
*** Spikerush *SuFW*
** Rice *W*
** Pickerelweed *Su*
** Naiad, veg. and sd. *Sp*
* Sawgrass *SuWSp*
* Paspalum *W*
* Duckweed, veg. *Su*
+ Wildmillet, Banana Waterlily, Widgeongrass, Arrowhead, Smartweed

Florida, 40 (25-11-4-0)
*** Smartweed *WSpSu*
*** Panicgrass *Su*
** Chufa, veg. *WSp*
* Bayberry *WSp*
* Cowlily *WSp*
+ Buttonbush, Holly, Sawgrass, Beakrush, Spikerush, Waterlily

GADWALL
Anas streperus

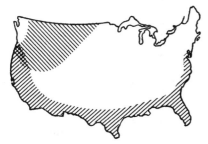

Specimens: 288	5	1	83
WINTER	SPRING	SUMMER	FALL
98%	80%	95%	97%

The gadwall is recognized as one of the world's most widely distributed ducks. It is found in Europe, Asia, Africa, and North America. We know it primarily as a bird of the West. The gray duck, as it is often called, is partial to fresh-water ponds and sloughs in the interior of the country, but in winter it may be found associated with other species along the coasts or southward.

Animal food: Only a very small proportion of animal food is eaten by the gadwall. Of this limited amount, about three-fourths consists of mollusks, particularly snails. Caddisfly adults and larvae, true flies and their larvae, bugs, beetles, dragonflies and damselflies and their nymphs, plus other miscellaneous insects make up the remaining quarter of the animal diet.

Plant food:
Southeast, 256 (254-2-0-0)
*** Widgeongrass, veg. and sd. *W*
*** Bulrush *W*
** Alga (incl. Muskgrass), veg. *W*
** Arrowhead, tuber *W*
** Naiad, veg. and sd. *W*
** Coontail, veg. and sd. *W*
* Pondweed, veg. and sd. *W*
+ Baldcypress, Axonopus, Buttonbush, Panicgrass, Spikerush, Sawgrass
West, 114 (29-3-1-81)
*** Pondweed, veg. and sd. *SuFWSp*
*** Alga, incl. Muskgrass, veg. *FWSp*
*** Horned-pondweed, veg. and sd. *SuFWSp*
** Widgeongrass, veg. and sd. *SuFWSp*
* Bulrush *SuFWSp*
* Wildmillet *FW*
+ Naiad, Wildbarley, Smartweed, Glasswort

BALDPATE
Mareca americana

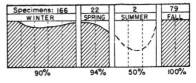

Specimens: 166	22	2	79
WINTER	SPRING	SUMMER	FALL
90%	94%	50%	100%

The baldpate, also known as widgeon, is one of our more abundant ducks. Though baldpates nest in the north-western part of the United States, their main breeding range extends northward through western Canada into Alaska. They winter near our southern borders, along both the Pacific and Atlantic coasts, as well as in Mexico.

In their feeding, baldpates resemble the coot in concentrating on vegetative parts of aquatic plants. Often they help themselves to vegetation that diving ducks bring to the surface. In some localities where alfalfa or garden crops are irrigated, baldpates become a nuisance by raiding these cultivated plants.

Animal food: The small amount of animal food in the baldpate's diet consists mostly of mollusks and aquatic insects and, to a small extent, other insects, sand fleas, and other small crustaceans.

Plant food:

Northeast (excl. Wis.), 35 (6-12-1-16)
- *** Pondweed, veg. and sd. *FW*
- *** Widgeongrass, veg. and sd. *FW*
- ** Naiad, veg. and sd. *SpF*
- ** Cutgrass, Rice *Sp*
- ** Muskgrass, veg. *Sp*
- ** Bulrush *SpF*
- * Wildcelery, veg. and sd. *SpF*
- * Wildrice *F*
- * Alga, veg. *SpF*

- * Wildmillet *Sp*
- * Burreed *F*
- \+ Eelgrass, Duckweed, Smartweed, Sedge

Southeast, 60 (52-8-0-0)
- *** Widgeongrass, veg. and sd. *W*
- ** Pondweed, veg. and sd. *W*
- ** Naiad, veg. and sd. *W*
- ** Bulrush *W*
- * Muskgrass, veg. *W*
- * Horned-pondweed, veg. and sd. *W*
- * Panicgrass *Sp*
- \+ Alligatorweed, Wildcelery, Coontail, Spikerush, Alga

West, 104 (73-2-1-28)
- *** Pondweed, veg. and sd. *SuFW*
- *** Widgeongrass *SuFW*
- ** Spikerush, veg. and sd. *FW*
- ** Alga, veg. *FW*
- ** Alfalfa, veg. and sd. *W*
- ** Eelgrass, veg. and sd. *W*
- * Bulrush *FW*
- * Wildmillet *W*
- * Watermilfoil, veg. and sd. *FW*
- \+ Smartweed, Barley, Muskgrass, Arrowgrass, Marestail

PINTAIL
Anas acuta

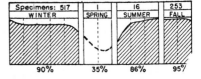

Specimens: 517	1	16	253
WINTER	SPRING	SUMMER	FALL
90%	35%	86%	95%

In point of total population, the pintail is the number two duck of this country. In the estimate of sportsmen it is one of the choicest species. Pintails breed throughout most of the Northwest, up through western Canada, and Alaska.

This attractive shoal-water species is most plentiful in the West. In winter large numbers concentrate along the Gulf coast of Texas and Louisiana—especially in the vicinity of rice fields. Winter flocks also occur on the Atlantic coast as far north as Chesapeake Bay. The handsome males, with distinctive long pointed tails are easily recognized in flight and on the water.

Animal food: The small amount of animal food eaten by the pintail includes mollusks (particularly univalves), crustaceans (especially crabs), aquatic beetles and their larvae, fly larvae, and also other aquatic insects. Among the miscellaneous animal food items are small fish, frogs, water mites, hydroids, and marine worms.

Plant food:

Northeast, 88 (47-1-5-35)
*** Bulrush *SuFW*
*** Smartweed *SuFW*
*** Pondweed, sd. and veg. *SuFW*
** Wildmillet *FW*
** Wildrice *FW*
 * Spikerush *FW*
 * Alga, veg. *F*
 * Naiad, veg. and sd. *F*
 + Corn, Wildcelery, Rice Cut-
    grass, Watershield, Sedge
Southeast, 376 (328-0-0-48)
** Widgeongrass, veg. and sd. *FW*

** Muskgrass, veg. *FW*
** Bulrush *W*
** Glasswort *FW*
 * Pondweed, sd. and veg. *FW*
 * Rice *W*
 * Corn *W*
 * Arrowhead, tuber *W*
 * Smartweed *W*
 * Wildmillet *W*
 + Waterlily, Naiad, Spikerush,
    Sawgrass, Chufa, Horned-
    pondweed, Watershield
West, 278 (127-0-11-140)
*** Pondweed, sd. and veg. *SuFW*
*** Bulrush *SuFW*
** Wildmillet *SuFW*
 * Widgeongrass, veg. and sd.
    SuFW
 * Smartweed *FW*
 * Spikerush *FW*
 * Barley *W*
 + Rice, Horned-pondweed, Alga,
    Bristlegrass, Arrowgrass,
    Marestail, Watermilfoil,
    Eelgrass

GREEN-WINGED TEAL
Anas carolinense

Specimens: 304	30	4	260
WINTER	SPRING	SUMMER	FALL
91%	86%	100%	86%

The green-winged teal is the baby of the duck family. It is smaller than the other two American teal. The greenwing is especially rapid in flight— its compact formations wheeling and changing direction with lightning precision. Despite its small size, this widespread, well-known species is a favorite with the hunter.

Frequently, and rather characteristically, the green-winged teal is seen foraging for food near the margins of sloughs, ponds, or lakes. It often tips for submerged food or sometimes takes items that diving ducks have brought to the surface.

Animal food: Half of its meager animal diet consists of insects, chiefly beetles, bugs, dragonfly and damselfly nymphs, caddisfly larvae, and diptera larvae. The other half consists of mollusks, mostly snails, and various small crustaceans.

Plant food: Seeds play an especially prominent role in the food of the greenwing.

Northeast, 104 (13-15-0-76)
*** Bulrush *SpF*
** Muskgrass, veg. *SpF*
** Wildrice *FW*
** Wildmillet *W*
** Sedge *WSp*
** Cyperus *WSp*
* Naiad, sd. and veg. *F*
* Smartweed *FWSp*
* Bristlegrass *Sp*
* Duckweed, veg. *FW*
* Pondweed *SpF*
* Spikerush *FW*
+ Pigweed, Widgeongrass, Wild-celery, Cordgrass, Horned-pondweed, Rice Cutgrass

Southeast, 170 (145-9-1-15)
*** Panicgrass *FWSp*
*** Bulrush *FWSp*
** Duckweed, veg. *FW*
* Wildmillet *WSp*
* Spikerush *WSp*
* Smartweed *WSp*

* Pondweed, sd. and veg. *W*
* Cyperus *W*
+ Muskgrass, Sawgrass, Water-hyssop, Buttonbush, Paspalum, Wildrice, Rice, Widgeongrass, Watermilfoil

West, 227 (98-6-4-119)
*** Pondweed, sd. and veg. *SuFWSp*
*** Bulrush *SuFW*
** Wildmillet *FWSp*
** Smartweed *FWSp*
** Spikerush *FW*
* Muskgrass, veg. *FW*
* Widgeongrass, veg. *SuWSp*
* Horned-pondweed, sd. and veg. *SuFWSp*
* Cyperus *FWSp*
* Sedge *FWSp*
* Cattail *W*
+ Duckweed, Barley, Arrowgrass, Pigweed, Sorghum

BLUE-WINGED TEAL
Anas discors

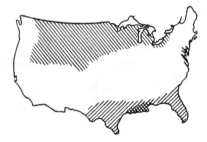

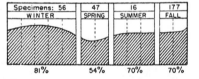

Specimens: 56	47	16	177
WINTER	SPRING	SUMMER	FALL
81%	54%	70%	70%

The blue-winged teal's breeding range includes the Prairie region of Canada and the northern part of the United States, but there are also many additional isolated localities where a few pair may be found nesting. It winters from the Gulf states southward into Central America and northern South America. The early fall migration of the bluewing and its adaptability to sloughs and small farm ponds may help to account for the fact that this species has fared better than some other ducks.

This summer teal is a quiet, relatively tame duck—a favorite game species. It is credited with great speed, but in migration its flight has been calculated at a modest 30 to 40 miles an hour. Probably its maximum speed is not much greater than this. The comparatively small size of teal doubtless contributes to the popular impression of their great speed.

Animal food: About a quarter of the total diet of the blue-winged teal consists of animal material, and of this, more than one-half is snails and other mollusks. Insects, especially larvae of caddisflies, dragonflies, and damselflies, bugs and beetles make up most of the balance. Crustaceans are a minor constituent.

Plant food: As compared with the diet of other ducks, seeds are especially prominent, though vegetative parts are also consumed freely.

Northeast, 113 (3-18-10-82)
*** Duckweed, veg. *SuF*
** Naiad, veg. and sd. *SpSuF*
** Pondweed, veg. and sd. *FWSp*
** Bulrush *SuFWSp*
* Smartweed *FWSp*
* Widgeongrass, veg. and sd. *FWSp*
* Wildrice *F*
* Cutgrass, Rice *SpSuF*
* Sedge *SpF*

* Spikerush *SpF*
+ Bristlegrass, Muskgrass. Arrowhead, Burreed, Watermilfoil, Wildmillet, Alga
Southeast, 91 (48-24-1-18)
*** Smartweed *SuFWSp*
** Widgeongrass, veg. and sd. *FWSp*
** Bulrush *FWSp*
* Spikerush *FW*
* Sawgrass *FW*
* Waterlily *FW*
* Cyperus *FW*
* Panicgrass *FWSp*
* Alga, veg. *Sp*
* Rice *F*
+ Buttonbush, Muskgrass, Duckweed, Wildmillet, Wildrice, Pondweed, Burreed
West, 47 (0-5-5-37)
*** Bulrush *SpSuF*
*** Smartweed *SpSuF*
** Widgeongrass, veg. and sd. *SuF*
** Bristlegrass *SpSu*
* Pondweed, veg. and sd. *F*
* Ragweed *SpSu*
* Muskgrass, veg. *F*
* Sedge *Sp*
* Spikerush *Su*
* Saltgrass *Su*
+ Buttercup, Cyperus

Reference: The Blue-winged Teal: Its Ecology and Management. Logan J. Bennett. Collegiate Press, Inc., 1938. 144 pp.

CINNAMON TEAL
Anas cyanoptera

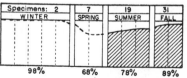

Specimens:	2	7	19	31
	WINTER	SPRING	SUMMER	FALL
	98%	68%	78%	89%

This small, rusty-colored westerner may be more properly called "ours" than most ducks, for the reason that

the major part of its breeding range is within the United States. Interestingly enough, cinnamon teal—exactly the same species—also live in temperate South America, over 2,000 miles to the south. No migration is known to occur between these two isolated colonies.

The cinnamon teal is a comparatively tame duck, of rapid flight. Most hunting of it must be done in Mexico where the species winters.

Animal food: About half of the limited animal diet consists of insects, and the other half mollusks. Among the insects eaten are beetles, bugs, dragonfly and damselfly nymphs, and fly larvae. The mollusks include both snails and bivalves.

Plant food: Like other teal, the cinnamon feeds commonly along the margins of lakes and ponds, picking up seeds that have drifted there as well as consuming vegetative parts of plants.

Mt.–Desert and Pacific, 59 (2-7-19-31)
*** Bulrush *SuFW*
*** Pondweed, sd. and veg. *SpSuF*
** Horned-pondweed, sd. and veg. *Su*
** Saltgrass *SpF*
** Sedge *Su*
* Widgeongrass, sd. and veg. *SuF*
* Smartweed *FSp*
* Dock *SpSu*
* Spikerush *SuFWSp*
+ Burreed, Duckweed, Cyperus, Watermilfoil

SHOVELLER
Spatula clypeata

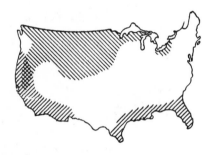

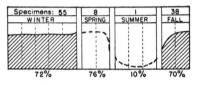

Specimens: 55	8	1	38
WINTER	SPRING	SUMMER	FALL
72%	76%	10%	70%

various aquatic insects, particularly water bugs, aquatic beetles, caddisfly larvae, and nymphs of dragonflies and damselflies; and crustaceans, especially ostracods and copepods.

This large-billed shoal-water duck is a moderately plentiful species. It is not nearly so abundant as some other ducks; yet it is far from being rare. Its widespread winter range extends along the Pacific, Gulf, and South Atlantic coasts.

The shoveller, or spoonbill as it is often called, feeds in the same varied habitats as other nondiving species. Often it employs its large bill to scoop up and sift organic material from mucky bottoms. A good part of its animal food is obtained this way.

Animal food: About one-fourth of the shoveller's food is animal as follows: mollusks, mostly fresh-water univalves;

Plant food:
Southeast, 43 (36-6-0-1)
*** Bulrush *W*
** Pondweed, veg. and sd. *W*
* Alga, veg. *Sp*
* Waterlily *W*
* Sawgrass *W*
* Duckweed, veg. *W*
* Spikerush *W*
* Widgeongrass, veg. and sd. *W*
* Wildmillet *W*
+ Muskgrass, Sedge, Naiad, Saltgrass, Horned-pondweed, Smartweed
West, 53 (18-0-0-35)
*** Pondweed, veg. and sd. *FW*
** Bulrush *FW*

** Spikerush *W*
** Saltgrass *W*
* Sedge *FW*
* Watermilfoil *F*

+ Marsilea, Smartweed, Widgeongrass, Duckweed, Alga,
Horned-pondweed

WOOD DUCK
Aix sponsa

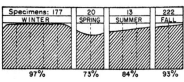

Specimens: 177	20	13	222
WINTER	SPRING	SUMMER	FALL
97%	73%	84%	93%

The wood duck is unique in several ways. Its drake is the most colorful of all our ducks. The species is distinctively what its name implies—a duck of the woods. It nests in cavities of trees and feeds to a large extent on fruits of woodland plants.

The range of wood ducks is confined almost entirely to the United States, though the breeding territory extends northward a short distance into Canada. Most of these ducks are found in the East, but a small contingent resides on the Pacific coast, and scattered pairs are found elsewhere. Not so very long ago the woody, also known as squealer, was a very abundant duck. Marked decreases in its population finally resulted in a closed season, effective from 1918 to 1941, by which time there was a partial recovery in numbers. Limited hunting is now permitted.

Animal food: Insects make up most of the small proportion of animal food in the wood duck diet. These are mainly beetles, true bugs, ants, and other *Hymenoptera*. Spiders, a few crustaceans, and mollusks also are eaten.

Plant food: In addition to the unique use of fruits and nuts of woody plants, the wood duck, more than any other species, eats quantities of seeds of the cowlily, waterlily, and watershield.

Northeast (excl. N.Y.), 87 (12-8-12-55)
*** Wildrice *SuFW*
*** Pondweed, sd. and veg. *SuF*
** Burreed *FWSp*
** Smartweed *FSp*
** Arrow-arum *FSp*
* Beech *FSp*
* Sedge *WSp*
* Duckweed, veg. *FW*
* Cowlily *Su*
* Oak *F*
* Wildcelery, veg. and sd. *FW*
* Arrowhead, veg. and sd. *FW*
* Grape *W*
* Watershield *SuF*
+ Waterlily, Dogwood, Ash, Pickerelweed, Skunkcabbage
New York, 57 (0-10-47-0)
*** Arrow-arum *SpSu*
*** Dogwood *Su*
** Duckweed, veg. and sd. *Sp*
** Pondweed, veg. and sd. *Sp*
** Burreed *Sp*

65

** Elm *Su*
* Cowlily *Su*
* Nightshade *Su*
Southeast, 107 (52-12-1-42)
*** Oak *FWSp*
** Hickory *W*
** Waterlily *FWSp*
** Duckweed, veg. *FW*
* Mannagrass *F*
* Ash *W*
* Blackgum *FSp*

* Water-elm *FW*
* Coontail, sd. and veg. *FW*
* Buttercup *F*
* Bidens *FW*
* Muskgrass, veg. *W*
+ Redroot, Hawthorn, Hornbeam,
Buttonbush, Sawgrass,
Fanwort, Smartweed,
Beakrush, Rice Cutgrass,
Lizardtail

REDHEAD
Aythya americana

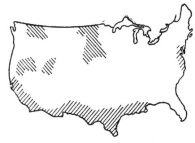

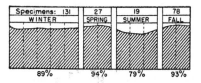

Specimens:	131	27	19	78
	WINTER	SPRING	SUMMER	FALL
	89%	94%	79%	93%

The redhead population has had its ups and downs. For a period of years its numbers steadily declined until finally a closed season was imposed to protect the survivors. In recent years the bird has made a definite comeback and has been restored to the hunting list. The drainage of many marshes where redheads nest in the Prairie and Mountain-Desert regions was a principal cause for the reduction of their population.

Redheads winter mainly in the Gulf region, in bays and lagoons along the coast of Texas and Mexico. They are also found in large rafts in Chesapeake Bay and Pamlico Sound.

Animal food: For a diving duck the redhead consumes a rather small proportion of animal food. This consists mainly of insects, especially grasshoppers and larvae of midges and caddisflies. Mollusks and snails are also eaten.

Plant food:
Northeast, 54 (14-11-0-29)
**** Pondweed, veg. and sd. *SpFW*
*** Wildrice *FWSp*
*** Wildcelery, veg. and sd. *FW*
** Bulrush *FWSp*
* Coontail, veg. and sd. *Sp*
* Naiad, veg. and sd. *FW*
* Smartweed *Sp*
+ Sedge, Widgeongrass, Burreed,
Spikerush, Muskgrass
Southeast, 83 (80-3-0-0)
*** Widgeongrass, veg. and sd. *W*
*** Pondweed, veg. and sd. *WSp*
** Waterlily, veg. and sd. *W*
* Naiad, veg. and sd. *WSp*
* Duckweed, veg. *W*
+ Bulrush, Muskgrass, Alga,
Coontail, Horned-pond-
weed, Spikerush, Water-
shield, Sawgrass
West, 118 (37-13-19-49)
**** Pondweed, sd. and veg. *SpSuFW*
*** Muskgrass, veg. *SpSuFW*
*** Bulrush *SuFWSp*
* Wildmillet *FW*
* Smartweed *FW*
* Alga *W*
* Widgeongrass, veg. and sd. *SuF*

66

* Horned-pondweed, veg. and sd.   + Saltgrass, Sedge, Waterweed,
    W   Spikerush

Reference: Production of the Redhead (*Nyroca americana*) in Iowa. Jessop B. Low. *Wilson Bul.* Vol. 52 (3), pp. 153–164, 1940.

RING-NECKED DUCK
Aythya collaris

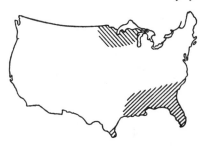

The ring-necked duck is a small diving species that has its main breeding territory in Canada. In the United States they nest in a limited area of the Prairie region immediately west of the Great Lakes. They winter in large numbers in the Southeast and to a lesser extent in other parts of the country, including the Pacific region. They are often found with rafts of scaup ducks.

Animal food: The animal food averages about a quarter of the total diet. Foremost are insects, chiefly nymphs of dragonflies and damselflies, caddisfly and midge larvae, various water bugs, and beetles. Next in importance are mollusks, particularly univalves, and then crustaceans, fish, spiders, and worms.

Plant food: The birds, while wintering in the Southeast, feed on watershield and waterlily seeds to a greater extent than other ducks.

Northeast, 35 (13-3-0-19)
  **** Pondweed, sd. and veg. *SpFW*
    ** Smartweed *FWSp*

    ** Wildrice *F*
     * Naiad, veg. and sd. *F*
     * Bulrush *FW*
     * Wildcelery, veg. and sd. *W*
     * Cutgrass, Rice *W*
     * Coontail, sd. and veg. *F*
     + Sedge, Wildmillet, Burreed, Muskgrass

Southeast, 167 (148-15-0-4)
  *** Watershield *FWSp*
   ** Coontail, sd. and veg. *FWSp*
   ** Duckweed, veg. *FW*
   ** Spikerush *WSp*
    * Waterlily *WSp*
    * Pondweed, sd. and veg. *W*
    * Arrowhead, tuber *W*
    * Bulrush *W*
    + Shoalgrass, Buttonbush, Waterprimrose, Alga, Muskgrass, Naiad, Chufa, Widgeongrass, Rice

West, 33 (11-4-9-9)
  *** Pondweed, sd. and veg. *SpSuFW*
  *** Muskgrass, veg. *FW*
    * Smartweed *FW*
    * Widgeongrass, veg. and sd. *SpSu*
    * Bulrush *F*
    * Burreed *SuW*
    * Sedge *SuF*
    * Wildmillet *W*
    * Watermilfoil *W*
    + Cowlily, Coontail, Alga

CANVASBACK
Aythya valisineria

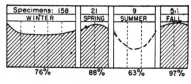

Specimens: 158	21	9	5ti
WINTER	SPRING	SUMMER	FALL
76%	88%	63%	97%

The canvasback, a species of medium abundance, is one of our most prized ducks. It breeds to a limited extent in our northwestern states and winters along our coasts or farther south. Large rafts of these heavy-bodied, flat-headed divers are frequently found in bays and other open-water areas. The canvasback is believed to be the fastest flying duck. It was clocked at 72 miles an hour from an airplane.

Animal food: For a diving duck, the proportion of the canvasback's animal food is rather small. It consists principally of bivalves and gastropods, dragonflies, damselflies, and various water bugs. The canvasback also eats some small fish and such miscellaneous animal matter as annelid worms, crabs, and other crustaceans.

Plant food: In the Northeast the canvasback's favorite food is wildcelery. Its partiality for this plant accounts for the duck's specific name. In other regions pondweeds replace wildcelery as the principal food.

** Wildrice *FWSp*
* Muskgrass *FWSp*
+ Bulrush, Watermilfoil, Naiad, Coontail, Arrowhead

Southeast, 64 (64-0-0-0)
*** Pondweed, veg. and sd.
*** Arrowhead, veg.
*** Waterlily, Banana, veg.
*** Bulrush
* Alga, veg.
+ Muskgrass, Naiad, Coontail, Widgeongrass

West, 109 (49-5-9-46)
***** (53%) Pondweed, veg. and sd. *SuFWSp*
* Widgeongrass, veg. and sd. *FW*
* Watermilfoil *SuFWSp*
* Burreed *SpSu*
+ Smartweed, Waterweed, Coontail, Sedge

Northeast, 71 (45-16-0-10)
**** Wildcelery, veg. and sd. *FWSp*
*** Pondweed, veg. and sd. *FWSp*

Reference: The Canvasback on a Prairie Marsh. H. Albert Hochbaum. American Wildlife Institute, 1944. 201 pp.

GREATER SCAUP DUCK
Aythya marila

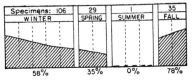

Specimens: 106	29	1	35
WINTER	SPRING	SUMMER	FALL
58%	35%	0%	78%

The greater scaup duck is a northern diving species that breeds in the subarctic. It winters along parts of our Atlantic and Pacific coasts and in the Great Lakes area.

Animal food: The greater scaup duck eats nearly as much animal material as plant. Mollusks of both the univalve and bivalve types are prominent in the diet. Various insects, particularly larval caddisflies, midges, and beetles are eaten; amphipods, mud crabs, and barnacles are also common food items.

Plant food:
Northeast, 87 (48-22-1-16)
*** Pondweed, sd. and veg. *SpFW*

** Wildcelery, veg. and sd. *FW*
** Naiad, veg. and sd. *SpFW*
* Coontail, veg. and sd. *SpW*
* Eelgrass, veg. and sd. *FW*
* Burreed *SpF*
+ Wildrice, Waterlily, Bulrush, Muskgrass
Southeast, 33 (25-3-0-5)
*** Widgeongrass, sd. and veg. *FW*
** Muskgrass, veg. *W*
* Wildcelery, veg. and sd. *FW*
* Pondweed, sd. and veg. *W*
* Naiad, veg. and sd. *FW*
+ Coontail, Glasswort, Bulrush
West, 51 (33-4-0-14)
*** Pondweed, sd. and veg. *FW*
** Muskgrass, veg. *W*
* Smartweed *Sp*
* Bulrush *F*
* Widgeongrass, sd. and veg. *SpW*
* Arrowhead, veg. *W*
+ Marsilea, Wildmillet

LESSER SCAUP DUCK
Aythya affinis

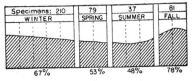

Specimens: 210	79	37	81
WINTER	SPRING	SUMMER	FALL
67%	53%	48%	78%

The lesser scaup duck, or little bluebill, is locally plentiful along our coasts in winter. It ranges farther south than the greater scaup duck. The lesser scaup duck occasionally breeds in our northern prairies, but its main breeding range is north of our borders. It is a diving duck typically seen on open water of inland lakes, coastal bays, or tidewater mouths of large rivers.

Animal food: The following items make up two-thirds or more of the animal food eaten by the lesser scaup duck: various mollusks, especially snails, nymphs of dragonflies and damselflies, larval caddisflies and midges, water boatmen, beetles, other insects, and crustaceans.

Plant food:

Northeast, 160 (67-31-3-59)
*** Wildcelery, veg. and sd. *SuFW*
*** Pondweed, sd. and veg. *FWSp*
** Wildrice *FWSp*
** Naiad, veg. and sd. *FWSp*
* Bulrush *FWSp*
* Arrowhead, veg. and sd. *WSp*
+ Sedge, Waterlily, Watermilfoil, Eelgrass, Smartweed, Coontail, Rice Cutgrass, Widgeongrass

Southeast, 148 (109-35-2-2)
*** Widgeongrass, sd. and veg. *SuFWSp*

** Horned-pondweed, sd. and veg. *Sp*
* Pondweed, sd. and veg. *WSp*
* Muskgrass, veg. *WSp*
* Smartweed *WSp*
* Wildcelery, veg. and sd. *WSp*
* Waterlily *W*
+ Arrowhead, Bulrush, Watershield, Coontail

West, 99 (34-13-32-20)
** Bulrush *SuFWSp*
** Widgeongrass, sd. and veg. *SuFW*
** Pondweed, sd. and veg. *SuFWSp*
* Muskgrass, veg. *SuFWSp*
* Watermilfoil *SuSp*
* Smartweed *SuWSp*
+ Sedge, Coontail, Spikerush

COMMON GOLDENEYE
Glaucionetta clangula

Specimens: 186	11	34	10
WINTER	SPRING	SUMMER	FALL
23%	11%	34%	23%

The common goldeneye, a northern diving duck, has its main breeding range north of the United States. Like the wood duck it usually nests in cavities of trees. Its principal wintering range is along our Atlantic and Pacific coasts where it may be found on open water, with other diving species. Though widespread, it is one of the less abundant species.

Animal food: About three-fourths of the goldeneye's diet is animal food. Of this, the major part consists of crustaceans, half of which are crabs. Aquatic bugs, caddisfly larvae, dragonfly and damselfly nymphs, fly larvae, Mayflies, beetles, and ants are the chief items in the remainder of the animal diet. Various mollusks and fish are also consumed in small amounts.

Plant food:

Northeast, 156 (124-7-19-6)
** Pondweed, sd. and veg. *SuFW*
* Wildcelery, veg. *FW*
+ Muskgrass, Widgeongrass, Eelgrass, Waterweed, Smartweed, Sedge

West, 85 (62-4-15-4)
*** Pondweed, sd. and veg. *SuFWSp*
+ Bulrush, Smartweed, Sedge, Wildmillet, Widgeongrass

BARROW GOLDENEYE
Glaucionetta islandica

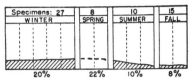

Specimens: 27	8	10	15
WINTER	SPRING	SUMMER	FALL
20%	22%	10%	8%

The Barrow goldeneye is restricted largely to the Pacific coast and the Northwest. It migrates only to a very limited extent within these regions. An interesting peculiarity of this somewhat uncommon bird is its habit of nesting high in the mountains—sometimes as high as 10,000 feet above sea level.

Animal food: Animal food dominates the diet of this species. The kinds of food are much the same as those eaten by the common goldeneye, but the order of preference seems to be insects, mollusks, and then crustaceans, rather than crustaceans, insects, and mollusks. These differences are probably explainable on the basis of distribution of the two species.

Plant food:
Northwest, 60 (27-8-10-15)
  * Pondweed, sd. and veg. *SuFWSp*
  + Alga, Widgeongrass, Horned-
     pondweed

BUFFLEHEAD
Bucephala albeola

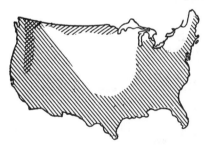

Specimens: 153	27	19	30
WINTER	SPRING	SUMMER	FALL
25%	19%	13%	24%

The bufflehead is a diving duck found on lakes, bays, large streams, and ponds. Its breeding range is largely north of the United States, but it winters in the southern half of the country and also in the Pacific Northwest. Though the bird is widespread in its range, its total population is relatively low.

Animal food: The chief item of food consists of insects, particularly larvae of caddisflies, nymphs of dragonflies and damselflies, larval and adult beetles, and water boatmen. Buffle-heads also eat various crustaceans and mollusks, both bivalves and univalves, but more commonly the latter. Occasionally they take fish.

Plant food: Though animals are the main food of buffleheads, they ordinarily supplement this fare with considerable quantities of aquatic plants and their seeds.

Northeast, 97 (64-15-0-18)
  ** Naiad, veg. and sd. *SpFW*
  * Pondweed, veg. and sd. *SpFW*
  * Wildcelery, veg. and sd. *W*
  * Wildrice, *W*
  + Widgeongrass, Coontail, Duck-
    weed, Alga, Smartweed,
    Bulrush, Burreed

West, 132 (89-12-19-12)
** Pondweed, veg. and sd. *SuFW*
 * Widgeongrass, veg. and sd.
     SpFW

+ Watermilfoil, Bulrush, Water-
    weed, Muskgrass

WHITE-WINGED SCOTER
Melanitta fusca

Specimens: 128	37	11	36
WINTER	SPRING	SUMMER	FALL
4%	7%	2%	16%

The whitewing, though considerably reduced in numbers as compared with former times, is probably the most abundant of the three North American scoters. It is also the largest but is held in low esteem as a gamebird.

Animal food: Like the other scoters,

the whitewing subsists largely on marine animal life: mollusks, especially rock clams, oysters, and mussels; crustaceans, particularly amphipods and barnacles; various insects, chiefly *Trichoptera;* and fishes.

Plant food:
Atlantic and Pacific Coasts, 212 (128-
    37-11-36)
  * Eelgrass, veg. *FWSp*
  + Pondweed

SURF SCOTER
Melanitta perspicillata

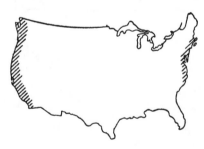

Specimens: 56	7	6	44
WINTER	SPRING	SUMMER	FALL
4%	0%	3%	23%

The surf scoter, like the American scoter, breeds in the Arctic but visits farther down our coasts in winter. This is a large, dark sea duck, commonly called coot by fishermen. It is not a popular gamebird.

Animal food: The food of the surf scoter is primarily mollusks, crusta-ceans, insects, fish, and echinoderms—much the same as the American scoter.

Plant food:
Atlantic and Pacific Coasts, 113 (56-
    7-6-44)
  * Eelgrass, veg. *FW*
  + Pondweed, Widgeongrass, Alga

AMERICAN SCOTER
Oidemia nigra

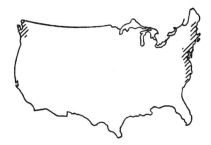

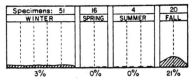

Specimens: 51	16	4	20
WINTER	SPRING	SUMMER	FALL
3%	0%	0%	21%

The American scoter is an arctic duck that enters our borders in winter along the North Atlantic coast and the Puget Sound region in the state of Washington. This black marine diver, locally known as coot or muscovie, is like other scoters in being regarded as a third-rate game species. This helps assure the bird a reasonably safe future.

Animal food : The food of the American scoter is almost entirely animal. It consists of mollusks (particularly mussels), crustaceans (especially barnacles), insects (chiefly caddisfly larvae), fishes, and echinoderms.

Plant food : The plant foods of this sea duck are, as might be expected, marine species.

Atlantic and Pacific Coasts, 91 (51-16-4-20)
* Eelgrass, veg. *FW*
+ Kelp, Muskgrass, Widgeongrass

RUDDY DUCK
Oxyura jamaicensis

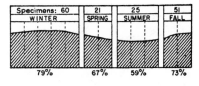

Specimens: 60	21	25	51
WINTER	SPRING	SUMMER	FALL
79%	67%	59%	73%

The ruddy duck, also known as butterball or bristletail, is a unique North American species—so unique that it is placed in a distinct family. Next to the bufflehead, it is our smallest diving duck and it has the additional distinction of an erect, stubby tail.

The ruddy duck occurs throughout the country, nesting in some of our western states and wintering in bays and estuaries along our coasts. During the twenties the population of ruddy ducks dropped alarmingly, and a closed season was imposed for this species. Since then its numbers have increased, and about ten years ago the hunting ban was lifted.

Animal food : In some localities the ruddy feeds exclusively on animal food. In general, however, the animal content averages about one-third of the total. It is formed chiefly of insects, such as midge and horsefly larvae, caddisfly larvae, and water boatmen. Various mollusks and crustaceans are also eaten.

** Bulrush *FWSp*
 * Naiad, veg. and sd. *FWSp*
 * Muskgrass, veg. *FWSp*
 * Widgeongrass, sd. and veg. *FWSp*
   + Smartweed, Arrowhead, Coontail

West, 76 (26-3-25-22)
 *** Pondweed, sd. and veg. *SuFWSp*
 *** Bulrush *SuFWSp*
 ** Widgeongrass, sd. and veg. *SuFWSp*
   + Horned-pondweed, Smartweed, Watermilfoil, Cyperus, Coontail, Muskgrass, Sedge

Plant food:
East, 81 (34-18-0-29)
 *** Pondweed, sd. and veg. *FWSp*
 ** Wildcelery, veg. and sd. *FW*

Reference: Nesting of the Ruddy Duck in Iowa. Jessop B. Low. *Auk,* Vol. 58(4), pp. 506–517, 1941.

Coot: *Rallidae*

COMMON COOT
Fulica americana

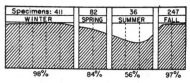

Specimens: 411	82	36	247
WINTER	SPRING	SUMMER	FALL
98%	84%	56%	97%

The coot, or mud hen, is closely related to the gallinules and rails. This slate-gray, whitish-billed, duck-like bird breeds over most of the country and winters mainly in the Gulf states and along the Pacific coast. It feeds primarily on the water surface, and though not web-footed like ducks, it can and does dive for food.

According to waterfowl inventories of the past ten years, the total number of coots is exceeded by only two duck species: the mallard and pintail. It is not regarded as a choice gamebird, and in many places is shot simply to eliminate it as a food competitor of ducks. **Animal food:** Most of the animal food (taken in limited quantity except in summer) consists of insects, principally aquatic beetles and bugs, dragonflies, and damselflies. A considerable number of univalves and bivalves are also eaten. The rest of the animal food is mostly crustaceans and spiders. **Plant food:** Coots concentrate on submerged aquatic vegetation. They eat seeds considerably but not to quite the same extent as ducks.

Northeast, 269 (40-30-16-183)
 *** Naiad, veg. and sd. *SuFWSp*
 *** Pondweed, veg. and sd. *SuFWSp*
 *** Bulrush *FWSp*

+ Sedge, Burreed, Spikerush, Smartweed

Southeast, 356 (293-35-2-26)
**** Duckweed, veg. and sd. *SuFW*
*** Widgeongrass, veg. and sd. *SuFWSp*
*** Muskgrass, veg. *SuFWSp*
** Pondweed, veg. and sd. *SuFWSp*
** Naiad, veg. and sd. *FWSp*
* Spikerush, sd. and veg. *FWSp*
+ Cyperus, Alga, Bulrush

West, 166 (78-17-32-39)
**** Pondweed, veg. and sd. *SuFWSp*
*** Muskgrass, veg. *SuFW*
*** Bulrush *FW*
** Alga, veg. and sd. *SuFW*
* Widgeongrass, veg. and sd. *SuFW*
+ Cyperus, Spikerush, Naiad, Rice, Coontail, Duckweed, Burreed

*** Wildrice *FW*
** Muskgrass, veg. *SuFWSp*
** Alga, veg. *SuFWSp*
* Coontail, veg. and sd. *SuFW*
* Duckweed, veg. *SuFW*
* Waterweed, veg. *SuF*
* Wildcelery, veg. *SuFW*

Reference: Food Habits of the American Coot with Notes on Distribution. John C. Jones. *U.S. Fish and Wildlife Service Res. Bul.* 2, 1940. 52 pp.

Gulls and Terns: *Laridae*

TERNS. In the United States there are about a dozen species of terns. These graceful fliers, like their larger relatives the gulls, are especially plentiful along the coasts. Only a few, like the black, common, and Forster terns, are typical of inland lakes.

The black and gull-billed terns feed primarily upon: Mayflies, dragonflies, caddisflies, beetles, and spiders. All other terns eat fish as their staple food. Besides small fish, shrimps, crabs, aquatic insects, squid, and even mussels are taken. These attractive birds have no significant economic value nor do they inflict any appreciable damage to our fisheries.

GULLS. About twenty species of gulls are present in the United States. They are common along our marine coasts, but some also occur inland—especially about the Great Lakes.

Gulls spend much time on shore, but most of their feeding (except for species like the Franklin gull) is done on the water. They are primarily fish eaters and scavengers. Shrimps, clams, sea urchins, bird eggs, and insects are also eaten. The species of gulls that roam inland feed extensively on insects—particularly on grasshoppers, crickets, and ants. It was these insect-eating gulls that saved the crops of pioneer Mormons. Desirable fish constitute only a minor part of the diet of gulls, the country over. In contrast, the public service rendered in scavenging marine garbage and other waste is very considerable.

Plant food is taken only to a limited extent. The Franklin, herring, and ring-billed gulls (treated below) subsist more extensively on plants than do the other species.

HERRING GULL
Larus argentatus

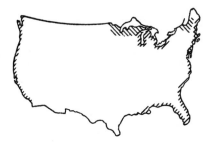

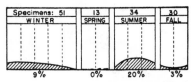

Specimens: 51	13	34	30
WINTER	SPRING	SUMMER	FALL
9%	0%	20%	3%

The herring gull is one of the most common gulls found along our seaboards and about large inland lakes. It is also one of the largest. When people talk about sea gulls, they usually refer to this conspicuous white or grayish species. The herring gull nests in a large area that extends from the Arctic to Long Island. It winters all along the Atlantic, Pacific, and Gulf coasts.

Animal food: The gull's animal diet consists mainly of small fish, crustaceans, mollusks, and a few insects. With what seems an unusual show of intelligence, herring gulls drop large mollusks from the air onto the rocks to break them. Then the birds descend to eat. Gulls have been reported feeding on young birds and bird eggs and even attacking young lambs.

Plant food: A considerable part of the plant food of the herring gull is obtained in connection with its role as a scavenger. In New England, however, it frequently alights in blueberry patches and feeds on the fruit.

United States, 128 (51-13-34-30)
* Garbage *WSpSuF*
* Blueberry *Su*
+ Crowberry, Alga

Reference: On the Habits and Behavior of the Herring Gull. R. M. Strong. *Auk*, Vol. 31 (1 & 2) 1914. 27 pp.

RING-BILLED GULL
Larus delawarensis

The ring-billed gull usually nests north of the United States but is a common winter visitor along our coasts and lake shores. Like the herring gull, it is a professional scavenger; much of the small quantity of plant food it eats is marine garbage.

Animal food: The principal items of its diet are fish, beetles, grasshoppers, and crickets, true bugs, amphibians, and mollusks.

Plant food:
United States, 61 (13-11-18-19)
* Garbage *W*
+ Sago Pondweed, Gooseberry

FRANKLIN GULL
Larus pipixcan

This gull breeds in the prairies of the United States and Canada and winters along our Gulf coast or farther south. It fares very largely on an animal diet. Examination of the contents of 124 birds showed no more than 1% of plant food in any season except spring when the plant total rose to 14%.

Animal food: The animal diet consists chiefly of grasshoppers and crickets, bees, true bugs, dragonflies and damselflies, spiders, and fish.

Plant food:

United States, 124 (15-12-55-42)
  * Wheat *Sp*
  + Oats, Duckweed

SKIMMER. The black skimmer is a unique relative of the terns and gulls. The lower half of its bill is knife-like and serves efficiently to capture fish, shrimp, and other small crustaceans, which comprise most of its all-animal diet. Our single species nests along the Atlantic and Gulf coasts from southern New England to Texas and winters from the Carolinas to South America.

CHAPTER SIX

Marshbirds and Shorebirds

T HE WATER-MARGIN habitat, whether brackish or fresh, marsh-covered or bare, is productive of much invertebrate life that is attractive to birds. The prevalence of crustaceans, marine worms, insects, and mollusks explains why so many birds of different families concentrate on this restricted environment.

The marshbird and shorebird category, as construed here, includes at least three major subgroups: the long-legged, shallow-water waders (herons, egrets, ibises), the marsh dwellers (rails, gallinules, cranes), and the shorebirds (sandpipers, plovers, and numerous other species that run along the beaches in search of food). Phalaropes are rather anomalous members of the shorebird group since they spend a great deal of time swimming in shallow water.

Birds of the marsh and shore-line habitat have little direct economic importance, positive or negative. Nor, except for the rails, are they prized as gamebirds. They are, however, an interesting part of the typical life of wet, marginal areas. Most of them subsist largely on animal food, but the rails, cranes, and gallinules are exceptions to this rule. Some long-legged, wading species eat fish extensively and have been denounced for this reason. Food-habits studies on herons and other waders have shown that generally they do little real damage. If, however, a heron invades a fish-hatchery pond, it can do considerable damage in a fairly short time.

The birds treated in this chapter are

Herons	Limpkin	Sandpiper Family (Snipes,
Egrets	Rails	Curlews, Willet, Sand-
Bitterns	Gallinules	pipers, etc.)
Ibises	Oystercatchers	Avocet
Spoonbills	Plovers	Stilt
Cranes	Turnstones	Phalaropes

General References: Life Histories of North American Marsh Birds. Arthur Cleveland Bent. *U.S. National Museum Bul.* 135, 1926. 490 pp.

Life Histories of North American Shore Birds. Arthur Cleveland Bent. *U.S. National Museum Bul.* 142, 1927, 420 pp.; and *Bul.* 146, 1929; 412 pp.

Birds in Relation to Fishes. Clarence Cottam and F. M. Uhler. *U.S. Fish and Wildlife Service Leaflet* 272, 1945. 16 pp.

Food Habits of a Group of Shorebirds: Woodcock, Snipe, Knot, and Dowitcher. Charles C. Sperry. *U.S. Dept. Int. Wildlife Res. Bul.* 1, 1940. 37 pp.

Herons, Egrets, Bitterns: *Ardeidae*

HERONS. Seven species of herons are native to the United States. These long-legged, large-winged waders subsist largely on fish, crustaceans, amphibians, and insects. Because of their fish-eating diet, herons have been widely persecuted. Generally, however, they consume relatively few pan fish—most of the fish eaten being enemies of the kinds desirable to man.

The great blue heron, commonest and best known of the group, is the one most severely and unfairly criticized. Examination of the stomach contents of 189 great blue herons from various parts of the country has helped to vindicate this picturesque and stately wader. The investigators concluded that "when not overabundant the bird is unquestionably a natural asset."

About 43% of the diet consisted of nongame or noncommercial fish, about 25% of useful species, 8% of insects, 8% of crayfish and other crustaceans, 5% of mice and shrews, and 4% of frogs, snakes, turtles, and the like.

The great white heron, another large species, ranges along the southern tip of Florida and the Florida Keys. It feeds almost entirely on fish, varying its diet by the occasional inclusion of a few crustaceans.

The green heron, a midget compared with its relatives, is a common inhabitant of eastern swamps and creeks. Stomach examination of 277 specimens showed that, except in the vicinity of hatcheries, the number of useful fish on which they feed is negligible. Crayfish make up nearly half the diet, small, nonvaluable fish about two-fifths, and aquatic insects nearly one-quarter.

The little blue heron becomes bluish as it develops into an adult. Until then it is white and is often confused with the egrets. This heron is widely distributed in the United States, breeding in the North and wintering in the South. Its food is mostly crayfish plus some worms, fish, grasshoppers, frogs, and lizards.

The Louisiana, or red-necked, heron is found along the Gulf and South Atlantic coasts. It is a colonial bird which sometimes collects in flocks of several thousand. Its favorite foods are insects, fish, snails, lizards, grasshoppers, and frogs.

The black-crowned night heron, found over most of the country, occasionally makes damaging raids on fish hatcheries. However, analysis of the stomachs of 117 of these black-capped night feeders revealed that of the 52% of fish in the diet, game fish and pan fish normally formed only a small part. Crayfish, crabs, and shrimps comprised about 22% of the total fare, aquatic insects 16%, frogs 6%, and mice and rats 3%.

The yellow-crowned night heron is limited largely to southern areas. In 120 stomachs of these birds only a single fish was found—and that one had no commercial or sport value. Crayfish and crabs made up almost the entire diet.

Reference: Birds in Relation to Fishes. Clarence Cottam and F. M. Uhler. *U.S. Fish and Wildlife Service Leaflet* 272, 1945. 16 pp.

EGRETS. Three species of egrets are found in the southern parts of the United States. These are the common or American, the snowy, and the reddish egrets. All have white plumage except the dark-colored reddish egret which also has a white phase. The feathers of these birds were once prized in the millinery trade, and until legal protection was established, early in this century, it appeared that egrets might be exterminated. Recently their numbers have been increasing, and they are once more extending their range northward.

These inhabitants of marshes and shallow lakes, bays, and streams feed largely on aquatic organisms. Crayfish, shrimps, aquatic insects, frogs, fish, crabs, and snails are their principal foods. Occasionally lizards, snakes, salamanders, mice, and moles are also eaten.

Reference: Birds in Relation to Fishes. Clarence Cottam and F. M. Uhler. *U.S. Fish and Wildlife Service Leaflet* 272, 1945. 16 pp.

BITTERNS. Two bitterns, the American and least, frequent swamps, marshes, and creeks across the United States. They are entirely animal feeders. Examination of stomachs of nearly 160 American bitterns showed that less than one-tenth of its food consisted of desirable fish. The main items eaten were insects, frogs, fish, crayfish, mice, and shrews.

The miniature least bittern eats less fish than the American. Insects, amphibians, and crustaceans are its principal fare.

Ibises, Spoonbills: *Ciconiidae and Threskiornithidae*

IBISES. Four species of ibis and wood ibis are found in southern swamps and along lake margins. Their range extends into Central and South America. This group includes the eastern glossy, the white-faced glossy, the white, and the wood ibis. The latter belongs to a distinct family which includes the storks. All these long-legged, curved-bill, heron-like waders feed almost entirely on an animal diet—mainly fish, aquatic insects, crayfish, crabs, and snails.

SPOONBILLS. The roseate spoonbill was facing extinction in the United States, a few decades ago, until legal protection was provided. The beautiful pink plumes, used commercially, were the main reason for its decimation. The spoonbill is native to our Gulf coast swamps and lakes—mainly in Florida and Texas—as well as to tropical America. It feeds in shallow water, submerging its bill and sometimes its head and neck in search for food. Fish are eaten commonly, but insects, snails, shrimps, and crayfish are also important food items.

Cranes: *Gruidae*

SANDHILL CRANE
Grus canadensis

There are three subspecies of the sandhill crane: the northern, western, and southern. They look too much alike to be distinguished except by careful study. The northern sandhill crane, a small brownish race, is found in the far north during the nesting season and winters from California and Texas southward into Mexico. Its numbers are still fairly considerable though much reduced as compared with former abundance. It is primarily a marshbird but often feeds in grain fields while wintering or migrating.

The western sandhill crane was once

very abundant. At one time it nested as far eastward as Ohio, but now most of its eastern nesting territory has been abandoned. These red-faced waders feed in upland fields as well as in marshlands. In some localities they cause damage to grain. The population of this race is now so low that there is fear of its extinction.

The southern sandhill crane, unlike the other two races, does not migrate. It occurs in Florida and ranges over the state line into southern Georgia. It is typically a marsh or lowland inhabitant as indicated by the principal foods used.

In addition to the sandhill crane there is another native species—one that is nearly extinct. It is the giant, white whooping crane (*Grus americana*). Probably less than 50 individuals of this majestic bird are still alive. Special efforts are being made to save this small remnant from extinction. We have very little information on its foods.

Animal food: Though sandhill cranes are largely vegetarian, they eat some animal food—especially when feeding in a marshy environment. Favorite items are grasshoppers, beetles, caterpillars, snails, frogs, and toads. Mice, lizards, snakes, and fish have also been recorded.

Plant food: These cranes are adapted to feeding on a wide range of plant foods. Besides eating seeds of grains and wild plants, they consume herbaceous foliage, underground stems, tubers, and roots.

West (northern subspecies), 29 (23-2-0-4)
**** Corn *WSp*
**** Sorghum *W*
*** Wheat *FWSp*
* Alfalfa, sd. and veg. *W*
+ Burreed

West (western subspecies), 12 (8-3-0-1)
**** Wheat *FWSp*
*** Corn *WSp*
*** Rice *FW*
** Grasses, sd. and veg. *FWSp*
* Oats *W*
+ Blueberry

Florida, 14 (4-10-0-0)
**** Chufa, tuber *WSp*
*** Bulrush, veg. *W*
** Waterlily, veg. and sd. *Sp*
** Baldcypress *Sp*
* Blueberry *Sp*
+ Cowlily

Reference: The Sandhill Cranes. Lawrence H. Walkinshaw. Cranbrook Institute of Science, Bloomfield Hills, Mich., 1949. 202 pp.

Limpkin: *Aramidae*

LIMPKIN
Aramus guarauna

The limpkin, a large, speckled, tropical wader is confined to the Okefenokee Swamp in Georgia and peninsular Florida west to the Wakulla River, near the St. Marks National Wildlife Refuge. This species, also known as the crying bird because of its weird calls, feeds almost exclusively on snails. Only the soft bodies of snails are consumed, the shells being left where found or dropped to the ground

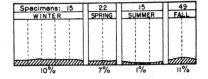

Specimens: 15	22	15	49
WINTER	SPRING	SUMMER	FALL
10%	7%	1%	11%

at nesting sites. The limpkin feeds mainly at night—a time when snails are most likely to be active.

Rails, Gallinules: *Rallidae*

RAILS. Six species of rails, or marsh hens, are present in the United States. The clapper rail, represented by several subspecies, is widely distributed over the country. So is the sora. The others are more localized in their range. These small, active marsh waders are popular gamebirds.

Rails are somewhat omnivorous but feed largely on animal material. The sora and yellow rails use plants more than other species. The food habits of the diminutive, obscure black rail are little known, and consequently it is not accorded an individual write-up. Indications are that it feeds on insects, crustaceans, and some plant material, including seeds.

KING RAIL
Rallus elegans

The king rail, locally called the fresh-water marsh hen, is primarily an inland bird. However, it winters along the South Atlantic and Gulf coasts. It is a popular gamebird.

Animal food: Insects, mostly beetles, grasshoppers, aquatic bugs, and drag-onfly nymphs, are the principal food of the king rail. Spiders, snails, crayfish, amphibians, and small fish are also eaten.

Plant food: Seeds and other parts of plants seem to be eaten only casually by this bird.

Northeast, 54 (5-10-9-30)
 * Arrowhead, tuber *FW*
 + Smartweed, Pondweed, Arrow-arum, Burreed, Common Ragweed, Bristlegrass, Wheat
Southeast, 47 (10-12-6-19)
 + Rice, Bulrush, Naiad, Widgeon-grass, Pondweed, Bayberry, Spikerush, Smartweed

CLAPPER RAIL
Rallus longirostris

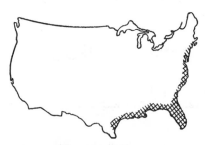

Specimens: 50	28	68	114
WINTER	SPRING	SUMMER	FALL
11%	1%	0%	3%

The clapper rail, or salt-water marsh hen, is a native of our Atlantic, Pacific, and Gulf coasts—and points southward. It is a permanent resident in all except the northernmost limits of its Atlantic coast range. The clapper's scant West Coast range is not mapped.

Animal food: The 96%, or more, of animal food consists mainly of decapods (shrimps, crayfish, crabs), various mollusks, aquatic insects, small fish, and clamworms.

Plant food:
East (*Coastal*), 278 (67-28-69-114)
 * Cordgrass *FW*
 + Bulrush, Sedge, Smartweed, Oak (acorn), Soybean

VIRGINIA RAIL
Rallus limicola

During its nesting season the Virginia rail ranges far beyond Virginia to Nova Scotia, Saskatchewan, and Nebraska. One race is recorded on the Pacific coast. It is typically an inland species that winters along the South Atlantic and Gulf coasts and farther south to Central America.

Animal food: Animal foods predominate in the diet. Beetles, snails, spiders, true bugs, and diptera larvae are the items that occur most frequently. Other animal foods commonly eaten are various crustaceans, dragonfly and damselfly 'nymphs, ants and other *Hymenoptera*, grasshoppers and crickets, bryozoans, and small fish.

Plant food: Seeds of marsh plants make up an appreciable portion of the diet.

Northeast, 98 (1-22-14-61)
  ** Wildrice *SuFSp*

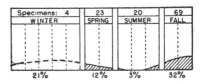

Specimens: 4	23	20	69
WINTER	SPRING	SUMMER	FALL
21%	12%	3%	32%

  * Bulrush *SuFSp*
  * Spikerush *SuFSp*
  + Sedge, Buttonbush, Cyperus, Pondweed, Cowlily, Smartweed
Southeast, 6 (2-1-0-3)
  * Cordgrass *F*
  + Spikerush, Sedge, Bulrush, Smartweed
West, 12 (1-0-6-5)
  * Bulrush *SuF*
  + Smartweed, Pondweed, Marestail, Burreed

SORA
Porzana carolina

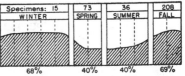

Specimens: 15	73	36	208
WINTER	SPRING	SUMMER	FALL
68%	40%	40%	69%

This and the rest of its animal diet are essentially the same as that of the Virginia rail.

Plant food:
Northeast, 251 (3-48-20-180)
  *** Sedge *SuFWSp*

The sora, a small but prized gamebird, has a wide distribution. It nests across the northern half of the United States and in Canada. Winters are spent along the southern fringe of our country and farther south into Central America. This rail is distinct in the large quantity of plant food it eats. The yellow rail is probably second in this regard.

Animal food: Beetles and other insects, snails, spiders, and crustaceans are the principal animal items taken.

*** Wildrice *SuF*
** Bulrush *SuFSp*
* Smartweed *SuF*
* Cutgrass *SuFSp*
* Spikerush *SuFSp*
* Wildmillet *FSp*
+ Duckweed, Burreed, Bitter Nightshade, Panicgrass, Cyperus
Southeast, 41 (11-15-0-15)
** Paspalum, Bull *F*
** Rice *F*
* Duckweed, veg. *W*

* Alga *WSp*
* Cordgrass *FW*
* Smartweed *W*
+ Panicgrass, Spikerush, Pondweed
West, 40 (1-10-16-13)
*** Bulrush *SuFSp*
*** Sedge *SuFSp*
* Wildmillet *F*
* Smartweed *SuFSp*
+ Alga, Buttercup, Dock, Pondweed, Saltgrass

YELLOW RAIL
Coturnicops noveboracensis

This small, elusive rail is rare. Little is known of its range, habits, and population. It nests in the northern states, particularly in the Northeast and in Canada, and winters along the Gulf and Atlantic coasts north to North Carolina.

Animal food: The animal food of this species is very similar to that of the other rails. Beetles, snails, grasshoppers, spiders, ants, fly larvae, true bugs, and various crustaceans are eaten.

Plant food: The limited data on food indicate variable proportions of plant-animal material. Seeds seem to be rather important in the diet.

East, 16 (4-4-1-7)
** Sedge *F*
** Smartweed *W*
* Nutrush *W*
* Bristlegrass *W*
+ Spikerush, Bulrush, Common Ragweed, Bayberry

PURPLE GALLINULE
Porphyrula martinica

This brightly colored marshland gamebird nests in the Southeast as far north as the Carolinas and Tennessee and winters primarily in South America. Seeds constitute a large part of its diet. Examination of 50 stomachs of purple gallinules showed proportions of plant food as follows: spring (15 birds), 35%; summer (29 birds), 71%; fall (6 birds), 83%.

Another species of water chicken, the grayish colored, red-billed Florida gallinule, also occurs in the Southeast as well as farther north and westward. Our very limited information on its diet indicates that it eats seeds and other plant material extensively and also feeds on aquatic insects, snails, and worms.

Animal food: Aquatic beetles and bugs

are the chief animal food items of the purple gallinule. The remainder consists mainly of various mollusks, ants and other *Hymenoptera*, spiders, flies and their larvae, caterpillars, and nymphs of dragonflies and damselflies.

Plant food:
Southeast, 50 (0-15-29-6)
*** Rice *SuFSp*
** Windmillgrass *Su*
** Paspalum, Knotgrass *SpSu*
** Duckweed *SuF*
* Wildmillet *Su*
* Signalgrass *SpSu*
* Spikerush *SpSu*
+ Bermudagrass, Sawgrass, Panicgrass, Widgeongrass, Giantcutgrass, Waterlily

Oystercatchers: *Haematopodidae*

OYSTERCATCHERS. The oystercatchers are birds of marine coasts. The common, or American, oystercatcher occurs along the Atlantic as far northward as New Jersey and is also present on the Pacific coast. Its dark counterpart, the black oystercatcher, ranges all along the Pacific from Lower California to the Aleutians.

These red-billed shorebirds feed on many forms of animal life besides oysters. Sixteen stomachs of the common oystercatcher contained limpets, shrimps, and other crustaceans together with some sea worms and oysters. Twenty-five black oystercatchers had been feeding largely on marine worms, barnacles and other crustaceans, mussels and limpets.

Plovers, Turnstones: *Charadriidae*

PLOVERS. Five of the eight species of American plovers nest and winter wholly or partly in the United States. These are the piping, snowy, Wilson, and mountain plovers and the killdeer, which is also a true plover. The other three, the black-bellied, semipalmated, and golden plovers, are not confined to the boundaries of any country or continent. The semipalmated and golden plovers nest in the Arctic, winter far south of the equator, and are seen here only when in transit. The black-bellied plover is similar except that it nests regularly on our East coast. The familiar killdeer, or killdee, is seen or heard from the Atlantic coast to the Pacific and from the Gulf region to Hudson Bay.

These medium-sized shorebirds move in small flocks along beaches, mud flats, and water margins. Their food consists almost entirely of animal organisms: insects of various kinds, marine worms, small crustaceans, and mollusks. In the case of the killdeer, insects (particularly beetles, caterpillars, grasshoppers, ants, and true bugs) constitute the major part of the diet.

TURNSTONES. Our two species of turnstones, the ruddy and the black, nest in the Arctic. The ruddy turnstone winters along the southern half of both the Atlantic and Pacific coasts and ranges on southward as far as Chile. The black turnstone is confined to the Pacific coast in winter and goes no farther south than Lower California.

As their name implies, these plover-like birds have the habit of overturning stones or other small objects in search of food. They feed principally on small crustaceans, mollusks, and insects.

Sandpipers and Allies: *Scolopacidae*

SANDPIPER FAMILY. This diverse family of shorebirds includes more than 30 species that occur regularly in the United States. The smaller members of the group generally bear the name sandpiper, while the larger species are called by various names such as snipe, curlew, willet, yellow-legs, knot, dowitcher, or godwit. The woodcock belongs in this family, but since it is a gamebird and nests in uplands, it is treated in Chap. Seven. By and large, the sandpiper group subsists on invertebrate animal life obtained along the shore. A few of the sandpipers proper, as well as the Wilson snipe, knot, dowitchers, and godwits, eat sufficient quantities of plant material to justify their separate treatment below.

Three species of curlews are found in the United States, but one, the Eskimo

curlew, is practically extinct. The Hudsonian curlew nests in the Arctic, winters in South America, and is seen along the Atlantic and Pacific coasts during migrations. The long-billed curlew (all three species of curlew have a long curved bill) is the only one that is resident within our borders in fair numbers. It nests in the Northwest and winters in California and Texas. It formerly wintered on the Atlantic coast. The curlews are almost exclusively animal feeders, but locally some of them feed on blueberries in the fall. Most of their diet is obtained along the shore. Snails and other small mollusks, various insects, crayfish, crabs, and other crustaceans, worms and spiders are the principal items eaten.

During the summer, the willet is found in many widely separated localities in the United States, but it is more common in alkaline districts of the West and along seaboards than in fresh-water areas. It winters in the warmer parts of the country and south of our borders into South America. The food of the willet consists primarily of aquatic insects, marine worms, and small crabs, mollusks, and fish.

Both species of yellow-legs, the greater and the lesser, do practically all their nesting north of the United States. The lesser yellow-legs, in migrating, passes on south of our borders into South America so we see it only in transit. The greater yellow-legs winters largely south of the United States, but some individuals remain as far north as Maryland on the Atlantic coast and Oregon on the Pacific coast. Yellow-legs commonly feed while wading in shallow water. The greater yellow-legs eats many small fish as well as insects, snails, worms, and crustaceans. The lesser yellow-legs feeds less on fish but more on insects—particularly ants, flies, and grasshoppers. Crustaceans, snails, and worms are also eaten.

The small, active birds known as sandpipers are common enough along our coastal beaches and lake margins to be familiar to almost everyone. But it takes skill and training to distinguish the species. The greatest number of sandpipers are found along our marine coasts and on the borders of brackish western lakes. Two species, the spotted and solitary sandpipers, are particularly common about eastern inland lakes. These shorebirds feed largely or almost entirely on animal life. Their diet includes numerous insects such as nymphs of caddisflies and dragonflies, beetles, ants and other *Hymenoptera*. Small crustaceans, mollusks, and marine worms are also eaten extensively. Only a few species such as the pectoral, white-rumped, stilt, and semipalmated sandpipers feed on appreciable amounts of plant food.

WILSON SNIPE
Capella gallinago

The Wilson snipe, better known in many parts of the country as the jacksnipe, is a popular gamebird, now protected by a closed season. This species and the woodcock are the only members of the shorebird family (*Scolopacidae*) that have been widely hunted in recent years. The Wilson

Specimens: 232	97	16	435
WINTER	SPRING	SUMMER	FALL
17%	22%	5%	19%

snipe offers a difficult target for the sportsman because of its erratic, zigzag flight. It is characteristic of marshes or coastal flats covered with low vegetation.

Animal food: The principal items of the animal diet are fly larvae, beetles, especially aquatic forms, various crustaceans, earthworms, fresh-water snails, and small fishes.

Plant food:

Northeast, 522 (40-75-11-396)
* Smartweed *SuFWSp*
* Bulrush *SuFWSp*
+ Bogbean, Sedge, Wildmillet, Burreed, Bristlegrass, Pondweed, Common Ragweed, Cyperus

Southeast, 168 (90-76-0-2)
* Bulrush *WSp*
* Panicgrass *WSp*
+ Sawgrass, Smartweed, Wildmillet, Cyperus, Spikerush, Centella, Bristlegrass, Common Ragweed, Pondweed, Burreed

West, 45 (11-16-4-14)
* Bulrush *SuFWSp*
* Sedge *F*
+ Burreed, Sunflower, Bogbean, Smartweed, Bristlegrass, Wildmillet

AMERICAN KNOT
Calidris canutus rufus

The knot is a transient or migrant visitor within our boundaries. It nests in the Arctic and winters in South America.

Animal food: Mollusks, principally univalves, constitute over half the animal diet. Insects and crustaceans follow in that order. Fly larvae and beetles make up most of the insects eaten.

Specimens:	59	87	67
WINTER	SPRING	SUMMER	FALL
	0%	6%	24%

Plant food:

East, 213 (0-59-87-67)
* Widgeongrass *F*
+ Eelgrass, Bogbean, Pondweed, Bulrush

PECTORAL SANDPIPER
Erolia melanotos

The fact that this sandpiper, the grass bird, frequents grassy parts of marshes may help explain the occasional large quantities of unidentified vegetable debris found in the stomachs of some of the specimens examined. It is, however, primarily an animal feeder.

The pectoral sandpiper is a common visitor to this country. It nests in the Arctic and winters in South America, migrating principally through the Mississippi Valley though it is also fairly common on the Atlantic coast. **Animal food:** The diet of this bird consists largely of insects, crustaceans, mollusks, and worms—practically the same as the least sandpiper.

Plant food:
United States, 68 (2-31-10-25)
  + Smartweed, Pondweed, Bulrush, Bristlegrass, Watermilfoil, Widgeongrass, Clover, Panicgrass

WHITE-RUMPED SANDPIPER
Erolia fuscicollis

The white-rumped sandpiper is a transient, passing mainly through the Mississippi Valley area on its migrations to and from nesting territory in the Arctic and its winter home in South America. This small shorebird frequents marshes and marshy shores in preference to sandy beaches.
Animal food: It feeds upon various insects, crustaceans, mollusks, clamworms, and small fish. More than 90% of its food is animal.

Plant food:
East, 13 (0-0-4-9)
  * Widgeongrass *SuF*
  + Sedge

DOWITCHER
Limnodromus griseus

Specimens: 13	34	124	3
WINTER	SPRING	SUMMER	FALL
1%	10%	20%	3%

Dowitchers winter along our southern coasts—including Southern California—but some go farther south into Central and South America. They nest in the far north from Hudson Bay to Alaska. Two subspecies are recognized: the eastern and the long-billed dowitchers.

These snipe-like shorebirds feed in shallow water or on mud flats, drilling their long bills repeatedly into the sand or mud in search of small marine animal life.

Animal food: The food of the dowitcher is largely animal: mainly fly larvae and beetles, marine worms, and mollusks—especially univalves. The balance consists chiefly of small crustaceans.

Plant food: Seeds of aquatic plants are eaten only to a limited extent.

East, 174 (13-34-124-3)
  * Pondweed *SuSp*
  * Bogbean *Su*
  + Bayberry, Widgeongrass, Bulrush, Smartweed, Watermilfoil

West, 69 (0-16-12-41)
  ** Pondweed *SuFSp*
   * Bulrush *SuFSp*

+ Sedge, Widgeongrass, Horned-
pondweed, Spikerush, Saltgrass

STILT SANDPIPER
Micropalama himantopus

Not many people see this sandpiper which visits the United States only briefly on its migrations between the Arctic and its winter territory in South America.

Animal food: More than 90% of the stilt sandpiper's diet is animal food. Along the coasts, it feeds mainly on crustaceans, mollusks, clamworms, and fly larvae. Inland, it eats many insects, particularly grasshoppers.

Plant food:
East, 15 (0-0-10-5)
+ Pondweed, Widgeongrass, Wa-
termilfoil, Bulrush, Sedge
West, 17 (0-5-8-4)
+ Pondweed, Sedge, Marestail,
Bulrush, Spikerush, Smart-
weed, Coontail, Vervain

SEMIPALMATED SANDPIPER
Ereunetes pusillus

This tiny, hardy, shorebird which nests in the Arctic is resident in a few of our southeastern coastal states during winter months, but most of its winter range is south of us—far down in South America. It is one of the most abundant shorebirds on the East coast during its migration.

Animal food: The principal items of food are insects, especially flies and their larvae, beetles, ants and other *Hymenoptera*, and caddisflies. Clamworms, various crustaceans, and mollusks of both the univalve and bivalve types are also prominent in the diet.

Plant food: Seeds of marsh and aquatic plants are eaten to a limited extent.

Atlantic Coast, 400 (0-30-193-177)
  * Bulrush *SuFSp*

Specimens: 0	30	193	177
WINTER	SPRING	SUMMER	FALL
0%	2%	2%	8%

+ Widgeongrass, Muskgrass,
Sedge, Pondweed, Bogbean,
Cattail

MARBLED GODWIT
Limosa fedoa

The marbled godwit still nests in our prairie states and Canada, though it is not nearly as plentiful as it was a hundred years ago. The bird is uncommon in the East, even during migrations.

Its wintering grounds are mainly south of our borders in Mexico and Central America.

The proportion of plant food averages about 50%. In 95 birds from the

West, the plant ratio was as follows: winter (4 birds) 50%; spring (14 birds) 24%; summer (56 birds) 45%; fall (21 birds) 65%.

Animal food: Insects are the principal animal food, especially fly larvae and beetles. Various crustaceans and mol-lusks, particularly univalves, are also eaten.

Plant food:

West, 95 (4-14-56-21)

**** Pondweed, Sago, sd. and veg.
SuFWSp

\+ Bulrush

HUDSONIAN GODWIT
Limosa haemastica

The Hudsonian godwit is a transient in the United States during spring and fall migrations. These snipe-like birds of mud flats, marshes, and shores nest north of our boundaries and winter in southern South America.

Nearly half of the food of the Hudsonian godwit is from plants. It is mainly seeds and fruits.

Animal food: The animal food consists mostly of insects, particularly fly larvae, and also snails, crustaceans, and clamworms.

Plant food:

North, 18 (0-7-5-6)

*** Bulrush *F*

** Cranberry, Small *Su*

\+ Smartweed, Bogbean

Avocet, Stilt: *Recurvirostridae*

AVOCET
Recurvirostra americana

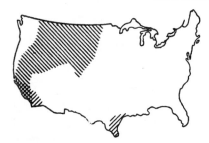

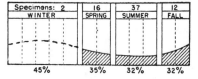

Specimens: 2	16	37	12
WINTER	SPRING	SUMMER	FALL
45%	35%	32%	32%

This western bird is common in alkali areas of the Mountain–Desert and Prairie regions. Like the godwits it has a long upward-turned bill, but in contrast to the godwits, the avocet is brightly patterned in black, white, and buff.

Animal food: Its food, which is mainly animal, consists chiefly of various insects, crustaceans, mollusks, and clamworms.

Plant food: The plant materials eaten by the avocet are almost entirely pondweed seeds.

West, 67 (2-16-37-12)

*** Pondweed *SuFWSp*

\+ Bulrush, Alga

STILT. The black-necked stilt is a noisy, eccentric, semitropical shorebird that nests along the Gulf coast and in the Southwest. It also winters in the Gulf region as well as farther south.

Insects, mollusks, small fish, and crustaceans are the stilt's main food. Among the insects eaten, beetles are most plentiful. Dragonfly and caddisfly nymphs, water bugs, and Mayflies also are important foods. Snails are the mollusks eaten most frequently.

Phalaropes: *Phalaropodidae*

PHALAROPES. The phalaropes total three species. One of them, the Wilson phalarope, nests in the western part of the United States. The other two, the northern and red phalaropes, are seen in this country only during migration. They nest in the Arctic and winter in South America.

The phalaropes are swimming sandpipers, a characteristic which helps to distinguish them in the field. They have the peculiarity of spinning about like tops while feeding on the water surface. It is an interesting fact that the females have much brighter plumage than the males—something unusual among birds. Also the eggs are incubated and the young cared for almost entirely by the males.

The food of phalaropes is primarily insects among which aquatic bugs, beetles, Mayflies, caddisflies, and dragonflies are prominent. Brine shrimps, water fleas, and snails are also taken commonly.

CHAPTER SEVEN

Upland Gamebirds

T o a large group of American sportsmen, upland gamebirds are important above all others—and with good reason. They provide a very large share of the bag for which hunters tramp afield. But the birds of this group also interest many more people who simply find them pleasing to see and hear. One cannot help enjoying the swift, graceful winging of doves, the cackling flight of pheasant over shocks of grain, the busy quail's cheery call, the drumming of grouse, or the peculiar notes and erratic flight of the woodcock.

Our principal upland gamebirds are the grouse (including prairie chickens), the quail (including partridge), the ringed-necked pheasant, wild turkey, woodcock, and the doves and pigeons. The woodcock is admittedly a ringer in this category. It is closely allied to the shorebirds, but its habitat includes upland fields and lowland woods. Furthermore, it is a well-known game species. Grouse, quail, pheasant, and wild turkey are all gallinaceous birds—they belong to the natural order *Galliformes* of which the barnyard hen is a common representative.

The upland gamebirds, exclusive of the woodcock, are primarily plant feeders. Doves take almost no animal food at all, grouse very little (except when young), while the animal food of quail and the wild turkey generally averages less than a quarter of the total diet. Wildlife technicians have given the diet of these game-birds their special attention. In some cases, a knowledge of the bird's food—especially of the plants used—has been instrumental in maintaining, restoring, or extending the range of the species.

General Reference: Life Histories of North American Gallinaceous Birds. Arthur Cleveland Bent. *U.S. National Museum Bul.* 162, 1932. 490 pp.

Grouse, Prairie Chicken: *Tetraonidae*

GROUSE. Eight species of these northern birds are found in the United States. Some, like the ruffed, blue, spruce, Franklin, and sharp-tailed grouse, are inhabitants of upland woods or brushy areas—often on mountains. Certain others, like the two species of prairie chicken and the sage grouse, live in comparatively open, level terrain. Subarctic relatives of the grouse are the ptarmigans.

Adult grouse are largely (more than 90%) vegetarian. Buds, leaves, fruits, and seeds are consumed to varying extents by the different species. In summer, insects are eaten to a limited degree as a supplement to the plant diet.

BLUE GROUSE
Dendragapus obscurus

According to present classification, two closely related western grouse, the dusky and the sooty, are treated as subspecies of the blue grouse. The dusky blue grouse (*Dendragapus obscurus obscurus*) is confined largely to the Rocky Mountains. The sooty blue grouse (*D. obscurus fuliginosus*) occurs

92

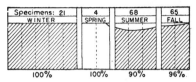

Specimens: 21	4	68	65
WINTER	SPRING	SUMMER	FALL
100%	100%	90%	96%

in the Pacific coast mountain ranges. Both are partial to woodland habitats —particularly coniferous forests. Several other subspecies of blue grouse are also recognized. The blue grouse is a popular gamebird, but its limited population has necessitated severe restrictions on open seasons and bag limits.

Animal food: Only in summer and early fall does the blue grouse feed to any considerable extent (10%) on animal food. The animal diet consists almost entirely of insects. In the early summer, scarabaeid beetles, leafhoppers, and sawfly larvae head the list of those taken; in late summer short-horned grasshoppers, ants, and leaf beetles are the most important.

Plant food: Leaves, twigs, and other vegetation are the principal food of this grouse; fruits and seeds are eaten to a lesser extent. In summer a variety of herbaceous plants are used, but in winter the leaves of conifers are the staple food.

Northern Rocky Mts., 158 (21-4-68-65)
**** Douglasfir *WSpSuF*
 ** Pine, lf. and sd. *WSpSuF*

 ** Eriogonum, lf. *SuW*
 ** Blueberry, lf. and fr. *SuF*
  * Cherry, Wild, bud and lf. *SuWSp*
  * Bearberry *Su*
  * Pussytoes, lf. *Su*
  * Gooseberry *F*
  * Spruce, lf. *W*
  * Willow, lf. and bud *SuW*
  * Mountain-ash *F*
  * Wallflower, lf. *F*
  * Vetch, lf. *Su*
  + Serviceberry, Wild Rose, Dandelion, Hawkweed, Gilia, Strawberry, Sedge, Shepherds-purse, Poplar

Pacific Northwest, 154 (24-39-59-32)
*** Fir, lf. *FWSp*
*** Douglasfir, lf. *WSpSuF*
 ** Cats-ear, flw. *Su*
 ** Blueberry, fr. and lf. *SuF*
 ** Bearberry *SuF*
  * Hemlock, lf. *WSp*
  * Pine, lf. *WSp*
  * Spruce, lf. *WSp*
  * Larch *SuF*
  * Clover, lf. *SuF*
  * Sedge *F*
  * Eriogonum, lf. *Su*
  + Sheepsorrel, Mountain-ash, Thimbleberry, Salal, Willow, Serviceberry, Aspen, Mountain-mahogany, Currant, Balsamroot

SPRUCE GROUSE
Canachites canadensis

The spruce grouse is a northern wilderness species that barely enters our country in northern New England and Minnesota. Our knowledge of the food habits of this tame, woodland grouse is based largely on specimens taken in Canada. The diet is almost exclusively vegetarian and consists primarily of conifer needles.

Canada and Northwest, 48 (12-4-12-20)
**** Pine, Jack, lf. *FWSp*
**** Spruce, White, lf. *F*
 *** Blueberry, lf. and fr. *Su*

*** Larch, lf. *SuF*
** Birch, bud and sd. *F*
** Fir, lf. *FW*
** Bearberry *Sp*
* Salal *F*

* Moss, capsule *Su*
* Sedge *Su*
* Beech *F*
+ Christmasfern, Woodfern, Bunchberry

FRANKLIN GROUSE
Canachites franklinii

The Franklin grouse is really a spruce grouse, though a distinct western species. Its main range is in the Northwest, north of the Canadian boundary, but it extends into the Rocky Mountain areas of Oregon, northern Idaho, and western Montana. In this country the bird is limited in population as well as in range. The principal data on its foods are from British Columbia.

Animal food: Only a trace—much like the spruce grouse.

Plant food:
British Columbia, 14 (0-0-6-8)
*** Blueberry *SuF*
*** Willow, lf. *SuF*
*** Mushroom *SuF*
*** Thimbleberry *SuF*
*** Crowberry *F*
** Pine, Lodgepole, lf. *F*
** Spruce, lf. *Su*
** Snowberry *SuF*
* Bunchberry *Su*
+ Bearberry

RUFFED GROUSE
Bonasa umbellus

Specimens: 1243	162	166	757
WINTER	SPRING	SUMMER	FALL
100%	98%	93%	98%

The ruffed grouse is the principal woodland gamebird of the North. It is typical of the wilder areas of our northern wooded states and also occurs throughout much of Canada and Alaska.

Unfortunately, in Canada and the North Central states the population of ruffed grouse is subject to periodic crash declines. During the mid-forties, the species passed through a low phase of these cycles but, since then, ruffed grouse numbers have increased and recently arrived at peak level.

Animal food: The adult diet is practically devoid of animal food. The young, however, eat quantities of insect larvae, beetles, flies, snails, spiders, and ants. They also consume seeds, especially of sedges.

Plant food: Though ruffed grouse are recognized primarily as browsers—eating foliage of woody plants, twigs,

94

catkins, and buds—they also relish fleshy fruits.

Northeast (mainly New York), 3267 (3267-0-0-0)
*** Aspen, bud and flw.
** Clover, lf.
** Hazelnut, bud and flw.
** Birch, flw.
* Greenbrier, fr. and lf.
* Sumac
* Grape
* Apple
* Hawthorn, fr. and bud
* Blackberry and Raspberry, fr. and bud
* Strawberry, lf.
* Willow, bud
* Cherry, Wild, bud and flw.
+ Dogwood, Dandelion, Oak, Hop-hornbeam, Blueberry, Wintergreen, Sedge, Hornbeam, Peavine, Sheepsorrel, Serviceberry

Virginia Alleghenies, 394 (394-0-0-0)
*** Oak
*** Grape
*** Greenbrier, fr. and lf.
* Wintergreen, fr. and lf.
* Mountainlaurel, lf. and bud
* Rose, Wild
* Sheepsorrel
* Pussytoes, lf.
* Blueberry, fr. and bud
* Hazelnut, bud and flw.
* Dogwood, bud and fr.
* Ferns, lf.
* Viburnum
+ Aster, Hawthorn, Partridgeberry, Sumac, Azalea, Menziesia, Trailing-arbutus, Serviceberry

Maine, 265 (47-23-7-188)
**** Aspen, bud *FWSp*
** Blueberry, fr. and bud *SuW*
** Clover, lf. *SuF*
** Hazelnut, flw. and bud *FWSp*
** Willow, bud and lf. *WSp*
* Apple, fr., bud, and lf. *FW*
* Birch, flw. and bud *FWSp*
* Raspberry *Su*
* Elderberry *Su*
* Sheepsorrel, lf. *Su*

* Maple, Red *Su*
* Wintergreen *SuFWSp*
* Hawthorn *F*
* Cherry, Wild, fr. and bud *W*
* Strawberry, Wild, fr. and bud *W*
+ Pyrola, Sumac, Viburnum, Serviceberry, Hawkweed, Goldthread, Beech, Cinquefoil, Woodfern

Pennsylvania, 207 (November)
*** Aspen, Large-toothed
*** Grape
** Hawthorn
** Dock
** Oak
* Blackberry
* Hop-hornbeam
* Blueberry and Huckleberry
* Cherry, Wild Black
* Witch-hazel
* Mountainlaurel
* Pear
* Wintergreen
* Birch
* Ferns
* Foamflower
* Hazelnut

Ohio, 42 (42-0-0-0)
*** Greenbrier, fr. and lf.
*** Aspen
** Dogwood
** Grape
** Sumac
** Beech, bud and fr.
** Witch-hazel
* Oak
* Bittersweet
* Fern, Rattlesnake, lf.
* Miterwort, lf.
* Apple, fr., bud, and lf.
* Hawthorn, fr. and lf.
+ Avens, Vetch, Pyrola

Wisconsin, 70 (9-3-1-57)
*** Aspen, Quaking, bud *WSp*
*** Hazelnut, catkin *FWSp*
*** Clover, White, lf. *F*
** Cherry, Wild *F*
** Blackberry *Su*
* Birch, catkin *FWSp*
* Dogwood *F*
+ Beadruby, Sumac, Nightshade, Elderberry, Strawberry, Rose

References: The Ruffed Grouse, Life History, Propagation, Management. Gardiner Bump and others. New York State Conservation Department, 1947. 915 pp.

The Ruffed Grouse, Its Life Story, Ecology and Management. Frank C. Edminster. The Macmillan Company, New York, 1947. 385 pp.

Early Winter Food of Ruffed Grouse on the George Washington National Forest. A. L. Nelson, Talbott E. Clarke, and W. W. Bailey. *U.S. Dept. Agr. Circ.* 504, 1938. 37 pp.

Food of Maine Ruffed Grouse by Seasons and Cover Types. Charles P. Brown. *Jour. Wildlife Mgt.*, Vol. 10(1), pp. 17–28, 1946.

Studies of the Eastern Ruffed Grouse in Michigan. Lee W. Fisher. *Mich. State Col. Tech. Bul.* 166, 1939. 46 pp.

PRAIRIE CHICKEN
Tympanuchus cupido

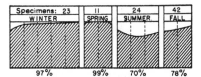

Specimens: 23	11	24	42
WINTER	SPRING	SUMMER	FALL
97%	99%	70%	78%

Animal food: The largest portion of the animal diet consists of grasshoppers. Beetles, bugs, caterpillars, and ants and other *Hymenoptera* make up the balance of the fare.

Plant food: The plant food is mainly seeds and fruits, but the birds also browse on buds and leaves.

This prairie chicken has two living subspecies, the greater and Attwater prairie chickens, and an extinct one, the heath hen of the Northeast. The last surviving heath hen died in 1932.

The greater prairie chicken (*T. cupido pinnatus*) was once abundant in the former grassy prairies. Its numbers were much reduced by market hunting and by agricultural invasion of their native habitat. Nevertheless, small colonies are still found in many localities of their original range. In the relatively unexploited Nebraska sandhills, fair-sized flocks are sometimes encountered.

The Attwater prairie chicken (*T. cupido attwateri*) is limited to southwestern Texas. According to Lehmann, its range has been reduced more than 93% and its numbers decreased more than 99% within the past 75 years. Fortunately, the few thousand remaining individuals of this Gulf coast bird appear to have a good chance to survive under present management.

Northern Prairies, 74 (16-6-17-35)
*** Corn *SuFWSp*
*** Oats *SpSuF*
*** Knotweed *SuFWSp*
*** Rose, Wild *SuFWSp*
 ** Wheat *SuFWSp*
  * Clover *SuF*
  * Bristlegrass *SuF*
  * Oak *FW*
  * Birch, bud and flw. *W*

+ Sorghum, Roughleaf Dogwood,
  Barley, Curly Dock, Snow-
  berry, Beaked Hazelnut,
  Greenbrier, Buckwheat,
  Sumac

Southeastern Illinois, 10 (0-0-10-0)
*** Blackberry (Dewberry)
*** Buttonweed
** Spurge, Flowering
** Ragweed, Giant
** Goldenrod, lf.
* Wheat
* Partridgepea
* Dogwood, panicle
* Cherry, Wild Black
+ Prairie Rose, Smartweed, Bris-
  tlegrass

Wisconsin, 15 (0-0-15-0)
**** Oats
*** Clover, White

** Aspen, Quaking
* Blackberry
* Knotweed
* Sedge
+ Bristlegrass, Buckwheat, Cherry,
  Dogwood, Dandelion, Spi-
  rea, Bluegrass, Jewelweed,
  Violet, Solomonseal, Vi-
  burnum

Texas, 23 (11-5-4-3)
**** Ruellia *SuFWSp*
** Ragweed, Western *W*
** Blue-eyed Grass *Sp*
** Blackberry *Sp*
* Falsegarlic *WSp*
* Buttonweed *FSp*
* Corn *Sp*
* Doveweed *SuW*
+ Gaura, Grape

References: The Prairie Chicken in Illinois. Ralph E. Yeatter. *Ill. Nat. Hist. Survey Bul.*, Vol. 22(4), pp. 377–416, 1943.
The Ecology of the Prairie Chicken in Missouri. Charles W. Schwartz. *Univ. of Mo. Studies*, Vol. 20(1), 1945. 99 pp.
The Attwater Prairie Chicken, Its Life History and Management. Valgene W. Lehmann. *U.S. Fish and Wildlife Service North American Fauna* 57, 1941. 63 pp.

LESSER PRAIRIE CHICKEN
Tympanuchus pallidicinctus

This lighter colored, western prairie chicken is a resident of the plains area, where in former times large numbers were reported. More recently, it was threatened with extinction until game laws intervened. The lesser prairie chicken lives on the open range but makes good use of available grain crops. Our data on its foods are very limited.

Animal food: Grasshoppers constitute by far the largest item in the animal diet. Beetles, bugs, and caterpillars comprise, for the most part, the balance.

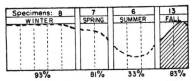

Plant food:
Oklahoma, 34 (8-7-6-13)
***** (52%) Oak *FWSp*
** Wheat *FW*
* Sumac, Dwarf *W*
* Gromwell *SpSu*
+ Sorghum, Partridgepea

SHARP-TAILED GROUSE
Pedioecetes phasianellus

The three subspecies of sharp-tailed grouse occupy an extensive territory from Alaska and northwestern Canada into northwestern United States. In this country the Columbian subspecies occurs in the Far West, the prairie

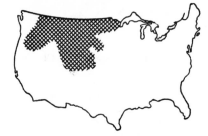

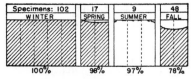

Specimens: 102	17	9	48
WINTER	SPRING	SUMMER	FALL
100%	96%	97%	78%

sharptail in the prairies, and the northern sharptail near the northern Great Lakes. The latter subspecies is the one that ranges farthest north in Canada and Alaska. Recently, it has become re-established in good numbers in Wisconsin and Michigan—beyond the range indicated on the map.

The sharptail is primarily an open woodland or brushland grouse. Even the prairie sharptail, which forages for food in open places, usually keeps fairly close to thickets and trees.

Animal food: The limited amount of animal food is taken mainly in the fall. It consists for the most part of grasshoppers, crickets, and beetles.

Plant food: The sharptail is varied in its plant diet, feeding almost equally on foliage, buds, seeds, and fruits.

Great Lakes Area, 188, fall and winter, plus droppings
**** Birch, White, sd. and bud
*** Mountain-ash, fr. and bud
*** Clover, White, lf.
** Alder, bud and flw.
* Cranberry
* Willow, bud and lf.
* Rose, Wild
* Raspberry
* Oats
* Cherry, Pin, bud
* Aspen, bud
* Knotweed
* Wheat
* Corn
* Dandelion
* Chokeberry
+ Sedge, Hazelnut, Bunchberry, Viburnum, Vetch, Goldenrod, Snowberry, Bearberry

Western Nebraska, 29, fall
*** Dandelion, sd. and lf.
*** Rose, Prairie
*** Clover, White, lf.
*** Sweetclover, lf.
* Snowberry, fr. and lf.
* Groundcherry, lf. and fr.
* Poison-ivy

Utah, fall, winter, and spring observations
**** Wheat *FWSp*
*** Grasses, sd. and veg. *FWSp*
*** Sunflower *FW*
*** Cherry, Choke *W*
** Alfalfa, veg. *Sp*
** Maple, bud *W*
* Sagebrush *W*
* Wyethia *W*
+ Yarrow, Dandelion, Rosinweed, Wild Rose, Willow

North Dakota (McHenry Co.), 34 (15-0-0-19)
**** Rose, Wild *FW*
*** Cherry, Wild, bud and sd. *FW*
*** Willow, bud *W*
** Poplar, bud *W*
* Corn *FW*
* Hawthorn *F*
+ Poison-oak, Oats, Wheat, Dandelion, Snowberry, Knotweed, Gromwell, Serviceberry, Bristlegrass, Ragweed

References: Winter and Spring Studies of the Sharp-tailed Grouse in Utah. William H. Marshall and Max S. Jensen. *Jour. Wildlife Mgt.*, 1937. 12 pp.

A Study of the Sharp-tailed Grouse. L. L. Snyder. University of Toronto. *Contribution Royal Ontario Museum of Zoology No. 6*, 1935. 66 pp.

SAGE GROUSE
Centrocercus urophasianus

Specimens: 38	39	106	29
WINTER	SPRING	SUMMER	FALL
92%	98%	91%	98%

this bird's food consists of the leaves and flower clusters of different species of sagebrush.

The sage grouse, also known as sage hen, is the largest member of the grouse family. It is a native of the northwest sagebrush country, and its existence is tied in very closely with the plant for which it is named. Its protective coloration, feeding, and nesting are all adapted to this plant; so it is not surprising that the range of the sage grouse is definitely limited by the distribution of sagebrush. A few scattered sage grouse are found in parts of southwestern Canada. Before the West was fully settled, these large gamebirds were abundant. Under present range conditions they would have probably disappeared entirely had there been no protective regulations.

Animal food: The small amount of animal food consists of a great variety of insects, chiefly ants and beetles (particularly ladybird beetles) and true bugs, such as the chinchbug.

Plant food: Nearly three-fourths of

Northern Desert, 203 (32-39-104-28)

***** (71%) Sagebrush, lf. and flw. *SuFWSp*

** Dandelion, lf. and flw. *SuFWSp*

* Alfalfa, veg. and sd. *SuFWSp*

* Clover, White, lf. and sd. *SuFWSp*

+ Gilia, Pussytoes, Agoseris

Reference: Life History, Habit and Food of the Sage Grouse. George L. Girard. University of Wyoming Press, 1937. 55 pp.

Quail, Pheasant: *Perdicidae and Phasianidae*

QUAIL. Six native species of quail and one introduced species, the Hungarian partridge, are present in different parts of the United States. They probably deserve to be ranked as our most important group of resident gamebirds.

Quail are largely seed eaters, feeding mainly on weeds and wild legumes. Insects, some of them injurious, constitute as much as a quarter of the summer diet of some species.

HUNGARIAN PARTRIDGE
Perdix perdix

The Hungarian, or European, partridge has been introduced into a number of states. In some localities it has had only temporary success, but in the upper Mississippi and Missouri Valley regions and Pacific Northwest, the birds have become well established. There is some possibility that where this oversized quail succeeds especially well—as in Alberta—it may compete directly with some of the native game species, such as the prairie chicken. **Animal food:** The small amount of animal food used includes insects and other invertebrates found on low vegetation in open places. Primarily these are grasshoppers and crickets, bugs, beetles, ants and other *Hymenoptera*, flies and their larvae, moths and butterflies and their larvae, centipedes and millipedes, and daddy longlegs. **Plant food:** Like other quail, the "hunkie" feeds primarily on seeds

Northeast, 43 (22-8-5-8)
*** Grass or Grain, lf. *WSp*
*** Corn *FWSp*

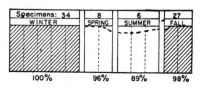

Specimens: 34	8	6	27
WINTER	SPRING	SUMMER	FALL
100%	96%	89%	98%

*** Wheat *SpSuFW*
*** Bristlegrass *FW*
*** Ragweed *FW*
  * Dandelion *SpSu*
  * Buckwheat *W*
  * Knotweed *FW*
  + Barley, Oats
Northwest (*Dak. to Wis.*), 32 (12-0-1-19)
**** Wheat *FW*
*** Barley *FW*
*** Oats *FW*
 ** Knotweed *FW*
 ** Bristlegrass *FW*
 ** Bromegrass *W*
 ** Tarweed *FW*
  * Alfalfa *Su*
  * Clover, lf. *W*
  * Grass, blade *F*
  + Fiddleneck, Sunflower, Buckwheat

References: The Hungarian Partridge in the Great Lakes Region. Ralph E. Yeatter. *Univ. of Mich. Bul.* 5, 1934. 92 pp.
The Hungarian Partridge in Wisconsin. Robert A. McCabe and Arthur S. Hawkins. *Amer. Mid. Nat.*, 1946. 75 pp.

BOBWHITE QUAIL
Colinus virginianus

As far as most sportsmen in the Southeast are concerned, this is *the* gamebird. Indeed, in this region the unqualified expression "bird" or "birds" generally means bobwhite quail. In the Northeast, high winter mortality prevents the bobwhite from being as important a game species, and in some states a completely closed season is observed. The introduction of this species into the Pacific Northwest has met with some success.

The bobwhite is one native American gamebird species that has prospered during the growth and development of this country. Farming areas have furnished an ideal habitat for it. Furthermore, the bobwhite and the ringnecked pheasant are the only two gamebirds that have been propagated artificially on a large scale. Even in states where gamebirds are plentiful, pen-reared birds are raised and released by the thousands. The modern

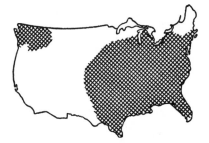

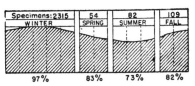

Specimens: 2315	54	82	109
WINTER	SPRING	SUMMER	FALL
97%	83%	73%	82%

trend, however, is away from this costly practice toward the more permanent gamebird production benefits resulting from improvement of food and cover resources of the environment. A number of state conservation departments are finding that sportsmen's money invested this way yields more than does artificial propagation and release.

The dietary needs of the bobwhite have received more study than any other wild bird in America. Special attention has been given to the food requirements of young growing chicks. **Animal food:** Beetles make up nearly one-half of the animal food, particularly ground beetles, leaf beetles, and weevils. Grasshoppers and crickets, various bugs, caterpillars, and other insects are consumed in large numbers. Spiders, snails, centipedes, sowbugs, and other invertebrates make up the balance. Young birds feed almost exclusively on the above animal diet. **Plant food:** Seeds are prominent in the diet, though tender leaves and fleshy fruits are also sampled.

Northeast, 175 (124-2-25-24)
- **** Ragweed *SuFW*
- *** Corn *FW*
- *** Smartweed *FW*
- ** Bristlegrass *SuFW*
- ** Wheat *SuFW*
- * Grape *FW*
- * Hogpeanut *FW*
- * Blackberry *Su*
- * Ash *FW*
- * Poison-ivy *W*
- * Sumac *W*
- * Oak *FW*

+ Panicgrass, Dock, Jewelweed, Black Locust, Spicebush, Partridgepea, Lespedeza, Flowering Dogwood, Crabgrass, Sassafras, Paspalum

Southeast (excl. Tex. and Okla.), 7,668 (7,639-0-29-0)
- **** Lespedeza, Common and Korean *W*
- ** Beggarweed *W*
- ** Oak *W*
- ** Partridgepea *W*
- ** Cowpea *SuW*
- ** Ragweed *SuW*
- * Pine *W*
- * Milkpea *W*
- * Paspalum, Bull *SuW*
- * Soybean *SuW*
- * Dogwood, Flowering *W*
- * Corn *SuW*
+ Wheat, Native Lespedeza, Wildbean, Sweetgum, Panicgrass, Vetch, Sorghum, Japanese Honeysuckle, Violet, Blackberry, Doveweed, Hickory, Black Locust,

Ash, Blackgum, Nutrush, Sumac, Carolina Geranium, Peanut

Northeastern Prairies, 105 (53-0-10-42)
**** Ragweed *FW*
**** Corn *FW*
*** Bristlegrass *FW*
** Sunflower *FW*
* Wheat *FW*
* Sorghum *FW*
* Knotweed *FW*
* Panicgrass *FW*
* Poison-ivy *W*
+ Doveweed, Sumac, Oak, Snowberry, Grape, Ash, Wild Rose

Texas and Oklahoma, 699 (699-0-0-0)
*** Sorghum
** Doveweed
** Oak
** Panicgrass
** Ragweed
** Corn
** Sunflower
* Milkpea, Downy
* Lespedeza
* Wildbean
* Sumac
+ Groundcherry, Spurge, Beggarweed, Wheat, Thistle, Crabgrass, Crownbeard, Chervil, Clover, Stillingia, Bidens

References: The Bobwhite Quail, Its Habits, Preservation and Increase. Herbert L. Stoddard. Charles Scribner's Sons, 1931. 559 pp.
Bobwhites on the Rise. Verne E. Davidson. Charles Scribner's Sons, 1949. 150 pp.
The Bobwhite Quail in Eastern Maryland. Kenneth A. Wilson and Ernest A. Vaughn. Game and Inland Fish Commission of Maryland, 1944. 138 pp.
Quail-food Plants of the Southeastern States. Alec C. Martin. *U.S.D.A. Circ.* 348, 1935. 16 pp.

SCALED QUAIL
Callipepla squamata

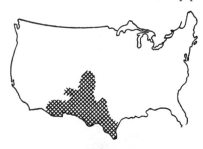

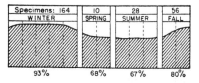

The scaled quail is a desert bird that has two distinct subspecies: the Arizona scaled quail (*C. squamata pallida*) of the Southwest and the chestnut-bellied scaled quail (*C. squamata castanogastris*) of southern Texas and northeastern Mexico.

The Arizona scaled quail occupies habitats that are even more barren than those used by either the Gambel or Mearns quail. It is found in rocky areas where cactus or other thorny shrubs prevail. The hunter finds it an elusive target. The birds, instead of flying when approached, usually scamper from sight with incredible speed.

The chestnut-belly, a brownish edition of the scaled quail, has very limited distribution in this country. It ranges southward from the lower Rio Grande section of Texas and thrives in areas supporting pricklypear cactus. Our information on its foods are limited to a small series of birds taken in Texas.

Animal food: The animal diet of the scaled quail, as judged by the Arizona subspecies, is twice that of the bobwhite and is greater than that of any other quail. It consists mainly of beetles, grasshoppers, ants, true bugs, leafhoppers, and spiders.

Plant Food:
Southwest, 258 (164-10-28-56)
  ** Sorghum *SuFW*
  ** Tansymustard *Sp*
  ** Snakeweed *W*
  * Deervetch *SuWSp*
  * Pigweed *SuFW*
  * Wheat *SuF*
  * Sunflower *FW*
  * Morning-glory *FW*
  * Evolvulus *SuFW*
  * Pricklypear *SuFW*
  * Mesquite *SuFWSp*
  * Filaree *SuW*
  * Oats *FW*

  + Vetch, Sage, Nightshade, Dove-
    weed
Southwest Texas, 32 (32-0-0-0)
  **** Wildprivet
  **** Acacia, Catclaw
  ** Lupine
  * Chervil
  * Bean
  * Doveweed
  * Clover
  * Neptunia
  * Capul
  * Hackberry
  * Pricklypear
  + Locoweed, Sorghum, Mesquite,
    Ground Spurge

Reference: Some Plants Valuable to Quail in Southwestern Texas. Valgene W. Lehmann and Herbert Ward. *Jour. Wildlife Mgt.*, Vol. 5(2), pp. 131–135, 1941.

CALIFORNIA QUAIL
Lophortyx californica

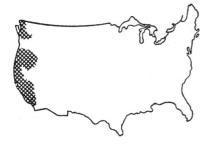

Specimens: 354	30	179	239
WINTER	SPRING	SUMMER	FALL
99%	95%	95%	99%

Animal food: The small percentage of animal food taken consists of a miscellany of insects, including ants and other *Hymenoptera*, beetles, grasshoppers, and crickets.

Plant food: In the late winter and spring, tender leaves, especially of burclover and filaree, constitute the major part of the diet. But in other seasons, seeds, particularly of legumes, are the staple food.

The California quail includes (according to recent classification) four subspecies. Of these, the valley California quail (*L. californica californica*) has the widest range and is by far the best known. Its range extends from California to parts of Oregon, Washington, and Nevada. Another subspecies occurs in a narrow coastal strip in central and northern California, one is confined to Santa Catalina Island, and the fourth occurs in Inyo County and vicinity.

The habitat of this jaunty, plume-topped quail varies from chaparral-covered upland to foothill slopes and valley floors. It is the principal upland gamebird in California.

California, 802 (354-30-179-239)
  *** Filaree, sd. and lf. *SpSuFW*
  ** Turkeymullein *SpSuFW*
  ** Barley *SuFW*
  ** Clover *SpSuFW*
  ** Lupine *SpSuFW*
  ** Burclover, lf. and sd. *SpSuFW*
  ** Deervetch *SuFW*
  * Oak *FW*
  * Poison-oak *FW*
  * Star-thistle *F*
  * Pigweed *SuF*

* Oats *SuF*
* Ryegrass *SuF*
* Bromegrass *SuFW*
+ Chickweed, Tarweed, Annual Bluegrass, Redmaids, Fiddleneck, Buttercup, Popcornflower, Gilia, Loco-

weed, Ceanothus, Toadrush, Wild Strawberry

Nevada, 189 (102-27-35-25)
*** Wheat *SuFWSp*
*** Burclover, sd. and lf. *SuFWSp*
** Alfalfa, lf. and sd. *SuFWSp*
** Barley *SuFWSp*
** Bassia *FW*
** Poplar *Su*
** Sweetclover *FWSp*
** Corn *WSp*
* Buffaloberry *SuFW*
* Russianthistle *FWSp*
* Bristlegrass *SuFW*
* Locust, Black *FW*
* Goosefoot *SuF*
* Violet *Su*
+ Pigweed, Ricegrass, Tansymustard, Dandelion, Greasewood, Wildmillet

Reference: A Life History of the California Quail. Lowell E. Summer, Jr. *Calif. Fish and Game*, Vol. 21, pp. 167–256 and 275–342, 1935.

GAMBEL QUAIL
Lophortyx gambelii

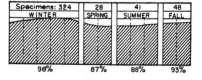

| Specimens: 324 | 28 | 41 | 48 |
WINTER	SPRING	SUMMER	FALL
98%	87%	88%	93%

The Gambel quail is a close relative of the California quail—another species of the same genus. It occupies an adjoining range in the desert regions of the Southwest.

Like the California quail, the Gambel quail is a jaunty plumed gamebird—the most important one in its region. It is a characteristic bird of river valleys and bottom lands and is partial to areas where mesquite, willows, or other shrubs provide some protective cover.

Animal food: Beetles, true bugs, grasshoppers, crickets, leafhoppers, ants, and spiders constitute the principal items in the meager animal diet.

Plant food: The Gambel quail is primarily a seed eater.

Southwest, 441 (324-28-41-48)
*** Mesquite *SuFWSp*
*** Deervetch *SuFWSp*
** Russianthistle *SuFW*
** Lupine *WSp*
** Alfalfa, sd. and lf. *W*
** Tansymustard *Sp*
** Spiderling *SuFW*
** Spurge *SpSuF*
** Bassia *FW*
* Crownbeard *W*
* Filaree, sd. and lf. *SuFW*

* Evolvulus *SuFWSp*
+ Pricklypear, Morning-glory, Mescat Acacia, Bristlegrass, Locoweed, Cupgrass, Mentzelia, Mistletoe, Sunflower, Sweetclover, Lycium, Horse-purslane, Brickellia, Corn

Reference: Life History of the Gambel Quail in Arizona. David M. Gorsuch. *Univ. Ariz. Biol. Science Bul.* 2, 1934. 89 pp.

MOUNTAIN QUAIL
Oreortyx picta

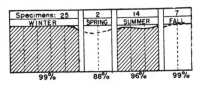

Plant food: Seeds are the principal plant food.

As its name implies, this species is primarily an upland one, living on mountains and hills of the Pacific region and adjoining states. In winter, those on the higher mountains migrate on foot to lower levels to escape deep snows. This migration, though limited in extent, is unusual among quail.

Animal food: The small amount of animal food consists chiefly of ants, ground beetles, leaf beetles, leafhoppers, grasshoppers, fly larvae, and aphids.

Pacific, 48 (25-2-14-7)
  *** Lupine *SuFW*
  *** Clover, sd. and lf. *FW*
  ** Bromegrass *SpF*
  ** Oak *W*
  ** Wheat *Su*
  ** Jointfir *F*
  * Deervetch *SuFW*
  * Barley *Su*
  * Filaree, sd. and lf. *SuFW*
  * Sumac *W*
  + Collomia, Collinsia, Fiddleneck, Cedar, Ceanothus, Knotweed, Tarweed, Bluegrass, Blue-eyed Grass

MEARNS QUAIL
Cyrtonyx montezumae

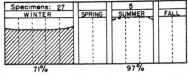

This small, oddly marked quail is limited both in numbers and impor-

tance. It occurs typically in rocky ravines of the semiarid mountains and hills in the Southwest and northern Mexico. Like other quail, the Mearns, or Montezuma, quail has adapted itself to the use of field crops where agriculture has invaded its native range.

Animal food: Among the items that make up the limited animal diet are beetles (particularly ground beetles, darkling beetles, and weevils), caterpillars, fly larvae, spiders, and centipedes.

Plant food:
Southwest (Tex., Ariz., and N. Mex.)
39 (34-0-5-0)

**** Chufa, tuber *W*
*** Oak *W*
** Sunflower *W*
** Brodiaea, bulb *W*
** Woodsorrel, bulb *Su*
* Pricklypear *W*
+ Caltrop, Corn, Spurge, Eriogonum, Morning-glory

RING-NECKED PHEASANT
Phasianus colchicus

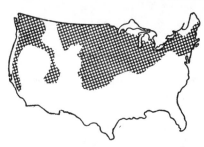

Specimens: 358	27	40	99
WINTER	SPRING	SUMMER	FALL
99%	93%	84%	84%

Except in places where their abundance has caused a local problem for the farmer, the introduction of the ring-necked pheasant is regarded as highly successful. This beautiful foreign bird is so well-established in many of our northern states that it has become an accepted member of our American gamebird group.

It thrives in the grain-producing agricultural regions. In some northern states, the artificial propagation of pheasants has been, and still is, a large program. In suitable range, however, the bird maintains its numbers without this costly practice. In general, introductions in the South have failed.

Animal food: Prominent in the animal foods eaten are caterpillars, beetles and their larvae, grasshoppers, crickets, fly larvae, and ants. Pheasants are also known to eat earthworms, toads, snails, spiders, millipedes, and egg shells (probably their own).

Plant food:
Northeast (excl. N.Y.), 819 (550-79-61-129)

**** Corn *SuFWSp*
** Ragweed *FW*
* Skunkcabbage *WSp*
* Grape *SuFW*
* Oats *SpSu*
* Oak *FWSp*
* Elderberry *Su*
* Buckwheat *SuFW*
* Cherry, Wild *FW*
* Wheat *SuFW*
+ Nightshade, Bristlegrass, Sumac, Burdock, Soybean, Dogwood

New York (Lake Plains Region), 153 (40-35-78-0)
*** Corn *WSp*
*** Blackberry *Su*
** Apple *WSp*
** Grape *Sp*
** Wheat *SuW*
* Sumac *W*
* Oats *Sp*

* Strawberry *Su*
* Barley *Sp*
* Beans *W*
+ Sedge

Northwest (*excl. Mont.*), 484 (90-75-260-59)
** Barley *SuFWSp*
** Wheat *SuFWSp*
* Oats *SuFWSp*
* Corn *SuFW*
* Ragweed *FW*
* Bristlegrass *SuFW*
* Russianthistle *SuF*
* Dandelion *SpSu*
* Knotweed *FW*
* Sunflower *FW*

+ Burclover, Sweetclover, Wild Rose, Groundcherry, Bean, Wild Cherry, Oak, Snowberry

Montana, 500 (126-104-153-117)
*** Wheat
*** Barley
** Corn
** Oats
* Oats, Wild
* Snowberry
* Bean
+ Bristlegrass, Sunflower, Wild-lettuce, Dandelion, Sorghum, Alfalfa, Sweetclover, Russianthistle

References: The Ring-necked Pheasant. W. L. McAtee (editor). American Wildlife Institute, 1945. 320 pp.

Wisconsin Pheasant Populations. Irven O. Buss. *Wis. Conserv. Dept. Pub.* 326, 1946. 184 pp.

Hunting as a Limitation to Michigan Pheasants. Durward L. Allen. *Jour. Wildlife Mgt.*, Vol. 11(3), pp. 232–243, 1947.

Wild Turkey: *Meleagrididae*

WILD TURKEY
Meleagris gallopavo

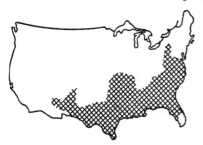

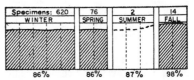

The wild turkey was the king of upland gamebirds in the early days when the East was being settled. It continued to be the leading species for sport and food for some time thereafter. Now, its numbers are so reduced that it is of secondary importance as a game species. Fair-sized populations of wild turkey are still found in some parts of the Alleghenies, in wooded coastal tracts along the Atlantic and Gulf seaboards, and inland in the Southeast as well as in Missouri, Texas, New Mexico, and Arizona. In most places, however, its numbers are continuing to decline. Only in extensive tracts of wild, wooded country does this prime bird have any real prospect of thriving.

The wild turkey has four subspecies in this country: the eastern wild turkey found through most of the Southeast, the Florida turkey in Florida, the Rio Grande form in Texas, and the Merriam subspecies in mountains of the Southwest. Three subspecies also occur in Mexico. From one of these, Indians developed the domesticated turkey long before America was discovered.

The wild turkey is a great hiker; it runs better and more often than it flies. It is wary, nervous, and constantly on the move. In summer, turkeys live in family flocks. The sexes commonly separate in fall and winter.

Semiwild turkeys are now propagated in some states and released for hunting. On the whole, these have been found poor substitutes for the genuine wild bird.

Animal food: The following items are the most common animal food: beetles, grasshoppers, crickets and walking sticks, ants, wasps and bees, flies (especially larvae of Marchflies), crayfish, spiders, snails, millipedes and centipedes, caterpillars, and true bugs. There are also a few records of salamanders being eaten.

Plant food: The plant food is mainly seeds and wild fruits, but there is some minor use of leaves and buds, especially in winter. Turkeys are particularly fond of nuts such as acorns and beechnuts (one crop contained 221 large acorns), but they also consume large quantities of small seeds.

Pennsylvania, 20 (20-0-0-0) plus droppings from all seasons
**** Oak *SuFWSp*
*** Grass, lf. *SpSuF*
** Grape, Wild *SuFW*
* Huckleberry *SuFWSp*
* Dogwood, Flowering *FW*
* Wheat *W*
* Corn *W*
+ Grapefern, Crabgrass, Viburnum, Blueberry, Bristle-

grass, Sedge, Sassafras, Sheepsorrel

Allegheny Mts. (Md. and Va.), 331 (331-0-0-0) plus droppings from all seasons
*** Grape *FW*
** Oak *FW*
** Crabgrass, sd. and lf. *SuF*
* Blackberry *Su*
* Dogwood *FW*
* Bluegrass, lf. and sd. *Sp*
* Buttercup *Sp*
* Bristlegrass *Su*
* Corn *W*
* Wheat *F*
+ Ash, Greenbrier, Eupatorium, Poison-ivy, Blackgum, Nimblewill Muhlygrass, Blueberry, Persimmon, Vetch

Virginia, 593 (593-0-0-0)
**** Oak
*** Dogwood
** Corn
** Grape
* Beech
* Blackgum
* Poison-ivy
* Greenbrier, fr. and lf.
* Lespedeza, Korean
+ Panicgrass, Ash, Japanese Honeysuckle, Peanut, Eupatorium, Goldaster, Partridgeberry, Sedge, Persimmon, Blueberry, Grapefern

Southeast (mainly Atlantic Coastal Plain), 342 (266-76-0-0)
**** Oak *WSp*
** Dogwood *WSp*
* Greenbrier, sd. and lf. *WSp*
* Blackgum *WSp*
* Beech *WSp*
* Oats *WSp*
* Chufa, tuber *WSp*
* Hickory *WSp*
* Holly *WSp*
* Pine *W*
* Poison-ivy *W*
+ Jack-in-the-pulpit, Goldaster, Partridgeberry, Rice, Bayberry, Grape, Corn

Missouri, 3,244 droppings from all seasons
*** Crabgrass, sd. and lf. *SuF*
*** Oak *FW*
** Paspalum *SuF*
** Panicgrass *SuF*
** Dogwood *FW*
* Grape *FW*
* Chufa *SuF*
* Clover *SuF*
* Buttercup *SpSu*
* Lespedeza *SuF*
\+ Bristlegrass, Blackberry, Hackberry, Blueberry, Pine, Cherry, Beggarweed
Texas, 64 (21-0-3-40)
*** Oak *FW*
*** Sorghum *SuFW*
** Sumac *W*
** Elm *Su*
** Oats *Su*
* Cedar *W*
* Hackberry *FW*

* Triodia *FW*
* Dropseedgrass *SuFW*
\+ Panicgrass, Bristlegrass, Ozarkgrass, Blue-eyed Grass, Zexmenia, Pricklypear, Corn, Locoweed, Nimblewill Muhlygrass, Wheat, Broomsedge
Arizona and New Mexico, 61 (23-0-0-38)
*** Pine *W*
** Oak *FW*
** Ragweed *F*
** Goldeneye *FW*
** Muhlygrass *FW*
* Dropseedgrass *FW*
* Gramagrass *F*
* Fescuegrass *F*
* Filaree, lf. *FW*
* Eriogonum *F*
* Peavine *FW*
\+ Bromegrass, Dandelion, Barley, Oats, Cedar, Silktassel, Lupine

References: The Wild Turkey in Virginia. Henry S. Mosby and Charles O. Handley. Commission of Game and Inland Fisheries, 1943. 281 pp.

History and Management of Merriam's Wild Turkey. J. Stokley Ligon. New Mexico Game and Fish Commission, 1946. 84 pp.

The Merriam Turkey on the San Carlos Reservation. Adolph Murie. *Jour. Wildlife Mgt.*, Vol. 10(4), 1946.

Early Winter Food Preferences of the Wild Turkey on the George Washington National Forest. A. C. Martin, Franklin H. May, and Talbott E. Clarke. *Trans. 4th N. Amer. Wildlife Conf.*, 1939.

Food Habit Trends of the Wild Turkey in Missouri. Paul D. Dalke and others. *Jour. Wildlife Mgt.* Vol. 6(3), 1942.

The Ecology and Management of the Wild Turkey in Missouri. Paul D. Dalke, A. Starker Leopold, and David L. Spencer. *Missouri Conservation Commission Tech. Bul.* 1, 1946. 86 pp.

The Wild Turkey in Alabama. Robert J. Wheeler, Jr. Alabama Dept. of Conservation, 1948. 92 pp.

Woodcock: *Scolopacidae*

AMERICAN WOODCOCK
Philohela minor

The woodcock is not only outstanding as a game species but is also one of our oddest birds. The plump body, short thick neck, and heavy long bill give it a unique appearance. During the breeding season, additional peculiarities are the woodcock's eccentric spiral flight and peculiar call. This popular eastern gamebird inhabits grassy fields and meadows as well as lowland woods. It nests on the ground in brushy fields or in the margins of woods.

Animal food: Two-thirds of its animal diet, which averages about nine-tenths of all it eats, consists of earthworms. The balance is made up of insects (mostly flies, beetles, and caterpillars), together with crustaceans, millipedes, centipedes, and spiders.

Plant food: The small quantity of plant food includes a variety of seeds.

Specimens: 36	17	31	164
WINTER	SPRING	SUMMER	FALL
9%	13%	2%	6%

East, 248 (36-17-31-164)
  + Bristlegrass, Blackberry, Panic-grass, Sedge, Ragweed, Knotweed, Violet

References: The American Woodcock. Olin S. Pettingill, Jr. Boston Society of Natural History. 1936. 360 pp.

Ecology and Management of the American Woodcock. Howard L. Mendall and Clarence M. Aldous. Maine Cooperative Wildlife Research Unit, 1943. 202 pp.

Doves, Pigeons: *Columbidae*

DOVES AND PIGEONS. Aside from the semidomesticated common pigeon, or rock dove, we have four principal members of the dove group in the United States: the band-tailed pigeon, mourning dove, white-winged dove, and ground dove. In former times the extinct passenger pigeon would also have been listed here. Four additional species barely enter the southern borders of the country. They are the white-crowned pigeon, the red-billed pigeon, the white-fronted dove, and the Inca dove. Still other doves and pigeons occur farther south in Mexico, Central America, and South America. Most species are migratory in some degree.

Doves and pigeons are vegetarians. Ours are mainly ground feeders and make seeds their staff of life—except for the band-tailed pigeon which subsists primarily on fruits. Since all species have a practically 100% plant diet throughout the year, ratio diagrams have been omitted.

BAND-TAILED PIGEON
Columba fasciata

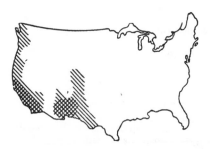

This large western pigeon has sometimes been mistaken for the extinct passenger pigeon whose fate it seemed about to share at one time. Regulation of hunting has enabled the bird to survive, and in some localities these pigeons have increased in numbers to the extent that their roving flocks have become an economic problem to the farmer.

The center of range of the band-tail is in Mexico, but it goes as far north as southern British Columbia in summer. It eats practically no animal food, subsisting largely on acorns, fleshy fruits, and seeds.

Southern Mt.–Desert, 133 (3-2-66-62)
**** Oak *F*
*** Pine *FW*
*** Cherry, Cult. and Wild *Su*
** Wheat *F*
* Centuryplant *Su*
* Mulberry *Su*
* Hackberry *Su*
* Sumac, Emory *Su*
* Grape, Canyon *Su*
* Sotol *Su*
* Bearberry *Su*

+ Mistletoe, Aralia, False Solomonseal, Cedar
Pacific, 510 (220-47-105-138)
*** Oak *WSp*
*** Cherry, Cult. and Wild *SpSuF*
** Dogwood, Pacific *F*
** Oats *SpSu*
** Elderberry *SuF*
** Wheat *SpSuF*
* Madrone *WSpSu*
* Buckthorn, Cascara *SuF*
* Garden Pea *SpSuF*
* Salal *F*
* Thimbleberry *Su*
* Bearberry *Su*
+ Pine, Hawthorn, Barley, Blueberry

MOURNING DOVE
Zenaidura macroura

If one were to seek out the typical bird of this country, it might well be the mourning dove. It is truly American since it nests in every single state. This gentle, unobtrusive bird is so adaptable that it is equally at home in wooded areas of the East, in the open prairies, and in western mountain regions. Two subspecies are recognized: an eastern and a western.

Though the mourning dove lays only two eggs, it usually raises two broods a year and, in the South, sometimes three. Its life history has been intensively studied in recent years—partly to determine the periods in which open hunting seasons will conflict least with late nesting. No one wants the mourning dove to go the way of the passenger pigeon—and under present management, it is not likely to do so.

In the fall, mourning doves can often be seen in small or large flocks preparatory to migration. During winter months, they concentrate in the southern half of the country. It is in the South, therefore, that mourning doves are particularly important as gamebirds.

The favorite feeding places of this bird are fields, orchards, or other open weedy areas where seeds can be gleaned readily. It also visits watering places frequently.

Animal food: Only traces of insect or other animal food are eaten. The data compiled for this study totaled 100% plant food in each of the four seasons.

Plant food:
Northeast, 184 (8-31-82-63)
*** Bristlegrass *SuFWSp*
*** Corn *SuFWSp*

111

*** Wheat *SuFWSp*
** Buckwheat *FSp*
** Ragweed *SuFWSp*
** Pokeweed *FWSp*
 * Knotweed *SuF*
 * Crabgrass *FW*
 + Pigweed, Wintercress, Spurge, Doveweed, Woodsorrel, Panicgrass, Acalypha, Bluecurls, Violet, Carolina Geranium

Southeast, 219 (42-51-10-116)
*** Corn *SuFWSp*
*** Bristlegrass *SuF*
** Crowfootgrass *FWSp*
** Cowpea *SuFWSp*
** Crabgrass *SuFWSp*
** Ragweed *FW*
 * Oats *Su*
 * Pine *FW*
 * Doveweed *SuFWSp*
 * Pokeweed *FW*
 * Panicgrass *SpSu*
 * Paspalum, Bull *SuFWSp*
 * Wheat *SpSu*
 * Geranium, Carolina *SpSu*
 * Chickweed *SpSu*
 + Vetch, Woodsorrel, Wildbean, Peanut, Spurge

Prairies, 142 (9-7-106-20)
*** Pigweed *SuWSp*
*** Corn *SuFWSp*
*** Doveweed *SuF*
*** Bristlegrass *SuFSp*
** Spurge *SuFSp*

** Wheat *Su*
** Knotweed *Su*
** Sunflower *SuFW*
 * Panicgrass *Su*
 + Sorghum, Woodsorrel, Acalypha, Goosefoot, Ragweed, Paspalum

Mt.–Desert, 167 (1-15-59-92)
**** Wheat *SpSuF*
*** Doveweed *SuF*
** Pigweed *SuFWSp*
** Sunflower *SuF*
 * Horse-purslane *F*
 * Barley *SuF*
 * Bristlegrass *SuF*
 * Knotweed *SuF*
 + Spurge, Beeplant, Filaree, Ricegrass, Sorghum, Acacia, Caltrop, Goosefoot, Wild Heliotrope, Castorbean

Pacific, 70 (1-1-23-45)
**** Turkeymullein *F*
*** Fiddleneck *SuF*
** California-poppy *Su*
** Star-thistle *SuF*
** Redmaids *SuF*
** Mustard *SuF*
** Wheat *SuF*
 * Sunflower *SuF*
 * Tarweed *SuF*
 * Pigweed *SuF*
 * Chickweed *SuF*
 + Bristlegrass, Sorghum, Filaree, Minerslettuce, Knotweed, Deervetch

References: The Mourning Dove in Alabama. George C. Moore and Allen M. Pearson. Alabama Cooperative Wildlife Research Unit. 1941. 36 pp.
Ecology and Management of the Mourning Dove in Cass County, Iowa. H. Elliott McClure. *Iowa Agr. Exp. Sta. Res. Bul.*, Vol. 310, pp. 356–415, 1943.

WHITE-WINGED DOVE
Zenaida asiatica

The principal range of the white-winged dove is in Mexico, but the birds are not uncommon in the southern parts of the border states. The larger western subspecies of the white-winged dove occurs in southern New Mexico, Arizona, and California. The eastern subspecies is found in southern Texas and sometimes farther eastward. The whitewings are typically desert birds, feeding and nesting in farmed valleys but ranging far and wide through the arid countryside. There are restricted open seasons on these doves in Texas and Arizona. Locally, they sometimes cause damage to crops.

Animal food: Ants, snails, and beetle larvae appear among the animal food

items, but as in the mourning dove, only in very small quantities.

Plant food: Seeds and other plant materials constitute practically 100% of the diet throughout the year.

Texas, 431 (0-0-77-354)
**** Doveweed *SuF*
*** Sunflower *Su*
** Corn *SuF*
** Sorghum *SuF*
* Bristlegrass *Su*
* Pricklyash *F*
+ Nettlespurge, Tragia, Melons, Hackberry, Acacia, Southern Buckthorn, Pricklypear, Nightshade, Panicgrass

Arizona, 310 (0-40-227-43)

**** Barley *SpSuF*
*** Wheat *SpSu*
** Giantcactus *Su*
** Acacia *Sp*
** Sorghum *F*
** Doveweed *F*
* Lycium *Sp*
* Desert-willow *Sp*
* Oak *SpSuF*
* Condalia *Sp*
* Pricklypoppy *SuF*
* Melons *SuF*
+ Sunflower, Coachwhip, Calliandra, Jojoba, Hopseedbush, Grape, Horse-purslane, Jujube, Corn, Wildoats, Pricklypear, Mesquite

Reference: The White-winged Dove in Arizona. Lee W. Arnold. Arizona Game and Fish Commission, 1943. 103 pp.

GROUND DOVE
Columbigallina passerina

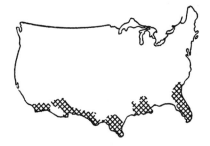

The small, brownish ground dove, a native of our southern border region, is too limited in numbers—and possibly in size—to justify an open hunting season. An eastern and a western race of the bird have been described in this country. Texas is the western boundary of one subspecies and eastern limit of the other.

We have appreciable food-habits information on only the eastern subspecies. It is almost entirely vegetarian, the plant food totaling 100% in each season except in winter when it drops to 99%.

Animal food: A few insects are eaten; mollusk fragments were recorded in one dove.

113

Plant food: These birds are ground feeders, and for the most part, eat weed seeds that have fallen or are available on low plants.

Eastern Gulf States, 41 (18-13-5-5)
*** Doveweed *SuF*
*** Paspalum *SuF*
 ** Panicgrass *SuFW*
 ** Bristlegrass *F*
 ** Cyperus compressus *WSp*

 ** Pine *FW*
  * Crowfootgrass *WSp*
  * Pigweed *WSp*
  * Sorghum *Sp*
  * Ragweed *W*
  * Chickweed *Sp*
  * Caperonia *Sp*
  * Spurge *FW*
  + Crabgrass, Woodsorrel, Goose-grass, Nutrush, Violet, Wheat, Corn, Purslane

CHAPTER EIGHT

Songbirds

T HIS GROUP IS designated by the name song-birds though some of its members hardly deserve it. Among the unmelodious species are crows, grackles, starlings, nighthawks, and shrikes. The group includes practically all the birds that are not covered in other categories.

The majority of our songbirds are migratory, staying with us only part of the year. Many species that winter in Central or South America nest in the United States and Canada. Conversely, many northern or arctic songbirds come south across our northern boundaries only for the winter months. Still other songbirds are more truly citizens of this country, remaining here throughout the year.

Besides their aesthetic importance to man—making life more enjoyable—song-birds are also economically significant. Many species help to control insects that are injurious to farm crops, orchards, forest trees, and gardens. The actual value of this service, apart from other means of control, is difficult or almost impossible to appraise. It can be easily overestimated or underestimated. Only if birds were completely absent for a couple of years might we be in position to know how much they curb destructive insects.

Unfortunately some songbirds have economic importance of another sort which is not so difficult to appraise. They do local damage to fruit orchards or grain crops. Deterrents of various kinds can be used to discourage such marauders. Occasionally, when these measures fail, more drastic steps must be taken. Most songbirds, however, are protected by international treaties and may not be killed without prior authorization.

General References: A Field Guide to the Birds. Roger Tory Peterson. Houghton Mifflin Company, Boston, 1947. 290 pp.
A Field Guide to Western Birds. Roger Tory Peterson. Houghton Mifflin Company, Boston, 1941. 240 pp.
Natural History of the Birds of Eastern and Central North America. Edward Howe Forbush and John Richard May. Houghton Mifflin Company, Boston, 1939. 554 pp.
Audubon Bird Guide, Eastern Land Birds. Richard H. Pough. Doubleday and Co., Inc., Garden City, N.Y., 1946. 312 pp.

Cuckoos, Road-runner: *Cuculidae*

CUCKOOS. Two species of cuckoos, the yellow-billed and black-billed, are common in the East. A yellowbill subspecies, the California cuckoo, is native in the West. A third species, the Maynard cuckoo, occurs in the Florida Keys.

115

These long-tailed, secretive birds are heard more than they are seen. Farmers call them raincrows on the assumption that their series of chuck-like calls presage rain. Unlike European cuckoos, our American species generally build their own nests and rear their young.

The yellow-billed and black-billed cuckoos are essentially alike in their food habits. Both are wholly insectivorous. About two-thirds of the diet consists of caterpillars—including the hairy or bristly kinds not eaten by most birds. Bugs, grasshoppers, and numerous other insects are also captured.

ROAD-RUNNER
Geococcyx californianus

This bizarre, long-tailed, ground-dwelling relative of the cuckoos is a resident of brushy places in the southwestern states and Mexico. It runs much more than it flies.

The road-runner, also known as chaparral cock, eats practically no plant materials. Its fare, as indicated by 104 examined specimens, includes grasshoppers and other large ground insects, spiders, lizards, small snakes, mice, and occasionally small birds or their eggs.

Whip-poor-wills, Nighthawks: Caprimulgidae

WHIP-POOR-WILL GROUP. These large-mouthed, bewhiskered nocturnal birds are represented by three species in the United States: the chuck-will's-widow in the Southeast, the whip-poor-will in the East and Southeast, and the poor-will in the West. All migrate in the fall—some wintering in our southern states and others traveling farther south.

The birds are seldom seen, though often heard, because they rest in the daytime and are active at night. They are almost entirely insectivorous, though the chuck-will's-widow occasionally feeds on small birds. The insects eaten most commonly include beetles, flying ants, moths, flies, grasshoppers, and mosquitoes.

NIGHTHAWKS. Nighthawks (known as bull-bats in the South) may be seen almost everywhere in the United States during summer evenings. They are equally at home over cities, fields, woodlands, and deserts. The common nighthawk ranges over Canada and the United States and winters in South America. Our only other species, the lesser, or Texas, nighthawk, is a smaller, southwestern bird that ranges from Texas and Utah to California.

The nighthawks are insectivorous—feeding on a great variety of insects such as flying ants, May beetles (also known as June beetles), flies, leaf chafers, mosquitoes, moths, and grasshoppers.

Swifts: Micropodidae

SWIFTS. Four species of swifts spend their summers in the United States: the chimney swift in the East, and the black, Vaux, and white-throated swifts in the West. All migrate southward in the fall—to Mexico and Central or South America.

These agile, swallow-like fliers spend most of the daylight hours on the wing, capturing their fare of insects. Prominent items are caddisflies, Mayflies, craneflies, various other flies, beetles, wasps, ants, bees, and true bugs. No plant food is eaten.

Hummingbirds: Trochilidae

HUMMINGBIRDS. These are the smallest birds in the world. And they are remarkable in other respects. Most hummingbirds are ornately decorated in beautiful iridescent colors. They have extraordinary flight ability—darting, balancing stationary in the air, or even flying backward, like aerial gymnasts. Their long, needle-like bills represent an unusual specialization for feeding in tubular flowers.

Hummingbirds are most abundant in the tropics. Of the 400 or more species in the Americas, about 15 come fairly regularly to the United States in spring and summer. A few even winter along our southern borders. In the East there is only one common species, the rubythroat, though the rufous hummer, mainly a western species, winters in limited numbers along the Gulf coast. The majority of our species are found in the Southwest. Only good ornithologists are able to identify the different species readily.

Not much is known about the food of hummingbirds beyond the probability that they get both nectar and insects from certain flowers. The fact that they are attracted by tubes of sugar water set out in gardens supports the assumption that nectar plays a part in their dietary role. However, stomach examinations of about 230 specimens—some of them collected immediately after visiting flowers—showed almost nothing but insects. Presumably the nectar is digested readily or escapes detection for other reasons. At any rate, the relative proportion of nectar and insects in the diet of hummingbirds is difficult to appraise and remains uncertain. Insects appearing most commonly in stomach examinations are small flies, ants, bees, and beetles. Besides taking nectar from flowers the hummers drink sap oozing from trees and also sip the juice from some fruits.

Plants known to be visited by hummingbirds are listed below in two categories: cultivated and wild. The species patronized most frequently are placed near the top of the lists.

Cultivated Plants Visited by Hummingbirds

(Throughout the United States, but particularly in the warmer parts)

Gladiolus (*Gladiolus*)
Petunia (*Petunia*)
Butterflybush (*Buddleia*)
Sage (*Salvia*)
Iris (*Iris*)
Fuchsia (*Fuchsia*)
Nasturtium (*Tropaeolum*)
Columbine (*Aquilegia*)
Orange, Grapefruit, Lemon (*Citrus*)
Canna (*Canna*)
Mimosa (*Albizzia*)
Acacia (*Acacia*)
Geranium (*Pelargonium*)
Begonia (*Begonia*)
Hollyhock (*Althaea*)
Althaea (*Hibiscus syriacus*)
Hibiscus (*Hibiscus*)
Larkspur (*Delphinium*)

Horsechestnut (*Aesculus hippocastanum*)
Clematis (*Clematis*)
Morning-glory (*Ipomoea*)
Lilac (*Syringa*)
Lantana (*Lantana*)
Phlox (*Phlox*)
Four-o'clock (*Mirabilis*)
Rose (*Rosa*)
Chinaberry (*Melia azedarach*)
Oleander (*Nerium*)
Eucalyptus (*Eucalyptus*)
Scarlet Runner Bean (*Phaseolus coccineus*)
Lima Bean (*Phaseolus lunatus*)
Portulaca (*Portulaca*)
Passionflower (*Passiflora*)

Wild Plants Visited by Hummingbirds

(In the East and Prairies. The ruby-throated hummingbird is the only species in this region, except for Florida)

Jewelweed (*Impatiens*). This is the wild plant most attractive to the ruby-throated hummingbird

Paintedcup (*Castilleja*)
Morning-glory (*Ipomoea, Convolvulus*)

Wild Plants Visited by Hummingbirds. *(Continued)*

Japanese Honeysuckle (*Lonicera japonica*)
Trumpetcreeper (*Tecoma radicans*)
Beebalm (*Monarda*)
Thistle (*Cirsium*)
Black Locust (*Robinia*)
Cardinal Flower (*Lobelia cardinalis*)

Vervain (*Verbena*)
Tuliptree (*Liriodendron tulipifera*)
Coralberry (*Symphoricarpos orbiculatus*)
Evening-primrose (*Oenothera*)
Turkscap Lily (*Lilium superbum*)

(In the Southwest)

Figwort (*Scrophularia*)
Penstemon (*Penstemon*)
Agave (*Agave*)
Ocotillo (*Fouquiera splendens*)
Aloe (*Aloe*)
Chuparosa (*Beloperone*)
Wild Tobacco (*Nicotiana*)
Paloverde (*Parkinsonia microphylla*)
Yucca (*Yucca*)
Manzanita (*Arctostaphylos*)
Larkspur (*Delphinium*)
Gilia (*Gilia*)

Currants and Gooseberries (*Ribes*)
Evening-primrose (*Oenothera*)
Columbine (*Aquilegia*)
Catmint (*Nepeta*)
Walkingstick Cactus (*Opuntia imbricata*)
Desert-willow (*Chilopsis*)
Creosotebush (*Larrea*)
Wolfberry (*Lycium andersoni*)
Beeplant (*Cleome*)
Morning-glory (*Ipomoea*)
Paintedcup (*Castilleja*)

(In the Pacific, particularly in California)

Penstemon (*Penstemon*)
Tarweed (*Madia, Hemizonia*)
Tree Tobacco (*Nicotiana glauca*)
Manzanita (*Arctostaphylos*)
Godetia (*Godetia*)
Lousewort (*Pedicularis*)
Delphinium (*Delphinium*)

Elderberry (*Sambucus*)
Jimsonweed (*Datura*)
Thistle (*Cirsium*)
Firechalice (*Zauschneria*)
Milkweed (*Asclepias*)
Fireweed (*Chamaenerion*)
Gentian (*Gentiana*)

Reference: The Feeding and Related Behavior of Hummingbirds with Special Reference to the Black-chin, *Archilochus alexandri* (Bourcier and Mulsant). Frank Bene, *Boston Soc. Nat. Hist. Memoirs*, Vol. 9 (3), pp. 399–478, 1946.

Kingfishers: *Alcedinidae*

KINGFISHERS. Two species of kingfishers are in the United States. The belted kingfisher covers most of this country and Canada. It moves south of our boundaries for the winter. The diminutive Texas kingfisher occurs only in southern Texas and Arizona and in Mexico.

Kingfishers are almost entirely animal feeders. They subsist mainly on fish but also eat crabs, crayfish, mussels, frogs, and lizards. The Texas kingfisher consumes insects frequently.

Woodpeckers, Flickers, Sapsuckers: *Picidae*

WOODPECKERS. Twenty-three species of woodpeckers have part or all of their range in the United States. This total includes three species of flickers and two sapsuckers. All these interesting, specialized birds have the common characteristic of a heavy bill supplemented by strong neck muscles for drilling purposes. By this means woodpeckers probe into wood for much of their food and also sculpture their nesting holes in dead trees.

Woodpeckers of one kind or another are present in practically all parts of the country—even in the deserts where giant cactus substitutes for real trees. Most species have only a limited migration, if any, but the sapsucker is a marked exception to this. Flickers also migrate for considerable distances.

Most woodpeckers do no economic harm to man. Generally their borings are in wood that is already dead. Sapsuckers, however, inflict major damage when they drill many holes into live wood. The California woodpecker sometimes becomes a nuisance when it riddles posts, bark of trees, and other timber with holes into which acorns are stuffed for future reference. Some woodpeckers feed mainly on insects, while others are more partial to seeds, nuts, and fleshy fruits.

References: Woodpeckers in Relation to Trees and Wood Products. W. L· McAtee. *U.S. Dept. Agr. Biol. Survey Bul.* 39, 1911. 99 pp.
Food of the Woodpeckers of the United States. F. E. L. Beal. *U.S. Dept. Agr. Biol. Survey Bul.* 37, 1911. 64 pp.
Economic Status of the Common Woodpeckers in Relation to Oregon Horticulture. Johnson Andrew Neff. Free Press Print, Marionville, Mo., 1928.

RED-SHAFTED FLICKER
Colaptes cafer

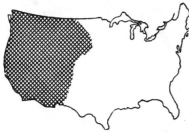

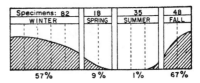

Animal food: The insect diet of this bird is very similar to that of the yellow-shafted flicker: ants, beetles, grasshoppers, crickets, etc.

The red-shafted flicker, like its eastern relative the yellow-shafted flicker, obtains much of its food on the ground —mainly ants and other terrestrial insects. It is interesting to note that these birds seem to specialize on somewhat poisonous foods. They are partial to the fruits of poison-ivy or poison-oak and to ants—the latter containing formic acid. In winter the diet swings strongly to the vegetarian side.

Plant food:
Pacific (mainly Calif.), 185 (85-11-39-50)
** Oak *FWSp*
** Poison-oak *FW*
* Grape *FW*
* Apple *FW*
* Elderberry *SuFW*
* Corn *SuFW*
+ Sumac, California Peppertree, Pine, Walnut, Prune

YELLOW-SHAFTED FLICKER
Colaptes auratus

The yellow-shafted flicker, or yellow-hammer, is common throughout the East except in the northern states during the winter. This is the bird that makes a stacatto "br-r-r-r-r-r" on metal roofs or other suitable sounding boards. We see them hopping on lawns looking for ants or tapping on trees in search of beetles and other insects.

Animal food: Half of the animal diet consists of ants and beetles. Ground beetles make up a large part. Grass-

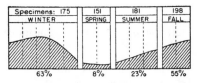

Specimens: 175	151	181	198
WINTER	SPRING	SUMMER	FALL
63%	8%	23%	55%

+ Oak, Sumac, Blackberry, Greenbrier, Grape, Corn, Blueberry, Serviceberry, Holly, Redcedar, Bayberry

hoppers, crickets, cockroaches, caterpillars, bugs, and various other insects supply the balance.

Plant food: In fall and winter more than half of the total food of this flicker consists of wild fruits.

East and Eastern Prairies, 705 (175-151-181-198)
  *** Poison-ivy *FW*
  * Blackgum *FW*
  * Virginia-creeper *SuFW*
  * Hackberry *W*
  * Dogwood *SuFW*
  * Cherry, Wild *SuF*

PILEATED WOODPECKER
Dryocopus pileatus

Specimens: 52	15	19	30
WINTER	SPRING	SUMMER	FALL
38%	6%	18%	49%

part of the remainder consists of beetles, particularly the larvae of woodboring species.

Plant food:
East, 88 (50-10-14-14)
  ** Grape *SuFW*
  ** Blackgum *FW*
  * Virginia-creeper *W*
  * Sassafras *Su*
  * Holly *W*
  + Dogwood, Greenbrier, Viburnum, Poison-ivy, Palmetto
Oregon, 28 (2-5-5-16)
  *** Elderberry *SuF*
  *** Buckthorn, Cascara *SuF*
  ** Cherry, Western Choke *SuF*

The pileated woodpecker, next to the nearly extinct and closely related ivorybill, is the largest of our woodpeckers. This magnificent bird ranges well up into Canada but is now rare in many parts of its original territory. It usually nests in mature stands of timber, preferring dead limbs of large trees.

Animal food: Ants constitute more than half of the animal diet. A major

RED-BELLIED WOODPECKER
Centurus carolinus

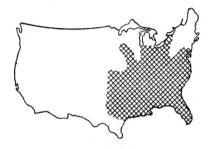

Specimens: 192 WINTER	27 SPRING	17 SUMMER	35 FALL
82%	44%	60%	83%

brates such as small tree frogs and lizards.

This is a common, striped-back species of the East. Its chattering calls may be heard throughout the year in deciduous woodlands and in large trees near dwellings. The red-belly is primarily a feeder on acorns and fruits. **Animal food:** Beetles (including woodboring larvae), ants and other *Hymenoptera*, grasshoppers, crickets, caterpillars, and bugs make up most of the animal diet. There are also records of these woodpeckers feeding upon verte-

Plant food:
East, 271 (192-27-17-35)
*** Oak *FWSp*
** Grape *SuFW*
** Corn *FWSp*
* Mulberry *Sp*
* Virginia-creeper *SuFW*
* Cherry *Su*
* Pine *FW*
* Poison-ivy *FW*
* Bayberry *FW*
* Hickory *W*
+ Dogwood, Beech, Hazelnut, Blackgum, Elderberry, Palmetto

GOLDEN-FRONTED WOODPECKER
Centurus aurifrons

The zebra-backed woodpecker of Texas and Mexico is similar and closely related to the red-bellied woodpecker of the East. We have scant information on its foods. The stomach contents of the 11 specimens collected in summer averaged 45% plant material. **Animal food:** This woodpecker feeds principally on grasshoppers, caterpil-

lars, beetles, ants and other *Hymenoptera*, and on bugs and spiders.

Plant food:
Texas, 11 (0-0-11-0)
*** Hackberry
** Pricklypear
* Pokeweed
+ Skunkbush Sumac, Bluewood Condalia

RED-HEADED WOODPECKER
Melanerpes erythrocephalus

This handsome eastern and prairie woodpecker is a familiar sight on roadside telephone poles or fence posts. Frequently too, one finds individuals that have been hit by highway traffic. The

redhead, like the flickers and Lewis woodpecker, obtains a considerable proportion of its food on the ground. **Animal food:** The redhead feeds extensively on beetles, ants and other

121

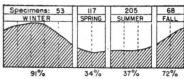

Specimens: 53	117	205	68
WINTER	SPRING	SUMMER	FALL
91%	34%	37%	72%

Hymenoptera, grasshoppers, caterpillars, and bugs. Hardly any wood-boring beetle larvae are taken.

Plant food:
East, 443 (53-117-205-68)
*** Oak *FWSp*
 ** Corn *FW*
  * Cherry, Wild *Su*
  * Mulberry *SpSu*
  + Blackberry, Elderberry, Apple, Grape

ANT-EATING WOODPECKER
Balanosphyra formicivora

The ant-eating woodpecker ranges from southern Oregon to southern California, thence across to south central Texas and south into Mexico. The subspecies commonly called the California woodpecker is the best known. It is notorious for the habit of storing acorns, its principal food item, in the bark of trees or in posts. The 90 specimens examined (35-0-33-22) had plant percentages as follows: winter 39%, summer 68%, and fall 88%.

Animal food: In spite of its name, this species eats fewer ants than most woodpeckers. Nor does it feed to any great extent upon wood-boring larvae. Bugs, flies and other *Hymenoptera*, beetles, grasshoppers, and caterpillars are some of the regular food items.

Plant food:
Pacific (mainly Calif.), 90 (35-0-33-22)
**** Oak *SuFW*
  ** Almond *FW*
   * Corn *SuW*
   * Walnut *F*
   + Elderberry, Fig, Wheat

LEWIS WOODPECKER
Asyndesmus lewis

This crimson-bosomed, gray-bibbed woodpecker of the West is unique among its kind. Besides the fact that the Lewis woodpecker seldom pecks or bores into wood in the typical woodpecker fashion, it also differs in its flight. It flies in an even, level plane as contrasted to the usual up-and-down course of other woodpeckers.

Animal food: Ants and other *Hymenoptera*, adult beetles, bugs, grasshoppers, and spiders constitute the main items of the animal diet. Caterpillars and wood-boring beetle larvae are

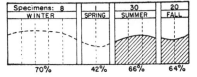

Specimens: 8	1	30	20
WINTER	SPRING	SUMMER	FALL
70%	42%	66%	64%

conspicuous by their absence from the stomachs examined.

Plant food:
Mt.–Desert and Pacific, 59 (8-1-30-20)
   *** Oak *FWSu*

** Elderberry *Su*
** Apple *SuF*
** Pine *FW*
** Cherry *SuF*
 * Hawthorn *SuF*
 * Currant *Su*
 * Serviceberry *SuF*
 * Dogwood, Western *SuF*
 + Poison-oak, Corn

YELLOW-BELLIED SAPSUCKER
Sphyrapicus varius

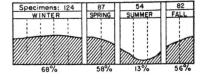

Specimens: 124	87	54	82
WINTER	SPRING	SUMMER	FALL
68%	58%	13%	56%

 * Cherry, Wild *F*
 * Dogwood *FW*
 * Virginia-creeper *FW*
 * Redcedar *FW*
 + Hackberry, Blackgum, Elderberry, Grape, Pokeweed, Sassafras, Apple

The yellow-bellied sapsucker is distributed over the wooded sections of the country. One subspecies occurs in the East and the eastern prairies, while three others are in the Far West.

Animal food: Beetles (larvae and adults), ants and other *Hymenoptera* are common in the sapsucker diet. Caterpillars, katydid eggs, spiders, and centipedes also occur.

Plant food:
East, 266 (77-80-42-67)
 **** Wood and sap from many kinds of trees including Maple, Birch, Fir, Hickory, Beech, Ash, Cedar, Tuliptree, Magnolia, Pine, Oak, Spruce, Elm *SpSuFW*
   * Holly, wood as well as fruit *FW*

Southern Prairies, 28 (28-0-0-0)
**** Wood and sap from various un-
      determined trees
**** Hackberry
  ** Holly
  ** Virginia-creeper
  ** Poison-ivy
   * Redcedar

Pacific (mainly Calif.), 37 (20-0-0-17)
 *** Undetermined fruits *FW*
  ** Wood and sap from trees *FW*
  ** Peppertree, California *FW*
  ** Poison-oak *FW*
   * Buckthorn *F*
   * Cactus *W*
   + Christmasberry

WILLIAMSON SAPSUCKER
Sphyrapicus thyroideus

This species nests in the Rockies, Sierras, and Cascade mountains and winters in California, the southwestern border states, and Mexico. The male and female of the Williamson sapsucker are so different in appearance that for some time they were assumed to belong to different species. Their borings are largely in pines and in other conifers.

In the 24 specimens (1-1-16-6) of Williamson sapsuckers examined for food contents, insects predominated, with ants and beetles the items taken most commonly. The plant material was practically all wood—mainly cambium and inner bark.

HAIRY WOODPECKER
Dendrocopos villosus

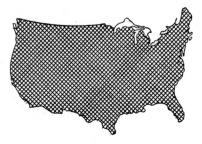

Specimens: 178	40	108	79
WINTER	SPRING	SUMMER	FALL
26%	20%	18%	24%

Animal food : Beetle larvae, ants, caterpillars, adult beetles, spiders, millipedes, and aphids constitute the major portion of the animal food.

Plant food :

East and Eastern Prairies, 405 (178-40-108-79)
   * Poison-ivy *FWSp*
   + Dogwood, Cherry, Pokeweed, Serviceberry, Corn, Blackgum, Virginia-creeper, Apple

The main difference between this species and its difficult-to-distinguish relative, the downy woodpecker, is its larger size and louder call notes. Both are alike in their food habits and in their widespread distribution, though the hairy woodpecker is generally the less common species. It has numerous geographic subspecies.

DOWNY WOODPECKER
Dendrocopos pubescens

The downy woodpecker has a range covering practically all the United States and most of the timbered area of Canada and Alaska. This smallest

Specimens: 411	104	175	138
WINTER	SPRING	SUMMER	FALL
29%	19%	14%	29%

** Poison-ivy *SuFWSp*
* Dogwood *FW*
+ Corn, Serviceberry, Oak, Virginia-creeper, Apple, Hophornbeam

of our woodpeckers is a common winter species, often seen with chickadees, titmice, or nuthatches.

Animal food: Wood-boring larvae of beetles and moths, adult beetles, and ants head the list of the downy's food items. Spiders, snails, surface-feeding caterpillars, and bugs (particularly aphids and scale insects) are also taken.

Plant food:
East and Eastern Prairies, 828 (411-104-175-138)

NUTTALL WOODPECKER
Dendrocopos nuttallii

The Nuttall woodpecker is a small striped-back, Pacific coast species ranging from southern Oregon to Mexico. It is a near relative of the downy and the hairy woodpeckers. Fifty-two specimens of this bird collected in California (12-2-24-14) had plant content averages as follows: winter 13%, spring 20%, summer 21%, and fall 35%.

Animal food: Beetles, caterpillars, bugs, ants and other *Hymenoptera* comprise the largest part of the animal diet.

Plant food: Much of the plant materials consumed by this bird are unidentifiable. Doubtless some of them consist of wood borings.

California, 52 (12-2-24-14)
** Poison-oak *SuF*
* Elderberry *SuF*

RED-COCKADED WOODPECKER
Dendrocopos borealis

This is a small, black-and-white-striped species of southeastern pine woods. Pine seeds are one of its principal foods. The 101 specimens of red-cockaded woodpeckers collected in the Gulf coast region (64-14-15-8) ate plant materials to the following limited extent: winter 22%, spring 4%, summer 12%, and fall 21%.

Animal food: It feeds largely on ants and beetles, most of the latter being wood-boring larvae. Grasshoppers, crickets, egg cases of roaches, caterpillars, termites, and spiders are also eaten commonly.

Plant food:
Gulf Coast, 101 (64-14-15-8)

*** Pine *W*   + Oak,   Bayberry,   Poison-ivy,
  * Corn *W*   Magnolia

WHITE-HEADED WOODPECKER
Dendrocopos albolarvatus

The contrasting black body and white head of this Pacific coast pine-forest species make it somewhat of a curiosity. Twelve white-headed woodpeckers captured in California, in winter, contained piñon pine seeds to the extent of 71%. The balance of the food was primarily ants. It also consumes beetles, bugs, various other insects and spiders.

California, 14 (12-0-2-0)
***** (71%) Pine, Piñon *W*

THREE-TOED WOODPECKERS. Two species of three-toed woodpeckers—the American and the arctic—occur in coniferous forests of our northern border states as well as in the Rocky Mountains south to Arizona and New Mexico. The major part of their range, however, is north of the United States in Canada and Alaska. These unique birds have only three toes, while other woodpeckers have four.

Examination of 70 stomachs of both species of three-toed woodpeckers showed almost no plant material except fragments of wood which were taken incidentally to the grubbing out of insects. Three-quarters of the food consists of wood-boring larvae of beetles and moths. Adult beetles, ants, and spiders make up most of the remaining one-fourth.

Flycatchers, Kingbirds, Phoebe: *Tyrannidae*

FLYCATCHERS. Most of the New World flycatchers nest in the United States and winter in Central America or northern South America. About 30 species of these agile, aerial feeders are summer residents in this country. Kingbirds, phoebes, and pewees are characteristic members of the flycatcher family.

Flycatchers subsist extensively on flies and on other winged insects. They help to control some of the insect pests of urban areas, farms, and forests. Flycatchers as a group are fairly uniform in their diet. True flies are actually the leading item. Mosquitoes, small moths, flying ants, and small beetles are also eaten commonly. In the main, flycatchers are entirely insectivorous, but a few of the larger species, notably the kingbirds, phoebe, and crested flycatcher, use small fruits as a minor part of their fare.

EASTERN KINGBIRD
Tyrannus tyrannus

Except for hummingbirds—which in the fall amuse themselves at the expense of other species—the eastern kingbird is really king of birds in the East. On rare occasion, one may hear their wings whistle as they chase and overtake a chimney swift or other bird. Crows are one of their most common targets. In the fall this kingbird migrates southward, wintering from Mexico to northern South America.

Animal food: Honeybees, ants, grasshoppers, and various beetles, bugs, and flies are the choice items.

Specimens:	156	497	48
WINTER	SPRING	SUMMER	FALL
	2%	18%	36%

Plant food:
East, 701 (0-156-497-48)
  * Sassafras *SuF*
  * Dogwood *SuF*
  * Cherry, Wild *SuFSp*
  + Pokeweed, Blackberry, Mulberry, Spicebush, Elderberry, Grape

ARKANSAS KINGBIRD
Tyrannus verticalis

The Arkansas kingbird occurs in practically all sections of the West and in recent years has extended its range eastward. Noisy groups of these aggressive birds are found commonly in groves of trees near buildings, in the Prairies as well as farther West. In winter most of them migrate to Mexico and Central America.

Animal food: Insects, in the following order, constitute most of the animal diet: bees and wasps, grasshoppers, beetles, bugs, and flies.

Plant food: Only the fruits of one kind of plant, elderberry, were found in appreciable amounts in 139 specimens examined.

West (mainly Calif.), 139 (0-30-103-6)
  * Elderberry *SuF*

CASSIN KINGBIRD
Tyrannus vociferans

This close relative of the Arkansas kingbird has a less extensive range in the United States. The Cassin kingbird nests from central California and southern Wyoming south into Mexico. It winters from California southward.

Animal food: Next to bees and wasps, this bird seems to prefer moths, and caterpillars (unusual for flycatchers), followed by beetles, bugs, and flies.

Plant food:
Southwest, 46 (24-0-8-14)
  ** Grape *FSu*
  * Elderberry *SuF*
  + Olive

GREAT CRESTED FLYCATCHER
Myiarchus crinitus

The great crested flycatcher summers throughout the East. It winters mainly in Central America and northern South America, though a few stay in southern Florida.

This pugnacious bird can often be

127

Specimens:	154	92	19
WINTER	SPRING	SUMMER	FALL

TRACE   7%   15%

seen or heard near the very top of large trees in woodlands or near dwellings. One of its peculiarities is its habit of including shed snake skin as one of the materials of its nest.

Animal food: Moths and caterpillars constitute the largest item of food. Beetles are next in importance, followed by *Orthoptera* (grasshoppers, crickets, and katydids). Bugs, wild bees, wasps, and true flies are taken

in considerable numbers. Incidental items include dragonflies, spiders, and various other invertebrates.

Plant food: Like another flycatcher, the kingbird, the crested flycatcher frequently feeds on fleshy fruits and particularly on those of sassafras.

East, 265 (0-154-92-19)
   * Sassafras *SuF*
   * Virginia-creeper *SuF*
   \+ Spicebush, Viburnum, Dogwood, Grape, Wild Cherry, Blueberry, Pokeweed, Mulberry, Blackberry

Reference: A Study of the Home Life of the Northern Crested Flycatcher (*Myiarchus crinitus boreus*). William Henry Mousley. *Auk*, Vol. 51, pp. 207–216, 1934.

EASTERN PHOEBE
Sayornis phoebe

Specimens: 120	89	78	68
WINTER	SPRING	SUMMER	FALL

21%   3%   5%   8%

by beetles, grasshoppers and crickets, moths and caterpillars, flies, bugs, and spiders.

The eastern phoebe is one of the earliest spring arrivals in the northeastern states. Its persistent call may be heard near bridges or other suitable nesting places, long before the leaves begin to appear.

Animal food: Bees, wasps, and ants top the list in the animal diet, followed

Plant food:
East, 355 (120-89-78-68)
   * Sumac *WSp*
   \+ Poison-ivy, Bayberry, Holly, Hackberry, Blueberry, Cherry, Blackberry, Elderberry, Sassafras

Horned Larks: *Alaudidae*

HORNED LARK
Eremophila alpestris

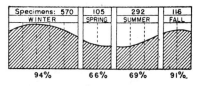

Specimens: 570	105	292	116
WINTER	SPRING	SUMMER	FALL
94%	66%	69%	91%

Though the range of the horned lark includes much of the United States, this shy, quiet, ground-dwelling bird is most abundant in the wide-open spaces of the West. One species alone is recognized, but it is split into 20 or more geographic subspecies. It is a true lark—a relative of the Old World skylark. Like the latter, the horned lark frequently flies high in the air while singing.

The horned lark feeds on seeds and insects that it finds on or near the ground. Weed seeds are its dietary mainstay, but in Southern California, commercial growers of vegetable and flower seeds have had to devise means of repelling the large flocks of horned larks which feed on the valuable seed crops.

Animal food: Beetles and their larvae, caterpillars, and grasshoppers make up a greater part of the animal diet.

Plant food:
East, 482 (285-67-114-16)
 **** Bristlegrass *SpSuFW*
 *** Ragweed, Common *SuFWSp*
 * Pigweed *FWSp*
 * Oats *SpSuFW*
 * Corn *SuWSp*
 * Smartweed *SuFWSp*
 * Sedge *SpFW*
 * Goosefoot *FWSp*
 * Wheat *SuWSp*
 * Crabgrass *FWSp*

 + Panicgrass, Clover, Woodsorrel, Sorghum, Dropseedgrass, Dock, Orchardgrass, Spurge
West (excl. Calif.), 381 (142-32-136-71)
 *** Bristlegrass *SpSuFW*
 ** Pigweed *SuFWSp*
 ** Knotweed *SuFW*
 ** Goosefoot *SuFWSp*
 * Ragweed, Common *W*
 * Sedge *SuFW*
 * Corn *SuFW*
 * Wheat *SpSuFW*
 * Oats *SpSuFW*
 * Sunflower *SuFWSp*
 * Purslane *SuF*
 + Saltbush, Panicgrass, Chickweed, Crabgrass, Shepherds-purse, Gromwell, Woodsorrel, Russianthistle, Dropseedgrass, Sorghum, Timothy
California, 337 (47-21-138-131)
 **** Redmaids *SpSuFW*
 **** Oats, Wild and Cult. *SuFWSp*
 ** Wheat *SuWSp*
 ** Filaree *SpSuFW*
 * Silene *SuFW*
 * Minerslettuce *SpSu*
 * Tarweed *SuF*

129

* Pigweed *SuF*
+ Fiddleneck, Eriogonum, Goosefoot, Chickweed, Turkey-

mullein, Mustard, Knotweed, Cyperus, Bromegrass, Fescuegrass

Reference: The Prairie Horned Lark. Gayle B. Pickwell. Academy of Science of St. Louis, 1931. 155 pp.

Swallows, Martin: *Hirundinidae*

SWALLOWS. Seven species of swallows, including the purple martin, spend their nesting season regularly in the United States. Most of them winter in Central or South America. The violet-green swallow is a western species, but the others (the tree, bank, rough-winged, barn, and cliff swallows as well as the martin) range over practically all the country.

All swallows are insectivorous—capturing practically all their food on the wing. The insects eaten most commonly are beetles of various sorts (including weevils, May beetles, and ground beetles), winged ants, wasps, bees, flies, bugs, moths, and dragonflies. Spiders are taken frequently and grasshoppers occasionally. Only one species, the tree swallow, feeds on plant products to an appreciable extent.

Reference: Food Habits of the Swallows, a Family of Valuable Native Birds. Foster E. L. Beal. *U.S. Dept. Agr. Bul.* 619, 1918. 28 pp.

TREE SWALLOW
Iridoprocne bicolor

The greenish-backed, white-breasted tree swallows summer in the northern half of the country and far northward toward the Arctic. In winter they migrate to our southern states, Mexico, and Central America.

The plant-food proportions for 362 tree swallows (22-88-207-45) were as follows: winter, 30%; spring, 1%; summer, 21%; fall, 29%.

Animal food: Flies, beetles, ants, bees and wasps, and bugs are the main food items; moths, grasshoppers, dragonflies, other insects, and spiders are also consumed.

Plant food: Tree swallows are partial to waxmyrtle or bayberry in the limited zones where it grows along the Atlantic and Gulf coasts. They feed on other fruits to only a small extent.

East (Coastal), 195 (22-43-119-11)
**** Bayberry *SuFWSp*
+ Virginia-creeper
East (Inland), 167 (0-45-88-34)
* Redcedar *SuF*
+ Dogwood

Reference: Studies of a Tree Swallow Colony. Lawrence B. Chapman. *Bird-Banding*, Vol. 10, pp. 61–72, 1939.

Jays, Magpies, Crows: *Corvidae*

JAYS. According to most recent classification, there are seven species of birds known as jays in the United States. They belong in five distinct genera. One of these, the piñon jay, is classed apart from the others as it is more closely related to the crows and to the Clark nutcracker.

Of our seven jays, three have very limited range. In the East the common blue jay is the only widespread species. The scrub, piñon, Steller, and Canada jays occupy extensive territories in the West.

Not all jays are blue or blue and white. One is greenish—the green jay of the southern Rio Grande region—while the small-billed Canada jays (whisky-jacks) are gray and white. The latter are confined largely to the northern states and Canada. Our food data for them are slight.

Only for some of the more common kinds of jays is there sufficient food-habits information to justify separate species accounts. However, these saucy opportunists show considerable uniformity in the type of food preferred. They fare primarily on acorns, grains, pine seeds, fruits, and insects. Jays are professional robbers, and in some areas they cause appreciable damage to crops. Many songbirds dislike and fear the jays because of their raids on nestlings or eggs.

In the main, jays are all-year residents, though some of them make short migratory jaunts in the fall and spring.

BLUE JAY
Cyanocitta cristata

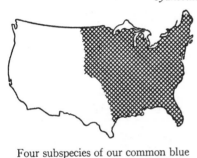

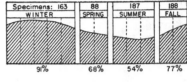

Specimens: 163	88	187	188
WINTER	SPRING	SUMMER	FALL
91%	68%	54%	77%

Four subspecies of our common blue jay range widespread east of the Rockies. These bold, handsome marauders are among our most familiar birds. Both winter and summer we hear their varied calls—some squeaky or tinkling, some harsh, and occasionally a cry like the red-shouldered hawk. In the fall some of the northern-state blue jays gather into small flocks and wander short distances southward.

Animal food: The blue jay's animal food is mainly large insects such as caterpillars, grasshoppers, and beetles. In breeding seasons, the eggs and young of small birds are part of the fare. It occasionally captures frogs or mice.

Plant food: As in most of the other jays, acorns are the staple food.

East (mainly Northeast), 626 (163-88-187-188)

**** Oak *FWSpSu*
 *** Corn *SuFWSp*
 * Beech *FWSp*
 * Blackberry *SuF*
 + Pecan, Wheat, Serviceberry, Blueberry, Mulberry, Wild Grape, Wild Cherry

Gulf States, 60 (41-11-5-3)
**** Oak *WSp*
 ** Pine *W*
 * Corn *WSp*
 * Grape *Su*
 + Blueberry, Holly

STELLER JAY
Cyanocitta stelleri

The Steller jay belongs to the same genus as the blue jay. It is a western cousin that inhabits inland mountains and coast ranges from Alaska to Cen-

131

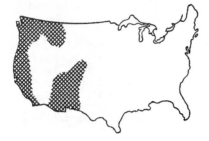

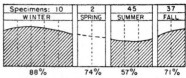

Specimens: 10	2	45	37
WINTER	SPRING	SUMMER	FALL
88%	74%	57%	71%

consists of insects—largely wasps, with some beetles and grasshoppers.

Plant food:
Pacific (mainly Calif.), 94 (10-2-45-37)
**** Oak *SuFW*
 ** Elderberry *SuF*
  * Cherry *SpSuF*
  * Oats, Wild *SuF*
  * Wheat *Su*
  * Raspberry *SuF*
  + Pine, Dogwood, Barley, Corn

tral America. The shrill challenging cries of this crested, black-headed, blue-bodied jay symbolize well the Far West.

Animal food: This jay's animal food

SCRUB JAY
Aphelocoma coerulescens

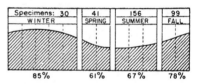

Specimens: 30	41	156	99
WINTER	SPRING	SUMMER	FALL
85%	61%	67%	78%

The scrub, or gray-back, jay is the most widespread of the western jays. Its territory is so far-flung as to include a small segment of the East—peninsular Florida (Florida scrub jay). The Woodhouse scrub jay is an especially widespread subspecies occupying much of the Mountain–Desert region.

Like other jays, the scrub jay often preys upon small songsters. Farmers and orchardists in some localities have reason to be unfriendly toward this colorful and interesting but wily bird. **Animal food:** The bulk of the scrub jay's animal food consists of insects, but the remains of egg shells and bird bones are encountered frequently in stomach analyses. The insects eaten are well distributed among the com-

mon orders, but grasshoppers are perhaps the most numerous. Wasps and bees are taken quite commonly, and the remainder of the invertebrate diet is divided among beetles, caterpillars, flies, bugs, and spiders. Occasionally lizards, frogs, and snails are eaten. **Plant food:** Acorns, pine seeds, and farm grains are principal plant foods of the scrub jay.

California, 326 (30-41-156-99)
**** Oak *FWSp*
*** Cherry, Cult., and Plum, Cult.
    SuF
  ** Pine *FWSp*
  ** Corn *SuFW*
  ** Raspberry *SuF*
  * Oats *SuFW*
  + Elderberry, Manzanita, Sumac
Southern Mt.–Desert, 9 (0-2-6-1) plus
  observations in various seasons

**** Pine, esp. Piñon Pine *SuF*
*** Oak *SuFSp*
 ** Wheat *SuF*
  * Gooseberry *Su*
  + Corn, Cherry, Serviceberry,
    Sumac
Florida, 16 (6-9-0-1)
**** Oak *FWSp*
  * Lippia *Sp*
  + Blueberry, Wheat, Huckleberry

Reference: A Preliminary Life History Study of the Florida Jay. Dean Amadon. American Museum of Natural History, New York, 1944. 22 pp.

MAGPIES. Our two species of these large noisy birds are disliked by Western ranchmen—since magpies sometimes prey on newborn, sickly, or recently branded livestock, as well as on poultry and wild birds and their eggs. In defense of magpies it may be argued that they render useful service as scavengers and also as destroyers of grasshoppers and other obnoxious insects. Actually they subsist mainly on insects—vertebrates and plant material are generally secondary foods except in winter when seeds and fruits constitute half or more of the diet.

Like their relatives the crows, magpies are very adaptable and are in no imminent danger of extermination because of man's prejudice. Thousands of these birds have been killed in Montana and elsewhere, but the dents in population are soon readjusted back to normal.

Magpies are all-year residents, commonly nesting in the same locality, year after year.

COMMON MAGPIE
Pica pica

Specimens: 92	62	109	51
WINTER	SPRING	SUMMER	FALL
56%	14%	37%	32%

The common, or American, magpie is the widespread species of the Northwest. Its range extends northward beyond our borders into Alaska.

Animal food: During the breeding season, weevils, ground beetles, *Hymenoptera*, grasshoppers, carrion, and small mammals constitute the main items of the animal diet. A second period of increased consumption of animal foods occurs in September occasioned by the annual crop of grasshoppers.

Plant food:
Mt.–Desert, 314 (92-62-109-51)
 ** Wheat *SpSuFW*
  * Cherry, Western Choke *SuFW*
  * Serviceberry *SuF*
  * Hackberry *FW*
  * Gooseberry *Su*
  + Apple, Skunkbush Sumac, Elderberry, Snowberry, Poison-oak, Cult. Cherry, Corn, Dogwood, Hawthorn, Pine, Nightshade

133

References: The Natural History of Magpies. Jean M. Linsdale. *Pacific Coast Avifauna No.* 25, 1937. 234 pp.
The Magpie in Relation to Agriculture. E. R. Kalmbach. *U.S. Dept. Agr. Tech. Bul.* 24, 1927. 22 pp.

YELLOW-BILLED MAGPIE
Pica nuttallii

This species is limited to the central valleys of California. Formerly it was also found along the coast.

Animal food: Insects, particularly grasshoppers, beetles, and hymenopterans, comprise the major portion of the animal diet. Spiders and carrion are also consumed in appreciable quantities.

Plant food:
California, 23 (10-0-2-11)
** Oats *SuF*
** Wheat *FW*
* Fig *Su*
* Oak *FW*
* Grape *F*
* Barley *SuF*
+ Fir, Poison-oak

RAVENS. Two species of ravens occur in the United States. The white-necked raven (*Corvus cryptoleucus*) is confined to the border region of the Southwest from Texas to Arizona and southward into Mexico. Food data for it are presented below.

The other species, *C. corax*, is widespread in higher elevations throughout most of the continent. In the East, however, it is found only locally in the Appalachians. Plant material is very secondary in its diet, the main food being insects such as beetles, grasshoppers, and cicadas together with some small mammals, birds and their eggs, scorpions, amphibians, and lizards. In the 27 specimens examined (5 collected in winter, 2 in spring, and 20 in summer) corn ranked as a 1-star item while melons, mesquite, and mistletoe were also found.

WHITE-NECKED RAVEN
Corvus cryptoleucus

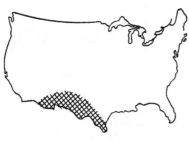

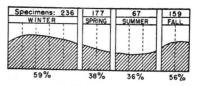

Specimens: 236	177	67	159
WINTER	SPRING	SUMMER	FALL
59%	38%	36%	56%

The white-necked raven often becomes an economic problem within its limited range in the United States. Field investigations on the activities of this bird showed that, though the reports of damage done were often much exaggerated, extensive losses were sustained in crops such as sorghum, corn, and melons. Apparently some of the damage can readily be avoided by good farming practices. This raven's food averages nearly 50–50, animal and plant.

Animal food: The principal animal food items are insects, particularly grasshoppers, beetles, moths, and caterpillars. Spiders, various other invertebrates, reptiles, amphibians, birds and bird eggs, and mammals (chiefly carrion) are also eaten. It is reported that on occasion feeble ewes are attacked.

Plant food:
Southwest (mainly Tex.), 707 (242-167-74-224)
**** Sorghum *FWSp*
** Corn *FWSp*

* Melons *SuF*
* Peanut *SuF*
* Pricklypear *Su*
+ Condalia, Hackberry, Martynia, Sunflower

Reference: The White-necked Raven in Relation to Agriculture. Shaler Eugene Aldous. *U.S. Fish and Wildlife Service Res. Rept.* 5, 1942. 56 pp.

CROWS. The crows of the United States include three species. The common crow occurs over most of the United States, the fish crow is confined to our eastern seaboards, and the western crow to the Pacific coast.

These large, black, loquacious birds are generally despised by sportsmen and farmers. In some localities crows are definitely destructive, but in other places they appear to do little or no real harm. Indeed, they often contribute a good deal of redeeming benefit to the farmer by destroying grasshoppers, other injurious insects, and mice. They are wary, adaptable birds and thus far have prospered in man's civilization despite many local campaigns of extermination directed against crow roosts. Their numbers are far greater now than in the days when the country was being settled.

More than half of the crow's food is taken from plants—farm crops, weed seeds, and fruits primarily. The balance of its fare is largely insects.

COMMON CROW
Corvus brachyrhynchos

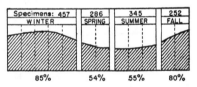

This species is present in practically all parts of the country and extends northward into Canada and southern Alaska. In the Canadian prairies, where there are important nesting grounds for ducks, the increasing crow population has created a special problem. Extensive studies have been made on the economic relationships of this bird. **Animal food:** Analyses of 1,340 stomachs show grasshoppers, scarab beetles, carrion, ground beetles, caterpillars, crustaceans, amphibians, and reptiles to be leading items. Other insects, spiders and myriapods, and eggs of domestic fowl are present in smaller quantities.

Plant food: Though agricultural crops are leading foods for the crow in each region, a considerable share of these are obtained by gleaning after the harvest.

East, 606 (220-137-135-114)
**** Corn *SuFWSp*
* Wheat *SuFWSp*
* Oak *SuFWSp*
* Mulberry *Su*
* Cherry, Wild *SuF*
* Buckwheat *SuFW*
* Oats *SpSuFW*
+ Pecan, Chufa, Sumac, Blackberry, Poison-ivy, Virginia-creeper, Bayberry, Serviceberry, Dogwood, Straw-

berry, Cowpea, Grape, Greenbrier

Prairies, 529 (174-126-214-15)
*** Corn *SuFWSp*
*** Wheat *SuFWSp*
** Sorghum *FWSp*
* Sunflower *FW*
* Oats *SpSuFW*
* Dogwood *SuFW*

* Sumac *FWSp*
\+ Serviceberry, Barley, Poison-oak, Melons, Mulberry, Oak, Hackberry

Mt.–Desert, 28 (5-7-12-4)
*** Wheat *SuFWSp*
** Oats *SpFW*
** Serviceberry *Su*
\+ Dogwood, Cherry

Pacific, 168 (55-14-1-98)
*** Corn *SuFWSp*
*** Wheat, *SuFWSp*
*** Walnut, English *FWSp*
*** Oats *SpFW*
*** Barley *FWSp*
* Chufa, tuber *WSp*
\+ Sunflower, Apple, Pine, Dogwood

References: The Crow in Its Relation to Agriculture. E. R. Kalmbach. *U.S. Dept. Agr. Farmers' Bul.* 1102, 1939. 21 pp.

Crow-Waterfowl Relationships. E. R. Kalmbach. *U.S. Dept. Agr. Circ.* 433, 1937. 36 pp.

FISH CROW
Corvus ossifragus

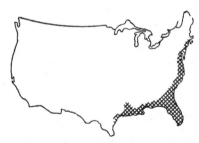

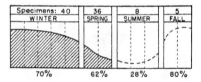

Specimens: 40	36	8	5
WINTER	SPRING	SUMMER	FALL
70%	62%	28%	80%

The weak croak-like calls of this tidewater species are the best field means of distinguishing it from the slightly larger common crow. Its range extends only a few miles inland along the Atlantic and Gulf coast tidewaters.

Contrary to common belief and the implications of its name, the fish crow apparently does not subsist primarily on fish. The winter, spring, and fall seasons show a predominance of plant food. In this connection, however, it should be noted that a major share of the specimens examined were collected in Florida.

Animal food: The fish crow's animal foods include weevils and other beetles (particularly scarab and ground beetles and their larvae), carrion, fish, crayfish, and eggs of birds and domestic fowl.

Plant food: The extensive use of greenbrier seeds is unique and surprising. Most of the specimens that fed heavily on greenbrier were collected in Florida.

Atlantic Coast, 89 (40-36-8-5)
**** Greenbrier *WSpSu*
** Blackberry *Su*
** Mulberry *Sp*
** Corn *W*
** Wheat *SpSu*
* Wildrice *W*
* Hackberry *W*

* Sawpalmetto *F*
+ Oats, Persea, Pokeweed, Blue-

berry, Grape, Bayberry, Fig, Sumac

PIÑON JAY
Gymnorhinus cyanocephalus

The piñon jay, or "blue crow," lives among the piñon pines and junipers in desert hills from Washington and Montana to Southern California and western Texas. It is different from most jays in appearance as well as in its habit of feeding in large flocks—like blackbirds. The name piñon jay is an apt one since a very large proportion of this bird's food consists of piñon pine seeds.

Animal food: Beetles, grasshoppers, caterpillars, and ants are the main items of its animal food.

Plant food:
Mt.–Desert, 17 (0-0-11-6) plus observations in various seasons
**** Pine, esp. Piñon Pine *FWSpSu*
** Wheat *SuW*
** Cedar *SuW*
* Corn *SuFW*
+ Sorghum, Beans, Barley, Oats

CLARK NUTCRACKER
Nucifraga columbiana

The Clark nutcracker is a picturesque resident of the higher altitudes of the West. It is particularly characteristic of the fir or spruce zones in the mountains from New Mexico and California north to Alaska. In winter it moves to lower altitudes.

Like the jays, the nutcracker is a common visitor at camps—probably due to curiosity as well as interest in food. In the small series of stomachs examined, pine seeds constituted about three-fourths of the total food. It is reported that the young are fed pine seeds exclusively.

Animal food: Grasshoppers, crickets, beetles, insect larvae, and small mammals comprise the animal diet of this bird.

Plant food:
Northwest, 16 (5-0-6-5)
***** (74%) Pine *SuFW*
* Fir *W*
* Wheat *W*
* Oats *W*
+ Corn, Oak, Lupine, Cedar

Chickadees, Titmice, Bush-tit: *Paridae*

CHICKADEES. The chickadee group in the United States consists of six widely distributed species. They are closely related to the equally pert and inquisitive titmice. Frequently one finds chickadees and titmice together, exploring the woods, feeding, and calling. Chickadees migrate only to a limited extent.

These birds feed largely on insects and seeds, the former dominating the diet. A considerable proportion of the food is difficult to identify because it is finely broken up.

BLACK-CAPPED CHICKADEE
Parus atricapillus

The black-capped chickadee nests and winters in the northern half of the United States and in southern Canada. Its "chick-a-dee-dee" is familiar to most of us.

Animal food: During winter, the blackcap consumes large numbers of eggs of moths, plant lice, katydids, and spiders. In warmer months the animal diet consists of moths, caterpillars, spiders,

137

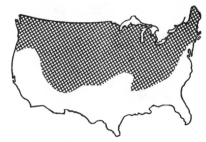

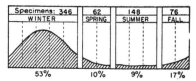

Specimens: 346	62	148	76
WINTER	SPRING	SUMMER	FALL
53%	10%	9%	17%

Corn, Chokeberry, Vir ginia-creeper

beetles (particularly weevils), flies, wasps, true bugs, plant lice, scale insects, leafhoppers, and treehoppers.

Plant food:
Northeast, 632 (346-62-148-76)
  ** Pine *FWSp*
  * Hemlock *W*
  * Birch *W*
  * Poison-ivy *W*
  + Blueberry, Bayberry, Ragweed,
      Sunflower, Serviceberry,

Reference: Annual Cycle of the Black-capped Chickadee. Eugene P. Odum. *Auk*, Vol. 59(4), pp. 499–531, 1942.

CAROLINA CHICKADEE
Parus carolinensis

The Carolina chickadee is a southern, slightly smaller and duller colored counterpart of the blackcap. It occurs throughout most of the Southeast.
Animal food: The animal food of the Carolina chickadee is almost identical with that of the blackcap. In winter, eggs of insects are a principal source of nourishment, while in summer a wide variety of adult insects are taken.
Plant food: In this chickadee as in others, a large share of the finely ground up plant material was unidentifiable.

Specimens: 88	57	47	18
WINTER	SPRING	SUMMER	FALL
55%	25%	11%	17%

Southeast, 210 (88-57-47-18)
  ** Pines *FWSp*
  * Poison-ivy *W*
  + Bayberry, Ragweed, Red Maple,
      Elm

MOUNTAIN CHICKADEE
Parus gambeli

The mountain chickadee is a native of the Rocky Mountains. Like the Hudsonian chickadee, this species frequents conifers. Its food is largely insects, except in winter, and includes nearly the same items as are eaten by the chestnut-backed and Hudsonian chickadees.

Plant food:
Mt.–Desert and Pacific, 112 (52-7-39-14)
  * Pine *W*
  * Poison-oak *W*
  + Oak

HUDSONIAN CHICKADEE
Parus hudsonicus

The Hudsonian, or boreal, chickadee, is a Canadian bird that barely gets within our northern borders. It is partial to conifers. Data on the foods of this species have been obtained from Canadian specimens as well as from birds collected in our northern states. Plant material is taken to a lesser extent than animal food, and it is often so finely broken that identification is difficult.

Animal food: The principal items in the animal diet are caterpillars, spiders, aphids, beetles, ants and other *Hymenoptera*.

Plant food: Conifer seeds supply practically all the plant food.

North, 110 (32-12-32-34)
* Spruce *FW*
* Fir *FW*
* Pine *WSp*
+ Hemlock and other unidentified conifer seeds

CHESTNUT-BACKED CHICKADEE
Parus rufescens

The chestnut-backed chickadee is largely a Pacific coast species but its range includes some of the northern Rocky Mountain area. It is found in relatively wild, timbered tracts from Alaska to western Montana and central California.

Animal food: The leading animal foods in its diet are the same as for the Hudsonian chickadee: caterpillars, spiders, aphids, beetles, ants and other *Hymenoptera*.

Plant food: Seeds of trees or shrubs constitute a supplement to the animal diet in the fall and winter months.

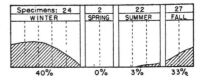

Specimens: 24	2	22	27
WINTER	SPRING	SUMMER	FALL
40%	0%	3%	33%

Pacific, 75 (24-2-22-27)
** Pine *FW*
* Poison-oak *W*
* Apple *SuFW*
+ Thimbleberry, Pacific Waxmyrtle

TITMICE. Two species of titmice divide most of the United States between themselves: the tufted titmouse in the East and the plain titmouse in the West. Two other species, the bridled and the black-crested titmice, barely extend over our southwestern boundaries from their main range in Mexico.

Titmice are so closely related to chickadees that recently they all were placed in the same genus, *Parus*. Like the chickadees, the titmice have little if any annual migration.

Acorns as well as other nuts and seeds make up much of the fare of titmice—especially in fall and winter. In the warmer months insects are the principal food. The bridled titmouse eats an especially large proportion of animal foods.

TUFTED TITMOUSE
Parus bicolor

The tufted titmouse, with its jaunty whistled notes, is one of the best-known birds of the East. It is particularly conspicuous in leafless winter woodlands when most other birds have flown southward.

Animal food: Caterpillars form more than half of the animal diet, wasps

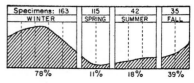

make up a large portion, and the balance consists of scale insects, ants, beetles, and spiders.

Plant food:
Northeast, 138 (76-12-27-23)
** Oak *W*
** Beech *W*
* Corn *FW*

* Apple *FW*
* Blackberry *SuW*
+ Elderberry, Mulberry, Blueberry, Grape, Serviceberry, Ragweed, Sunflower
Southeast, 171 (87-60-13-11)
** Oak *FW*
** Beech *FW*
* Blueberry *Su*
* Blackberry *SpSu*
+ Mulberry, Bayberry, Pine, Virginia-creeper, Hackberry

PLAIN TITMOUSE
Parus inornatus

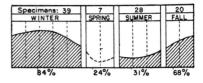

This western titmouse inhabits much of the Mountain–Desert and Pacific regions. The name "plain" fits this species very well since it lacks the ornamentation of our other titmice.
Animal food: The invertebrate portion of the plain titmouse's food consists

principally of caterpillars, various bugs, especially scales, beetles, ants and other *Hymenoptera*, and spiders.

Plant food:
California, 94 (39-7-28-20)
** Oak *W*
* Cherry *Su*
+ Oats, Apple, Pine, Star-thistle, Poison-oak, Walnut

BUSH-TIT
Psaltriparus minimus

This tiny grayish bird is a western relative of the chickadees and titmice. It ranges from British Columbia and western Wyoming to western Texas and Mexico. An additional species (formerly regarded as a subspecies) occurs in southern New Mexico and Texas.

Our information on the food of this active midget is confined largely to Pacific coast specimens.
Animal food: Most of the food of the bush-tit consists of various small insects and arachnids obtained on the foliage or twigs of woody plants. Prominent items are aphids, beetles,

140

caterpillars, scale insects, mealybugs, leafhoppers, treehoppers, true bugs, spiders, and pseudoscorpions.

Plant food: *Pacific (mainly Calif.),* 385 (138-18-89-140). Plant foods though considerable in winter (33%) and fall (27%) are difficult to recognize—mainly because items in stom-achs are finely comminuted. Records from stomach analyses indicate that galls—particularly leaf galls—constitute the bulk of plant food, though poison-oak fruits and a few kinds of seeds are consumed to a limited amount.

Nuthatches: *Sittidae*

NUTHATCHES. Nuthatches occur throughout the United States except in regions where trees are scarce or absent. We have four species in the country, one widespread, one in the Southeast, one in the Far West, and one in the North. They migrate limited distances only.

All nuthatches have the peculiar habit of creeping, head downward, on tree trunks or branches. Generally the foods eaten by nuthatches are broken up so finely that their identification in stomach examinations is difficult and some items remain undetermined. They are partial to conifer seeds—particularly pine.

WHITE-BREASTED NUTHATCH
Sitta carolinensis

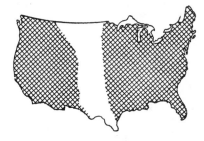

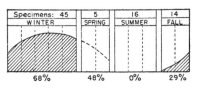

Specimens: 45	5	16	14
WINTER	SPRING	SUMMER	FALL
68%	48%	0%	29%

This is the most common nuthatch of the East. Some of its five subspecies are well represented in the West also. The whitebreast is the largest of our nuthatches, by more than an inch. It is partial to deciduous forests, where it feeds extensively on acorns. These or other nuts it frequently conceals in bark crevices for future use.

Animal food: Beetles, particularly weevils, ants and other *Hymenoptera*, spiders, moths, and caterpillars are leading items in the whitebreast's animal foods.

Plant food:
East and Eastern Prairies, 48 (32-4-5-7) plus observations
*** Oak *FW*

  ** Corn *WSp*
   * Pine *W*
  + Beech, Sunflower, Wheat, Sorghum, Hickory, Elderberry, Oats, Virginia-creeper
Pacific, 32 (15-0-10-7) plus observations
*** Oak *SuFW*
 ** Pine *FW*
  * Wheat *W*
 + Oats, Redmaids

RED-BREASTED NUTHATCH
Sitta canadensis

The redbreast nests well up into Canada as well as in the cooler parts of the United States. In winter it moves as far south as the Gulf. The high-pitched call of this species is distinctive. **Animal food:** Stomach examinations of the red-breasted nuthatch have been too few to give good indications of its animal diet. The insects eaten appear to be the more common bark inhabitants—similar to those taken by other nuthatches.

Plant food:
East, 7 (3-1-0-3) plus observations
**** Pine *FW*
 * Spruce, Black *F*
 * Maple, bud *Sp*
 + Corn, Wheat
Pacific, 8 (5-0-1-2)
**** Pine *W*
 * Cypress *W*
 + Elderberry

BROWN-HEADED NUTHATCH
Sitta pusilla

The brown-headed nuthatch is a resident of pine forests in the Southeast. This vociferous little bird is commonly found in small flocks. It forages among pines and makes pine seeds about half of its diet.
Animal food: The brown-headed nuthatch feeds on insects and other invertebrates that occur on the trunks and twigs of trees. Among these are ants and other *Hymenoptera*, moth eggs, caterpillars and cocoons, and scale insects.

Plant food:
Southeast, 16 (4-7-3-2)
***** (56%) Pine *FWSpSu*

PYGMY NUTHATCH
Sitta pygmaea

This smallest of nuthatches is a resident of the Far West. Like most other species, the pygmy nuthatch is partial to pine woods where it may be found in sizable flocks.
Animal food: The 30 stomachs examined showed the following animal food items in this approximate order: spittlebugs, ants and other *Hymenop-*tera, beetles, caterpillars, spiders, and true bugs.

Plant food:
California, 32 (6-1-24-1) plus observations
**** Pine *W*
 + Fir, Mustard, Clover

Creeper: *Certhiidae*

BROWN CREEPER
Certhia familiaris

The brown creeper is an inconspicuous species that is seldom noted except by bird students. These birds are widespread and fairly common in the northern states and Canada during the summer. They winter entirely within our boundaries.

The creeper, with its tail braced against the tree trunk, spirals upward searching for insects in crevices of the

142

bark. The food habits of the brown creeper need further study; only 12 stomachs have been examined.

Animal food: The chief animal food items in the few stomachs examined were spiders, small beetles, true bugs, caterpillars, ants and small *Hymenoptera*.

Plant food:
United States, 12 (3-1-3-5)
  * Pine *FSp*
  * Corn *W*
  + Panicgrass

Wren-tit: *Chamaeidae*

WREN-TIT
Chamaea fasciata

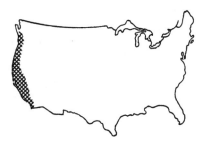

Specimens: 48	13	42	62
WINTER	SPRING	SUMMER	FALL
61%	6%	45%	76%

Wren-tits are native to our Pacific coast states. They conceal themselves, like wrens, in chaparral and other brushy growths.

Animal food: The animal food consists of invertebrates, principally ants and other *Hymenoptera*, beetles, bugs, caterpillars, and spiders.

Plant food: Fleshy fruits constitute about a half or more of the wren-tit's fare except during spring.

California, 165 (48-13-42-62)
  *** Poison-oak *FW*
  * Blackberry *Su*
  * Sumac, Laurel *FW*
  * Elderberry *Su*
  * Christmasberry *SuF*
  * Grape *SuF*
  * Waxmyrtle, Pacific *FW*
  + Salal, Snowberry, Pricklypear, Turkeymullein

Dipper: *Cinclidae*

DIPPER
Cinclus mexicanus

The dipper, or water ouzel, is one of our most interesting and unique birds. It is a true songbird, presumably related to wrens and thrushes and yet it has some of the aquatic habits of waterfowl. When searching for food, the dipper walks and swims under water—often in the turbulent current of mountain streams.

The dipper is the only one of its kind in the United States, but there are about 30 others in different parts of the world. Ours is a bird of the western mountains. Its range extends from New Mexico and Southern California to Alaska and Alberta.

The food of the dipper consists mainly of aquatic insects—especially beetles and caddisfly larvae. Moths, snails, some small fish, and fish eggs are also on the usual menu. Almost no plant materials are eaten.

143

Wrens: *Troglodytidae*

WRENS. Nine species of wrens are native to the United States. These active, vociferous birds have adapted themselves to a diversity of environments varying from brushy woodlands, garden shrubbery, marshes, and rocky canyons to cactus deserts. Most of the species migrate short distances, but some remain as all-year residents.

Plant material forms only a small part of the diet of wrens when it is used at all. Fruits and seeds are eaten to a limited extent by the two species treated below. Insects of many kinds and spiders are the main foods of wrens.

CAROLINA WREN
Thryothorus ludovicianus

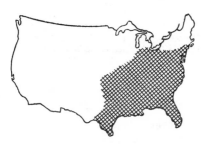

Specimens: 200	99	65	42
WINTER	SPRING	SUMMER	FALL
11%	2%	1%	3%

As indicated on its range map, the Carolina wren extends far beyond the Carolinas. The cheerful, ringing calls of this largest of our eastern wrens are heard commonly from the seclusion of brushy or viny lowlands—mainly in spring and summer.

Animal food: The Carolina wren's fare consists primarily of ants and other *Hymenoptera*, flies, and millipedes. Fragments of small vertebrate animals are commonly found in stomachs.

Plant food:
East, 406 (200-99-65-42)
  + Poison-ivy, Bayberry, Pine, Oak, Sweetgum

CACTUS WREN
Campylorhynchus brunneicapillus

The cactus wren is a native of southwestern deserts from western Texas to Southern California and down into Mexico. It makes its home among cactus, mesquite, or thorny shrubs and has the peculiarity of building extra or dummy nests that are not used.

The plant material eaten by the cactus wren does not exceed 11% in any season as judged by the 73 specimens examined.

Animal food: Beetles, grasshoppers, crickets, caterpillars, and bugs constitute the principal items of the animal diet.

Plant food:
California and Arizona, 73 (14-9-27-23)
  * Pricklypear *SuFW*
  * Elderberry *SuF*
  + Poison-oak, Fiddleneck, Filaree, Sumac

Mockingbird, Catbird, Thrashers: *Mimidae*

MOCKINGBIRD
Mimus polyglottos

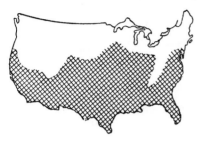

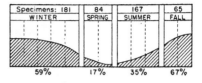

Specimens: 181	84	167	65
WINTER	SPRING	SUMMER	FALL
59%	17%	35%	67%

Mockingbirds are primarily southern in their distribution; only a sparse population is present along the northern fringes of their territory indicated on the range map.

Mockingbirds and their music are thoroughly enjoyed except perhaps on moonlight nights in spring and summer, when their persistent singing at all hours sometimes begins to pall. This bird's pugnacious activity often drives away other desirable species of songsters. This is especially noticeable at winter feeding stations.

The foods of these songsters vary markedly with the seasons. In spring and summer they are largely insectivorous; during fall and winter more than half of their food consists of fruits.

Animal food: Beetles, ants, bees, wasps, and grasshoppers are especially important items in the animal diet.

Plant food:
Southeast, 268 (122-34-77-35)
  ** Holly *W*
  ** Greenbrier *FWSp*
  ** Pokeweed *SuF*
  ** Virginia-creeper *SuF*
   * Elderberry *SuF*
   * Blackberry *Su*
   * Redcedar *FWSp*
   * Blackgum *W*
   * Grape *SuFW*

   * Sumac *FW*
   * Beautyberry *SuFW*
   * Hackberry *W*
   * Mulberry *SpSu*
  + Rattanvine, Chinaberry, Bayberry, Sassafras, Dogwood, Wild Cherry, Palmetto
Texas, 193 (59-50-54-30)
  *** Hackberry *SuFW*
   * Virginia-creeper *SuF*
   * Ehretia *Su*
   * Condalia, Bluewood *Su*
  + Blackberry, Holly, Wild Cherry, Pokeweed, Sumac, Poison-ivy
California, 67 (8-3-41-15)
  **** Grape *SuFW*
  *** Peppertree, California *FW*
  *** Fig *SuFW*
  ** Buckthorn, Cascara *SuF*
   * Cedar *W*
   * Poison-oak *W*
  + Elderberry, Nightshade, Laurel Sumac, Blackberry, Bearberry

CATBIRD
Dumetella carolinensis

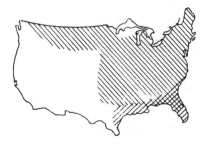

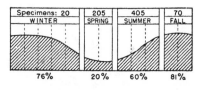

Specimens: 20	205	405	70
WINTER	SPRING	SUMMER	FALL
76%	20%	60%	81%

The catbird is one of our most familiar suburban species in the East. It is common in the vicinity of human habitations, often nesting in dense shrubbery. This is where one usually hears its cat-like calls and squeaky, varied melodies, or glimpses the dark gray bird moving furtively among the foliage.

The white man's invasion of the New World has probably been of distinct advantage to the catbird. It is fond of fruits from wild plants, ornamental shrubbery, orchards, and gardens. Generally the bird's toll from cultivated plants is not consequential. Early in the fall, shortly after the rearing of young, the catbird leaves for points south—some individuals going as far as Panama.

Animal food: Much of the catbird's diet represents activity directly beneficial to man. Ants, beetles, caterpillars, and grasshoppers constitute three-quarters of the animal food, the remainder being made up of bugs, miscellaneous insects, and spiders.

Plant food: Fleshy fruits dominate the menu more than in any other native bird.

Northeast, 522 (3-160-303-56)
*** Blackberry *SuF*
** Cherry, Cult. and Wild *SuF*
* Elderberry *SuF*
* Greenbrier *SpSu*
* Grape *SuF*
* Persimmon *F*

* Sumac *SpSuF*
* Blueberry *Su*
* Bayberry *SpSuF*
* Pokeweed *SuF*
* Dogwood *SuF*
* Serviceberry *SpSu*
* Sassafras *SuF*
+ Virginia-creeper, Mulberry, Nightshade, Holly, Spice-bush, Gooseberry

Southeast, 77 (17-17-29-14)
*** Blackberry *SpSuF*
** Holly *WSp*
** Bayberry *FW*
** Greenbrier *SuF*
** Poison-ivy *W*
* Sassafras *SuF*
* Pokeweed *F*
* Elderberry *SuF*
* Beautyberry *F*
* Blueberry *SpSu*
* Cherry, Wild *Su*
+ Huckleberry, Dogwood, Grape, Hackberry, Virginia-creeper, Chinaberry

West, 81 (0-8-73-0)
** Blackberry *Su*

** Buckthorn *Su*
** Buffaloberry *Su*
* Cherry, Wild *Su*
* Mulberry *SpSu*

* Gooseberry *Su*
+ Strawberry, Dogwood, Serviceberry, Mountain-ash, Blueberry

THRASHERS. Of our eight species of thrashers, one is very common in the East and northern prairies while the other seven are all western—especially southwestern. Besides the four species treated individually below, four others (Sennett, Bendire, Leconte, and Crissal) are summer inhabitants of the Southwest. All, except the sage thrasher, have curved bills but the Bendire thrasher's bill is nearly straight.

These large, retiring songsters are fond of brushy places. They sally out into open areas for seeds or insects but are always ready to run or fly back to cover. Insects predominate in their spring and summer menus, but in other seasons seeds and fruits are the principal food.

BROWN THRASHER
Toxostoma rufum

Specimens: 134	163	249	82
WINTER	SPRING	SUMMER	FALL
78%	28%	46%	71%

The rusty-brown, speckled-breasted brown thrasher nests in brushy or thicket-covered upland areas—often near dwellings. It is nearly as common in towns as in rural sections. This thrasher's choppy, repetitive song is often mistaken for that of the mockingbird.

Animal food: One-third of the animal diet consists of beetles; the other two-thirds includes a large variety of items without a predominance of any. Among these are grasshoppers and crickets, ants and other *Hymenoptera*, caterpillars, and spiders. Bones of lizards, salamanders, and frogs have also been found in several stomachs.

Plant food:

Northeast, 287 (0-111-128-48)
** Blackberry *Su*
** Cherry, Wild *SuF*
* Elderberry *SuF*

* Corn *SuFSp*
* Oak *Sp*
* Dogwood *F*
* Blackgum *F*
* Bayberry *FSp*
* Blueberry *Su*
+ Grape, Wild Strawberry, Poison-ivy, Sumac, Serviceberry, Mulberry, Sassafras, Redcedar, Greenbrier

Southeast (excl. Tex.), 186 (76-35-48-27)
** Blackberry *SpSuF*
** Oak *FW*
** Elderberry *SuF*
* Corn *WSp*
* Beautyberry *FW*
* Virginia-creeper *F*
* Sumac *SuFW*
* Pine *W*
* Blueberry *WSp*
* Bayberry *W*
* Holly *W*
* Grape *SuF*
+ Cherry, Flowering Dogwood, Hackberry, Greenbrier,

Blackgum, Rattanvine, Mulberry, Pokeweed

Texas, 75 (64-9-0-2)
*** Oak *FW*
** Holly *W*
** Hackberry *W*
* Viburnum *W*
+ Sumac, Poison-ivy, Corn, Grape, Beautyberry, Strawberry
Eastern Prairies, 88 (0-12-70-6)
** Cherry *Su*
* Dogwood *Su*
* Buckthorn, Lanceleaf *Su*
* Corn *Su*
* Mulberry *Su*
+ Grape, Gooseberry, Strawberry, Blackberry, Silver Buffalo-berry

CURVE-BILLED THRASHER
Toxostoma curvirostre

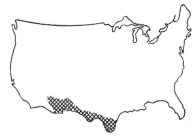

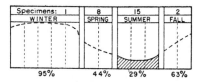

The curve-billed thrasher is confined to our southwestern border states and to northern Mexico. It is typical of arid areas where cactus and mesquite prevail. Incidentally, the bill of this species is curved no more than in several other thrashers. Only limited studies have been made on its food habits.

Animal food: The animal food items most commonly found in the few exam-ined stomachs of this species are beetles, ants and other *Hymenoptera,* caterpillars, crickets and grasshoppers, spiders, and millipedes.

Plant food:
Southwest, 26 (1-8-15-2)
** Pricklypear *SuFW*
** Wheat *Sp*
** Corn *Su*
* Condalia, Bluewood *Su*
* Chufa *F*
* Barley *W*
+ Nightshade, Hackberry, Bristle-grass

CALIFORNIA THRASHER
Toxostoma redivivum

The California thrasher is a common species within its relatively small range. It frequents the dense cover of manzanita and other chaparral on hill slopes. Like other thrashers, this one feeds largely on the ground, but it perches high on a bush or tree to sing.

Animal food: The animal diet consists primarily of beetles, ants and other *Hymenoptera,* moths and caterpillars, and spiders and myriapods.

Plant food:
California, 100 (31-5-38-26)
** Poison-oak *SuFW*
* Sumac, Laurel *SuF*

148

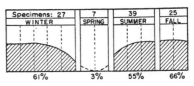

* Elderberry *Su*
* Oak *W*

* Raspberry *Su*
* Buckthorn *F*
* Grape *SuF*
* Bearberry *SuW*
+ Black Nightshade, Christmas-
  berry, Wheat, Prune, Mis-
  tletoe, Sorghum

SAGE THRASHER
Oreoscoptes montanus

The smaller size and straight, small bill help to explain why this thrasher is classed in a distinct genus from the others. It nests from Southern California, through much of the Rockies, to British Columbia, and winters in the Southwest and northern Mexico.

Animal food: Among the principal items of the extensive animal diet are beetles, grasshoppers and crickets, ants and other *Hymenoptera*, caterpillars and moths, spiders, bugs, and flies.

Plant food: In contrast to most thrashers, this bird eats only a very small proportion of plant food.

West, 33 (0-1-22-10) plus observations
* Serviceberry *F*
* Grape *F*
+ Gooseberry, Blackberry

Thrushes, Bluebirds, Robin: *Turdidae*

ROBIN
Turdus migratorius

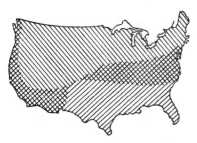

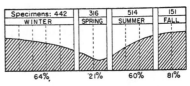

Robins occupy practically all parts of the United States as well as much of Canada and some of Alaska. In fall most of them come to our southern states, but a few hardy robins remain in the North.

This familiar songster has prospered with man's conversion of the American wilderness into an agricultural-industrial domain. It likes clearings as compared with dense woods and is particularly partial to lawns and orchards. Robins are noted for their destruction to cherries and other fruits—enough so, occasionally, to justify issuing of permits for killing them in certain localities. Their most obvious feeding activity in urban areas is pulling up earthworms.

Animal food: The chief items of animal food are caterpillars, beetles, (particu-

larly ground beetles, weevils, and dung beetles), and earthworms. The balance of the animal diet is made up largely of true bugs, flies, sowbugs, snails, spiders, termites, millipedes and centipedes.

Plant food:

Northeast, 770 (77-199-327-167) plus observations
*** Cherry, Cult. and Wild *SuF*
** Dogwood *FW*
** Sumac *WSp*
** Blackgum *FW*
* Grape, Wild and Cult. *SuFW*
* Redcedar *FWSp*
* Virginia-creeper *FWSp*
* Blackberry *Su*
\+ Mulberry, Apple, Holly, Poke-weed, Blueberry, Service-berry, Greenbrier, Corn, Elderberry, Viburnum, Hawthorn, Hackberry, Spicebush, Bittersweet, Ragweed

Southeast (*excl. Fla.*), 263 (215-29-17-2)
** Chinaberry *WSp*
** Blackberry *Su*
* Hackberry *WSp*
* Greenbrier *W*
* Cherry, Wild and Cult. *Su*

* Holly *W*
* Persimmon *W*
* Grape *FW*
* Corn *Sp*
\+ Redcedar, Mulberry, Rattan-vine, Beautyberry, Flower-ing Dogwood, Virginia-creeper, Blackgum, Sumac, Blueberry

Florida, 32 (32-0-0-0)
*** Holly
*** Palmetto
*** Blackgum
** Chinaberry
** Beautyberry
* Greenbrier
\+ Japanese Honeysuckle, Sumac

Eastern Prairies, 130 (39-29-52-10)
*** Hackberry *WSp*
*** Grape, Cult. and Wild *SuF*
** Cherry, Cult. and Wild *Su*
* Russianolive *Su*
* Sumac *WSp*
\+ Virginia-creeper, Greenbrier, Mulberry, Blackberry, Oats, Corn, Apple, Dog-wood, Bittersweet

Mt.–Desert, 113 (5-50-53-5)
*** Cedar *FW*
** Hackberry *F*
** Russianolive *W*
* Sumac *W*
* Currant *Su*
* Serviceberry *Su*
\+ Dogwood, Mistletoe, Wheat

Pacific, 114 (41-41-13-19)
*** Peppertree, California *WSp*
*** Grape, Cult. *FW*
** Prune *FW*
** Cherry, Cult. and Wild *SuF*
* Raspberry *Su*
* Apple *W*
\+ Mistletoe, Serviceberry, Wheat, Fig, Buckthorn

Reference: A Detailed Study of a Family of Robins. William E. Schantz. *Wilson Bul.* Vol. 51(3), pp. 157–169, 1939.

THRUSHES. Thrushes are shy, woodland birds that are present, in season, everywhere in the United States except the prairies and deserts. Only six species are native to this country. Some of our very finest songsters are among these drab-colored, freckle-breasted birds. Incidentally, the water-thrushes, though marked like thrushes, are classed with the warblers.

All thrushes migrate. Some, such as the oliveback, may travel from the northern part of this continent far southward into South America, while by contrast, many of the hermit thrushes winter as well as nest within our national boundaries. Thrushes are largely insectivorous in warm months, while in cooler seasons fleshy fruits become very important in their diet.

VARIED THRUSH
Ixoreus naevius

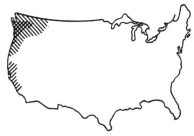

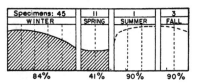

The varied thrush is classed in a genus by itself. It looks so much like a robin with a dark band across its breast that it is commonly called the banded robin. This distinctive bird occupies a limited zone in the Pacific Northwest during the summer and, in the fall, moves down the coast as far as Southern California.

Animal food: Principal invertebrates eaten are beetles, ants and other *Hymenoptera*, caterpillars, millipedes and centipedes, crickets, snails, and miscellaneous insects.

Plant food: A very large part of the diet of the varied thrush consists of wild fruit.

Pacific, 60 (45-11-1-3)
*** Oak *W*
** Madrone *W*
** Snowberry *FW*
** Raspberry *Su*
* Apple *W*
* Prune *W*
* Honeysuckle *W*
+ California Peppertree, Poison-oak, Buckthorn, Grape, Wheat, Filaree, Nightshade

WOOD THRUSH
Hylocichla mustelina

The wood thrush nests in the East but spends the colder months in southern Mexico and Central America. Its beautiful liquid notes add much to the

enjoyment of eastern woodlands in summer mornings and evenings. This rusty-backed thrush divides its feeding activity between insects and fruits.

Animal food: Beetles, ants and other *Hymenoptera*, caterpillars, spiders, and grasshoppers are the principal items of the animal diet. Also taken to a con-

siderable extent are flies, bugs, myriapods, sowbugs, snails, and earthworms.

Plant food:
Northeast, 176 (0-64-85-27) plus ob-
    servations
    ** Spicebush *F*
    ** Dogwood *SuF*
    * Cherry, Wild *SuF*

* Grape *F*
* Blackberry *Su*
* Blackgum *F*
* Mulberry *Su*
* Virginia-creeper *F*
+ Elderberry, Blueberry, Service-
    berry, Holly, Aralia, Jack-
    in-the-pulpit

Reference: A Nesting Study of the Wood Thrush. Hervey Brackbill. *Wilson Bul.*
Vol. 55 (2), pp. 73–87, 1943.

HERMIT THRUSH
Hylocichla guttata

Specimens: 180	171	49	184
WINTER	SPRING	SUMMER	FALL
60%	7%	15%	47%

This brown-tailed thrush is the only
one that occupies extensive areas of the
United States in winter as well as in
summer. Nesting in our northeastern
states and throughout the wooded
parts of the West, it winters in the
southern part of the country. The song
of the hermit thrush is regarded by
many as the most beautiful of all.

Though this thrush eats an assortment of fruits, it feeds on insects to a
greater extent than others.

Animal food: Beetles, ants, caterpillars,
flies, and bugs are the leading items in
the varied insect diet.

Plant food:
East, 472 (107-167-37-161) plus ob-
    servations
    ** Holly *FW*
    * Greenbrier *WSp*
    * Dogwood, Flowering *FW*
    * Serviceberry *Su*
    * Sumac *FWSp*
    * Grape *FW*

+ Virginia-creeper, Pokeweed,
    Hackberry, Japanese
    Honeysuckle, Elderberry,
    Wild Cherry, Bayberry,
    Rattanvine, Redcedar, Vi-
    burnum, Blackgum, Sas-
    safras, Spicebush, Blue-
    berry
Pacific, 112 (73-4-12-23)
    ** Peppertree, California *FWSp*
    ** Poison-oak *FW*
    + Grape, Mistletoe, Snowberry,
        Buckthorn, Nightshade,
        Dogwood, Raspberry, Blue-
        berry, Laurel Sumac

OLIVE-BACKED THRUSH
Hylocichla ustulata

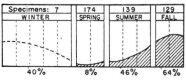

During the nesting season, the olive-backed thrush is largely a Canadian bird, but it ranges into some of our northern states—particularly in the Northwest. In the East it breeds as far southward as the Alleghenies of West Virginia. One subspecies, the russet-backed thrush, has a range extending down the Pacific coast to Southern California. All the olive-backed group winter in Mexico or Central America.

Animal food: Beetles, ants and other *Hymenoptera*, and caterpillars are the principal invertebrates in the animal diet. Flies, bugs, grasshoppers and other insects, as well as spiders, millipedes, snails, sowbugs, and earthworms are also consumed.

Plant food:

Northeast, 277 (1-132-35-109) plus observations

** Cherry, Wild *SuF*
* Dogwood *F*
* Elderberry *SuF*
* Virginia-creeper *F*
* Grape *F*
+ Pokeweed, Sumac, False Solomonseal, Blackberry, Sassafras, Serviceberry, Aralia, Greenbrier, Mountain-ash, Viburnum, Blackgum

Prairies, 11 (0-9-2-0)
*** Hackberry *Sp*
*** Serviceberry *Su*
* Holly *Sp*
* Rose *Sp*
* Greenbrier *Sp*

California, 154 (6-26-102-20)
** Cherry *SpSu*
** Elderberry *SuF*
** Buckthorn *FW*
** Poison-oak *FW*
* Raspberry *SpSu*
* Dogwood *F*
* Peppertree, California *F*
+ Grape, Prune, Apricot, Snowberry, Fig, Mulberry, Nightshade

GRAY-CHEEKED THRUSH
Hylocichla minima

These grayish-brown birds visit the United States only to a very limited extent. One subspecies, the Bicknell thrush, nests in alpine parts of New England and in southern Canada, but the other subspecies spends the summer near the limit of tree growth in northern Canada. In the fall, the gray-cheek migrates to South America.

Animal food: The principal items of animal diet are beetles, ants and other *Hymenoptera*, and caterpillars. Besides

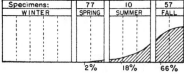

insects a few crayfish, sowbugs, and earthworms are consumed.

Plant food:

Northeast, 144 (0-77-10-57) plus observations

153

** Dogwood *F*
* Cherry, Wild *F*
* Blackgum *F*
* Grape *F*
* Blueberry *SuF*

+ Viburnum, Spicebush, Nightshade, Pokeweed, Greenbrier, Holly, False Solomonseal, Blackberry, Sassafras

VEERY
Hylocichla fuscescens

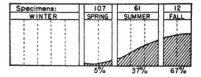

The veery, including its western form the willow thrush, nests in our northern states and Canada. Its attractive, somewhat eerie song is distinctive. In the fall, the veery leaves our continent for South America.

Animal food: Beetles, ants and other *Hymenoptera*, caterpillars, spiders, and grasshoppers constitute most of the animal diet. Also consumed in appreciable numbers are bugs, flies, sowbugs, and snails.

Plant food:
Northeast, 181 (1-104-64-12)
** Bunchberry *SuF*
* Serviceberry *Su*
* Elderberry *Su*
* Blackberry *Su*
* Pokeweed *F*
* Blueberry *Su*
* Spicebush *Su*
+ Virginia-creeper, False Solomonseal, Mountain-ash, Cherry, Strawberry, Sumac

BLUEBIRDS. There are three species of bluebirds in the United States, one in the East and two in the West. They migrate only a short distance southward in the fall. The popularity of these beautiful songsters is indicated by the large number of birdhouses prepared for them. Bluebirds generally are useful as well as attractive since they feed primarily on insects and consume many injurious species.

EASTERN BLUEBIRD
Sialia sialis

This is the familiar bluebird of the East—so frequently regarded in the Northeast as one of the first signs of spring. Actually, some individuals winter in all but the northernmost states of their range. The eastern bluebird nests commonly in apple orchards or in other trees near human habitations. It is a regular patron of birdhouses.

Animal food: Beetles, particularly ground beetles, May beetles, and weevils, grasshoppers and crickets, and caterpillars are the choice items of the animal diet. Various other insects and spiders, centipedes, sowbugs, and snails are also eaten.

Plant food: Fleshy fruits are the favorite plant items of the bluebird.

Northeast, 674 (273-116-172-113) plus observations
* Dogwood *FW*
* Redcedar *FW*

154

Specimens: 381	149	207	133
WINTER	SPRING	SUMMER	FALL
39%	7%	17%	38%

* Pokeweed *SuF*
+ Bayberry, Blackgum, Poison-
  ivy

* Sumac *WSp*
* Bayberry *FWSp*
* Virginia-creeper *FW*
+ Poison-ivy, Mistletoe, Poke-
  weed, Blackberry, Elder-
  berry, Wild Cherry, Serv-
  iceberry, Bittersweet, Jap-
  anese Honeysuckle, Grape
Southeast, 245 (145-53-30-17)
** Holly *W*
** Blueberry *Su*
* Dogwood, Flowering *FW*
* Virginia-creeper *FW*
* Hackberry *W*
* Sumac *SuFW*
* Elderberry *F*

Reference: A Study of Eastern Bluebirds in Arkansas. Ruth Harris Thomas. *Wilson Bul.*, 1946. 40 pp.

MEXICAN BLUEBIRD
Sialia mexicana

The Mexican bluebird, also known as the western or chestnut-backed bluebird, is distinct from both the eastern and mountain species in having reddish-brown coloration on its back as well as on its breast. It is also unique in being comparatively silent. The range of this western species is the Mountain–Desert and Pacific coast regions, from British Columbia into Mexico. In winter, it migrates southward to the warmer parts of its general territory.

Animal food: Grasshoppers constitute the largest and most regular item, followed by caterpillars, beetles (particularly ground beetles), and ants. Bees, wasps, flies, spiders, sowbugs,

Specimens: 56	20	65	64
WINTER	SPRING	SUMMER	FALL
26%	0%	4%	21%

snails, earthworms, and centipedes appear more or less as incidental items.

Plant food:
California, 215 (67-8-73-67)
** Grape, Cult. *FW*
* Mistletoe *W*
* Elderberry *SuF*
+ Fig, California Peppertree,
  Blackberry

155

MOUNTAIN BLUEBIRD
Sialia currucoides

The male mountain bluebird is the only one of our three species that is blue all over. This western bird nests throughout the Rocky Mountain region and in the adjoining Sierra and Cascade ranges. It winters in the milder parts of this territory.

Animal food: Beetles, particularly ground beetles, and weevils take first place in the diet, followed by grass-hoppers and crickets, ants, caterpillars, and bugs.

Plant food: Fruits constitute most of the small proportion of plant material in the diet.

West (mainly Rocky Mts.), 97 (33-12-38-14)
   * Grape *W*
   + Elderberry

TOWNSEND SOLITAIRE
Myadestes townsendi

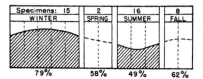

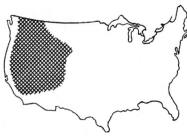

The Townsend solitaire is a melodious songster of isolated areas in the western mountains. Its range extends from our southwestern states to Alaska. The general appearance of the solitaire and its aerial pursuit of insects is suggestive of flycatchers, but its manner of running on the ground resembles that of the robin. It nests on the ground.

Animal food: The animal diet consists chiefly of beetles, moths and their caterpillars, spiders, and ants.

Plant Food:
West, 41 (15-2-16-8)
   *** Cedar *FWSpSu*
   ** Hawthorn *FW*
   ** Madrone *FW*
   ** Pine *FW*
   * Gooseberry *SuF*
   * Hackberry *FW*
   * Bearberry *FW*
   * Honeysuckle *SuF*
   * Poison-oak *FW*
   * Sumac *FW*
   + Bitter Cherry, Rose, Serviceberry

Gnatcatchers, Kinglets: *Sylviidae*

GNATCATCHERS. About 20 kinds of gnatcatchers are native to the New World. Two species occur in wooded parts of the United States. These tiny, active, cheerful birds are related to the kinglets and warblers rather than to flycatchers, as their name might imply. Their food is entirely insectivorous and generally consists of small, delicate species. Occasionally, however, they attack locusts (*Cicada*). Prominent in their fare are flies, gnats, and caddisflies.

KINGLETS. Kinglets, except for hummingbirds, are about the smallest of our native birds. Two species, the ruby-crown and golden-crown, are found commonly through all but the coldest parts of the United States in winter. Their ranges overlap, and occasionally both kinds are seen together. The nesting territory of these tiny songsters is mainly in cool latitudes.

Kinglets are partial to coniferous trees in their feeding. Usually one detects their distinctive notes before he sees them. Both species are insectivorous, but about one-tenth of the ruby-crown's fall and winter food is from plants. Insects eaten are principally wasps, bugs, flies, beetles, plant lice, and insect eggs.

RUBY-CROWNED KINGLET
Regulus calendula

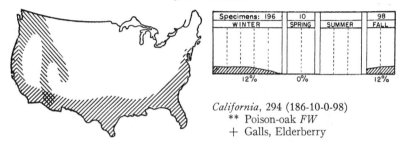

Specimens: 196	10		98
WINTER	SPRING	SUMMER	FALL
12%	0%		12%

California, 294 (186-10-0-98)
** Poison-oak *FW*
\+ Galls, Elderberry

Pipits: *Motacillidae*

PIPITS. Our two pipits, the American and Sprague, are hardy, ground-dwelling prairie birds that nest largely in Canada. A few spend the summers in our northern border states or in the higher altitudes of the West. Both species winter in southern parts of the United States or in Mexico and Central America.

Pipits are distinctive in their manner of walking (they do not hop) and in the way their tails bob up and down as they move about on the ground. During the breeding season the male sings high in the air, like the horned larks. They feed largely on insects, but in the fall and winter, weed seeds become a major part of their diet.

AMERICAN PIPIT
Anthus spinoletta

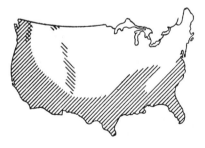

Specimens: 168	19	26	72
WINTER	SPRING	SUMMER	FALL
31%	TRACE	1%	16%

of pipits may often be seen feeding in open fields during winter.

Animal food: Beetles, caterpillars, flies and their larvae, grasshoppers and crickets, ants and other *Hymenoptera*, spiders, bugs, millipedes, and crustaceans constitute the main items of animal food.

The American pipit, mainly a bird of Canada in the summertime, nests also in the higher mountains of Oregon, Colorado, and New Mexico. It winters throughout the warmer sections of the country. Moderate-sized or large flocks

Plant food:
Northeast, 93 (18-15-15-45)
* Panicgrass *W*

157

    * Crabgrass *W*
    + Ragweed, Acalypha, Smartweed
Southeast, 110 (109-1-0-0)
   *** Spurge
    * Doveweed
    * Crabgrass
    * Wheat
    * Bristlegrass
    * Crowfootgrass

    + Pricklyash, Panicgrass, Corn,
      Pigweed
Pacific, 71 (46-2-2-21)
    ** Tarweed *FW*
    ** Redmaids *FW*
    ** Wheat *W*
    * Canarygrass *W*
    * Chickweed *FW*
    + Oats, Silene, Knotweed, Clover,
      Pigweed

SPRAGUE PIPIT
Anthus spragueii

The Sprague pipit nests in our northernmost states of the Great Plains and farther north into Canada and the Arctic. It winters in the Southeast—along our Gulf coast—or farther south. **Animal food:** In six of eleven stomachs examined, over 75% of the food consisted of grasshoppers or crickets. Ants and other *Hymenoptera*, weevils and various other beetles, small bugs, and caterpillars formed the remainder of the animal food.

Plant food:
Prairies, 11 (2-2-6-1)
    ** Doveweed *W*
    + Gromwell, Ragweed, Panicgrass

Waxwings: *Bombycillidae*

CEDAR WAXWING
Bombycilla cedrorum

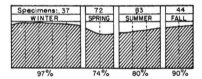

The unique, eccentric cedar waxwing, or cedarbird, is largely a native of the United States. It nests in our northern states and Canada and winters in the South. Another and somewhat larger species, the Bohemian waxwing, inhabits the northern parts of the continent and comes into the states only to a limited extent. Information on the Bohemian's food habits is slight but seems to follow the pattern of the cedar waxwing.

Fleshy fruits constitute nearly nine-tenths of the cedarbird's food. And in the Northeast, cedar berries are the outstanding staple.

Animal food: The chief items of animal diet are beetles, ants and other *Hymenoptera*, flies, bugs, caterpillars, grasshoppers, crickets, and Mayflies.

Plant food:
Northeast, 156 (17-38-60-41) plus observations
 **** Redcedar *FWSp*
  *** Cherry, Wild *SuF*
   ** Dogwood, Flowering *FW*
    * Blackberry *Su*
    * Hackberry *W*
    * Chokeberry *W*

* Mulberry *SpSu*
* Serviceberry *Su*
* Viburnum, Blackhaw *F*
* Pokeweed *F*
* Grape *FW*
+ Elderberry, Ragweed, Holly, Barberry, Blackgum, Poison-ivy, Greenbrier, Ash, Privet

Southeast, 9 (6-2-1-0)
  ** Mistletoe *W*
  ** Privet *W*
  * Persimmon *W*
  + Grape, Holly
West (excl. Pacific), 17 (4-2-11-0)
  **** Cherry *Su*
  *** Apple *W*
  *** Hawthorn *Sp*
  *** Russianolive *W*
  * Blackberry *Su*
  + Roughleaf Dogwood, Grape
Pacific, 54 (10-30-11-3)
  **** Peppertree, California *WSp*
  *** Cherry, Cult. *SpSuF*
  *** Grape, Cult. *F*
  ** Mistletoe *W*
  ** Strawberry *SpSu*
  * Gooseberry *SpSu*
  + Filaree

Phainopepla: *Ptilogonatidae*

PHAINOPEPLA
Phainopepla nitens

Specimens:	1	4	31	6
	WINTER	SPRING	SUMMER	FALL
	100%	94%	88%	100%

The phainopepla, or silky flycatcher, is a New World bird belonging in a family by itself. Its generic name is too long and awkward to serve well as a common name, but the designation silky flycatcher is misleading since the phainopepla is not related to the flycatchers.

Phainopeplas are inhabitants of warm climates. Our one species is limited to southwestern border states from Texas to California. Like their not-too-distant relatives, the wax-wings, these crested semitropical birds are fruit eaters. Insects make up only a small part of their fare.

Animal food: Ants are the animal item consumed most. Spiders, beetles, and miscellaneous insects are also eaten.

Plant food:
California and Arizona, 43 (1-5-31-6) plus observations
  **** Elderberry *Su*
  *** Grape *SuF*
  ** Buckthorn, California *F*
  ** Mistletoe *W*
  * Peppertree, California *W*
  * Mulberry *Sp*
  * Cherry, Wild *F*
  + Condalia, Nightshade

References: Distribution and Habitat Relationships of the Phainopepla. James E. Crouch. *Auk,* Vol. 60(3); pp. 319–333, 1943.

Breeding Notes on the Phainopepla. A. L. and R. M. Rand. *Auk*, Vol. 60(3), pp. 333–341, 1943.

Shrikes: *Laniidae*

SHRIKES. Shrikes are found in nearly every part of the country. One of our two species nests in Canada and Alaska and winters in the United States. The other, including the forms known as the migrant and loggerhead shrikes, is more southerly and nests as well as winters largely within our national boundaries.

Shrikes feed almost exclusively on animal life—both vertebrate and invertebrate. Especially prominent in their diet are large insects such as grasshoppers, beetles, caterpillars, and wasps. Small rodents and birds are also captured, and because of this the shrikes are regarded with some disfavor. Their habit of hanging prey—whether insect, rodent, or bird—upon barbed wire or on thorns of bushes has earned them the local name butcherbird.

Starlings: *Sturnidae*

STARLING
Sturnus vulgaris

The introduction of the European starling to this country (New York City in 1890 and 1891) has proved to be a regrettable and uncorrectable mistake. The species has become much more abundant here, especially in the East, than in Europe—possibly because its parasites have not caught up with it. Many thousands of these noisy birds flock into our eastern cities in fall and winter evenings. The starling has moved westward as far as the Rockies and is beginning to appear on the Pacific coast.

Though it has a redeeming feature in the destruction of insects, this European invader is a serious nuisance to city dwellers, fruit growers, and to many native birds. Woodpeckers, flickers, bluebirds, and purple martins often are driven from their nesting holes by it.

Another starling known as the crested mynah, or Chinese starling, has become established in and near Vancouver, British Columbia. Thus far it has not spread into the United States.

Animal food: The animal food items most commonly used are beetles, grasshoppers, millipedes, and caterpillars.

Plant food:

Northeast, 2,573 (713-411-1,047-402) plus observations

Specimens: 644	249	857	407
WINTER	SPRING	SUMMER	FALL

68% 7% 41% 39%

** Cherry, Wild and Cult. *SuF*
** Sumac *W*
* Bayberry *W*
* Mulberry *Su*
* Elderberry *SuF*
* Blackgum *F*
* Poison-ivy *FW*
* Apple *FW*
+ Virginia-creeper, H a c k b e r r y, Grape, Corn, R e d c e d a r, Pokeweed, Viburnum, Dogwood, Oak

References: The Starling's Family Life and Behavior. H. A. Allard. *Jour. Wash. Acad. Sci.*, 1940. 12 pp.
The European Starling in the United States. E. R. Kalmbach. *U.S. Dept. Agr. Farmers' Bul.* 1571, 1931 (revised). 26 pp.

Vireos: *Vireonidae*

VIREOS. Vireos are largely tropical birds. About a dozen species spend the nesting season in the United States. Practically all these greenish or yellowish woodland birds move south of our borders to Mexico, Central America, or South America in the fall. Because vireos are small and inconspicuous among forest foliage, the different species are difficult to identify. Their calls, however, are distinctive enough.

The food of vireos is primarily insects. Fleshy fruits comprise a minor but appreciable part of the fare of four species which are given individual treatment below. The others, including two important species, the widespread blue-headed vireo and the Bell vireo, are almost wholly insect eaters. Insects most commonly eaten by vireos include caterpillars, moths, bugs, beetles, wasps, ants, bees, and flies. Spiders are also taken.

WHITE-EYED VIREO
Vireo griseus

Specimens: 39	104	56	22
WINTER	SPRING	SUMMER	FALL
9%	12%	10%	32%

This little bird is noisy for its size. The explosive whistle of the white-eye often startles those who invade its brushy haunts. It feeds very largely on insects but supplements this diet with small quantities of fleshy fruits.
Animal food: Caterpillars and moths, bugs, beetles, ants, wasps, bees, flies, and spiders are chief items in the white-eye's diet.

Plant food:
Southeast, 221 (39-104-56-22)
  * Waxmyrtle, Southern *FW*
  + Blackberry, Holly, Virginia-creeper, Poison-ivy, Elderberry, Sassafras

RED-EYED VIREO
Vireo olivaceus

The common red-eyed vireo is probably the most abundant nesting bird in forests of the eastern United States. It is also one of our most persistent, cheerful woodland singers. Even at noon on hot summer days, these busy insect eaters continue their calls. The redeye migrates to South America in the fall. Its insect diet is varied with a fair amount of fleshy fruits.
Animal food: Caterpillars and moths, bugs, beetles, ants, wasps and bees, flies, and spiders are among the main food items of this species.

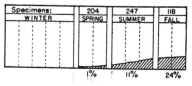

Specimens:	204	247	118
WINTER	SPRING	SUMMER	FALL
	1%	11%	24%

Plant food:
East, 569 (0-204-247-118) plus observations

* Dogwood *FW*
* Virginia-creeper *FW*
+ Spicebush, Sassafras, Elderberry, Blackberry, Magnolia, Blackgum, Cherry, Sumac

PHILADELPHIA VIREO
Vireo philadelphicus

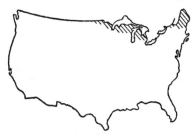

Specimens:	33	28	18
WINTER	SPRING	SUMMER	FALL
	3%	2%	18%

The uncommon Philadelphia vireo nests mainly in Canada but also occurs in some of the northeast border states. This species is generally considered the rarest of the vireos in eastern North America.

Animal food: Caterpillars, moths, beetles, wasps, ants, bees, flies, true bugs, and spiders make up most of this bird's food.
Plant food: Plant material (fruit) eaten by this species is insignificant except in the fall when it totals 12%.

Northeast, 79 (0-33-28-18)
* Bunchberry *F*
+ Rose, Grape

WARBLING VIREO
Vireo gilvus

Specimens:	159	143	45
WINTER	SPRING	SUMMER	FALL
	TRACE	8%	9%

The warbling vireo is an inconspicuous species that would be noted even less except for its persistent finch-like singing. The winter home of this species is uncertain beyond the fact that the bird has been recorded in Guatemala.
Animal food: Caterpillars comprise the largest portion of the animal food, fol-

lowed by beetles, true bugs, and other insects. It also consumes spiders and snails in appreciable numbers.

Plant food:
Northeast, 132 (0-81-42-9)
  ** Bunchberry *SuF*
  * Dogwood *F*
  + Pokeweed, Cherry, Sumac

Eastern Prairies, 30 (0-14-15-1)
  * Dogwood *Su*
  * Grape *Su*
Mt.–Desert, 43 (0-5-31-7)
  ** Dogwood *SuF*
  + Elderberry
Pacific, 142 (0-59-55-28)
  + Dogwood, Elderberry, Poison-
    oak, Snowberry

Warblers: *Parulidae*

WARBLERS. Our American warblers are more accurately known as wood warblers. They are distinct from the true warblers (*Sylviidae*) of the Old World.

More than 50 species of warblers enter the United States—mainly in spring and summer. Some nest well up in Canada or Alaska. Their winters are usually spent in the tropics—in Central America, northern South America, Mexico, and the West Indies. Only a few species such as the myrtle, parula, pine, Audubon, yellowthroat, and palm warblers remain in this country during winter.

Warblers are insectivorous woodland birds. Only the few species treated individually below consume significant amounts of plant material. Among the insects eaten most commonly are various kinds of caterpillars, beetles, wasps, ants, flies, bugs, plant lice, bees, cankerworms, and locusts. Spiders are also taken often. The actual value of warblers in helping to preserve our forests through insect destruction is an uncertain matter, difficult to appraise. While lack of knowledge limits a positive statement regarding the extent of benefit, it is safe to say that these lively, colorful songsters are rarely an economic liability to man.

MYRTLE WARBLER
Dendroica coronata

Specimens: 75	15		6
WINTER	SPRING	SUMMER	FALL
17%	TRACE		63%

Plant food:
East (mainly S.E.), 68 (58-9-0-1) plus observations

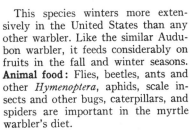

This species winters more extensively in the United States than any other warbler. Like the similar Audubon warbler, it feeds considerably on fruits in the fall and winter seasons. **Animal food:** Flies, beetles, ants and other *Hymenoptera*, aphids, scale insects and other bugs, caterpillars, and spiders are important in the myrtle warbler's diet.

163

* Redcedar *W*
* Bayberry *W*
* Poison-ivy *W*
+ Pine, Palmetto, Elm, Persimmon, Hornbeam

California, 28 (17-6-0-5)
* Poison-oak *FW*
* Fig *F*
+ Pacific Waxmyrtle

AUDUBON WARBLER
Dendroica auduboni

Specimens: 193	17	3	17
WINTER	SPRING	SUMMER	FALL
28%	0%	0%	24%

The Audubon warbler is a western species and one of the few that does not leave the country completely in any season. It resembles the myrtle warbler in habits, calls, and appearance. **Animal food:** Ants and other *Hymenoptera*, plant lice and other bugs, flies, caterpillars, and beetles make up the principal insect items. Spiders are also eaten in considerable numbers.

Plant food:
California, 383 (193-17-3-170)
* Sumac, Laurel *FW*
* Poison-oak *FW*
* Fig *F*
+ Elderberry, Grape, Pacific Waxmyrtle, California Peppertree

HERMIT WARBLER
Dendroica occidentalis

The hermit warbler has a restricted nesting territory in the mountains of California and Washington. It is found commonly among pines and, for warblers, is unusual in its consumption of pine seeds. The pine warbler is the only other one known to share in the use of this food.

Animal food: Listed among the animal items in the few stomach records available are beetles, bugs, flies, caterpillars, wasps, and spiders.

Plant food:
California, 5 (3-1-0-1) plus observations
*** Pine *W*

PINE WARBLER
Dendroica pinus

The mellow, warbling song of this pinewoods species may be heard the year round in the United States since it winters in the Southeast as well as in Mexico.
Animal food: Ants and other *Hymenoptera*, bugs, beetles, caterpillars, spiders, grasshoppers, and flies are the principal items of its animal diet.

Plant food:
East, 14 (7-5-2-0)
** Pine *FW*
* Dogwood, Flowering *FW*
+ Grape, Sumac, Panicgrass

CHAT
Icteria virens

The chat is our largest warbler. In fact it is so much larger than others of its family and is so different in other respects that we often forget it is a warbler. Its favorite territory is thicket-covered runs or brushy lowlands. Here in summer, one can hear its chuckles, whistles, and scolding notes—occasionally accompanied by aerial gymnastics.

Two subspecies nest in the United States: the yellow-breasted chat (*I. virens virens*) in the West and the long-tailed chat (*I. virens auricollis*) in the Mountain–Desert and Pacific regions. Winters are spent in Central America.

In 28 chats that have been examined, the food was largely insects. Nine birds taken in the spring season averaged 2% of plant food, while 19 in summer had 35% of plant material.

Animal food: Ants, wasps, beetles (principally ground beetles and weevils), caterpillars, grasshoppers, spiders, and true bugs stand out as the choice animal-food items.

Plant food: Fleshy fruits are the chief alternate to the chat's insect diet.

East, 16 (0-4-12-0)
*** Blackberry *Su*
* Blueberry *Su*
* Elderberry *Su*
\+ Pokeweed
Pacific, 12 (0-5-7-0)
** Madrone *Su*
* Thimbleberry *Su*
* Sumac *Su*
* Dogwood *Sp*
\+ Nightshade

English Sparrow: *Ploceidae*

ENGLISH SPARROW
Passer domesticus

The English sparrow, sometimes known as house sparrow, is no sparrow at all. It is one of the weaver finches. This semidomestic species was first brought from Europe in 1850, and within fifty years it had spread all over the country. In the fall, large flocks of English sparrows congregate in rural areas and sometimes do damage by threshing out quantities of kernels from shocked grain.

In former times when horses were the chief means of public conveyance, the sparrows obtained a large proportion of their food—especially oats—from manure. Since then, sorghum has become a major crop in this country and is widely used in the cracked-grain mixtures fed to poultry—and incidentally to English sparrows. Dietary transitions are evident to some degree in the tables given below for the East and Prairies. Only in these two regions (East and Prairies) were specimens of English sparrows adequate in number

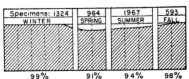

Specimens: 1324	964	1967	593
WINTER	SPRING	SUMMER	FALL
99%	91%	94%	98%

for comparisons of the past (1870–1909) with a more recent era (1910–1920). No extensive food-habits examinations for this bird have been made since 1920.

Animal food: The small amount of animal matter consumed consists chiefly of beetles (particularly dung beetles, May beetles, Japanese beetles, and weevils), and grasshoppers. To a lesser extent caterpillars and moths, fly larvae, bugs, ants, bees, wasps, and other insects are eaten.

Plant food:

East (1879–1909), 497 (94-121-213-69)
**** Oats, largely from manure SpSuFW
*** Corn, mainly cracked SuFWSp
*** Wheat SuFWSp
** Ragweed SuFWSp
* Crabgrass SuFWSp
* Knotweed SuFWSp
* Bristlegrass SuFWSp
+ Sorghum, Elm, Chickweed, Goosefoot, Annual Bluegrass, Timothy, Mulberry, Wildmillet

Prairies (1879–1909), 132 (21-43-50-18)
**** Corn SuFWSp
*** Oats SuFWSp
*** Bristlegrass SuFWSp
** Wheat SuFWSp
** Ragweed SuFWSp
* Sunflower SuFWSp
* Crabgrass SuFWSp
+ Sorghum, Elm, Knotweed and Smartweed

East (1910–1920), 1093 (282-214-393-204)
**** Corn, mainly cracked SuFWSp
*** Oats, largely from manure SpSuFW
*** Wheat SuFWSp
** Sorghum SuFWSp
** Crabgrass SuFWSp
* Ragweed SuFWSp
* Knotweed SuFWSp
* Bristlegrass SuFWSp
+ Elm, Chickweed, Goosefoot, Annual Bluegrass, Timothy, Mulberry, Wildmillet

Prairies (1910–1920), 365 (205-64-85-11)
**** Corn SuFWSp
*** Oats SuFWSp
*** Sorghum SuFWSp
*** Wheat SuFWSp
* Bristlegrass SuFWSp
+ Ragweed, Elm, Knotweed and Smartweed, Sunflower, Crabgrass

Mt.–Desert, 120 (2-64-50-4)
***** (62%) Wheat SuFWSp
*** Sunflower F
* Oats SpSuFW
+ Corn, Barley, Filaree, Pine

Pacific, 21 (5-3-7-6)
**** Wheat SuFWSp
**** Oats SpSuFW
** Corn Su
* Sorghum W
* Barley Su
+ Knotweed

Reference: The Economic Status of the English Sparrow in the United States. E. R. Kalmbach. *U.S. Dept. Agr. Tech. Bul.* 711, 1940. 66 pp.

Blackbirds, Orioles, Meadowlarks: *Icteridae*

BOBOLINK
Dolichonyx oryzivorus

The bobolink, a colorful member of the blackbird family, is a resident of Canada and northern United States for about three months in spring and summer. An equivalent period in winter is spent as a good neighbor in Brazil and Argentina—nearly 5,000 miles away. The remainder of the time, in fall and spring, is spent migrating leisurely between its southern and northern homelands.

Bobolinks nest in hayfields and meadows in our northern states. Before the summer is over the males lose their bright plumage and appear like large, buff-colored sparrows. Their distinctive "spink" notes, however, continue to be a good means of identification.

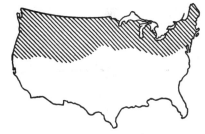

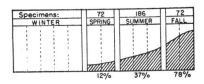

Specimens:	72	186	72
WINTER	SPRING	SUMMER	FALL

12%   37%   78%

In northeastern areas, the bobolinks enjoy feeding in wildrice marshes. When migrating through lowlands along the Gulf coast, they eat large quantities of cultivated rice and, for this reason, are often called ricebirds. **Animal food:** Caterpillars, grasshoppers, weevils and other beetles, ants, various other insects, spiders and centipedes are prominent in the bobolink's animal food.

Plant food: Seeds, cultivated or wild, are the main items of plant food.

Northeast, 258 (0-44-150-64)
  *** Wildrice *SuF*
  *** Bristlegrass *SuF*
   ** Oats *SpSuF*
    * Smartweed *SuFSp*
    + Dock, Panicgrass, Wheat, Ragweed, Barley

Southeast, 29 (0-20-0-9)
  *** Rice *FSp*
    * Panicgrass *FSp*
    * Smartweed *FSp*
    * Oats *Sp*
    + Cyperus, Bristlegrass
West, 44 (0-8-36-0)
  *** Oats *SpSu*
   ** Bristlegrass *SpSu*
    * Knotweed *Su*
    + Sunflower, Wheat, Eriogonum, Timothy

MEADOWLARKS. Our two species of meadowlarks divide the country nearly equally on an East-West basis. They inhabit practically every section of the country in summer—moving southward only short distances in the fall.

Most of us are familiar with this short-winged, pudgy bird of open fields and enjoy hearing its calls or seeing it flit and soar. Ordinarily, meadowlarks may be regarded as harmless, desirable members of our bird population. Locally, however, they may prove a serious nuisance. When flocks of the eastern meadowlarks move northward through the Carolinas, they pull a great deal of sprouting corn.

EASTERN MEADOWLARK
Sturnella magna

The eastern meadowlark has four geographic subspecies—one of them really western in territory as indicated by its name, Arizona meadowlark. A glance at the list of its principal plant foods will show that it is not solely a bird of meadows.

Animal food: Grasshoppers and crickets constitute the greater part of the animal diet, followed by beetles and caterpillars. The remainder consists of ants, wasps, and spiders and true bugs.

Plant food:
Northeast, 339 (79-84-99-77)
   ** Corn *FWSp*
    * Wheat *WSp*

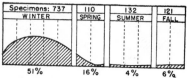

* Bristlegrass *W*
* Sunflower *W*
* Wheat *W*
* Oats *W*
+ Sorghum, Nightshade

* Bayberry *W*
+ Common Ragweed, Bristlegrass,
  Oats, Smartweed
Southeast, 589 (424-78-21-66)
** Corn *FW*
* Pine *W*
* Bristlegrass *W*
+ Oats, Oak, Bayberry, Wheat,
  Panicgrass, Sorghum, Sun-
  flower, Chokeberry
Eastern Prairies, 168 (67-40-53-8)
*** Corn *WSp*

WESTERN MEADOWLARK
Sturnella neglecta

crickets and grasshoppers, caterpillars,
ants, bees and wasps, bugs, and miscellaneous other items.

The more melodious, liquid song of
the western meadowlark serves as an
excellent field characteristic to distinguish this species from its eastern
cousin. The notes of this meadowlark
are one of the most common props for
outdoor shots in western movies. In
food habits, the two species are much
alike.

Animal food: The animal food of the
western meadowlark consists of beetles,

Plant food:
West (excl. Pacific), 283 (116-63-57-47)
*** Bristlegrass *FW*
* Corn *W*
* Sunflower *FW*
+ Wheat, Oats, Sorghum
Pacific, 116 (62-4-17-33)
*** Oats, Wild *SuFW*
** Wheat *SuFW*
+ Corn, Filaree, Tarweed, Fiddle-
  neck, California-poppy

BLACKBIRDS. Blackbirds, including grackles and cowbirds, are a very successful
bird group—sometimes too successful for the farmer. Ordinarily, the roving flocks

of these birds compensate in part at least for their damage to ripening corn or other crops by their beneficial activity in consuming destructive insects. Blackbirds are inclined to be opportunists in their feeding, taking whatever plant and animal foods are readily available. Seeds, insects, and fruits are principal dietary items. The proportions of plant and animal food vary with the species of blackbird and with the seasons.

YELLOW-HEADED BLACKBIRD
Xanthocephalus xanthocephalus

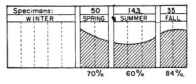

Plant food : The plant foods are largely gleaned seeds of farm crops and grainfield weeds.

This bird's bright-yellow head and breast remind one of an oriole. The yellowhead breeds in western marshlands of the United States and Canada. It winters largely in Mexico. Much of its feeding is done on farm lands adjoining marshes, and occasionally crop damage is reported.

Animal food : The animal food, roughly about one-third of the diet, is chiefly beetles, caterpillars, and grasshoppers.

West, 215 (0-44-137-34) plus observations
*** Bristlegrass *SuFSp*
*** Oats *SpSuF*
*** Corn *SuFSp*
* Ragweed, Common and Western *FSp*
* Wheat *Su*
* Sunflower *F*
* Sorghum *F*
\+ Knotweed, Dandelion, Barley

Reference : Incubation Studies of the Yellow-headed Blackbird. Reed W. Fautin. *Wilson Bul.*, 1941. 15 pp.

REDWING
Agelaius phoeniceus

Redwings are among the most widespread and well-known birds of the whole country. Fourteen subspecies are recognized in the United States. The tricolored redwing is a distinct species.

The red-blazoned black plumage of the male redwing and its liquid calls are familiar summertime features of most of our marshes and swamps. The species inhabits both coastal and inland swamps, building its nest among cattails or other wet-land plants. The

redwing is usually aggressive when crows or other animals approach its nesting area.

Feeding is done singly, in pairs, or in flocks. Sometimes redwings cause considerable damage when they feed on sprouting or maturing corn. In fall, they migrate in moderate or large-sized flocks, often in the company of other blackbirds. Winters are spent in the southern half of the United States.

Animal food : The animal food is primarily insects. Weevils and other

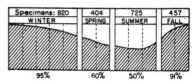

Specimens: 820 WINTER	404 SPRING	725 SUMMER	457 FALL
95%	60%	50%	91%

beetle, caterpillars, grubs, cankerworm, grasshoppers, and ants predominate. Snails, crustaceans, and spiders are eaten to a limited extent. **Plant food**: Seeds of weeds and farm crops make up most of the diet.

Northeast, 490 (40-121-281-48)
* *** Ragweed *SuFWSp*
* *** Bristlegrass *SuFWSp*
* ** Corn *SuFWSp*
* ** Oats *SpSuF*
* ** Wildrice *SuF*
* ** Smartweed *SuFWSp*
* * Wheat *SuFWSp*
* * Dock *F*
* \+ Panicgrass, Timothy, Paspalum

Southeast (excl. La.), 256 (137-43-29-47)
* *** Panicgrass *SuFWSp*
* *** Bristlegrass *SuFW*
* *** Corn *SuFWSp*
* ** Ragweed *FW*
* ** Doveweed *FW*
* ** Rice *WSp*
* * Smartweed *SuFWSp*
* * Sorghum *SuSp*
* * Wheat *Su*
* \+ Blackberry, Paspalum, Wildmillet

Louisiana Coast, 1110 (480-206-214-210)
* **** (63%) Rice *SuFWSp*
* * Caperonia *SuFWSp*
* * Paspalum *SuF*
* \+ Wildmillet, Dayflower, Giant Bristlegrass, Chufa, Ragweed

Prairies, 229 (35-27-99-68)
* **** Bristlegrass *SuFWSp*
* *** Corn *SuFWSp*
* *** Oats *SpSuF*
* ** Ragweed *FWSp*
* ** Panicgrass *W*
* * Knotweed *SuFWSp*
* * Wheat *Su*
* \+ Sunflower

Mt.–Desert, 125 (0-75-49-1)
* *** Wheat *SpSu*
* * Oats *Sp*
* * Sunflower *Sp*
* \+ Knotweed, Ragweed

California, 282 (69-18-56-139)
* **** Oats, Wild and Cult. *SpSuFW*
* ** Wheat *SpSuFW*
* ** Rice *FW*
* ** Barley *WSpSuF*
* ** Corn *SuF*
* * Knotweed *WSuF*
* * Redmaids *SpSuFW*
* \+ Filaree, Tarweed, Wildmillet, Bristlegrass

Reference: The Red-winged Blackbird: A Study in the Ecology of a Cattail Marsh. A. A. Allen. *Proc. Linnean Soc. of N.Y.*, pp. 24–25, and 45–128, 1914.

TRICOLORED REDWING
Agelaius tricolor

The tricolor is a close relative of the ordinary redwing with similar habits and habitat. Its limited range extends from southern Oregon through the central valley of California.

Animal food: The major items of its animal food are beetles, caterpillars, grasshoppers, and ants with other insects and snails being used to a lesser degree.

Plant food: Most of the specimens examined were collected from a rice-growing district, and this helps to explain the prominence of rice in the diet.

California, 21 (2-15-0-4)
* **** Rice *F*
* ** Barley *W*
* ** Corn *W*
* * Wildmillet *F*
* * Knotweed *F*
* * Filaree *Sp*
* + Bulrush

ORIOLES. Orioles are classed in the middle of the blackbird group—after the yellowhead, redwing, and tricolor and before the rusty, Brewer blackbird, grackle, and cowbird. Six species of orioles visit the United States regularly during spring and summer, wintering in Mexico and Central America. Two of these colorful songsters, the Baltimore and orchard orioles, are common throughout the East, while the Bullock oriole is almost equally plentiful in the West. The three other species are limited to parts of the Southwest, and on these we have very little food information. They are the hooded, Scott, and Audubon orioles. Orioles are mainly insectivorous, but they relish small quantities of fleshy fruits.

ORCHARD ORIOLE
Icterus spurius

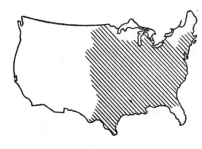

Specimens:	164	177	35
WINTER	SPRING	SUMMER	FALL

5%   8%   1%

Orchard orioles, true to their name, are found nesting commonly in orchards. They may be of importance to orchardists since their food consists chiefly of insects. This small species migrates southward early in the fall.

Animal food: Caterpillars are definitely the choice item on the diet, followed by bugs, grasshoppers, ants and other *Hymenoptera*, beetles, and spiders.

Plant food:
Northeast, 105 (0-59-46-0) plus observations
* * Mulberry *SpSu*
* * Cherry, Cult. *Su*
* + Blackberry, Grape (Cult.)

Southeast, 239 (0-99-105-35) plus observations
* ** Blackberry *SpSu*
* * Blueberry *SpSu*
* + Huckleberry, Mulberry, Grape (Cult.)

Eastern Prairies, 41 (0-1-40-0)
* ** Mulberry *Su*
* + Blackberry

171

HOODED ORIOLE
Icterus cucullatus

The hooded oriole ranges from southern Texas to southern California. Our food information on it is scant.

Animal food: A variety of insects including weevils, stinkbugs, grasshoppers, caterpillars, ants, bees, and leafhoppers are taken. Unlike the other orioles, the 11 stomachs on record do not show a preponderance of caterpillars.

Plant food:
California and Arizona, 11 (0-0-11-0)
  * Fig
  + Elderberry, Nightshade

BALTIMORE ORIOLE
Icterus galbula

Specimens:	75	125	
WINTER	SPRING	SUMMER	FALL

8%   20%

Plant food:
Northeast, 208 (0-80-126-2) plus observations
  * Mulberry *Su*
  * Serviceberry *Su*
  * Blackberry *Su*
  + Blueberry, Cherry (Cult. and Wild), Pear, Garden Pea, Corn, Grape, Apple

This brilliantly colored, melodious species is partial to areas where large trees are present in relatively open spaces. It is in such locations, often in tall elms, that the Baltimore oriole builds its hanging nest. Sometimes these orioles can be induced to nest near one's home by making string or horsehair available as nest-building material. Their summer range extends beyond our northeastern states into southern Canada.

Animal food: Caterpillars constitute the leading food item. Among the other animal items are beetles, bugs, ants, wasps, spiders, and grasshoppers.

BULLOCK ORIOLE
Icterus bullockii

The Bullock oriole is the western counterpart of the Baltimore. Like the latter it selects tall, spreading trees as the site for its hanging nest. Locally, the Bullock oriole is guilty of raiding cultivated fruits, but the damage caused is generally minor.

Animal food: Caterpillars, beetles, ants and wasps, grasshoppers and other insects occur prominently in the diet.

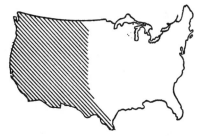

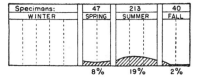

Specimens:	47	213	40
WINTER	SPRING	SUMMER	FALL
	8%	19%	2%

California, 164 (0-39-125-0)
 * Cherry, Cult. *SpSu*

Plant food:
Southwest, 136 (0-8-88-40)
 + Wheat, Condalia, Hackberry, Dogwood, Elderberry, Oats
 * Fig *Su*
 * Raspberry *Su*
 + Sorghum, Peach, Apricot, Elderberry, Grape, Mulberry

RUSTY BLACKBIRD
Euphagus carolinus

Specimens: 42	56	4	30
WINTER	SPRING	SUMMER	FALL
60%	31%	4%	36%

crustaceans, snails, and salamanders.
Plant food: The plant foods are largely grains and weed seeds gleaned from farmlands.

The rusty is mainly a Canadian bird in summer—its nesting range barely extending over the international boundary into the Northeast. It winters in the Southeast and adjoining Prairies, and here it is most commonly seen in swampy or lowland woods. The rusty blackbird also feeds in open farmland but is not ordinarily regarded as a pest species. This may be due to the fact that its numbers are fewer than some of the other blackbirds and partly because its feeding in fields is largely gleaning of waste grain.

Animal food: Aquatic beetles, and their larvae, constitute the largest part of the animal diet. Grasshoppers and caterpillars are also taken to a large extent. The balance of its animal food consists of various aquatic insects, ants, some bugs and flies, spiders, centipedes, and other small animals such as

Northeast and Canada, 90 (23-39-4-24)
 *** Corn *FW*
 ** Wildrice *W*
 ** Oats *W*
 ** Bristlegrass *W*
 * Wheat *FW*
 * Ragweed *W*
 + Grape, Blackberry, Elderberry, Oak, Beech
Southeast, 9 (9-0-0-0)
 *** Rice
 *** Wheat
 *** Oats
 ** Ragweed
 ** Grape
 * Panicgrass
Prairies, 49 (19-24-0-6)
 *** Corn *FWSp*
 *** Bristlegrass *FWSp*
 * Oats *WSp*
 * Ragweed *W*

173

BREWER BLACKBIRD
Euphagus cyanocephalus

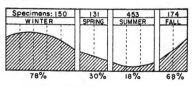

Specimens: 150 WINTER	131 SPRING	453 SUMMER	174 FALL
78%	30%	18%	68%

aphids, other insects, and a few spiders, centipedes, sowbugs, and snails.
Plant food: Seeds from farm crops are the chief plant foods.

The Brewer blackbird is, in a sense, the grackle of the West. Its range begins where the grackles stop—about midway across the country. However, small numbers of this species also winter in the southeastern states. Brewers are typical grackle-like blackbirds, not only in appearance, but also in notes and habitat. They are common in moist meadows and about marshes. Some also live in towns.
Animal food: Beetles and caterpillars comprise the main animal food items. They also take grasshoppers, crickets,

West (excl. Calif.), 399 (27-53-273-46)
*** Corn *WSp*
** Oats *SpSuFW*
* Wheat *SpSu*
+ Sunflower, Bristlegrass, Knotweed, Dandelion
California, 279 (45-28-133-73)
**** Oats, Wild and Cult. *SuFWSp*
* Cherry, Cult. *SpSu*
* Wheat *SuFW*
* Barley *FW*
* Filaree *SpWF*
* Corn *SpSuF*
* Rye *F*
+ Chickweed, Tarweed

GRACKLES. According to the most recent ornithological interpretations, there are only two species of grackles in the country: the boat-tailed and the one now designated as the common grackle. The boattail is confined to coastal areas in the Southeast. The other grackle, in summer, occurs as far west as the Rockies and moves southward into the southeastern states for the winter.

In spring and summer the grackle's food (both species) is about two-thirds animal and one-third plant, but in fall and winter this proportion is reversed. The gregarious habits of these blackbirds—frequently ranging in flocks of hundreds—cause them to become local nuisances, both to the farmer and the city dweller.

BOAT-TAILED GRACKLE
Cassidix mexicanus

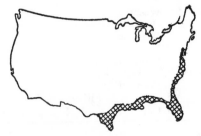

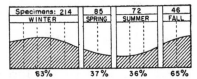

Specimens: 214 WINTER	85 SPRING	72 SUMMER	46 FALL
63%	37%	36%	65%

The giant of our grackles, the boattail, is partial to tidal mud flats, brackish marshes, and lowland ponds in the Southeast. Small numbers of these

174

birds, however, are found as far north as southern Delaware along the Atlantic coast. Their habitat is reflected in the foods listed below. Besides its greater size, the boattail may be distinguished from other grackles by its loud, whistle-like notes.

Animal food: Insects (particularly beetles and grasshoppers), crustaceans (chiefly crayfish, crabs, and shrimp), a few lizards, toads, frogs, and small mammals are the main items of animal food.

Plant food:
Southeast, 417 (214-85-72-46)
  **** Corn *SuFWSp*
  *** Rice *SuFWSp*
    * Chufa, tuber *WSp*
    * Fig *SuF*
    + Bristlegrass, Oats, Bayberry, Grape

COMMON GRACKLE
Quiscalus quiscula

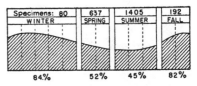

These are the familiar crow blackbirds that move northward in noisy flocks early in the spring—usually before snows are entirely past. In summer we often find grackles nesting in Norway spruces and other conifers in cities and towns. In the fall, prior to migrating, long lines of grackles may be seen (and heard) flying to or from their night roosts.

The principal distinction between the two color forms of the common grackle—the purple and bronzed—is in the shade of the iridescent color reflected from their plumage. These two forms are not always clearly distinguishable. They are now recognized as belonging to the same species, though at times in the past they have been classed as distinct. The bronzed form ranges mainly west of the Alleghenies, while the purple subspecies occurs east of this boundary. A third form is the Florida grackle which ranges from South Carolina to Florida.

Animal food: Leading items of animal food are insects (especially bees, grasshoppers, and crickets), spiders, myriapods, crustaceans (particularly crayfish and sowbugs), earthworms, snails, some vertebrates such as toads, salamanders, and mice, and birds' eggs.

Plant food: Most of the plant foods which, except for the summer season, are the major constituents of the diet, are farm crops. Often this feeding represents damage, but at other times it consists of harmless gleaning.

Northeast, 1235 (63-267-786-119)
  **** Corn *SuFWSp*
   ** Oats *SpSuF*
   ** Wheat *SuFWSp*
   ** Oak *FWSp*
    * Ragweed *FWSp*
    * Blackberry *Su*
    + Cherry (Cult. and Wild), Bristlegrass, Beech, Mulberry,

Gromwell, Wild Grape, Apple
Southeast, 125 (33-52-35-5)
**** Corn *SuFWSp*
*** Oak *FWSp*
  * Sorghum *SuSp*
  * Blackberry *Su*

+ Mulberry, Bristlegrass, Rice
Prairies, 638 (2-235-345-56)
***** (55%) Corn *SuFWSp*
  ** Oats *SpSuFW*
  + Bristlegrass, Wheat, Sunflower, Blackberry

COWBIRD
Molothrus ater

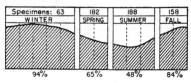

The cowbird is a unique member of the blackbird family. Birds of this genus are the only ones in North America that regularly lay eggs in other birds' nests. Apparently this social parasite is too lazy or too smart to take care of its own domestic duties. At least 158 different species of birds are known to have been victimized by the cowbird.

Many kinds of birds seem to recognize the cowbird as an enemy. Robins and catbirds destroy and remove cowbird eggs that are laid in their nests. If all species did this, the cowbird would soon pass out of existence—unless it changed its habits. Vireos and some warblers finding a cowbird egg in their nest generally cover the unwelcome egg with an additional nest floor. Chats abandon their nests when they find cowbird eggs present.

When the cowbird egg hatches, the nestling is cared for by the foster parents along with the legitimate offspring. In fact the parents often neglect their own young in the effort to satisfy the voracious large cowbird nestling. The young cowbird eventually joins others of its kind and continues the parasitic cycle.

There are four subspecies of cowbird—their range extending well up into Canada and down into Mexico. Other species occur south of our borders, one of them barely entering the United States along our southwestern boundary. In migration, cowbirds commonly flock with other blackbirds.

Animal food: Grasshoppers constitute the main animal food item, while beetles, caterpillars, other insects, spiders, and myriapods make up the balance.

Plant food: Weed seeds are leading food items in the cowbird dietary.

Northeast, 290 (17-76-88-109) ·
*** Bristlegrass *SuFWSp*
*** Ragweed *FWSp*
*** Oats *SuFSp*
  ** Corn *SuFW*
  * Crabgrass *FWSp*
  * Wheat *SuFSp*
  * Knotweed *SuFWSp*
  + Paspalum, Smartweed, Sheep-sorrel
Southeast, 91 (42-0-16-33)
*** Bristlegrass *SuFW*
*** Panicgrass *SuFW*
  ** Ragweed *FW*
  ** Oats *Sp*
  ** Wheat *SuFW*
  ** Doveweed *SuF*
  * Corn *W*
  * Paspalum *W*
  + Sorghum, Wildmillet, Crabgrass
West, 208 (4-106-84-14)
**** Bristlegrass *WSpSu*

** Oats *SpSu*
 * Timothy *W*
 * Ragweed *SuSp*

 * Corn *SuWSp*
+ Sunflower, Knotweed, Panicgrass

Reference: The Cowbirds. Herbert Friedmann. Charles C. Thomas, Publisher, Springfield, Ill., 1929. 421 pp.

Tanagers: *Thraupidae*

TANAGERS. Four species of tanagers visit parts of the United States during the nesting season. They winter south of our borders—in Mexico, Central or South America. The hepatic tanager breeds only along our southwestern border states (western Texas to Arizona), and we lack accurate information on its foods.

The brilliantly colored tanagers are primarily insect eaters, though one-fourth to one-third of the western tanager's diet is from plants. Fleshy fruits are the only items that compete with insects in their fare.

WESTERN TANAGER
Piranga ludoviciana

The western tanager replaces, in its territory, the scarlet tanager of the East. It nests throughout the Mountain–Desert and Pacific regions and winters in Mexico.

Cultivated cherries were the principal fruit eaten by 52 specimens examined. However, this colorful songster is not regarded as a serious menace to fruit crops.

Animal food: The nonplant part of this species' diet closely resembles that

of the scarlet tanager. Wasps, bees, ants, beetles, and bugs head the varied list of insect items.

Plant food:
Pacific, 52 (0-0-52-0)
 *** Cherry, Cult.
   * Raspberry
   * Mulberry
   * Elderberry
   * Serviceberry

SCARLET TANAGER
Piranga olivacea

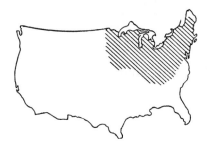

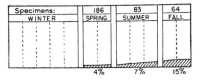

Specimens:		186	83	64
WINTER		SPRING	SUMMER	FALL
		4%	7%	15%

The scarlet tanager is the most brilliant bird of the Northeast and southern Canada. Seldom, however, does it expose itself to clear view. This beautiful species migrates to South America in the fall.

Animal food: *Hymenoptera* (wasps,

177

bees, and ants), beetles, bugs, caterpillars, and moths constitute the main
items of the animal diet.

Plant food:
Northeast, 327 (1-184-80-62) plus observations

* Blackberry *Su*
+ Dogwood, Elderberry, Grape,
  Huckleberry, Serviceberry,
  Bayberry, Sumac, Cherry,
  Mulberry, Blackgum

SUMMER TANAGER
Piranga rubra

The summer tanager is present
thoughout most of the southern half
of the United States in summer. We
have only slight food information for
it, but a summary from 11 specimens
taken in the Southeast is given below.
Except for one of these 11 birds, the
plant percentage ran quite low.

Animal food: Beetles, ants, wasps,
bees, caterpillars, and bugs are important parts of the insect fare.

Plant food:
Southeast, 11 (0-9-1-1) plus observa-
tions
*** Blackberry *SpSu*
+ Mulberry, Cherry, Grape

Sparrows, Finches, Buntings, Grosbeaks, Towhees: *Fringillidae*

CARDINAL
Richmondena cardinalis

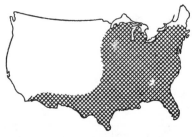

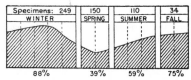

The cardinal, or redbird, is one of
the few songbirds that stay put. It is
a familiar part of the eastern countryside, winter and summer. Cardinals
are related to the grosbeaks—sharing
with them the characteristics of heavy
bill and beautiful song. Their clear,
whistle-like "cheer, cheeer, cheer" in
late winter months is one of the most
pleasing of all outdoor sounds. Red-
birds are likely to be attracted to
residential areas planted with fruit-
bearing shrubs or trees. Sunflower
seeds, unsalted peanuts, and melon
seeds are relished by them at winter
feeding stations.

Animal food: Caterpillars, grasshoppers, true bugs, and beetles comprise
the greatest part of the animal diet.
Plant food: The plant part of the
cardinal's diet shows a surprising diversity: wild fruits, weed seeds, and
cultivated grains are eaten.

Northeast, 141 (85-12-31-13)
*** Grape *SuFW*
*** Smartweed *SuFW*
** Corn *SuFW*
** Dogwood *SuFW*
* Oats *Su*
* Sedge *SpSuW*
* Mulberry *SpSu*
* Sumac *W*
* Vervain *W*
* Tuliptree *W*
+ Viburnum, Nightshade, Service-
  berry, Ragweed, Green-

** Corn *SuFW*
* Sedge *SuFWSp*
* Panicgrass *W*
+ Ragweed, Wild Cherry, Dog-
   wood, Oats, Goosegrass,
   Plantain, Smartweed,
   Knotweed
Southern Prairies, 266 (98-121-40-7)
*** Grape *SuFWSp*
** Corn *SuWSp*
* Doveweed *SuFW*
* Bristlegrass *SuFWSp*
* Dogwood *W*
* Mulberry *SpSu*
* Knotweed *W*
* Hackberry *W*
+ Oats, Sedge, Blackberry, Panic-
   grass

brier, Ash, Blackberry,
Bristlegrass
Southeast, 136 (66-17-39-14)
*** Bristlegrass *SuFW*
** Blackberry *Su*
** Grape *FW*

PYRRHULOXIA
Pyrrhuloxia sinuata

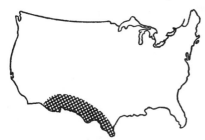

Specimens:			57	15
WINTER	SPRING	SUMMER	FALL
			75%	73%

The pyrrhuloxia, like the phainopepla, is unfortunate in not having a
good common name. This crested,
cardinal-like bird of the Southwest is
an all-year resident within its range. It
is a seed eater, feeding largely on weedy
plants. Only for the subspecies known
as the Texas pyrrhuloxia do we have
significant food data.
Animal food: Insects eaten are chiefly
grasshoppers, caterpillars, and beetles
(particularly weevils). Stinkbugs, cicadas, and miscellaneous other insects
are also captured.

Plant food:
Texas, 72 (0-57-15-0)
**** Bristlegrass *SuF*
*** Doveweed *SuF*
** Sandbur *SuF*
** Panicgrass *SuF*
* Sorghum *Su*
+ Pigweed, Goosefoot, Sunflower,
   Carpetweed, Paspalum

GROSBEAKS. Five species of birds in the United States are called grosbeaks.
All of them have heavy bills—as their name implies. All are seed eaters and
attractive songsters. In other respects, however, the grosbeaks are not a natural,
compact, closely related group. This is indicated by their classification into four
different genera, some of which are not contiguous. Three species of grosbeaks
are warm-climate birds that spend the winters south of our borders while two, the
evening and pine grosbeaks, are northerners, more closely allied to the finches, and
partial to cool, coniferous forests.

Reference: Food Habits of the Grosbeaks. W. L. McAtee. *U.S. Dept. Agr. Biol. Survey Bul.* 32, 1908. 92 pp.

ROSE-BREASTED GROSBEAK
Pheucticus ludovicianus

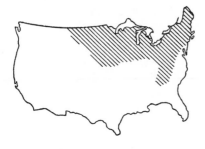

Specimens:	82	58	11
WINTER	SPRING	SUMMER	FALL
	41%	41%	76%

In spring the rose-breasted grosbeak comes north to the United States and Canada from its winter home. This attractive singer—with a song resembling that of the robin—nests in the Northeast and in Canada.

Animal food: Nearly half of the animal diet is composed of beetles. Ants, bees, wasps, caterpillars, and scale insects make up appreciable amounts; the balance consists of various other invertebrates.

Plant food:
Northeast and Northern Prairies, 165 (0-96-58-11) plus observations
** Elderberry *SuF*
** Cherry, Wild, flw. and fr. *SpSu*
* Wheat *SpSu*
* Smartweed *SuF*
* Blackberry *SuF*
* Corn *SpSuF*
* Garden Pea *Sp.Su*
* Elm, flw. *Sp*
* Beech, flw. *Sp*
* Hickory, flw. *Sp*
+ Oats, Serviceberry, Mulberry, Hop-hornbeam, Pokeweed, Oak, Pigweed

BLACK-HEADED GROSBEAK
Pheucticus melanocephalus

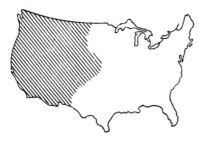

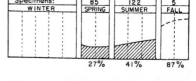

Specimens:	85	122	5
WINTER	SPRING	SUMMER	FALL
	27%	41%	87%

This is a close relative of the rose-breasted grosbeak and takes its place in the West. The blackhead is fond of fruits, cultivated as well as wild, but its toll is generally minor—especially when reckoned with the good it does in destroying harmful insects.

Animal food: A great variety of insects and other invertebrates particularly beetles, bugs, grasshoppers, caterpillars, ants, bees, wasps, spiders, and snails are eaten by the black-headed grosbeak.

Plant food:
California, 212 (0-85-122-5)
*** Fig *SuF*
** Elderberry *Su*
** Cherry, Cult. *SpSu*
* Oats *SpSuF*

| * Raspberry *Su* | + Wheat, Prune, Milkthistle, Red- |
| * Filaree *Sp* | maids |

Reference: Breeding Behavior of the Black-headed Grosbeak. Henry G. Weston, Jr. *Condor*, Vol. 49, pp. 54–73, 1947.

BLUE GROSBEAK
Guiraca caerulea

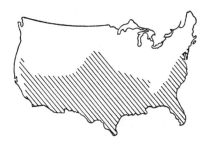

Specimens:	15	17	2
WINTER	SPRING	SUMMER	FALL

34%   43%   83%

Plant food: Bristlegrass seeds are important food for the blue grosbeak in all regions. Cultivated and wild grasses are its chief source of food.

The blue grosbeak resembles its first cousin, the indigo bunting, in more than color. Both are partial to brushy areas, and both nest mainly in the southern two-thirds of the country. The blue grosbeak ranges all the way across the continent. In the fall it migrates to Central America—like the indigo bunting.

Animal food: Beetles, bugs, caterpillars, grasshoppers, ants, and numerous other kinds of insects are eaten by this bird.

East, 8 (0-2-4-2)
**** Wheat *Su*
 *** Bristlegrass *F*
  ** Panicgrass *Su*
Northern Prairies, 9 (0-1-8-0)
**** Corn *SuSp*
  ** Oats *Su*
   * Bristlegrass *Su*
Southwest, 17 (0-12-5-0)
 *** Bristlegrass *Su*
  ** Wheat *Sp*
  ** Corn *SuSp*
   * Burclover *Su*
   + Dropseedgrass

EVENING GROSBEAK
Hesperiphona vespertina

The evening grosbeaks are primarily Canadian citizens. However, one of the western subspecies nests in the Rocky Mountains as far south as Arizona. In winters of some years, large flocks of these quiet, finch-like birds leave their wilderness isolation and are seen in our northern states. They feed almost exclusively on the fruits and seeds of trees but are greatly attracted by sunflower seeds at feeding stations.

Animal food: Like the other grosbeaks, the two main insect food items are beetles and caterpillars. Also included in the diet are ants, bees, wasps, bugs, spiders, and other invertebrates.

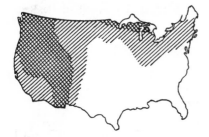

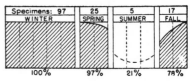

| Specimens: 97 | 25 | 5 | 17 |
| WINTER | SPRING | SUMMER | FALL |

100%   97%   21%   78%

Plant food:
Northeast, 74 (65-8-0-1)
**** Maple *WSp*
**** Dogwood *WSp*
*** Cherry, Wild *WSp*
  * Mountain-ash *W*
  + Ash, Blackberry

Northwest, 70 (32-17-5-16)
*** Pine, Ponderosa *WSp*
*** Cherry, Wild *WSp*
*** Cedar *FWSp*
 ** Manzanita *W*
 ** Dogwood *FW*
 ** Russianolive *W*
  * Boxelder *FSp*
  * Hackberry *WSp*
  * Snowberry *W*
  * Serviceberry *W*
  + Sumac, Ash

PINE GROSBEAK
Pinicola enucleator

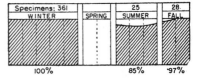

| Specimens: 361 | | 25 | 28 |
| WINTER | SPRING | SUMMER | FALL |

100%   85%   97%

The pine grosbeak looks like, and is, a finch. It is a round-the-world species that lives mainly in northern coniferous forests. In the United States it occurs in our higher western mountains and in northern states of the East. When alpine food supplies become scarce the birds move into the lowlands or southward.

Animal food: Beetles, caterpillars, *Hymenoptera* and other insects, and invertebrates make up the animal diet of this grosbeak.

Plant food: Like most of the other grosbeaks, this one feeds largely on fruits of trees. Occasionally, however, it forages on weed seeds.

Northeast, 314 (274-1-12-27)
**** Pine *W*
*** Blackberry *FW*
 ** Redcedar *W*
 ** Mountain-ash *W*
 ** Maple *W*
  * Ragweed *W*
  * Dogwood *W*
  * Ash *W*
  * Crowberry *FW*
  + Wintercress, Hawthorn, Huckleberry, Spruce
Pacific, 103 (87-2-13-1)
**** Snowberry *W*
 ** Willow *W*
 ** Dogwood *SuW*
  * Honeysuckle *Su*
  * Pine *Su*
  * Minerslettuce *Su*
  + Strawberry, Ash

BUNTINGS. Under the name buntings are three distinct bird groups belonging to the very large *Fringillidae* family. The lark bunting and snow bunting are treated farther on, near the end of the family (pages 193 and 211). They are distinct from the colorful and melodious group of buntings that include the indigo, lazuli, painted, and beautiful buntings. The latter are relatives of the grosbeaks and cardinals, and in the main they favor temperate, semitropical, and tropical climates—nesting in parts of the United States and wintering in Mexico and Central America. The beautiful bunting's range in this country is confined to Southern California, and on this species we have no food data. Information on foods of the other three closely related species is scant, but on the whole these birds fare on seeds and insects with some preponderance of the former.

INDIGO BUNTING
Passerina cyanea

The indigo bunting, arriving from Central America and Cuba in the spring, is a common summer bird in the eastern United States. Frequently we see and hear the male indigo on roadside telephone wires, along country lanes, or near field borders. Its cheery song and flash of bright blue—a more brilliant hue than that of the bluebird—are familiar; yet it is one of the least known birds as regards its feeding. Only three stomach analyses of indigo buntings are available, and

records of field observations are scant.
Animal food: The animal food—apparently a considerable part of the summer diet—consists largely of insects, particularly caterpillars, beetles, and grasshoppers.
Plant food: In the three specimens examined, seeds constituted a large proportion of the food. Seeds of ragweed and bristlegrass and farm grains, including wheat and oats, are relished. Also the fleshy fruits of blackberry and elderberry are eaten.

LAZULI BUNTING
Passerina amoena

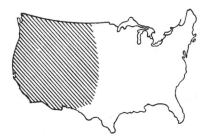

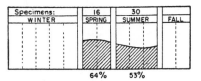

Specimens:	16	30	
WINTER	SPRING	SUMMER	FALL

64% 53%

The lazuli bunting is a western relative of the indigo bunting. Its markings, especially on the breast, differ from those of the eastern bird, but their habits and song show resemblance. After spending the nesting season in western parts of North America, the lazuli bunting returns to Mexico and Central America.
Animal food: Grasshoppers, caterpil-

lars, and beetles, plus a goodly number of true bugs, bees, and ants are the main animal items.
Plant food: Seeds of weedy plants constitute more than one-third of the spring and summer food.

Pacific (mainly Calif.), 46 (0-16-30-0)
 *** Oats, Wild *SpSu*
 ** Minerslettuce *SpSu*
 ** Needlegrass *Su*
 * Canarygrass *SpSu*
 * Bluegrass, Annual *Sp*
 + Melicgrass, Velvetgrass, Filaree, Chickweed

PAINTED BUNTING
Passerina ciris

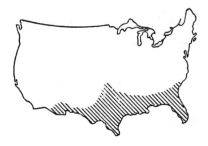

The male painted bunting with its combination of scarlet, purple, and green is one of our most ornate songbirds. This bird is a summertime resident of swamps and woodland groves of the deep South. A few remain in southern Florida, while the remainder migrate to Mexico, Central America, and Cuba for the winter.

Animal food: Grasshoppers, beetles (mostly weevils), caterpillars, and true bugs—occasionally spiders and snails—together with other animal items constitute about 14% of the summer food.

Plant food: Eighty-six per cent of the summer food of the painted bunting is of plant origin, 70% being seeds of bristlegrass.

Texas, 102 (0-0-102-0)
***** (70%) Bristlegrass *Su*
　* Panicgrass *Su*
　+ Pigweed, Woodsorrel, Spurge, Sedge

DICKCISSEL
Spiza americana

Specimens:	5	180	
WINTER	SPRING	SUMMER	FALL

38%　　20%

Though the summer range of this pert bird is depicted as extending through much of the East, the dickcissel is really common only in the Middle West. In the eastern part of the Prairies, its cheerful chirpings from telephone wires or fence posts are among the most familiar sounds as one drives along the highways. The dickcissel winters in South America.

Animal food: Almost half of the animal food consists of grasshoppers, katydids, and crickets. Beetles, especially ground beetles, weevils, and dung beetles, ants, caterpillars, and a few flies and bugs constitute most of the other half of its animal diet.

Plant food: Bristlegrass seeds comprise most of the limited quantity of plant food of the dickcissel while it is in this country.

Prairies, 185 (0-5-180-0)
**** Bristlegrass *Su*
　* Oats *Su*
　+ Panicgrass, Wheat, Corn

FINCHES. Aside from goldfinches, there are six species of finches in the country. They belong to two distinct but closely related genera. The purple, Cassin, and house finches are in the genus *Carpodacus*, while the three species of rosy finch are named *Leucosticte*. For one of the latter, the black rosy finch, food data are lacking. All six species are exclusively western, except for the purple finch which has an eastern as well as a western subspecies. Goldfinches are closely related to these two groups of finches but are given separate treatment in this chapter.

The house finch is an all-year resident within its range, but the other finches migrate—generally a comparatively short distance. Their food is largely from the plant kingdom—seeds, buds, and fruits—but insects are also eaten. The house finch, with habits like the English sparrow, becomes a nuisance in some localities, and other finches occasionally become destructive by disbudding orchard trees. On the credit side are the melodious, warbling songs of these birds and their attractive appearance.

PURPLE FINCH
Carpodacus purpureus

The purple finch is a northern bird in summer, nesting mainly in Canada and in a few of our northern states. The winters are spent in the South.

Our information on purple finch foods is confined largely to the East. These rosy-colored, warbling songsters obtain a large share of their springtime food by eating buds or tree flowers. Sometimes this habit becomes a detriment in orchard areas. In the fall and winter they feed a great deal on the dry seed-like fruits of tuliptree and ashes.

Animal food: Insects are eaten very sparingly. Generally they are aphids or caterpillars.

Plant food: Buds, fruits, and seeds constitute practically 100% of the food of the eastern purple finch.

East, 27 (16-4-0-7) plus many observations
*** Elm, bud and sd. *Sp*
** Tuliptree *FW*
** Apple, bud *Sp*
** Cherry and Peach, bud and fr. *SpF*
** Pear, bud *Sp*
** Redcedar *F*
* Maple, bud and fr. *Sp*
* Sycamore *F*
* Ragweed *F*
* Aspen, bud *Sp*
* Dogwood *F*
* Honeysuckle *F*
* Sweetgum *F*
* Cocklebur *F*
* Ash *W*
\+ Hop-hornbeam, Beech, Birch, Blackgum, Bidens, Grape, Poison-ivy

HOUSE FINCH
Carpodacus mexicanus

Specimens: 388	138	406	231
WINTER	SPRING	SUMMER	FALL
99%	92%	96%	100%

In the West, the house finch, also known as the linnet, replaces to some extent the English sparrow as a common species about dwellings, orchards, and farms. It is especially plentiful in California where it often becomes a local nuisance. Sometimes hundreds of the birds roost in vines on a single dwelling. They are fond of cultivated fruits and are capable of causing damage to crops. As compared with the male English sparrow, this bird has the asset of a warbling melody and bright reddish coloring.

185

Animal food: The few animal items included in the diet are principally aphids and caterpillars.

Plant food: Though linnets eat cultivated fruits their main diet consists of weed seeds.

California, 849 (270-130-312-137)
**** Filaree *WSpSuF*
*** Turkeymullein *SuFW*
*** Mustard *SpSuFW*
** Knotweed *SuFW*
** Fig *SuFW*
** Prune *SuF*
** Pigweed *SuFW*
* Star-thistle *SuFWSp*
* Chickweed *SpSu*
* Wildradish *SpSuF*
* Tarweed *SuFW*
+ Minerslettuce, Elderberry, Corn Spurry, Sedge, Eriogonum, Apple, Pine

GRAY-CROWNED ROSY FINCH
Leucosticte tephrocotis

The gray-crowned rosy finch is a western species, present mainly in mountains of the Northwest and in Canada. The food information on this species has been obtained from 40 specimens from the Pacific region. In these, the plant material averaged as follows: Winter, 100% (4 birds); summer, 67% (34 birds); fall, 100% (2 birds).

Animal food: The animal diet is quite evenly divided among ants and other *Hymenoptera*, beetles, bugs, and caterpillars. Spiders, grasshoppers, and other invertebrates are also eaten.

Plant food: This bird is a feeder on a diversified assortment of seeds.

Pacific (mainly Calif.), 40 (4-0-34-2)
**** Lewisia *SuF*
*** Oats *W*
** Pine *Su*
** Wheat *W*
* Peppergrass *Su*
* Sedge *Su*
* Timothy *W*
* Cinquefoil *Su*
+ Penstemon, Fescuegrass, Knotweed, Redmaids, Rockcress

BROWN-CAPPED ROSY FINCH
Leucosticte australis

The brown-capped rosy finch breeds in the high mountains of Colorado, while in winter it is found in valleys of both Colorado and New Mexico. It is similar to the gray-crowned rosy finch but is lighter colored and has a brown cap. Only seven specimens

have been examined for food-habits information.

Animal food: The limited data show that miscellaneous insects and spiders probably make up most of the animal diet. In the birds collected in winter there was no animal material, but in the five collected in summer it came to just about half of the total.

Plant food: Like the gray-crowned rosy finch, this species is primarily an eater of seeds of weeds and other herbs.

Southern Mt.–Desert, 7 (2-0-5-0)

```
**** Knotweed W
 *** Chickweed Sp
  ** Gramagrass W
   * Pigweed W
   * Lovegrass W
   + Strawberry, Fescuegrass, Goose-
     foot
```

COMMON REDPOLL
Acanthis flammea

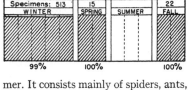

The common redpoll is a subarctic bird that comes as far south as our northern states in winter. Our information on its winter food indicates that it is almost entirely vegetarian, feeding on weed seeds and on the seeds of alders and birches.

Animal food: Animal food is negligible during the winter months, but may amount to considerable in the sum-

mer. It consists mainly of spiders, ants, and flies.

Plant food:
North, 501 (468-12-1-20)
```
**** Ragweed WSp
 *** Alder FW
 *** Birch W
 *** Goosefoot W
 *** Smartweed WSp
  ** Pigweed WSp
   * Timothy WSp
   * Eriogonum W
   * Bristlegrass FW
   + Sedge, Selfheal, Russianthistle
```

PINE SISKIN
Spinus pinus

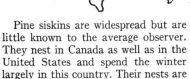

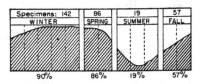

Pine siskins are widespread but are little known to the average observer. They nest in Canada as well as in the United States and spend the winter largely in this country. Their nests are

generally built in pines or other conifers. Pine siskins feed on pine and alder seeds, but a larger proportion of their food consists of weed seeds.

Animal food: Caterpillars, plant lice (aphids), spiders, bugs, and fly larvae are the main animal-food constituents of the diet.

Plant food:
West (mainly Calif.), 105 (41-35-19-10)
**** Filaree *SpFW*
  ** Pine *WSp*
   * Alder *W*

  * Star-thistle *F*
  * Eucalyptus *FW*
  * Minerslettuce *WSp*
  * Sunflower *F*
  + Chickweed, Douglasfir, Silene

GOLDFINCHES. Three species of goldfinch are recognized within our national limits. The green-backed and Lawrence are in the Southwest, and the common goldfinch is widespread over practically all the country.

These cheerful, friendly little relatives of the domesticated canary are locally called thistle birds or wild canaries. They can often be seen in the open countryside, feeding on heads of thistles, goldenrods, dandelions, or other weeds. One may also hear them overhead, each dip in flight accompanied by three or four notes. Goldfinches nest later than most birds—often not until late in summer They migrate only short distances.

COMMON GOLDFINCH
Spinus tristis

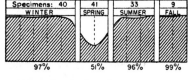

The common goldfinch is present in most regions of the country. The eastern race, often called the eastern goldfinch, is the most widespread. Food data for this and a California subspecies known as the willow goldfinch are given below.
Animal food: The small quantity of animal food taken by these birds consists mostly of aphids and caterpillars.
Plant food: Goldfinches are primarily seed eaters. They make a practice of hulling the seeds and cutting off any plumes or other nonnutritious attachments.

East, 39 (6-20-12-1) plus many observations

*** Ragweed *SuFWSp*
*** Thistle *W*
*** Shepherds-purse *Su*
*** Sweetgum *W*
  * Goosefoot *Su*
  * Sunflower *FW*
  * Dandelion *FW*
  * Velvetgrass *Su*
  * Alder *W*
  * Goldenrod *W*
  + Chickweed, Leafcup, Sowthistle, Wildlettuce, Honeysuckle, False-nettle, Tuliptree, Evening-primrose, Coneflower, Pine, Timothy, Elm, Maple
California, 84 (34-21-21-8)
*** Sunflower *SuFWSp*
*** Star-thistle *SuFW*
*** Filaree *WSp*
  * Tarweed *F*
  + Oak

GREEN-BACKED GOLDFINCH
Spinus psaltria

The green-backed, or Arkansas, goldfinch is a bird of the Southwest. The food data presented here were obtained entirely from California.

188

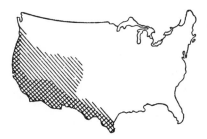

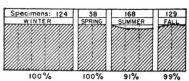

+ Mayweed, Filaree, Sunflower, Minerslettuce, Oats, Nightshade, Sage, Silene

Animal food: Aphids and caterpillars are principal animal items of its diet. **Plant food:** Weed seeds are the staple food.

California, 417 (124-38-129-126)
***** (54%) Star-thistle *SuFW*
 ** Pigweed *FW*
  * Turkeymullein *FW*
  * Tarweed *SuF*

LAWRENCE GOLDFINCH
Spinus lawrencei

Animal food: There are no records of animal food taken by this species.
Plant food: As in the case of other goldfinches the principal foods are weed seeds.

Mt.–Desert and Pacific, 29 (3-12-5-9) plus observations
**** Pigweed *FWSp*
 *** Fiddleneck *SpSu*
  ** Star-thistle *SuFW*
  ** Chamise *F*
   * Redmaids *SuF*
   * Russianthistle *FW*
   * Chickweed *W*
   + Peppergrass, Knotweed, Shepherds-purse, Cryptantha

The Lawrence goldfinch is a native of arid areas in Southern California and Arizona. This small species has less yellow coloring on its plumage than either the common or green-backed goldfinches.

CROSSBILLS. Two species of crossbills, the red and the whitewing, inhabit the northern parts of the continent. They winter to a limited extent in our northern states.

Crossbills are members of the sparrow family—their nearest relatives being the goldfinches and pine siskins. Their remarkable bill tips curve and cross over each other—a peculiarity which facilitates the extraction of seeds from cones of spruce, fir, pine, and other conifers. In this regard the crossbills have a distinct advantage over many other northern birds.

RED CROSSBILL
Loxia curvirostra

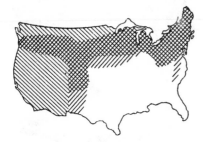

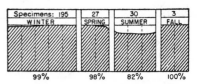

The red crossbill is almost exclusively a bird of the coniferous forests. Conifer seeds constitute more than nine-tenths of its food. In winters following failure or poor production of spruce seeds in subarctic forests, these reddish (adult males) or greenish birds enter our northern states in large numbers.
Animal food: The invertebrates most

in evidence in examined stomachs are spiders, caterpillars, fly larvae, beetles and their larvae, *Hymenoptera*, plant lice, and spittlebugs. Most of these are obtained from spruces, pines, or other conifers.

Plant food:
United States, 255 (195-27-30-3)
***** (66%) Pine *FWSpSu*
  * Larch *F*
  * Hemlock *W*
  * Spruce *FSpSu*
  + Fir, Douglasfir, Ragweed

Reference: A Monographic Study of the Red Crossbill. Ludlow Griscom. Boston Society of Natural History, 1937. 133 pp.

WHITE-WINGED CROSSBILL
Loxia leucoptera

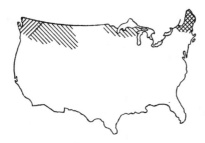

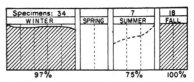

The white-winged crossbill is a bird of evergreen forests in Canada and Alaska. Its range barely enters northern United States. Like the red crossbill, the whitewing obtains most of its food from the cones of evergreens.
Animal food: The few available records show caterpillars and other larvae as the principal animal food.

Plant food: It is interesting to note that these crossbills vary their conifer seed diet to a limited extent by the use of weed seeds.

Northeast, 59 (34-0-7-18)
**** Spruce *SuFW*
  *** Pine *W*
  ** Hemlock *W*
  * Sunflower *W*
  * Fir *F*
  * Ragweed *W*
  + Redcedar, Bristlegrass, Huckleberry

190

TOWHEES. There are five species of towhees in the United States: one in the East and four in the West. They migrate to only a limited extent.

These long-tailed birds are addicted to brushy places. They like to feed on the ground, often scratching among fallen leaves for seeds and insects. Sometimes, however, they emerge short distances from hedgerows or similar cover to forage in open fields. More than half of their food is of plant origin.

GREEN-TAILED TOWHEE
Chlorura chlorura

The green-tailed towhee with its brown cap, greenish back and tail, and white throat is so distinct that it is classed in a separate genus. Its range includes most of the Pacific and Mountain–Desert regions. Only a limited amount of food-habits information is available on the greentail.

Animal food: The few stomach examination records reveal a diet very similar to that of the other towhees, with beetles, ants and other *Hyme-*

noptera, caterpillars, and grasshoppers comprising the principal animal items.

Plant food:
Mt.–Desert, 10 (0-3-5-2) plus observations
* Pigweed *Sp*
* Elderberry *F*
* Minerslettuce *Sp*
* Serviceberry *Su*
+ Filaree, Dandelion, Ricegrass

EASTERN TOWHEE
Pipilo erythrophthalmus

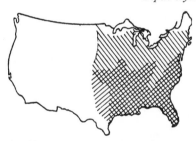

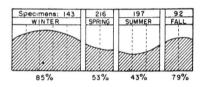

Specimens: 143	216	197	92
WINTER	SPRING	SUMMER	FALL
85%	53%	43%	79%

The eastern, or common, towhee is one of our most popular birds. Its calls and song, sprightly actions, and bright plumage have earned it a variety of common names among which are chewink, joree, ground robin, and low-ground-Stephen. It seldom ventures from woody cover except when feeding.

Animal food: The animal diet consists mostly of beetles, moths and caterpillars, grasshoppers, crickets, ants, bees, wasps, bugs, and spiders.

Plant food:
Northeast, 410 (18-150-163-79) plus observations

*** Ragweed *SuFWSp*
** Oak *FWSpSu*
** Smartweed *SuFWSp*
** Corn *SuFWSp*
* Blackberry *SpSuF*
* Blueberry *SuF*
* Sedge *SpSu*
* Bristlegrass *SuFWSp*
+ Bayberry, Strawberry, Huckleberry, Chickweed, Serviceberry, Oats, Grape, Wild Black Cherry, Sweetbay Magnolia, Apple
Southeast, 648 (143-216-197-92)
** Blackberry *SpSu*
** Oak *FWSp*
** Panicgrass *SuFWSp*
** Ragweed *FW*
** Waxmyrtle *FWSp*
* Blueberry *SuWSp*

* Corn *SuWSp*
* Grape *SuWSp*
* Pine *FW*
* Paspalum *SuWSp*

* Smartweed *FWSp*
+ Beautyberry, Hackberry, Holly, Magnolia, Sedge, Sweetgum

SPOTTED TOWHEE
Pipilo maculatus

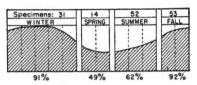

The spotted towhee occupies limited zones in the Pacific region. However, subspecies known as the arctic and spurred towhees occur extensively in the Mountain–Desert region. The spotted towhee is similar in habits and appearance to its eastern red-eyed cousin but is distinct in having white spots on its otherwise dark back.

Animal food: The chief items of the animal diet are beetles, ants and other

Hymenoptera, caterpillars and moths, grasshoppers, crickets, bugs, and flies.

Plant food:
Pacific (mainly Calif.), 150 (31-14-52-53)
** Oak *FWSp*
** Raspberry *SuF*
* Star-thistle *SuF*
* Oats *SuF*
* Wheat *SpSuF*
* Minerslettuce *SuF*
* Redmaids *SpSu*
* Poison-oak *SuFW*
+ Nightshade, Tarweed, Eriogonum, Filaree, Barley, Fig, Laurel Sumac, Gooseberry, Snowberry, Dock

BROWN TOWHEE
Pipilo fuscus

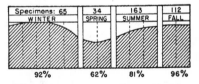

The brown towhee of California and the Southwest is neither colorful in appearance or in action. It is a common species that is seldom heard to make more than a muffled chirp. It frequently leaves protective shrubbery

to come out into field and orchard margins for food.

Animal food: Principal insect items are beetles, caterpillars and moths, grasshoppers, crickets, ants and other *Hymenoptera*, and bugs.

Plant food:
California, 374 (65-34-163-112)
*** Oats, Wild and Cult. *SpSuFW*

* Bluegrass, Annual *Sp*
* Star-thistle *SuFW*
* Nightshade *SuFW*
* Filaree *SuFWSp*
* Elderberry *SuFW*
* Pigweed *SuFW*
* Chickweed *WSpSu*
+ White Sage, Redmaids, Corn, Blackberry, Laurel Sumac, Turkeymullein, Mayweed, Fiddleneck, Smartweed, Eriogonum, Nettle, Wild Geranium

** Barley *SuFWSp*
** Ryegrass *SuFW*
* Fescuegrass *SuFW*
* Tarweed *SuF*
* Minerslettuce *SpSu*
* Bromegrass *SuW*

ABERT TOWHEE
Pipilo aberti

The Abert towhee, like its close relative the brown towhee, is a drab-colored species. Its range includes the Southwest from southwestern New Mexico and southern Utah and Nevada to Southern California. In this region the Abert towhee is a common inhabitant of mesquite thickets or other desert shrubbery.

Animal food: The few examination records indicate a diet closely resembling that of the other towhees, namely, beetles, caterpillars, ants and other *Hymenoptera*, moths, grasshoppers, crickets, and bugs.

Plant food:
Arizona, 10-(2-7-1-0)
** Fiddleneck *Sp*
** Crownbeard *Sp*
** Bristlegrass *W*
* Barley *Sp*
* Canarygrass *Sp*
+ Pigweed, Poplar, Wheat, Oats

LARK BUNTING
Calamospiza melanocorys

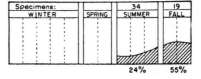

Specimens:			34	19
WINTER	SPRING	SUMMER	FALL	
			24%	55%

The black plumage and white wing patch of the male lark bunting are unique in the sparrow group to which this bird belongs. It is a summer resident of the Great Plains region of the United States and Canada—preferring uncultivated areas of the open range. In the fall and winter it migrates southward into Mexico.

Animal food: Grasshoppers comprise over half of the animal diet. Beetles, mostly weevils, account for a large proportion as do true bugs (mostly stinkbugs). The balance consists of wild bees, ants, and miscellaneous insects.

Plant food: Seeds of wild plants are the principal plant food.

Prairies, 53 (0-0-34-19)
  ** Purslane *F*
  ** Sorghum *F*
  ** Needlegrass *SuF*
   * Pigweed *SuF*

  * Vervain *SuF*
  + Knotweed, Oats, Panicgrass,
     Gromwell, Goosefoot,
     Dropseedgrass

SPARROWS. The true sparrows are classed with the towhees, lark and snow buntings, juncos, and longspurs on a top branch of the ornithological family tree—in the subfamily *Emberizinae*. There are about 36 species of sparrows in the United States. Twenty-eight of the more common ones are treated in this chapter.

This large clan of plain, grayish or brown-streaked songbirds forms a very successful and important part of the North American avian population. Sparrows are adapted to various environments and are present almost everywhere on the continent. The majority of species (field, vesper, savannah, etc.) are partial to fields or open areas. Others such as the fox and white-throated sparrows frequent bushy areas, while still others prefer brackish marshes, swamps, or even sagebrush plains. Though a few species are very localized, many are wide ranging, some even inhabiting parts of the Arctic during the summer.

All sparrows have fairly heavy bills well adapted to crushing seeds. Plant materials generally predominate in the diet except during the warm months when insects are plentiful. None of the true sparrows (the English sparrow is a weaver finch) cause significant damage to crops. On the other hand, they eat destructive insects, and some of them are our most familiar, best-loved songsters.

IPSWICH SPARROW
Passerculus princeps

The Ipswich sparrow is remarkable in the fact that its nesting home is limited to Sable Island, Nova Scotia—a relatively small island about 25 miles long, approximately 100 miles off the coast of Nova Scotia. The birds winter among the sand dunes of the Atlantic coast from Maine southward—a few going as far as Georgia. The winter food consists very largely of seeds of dune or beach plants. In summer, however, insects dominate the diet.

Animal food: The animal food is made up of beetles, wasp-like insects, bugs, caterpillars, flies, spiders, and snails. Tiger beetles, a rather unusual element of sparrow fare, are also eaten owing,

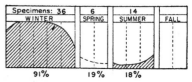

probably, to the abundance of these active insects upon the sand dunes.

Plant food:
Northeast, 56 (36-6-14-0)
  **** Beechgrass *W*
   ** Saltbush, Fat-hen *W*
    * Lovegrass *W*
   + Panicgrass, Bayberry, Smart-
     weed, Bunchberry, Pin-
     weed

SAVANNAH SPARROW
Passerculus sandwichensis

This small bird of grassy fields and open areas ranges in spring and summer from the upper half of the United States as far northward as the Arctic and winters in the warmer parts of this country southward to Central America. The savannah sparrow has 11 subspecies, some of which are quite local and distinctive in their feeding. Among these is the large-billed sparrow which

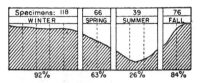

Specimens: 118	66	39	76
WINTER	SPRING	SUMMER	FALL
92%	63%	26%	84%

reverses the usual procedure by coming northward in winter from Lower California to Southern California. It feeds extensively on crabs, sowbugs, and snails as well as on various insects. The plant foods of this and other subspecies are included in the tables of data below.

Animal food: Leading items of the savannah sparrow's animal diet are beetles, caterpillars, grasshoppers, ants and other *Hymenoptera*, bugs, flies, and various other insects. Spiders and snails are also taken locally.

Plant food:
Northeast, 113 (7-45-29-32)
*** Bristlegrass *SuFSp*
*** Crabgrass *SuFWSp*
** Ragweed *FWSp*
** Panicgrass *FWSp*
* Wildmillet *FSp*
* Chickweed *SpSuF*
* Smartweed *FWSp*
+ Pigweed, Woodsorrel, Wheat
Southern Prairies, 58 (39-12-3-4)
**** Panicgrass *FWSp*
*** Goosegrass *W*
** Pigweed *W*

* Woodsorrel *W*
* Sedge *W*
* Bristlegrass *WSp*
* Sunflower *WSp*
* Ragweed *WSp*
* Goosefoot *F*
* Dropseedgrass *W*
* Chickweed *Sp*
+ Smartweed, Wheat
California, 128 (72-9-7-40)
*** Knotweed *FW*
*** Turkeymullein *FW*
*** Pigweed *SuFW*
** Oats *FW*
* Canarygrass *FW*
* Bluegrass, Annual *SpF*
* Rabbitfootgrass *FW*
* Ryegrass *FW*
* Minerslettuce *WSpF*
* Chickweed *SpSuFW*
* Bromegrass *W*
* Barley *FW*
* Redmaids *F*
* Sheepsorrel *W*
* Tarweed *FW*
+ Filaree, Mayweed, Goosefoot
Southern California and Mexico (large-billed sparrow), 30 (30-0-0-0)
*** Oats, Wild
** Nightshade
** Barley
* Sandverbena
* Filaree

GRASSHOPPER SPARROW
Ammodramus savannarum

This diminutive, stubby-tailed bird of grassy areas is widely distributed from coast to coast in nesting season. It winters along our southern borders as well as farther south. Grasshopper sparrows are notable destroyers of grasshoppers.

Animal food: Besides grasshoppers, they also eat caterpillars, ants, bugs, spiders, snails, and various other invertebrates.

Plant food:
Northeast, 35 (1-5-25-4)
*** Bristlegrass *SpSuF*
** Sheepsorrel *SuF*
** Oats *Su*
* Smartweed *F*

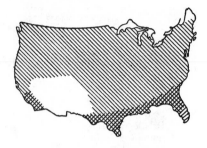

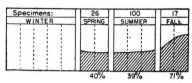

40%   39%   71%

** Ragweed *SpSu*
** Panicgrass *SpSu*
 * Woodsorrel *SpSu*
 + Sunflower, Sedge
California, 8 (0-0-0-8)
*** Knotweed
*** Campion
*** Oats
 * Pigweed

 + Panicgrass, Plantain, Wood-
    sorrel
West (excl. Calif.), 60 (0-6-53-1)
**** Bristlegrass *SpSu*

HENSLOW SPARROW
Passerherbulus henslowii

The Henslow sparrow occupies the eastern two-thirds of the United States. Like the grasshopper and savannah sparrows, this one is a small, elusive inhabitant of weedy meadows and grassy fields. Except for its sharp, somewhat metallic notes it would be rarely detected.

Animal food: Beetles, grasshoppers, bugs, leafhoppers, caterpillars, ants and other *Hymenoptera* were the most common insects found in the stomachs examined.

Plant food:
Northeast, 23 (3-3-13-4)
*** Ragweed *F*
 * Bristlegrass *SuF*
 * Blackberry *Su*
 + Panicgrass, Sheepsorrel, Smart-
    weed

Reference: The Life History of Henslow's Sparrow. A Sidney Hyde. University of Michigan Press, Ann Arbor, 1939. 75 pp.

SHARP-TAILED SPARROW
Ammospiza caudacuta

The sharp-tailed sparrow is represented by three subspecies in distinct areas of the continent. One is a salt-marsh bird of the Atlantic coast, another occurs in the Prairie states and provinces, while the third is confined to the southern margin of James Bay, Canada. Our food information is limited to the Atlantic coast form. In winter, all three races migrate to the Gulf coast.

Animal food: These sparrows feed on an unusually large number of leafhop-pers, also true bugs, flies and their larvae, and various other insects. Birds of this species that confine their activities to the seashore feed extensively on sand fleas.

Plant food:
Atlantic Coast, 55 (0-1-21-33)
**** Cordgrass *F*
 ** Wildrice *F*
 + Panicgrass, Fat-hen Saltbush,
    Clover, Dandelion

196

SEASIDE SPARROW
Ammospiza maritima

Seaside sparrows confine their range to brackish marshes of the Atlantic and Gulf coasts. Each of the seven subspecies has its limited territory along particular sections of the coast, and all races except the northernmost one are permanent residents in their summer range.

Animal food: Leafhoppers, true bugs, flies and their larvae, various other insects that live near the seashore, small crabs, and sand fleas are eaten.

Specimens:	22	24	6
WINTER	SPRING	SUMMER	FALL
	6%	0%	60%

Plant food:
Atlantic and Gulf Coasts, 13 (0-4-3-6)
*** Cordgrass *F*
** Saltbush *FSp*
* Smartweed *F*
* Bristlegrass *Sp*

VESPER SPARROW
Pooecetes gramineus

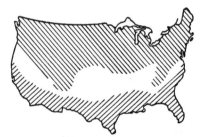

Specimens: 14	91	91	44
WINTER	SPRING	SUMMER	FALL
92%	59%	44%	64%

In addition to nesting in the northern half of the United States, vesper sparrows range into southern Canada. These plaintive songsters are characteristic of field borders where they may be seen commonly on fences.

Animal food: Beetles, grasshoppers, caterpillars, bugs, ants and other *Hymenoptera* are favorite foods.

Plant food:
East, 128 (4-70-43-11)
*** Ragweed *FWSp*
*** Bristlegrass *SuFSp*

** Smartweed *SuFSp*
* Panicgrass *SuFWSp*
* Oats *SuF*
* Pigweed *SuSp*
+ Goosefoot, Timothy, Purslane, Paspalum, Dock
Mt.–Desert, 112 (10-21-48-33)
** Pigweed *FWSp*
** Oats *SuW*
** Bluegrass *Su*
* Wheat *SpSu*
* Knotweed *F*
* Panicgrass *FSp*
* Goosefoot *SuFW*
* Sunflower *SuFW*
+ Bromegrass, Minerslettuce, Dandelion, Soapwort

LARK SPARROW
Chondestes grammacus

Lark sparrows (eastern and western forms) are native to all regions of the country except in parts of some Atlantic, Gulf coast and Great Lakes states. These ground feeders of open, upland areas resemble the closely related vesper sparrow, in having a white-margined tail and a melodious song. This sparrow is unique in its prominent chestnut and white head stripes.

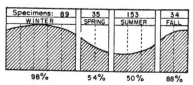

Specimens: 89	35	153	34
WINTER	SPRING	SUMMER	FALL
98%	54%	50%	88%

* Sunflower *W*
+ Smartweed, Oats, Corn, Pigweed

Mt.–Desert, 41 (0-15-24-2)
*** Wheat *SpSu*
* Panicgrass *SuFSp*
* Oats *Su*
* Bromegrass *Sp*
+ Filaree, Pigweed

California, 95 (26-10-31-28)
*** Redmaids *SpSuFW*
*** Oats *SuFW*
** Knotweed *SuFW*
** Wheat *SuF*
* Tarweed *SuFW*
+ Turkeymullein, Filaree, Chickweed, Pigweed

Animal food: More than half of the animal diet consists of grasshoppers. The balance consists mostly of beetles and caterpillars.

Plant food:
Prairies, 175 (63-10-98-4)
*** Bristlegrass *SuF*
*** Panicgrass *SuFW*
*** Ragweed *WSp*
* Wheat *W*
* Doveweed *SuW*
* Sorghum *W*

RUFOUS-CROWNED SPARROW
Aimophila ruficeps

This bird of the Southwest and central valleys of California inhabits brushy localities of that arid territory. It is an all-year resident. Like its relative, the lark sparrow, the rufous-crowned sparrow is a ground species that runs from intruders rather than taking immediate flight.

Animal food: Grasshoppers, beetles, ants, and bugs constitute the main items of the animal diet.

Plant food:
California, 25 (0-0-25-0)

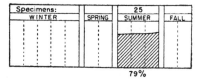

Specimens:		25	
WINTER	SPRING	SUMMER	FALL
		79%	

*** Oats, Wild
** Filaree
** Minerslettuce
* Chickweed
* Dock
+ Pigweed

PINE-WOODS SPARROW
Aimophila aestivalis

Pine-woods sparrows are primarily southeastern. They range as far north as Illinois, southwestern Pennsylvania, and Virginia in summer but retire to the Gulf or South Atlantic states for winter.

This sparrow is partial to open grassy areas interspersed with pines and some brush. Its feeding and nesting is done on the ground, but the male bird usually ascends a tree in the mornings and evenings to pour out its loud, high-pitched, distinctive song. Seven specimens collected in winter showed a 76%

Animal food: Beetles, grasshoppers and their eggs, spiders, caterpillars, wasps, leafhoppers, and snails seem to be the choice items of the animal diet.

Plant food:
Southeast, 20 (7-8-5-0)
  *** Panicgrass *WSp*
    * Paspalum *W*
    * Crabgrass *WSp*
    * Yellow-stargrass *Sp*
    * Blueberry *SpSu*
    * Bristlegrass *W*
    * Nutrush *WSp*
    + Pine, Three-awn, Mockstrawberry, Doveweed

preponderance of plant food, but eight obtained in spring and five in summer ate insects to a total of slightly more than 80% of their diet.

BOTTERI SPARROW
Aimophila botterii

This is a desert sparrow that ranges from southern Texas to southeastern Arizona and south into Mexico. The 14 examined specimens were collected in summer and contained only about 15% plant food. The remainder of the diet was insects.

Animal food: Grasshoppers, beetles, bugs, spiders, caterpillars, mantids, and various other invertebrates are eaten.

Plant food:
Texas and Arizona, 14 (0-0-14-0)
  * Panicgrass
  * Acalypha
  * Leaf-flower
  * Purslane
  + Hall's Bulrush, Ruellia

BELL SPARROW
Amphispiza belli

The range of these light-colored birds, also known as sage sparrows, extends through the Mountain–Desert and Pacific regions from southeastern Washington and western Montana south into Mexico. From our limited food-habits data, it appears that the Bell sparrows are largely seed eaters— even the six specimens taken in summer showed plant items totaling 83% of their diet.

Animal food: Beetles, ants and other *Hymenoptera*, grasshoppers, and bugs were leading insect items.

Plant food:
California, 11 (0-1-6-4)
  **** Oats, Wild *F*
  **** Turkeymullein *Su*
   *** Eriogonum *Su*
    * Filaree *Su*

JUNCOS. Technically, juncos are sparrows. Despite their unique coloration and distinct common name, they are classed among the other members of the sparrow subfamily. These dainty, twittering snowbirds are found practically everywhere in the United States during winter. In summer they nest in our northernmost states and in the higher mountain ranges, as well as farther north in Canada.

Five species are recognized in the country. They differ in markings, but all have a light-colored bill and conspicuous white feathers on the margins of their tails, and all are similar in habits. The slate-colored junco is the most common in the East, and the Oregon junco is the principal western species.

Juncos, like many other members of the sparrow family, are primarily ground-feeding seed eaters. They are partial to seeds of common weeds. In summer, insects constitute about half or more of their diet.

SLATE-COLORED JUNCO
Junco hyemalis

Specimens: 48	27	35	138
WINTER	SPRING	SUMMER	FALL
76%	40%	93%	92%

To most easterners the name "snow-bird" refers to the slate-colored junco. This hardy bird nests in the higher Appalachian ranges northward into Canada. In the fall, when cool weather arrives, the first flocks of these juncos spread out through the East and remain until warm spring weather recreates the urge to move back to their nesting territory. During winter, one may frequently encounter flocks of juncos numbering 100 or more.

Animal food: Caterpillars, beetles, and ants seem to be the choice items of the animal diet, the balance being made up of wasps, bugs, grasshoppers, other insects, and spiders.

Plant food:

Northeast, 198 (114-26-27-31) plus observations
*** Ragweed *FWSp*
** Bristlegrass *FWSp*
** Crabgrass *FWSp*
** Dropseedgrass *WSp*
* Violet *SuF*
* Smartweed *FW*
* Goosefoot *FWSp*

* Panicgrass *FW*
* Timothy *SuFW*
* Pigweed *FWSp*
* Woodsorrel *SuFW*
+ Broomsedge, Corn, Paspalum, Bluet, Sedge, Honeysuckle, Poison-ivy, Sumac, Purple-top, Vervain, Sweetgum, Goldenrod, Nimblewill Muhlygrass, False-nettle, Pine, Chinese Lespedeza

Prairies, 50 (24-22-0-4)
*** Bristlegrass *FW*
*** Ragweed *FWSp*
*** Dropseedgrass *FW*
** Pigweed *FWSp*
** Goosefoot *WSp*
* Knotweed *WSp*
* Wheat *WSp*
* Crabgrass *FWSp*
* Panicgrass *FWSp*
+ Sedge, Vervain

OREGON JUNCO
Junco oreganus

The Oregon junco's range covers most of the Mountain–Desert and Pacific regions. This common western junco probably typifies fairly well the

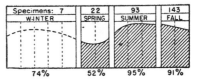

Specimens: 7	22	93	143
WINTER	SPRING	SUMMER	FALL
74%	52%	95%	91%

diet of the three other lesser known western species: the white-winged, gray-headed, and Arizona juncos.

Animal food: Beetles (especially weevils), ants, caterpillars, grasshoppers, leafhoppers, together with some spiders, wasps, and flies are the chief items in the animal diet of this junco.

Plant food:
California, 265 (143-7-22-93)
*** Oats *FW*

*** Chickweed *WSpSuF*
** Barley, Wild and Cult. *FW*
** Pigweed *FW*
** Redmaids *SpSu*
** Minerslettuce *SpSu*
* Cryptantha *Su*
* Goosefoot *FW*
* Knotweed *FW*
* Filaree *FW*
* Melicgrass *FW*
+ Pine, Silene, Wheat, Eriogonum, Annual Bluegrass, Starthistle, Mayweed, Scarlet Pimpernel, Sheepsorrel, Woodsorrel, Galls, Poison-oak, Tarweed

TREE SPARROW
Spizella arborea

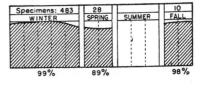

Specimens: 483	28	SUMMER	10
WINTER	SPRING		FALL
99%	89%		98%

The tree sparrow is a northern bird that visits the United States only in winter. It breeds in Canada and as far north as the Bering Sea. Commonly one sees tree sparrows feeding with groups of juncos. Weed seeds constitute more than nine-tenths of the food of these attractive songsters while they are with us in late fall and winter.

Animal food: The small amount of animal food consists mostly of beetles, ants and other *Hymenoptera*, caterpillars, bugs, grasshoppers, and spiders.

Plant food:
Northeast, 125 (107-9-0-9) plus observations
*** Bristlegrass *FWSp*
*** Crabgrass *W*
*** Panicgrass *FWSp*
** Sedge *FW*
* Goosefoot *W*
* Cyperus *FW*
* Broomsedge *W*
* Dropseedgrass *W*
* Sheepsorrel *FWSp*
* Pigweed *W*
* Ragweed *W*
* Cutgrass, Rice *W*
+ Smartweed, Birch, Corn, Chickweed, Purpletop, Golden-

rod, Aster, Vervain, Nim-
blewill Muhlygrass
Eastern Prairies, 396 (376-19-0-1)
**** Bristlegrass *WSp*
  ** Pigweed *WSp*
  ** Crabgrass *WSp*
   * Panicgrass *WSp*

 * Dropseedgrass *WSp*
 * Knotweed *WSp*
 * Ragweed *WSp*
 * Goosefoot *WSp*
 * Timothy *Sp*
 * Oats *Sp*
 + Corn, Sunflower, Woodsorrel

Reference: Distribution of the American Tree Sparrow. A. Marguerite Baum-
gartner. *Wilson Bul.*, Vol. 51(3), pp. 137–149, 1939.

CHIPPING SPARROW
Spizella passerina

Specimens: 10	119	217	67
WINTER	SPRING	SUMMER	FALL
98%	34%	41%	80%

 * Panicgrass *SuFWSp*
 * Oats *SpSu*
 * Timothy *SuFWSp*
 + Chickweed, Pigweed, Ragweed,
   Spurge, Goosefoot, Or-
   chardgrass, Smartweed,
   Purslane, Broomsedge
Mt.–Desert and Pacific, 136(2-20-91-23)
 *** Filaree *Su*
  ** Pigweed *SuF*
   * Bristlegrass *F*
   * Panicgrass *Su*
   * Oats *Su*
   * Chickweed *Su*
   + Needlegrass, Bluegrass, Red-
     maids, Minerslettuce

Beyond its extensive range in this
country, the chipping sparrow also
nests throughout much of Canada.
Practically all its wintering population
concentrates in our southern states.
Doubtless this species is much more
abundant now than in early Colonial
days. It is one of the most common
native species in the vicinity of human
habitations, nesting in shrubbery or
trees near dwellings.

Animal food: A great variety of insects
is consumed. Particularly prominent
are grasshoppers, caterpillars, beetles,
leafhoppers, true bugs, ants, and wasps.
Spiders also are eaten.

Plant food:
East, 277 (8-99-126-44) plus observa-
  tions
 *** Crabgrass *SuFWSp*
  ** Bristlegrass *SuFWSp*

CLAY-COLORED SPARROW
Spizella pallida

The clay-colored sparrow is mainly
Canadian and Mexican. It nests in a
few of our northern Prairie states and

winters from southern Texas and New
Mexico southward.

Only limited information is at hand

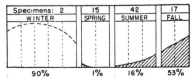

Animal food: Of the 13 stomachs examined, 10 contained beetles, two moths, two leafhoppers, and spiders and *Hymenoptera*, one each.

Plant food:
Eastern Prairies, 13 (0-9-2-2) plus
    observations
  **** Bristlegrass *Sp*
   *** Thistle *Su*
   *** Pigweed *Sp*
   *** Panicgrass *Sp*
    ** Crabgrass *Sp*
    ** Goosefoot *F*
     * Elm, bud *Sp*

on its food. More than three-fourths of the material in the few specimens examined consisted of seeds.

BREWER SPARROW
Spizella breweri

Specimens: 2	15	42	17
WINTER	SPRING	SUMMER	FALL
90%	1%	16%	53%

Animal food: Beetles and their larvae, bugs, grasshoppers, ants, bees, wasps, aphids and other *Homoptera*, caterpillars, and spiders constitute the main portion of the animal diet.

Plant food:
West, 76 (2-15-42-17)
   * Pigweed *SuFW*
   * Gramagrass *SuF*
   * Purslane *Su*
   + Goosefoot, Timothy, Dropseed-
     grass, Dandelion

This light-colored western species has its principal breeding range in the Mountain–Desert region, nesting in sagebrush or other shrubs on desert mesas or mountain slopes. The majority of Brewer sparrows winter south of the United States, but some remain within our southwestern boundary.

FIELD SPARROW
Spizella pusilla

Specimens: 27	59	50	39
WINTER	SPRING	SUMMER	FALL
90%	54%	49%	82%

The field sparrow is primarily a bird of the East. It does not extend farther west than the Prairies. This pink-billed inhabitant of grassy fields and fence rows is very common within its range. Many people, who otherwise would not know the bird at all, are familiar with its morning and evening song—a plaintive series of descending and accelerating notes. Weed seeds are its principal food.

Animal food: Insects eaten consist chiefly of beetles, grasshoppers, and caterpillars. Various other invertebrates, including ants and other *Hymenoptera*, leafhoppers, true bugs, and spiders are also consumed.

Plant food:

Northeast, 137 (21-50-33-33) plus observations

*** Bristlegrass *SuFWSp*
*** Crabgrass *SuFWSp*
** Broomsedge *FWSp*
** Panicgrass *SuFWSp*
* Oats *SpSuF*
+ Dropseedgrass, Sheepsorrel, Pigweed, Ragweed, Woodsorrel, Timothy, Goosefoot

Prairies, 38 (6-9-17-6)
*** Bristlegrass *SuFWSp*
** Panicgrass *SuFSp*
** Dropseedgrass *WSp*
** Crabgrass *SuFSp*
+ Vervain, Goosefoot, Wheat, Redtop, Gromwell

HARRIS SPARROW
Zonotrichia querula

Specimens: 75	21		5
WINTER	SPRING	SUMMER	FALL
94%	80%		99%

The Harris sparrow is a black-faced, pink-billed winter visitor to our central and southern prairies. It is a northern bird that nests far up in Canada. While in this country it feeds heavily on ragweed and other weed seeds.

Animal food: In addition to various insects, including unusually large numbers of leafhoppers, the Harris sparrow eats spiders and snails.

Plant food:

Eastern Prairies, 101 (75-21-0-5)
**** Ragweed *FWSp*
** Knotweed *WSp*
** Bristlegrass *FWSp*
** Corn *FWSp*
* Goosefoot *WSp*
* Oats *W*
+ Sunflower, Panicgrass, Timothy, Wheat

WHITE-CROWNED SPARROW
Zonotrichia leucophrys

Specimens: 22	80	15	303
WINTER	SPRING	SUMMER	FALL
99%	75%	64%	96%

The white-crowned sparrow is, in some degree, a western counterpart of its relative, the white-throated sparrow, although small numbers of the

whitecrown occur regularly east to the Atlantic coast. Both nest in Canada as well as in this country, both have a similar pattern of black and white stripes on the head, and their songs and general habits are also somewhat similar. The food-habits data recorded from the Northeast represent migrating birds.

Animal food: Parasitic *Hymenoptera*, ants, caterpillars, beetles, grasshoppers, bugs, and spiders constitute the main items of the animal diet.

Plant food:
Northeast, 26 (0-13-0-13)
  *** Oats *SpF*
  *** Bristlegrass *FSp*
  ** Panicgrass *F*
  ** Smartweed *F*
  * Chickweed *SpF*
  * Dock *F*
  * Crabgrass *F*
  * Pigweed *F*
  * Ragweed *FSp*
  + Goosefoot, Elderberry, Vervain
Eastern Prairies, 41 (32-3-0-6)
***** (52%) Ragweed *FW*

  ** Goosefoot *FW*
  ** Sunflower *FW*
  ** Pigweed *W*
  ** Oats *W*
  * Panicgrass *FW*
  * Bristlegrass *W*
  * Dropseedgrass *W*
  + Doveweed, Wheat, Corn, Knotweed
Mt.–Desert, 16 (0-3-0-13)
  *** Pigweed *F*
  *** Sunflower *F*
  *** Knotweed *F*
  *** Goosefoot *F*
  ** Oats *Sp*
  * Russianthistle *F*
  * Dropseedgrass *F*
  * Blackberry *F*
Pacific (mainly Calif.), 540 (193-61-15-271)
  *** Pigweed *FW*
  ** Oats *SuFW*
  * Bluegrass, Annual *SpSuF*
  * Mayweed *FW*
  * Chickweed *SpSuFW*
  * Minerslettuce *SpSuF*
  * Tarweed *F*
  * Star-thistle *SuFWSp*
  * Nightshade *FW*
  * Goosefoot *FWSp*
  * Blackberry *SpSu*
  + Fescuegrass, Ryegrass, Redmaids, Spurry, Filaree, Elderberry, Sorghum, Poison-oak, Bromegrass, Knotweed

GOLDEN-CROWNED SPARROW
Zonotrichia coronata

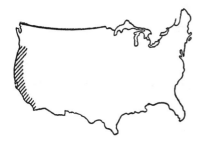

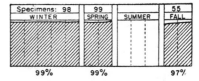

Specimens: 98	99		55
WINTER	SPRING	SUMMER	FALL
99%	99%		97%

This large, golden-crowned northern visitor to our Pacific coast is unique in

the extent to which plant material is eaten—nearly 100%. Flowers make up an unusually large part of its diet.
Animal food: The small amount of animal matter in the diet consists mainly of ants, wasps, bees, caterpillars, and beetles.

Plant food:
California, 183 (98-30-0-55)
**** Flowers of various plants *WSp*
*** Fescuegrass *FW*
** Oats *FWSp*
 * Star-thistle *FW*
 * Poison-oak *FW*
 * Ryegrass *FW*
 * Bromegrass *FW*

 * Tarweed *FW*
 * Pigweed *FW*
 * Chickweed *Sp*
 * Knotweed *FW*
 * Nightshade *F*
 * Wheat *FW*
 * Turkeymullein *FW*
 + Mayweed, Barley, Buttercup,
   Filaree

WHITE-THROATED SPARROW
Zonotrichia albicollis

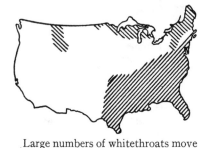

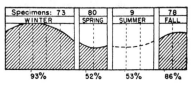

Specimens: 73	80	9	78
WINTER	SPRING	SUMMER	FALL
93%	52%	53%	86%

.Large numbers of whitethroats move from Canada and the northernmost states to the Southeast in the early fall and remain until late in spring. Their chirping call notes and plaintive, high-pitched songs are heard in bushes and shrubs especially toward spring. Seeds of ragweed and smartweed are the two main plant foods.

Animal food: Ants, parasitic *Hymenoptera*, beetles, bugs, flies, caterpillars, spiders, millipedes, and snails are the most commonly consumed animal items.

Plant food:
Northeast, 200 (39-74-9-78) plus observations
**** Ragweed *FWSp*
*** Smartweed *FWSp*
 * Bristlegrass *FWSp*
 * Oats *SpF*
 * Corn *WSp*
 * Panicgrass *FWSp*
 * Poison-ivy *W*
 * Grape *FW*
 + Pigweed, Blackberry, Elderberry, Blueberry, Greenbrier, Chickweed, Wild Cherry, Wild Strawberry, Aralia, Holly, Honeysuckle, Dogwood

FOX SPARROW
Passerella iliaca

Fox sparrows are largely northern birds (Canadian and Alaskan) that winter in the United States or farther south. Like towhees and whitethroated sparrows, they are commonly found in brushy places, scratching among the dead leaves on the ground. They also feed along the margins of fields and consume weed seeds extensively.

Animal food: The animal food, during the winter months in this country,

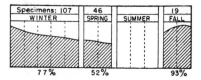

Specimens: 107	46		19
WINTER	SPRING	SUMMER	FALL
77%	52%		93%

consists mainly of millipedes and ground beetles.

Plant food:
East, 72 (54-11-0-7) plus observations

****	Smartweed *WSp*
***	Ragweed *FWSp*
***	Hawthorn *WSp*
**	Blackberry *WSp*
*	Birch *W*
*	Bristlegrass *W*
*	Virginia-creeper *W*
+	Barley, Timothy, Pear, Dock, Greenbrier, Grape, Corn, Poison-ivy

West, 100 (53-35-0-12)

***	Ragweed *FWSp*
***	Bearberry *FSp*
***	Grape *W*
**	Knotweed *WSp*
*	Raspberry *FW*
*	Pigweed *FW*
*	Hackberry *W*
*	Poison-oak *F*
+	Nightshade, Tarweed, Chickweed, Barley

LINCOLN SPARROW
Melospiza lincolnii

Specimens: 9	19		20
WINTER	SPRING	SUMMER	FALL

83%   31%   93%

This retiring, obscure northern relative of the song sparrow may occasionally be found farther eastward than its principal range, as mapped. A few individuals pass through the Northeast and the Prairies during fall and spring migrations. The principal fare of the Lincoln sparrow is weed seeds.

Animal food: Leading items of the animal diet are beetles, ants and other *Hymenoptera*, bugs, grasshoppers, spiders, and millipedes.

Plant food:

Northeast, 13 (0-8-0-5)

***	Panicgrass *F*
**	Crabgrass *F*
**	Ragweed *FSp*

**	Sedge *Sp*
*	Bristlegrass *F*
*	Goosefoot *Sp*
*	Pigweed *Sp*
+	Wildmillet, Chickweed

Eastern Prairies, 13 (0-7-0-6)

***	Bristlegrass *FSp*
***	Pellitory *F*
***	Panicgrass *FSp*
**	Corn *Sp*
*	Ragweed *Sp*
*	Goosefoot *FSp*
*	Sunflower *F*

California, 17 (9-1-0-7)

****	Pigweed *FW*
***	Barley *W*
**	Sedge *FW*
**	Rabbitfootgrass *F*
*	Chickweed *F*
*	Goosefoot *Sp*
*	Mayweed *F*
*	Knotweed *W*
+	Star-thistle, Clover

SWAMP SPARROW
Melospiza georgiana

The well-named swamp sparrow is usually found near wet, brushy places in the East. Frequently, however, these dark-backed songsters forage into adjoining field borders for weed seeds and insects.

Animal food: Beetles, ants and other *Hymenoptera*, caterpillars, grasshop-

207

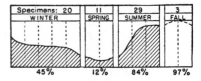

Specimens: 20	11	29	3
WINTER	SPRING	SUMMER	FALL
45%	12%	84%	97%

*** Smartweed *SuFSp*
** Panicgrass *SuFW*
** Vervain *FWSp*
* Cutgrass, Rice *F*
* Crabgrass, Hairy *F*
* Dock *F*
+ Bristlegrass, Acalypha, Night-shade, Boehmeria, Rag-weed, Goosefoot, Straw-berry, Timothy, Eupato-rium, Bidens, Goldenrod, Elderberry

pers, and crickets appeared most commonly as items in the insect part of the diet.

Plant food:
Northeast, 73 (30-11-29-3) plus observations
*** Sedge *SuFWSp*

SONG SPARROW
Melospiza melodia

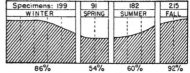

Specimens: 199	91	182	215
WINTER	SPRING	SUMMER	FALL
86%	54%	60%	92%

and crickets, caterpillars, ants and other *Hymenoptera*, and bugs are the chief food items of the animal diet.

Plant food:
Northeast, 342 (116-66-97-63) plus observations
*** Smartweed *SuFWSp*
*** Bristlegrass *SuFWSp*
*** Ragweed *FWSp*
** Panicgrass *SuFWSp*
* Crabgrass *FW*
* Oats *SuFW*
* Pigweed *FWSp*
* Dock *SuF*
* Goosefoot *FWSp*
* Timothy *FW*
* Sedge *W*
+ Corn, Vetch, Wildrice, Ver-vain, Bulrush, Nimblewill Muhlygrass
Pacific (*mainly Calif.*), 345 (83-25-85-152)

This alert, jaunty sparrow is one of the commonest, best-known and most loved songsters in the United States. It is nearly equally at home in town or country and is found in virtually all regions except the deserts and arid plains. Twenty-one subspecies are recognized within our borders—some of them ranging far north into Canada or Alaska in the nesting season. Some individuals in temperate latitudes remain as all-year residents.

Song sparrows are rather shy and usually seclude themselves in brushy cover. Their feeding, however, is generally done near the margins of open areas where weeds abound.

Animal food: Beetles, grasshoppers

*** Pigweed *SuFW*
** Knotweed *SuFW*
* Nightshade *SuFW*
* Minerslettuce *SpSuF*
* Oats *SuFW*
* Star-thistle *SuFW*
* Chickweed *SpSuFW*
+ Bromegrass, Goosefoot, Filaree, Tarweed, Panicgrass, Blackberry, Dock, Elderberry, Spurry, Wheat

Reference: Studies in the Life History of the Song Sparrow, I and II. Margaret Morse Nice. Linnaean Society of New York, 1937. 247 pp.

LONGSPURS. The longspurs are hardy inhabitants of wide open spaces. Four species occur in the United States. The Lapland and Smith longspurs are arctic-nesting species that enter our country only in winter. The other two, the McCown and chestnut-collared longspurs are comparative southerners, nesting in the plains of Canada and northern United States and wintering in our southern plains and Mexico.

Like the pipits and horned larks, the longspurs are unique in possessing long rear toenails. Their chestnut and black markings are somewhat suggestive of the English sparrow.

In seasons other than summer, the longspurs are nine-tenths or more vegetarian—seeds of wild grasses and weeds being their main fare.

McCOWN LONGSPUR
Rhynchophanes mccownii

Animal food: Beetles and grasshoppers are eaten commonly, as are other insects and spiders.

Plant food:
Prairies, 20 (0-7-9-4)
*** Knotweed *SpSu*
*** Sunflower *F*
*** Wheat *SpSu*
** Buffalograss *Sp*
** Goosefoot *FSp*
** Gramagrass *F*
** Needlegrass *SuF*
* Bristlegrass *Su*
+ Pigweed, Ragweed, Sedge

Of the 20 examined specimens of this species, 7 were collected in the spring, 9 in summer, and 4 in the fall with the following plant proportions in the diet for those seasons: 96%, 65%, 90%.

LAPLAND LONGSPUR
Calcarius lapponicus

The winter range depicted for the Lapland longspur represents its inclusive limits within this country. In relatively mild winters, flocks of these birds do not pass far beyond our Canadian border states.

209

| Specimens: 512 | 71 | 17 |
| WINTER | SPRING | SUMMER | FALL |

100% 93% 94%

**** Bristlegrass *FWSp*
*** Crabgrass *W*
** Sedge *FSp*
** Wheat *WSp*
** Pigweed *WSp*
* Panicgrass *WSp*
* Ragweed, Common *FW*
+ Goosefoot, Knotweed, Drop-seedgrass, Common Purslane

Animal food: The small amount of animal food is composed almost entirely of insects. The winter diet in Texas consists of weevils, ground beetles, leaf beetles, and grasshoppers.

Plant food:
Northeast and Northern Prairies, 600 (512-71-0-17)

SMITH LONGSPUR
Calcarius pictus

This arctic-breeding longspur winters in the United States from Kansas to Texas. It passes through Illinois on migrations, and it was there that the specimens reported below were obtained.

Animal food: Beetles (particularly ground beetles), caterpillars, and spiders are prominent among the invertebrates eaten by this species.

Plant food:
Illinois, 21 (0-21-0-0)
**** Dropseedgrass
*** Bristlegrass
*** Panicgrass
** Wheat
* Timothy
+ Clover, Crabgrass, Common Ragweed, Bulrush, Wildmillet, Sedge

CHESTNUT-COLLARED LONGSPUR
Calcarius ornatus

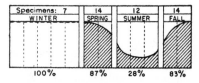

| Specimens: 7 | 14 | 12 | 14 |
| WINTER | SPRING | SUMMER | FALL |

100% 87% 28% 83%

This inhabitant of western prairies divides its affiliations between Canada, Mexico, and the United States. Some chestnut-collared longspurs remain within our borders the year round.

Animal food: The chestnut-collar eats many beetles, grasshoppers, and spiders, as well as numerous other kinds of invertebrates.

Plant food:
Western Prairies, 43 (7-12-11-13)
*** Dropseedgrass *FW*
*** Wheat *SpSu*

** Sunflower *F*
** Needlegrass *FSp*
 * Panicgrass *SuW*
 * Three-awn *F*

 * Pigweed *F*
 * Bristlegrass *Su*
 * Gramagrass *F*
 + Goosefoot, Sedge

SNOW BUNTING
Plectrophenax nivalis

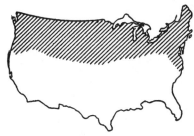

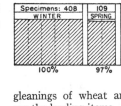

Specimens: 408	109	6	22
WINTER	SPRING	SUMMER	FALL
100%	97%	100%	85%

The eastern snow bunting is the only "snowflake" that visits the United States. It enters our northern borders in late fall and, unless snows become especially deep, remains in our northern states (and southern Canada) until early spring. In severe winters it moves farther southward where snow does not prevent feeding on weed seeds or waste grain. The snow bunting is more or less a bird of the world. It nests in polar or arctic regions and in winter moves southward on various continents.

Animal food: Fly larvae and pupae, particularly of the cranefly, caterpillars, beetles, and true bugs constitute the major portion of the animal diet. Crustaceans are also consumed, particularly sand fleas.

Plant food: Seeds constitute nine-tenths or more of the total diet of the snow bunting. In the East, weed seeds are the principal food, but in the West, gleanings of wheat and other grains are the leading items.

Northeast, 425 (366-31-6-22)
*** Bristlegrass *W*
*** Ragweed *WSp*
*** Pigweed *W*
 ** Sandgrass *W*
 ** Goosefoot *W*
 ** Oats *WSp*
  * Knotweed *W*
  * Beechgrass *W*
  * Sedge *W*
  * Wildrye *Su*
  * Buttercup *F*
  * Dropseedgrass *W*
  * Wheat *W*
  + Fescuegrass, Panicgrass, Bulrush
Northwest, 120 (42-78-0-0)
***** (53%) Wheat *WSp*
 *** Sedge *Sp*
  ** Barley *Sp*
   * Oats *WSp*
   * Pigweed *W*
   + Bromegrass, Timothy, Knotweed, Cinquefoil, Goosefoot

211

CHAPTER NINE

Birds of Prey

P<small>ARASITISM, AS APPRAISED</small> by some biologists, is the most specialized form of organic existence. Following this criterion, the birds of prey, although not considered parasites, should rate a place near the top of the avian scale.

Aside from its bearing on evolutionary classification, predation by birds and mammals is significant as a sort of natural safety valve, providing a balancing check on wildlife populations. Predaceous animals help to keep the lid on population growth of species which, if uncurbed, might eventually bring catastrophe to themselves and other inhabitants of their environment by exhausting food resources or through epidemic diseases resulting from abnormal crowded conditions. Game managers have found that in some instances predators actually benefit the species on which they prey by weeding out weak or sickly individuals. Gamebird sportsmen in some parts of the Southeast have begun to recognize an abundance of hawks and owls as a blessing in disguise. These predators feed on and often help to limit the number of cotton rats, which in turn are serious enemies of the bobwhite quail. By helping to keep populations of certain species in balance, birds of prey (and other predators) benefit many desirable forms of wildlife—and incidentally benefit all of us.

Applying the word predation literally, we might speak of flycatchers, warblers, swallows, chimney swifts, and whip-poor-wills as birds of prey. These and numerous other species feed entirely on invertebrate animal food. There is little essential difference between a swallow swooping after a fly and a hawk diving on a pigeon. However, the term "birds of prey" has been applied only to species which feed on vertebrates. Sometimes the name is limited to the natural order *Falconiformes* which includes the hawks, eagles, and vultures, but it is often extended to include the owls (*Strigiformes*) as well. It is in this broader, more inclusive sense that the designation "birds of prey" is used here. Despite the economic importance of this carnivorous group of birds and the public's widespread interest in it, only a brief treatment of these two orders of birds is justified in a book which treats primarily of wildlife and plant relationships.

Hawks and their kin and owls make no direct use of plants in their diets. Yet plants are vitally important to them. The local and regional distribution of various species of these birds is largely dependent on the flora. For one thing, the character of the vegetation controls the abundance and distribution of plant-eating prey such as rats, mice, rabbits, birds, grasshoppers, and the like. Further than this, plants—especially large trees—furnish the favorite nesting sites for a majority of birds of prey. Bottom-land woods are preferred for nesting by several kinds of hawks and owls. Still another plant feature that is important to some species but not to others is the use of foliage as a screen for predaceous operations—

shielding the attackers from the view of their intended victims. Thus factors associated with the native vegetation limit certain hawks or owls to eastern woodlands, others to the prairies or deserts, and still others to coniferous northern forests.

Birds of prey range in size from the elf owl, which is smaller than the robin, to the nearly extinct California condor—regarded as our largest bird. The condor's wingspread occasionally exceeds 10 feet, while in eagles and vultures it usually ranges between 6 and 8 feet. Naturally the size and build of a bird has much to do with its food habits. The larger species are capable of handling large prey, while smaller species usually select victims proportionate to their size. Thus, while eagles feed on medium-sized fish, ground squirrels, rabbits, ducks, and occasionally lambs or fawns, many hawks and owls specialize on mice, rats, and small birds, and still others—like the sparrow hawk—fare largely on insects. Certain raptors like the falcons or darters are built for speed and are capable of easily

overtaking their victims on the wing. Some, like the vultures, eagles, broad-winged hawks, and kites, are able to soar effortlessly for many miles while searching for food. The owls are especially equipped with broad, silent wings and keen instincts for hunting nocturnal prey such as mice and rats. Members of the birds-of-prey group generally have strong talons and bills for holding and tearing flesh.

A common peculiarity of both hawks and owls is their habit of regurgitating pellets of fur, feathers, and bones. The pellets are disgorged at fairly regular intervals after feeding and may be found in quantities at roosting or nesting sites. Examination of the contents of these souvenirs of former meals has afforded an important means of food-habits study for this group of birds.

The economic role of birds of prey, especially of the hawks, has received considerable study. Thousands of stomach and pellet examinations have been made and have established beyond reasonable doubt the fact that the majority of hawks, owls, and vultures perform a harmless or even useful role, as predators and scavengers. Dr. A. K. Fisher sums it up in his book, *Hawks and Owls of the United States in Their Relation to Agriculture*, by stating: "Owls are among the most beneficial of all birds, inflicting very little damage upon the poulterer and conferring vast benefits upon the farmer. . . . All hawks, with one or two exceptions, are to some extent beneficial to the farmer." Only a few species are potentially destructive to man's interests. It is a generally accepted viewpoint that only

213

certain individuals of these few species are objectionable and need to be dealt with directly.

If certain individual goshawks, horned owls, Cooper, sharp-shinned, or red-tailed hawks acquire a taste for chicken and establish headquarters near poultry, they can do real damage. If certain ones become locally destructive to gamebirds, they need to be dispatched with a shotgun, just as when a dog develops a mania for killing poultry or sheep, it too must be put out of the way. But it does not follow that all dogs or all hawks and owls should be killed. Unfortunately, in the case of birds of prey, a relatively small number of individuals or a few species have caused the entire group to be branded with an undeserved reputation. The fact that various species of hawks and owls are not readily distinguished by the layman has also contributed to the general condemnation of the group as a whole.

Disease and climatic and nutritional deficiencies, as population control factors, are much more important than predation for both wild and domesticated birds. Furthermore, in general principle it is true that only when the prey are thriving and plentiful are predators likely to be abundant. Conversely, predators usually become scarce when their potential victims are at low ebb. This has been clearly shown in the long records of the relationship of lynx to snowshoe hare populations in Canada.

The credit side of the ledger for birds of prey is hard to evaluate specifically. There is no doubt that they exercise part of the broad controlling influence that holds populations of wildlife and, to some extent, insects in check. During plagues of mice, an influx of birds of prey has been noted. In feeding upon such pests as meadow mice, cotton rats, Norway rats, ground squirrels, and grasshoppers, hawks and owls exert a helpful influence toward keeping man's enemies in check. Even vultures, as scavengers, help by disposing of carrion from along highways and in the fields. It is reported that, after the great slaughter of buffalo in 1882, thousands of turkey vultures were attracted into Montana and nearby states where they are usually scarce.

Whatever their economic worth in dollars and cents, the birds of prey offer an additional value which cannot be expressed in monetary terms. Many people would feel something important missing from the outdoor world if there were no longer the opportunity to see eagles, hawks and vultures soaring aloft, or ospreys diving for fish, or if the shrill cries of the redtail and the booming and chuckles of the great horned owl were silenced forever. Birds of prey, like all other species, have a natural place in the wildlife scheme.

The birds-of-prey assemblage, as construed here, includes two orders that are not closely related: the hawks and their allies in one order and owls in the other. The hawk-eagle-vulture order includes 40 species native to the United States, while owls number 17. A brief survey of the principal representatives of these two orders follows:

Order *Falconiformes*: Vultures, Hawks, Eagles

VULTURES. Three kinds of vultures occur in the United States: the common, widespread turkey vulture or turkey buzzard, the black vulture of the Southeast,

and the California condor of Southern California. The latter species is nearing extinction—only about 100 or less individuals are still known to be alive in California. All vultures eat carrion of any kind or quality available.

KITES. There are four species of kites in the United States. One, the everglade kite, is confined to peninsular Florida southward, while the others are largely southern or southeastern. However, the swallow-tailed kite has bred locally as far northward as Minnesota. Except for the everglade kite, these graceful, white-marked birds are largely similar to each other in their dietary preferences. Their food consists of lizards, snakes, frogs, grasshoppers, and other large insects. The everglade kite appears to subsist almost exclusively on fresh-water snails.

ACCIPITER HAWKS. In this genus (*Accipiter*) belong the three species of hawks which are generally regarded as the most destructive and objectionable. They are the goshawk, sharp-shinned, and Cooper hawk. The goshawk is largely northern, while the other two are widespread in wooded or semi-open regions of the country. Besides poultry and gamebirds (quail, grouse, doves) hawks of this group feed on a great variety of small birds and to a lesser degree on rodents.

BUTEO HAWKS. Ten species of these rather large hawks are present in the country. The red-tailed, red-shouldered, broad-winged, Swainson, and rough-legged hawks are among the better known and more important members of the

215

genus. Rodents of various kinds—many of them destructive—are the staff of life of these hawks. In addition, rabbits, snakes, lizards, and small birds are also eaten. Insects are taken commonly by the Swainson and broad-winged hawks. In some localities the redtail becomes a nuisance as a chicken thief.

EAGLES. The eagle, commonly spoken of as the king of birds, is represented in the United States by two species: the golden and bald. The latter has been symbolized as our national bird. It is widely distributed throughout the country, while the golden eagle is largely western. The food of the bald eagle is largely fish, some of it purloined from ospreys. In the Northwest it has been accused of being destructive to salmon. Some rodents and birds are also captured. Frequently this species flushes rafts of ducks and attacks crippled individuals that happen to be present.

MISCELLANEOUS HAWKS. There are three additional genera of importance in the order. The marsh hawk is a widespread, long-tailed, white-rumped marsh harrier that subsists on rodents, amphibians, reptiles, and birds. The osprey is a white-bellied, fish-eating relative of the eagles. The Audubon caracara, a native of Florida, southwestern Arizona, and farther south, is a long-legged, eagle-headed hawk that often competes with vultures for carrion. It also feeds on lizards, snakes, frogs, crayfish, and young birds.

Order *Strigiformes:* Owls

Owls range in size from the great horned owls, which are as large and powerful as the bigger hawks, to diminutive western representatives such as the elf owls

and pygmy owls which are as small as some songbirds. Generally the size of their prey is somewhat in proportion to their own size. Small owls usually feed on small rodents and on large insects. However, it is common for species such as the horned owl, the barred owl, and the spotted owl to feed not only on medium large prey such as rabbits, rats, squirrels, gamebirds, and other birds but also, to a limited extent, on crayfish, frogs, and large insects. The principal kinds of owls in the country are

Barn Owl	Pygmy Owls (2 spp.)	Great Gray Owl
Screech Owls (3 spp.)	Elf Owl	Long-eared Owl
Horned Owl	Burrowing Owl	Short-eared Owl
Snowy Owl	Barred Owls (2 spp.)	Saw-whet Owl
Hawk Owl		

General References: Hawks and Owls of the United States. A. K. Fisher. *U.S. Dept. Agr. Bul.* 3, 1893. 201 pp.

Food Habits of Common Hawks. W. L. McAtee. *U.S. Dept. Agr. Circ.* 370, 1935. 36 pp.

The Hawks of North America. John B. May. National Association of Audubon Society, 1935. 140 pp.

Life Histories of North American Birds of Prey. *U.S. National Museum Bul.* (2 parts), 167, 1937, 409 pp.; and 170, 1938, 482 pp.

CHAPTER TEN

Fur and Game Mammals

T HIS SOMEWHAT MISCELLANEOUS and arbitrary category consists primarily of mammals that are large enough to be valuable for fur or game, or both. However, the armadillo and a few other species of negligible importance for either fur or flesh are also included. Excluded are the large ruminants such as deer, elk, moose, and bison, which, because of their wholly herbivorous diet, are treated separately in Chap. Thirteen, Hoofed Browsers. The fur and game segment of our native wildlife has been of tremendous economic importance since the earliest days of settlement. Species or groups treated in this chapter are

Opossum	Foxes	Muskrat
Bears	Coyote	Mountain Beaver
Raccoon	Wolves	Porcupine
Ring-tailed Cat	Puma	Pika
Martens	Lynx and Bobcat	Hares and Rabbits
Weasels	Seals and Sea Lions	Armadillo
Wolverine	Woodchuck and Mar-	Manatee
Otters	mots	Whales, Dolphins, and
Skunks	Tree Squirrels	Porpoises
Badger	Beaver	

The feeding habits of these mammals vary from a carnivorous diet as in the wolves, puma, lynx, seals, wolverine, otters, and weasels to the completely vegetarian diet of the woodchuck, beaver, muskrat, mountain beaver, porcupine, pika, hares and rabbits, and manatee. The others are intermediate—subsisting on both plant and animal material.

General References: Lives of Game Animals. Ernest Thompson Setson. Doubleday & Company, Inc., New York, Vol. I, 1925. 640 pp. Vol. II, 1926. 746 pp.
American Mammals. W. J. Hamilton, Jr. McGraw-Hill Book Company, Inc., New York, 1939.
Field Book of North American Mammals. H. E. Anthony. G. P. Putnam's Sons, New York, 1928.
Wild Animals of North America. E. W. Nelson. National Geographic Society, 1930.
Mammals of North America. Victor H. Cahalane. The Macmillan Company, New York, 1947.

Opossum: *Didelphiidae*

OPOSSUM
Didelphis virginiana

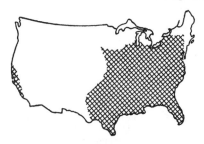

Specimens: 189 WINTER	32 SPRING	58 SUMMER	27 FALL
17%	5%	13%	17%

The opossum, a grayish, long-haired, pointed-nosed, rat-tailed night prowler, belongs to a primitive order of mammals—the marsupials. Included in the group are the kangaroos and a number of other remarkable animals that carry their nearly embryonic young in a special external pouch. Most of the marsupials are native to the Australian region, but the opossum's center of population is Central and South America.

Only two species of opossum are present in the United States. The Virginia opossum is a particularly common and popular game animal in the Southeast. It occurs in woodlands, particularly bottom lands, throughout the East except in the northernmost states and was introduced successfully into Southern California some years ago. This species is the most northerly of all opossums and also the largest. The range of the other native species, the Texas opossum, is confined to south Texas and Mexico.

The opossum is omnivorous and takes almost any available animal food or any kind of fleshy fruit—even including overripe garbage.

Animal food: The animal portion of the opossum's varied diet includes both terrestrial and aquatic invertebrates, especially insects, and small, cold-blooded and warm-blooded vertebrates, found dead or alive, plus bird eggs and young in season. It appears that no available meats are too unsavory for the opossum to eat.

Plant food: Fleshy fruits, acorns, and corn are often eaten, but in general plant material constitutes a minor part of the diet.

Northeast, 129 (112-14-3-0)
  * Grape *W*
  + Oak, Pokeweed, Apple, Corn, Oats, Pawpaw, Strawberry
Southeast, 140 (54-13-49-24)
  * Grape *SuFW*
  * Persimmon *FW*
  + Blackgum, Oak, Mulberry, Corn, Blueberry, Wild Cherry, Clubmoss (Groundpine)
Missouri, 68 (50-18-0-0)
  ** Corn *W*
  * Mulberry *Sp*
  + Pokeweed, Greenbrier, Hackberry, Groundcherry, Grape, Blackberry
Oklahoma and Texas, 37 (23-5-6-3)
  * Oak *W*
  * Hackberry *W*
  + Redcedar. Mulberry, Pokeweed

Reference: Some Aspects of the Life History and Ecology of the Opossum in Central Missouri. Harold C. Reynolds. *Jour. Mammalogy*, Vol. 26 (4), pp. 361–379, 1945.

Bears: *Ursidae*

BEARS. Two genera of bears have been recognized in the United States: the black bears (*Euarctos*) and the grizzly or big brown bears (*Ursus*). However, some mammalogists now lump the two into one genus, *Ursus*.

The black bears may be construed as one or three species depending on whether the Florida and Louisiana forms are regarded as distinct. They live in extensive forested areas throughout the country and in most places are holding their own fairly well.

The grizzly and big brown bears are wholly western—but are also present in Canada and Alaska. They have been greatly reduced in range and total population. It is believed that very few species—possibly only one—of these lumbering land mammals are now living, while ten or more species are known to be extinct.

Bears are omnivorous, eating flesh, berries, acorns, honey, and occasionally fruits. We have substantial information on foods for the black bear only.

BLACK BEAR
Euarctos americanus

These large, powerful animals are still common in extensive forested tracts where human populations are low—particularly in mountains and swamp lands. Generally the black bear is as shy of people as people are afraid of it. It relies on its nose more than its ears and eyes for locating food and avoiding danger. Though the black bear is largely vegetarian, it always appreciates meat.

Animal food: This bear eats insects, fish, small mammals, and any other animals it can capture. It occasionally picks off weak or wounded deer, and antelope or their young, and is not averse to carrion. Campers' food stores are often raided, and there are times when it preys upon the local livestock.

Plant food: Berries and other fleshy fruits, as well as acorns, beechnuts, and pine seeds are staple foods of the black bear. Honey is sought as a prized delicacy.

Pennsylvania, droppings
**** Oak *F*
**** Cherry, Wild *Su*
**** Beech *F*
** Apple *F*
** Grape *F*

Virginia and West Virginia, 16 (16-0-0-0)
**** Oak
*** Blueberry

** Apple
** Blackgum
** Grape
** Chokeberry
 * Greenbrier
 + Holly, Sedge
Minnesota, summer droppings
**** Blueberry

** Hawthorn
Western stock ranches, 50 (season unspecified)
** Pine, Piñon
 * Serviceberry
 * Cherry, Wild
 * Buffaloberry
 + Dogwood, Horsetail

References: The Black Bear in New Hampshire. Clark L. Stevens. Forestry Club, University of New Hampshire, 1943. 30 pp.

Notes on Early Winter Food Habits of the Black Bear in George Washington National Forest. Clarence Cottam, A. L. Nelson, and Talbott E. Clarke. *Jour. Mammalogy*, Vol. 20(3), pp. 310–314, 1939.

The Food Habits of the Black Bear in Pennsylvania. Logan J. Bennett, P. F. English, and R. L. Watts. *Jour. Mammalogy*, Vol. 24(1), pp. 25–31, 1943.

Raccoons: *Procyonidae*

RACCOON
Procyon lotor

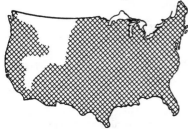

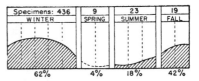

Plant food: Only in the prairies are acorns conspicuous by their absence from the diet. Corn and fleshy fruits are also favorite foods.

The raccoon is present in practically all parts of the country but is most abundant in the Southeast. These ring-tailed, black-masked animals are partial to open woodlands but are common visitors on farms, where sometimes they make serious raids on ripening corn. Raccoons also like to explore along stream margins looking for frogs, crayfish, salamanders, and other tidbits. In the fall and winter their dietary mainstay is acorns.

Animal food: Although having a predilection for such items as frogs, crayfish, and grasshoppers, a raccoon will prey upon practically all large insects and almost any small vertebrates (including muskrats and rabbits) found within its bailiwick.

Northeast, 188 (180-1-3-4) plus many droppings
**** Oak *W*
**** Corn *W*,
 ** Persimmon *W*
  * Pokeweed *W*
  * Grape *W*
  + Beech, Hazelnut, Holly, Pawpaw, Greenbrier, Hackberry, Hickory
Southeast, 136 (120-8-5-3)
 *** Oak *W*
 *** Palmetto *W*
  ** Greenbrier *W*
  ** Grape *W*
  ** Persimmon *W*
   * Corn *W*
   + Holly, Pecan

221

Eastern Texas, 90 (83-0-7-0) plus many
droppings
**** Oak
*** Persimmon
** Grape
* Hawthorn
* Holly
* Mulberry
+ Beautyberry, Yaupon, Black-

berry, Greenbrier, Poke-
weed, Rattanvine
Iowa, 363 scats and 2 stomachs, all
seasons
**** Corn *FW*
* Grasses *Sp*
* Blackberry and Raspberry *Su*
* Gooseberry *Su*
+ Hickory, Smartweed, Grape,
Nightshade, Wild Cherry,
Clover
Pacific, 73 (53-0-8-12)
** Oak *W*
* Cherry, Hollyleaf *W*
* Buckthorn *W*
+ Manzanita, Fairybells, Fig, Bar-
ley, Alfalfa, Nightshade,
Grape, Blueberry

Reference: Raccoons: Their Habits and Management in Michigan. Frederick W.
Stuewer. Ecological Monographs, Vol. 13 (2), 1943. 55 pp.

RING-TAILED CAT
Bassariscus astutus

The ringtail, also known as coon cat,
civet cat, and cacomistle, is a close
relative of the raccoon. The relationship is evident in their similarly marked
tails and varied diets, as well as in their
nocturnal habits. Ring-tailed cats are
widespread in Mexico and range within
our borders from Texas and California
to Oregon and Utah. They inhabit
crevices or caves in rocky ledges, but
in Texas they live on brushy or cactus-
covered plains. The food data in this
report are based entirely on specimens
from Texas.
Animal food: The animal food of the
ringtail is chiefly small birds, a few
insects, and small mammals such as
mice and rabbits.
Plant food: Plant food is generally

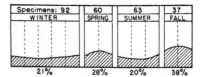

secondary in the diet but fruits are
eaten considerably in the fall.

Texas, 252 (92-60-63-37)
** Persimmon *SuF*
** Redcedar *WSp*
* Hackberry *FWSp*
* Mistletoe *W*
+ Pricklypear, Barberry, Buck-
thorn, Sophora, Condalia,
Mesquite, Grape, Oak,
Plum, Groundcherry

Weasels, Skunks, and Otters: *Mustelidae*

MARTENS. Two species of martens (aside from the fisher) occur in wilderness
forests of our northern states. The value of marten and fisher pelts has caused
the animals to become scarce or extinct in many parts of their former range.
These active, agile relatives of the weasel feed on almost any available kind of
animal that is not too large for them to kill. Rodents, including squirrels, rabbits,
chipmunks, conies, and mice are the principal fare. Weasels, mink, birds of various
kinds and their eggs, frogs, fish, and insects are also eaten. Occasionally fleshy
fruits are taken. Mountain-ash fruits constitute a small percentage of the winter

food of the Pacific marten, as judged by dropping analyses and 25 examined stomachs.

The fisher is a close relative of the marten (belonging to the same genus) but is larger and more powerful. It frequently includes the marten among its prey. The principal range of the fisher is in Canada since the species has disappeared from most of its former territory in the northern half of the United States. The diet of this tree-dwelling mammal is similar to that of the marten, but includes some larger prey such as the porcupine.

WEASELS. The weasel genus (*Mustela*) includes among its numerous widely distributed species the smallest of all carnivores. The valuable ermine, mink, and ferret belong here as well as the forms more regularly known as weasel. Regardless of size they are all vicious predators, often killing beyond their possible dietary needs as though it were a pleasurable pastime.

These bloodthirsty animals are seldom if ever interested in plants as food. The prey most commonly taken are rabbits, mice, squirrels, gophers, and other rodents, birds and their eggs, snakes, frogs, and fish.

WOLVERINES. The wolverine is the largest representative of the weasel family. It is a shaggy-haired, short-legged, powerful resident of northern wilderness forests in Canada and of a few of our northern states. Two species are recognized within our boundaries. The animal has been exterminated in much of its former range.

Besides feeding on trapped animals and other carrion, the wolverine subsists on rabbits, gophers, rats, mice, marmots, and occasionally on birds. No plant food is taken.

OTTERS. Two kinds of otter occur in the United States, both of them aquatic, fish-eating members of the weasel family and both with especially valuable pelts.

The sea otter is a rare, nearly extinct species that formerly was plentiful along the Pacific coast from Lower California to Alaska. Early fur hunters reduced the sea otter population to a low ebb from which it has never recovered. Their food is marine animal life: primarily fish, sea urchins, crustaceans, and mollusks.

The land otter is widely distributed along streams and bays of North and South America as well as in the Old World. Its numbers, however, are also limited, especially near areas inhabited by man. Their food is mainly crayfish and fish, but snakes, water beetles, and frogs are also eaten.

SKUNKS. Skunks are present in practically all parts of the United States. The number of species and subspecies recognized has fluctuated considerably as different authorities have made new studies and revisions of the group. Now, many of the former species are classed as subspecies. There are three genera involved: the spotted (*Spilogale*), striped (*Mephitis*), and hog-nosed (*Conepatus*) skunks.

The diet of skunks is largely insectivorous, but amphibians, reptiles, rodents, and other small forms of animal life are also consumed. Fruit usually constitutes a small proportion of the diet. Data on the foods of five species are given below.

ALLEGHENY SPOTTED SKUNK
Spilogale putorius

These are the smallest of our skunks, and by many, their pelts are regarded as the most attractive. The Allegheny spotted skunk is the principal eastern representative of the group. Most other species of spotted skunks are western. **Animal food:** This southeastern skunk eats whatever small forms of animal life are available. In winter and spring it depends largely on mice, chipmunks, and other small mammals. During the rest of the year, insects, especially beetles, are important food. Other invertebrates such as crayfish, spiders, and centipedes are eaten, and occasionally small snakes, salamanders, lizards, birds and their eggs.
Plant food: Plant materials constitute only a small proportion of the usual fare.

East, 18 (15-2-0-1)
  * Fleshy Fungus *W*
  * Persimmon *W*
  + Blueberry

PRAIRIE SPOTTED SKUNK
Spilogale interrupta

The prairie spotted skunk ranges from Iowa and southern Minnesota south through most of Oklahoma and eastern Arkansas into northeastern Texas. It is closely related to the Allegheny spotted skunk.
Animal food: Its winter diet consists primarily of small mammals, particularly mice, but also includes rats and carrion. In summer the food is largely beetles, together with other insects and millipedes, and some young rabbits, birds, and mice.
Plant food: This species eats plant materials only as supplemental food.

Iowa, many droppings from all seasons
  * Grape *SuF*
  * Mulberry *Su*
  + Grasses, Wheat, Horse-nettle, Oats

STRIPED SKUNK
Mephitis mephitis

This is the familiar, widely distributed species with distinct black

| Specimens: 61 | 21 | | |
WINTER	SPRING	SUMMER	FALL
11%	0%		

and white bands down the back clearly advertising the fact that it is a skunk.
Animal food: These skunks have a varied diet that is influenced largely by local availability of invertebrate and vertebrate organisms. They feed on adult and larval insects—especially

on grasshoppers, grubs, crickets, beetles, and wasps. Spiders are commonly taken as are toads, frogs, lizards, mice, gophers, and eggs of turtles and birds. **Plant food:** Plant materials ordinarily constitute only a small part of the diet. Fleshy fruits are the principal plant item taken.

Northeast, 82 (61-21-0-0)
  ** Grape *W*
   * Blueberry *W*
   + Cherry, Nightshade, Oats
Southeast, 39 (7-5-21-6)

*** Peanut *SuFW*
  * Blackberry *Su*
  + Persimmon
Iowa, 143 fall scats
  * Groundcherry
  + Grasses, Hawthorn, Oats, Cantaloupe
Texas, 49 (20-14-15-0)
  * Pricklypear *W*
  + Hackberry
California, 31 (27-0-0-4)
  ** Nightshade *F*
   * Grape *W*
   * Manzanita *W*

NORTHERN HOODED SKUNK
Mephitis macroura

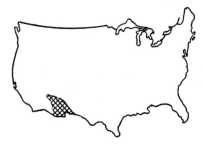

The northern hooded skunk is restricted to southern Arizona (and Mexico). Though only three stomach specimens of this distinct subgenus have been examined, the resulting data, though too scant to be reliable, are interesting. More than 75% of the food of these three consisted of plant material.

Animal food: Horned toads, beetle larvae, other insects, and lizards were the principal animal food items in the three specimens examined.

Plant food:
Arizona, 3 (2-0-0-1)
  **** Mesquite *FW*
   *** Manzanita *W*

HOG-NOSED SKUNK
Conepatus mesoleucus

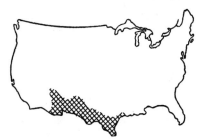

The hognose is much like the common skunk except for its hog-like muzzle, smaller tail, and single broad band of white. This southwestern species uses its hog-like nose in rooting up insect larvae.

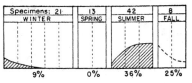

Specimens: 21	13	42	8
WINTER	SPRING	SUMMER	FALL
9%	0%	36%	25%

Animal food: Theirs is a grubby diet for a grubby animal: larval and adult beetles, grasshoppers, crickets, and many other insects. Small mammals and other vertebrates are minor constituents.

Plant food: As indicated in the diagram, plant material plays a more important role in the diet of the hognose than in most other skunks.

Texas, 84 (21-13-42-8)
** Persimmon *SuF*

* Pricklypear *SuF*
\+ Hackberry, Mulberry

BADGER
Taxidea taxus

The badger is a native of the Prairies and other open or semiopen regions from northern Mexico to the far North. Now, however, this low-geared, burrowing animal is much reduced in numbers and is absent from most of its original range—along with the prairie dogs that formerly furnished a considerable part of its food. The badger's prey consists largely of ground squirrels, pocket gophers, prairie dogs, rabbits, and mice, together with occasional insects, lizards, and grouse.

Foxes, Coyote, and Wolves: *Canidae*

RED AND KIT FOXES (Vulpes). Besides inhabiting the territory shown in the range map, red foxes and kit foxes occupy an extensive range in Canada and Alaska. Red foxes are distinct in their rusty-orange color, bushy tails, and dark-fronted forelegs. They are wily creatures and have prospered in spite of man's invasion of their habitats and the extensive use of their pelts. Black, silver, and cross foxes are simply color variations of the red fox. Some of these color phases are particularly prized for furs and are now produced under semidomestication on fur farms. Kit foxes are smaller, lighter colored inhabitants of the plains and deserts.

The food of these foxes consists mainly of mice, and other small rodents, and rabbits, together with occasional birds, insects, reptiles, and amphibians. Fleshy fruits are also commonly eaten when available. Only for the eastern red fox (treated below) are appreciable food data available.

EASTERN RED FOX
Vulpes fulva

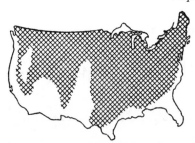

Specimens: 130	5	11	25
WINTER	SPRING	SUMMER	FALL
4%	0%	31%	23%

The range of this fox is not clearly defined. In recent years it has become fairly common in Piedmont sections of the Southeast as well as throughout most of the Northeast. Farther west, in the prairie country, it is represented by a subspecies known as the plains or royal red fox.

Animal food: The varied animal diet reflects the relative availability of different foods at various times and places. Ubiquitous mice are of first importance, and rabbits are a staple where available. Other small mammals as well as birds and cold-blooded vertebrates also fall prey. The larger insects, especially grasshoppers, are eaten in season, and carrion too, if relatively fresh.

Plant food: Fleshy fruits and seeds average about one-quarter of the summer and fall diet.

East (excl. Mass. and Ala.), 139 (121-
   2-2-14)
   * Cherry, Wild Black *F*
   + Apple, Blackberry, Grasses, Per-
      simmon, Pear, Corn, Pea-
      nut, Blueberry
Massachusetts, 57 (0-0-0-57) and 164
   winter scats

*** Apple *FW*
   + Grass, Blueberry, Corn, Choke-
      cherry, Grape
Alabama, 32 (9-3-9-11)
   *** Persimmon *F*
   * Corn *SuF*
   + Peanut, Cherry

Reference: The Fox in New York. Clayton B. Seagers. *N.Y. State Conserv. Dept.
Educ. Bul.,* 1944. 85 pp.

GRAY FOX
Urocyon cinereoargenteus

Specimens: 567	120	344	276
WINTER	SPRING	SUMMER	FALL
15%	6%	10%	18%

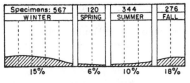

In general habits and, to some extent, appearance, the gray fox is much
like the red fox. Occasionally individuals have been known to climb small
trees. A closely related species ›(*U.
littoralis*) occurs on islands off the
coast of Southern California.

Animal food: The animal part of
the diet includes small animals of
all kinds: birds, mice, rabbits, and
other mammals.

Plant food: Fruit and other plant
products constitute a small but fairly
consistent part of the fox's fare.

Northeast, 89 (84-1-2-2)
   * Apple, *W*
   + Pokeweed, Corn, Persimmon,
      Grape, Wild Black Cherry,
      Pear, Hawthorn

Southeast, 1108 (489-73-302-244)
   * Persimmon, *FW*
   * Peanut *SuFWSp*
   * Cherry, Wild *SuSP*
   + Apple, Grape, Corn, Beech,
      Blackberry, Oak, Blueberry
Southwest (mainly Tex.), 210 (94-46-
   40-30)
   * Hackberry *FW*
   * Persimmon *SuF*
   + Cedar, Pricklypear, Peanut,
      Condalia, Oak

Reference: The Fox in New York. Clayton B. Seagers. *N.Y. State Conserv. Dept.
Educ. Bul.,* 1944. 85 pp.

COYOTE
Canis latrans

The coyote is one of the few mammals that has increased its range in
the past two centuries—and this in

the face of vigorous campaigns for its
reduction. Formerly it was primarily
an animal of the West, particularly

of the plains and deserts, but now it is found as far east as Ontario.

The coyote is a problem to western ranchmen and farmers. As part compensation, however, it helps to control jack rabbits, ground squirrels, and other rodents. This wily, small prairie wolf is almost entirely carnivorous, but occasionally it feeds on fleshy fruits. The plant material in 8,263 specimens taken in all seasons averaged less than 2% of the whole diet. In summing up the coyote diet, Seton says: "While a hunter by profession and by choice, there is nothing in the way of fish, flesh, or fowl, dead or alive, ancient or modern, that the coyote disdains for food."

Reference: Food Habits of the Coyote. Charles C. Sperry. *U.S. Fish and Wildlife Service Res. Bul.* 4, 1941. 69 pp.

WOLVES. When this country was being settled, wolves were common except in some of the most arid parts of the West. Now their domain is limited to a few regions such as the western mountains, forested areas in northern border states from Michigan westward, and some localities in the Gulf states. Two species are recognized: the widespread gray, or timber, wolf (*Canis lupus*) and the black, or red, wolf (*C. niger*).

Wolves are almost entirely carnivorous. Their destructiveness to western livestock has necessitated extensive programs of control. These predators feed on livestock and poultry when opportunity offers, but their fare consists more regularly of rabbits, carrion, rodents, and deer.

Reference: The Wolves of North America. Stanley P. Young and Edward A. Goldman. American Wildlife Institute, 1944. 636 pp.

Cats: *Felidae*

PUMA, OR MOUNTAIN LION. This large member of the cat family is variously known as a mountain lion, puma, cougar, and panther. A number of different species have been recognized in different parts of the country, but it appears that they can all be regarded as subspecies of *Felis concolor*.

The puma was formerly present in practically all parts of the United States. Now it is confined almost entirely to mountains of the West. This powerful predator is unpopular with western ranchers because of its tendencies to kill horses, cattle, and sheep. Its food is almost entirely flesh. Besides domestic animals, it feeds on deer, squirrels, rabbits, porcupines, gophers, and rats.

Three other species of cats (*Felis*), the jaguar, ocelot, and jaguarundi, occur sparingly along our Mexican border. They are largely tropical in distribution and are also completely carnivorous in their diet.

Reference: The Puma, Mysterious American Cat. Stanley P. Young and Edward A. Goldman. American Wildlife Institute, 1946. 358 pp.

LYNX AND BOBCAT. The short-tailed, chunky cat known as lynx, bobcat, or wildcat has two principal species in the United States. The one commonly known as Canada lynx is a northern animal which, in this country, is limited largely to the Rocky Mountains and to a few of our Canadian boundary states in the East. The other form, generally called bobcat or wildcat, is much more widespread over the United States. Both the lynx and the wildcat are powerful, stealthy, carnivorous prowlers—often spending considerable time in trees. Rabbits, squirrels, and other small mammals, as well as birds and occasionally deer, are taken as prey.

Seals and Sea Lions: *Otariidae and Phocidae*

SEALS AND SEA LIONS. These marine mammals are regarded as near relatives of the carnivores. They are well-adapted for aquatic life and subsist wholly on fish and other marine organisms. On coastal rocks and beaches where they rest and raise families, they are rather helpless.

The harbor seal is a small, widely distributed member of the group. One species occurs along the North Atlantic coast, from New England northward, and another is fairly common along the Pacific coast. Eskimos make use of this seal for meat, rawhide, and clothing. Examination of 137 harbor seal stomachs indicated that fish was their principal fare—particularly gadid, herring, and flounder. Shrimp and octopus are also eaten.

Fur seals are northern animals that come southward as far as California in winter. Their breeding grounds are on the Pribilof Islands, Alaska, where the animals are now given protection with only a restricted number being removed annually for furs. Analyses of the stomachs of fur seals show that they subsist largely on herring, pollack, salmon, and other fish as well as on squid and crustaceans.

Sea lions are closely related to the fur seals and, like the latter, occur along the Pacific coast. Their hides, though not so valuable as those of the fur seal, have been in demand since the early days of settlement. Also their flesh has been sought for both food and seal oil. As a consequence the population of these animals has been greatly reduced. Two species occur along our West coast. The northern, or Steller, sea lion comes as far south as California in winter, and the California sea lion ranges along the coast from Mexico to Northern California. The food of the sea lion consists mainly of fish—especially pollack, salmon, and halibut. Squid and crustaceans are also eaten.

Elephant seals or sea elephants are now almost extirpated from their former range along the coast of California. Their population is chiefly limited to a small herd near Guadalupe Island in Lower California.

Woodchuck, Marmot, and Tree Squirrels: *Sciuridae*

WOODCHUCK AND MARMOT. Three principal species of the genus *Marmota* occur in the United States: the woodchuck or groundhog (*M. monax*) mainly in the East, the whistler or hoary marmot (*M. caligata*) in the Northwest, and the yellow-bellied marmot or rockchuck (*M. flaviventris*) throughout most of the Rocky Mountain region. These large, burrowing rodents are wholly vegetarian and subsist largely, though not entirely, on herbaceous plants. Appreciable information on foods is available only for the woodchuck and the yellow-bellied marmot.

WOODCHUCK
Marmota monax

The woodchuck, or groundhog, is an unpopular animal despite its legendary fame as the determiner of weather. Frequently it is a nuisance to farmers or truck gardeners—partly due to crops eaten and partly because of their dens that endanger livestock and machinery.

The woodchuck ranges over much of Canada and northeastern United States. It makes its dens in fields, fence rows, and woodlands bordered by clearings. Only a limited amount of information has been collected to date on foods used or preferred by the woodchuck.

Northeast, observations
- *** Clover
- ** Grasses
- ** Vegetables
- * Soybeans
- * Alfalfa
- + Honeysuckle

Reference: The Life History of the Rufescent Woodchuck. W. J. Hamilton, Jr. *Carnegie Museum*, Vol. 23, 1934. 93 pp.

YELLOW-BELLIED MARMOT
Marmota flaviventris

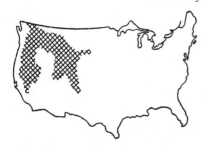

The yellowbelly, or rockchuck, has its favorite denning habitat among rock piles in grassy mountain meadows. It occurs in various parts of the Far West—particularly in the Rockies. Colonies of these animals often make dens in the same vicinity. The fact that the food of the yellowbelly includes woody as well as herbaceous plants is indicated by the 17 specimens examined.

Western Prairies and Mt.–Desert, 17 (0-2-15-0)
- **** Grasses *Su*
- ** Locoweed *Su*
- ** Apple *Su*
- ** Serviceberry *Su*
- ** Blackberry *Su*
- * Alfalfa *Su*

Reference: Revision of the North American Marmots. Arthur H. Howell. *No. Amer. Fauna* 37, 1915. 80 pp.

TREE SQUIRRELS. Three main groups of arboreal squirrels live in wooded areas of the United States. These are the red squirrels and chickarees (*Tamiasciurus*), the gray and fox squirrels (*Sciurus*), and the flying squirrels (*Glaucomys*). In contrast to the ground squirrels and rock squirrels, these tree squirrels (as their name implies) spend a large share of their time aloft and get most of their food from trees. They also have value as game species and are larger and more attractive animals than their ground-dwelling cousins.

For present purposes the unqualified name "squirrels" refers to tree squirrels.

RED SQUIRREL
Tamiasciurus hudsonicus

The red squirrel (Map below, eastern part) ranges from the higher mountains of the South and from our northern states through Canada up to Alaska. It is typical of coniferous forests but is also found in hardwood areas.

Animal food: The red squirrel seems to have a strong predilection for flesh. It eats insects, young birds, and eggs and also robs meat-baited traps.

Plant food: Seeds and fruits of both conifers and hardwoods are prominent in the diet of this species.

East, observations
*** Hickory *FW*
** Serviceberry *Su*
** Beech *FW*

** Oak *FWSp*
** Maple *SuF*
** Fungus *SpSuF*
** Spruce *W*
* Cherry, Wild *Su*
* Pine *FW*
* Fir *W*
* Tuliptree *F*
* Walnut, Black *F*

West, fall and winter observations
** Douglasfir
** Pine
* Fir
* Spruce
* Hemlock
* Viburnum
* Apple
* Hazelnut

References: Observations on the Life History of the Red Squirrel in New York. W. J. Hamilton, Jr. *Amer. Mid. Nat.*, Vol. 22 (3), 1939. 13 pp.
The Red Squirrel: Its Life History and Habits. Robert T. Hatt. *Roosevelt Wild Life Annals, N.Y. State Col.*, Vol. 2(1), 1929. 143 pp.

DOUGLAS CHICKAREE
Tamiasciurus douglasii

Range of genus *Tamiasciurus*

The Douglas chickaree, or Douglas squirrel, found in coniferous forests of the Pacific coast region, inhabits

the coastal strip mapped. It is rusty-reddish on the underparts where the red squirrel is normally whitish. Most of its food consists of conifer seeds.

Pacific, observations
*** Pine
*** Fir
** Hemlock
* Salal
* Hazelnut
* Ash
* Mountain-ash
* Incense-cedar
* Douglasfir

231

FREMONT CHICKAREE
Tamiasciurus fremonti

The Fremont chickaree is a common species in the southern Rocky Mountains from Wyoming and Utah to New Mexico and Arizona (Map on page 231). Unlike the Douglas chickaree, it always has whitish underparts. Limited observations indicate that Douglasfir seeds are a staple in its diet.

EASTERN GRAY SQUIRREL
Sciurus carolinensis

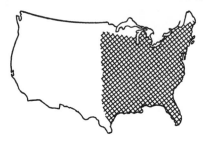

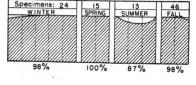

Specimens: 24	15	13	46
WINTER	SPRING	SUMMER	FALL
98%	100%	87%	98%

Gray squirrels are familiar to practically everyone in the East—city dweller and farmer alike. They are still common throughout most of their range but, according to old reports, were so plentiful during Colonial days that they caused serious damage to the settler's corn and other crops. In 1749 a bounty of three pence yielded a toll of 640,000 gray squirrels in Pennsylvania. Damage is still reported, but usually it is not serious.

The gray squirrel is partial to hardwood forests where acorns, hickory nuts, and beechnuts are available. It does a great deal of food storing. Occasionally one encounters a black phase of this species.

Animal food: Weevil fragments found regularly in gray squirrel stomachs are probably ingested accidentally with acorns. Certain insect foods, however, such as caterpillars and cocoons, beetles, and ants are occasionally eaten. Some individuals eat birds' eggs and nestlings on occasion.

Plant food:
East, 98 (24-15-13-46) plus observations
**** Oak, acorns and flw. *SuFWSp*
*** Hickory *FWSpSu*
** Beech *FW*
** Maple *SuFW*
* Walnut, Black *FW*
* Hornbeam *F*
* Pine *FW*
* Blackgum *F*
* Dogwood, Flowering *F*
* Mulberry *Su*
* Sweetgum *F*
* Fungus *SuFWSp*
* Spruce *W*
+ Sedge, Cherry, Blackberry, Tuliptree, Elm

Reference: Fox Squirrels and Gray Squirrels in Illinois. Louis G. Brown and Lee E. Yeager. *Ill. Nat. Hist. Surv. Bull.*, 1945. 87 pp.

WESTERN GRAY SQUIRREL
Sciurus griseus

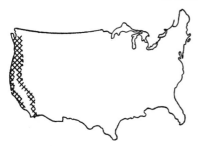

These broader tailed relatives of the eastern gray squirrel are natives of the Pacific coast. They occur rather sparingly within their range and are most likely to be found in groves of pine or oak. Information on the animal food of this species is lacking, but presumably it is, as in the eastern gray squirrel, very limited in quantity.

Food data are scant on other notable gray squirrels of the West, including the long-eared Abert and Kaibab squirrels. These are believed to feed largely on the seeds of yellow pine.

California, observations
**** Pine *W*
**** Oak *W*
 * Mulberry *Sp*

EASTERN FOX SQUIRREL
Sciurus niger

Specimens: 16	10	35	11
WINTER	SPRING	SUMMER	FALL
100% 0	79%	96%	100%

Plant food:
Northeast (excl. Ohio and Mich.), 72 (16-10-35-11)
 *** Corn *SuFWSp*
 *** Oak *SuFWSp*
 ** Hickory *FWSpSu*
 ** Elm, bud and sd. *SpSu*
 ** Wheat *SuW*
 * Beech *FW*
 * Blackberry *Su*
 * Grape *SuF*
 + Blackgum, Fungus, Blueberry, Mulberry
Ohio, 78, all seasons
 *** Hickory *SuFWSp*
 *** Beech *SuFWSp*
 *** Oak *FWSpSu*
 *** Corn *SuFWSp*
 ** Maple, bud and sd. *WSpSuF*
 ** Elm, bud and sd. *WSpSu*
 ** Walnut, Black *FWSpSu*
 ** Wheat *SuFWSp*
 * Hazelnut *W*
 * Mulberry *Su*

This, the largest of our squirrels, is of special interest as a game species. Fox squirrels weigh two to three pounds —about twice as much as gray squirrels. The eastern fox squirrel occurs throughout most of the East and as far west as western Texas. Two additional fox squirrels are present in the southern parts of Arizona and New Mexico.

Animal food: Two or three per cent of insect food—various stages of beetles and lepidoptera—seems a normal part of the diet in spring and summer. However, two specimens collected in Georgia in April contained 100% insect material, about half noctuid larvae and half May beetles.

* Witch-hazel *W*
* Blackgum *Su*
* Dogwood *W*
* Buckeye *FWSp*
* Blackberry and Raspberry *SuF*
+ Apple, Huckleberry, Butternut, Willow, Soybean, Tuliptree, Hop-hornbeam, Fungus, Bittersweet, Wild Cherry, Sycamore

Michigan, observations, all seasons
**** Oak *FWSpSu*
*** Hickory *SuFWSp*
*** Corn *SuFWSp*
** Beech *FW*

** Walnut *FW*
** Maple, bud, flw., and fr. *SpSu*
** Elm, bud, flw., and fr. *SpSu*
* Ash *SuF*
* Basswood, bud and fr. *SpFW*
* Serviceberry *Su*
* Cherry, Wild *SuF*
* Dogwood *SuF*
* Blackberry and Raspberry *Su*
+ Willow, Strawberry, Blueberry, Elderberry, Black Locust, Chokeberry, Wheat, Oats, Buckwheat, Hop-hornbeam, Osage-orange, Greenbrier, Pine, Hackberry

References: Michigan Fox Squirrel Management. Durward L. Allen. Michigan Department of Conservation, 1943. 404 pp.
Fox Squirrels and Gray Squirrels in Illinois. Louis G. Brown and Lee Y. Yeager. *Ill. Nat. Hist. Surv. Bul.*, 1945. 87 pp.

FLYING SQUIRREL
Glaucomys volans

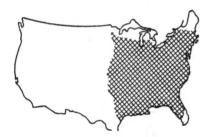

These small to medium-sized squirrels are less known because, in contrast to most squirrels, they are nocturnal. In addition to the eastern species, another flying squirrel (*G. sabrinus*) occurs in Canada and in the Far West. There is very little information on their food habits.

Animal food: Insects such as moths and beetles form a minor part of the diet. Birds and their eggs have been reported eaten, but the extent of this depredation remains to be ascertained.

Plant food:
Northeast, 12 (7-2-3-0), plus observations
*** Beech *FW*
** Oak *FW*
* Hackberry *FW*
* Maple, sap *FW*

Reference: Revision of the American Flying Squirrels. Arthur H. Howell. *No. Amer. Fauna* 44, 1918. 64 pp.

Beaver: *Castoridae*

BEAVER
Castor canadensis

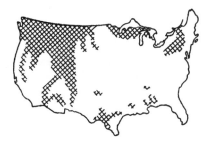

The beaver was formerly plentiful from Alaska and northern Canada to the Mexican boundary, wherever fresh water and trees were present. The valuable pelts of this large, amphibious, flat-tailed rodent were a principal stimulus to the early exploration and settlement of wilderness areas of the United States. Now its numbers and range within the United States are much reduced.

The beaver is entirely vegetarian. It subsists chiefly on the bark or wood of twigs, branches, and tree trunks.

Northeast, observations
- *** Poplar (incl. Aspen)
- ** Willow
- ** Birch
- ** Hazelnut
- ** Waterlily
- ** Cowlily

** Serviceberry
* Maple
* Alder
* Ash

Southeast, observations
- *** Sweetgum
- ** Pine
- ** Ash

Missouri, observations
- — Corn
- — Dogwood
- — Oak
- — Alder
- — Birch, River
- — Willow
- — Elm
- — Maple
- — Sycamore
- — Redcedar

West, observations
- **** Poplar (incl. Aspen)
- *** Willow
- ** Douglasfir
- ** Pine
- ** Birch
- ** Waterlily

References: The Beaver, Its Work and Ways. E. R. Warren. The Williams & Wilkins Company, Baltimore, 1927. 177 pp.

A Study of Beaver Colonies in Michigan. Glenn W. Bradt. *Jour. Mammalogy*, Vol. 19 (2), pp. 139–162, 1938.

Beaver Habits and Experiments in Beaver Culture. Vernon Bailey. *U.S. Dept. Agr. Tech. Bul.* 21, 1927. 40 pp.

Muskrat: *Cricetidae*

MUSKRAT
Ondatra zibethicus

Muskrats in the United States are now regarded as all belonging to one species. Like the beaver, the muskrat is amphibious, but is partial to marshy

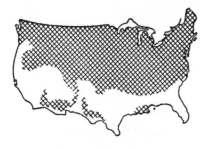

areas instead of open streams. Both of these valuable fur animals have been trapped heavily, but the muskrat has survived more successfully probably because of its greater fecundity and wider adaptability. Muskrat houses, if not the muskrats themselves, are a common sight in many parts of the country.

Animal food: The muskrat is essentially vegetarian, but there is minor use of animal food including fish, freshwater mussels, insects, crayfish, and snails. The percentage of animal food is very low.

Plant food: Plant material eaten by the muskrat consists largely of the stems, leaves, and rootstocks of marsh plants.

Northeast, 45 (45-0-0-0) plus observations
- **** Cattail
- *** Bulrush
- ** Burreed
- * Waterstarwort
- * Pondweed
- * Arrowhead
- * Corn
- + Willow, Pear, Buttercup, Oak, Spikerush, Horsetail, Pickerelweed

Maryland, Patuxent Refuge, all season observations
- *** Burreed
- ** Cutgrass, Rice
- ** Arrowhead
- * Waterlily
- * Panicgrass

Louisiana, all season observations
- *** Bulrush
- ** Cattail
- ** Panicgrass
- * Cordgrass
- * Rush, Needlegrass
- + Sawgrass, Rice Cutgrass, Reedgrass, Giant Bristlegrass

Iowa, winter observations
- ** Cattail
- * Grasses
- + Corn

References: The Muskrat in New York. Dr. Chas. E. Johnson. *Roosevelt Wild Life Bul.*, Vol. 3(2), pp. 194–322, 1925.

The Muskrat. David E. Lantz. *U.S. Dept. Agr. Farmers Bull.* 396, 1910. 58 pp.

The Muskrat in the Louisiana Coastal Marshes. Ted O'Neil. Louisiana Dept. of Wild Life and Fisheries, 1949. 152 pp.

Mountain Beaver: *Aplodontiidae*

MOUNTAIN BEAVER
Aplodontia rufa

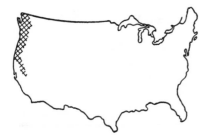

This burrowing rodent is not a real beaver, nor is it beaver-like in appearance or habitat. This single species is confined to humid forests of the Pacific Northwest. It is completely vegetarian, feeding on the leaves, stems, and sometimes bark of a great variety of plants that occur in the vicinity of its tunnels.

Pacific, observations, various seasons
- * Rhododendron

* Ceanothus	+ Gooseberry, Dogwood, Poplar,
* Brakefern	Stonecrop, Lupine, Grasses,
* Woodfern	Iris

Reference: Mountain Beavers in the Pacific Northwest. Theo. H. Scheffer. *U.S. Dept. Agr. Farmers Bul.* 1598, 1929. 18 pp.

Porcupine: *Erethizontidae*

PORCUPINE
Erethizon dorsatum

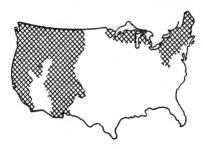

The porcupines of North America are all one species. The common eastern form ranges from Labrador to Pennsylvania and the Great Lakes, while the western races occur from Alaska to Mexico.

Next to the beaver, this is our largest native rodent. Though it is an interesting animal, the porcupine is an unpopular nuisance in several ways. Its barbed quills are painful to man and beast, and its winter girdling of trees while feeding on bark is a vexing problem to foresters.

Porcupines are vegetarian. In winter their diet consists almost wholly of the inner bark of trees. In other seasons they make use of a wide variety of herbaceous plants.

Northeast (excl. Vt.), observations, various seasons
*** Hemlock
** Cowlily
* Waterlily
* Basswood

* Poplar
* Pine
* Maple
* Birch
* Beech, nuts and bark
* Arrowhead
+ Ash, Fir
Vermont, winter observations
*** Maple, Sugar and Striped
*** Beech
*** Hemlock
** Spruce, Red
** Fir, Balsam
** Birch, Yellow
* Ash
* Apple
Mt.–Desert, 15 plus observations, all seasons
** Pine, wood
* Oak, acorns
+ Ceanothus, Clover, Dandelion, Sedge, Goldenrod, Knotweed, Poplar

Reference: Ecology and Life History of the Porcupine as Related to Forests of Arizona and Southwestern United States. Walter P. Taylor. *Univ. Ariz. Bul.*, 1935. 177 pp.

Pikas: *Ochotonidae*

PIKAS
Ochotona

and *O. schisticeps*, are recognized in this country.

Pikas are vegetarian. They have the unusual habit of storing quantities of hay-like herbage within their rocky recesses for winter. Probably a great variety of plants are used. The list below indicates a few of the typical components.

Pikas, also known as conies, are small, short-eared, tail-less, guinea-pig-like inhabitants of rocky places in the higher altitudes of the Rockies and other western mountains. They usually live at altitudes of 8,000 to 13,500 feet. Two species, *O. princeps*

Pacific, observations, various seasons

    * Stonecrop
    * Fireweed
    * Dryad
    + Sweetgrass, Sedge, Crowberry, Willow, Cinquefoil, Blueberry, Fescuegrass, Avens, Fir, Pine

Hares and Rabbits: *Leporidae*

HARES. In a broad sense, the hares include the varying hares, the arctic hare, and the jack rabbits. As used here, the term refers to the northerly members of the genus *Lepus* that are commonly designated varying hares or snowshoe rabbits. With the exception of the subspecies known as the Washington hare, this group of rabbits changes color with the season: white in winter and brownish the rest of the year. Another peculiarity is their periodic crash declines in population. It has been variously estimated that these drastic drops in population run in cycles of 7 or 10 years.

The principal distribution of varying, or snowshoe, hares is in Canada and Alaska with limited fringes of their range extending down into the higher altitudes and cooler regions of the United States. Hares are valuable game animals but are destructive to young woody plants. One species and a number of subspecies are recognized. Our information on food habits of these hares is limited to a few local studies. They feed entirely on vegetation—herbage (in summer) and live bark or twigs (winter).

VARYING, OR SNOWSHOE, HARE
Lepus americanus

This hare, also known as the snowshoe rabbit because of its large hind feet, is a principal source of food for the Canada lynx as well as for the fox, fisher, and marten. Northern woodsmen also rely on it for some of their meat supply. When these medium-large, north-woods rabbits undergo

declines in population, their carnivorous enemies also become reduced in numbers. When varying hares are abundant, they cause much damage by browsing or barking young forest trees.

Northern New York, observations, mainly winter

**** Pine, White and Red
*** Spruce, White
** Birch, Paper
** Aspen
Minnesota, 54 (8-15-9-22) plus observations
*** Aspen *WSp*

*** Willow *SuWSp*
*** Grasses *SpSuF*
** Hazelnut *W*
** Ferns *W*
* Birch *WSp*
* Alder *WSp*
* Sumac *FW*
* Strawberry *SpW*
* Clover *SuFW*
* Dandelion *SpW*
* Beadruby *W*
+ Maple, Oak, Wild Cherry, Pine
Utah, winter observations
** Douglasfir
** Willow
* Snowberry
* Maple
* Serviceberry

References: Notes on the Life History of the Snowshoe Hare. C. M. Aldous. *Journ. Mammalogy*, Vol. 18 (1), pp. 46–57, 1937.
The Snowshoe Hare, Its Life History. Joye H. Severaid. Maine Department of Inland Fish and Game, 1942. 95 pp.
Observations on the Snowshoe Hare. Wallace B. Grange. *Jour. Mammalogy*, Vol. 13 (1), 1932. 19 pp.

JACK RABBITS. Four species of jack rabbits are native to open, arid areas in our western plains and deserts. Two species of the antelope jack rabbit group barely extend into our country from Mexico, but the other two have wide ranges in the West. The kangaroo-like hind legs of jacks enable them to attain great speed for escaping from enemies. Often when running at full tilt, their long, bounding leaps measure more than 10 feet. Another notable characteristic—and one that accounts for its name—is its long jackass-like ears. These rabbits are close relatives of the varying hare—belonging to the same genus *Lepus*.

Jacks are one of the dietary mainstays of the coyote, and reduction of coyote numbers has, on occasion, resulted in excessive populations of rabbits. Like other members of the family, jack rabbits are entirely vegetarian. Shrubs, grasses, and weedy plants are their principal fare. Almost any available green plants are likely to be eaten.

References: The Life Histories and Ecology of Jack Rabbits. Charles T. Vorhies and Walter P. Taylor. *Univ. Ariz. Exp. Sta. Rept.*, pp. 471–587, 1933.
The Jack Rabbits of the United States. T. S. Palmer. *U.S. Biol. Surv. Bul.* 8, 1896.

WHITE-TAILED JACK RABBIT
Lepus townsendii

This so-called prairie hare is *the* jack rabbit of the Northwest. Its conspicuous white tail—suggestive of the tail of the white-tailed deer—is its chief distinction. Seton rated the white-tailed jack next to the antelope as the

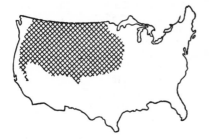

speediest animal of the northern plains. In some parts of its range it is disappearing and is being replaced by the black-tailed jack rabbit—presumably because of the effects of grazing and other phases of agriculture.

Utah, winter observations
*** Snakeweed
*** Rabbitbrush
+ Sagebrush

ANTELOPE JACK RABBIT
Lepus alleni

This is one of the two species of the antelope or white-sided jack rabbits that range only a short distance into our Southwest from the Mexican tablelands. On the other species, *L. gaillardi*, we have no food-habits data at all. This group of jack rabbits is noted for its use of pricklypear cactus as a source of water.

Arizona, 177 (38-12-81-46)
**** Grasses *SpSuFW*
**** Mesquite *SpSuFW*
*** Gramagrass *SpSuFW*
* Bristlegrass *SpSuFW*
* Pricklypear *SpSuFW*
* Purslane *Su*
* Spiderling *F*
+ Panicgrass, Three-awn, Trichloris

BLACK-TAILED JACK RABBIT
Lepus californicus

** Gramagrass *SpSuFW*
** Alfalfa *SpF*
* Eriogonum *W*
* Spiderling *SuF*
* Pricklypear *Su*
+ Panicgrass, Three-awn, Cottontopgrass, Bristlegrass, Purslane

The blacktail's alternative name, California jack rabbit, is somewhat misleading since, as indicated on the range map, this species occupies a large share of the West—especially the Southwest. In early days, as many as 35,000 of these jack rabbits were killed in a one-day drive.

Arizona and New Mexico, 65 (17-3-33-12)
**** Mesquite *SpSuFW*
*** Grasses *SpSuFW*

Utah, winter observations
** Sagebrush
** Greasewood
** Saltbush
** Rabbitbrush
California, April observations
** Filaree

COTTONTAILS
Sylvilagus

Common cottontail (*S. floridanus*)

New England cottontail (*S. transitionalis*)

Cottontails are present in practically all parts of the United States. That is why rabbit hunting is a principal outdoor sport throughout the country. Besides this recreational value and a limited use as a source of fur, cottontails are the staple food of many valuable fur animals. Nine species of cottontails are recognized—excluding the related pygmy rabbit of the Great Basin desert.

Range maps have been drawn for four important species on which food-habits data are available. In some instances two or more species of cottontails were involved in the data compilations for a particular region, and consequently the information is presented according to regions (and states) instead of by species of rabbits.

In summer, cottontails subsist largely on tender herbaceous plants, but in winter they frequently resort to twigs and bark of young trees. Sometimes rabbit damage to orchards is serious.

Connecticut, 76 (0-13-49-14) plus many observations
  ** Crabgrass *SpSuFW*
  ** Bluegrass *SpSuFW*
  ** Garden Crops *SuF*
  ** Clover *SpSuFW*
  ** Blackberry *SuFWSp*
  ** Plantain *SpSuF*
  ** Sheepsorrel *SpSu*
  * Panicgrass *SpSuFW*

  * Goldenrod *SuF*
  * Birch, Gray *WSp*
  * Maple, Red *WSp*
  * Cherry, Wild *WSp*
  * Blueberry *SuFWSp*
  + Wildmillet, Bristlegrass, Chickweed, Apple, Wild Strawberry, Willow, Dogwood, Oak, Winterberry, Sumac, Paspalum
Ohio, observations on farm, all year
  *** Wheat *SpSuFW*
  ** Alfalfa *SpSuFW*
  ** Clover, Red *SpSuFW*
  ** Soybean *SpSuFW*
  * Oats *SpSu*
  * Carrot *SuF*
  + Alsike Clover, Corn, Rye, Bluegrass, Redtop
Michigan, winter observations
  **** Sumac
  ** Plantain
  ** Dogwood
  ** Blackberry
  * Yarrow
  * Cherry, Wild

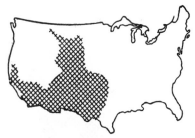

Rocky Mountain cottontail (*S. nuttallii*)

  * Elderberry
  * Oak
  * Apple
  + Sassafras, Willow, Hickory, Grape, Buckthorn, Wild Rose

Iowa, winter observations

  *** Sumac, Smooth
  ** Basswood
  ** Apple
  * Dogwood, Red-osier
  + Hawthorn, Oak, Elderberry, Willow, Raspberry, Elm

Utah, winter observations

  − Cherry, Black Choke
  − Snakeweed, Broom
  − Bitterbrush
  − Oregon-grape
  − Sagebrush

Audubon cottontail (*S. auduboni*)

  − Grasses
  − Birch
  − Aspen

Arizona, 4 (0-0-4-0)

  **** Mesquite
  *** Pricklypear

California, San Joaquin Exp. Range, numerous observations, all seasons

  − Filaree
  − Bromegrass
  − Fescuegrass
  − Popcornflower
  − Clover
  − Deervetch
  − Tarweed
  − Turkeymullein
  − Spikerush
  − Rush

References: The Cottontail Rabbits in Connecticut. N. W. Hosley, editor. *Conn. Geological and Natural History Survey Bul.* 65, 1942. 96 pp.

Cottontails in Michigan. Paul Hickie. Michigan Department of Conservation, 1940. 104 pp.

Natural History Observations on the Audubon Cottontail. Lloyd G. Ingles. *Jour. Mammalogy*, Vol. 22 (3), pp. 227–250, 1941.

Rabbits in Relation to Crops. F. E. Garlough, J. F. Welch, and H. J. Spencer. *U.S. Fish and Wildlife Service Conserv. Bul.* 11, 1942. 20 pp.

Armadillo: *Dasypodidae*

ARMADILLO. Armadillos are mainly tropical or South American, but one species, the nine-banded armadillo, ranges northward over the Mexican border into southern Texas and occasionally into adjoining states. This unique, armor-plated creature subsists largely (about three-fourths of its diet) on insects obtained on the ground. Nearly half of the insects eaten are beetles. Fleshy fruits are a minor supplement. The balance of the diet consists of spiders, centipedes, millipedes, and other invertebrates as well as a few reptiles and amphibians.

Reference: The Armadillo, Its Relation to Agriculture and Game. E. R. Kalmbach. Game, Fish and Oyster Commission, Austin, Tex., 1943. 61 pp.

FLORIDA MANATEE. This rare, whale-like marine mammal occupies coastal bays and lagoons from Florida south to the West Indies. One other species is present in South America. A third species, the Steller sea cow, inhabited a few islands in the North Pacific Ocean until about two centuries ago when it was exterminated by whalers and sailors.

The manatee or sea cow, is a vegetarian that browses on submerged aquatics. Little is known about the specific plants which are its chief sources of food. Presumably it feeds on the plant known as manateegrass (*Cymodocea manatorum*).

WHALES, DOLPHINS, PORPOISES. These marine mammals are typically oceanic and a majority of them are animal eaters. Belonging in a sense to the world, rather than to particular countries, they have had little protection from any source until recently, and as a consequence, some of the more valuable whales have been greatly reduced in numbers.

Whales include several distinct families as well as a number of genera and species. Some have teeth, while others have, instead, special structural arrangements for straining minute organisms out of sea water. It is an interesting contrast that certain kinds of these largest animals in the world feed on minute forms of life including diatoms and other unicellular plants. Certain others, like the sperm whale, feed largely on squid and octopuses. Whales are present in both the Atlantic and Pacific oceans and in other oceans throughout the world. Their oil, whalebone, ambergris, and blubber have much economic value.

Porpoises and dolphins belong to the same order (*Cetacea*) as whales. They are numerous and are widely distributed but lack the economic importance of their larger cousins.

CHAPTER ELEVEN

Small Mammals

T HE SMALL-MAMMAL assemblage consists mainly of rodents (order *Rodentia*) though it excludes some of the large species such as the beaver, mountain beaver, tree squirrels, muskrat, and porcupines. Two other rather small orders are included, namely, the moles and shrews (*Insectivora*) and bats (*Chiroptera*). The principal groups or species treated in this chapter are

Moles	Pocket Mice	Lemming Mouse
Shrews	Kangaroo Rats	Meadow Mice
Bats	Grasshopper Mice	Pine Mouse
Ground Squirrels	White-footed Mice	House Mouse
Prairie Dogs	Cotton Rat	House Rat
Chipmunks	Wood Rats	Jumping Mice
Pocket Gophers		

In general, small mammals have no appreciable value as either fur or game, but some have decided negative importance as pests to man. What these creatures lack in size they more than make up in population numbers. The familiar domestic rat and house mouse are outstanding nusiances. Western ground squirrels also cause extensive damage in agricultural areas. In defense of rodents as a group it may be stated that most species cause little or no economic damage while some like the beaver and muskrat (treated in Chap. Ten) are of positive economic value.

Moles, shrews, and bats live almost entirely on insects, but the rodent constituents of the small-mammal group are largely vegetarian. Grasshopper mice are an exception since insects constitute much of their fare. Other rodents feed on animal food (insects, small vertebrates, etc.) but do so only to a limited extent. Gophers and similar subterranean burrowers subsist mainly on roots or other vegetative parts of plants, but most rodents prefer more nutritious plant parts such as seeds and nuts.

References: Lives of Game Animals. Volume IV. Ernest Thompson Seton. Doubleday & Company, Inc., New York, 1928.

American Mammals. W. J. Hamilton, Jr. McGraw-Hill Book Company, Inc., New York, 1939.

Field Book of North American Mammals. H. E. Anthony. G. P. Putnam's Sons, New York, 1928.

Wild Animals of North America. E. W. Nelson. National Geographic Society, 1930.

Mammals of North America. Victor H. Cahalane. The Macmillan Company, New York, 1947.

Moles: *Talpidae*

MOLES. Moles resemble gophers in their habit of tunneling underground but belong to a distinct order known as the Insectivores. These long-snouted burrowers differ from rodents in their minute eyes, large forefeet, short neck, and fine, close fur.

About eight species of moles, belonging to five different genera, are present in various regions of the country except the Mountain–Desert region and arid western prairies. In the East are the common (*Scalopus*), the star-nosed (*Condylura*), and the hairy-tailed moles (*Parascalops*). The two other genera, the western moles (*Scapanus*) and shrew mole (*Neurotrichus*), occur only in Pacific coast states.

The food of moles is largely grubs, other larval stages of insects, and earthworms, but underground parts of plants—particularly bulbous or fleshy-rooted species—constitute an important supplement to the animal part of the diet. Adequate food data are available for only two species, the common and the Townsend moles.

Reference: A Review of the American Moles. Hartley H. T. Jackson. *No. Amer. Fauna* 38, 1915. 100 pp.

COMMON MOLE
Scalopus aquaticus

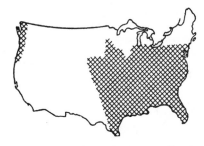

Specimens: 104	53	46	67
WINTER	SPRING	SUMMER	FALL
10%	18%	8%	3%

Plant food:
East, 270 (104-53-46-67)
 * Corn *WSp*
 + Peanut, Wheat, Sedge, Sweet Potato

This prevalent, eastern mole is similar to the western moles of the genus *Scapanus* but is less heavily furred and generally does not throw out as many mounds of soil from its burrows.

Animal food: Earthworms and white grubs are basic foods, supplemented by other insect larvae, pupae, and adults occurring in the soil. Spiders and centipedes are also devoured occasionally.

Reference: The Common Mole of Eastern United States. Theo. H. Scheffer. *U.S. Dept. Agr. Farmers Bul.* 583, 1917. 12 pp.

TOWNSEND MOLE
Scapanus townsendii

The Townsend, or Oregon, mole is one of three species of the genus *Scapanus*, commonly known as western moles. The specimens examined

245

for food-habits information were taken mainly in connection with studies of mole damage on Oregon and Washington farms raising bulbous flowering plants. Not only were bulbs eaten extensively, but further physical damage was done to hills in which the bulbs were not consumed.

Animal food: The animal portion of food is largely earthworms with small amounts of soil-inhabiting arthropods eaten regularly, and occasionally insects in quantity.

Specimens: 58	1	17	22
WINTER	SPRING	SUMMER	FALL

| 20% | 0% | 33% | 14% |

Plant food:
Washington and Oregon, 98 (58-1-17-22)
* Tulip, bulb *W*
* Tigerflower, bulb *F*
* Other bulbs and tubers *W*
* Carrot, root *Su*
* Corn *Su*
+ Garden Parsnip, Oats

Shrews: *Soricidae*

SHREWS. These mouse-like insectivores include the smallest members of the mammal group. They have velvety, mole-like fur and spend most of their time in

burrows. Shrews are widespread in the United States and are represented by about 30 species in six genera. They occur in many different kinds of habitats. The long-tailed shrews (*Sorex*) include more species than the other genera.

Shrews feed primarily upon insects and other invertebrates, but plant materials —generally undetermined—often constitute a part of the diet. Among their principal food items are earthworms and larval and adult stages of various insects including beetles, caterpillars, ants, and flies. Snails, spiders, grasshoppers, and mice are also eaten.

Reference: A Taxonomic Review of the American Long-tailed Shrews (Genera *Sorex* and *Microsorex*). Hartley H. T. Jackson. *No. Amer. Fauna* 51, 1928. 238 pp.

Bats: Order *Chiroptera*

BATS. Bats are distinctive in being the only mammals capable of true flight. About 35 species of these nocturnal creatures are widely distributed in the United States. Most of our bats are small to moderate in size and are wholly insectivorous. In the South Pacific, however, some large, fruit-eating species, known as flying foxes, attain a wingspread of five feet. In addition, there are the vampire

bats of tropical America which feed entirely upon blood taken from living animals.

Our native bats are generally not numerous enough to have significant economic importance. They are not harmful and may be definitely beneficial. Among the insects eaten most commonly are various kinds of flies, moths, flying ants, caddisflies, mosquitoes, ground beetles, and bugs.

Ground Squirrels, Prairie Dogs, Chipmunks: *Sciuridae*

GROUND SQUIRRELS. This large and abundant group of western rodents was formerly divided into four genera. Now, however, according to the latest revision, the 22 species and 67 subspecies present in the United States are all placed in the one genus *Citellus*. Nine species are given individual treatment below, but for some of these the food data are quite limited. As in most rodents, the food of ground squirrels is chewed finely and is difficult to identify in stomach examinations. All species are very largely vegetarian in their diet but consume small quantities of insects or flesh as well.

As a group, ground squirrels are regarded as serious pests to agriculture and have been subject to extensive programs of control. They eat seeds, fruits, or vegetative parts of almost any kind of plants including forage or grain crops as well as weeds and grasses. Millions of dollars of damage are credited to these rodents annually in the state of California. They may also serve as agents for the spread of diseases often fatal to man such as spotted fever, bubonic plague, and tularemia.

Reference: Revision of the North American Ground Squirrels, with a Classification of the North American Sciuridae. Arthur H. Howell. *No. Amer. Fauna* 56, 1938. 256 pp.

CALIFORNIA GROUND SQUIRREL
Citellus beecheyi

Instead of being limited to California, as its name might imply, this Pacific coast species ranges from Washington south into Lower California. It is known locally, as the Beechy ground squirrel, digger squirrel, or, because of its partiality to rocky places, the rock squirrel. The California ground squirrel is a very abundant species that has been controlled by poisoned bait in order to reduce crop losses. Both bubonic plague and tularemia are spread by this species.

Many different kinds of plant foods are used, depending considerably on what is available in different seasons. Green herbage, seeds, nuts, bulbs, fleshy fruits, and flowers are taken, and frequently acorns, seeds, or bulbs are stored for future use. In addition to the foods listed in the table below, the California ground squirrel has been reported feeding on seeds of elderberry, jimsonweed, turkeymullein, bulbs of wild hyacinth, and various agricultural crops including nuts, fleshy fruits, grains, and forage.

California, extensive observations, all seasons
**** Filaree, veg. and sd. *WSpSuF*
*** Oak *SuFWSp*
** Tarweed, veg. and sd. *SuFWSp*
* Lupine, veg. and sd. *WSp*
* Popcornflower, veg. and sd. *WSp*
* Redmaids, veg. *WSp*
* Gilia, Birdseye, flw. *Sp*
* Eriogonum, veg. *Su*
* Bromegrass, Ripgut, veg. and sd. *SpSu*
* Oats, Wild, veg. and sd. *SpSu*
+ Fiddleneck, Phacelia, Windmill Pink, Godetia, Ceanothus, Loosestrife, Manzanita, Buckeye

References: The California Ground Squirrel. Jean M. Linsdale. University of California Press, Berkeley, 1946. 475 pp.
Natural History of the Ground Squirrels of California. Joseph Grinnell and Joseph S. Dixon. *Calif. State Comm. Hort.*, Vol. 7, pp. 597–708, 1918.

MANTLED GROUND SQUIRREL
Citellus lateralis

The wide-ranging mantled ground squirrel consists of a single species, *C. lateralis*, which has 14 subspecies in 11 western states. Another mantled

ground squirrel, *C. saturatus*, occurs in Washington and British Columbia.

The mantled ground squirrel is marked and colored very much like a chipmunk. Its habits are similar too— even to climbing trees and stuffing cheek pouches with food. These ground squirrels normally live on relatively open slopes of mountains and hills away from agricultural areas.

The food of this species consists mainly of seeds, nuts, and fleshy fruits, but insects and flesh are frequent minor items of the diet. Grasshoppers, beetles, and caterpillars are commonly eaten, and meat used as bait for traps is attractive to them. Some individuals vary their menu with carrion, young birds, eggs, and mice.

West, 24 (0-0-16-8)
*** Penstemon *SuF*
 ** Knotweed *F*
 ** Gooseberry *SuF*
 ** Phacelia *Su*
  * Bitterbrush *Su*
  * Pine *Su*
  * Onion *Su*
  * Manzanita *F*
  * Cinquefoil *Su*
  * Oak *F*
  * Dock *Su*
  * Collomia *Su*
  + Bedstraw, Blueberry, Service-berry, Turkeymullein

Reference: The Natural History and Behavior of the Western Chipmunk and the Mantled Ground Squirrel. Kenneth Gordon. Oregon State College Studies in Zoology, 1943. 104 pp.

COLUMBIAN GROUND SQUIRREL
Citellus columbianus

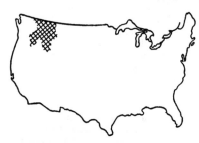

The Columbian ground squirrel covers a relatively limited range in southern Canada, western Montana, and eastern Oregon. It is found in a wide variety of situations, from farmlands or rough open areas to partly wooded slopes and mountain meadows. This species is regarded as one of the chief disseminators of Rocky Mountain spotted fever.

Animal food: A few grasshoppers, beetles, caterpillars, and other insects are eaten.

Plant food: A great variety of herbage, flowers, seeds, bulbs, and fruits are eaten by these squirrels. In addition to the items tabulated below, the following have been reported as fed upon: the bulbs of wild camas, wild onion, and glacierlily, flowers and other parts of false-hellebore, camas, lupine, buttercups, and wildlettuce, and fruits of currants, gooseberries, strawberries, and serviceberries. Grain and forage crops are also relished.

Northern Mt.–Desert, 22 (0-12-10-0)
 plus observations
 ** Wyethia, flw. *Sp*
 ** Other flowers *Sp*
 ** Tarweed *F*
 ** Turkeymullein *F*

248

** Oak *F*
** Filaree, veg. and sd. *F*

* Buffaloberry *Su*
* Gilia *Su*

RICHARDSON GROUND SQUIRREL
Citellus richardsoni

The Richardson ground squirrel, also known as the flickertail or yellow ground squirrel, is a northern species that ranges from southern Saskatchewan and Alberta into the Dakotas, Montana, Wyoming, and Nevada. It is partial to open grassy prairies and to the level flood plains of streams and lakes, but is also found among sagebrush and greasewood.

Animal food: Like other ground squirrels this one is almost entirely vegetarian. It feeds to only a limited extent on grasshoppers and caterpillars and occasionally takes mice and birds.

Plant food: Seeds and foliage of herbaceous plants are the mainstay of the Richardson ground squirrel. Seeds of wheat and other grains are also used extensively when available.

Northern Prairies, 35 (0-4-31-0)
** Goosefoot *Su*
** Wheat *Su*
* Bluegrass, blade *Su*
* Dandelion *Su*
* Sunflower *Su*
* Knotweed *Su*
* Cinquefoil *Su*

THIRTEEN-LINED GROUND SQUIRREL
Citellus tridecemlineatus

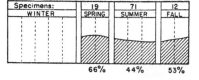

The thirteen-lined ground squirrel is widely distributed in the Prairie region of the United States and Canada, extending as far eastward as the Great Lakes states.

This species is regarded as less destructive economically than some of its relatives. Agricultural crops, particularly wheat, corn, and oats, are raided locally, but in the main these ground squirrels subsist on wild plants. On grazing ranges they are regarded as beneficial because of their fondness for grasshoppers and other insects.

Animal food: Animal food makes up a larger proportion of the diet than in most ground squirrels. Grasshoppers

are the number one animal item, though it also eats other insects and their larvae. Mice or birds are fed upon occasionally, sometimes as carrion.

Plant food: The seeds of many different kinds of wild and cultivated plants are eaten. Numerous other species besides those listed below are utilized to a limited extent.

Prairies, 102 (0-19-71-12) plus observations
*** Ragweed *FW*
** Knotweed *FSp*
** Bristlegrass *SuF*
** Sunflower *F*
** Clover *Su*
* Wheat *SpSu*
* Needlegrass *Su*
* Pricklypear *Su*
* Russianthistle *SuF*

249

FRANKLIN GROUND SQUIRREL
Citellus franklini

The Franklin ground squirrel, also known as gray gopher, is a comparatively eastern species, its range extending from the Canadian prairies to Oklahoma and Illinois. Generally the economic losses from this species are minor, because of its local distribution and usually limited numbers.

Animal food: While insects such as beetles, grasshoppers, and caterpillars are the principal animal foods, birds and their eggs, mice, and even young rabbits are sometimes eaten.

Plant food: Plant materials constitute about two-thirds of the diet. Seeds and foliage of weeds, grasses, and crop plants are the main items.

Northern Prairies, 30 (0-4-26-0) plus observations
 ** Cocklebur *Su*
 * Needlegrass *Su*
 + Basswood, Strawberry

ANTELOPE GROUND SQUIRREL
Citellus leucurus

The name antelope ground squirrel is, for present purposes, used exclusively for this particular species though two others, the Harris and Nelson ground squirrels, also belong to the antelope ground squirrel group. This species, has a far more extensive range in the United States than its two close relatives mentioned above.

These small, grayish, white-lined ground squirrels are desert inhabitants and therefore have little importance to agriculture. Their food consists largely of seeds and fruits of herbaceous or shrubby plants, but insects and small animals are also relished.

Mt.–Desert and California, 22 (6-3-6-7)
 *** Pricklypear *SuFW*
 ** Pine *F*
 ** Saltgrass *Sp*
 * Russianthistle *F*
 * Paloverde *W*
 * Four-o'clock *F*
 * Cedar *Su*
 * Yucca *W*
 + Saltbush

NELSON GROUND SQUIRREL
Citellus nelsoni

This ground squirrel has an isolated and very restricted range in the San Joaquin Valley of California. The name San Joaquin antelope squirrel has also been applied to it. Information on its foods is very limited, but apparently, like its related species, it depends largely on seeds of common plants.

California, 5 (0-2-0-3)
**** Turkeymullein *F*

**** Filaree *Sp*
*** Barley *F*

HARRIS GROUND SQUIRREL
Citellus harrisii

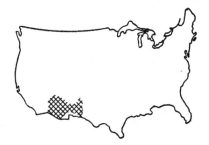

The Harris ground squirrel is a close relative of the antelope and Nelson ground squirrels. Like them, it has

little economic importance since deserts are its typical habitat. Though it subsists primarily on seeds of native shrubs and herbs, it also feeds on insects and flesh. Three specimens collected on the same day at Parker, Ariz., were full of fish remains.

Arizona, 17 (6-10-1-0)
***** (65%) Pricklypear, flw. and sd.
        SpSu
  ** Mesquite *Su*
  ** Gooseberry *W*
  ** Paloverde *W*
  ** Grasses *W*

PRAIRIE DOGS. Prairie dogs, like their burrowing relatives the ground squirrels, are native to the semiarid, open areas of the West. Four species of these chubby ground rodents are generally recognized. Food data for three species are presented below. The fourth, the Utah prairie dog, is restricted to Iron County, Utah.

These picturesque animals are not nearly so abundant as they were formerly—mainly because of campaigns for their reduction. Prairie dogs are almost entirely vegetarian in diet, and where their numbers are great they compete with cattle and other livestock in the use of range forage. Also, their burrows occasionally cause injury to horses and farm equipment. In places, however, they have been found to destroy weeds with resulting benefit to range grasses, especially gramagrass. Because of the public's strong interest in these animals, it would be regrettable if representative colonies of them were not protected in non-agricultural locations.

Reference: A Systematic Account of the Prairie-dogs. N. Hollister. *No. Amer. Fauna* 40, 1916. 37 pp.

BLACK-TAILED PRAIRIE DOG
Cynomys ludovicianus

This is by far the most widespread species of prairie dog and is the one with which most people are familiar. The black tip of its tail distinguishes it from the other species.
Animal food: Slight use is made of insects when they are available in abundance. Grasshoppers and noctuid larvae are prominent items.
Plant food: Almost any kind of green

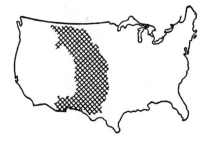

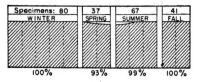

Specimens: 80	37	67	41
WINTER	SPRING	SUMMER	FALL
100%	93%	99%	100%

vegetation in the vicinity of their tunnels is eaten by these prairie dogs.

Western Prairies, 225 (80-37-67-41)
  ** Wheatgrass *SuFWSp*
  ** Russianthistle *FWSp*
   * Bromegrass *SuFWSp*
   * Fescuegrass *SuFWSp*

   * Bluegrass *SuFWSp*
   * Gramagrass *SuFWSp*
   * Barley, Little Wild *SuFWSp*
   * Pricklypear, lf. and fr. *SuFWSp*
   * Saltbush, lf. *WSp*
   * Cogswellia, lf. *Sp*
   * Globemallow, Scarlet, fr. *SuFWSp*
   * Sagebrush, lf. *FW*
   + Twinpod, Knotweed, Plantain, Sunflower, Tansymustard, Nightshade

WHITE-TAILED PRAIRIE DOG
Cynomys leucurus

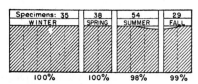

Specimens: 35	38	54	29
WINTER	SPRING	SUMMER	FALL
100%	100%	98%	99%

weeds and grasses are eaten commonly by this species.

This species and its allies, the Gunnison and Utah prairie dogs, inhabit higher altitudes than the blacktail. Plateaus or tableland areas among the Rocky Mountains are the usual sites for their towns.

Animal food: Such insects as are common in and around the burrows are taken in summer and early fall, particularly grubs and adult beetles, lepidopterous larvae, and grasshoppers.

Plant food: Shrubby plants as well as

Wyoming and Montana, 156 (35-38-54-29)
 **** Saltbush, lf. *SpSuFW*
 *** Russianthistle, lf. *SpSuFW*
  ** Wheatgrass *SuFWSp*
  ** Sagebrush, lf. and flw. *SpFW*
  ** Onion, bulb *SuF*
   * Bluegrass, *SuFWSp*
   * Pricklypear, fr. and sd. *FW*
   * Wheat, grain *F*
   * Globemallow *SuF*
   + Tansymustard, Hawksbeard, Blue Wildlettuce, Fescuegrass, Bromegrass

GUNNISON PRAIRIE DOG
Cynomys gunnisoni

This prairie dog is closely related to the whitetail but is slightly darker and is restricted to the southern Rocky Mountains.

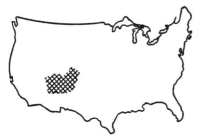

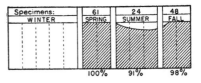

Specimens:	61	24	48
WINTER	SPRING	SUMMER	FALL

100% 91% 98%

*** Dandelion, flw. and bud *SpSu*
*** Russianthistle *FSuSp*
** Wheatgrass *SpSuF*
** Nightshade, lf. and fr. *SpSuF*
* Gramagrass *SpSuF*
* Dropseedgrass *SpSuF*
* Eriogonum, lf. *SpSuF*
+ Three-awn, Hilaria, Plantain, Greasewood, Morning-glory, Thistle, Microsteris, Alfalfa

Animal food: Insects constitute a slightly larger proportion of the summer diet of this species than in other prairie dogs. Grasshoppers, beetles, and lepidopterous larvae are especially common items.

Plant food:
Southwest, 133 (0-61-24-48)

CHIPMUNKS. Until recently, chipmunks were divided into two genera: eastern, *Tamias*, and the other mainly western, *Eutamias*. Now, all are placed in the single genus *Tamias*. The eastern chipmunk includes only a single species, while the western has about 16. These attractive, lively rodents are widely distributed but are absent from the Gulf region, much of the prairies—especially to the south—and from desert areas of the Southwest.

Chipmunks are at home both on the ground and in trees. In this regard as well as in others, they are intermediate between the tree squirrels and ground squirrels. Their dens consist of holes in the ground, and it is on the ground that they do most of their feeding.

Nuts and fruits of woody plants are prominent foods of chipmunks, but seeds of weeds and crop plants are also used extensively. The diet is mainly vegetarian, but insects and various other forms of animal life are also taken. The feeding activities of chipmunks are of practically no economic importance to man.

Reference: Revision of the American Chipmunks. Arthur H. Howell. *No. Amer. Fauna* 52, 1929. 157 pp.

WESTERN CHIPMUNKS
Eight species of *Tamias*

Aside from the information for the northwest and least chipmunks, treated below, there are some limited food data from eight other western species. Because of the scant data for the various species, the information from these eight has been combined. The tabulation shows that seeds and fruits are their primary food, but a limited number of insects are eaten.

Mt.–Desert and Pacific, 48 stomachs and cheek pouches (0-0-30-18)

**** Pine *SuF*
** Pricklypear *SuF*

** Manzanita *SuF*
** Sedge *Su*
* Ceanothus *SuF*
* Bromegrass *SuF*
* Fungus *SuF*
* Serviceberry *Su*
* Sumac *Su*

* Oak *Su*
* Cherry, Wild *Su*
* Cedar *Su*
* Gooseberry *Su*
* Fir *F*
+ Needlegrass, Knotweed, Black-
  berry, Fireweed

NORTHWEST CHIPMUNK
Tamias amoenus

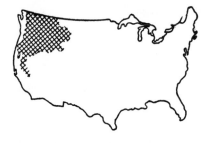

This richly colored, bright-striped species of the Northwest is similar and closely related to the least chipmunk. The northwest chipmunk eats some insects, both adults and larvae, but it subsists mainly on seeds of herbaceous and woody plants.

Pacific Northwest, 29 cheek pouches (0-5-18-6)
*** Pine *F*
** Fireweed *SuSp*
** Serviceberry *Su*
** Tarweed *SuSp*
** Bromegrass *SuF*
* Bitterbrush *Su*
* Ceanothus *SuF*
* Needlegrass *Su*
* Geranium, Wild *Su*
* Buffaloberry *Su*
* Selfheal *Su*
* Dandelion *Sp*
+ Sedge

Reference: The Natural History and Behavior of the Western Chipmunk and the Mantled Ground Squirrel. Kenneth Gordon. Oregon State College Studies in Zoology, 1943. 104 pp.

LEAST CHIPMUNK
Tamias minimus

The least chipmunk is a small, brightly colored, widespread species. It is probably the most common of the 16 western chipmunks. Its various subspecies include the Lake Superior chipmunk which occurs as far east as Michigan.

During the warm seasons, nearly half of this chipmunk's food consists of insects. In the main, however, seeds and fruits are its principal fare.

Minnesota, 71 stomachs and 31 pouches, August and September
*** Blackberry
*** Blueberry
** Smartweed
** Pearlberry
* Geranium, Wild
Western Prairies and *Mt.–Desert*, 32 cheek pouches and stomachs (0-0-24-8)

*** Bitterbrush *F*
*** Wheat *F*
** Sedge *SuFW*
** Gooseberry *Su*
** Knotweed *SuF*
** Cinquefoil *FW*
** Cherry, Wild *SuF*
** Ragweed *F*

* Buffaloberry *Su*
* Dandelion *Su*
* Bromegrass *Su*
* Sunflower *Su*
* Sagebrush *Su*
* Ricegrass *Su*
* Goosefoot *Su*

EASTERN CHIPMUNK
Tamias striatus

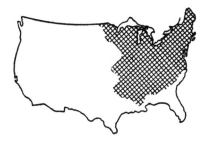

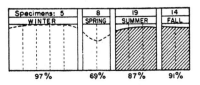

Specimens: 5	8	19	14
WINTER	SPRING	SUMMER	FALL
97%	69%	87%	91%

The wide-ranging eastern chipmunk is partial to fences and stone walls—in or near open woods, but may be found in a wide variety of situations. The chipmunk is a busy storer of reserve food supplies and may often be seen with its cheeks stuffed with food destined for its underground cache.

Animal food: Though chiefly vegetarian, the eastern chipmunk is known to eat mice, insects, small birds and eggs, snails, and occasionally small snakes.

Plant food: Seeds or nuts of woody plants are the principal fare, but corn, wheat, and other crop plants as well as seeds of weedy plants are taken.

Northeast, 46 (5-8-19-14)
** Maple *SpSuF*
** Hickory *FW*
** Oak *FW*
** Hazelnut *SuF*
** Basswood *SuFSp*
** Beech *FSp*
* Cherry, Wild *SuSp*
* Corn *SuF*
* Blackberry *Su*
* Viburnum *F*
* Wheat *SuF*
* Chinkapin *SuSp*
* Dogwood, Flowering *F*
+ Aralia, Buttercup, Sweetgum, Strawberry

Reference: The Habits and Life History of the Eastern Chipmunk. Elsa G. Allen. *N.Y. State Museum Bul.*, 1938. 122 pp.

Pocket Gophers: *Geomyidae*

POCKET GOPHERS. Pocket gophers, like their insectivore counterparts, the moles, are our only rodents that are well adapted to continuous subterranean life. Their long foreclaws, stocky body, small ears, and short tail and even their feeding habits are all suited to an existence in underground burrows.

There are two principal genera of gophers, *Geomys*, eastern, and *Thomomys*, western, with many species and hundreds of subspecies. Their range covers most of the United States except the Northeast.

The diet of pocket gophers is entirely vegetarian and consists largely of roots, rootstocks, and bulbs. Seeds and nuts are also eaten when available near the burrow doors. They are sometimes stored in caches for future use. Finely chewed roots and underground stems of plants are difficult to identify, and for this reason the listings presented below are short. Apparently the animals can and do subsist on almost any plants which grow in the vicinity of their burrows. On farms and orchards, gophers are often destructive and require control.

References: The Pocket Gopher. Theo. H. Scheffer. *U.S. Dept. Agr. Bul.* 172, 1910. 35 pp.
Distribution and Variation of Pocket Gophers in the Southwestern United States. Wm. B. Davis. *Texas Agr. Exp. Sta. Bul.* 590, 1940. 38 pp.

BOTTA POCKET GOPHER
Thomomys bottae

The Botta pocket gopher (named after an early European naturalist) becomes very destructive locally in the Southwest. The information presented below is based on foods found in cheek pouches or in food caches.

California, San Joaquin Exp. Range, 52 nests, 2 cheek pouches, and

89 storage chambers, collected mainly in December
*** Bromegrass
*** Oak
*** Brodiaea, bulb
*** Filaree, veg. and sd.
  * Bermudagrass, root
  * Fescuegrass, veg. and sd.
  + Wildbarley, Popcornflower, Toad Rush, Fiddleneck

WESTERN POCKET GOPHER
Thomomys talpoides

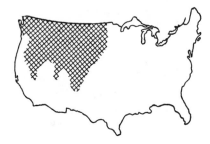

tion on foods of this species is based largely on studies in Montana and Utah. In an additional series of 31 stomachs from North Dakota, the contents were "mainly roots and unidentifiable vegetable pulp."

Montana, 158 (56-27-50-25)
  * Sagebrush *WSp*
  * Grasses *SpF*
  + Saltbush, Goosefoot, Pricklypear, Dandelion, Winterfat, Russianthistle
Utah, Manti National Forest, 7 caches
***** (67%) Dandelion, root
*** Springbeauty, bulb
*** Starwort, tuber
  * Dogtooth-violet, bulb
  + Oniongrass, Indianpotato, Saxifrage, Peavine

This species lacks a well-established common name. The designation "western" is not too suitable since there are other western pocket gophers. It is, however, one of the more important, widespread western species, covering the area shown on the map plus the Prairie region of Canada. Our informa-

BROWN POCKET GOPHER
Thomomys fuscus

The brown pocket gopher is a northwestern species ranging from western

Montana to Washington and Oregon. A large proportion of the stomach contents were unidentified beyond the point that they were "roots and other vegetative material."

Montana, 171 (64-30-49-28)
 * Grasses, stem and lf. *SpF*

 * Goosefoot *FSp*
 * Sagebrush *FW*
 * Russianthistle *Sp*
 + Pussytoes, Saltbush, Prickly-pear, Falsemallow

EASTERN POCKET GOPHERS
Geomys

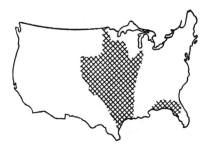

This genus of about 10 species occurs principally in the eastern part of the Prairies and along parts of the Gulf coast. There are, however, no pocket gophers at all in the eastern United States east and north of the range shown on the map. A closely related genus, the chestnut-faced pocket gopher (*Cratogeomys*), adjoins the eastern pocket gopher in the southwest, from Texas and eastern New Mexico to southeastern Colorado.

Little definite information is available on the foods of the eastern pocket gophers. They are recognized as being destructive to alfalfa and other farm crops in the Prairies and are known also to feed on foliage, stems, seeds, and underground parts of a great variety of plants including sunflowers, gayfeather, potatoes, corn, wheat, red clover, as well as on many garden vegetables. Their diet is entirely vegetarian.

Pocket Mice and Kangaroo Rats: *Heteromyidae*

POCKET MICE AND KANGAROO RATS. This family of burrowing rodents is strictly American and is confined to the arid parts of the West. The group is characterized by special, fur-lined cheek pouches, long hind legs, and a long, often tufted, tail. It includes four genera as follows:

Texas spiny mouse (*Liomys*) 1 sp.
Pocket mice (*Perognathus*)... 26 spp.
Kangaroo rats (*Dipodomys*).. 20 spp.

Dwarf pocket rats (*Microdipodops*)................. 4 spp.

The direct economic significance of these rodents is comparatively slight—mainly because they inhabit deserts and semiarid areas. They are almost entirely vegetarian, subsisting mainly on seeds, but occasionally consuming some foliage and a few insects. The food-ratio diagram for 106 kangaroo rats of different species helps to indicate their relative use of plant and animal food.

Reference: Life History of the Kangaroo Rat. Charles T. Vorhies and Walter P. Taylor. *U.S. Dept. Agr. Bul.* 1091, 1922. 40 pp.

POCKET MICE
Perognathus

As their name "mice" implies, these attractive rodents of the deserts and prairies are smaller than their relatives, the kangaroo rats or pocket rats. They are almost exclusively seed eaters, storing seeds temporarily in their ex-

ternal cheek pouches and then trans-
ferring them to underground storage
deposits. Insects are rarely eaten.

Western Prairies and Mt.–Desert, 59
(11-6-27-15)
   *** Mesquite *SuFW*
   ** Locoweed *SuSp*
   ** Creosote *SuSp*
   ** Beeplant *Su*
   ** Pigweed *SuF*

  ** Cedar *SuW*
   * Fescuegrass *SuSp*
   * Saltbush *W*
   * Pricklypears *SuFW*
   * Bromegrass *Sp*
   * Morning-glory *FW*
   * Bristlegrass *F*
   * Sunflower *F*
   * Plantain *SuW*
   * Deervetch *Su*
   * Barley *F*
   * Russianthistle *F*
   + Nightshade, Knotweed, Sage-
      brush
California, 19 (3-0-8-8)
  *** Poison-oak *FW*
  *** Filaree *SuF*
  *** Deervetch *SuW*
   * Ryegrass *F*
   * Oats *Su*
   * Nightshade *Su*
   * Bitterbrush *Su*
   + Saltbush, Knotweed

CALIFORNIA KANGAROO RATS
Dipodomys

Special studies on kangaroo rats in
the San Joaquin Valley of California
provided the information presented
below.

California, San Joaquin Exp. Range,
264 burrow deposits plus 117
cheek pouches in summer, fall,
and January

**** Bromegrass, sd. and lf. *WSuF*
**** Filaree, sd. and lf. *WSuF*
  ** Fescuegrass, sd. and lf. *WSuF*
   + Deervetch, Redmaids, Wildbar-
     ley, Turkeymullein, Pine,
     Popcornflower, Minerslet-
     tuce, Oak, Lupine

BANNER-TAILED KANGAROO RAT
Dipodomys spectabilis

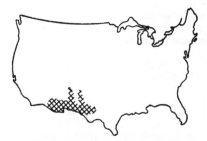

This southwestern species is also
known as the large kangaroo rat be-

cause of its greater size, or as the
spectacled kangaroo rat because of the
distinct dark marking around the eyes.
Its extensive mounds, as much as 3
feet high and 15 feet in diameter, are
often located along stream courses in
the deserts. Seeds are eaten almost
exclusively, but foliage is also taken
to a limited extent.

Arizona, 157 dens (73-17-34-33)
**** Gramagrass
 *** Three-awn
   * Locoweed

* Mesquite
* Snakeweed
* Deervetch
* Triodia
* Bladderpod
+ Goldenweed, Pigweed, California-poppy, Filaree, Dock, Peppergrass, Lovegrass, Spiderling, Plantain, Nightshade, Carpetweed

Reference: Sources of Water Supply for Desert Animals. Vernon Bailey. *Scientific Monthly*, Vol. 17(1); pp. 66–86, 1923.

MERRIAM KANGAROO RAT
Dipodomys merriami

This is a comparatively small kangaroo rat occurring in the same region as the bannertail and also farther west. Weed seeds constitute a large proportion of its food.

Southwest, 35 (2-13-9-11)

*** Pigweed *Sp*
** Fescuegrass *Su*
** Plantain *SpSu*
 * Spiderling *SuF*
 * Mesquite *Su*
 * Paloverde *F*
 * Goosefoot *SpSu*
 * Creosote *Su*
 * Russianthistle *F*
 * Purslane *F*
 * Filaree *SpF*
 * Spurge *Sp*
 * Lupine *Sp*
 * Penstemon *Su*
 * Manzanita *F*
 * Gramagrass *F*
 + Pricklypear, Puncturevine, Datura, Barley

ORD KANGAROO RAT
Dipodomys ordii

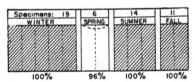

Specimens: 19	6	14	11
WINTER	SPRING	SUMMER	FALL
100%	96%	100%	100%

interesting animals are like the kangaroo in using only their hind legs and tail for hopping about.

West, 60 (19-16-14-11)
*** Sorghum *W*
 * Purslane *FW*
 * Crownbeard, Golden *FW*

The Ord kangaroo rat has a comparatively wide range in the plains and deserts of the Southwest. These

259

* Pigweed *W*
* Pricklypear *Sp*
* Squirreltailgrass *Su*
* False Buffalograss *Su*
* Lycium *Su*
* Puncturevine *F*
* Bursage *FSp*

* Saltbush *Sp*
* Pluchea *Sp*
* Ragweed *Sp*
+ Wislizenia, Cyperus, Bristlegrass, Saltcedar, Deervetch, Dalea

Cricetid Family of Native Mice and Rats: *Cricetidae*

One of the most diverse and abundant groups of small mammals is this family which includes our native mice and rats. Many of the species are of only minor economic importance; others are limited in population or in range. The genera of the family are listed systematically below with a dagger (†) preceding those for which no food data are available.

Grasshopper mice (*Onychomys*)	2 spp.	Lemming mice (*Synaptomys*)	2 spp.
†Harvest mice (*Reithrodontomys*	7 spp.	†Lemming mice (*Phenacomys*)	4 spp.
†Baiomys mouse (*Baiomys*)	1 sp.	†Red-backed mice (*Clethrionomys*)	10 spp.
White-footed mice (*Peromyscus*)	14 spp.	Meadow mice (*Microtus* and *Lagurus*)	31 spp.
†Rice rats (*Oryzomys*)	2 spp.	Pine mice (*Pitymys*)	3 spp.
Cotton rats (*Sigmodon*)	3 spp.	†Florida water rat (*Neofiber*)	1 sp.
Wood rats (*Neotoma*)	10 spp.	Muskrat (*Ondatra*)	1 sp.

Included in this large group are the common field and meadow mice, which because of their great numbers can be injurious to farm crops and orchards. The only species of positive economic value is the muskrat, treated with the Fur and Game Mammals in Chap. Ten.

GRASSHOPPER MICE. This genus of two native species inhabits plains and other open areas of the West. Like their relatives, the white-footed mice, the grasshopper mice are whitish underneath but have proportionately shorter, thicker tails. They are primarily insectivorous, feeding on seeds and other plant materials only to a limited extent.

References: Life History and Habits of Grasshopper Mice. Vernon Bailey and Charles C. Sperry. *U.S. Dept. Agr. Bul.* 145, 1929. 19 pp.
A Systematic Account of the Grasshopper Mice. N. Hollister. *Proc. U.S. Nat. Museum*, Vol. 47, pp. 427–489, 1914.

WHITE-BELLIED GRASSHOPPER MOUSE
Onychomys leucogaster

This wide-ranging species has about 11 geographic subspecies in the arid and semiarid treeless plains and foothills of the West. Our information on the foods of the white-bellied grasshopper mouse is based on specimens obtained in the northern part of its range.

Animal food: These mice have a huge appetite for grasshoppers and crickets. Beetles, cocoons, caterpillars, cicadas, larvae and pupae of flies, spiders, and scorpions are also eaten. Mice, young of other small rodents, and lizards are killed and eagerly devoured.

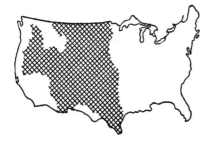

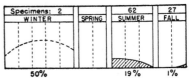

Plant food:
Northern Prairies, 91 (2-0-62-27)
   ** Wheat *SuW*
    * Bromegrass *Su*
    + Bristlegrass, Barley, Needle-
      grass

TROPICAL GRASSHOPPER MOUSE
Onychomys torridus

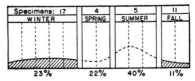

The tropical grasshopper mouse is not only more southerly in its range but is also smaller in size and longer tailed than its relative, the white-bellied grasshopper mouse. Its seven subspecies live in the open desert of the Southwest.

Animal food: As in the whitebelly, insects of various kinds constitute a major part of the diet.

Plant food:
West, 37 (17-4-5-11)
   * Wheat *W*
   * Russianthistle *F*

WHITE-FOOTED MICE
Peromyscus

The 14 species and 57 subspecies of white-footed mice in the United States are only a small part of this large North and Central American genus. It is estimated that there are about 150 species and subspecies in the New World. Their range in the United States extends across both forested and open country.

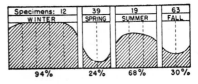

The versatile diet of the white-footed mouse, also known in some localities as deer mouse, reflects the local availability of foods, both plant and animal, at various seasons.

Animal foods: Large insects such as grasshoppers, beetles, moths, crane-flies, caterpillars and cocoons, and a host of other insects are commonly eaten. Snails and centipedes also contribute to the fare, and even small mammals and birds are eaten on occasion.

Plant food: Seeds, fruits, and roots or tubers are the principal plant parts used as food.

261

East, 72 (16-41-9-6) plus observations
** Oak *FW*
** Blueberry *Su*
* Knotweed *F*
* Maple *SuF*
* Pine *FW*
* Tuliptree *F*
* Hogpeanut, tuber *SuF*
* Cherry, Wild *F*
* Corn *F*
+ Dogwood, Springbeauty, Violet, Toothwort, Fir, Magnolia, Dock, Hickory, Jewelweed, Rhododendron, Beech

West, 80 (2-0-10-68) plus observations
** Cedar *FW*
** Pine *FW*
* Oak *FW*
* Russianthistle *F*
* Corn *F*
+ Sunflower, Groundcherry, Three-awn, Knotweed, Maple

COTTON RAT
Sigmodon hispidus

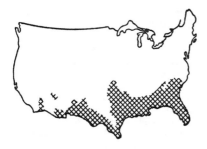

In their favorite habitats (grassy clearings, croplands, and fields overgrown with broomsedge) these small-eared, long-tailed rodents are probably the most abundant small mammals of the Southeast. There are two additional species near our southwestern border and numerous others in Mexico and farther southward into South America.

Information on the diet of the cotton rats is limited to field observations. Their diet is largely vegetarian, consisting of stems, foliage, and seeds of various agricultural and wild plants. Among crop plants damaged are sweet potatoes, corn, peanuts, tomatoes, sugarcane, squash, carrots, and cotton. Sometimes these depredations entail serious economic losses.

WOOD RATS. One of the distinctive traits of wood rats or pack rats, as they are frequently called, is their habit of making large nests of twigs, leaves, and other materials. Two species of wood rats occur in the East and eight in the West.

Ordinarily wood rats do not invade human habitations. They have relatively little economic importance and do not use farm crops to any great extent. The diet of wood rats is almost entirely vegetarian: the plant materials used are quite diverse—principally foliage, seeds, nuts, and underground parts.

References: Biotic Relations of the Wood Rat. Elden H. Vestal. *Journ. Mammalogy,* Vol. 19 (1), pp. 1–36, 1938.
A Life History Sketch of the Allegheny Wood Rat. Earl L. Poole. *Journ. Mammalogy,* Vol. 21 (3), pp. 249–270, 1940.

EASTERN WOOD RAT
Neotoma floridana

The name "eastern" as applied to this wood rat is not so much of a misnomer as "Florida" in its specific name. Its principal abundance is in the lower Mississippi Valley region and adjoining prairies.

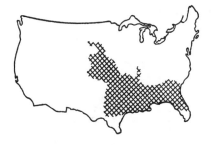

Animal food: Insects are occasionally picked up, but they constitute a very minor part of the diet.

Plant food:
Southern Prairies, 14 (1-1-7-5) plus
  observations
  ** Oak
   * Greenbrier
   * Goldenrod, rootstock
   * Pricklypear
   * Cedar
   + Sumac, Mesquite, Walnut

WHITE-THROATED WOOD RAT
Neotoma albigula

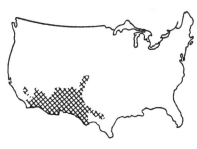

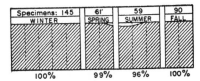

Specimens: 145	61'	59	90
WINTER	SPRING	SUMMER	FALL
100%	99%	96%	100%

trace, rarely more than 1%. Beetles and ants occur most often.

Plant food: The whitethroat appears partial to seeds and fruits though it also feeds on green parts of plants.

This southwestern species adjusts to local availability of material that can serve as shelter. In rocky hills they use rock piles as homes, in wooded areas they build piles of sticks, and in the desert nests are often made from cacti or other thorny shrubs.

Animal food: Though insects are found in many stomachs, they usually are a

Arizona, 355 (145-61-59-90) plus observations
  **** Mesquite, pod and lf. FWSpSu
  **** Pricklypear, fr. SuFWSp
    ** Giantcactus, fr. Su
     * Acacia, Catclaw
     * Carpetweed, plant F
     + Spiderling, Sagebrush, Eriogonum

Reference: Life History and Ecology of the White-throated Wood Rat. Charles T. Vorhies and Walter P. Taylor. University of Arizona, 1940. 74 pp.

COOPER LEMMING MOUSE
Synaptomys cooperi

The lemming mouse is largely boreal; yet one species, the Cooper lemming mouse, has a range extending throughout practically all the Northeast. This seldom-seen mouse is found in a wide variety of situations including bogs and lake margins as well as hillsides and open pastures.

The habits of the Cooper lemming mouse are little known. As to its feeding, stomach examinations of 23 specimens and field observations indicate that the green blades of grasses supply about nine-tenths of the food. Sedges, white clover, buttercups, sunflower tubers, mosses, and fleshy fungi are also eaten.

MEADOW MOUSE
Microtus

The meadow mouse, also called field mouse or meadow vole, is represented by numerous species and subspecies. It is one of our most abundant rodents. These mice are partial to open areas including meadows, farms, wastelands, and clearings in woods. On agricultural lands they sometimes cause damage to grain crops, pastures, and orchards—especially when the species has reached a population peak.

Meadow mice are almost entirely vegetarian. They subsist on foliage, roots, twigs, and bark and, to a limited extent, on seeds. Stomach analyses of their finely chewed food have given only meager data to supplement observations. Among the items noted in

use are the following: corn, barley, wheat, oats, clover, alfalfa, bluegrass, broomsedge, bulrush, dock, strawberry, buttercup, goldenrod, rosinweed, ragweed, sunflower, willow, maple, poplar, oak, and apple.

PINE MOUSE
Pitymys pinetorum

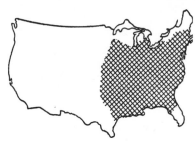

This close relative of the meadow mouse differs in having a shorter tail, shorter, denser fur, and is more subterranean in its habits. The pine mouse is partial to woodlands and brushy areas. It also invades orchards and gardens. In the former it frequently

does damage to the roots and bark of apple or other trees.

Pine mice feed both aboveground and below the surface on roots, underground stems, leaves, seeds, and fruits. Apparently they are largely vegetarian, but snails are eaten frequently. Among garden vegetables consumed are carrots, beets, rhubarb, beans, celery, parsnips, turnips, rutabaga, potatoes, and corn. Other plants used for food include: clover (stem and leaves), hawthorn (fruit), violet (rootstock), buttercup (stem), grasses, wildcarrot (root and leaves), dandelion (root and leaves), apple (root, stem, and fruit), goldenrod (rootstock), persimmon (seeds), groundcherry (fruit), yarrow (leaves), dutchmans-breeches (tuber), and sheepsorrel (leaves).

Introduced Mice and Rats: *Muridae*

HOUSE MOUSE. The well-known house mouse consists of a single widespread species that originally came from the Old World. Besides being uninvited tenants in our homes, house mice live wild in the fields in many places.

There is no question about the economic status of house mice. Everyone agrees that they are destructive pests. Their food consists of almost anything that man relishes. They are partial to cereal products, cooked or raw, and, as everyone knows, to cheese. Peanut butter is particularly attractive to them.

HOUSE RAT. Man has been waging war against rats for centuries, but they are still numerous wherever men congregate, on sea as well as on land. These rodent immigrants from the Old World not only cause millions of dollars of annual loss or damage to various stored products, but also spread several serious diseases that affect mankind. To most people the name "rodent" has become synonymous with the despicable rat. This, unfortunately, has led to serious prejudice against many harmless members of the rodent group.

The common house rat is more specifically known as the Norway rat (*Rattus norvegicus*). Two other forms, the black rat and the Alexandrine or roof rat, are also present locally but are not nearly so plentiful.

Rats are omnivorous in their diet, eating any plant and animal foods that are available.

Jumping Mice: *Zapodidae*

JUMPING MICE. Jumping mice are widely distributed in the northern half of the United States and northward to the Arctic Circle but are not abundant enough to be important economically. The family includes two genera, *Zapus* and *Napaeozapus*, with nine native species in the former and one in the latter.

These small acrobatic mice are characterized by long hind legs and long, slender tails. They are partial to meadows and other grassy areas. Little is known about their foods, but it is reported that they are largely vegetarian, feeding on foliage and stems as well as on seeds.

265

CHAPTER TWELVE

Hoofed Browsers

T HIS SMALL GROUP of mammals falls within a natural zoological unit—the order *Artiodactyla;* even-toed, hoofed mammals. All are ruminants (cud chewers) except the peccary. For our purposes the name "hoofed browsers" seems preferable. The group, as treated in this chapter, includes

Peccary	Black-tailed Deer	Bison
Elk	Moose	Bighorn
White-tailed Deer	Antelope	Mountain Goat
Mule Deer		

Hoofed browsers are almost exclusively plant eaters. The occasional insects noted in the contents of deer stomachs are probably consumed incidentally. Deer and elk feed largely on the more tender parts of woody plants, but other hoofed browsers such as bison, mountain sheep, and antelope forage extensively on grass and herbs. Acorns, persimmons, and other nuts or fruits are relished by deer, but it is the vegetative parts of plants, the foliage and twigs, that are the mainstay of the hoofed browsers' diet. Unless otherwise specified in this chapter's tables of food use, vegetative parts rather than seeds and fruits are the items eaten. Also, the ratio diagrams are omitted since these animals are 100% vegetarian in all seasons.

The significance of this big-game group is far out of proportion to the number of its species—even though some are now relatively rare and need protection. Deer are *the* big-game animals today, and it will be a long time before any other species challenges their importance to the hunter.

General References: Lives of Game Animals. Volume III. Ernest Thompson Seton. Doubleday & Company, Inc., New York, 1927.
American Mammals. W. J. Hamilton, Jr. McGraw-Hill Book Company, Inc., New York, 1939.
Field Book of North American Mammals. H. E. Anthony. G. P. Putnam's Sons, New York, 1928.
Wild Animals of North America. E. W. Nelson. National Geographic Society, 1930.
Mammals of North America. Victor H. Cahalane. The Macmillan Company, New York, 1947.

Peccaries: *Tayassuidae*

PECCARY
Pecari angulatus

The peccaries are New World animals. There are only two species, one of which, the collared peccary, occurs within the southern borders of the United States. This small pig-like animal formerly ranged as far northward

as Arkansas, but now it is limited to the southern parts of Texas, New Mexico, and Arizona. These interesting, shy inhabitants of thickets or lowland woods commonly travel in small bands.

The food of peccaries is likely to be quite diverse, depending on what is available. Like pigs, they are omnivorous, eating largely plant material but also consuming insects, worms, eggs, reptiles, toads, and other organisms. The food data available are based on local observations. More information on the natural foods of this animal is needed.

Texas and Arizona, fall observations
*** Oak, acorns
* Pricklypear, fr.

Deer Family: *Cervidae*

ELK (WAPITI)
Cervus canadensis

Three species of elk, or wapiti, have been recognized in the United States. One, the Arizona elk (*C. merriami*) of Arizona and New Mexico is now extinct, and the dwarf elk (*C. nannodes*) is restricted to a very small range in Kern County, Calif. The third species is the comparatively widespread, common elk (*C. canadensis*). Many zoologists prefer the less familiar name "wapiti" for this animal since elk, as used in Europe, refers to what we call moose.

This stately, large-antlered, northern deer occupies only a small fraction of its original range. In colonial days it was plentiful in the East and common in most other wooded parts of the country except in some sections of the South. Though its population is greatly depleted as compared with former times, this popular game animal is more than holding its own in areas where management has been provided. A colony of western elk recently established in Virginia is prospering.

Elk spend the summers in the mountains or hills and descend to the more protected lowlands for the winter. They frequent forests but are also partial to open areas in or near woodlands. Their food is entirely from plants:

267

browse from a wide variety of trees and shrubs and forage from grasses and other herbaceous plants.

Northern Mt.–Desert, 186 (131-23-11-21) plus observations
** Ceanothus, Snowbrush *WSp*
** Pine *WSp*
** Willow *WSp*
* Mountain-mahogany *W*
* Poplar *WSp*
* Wheatgrass *WSp*
* Bromegrass *W*

* Fescuegrass *W*
* Needlegrass *W*
* Sedge *WSp*
* Maple *W*
* Fir *W*
* Sagebrush *W*
* Douglasfir *W*
+ Muhlygrass, Koeleria, Wildrye, Melicgrass, Gramagrass, Serviceberry, Oak, Rabbitbrush, Birch, Spruce, Wild Cherry, Snowberry, Bitterbrush

References: Elk of the Northern Rocky Mountain Region. Raymond M. West. *U.S. Forest Service*, 1941. 32 pp.
The Elk of North America. Olaus J. Murie. Wildlife Management Institute; in press.

WHITE-TAILED DEER (VIRGINIA DEER)
Odocoileus virginianus

The genus *Odocoileus* is peculiar to the Americas. It includes the white-tailed, black-tailed, and mule deer, as well as other less-known species. The whitetail is the most widespread and important deer in the United States. As represented by its numerous subspecies, the white-tailed deer is present in practically all parts of the country except along the Pacific coast. This favorite game animal is, however, most abundant in the eastern woodlands. It is typically a forest dweller but often frequents glades or woodland openings while feeding. It also forages along forest margins and sometimes in orchards and farm land.

Whitetails have adapted themselves to present conditions so well that their abundance in some localities has produced special problems in wildlife management. When deer populations become excessive, damage to farms and forests may result, and in addition, their winter food may be reduced to the point where starvation results. Management programs are helping to maintain the white-tailed deer without the evils of overprotection.

Most of us have had opportunity to glimpse whitetails bounding away—a special treat, for the hunter and for anyone alert to beauty in nature. Deer are such choice game animals and are so widely distributed that they furnish sport for many thousands of hunters. Early records make it clear that they were extremely important as a source of food and clothing to eastern Indians and to our pioneer forefathers.

The whitetail is vegetarian, though Seton and others say they have been known to eat fish. A major proportion of the diet consists of twigs of shrubs and trees. Herbaceous plants, including weeds and grasses, are eaten frequently in summer. Acorns, blackgum fruits, persimmons, and other kinds of fruits are relished. Some of the plants browsed heavily by deer in the winter season represent necessity rather than choice. This is true in northern deer yards where the more palatable foods are depleted, and as a last resort, extensive use is made of starvation foods. It is for this reason that fir heads the list of foods eaten by deer in winter in Wisconsin and Minnesota. This also explains why, in some localities, pine, spruce, and alder are eaten in large quantities during the winter season. For a report on preference rating of deer foods in Wisconsin, see the listing on page 11.

Maine, Mt. Desert Is., observations, various seasons
*** Maple, Red and Striped
** Sweetfern
** Oak
** Blueberry
** Blackberry
* Arborvitae
* Huckleberry
* Spiraea
* Sumac
+ Viburnum, Poplar

New York, Ithaca region, winter observations
**** Maple
** Witch-hazel
** Sumac
** Aspen
* Birch
* Dogwood
* Viburnum
* Oak
* Ash
* Willow
* Basswood
* Cherry, Wild
* Hornbeam
* Apple
+ Blackberry, Serviceberry, Hazelnut, Hawthorn, Bush Honeysuckle, Beech, Sweetfern, Hop-hornbeam, White Pine, Sassafras, Meadowsweet, Hemlock, Elm, Blueberry

Pennsylvania, 27 (15-2-3-7) plus observations
*** Maple *SuFWSp*
** Sweetfern *WSpF*
** Hemlock *WSp*

** Willow *WSpF*
** Wintergreen *FW*
* Grasses *FW*
* Holly *Sp*
* Oak *FW*
* Mountainlaurel *W*
* Ceanothus *SuF*
* Fern, incl. Woodfern *W*
* Cherry, Wild *SuF*
+ Milkwort, Pine, Goldenrod, Apple, Chokeberry, Serviceberry, Poplar, Blackberry

Wisconsin and Minnesota, 570 (554-16-0-0)
*** Fir *WSp*
*** Arborvitae *WSp*
*** Poplar *W*
** Hemlock *WSp*
** Pine *WSp*
** Wintergreen *Sp*
* Alder *W*
* Willow *WSp*
* Bunchberry *W*
* Maple *W*
* Ferns *WSp*
+ Oak, Birch, Sweetfern, Leatherleaf, Fungus, Mountainlaurel, Labrador-tea, Spruce

Missouri, 19 (15-1-0-3)
**** Oak *FW*
*** Lespedeza *F*
*** Snowberry *FW*
** Grasses *WSp*
** Blackgum *W*
* Sumac *W*
* Pussytoes *W*
* Corn *W*
+ Greenbrier, Redcedar

North Carolina Mts., 73 (36-16-16-5)
*** Oak *SuFWSp*
*** Rhododendron *WSp*
** Greenbrier *SuFWSp*
** Maple *SuFWSp*
** Mountainlaurel *WSp*
** Galax *W*
* Grasses *SpSuF*
* Corn *SuF*
* Blueberry *W*
* Hollyfern *W*
* Pine *W*
* Apple *FW*
* Sourwood *FW*
* Dogwood *SuFW*

* Sedge *Sp*
+ Chestnut, Leucothoe, Fungus

North Carolina, Holly Shelter Refuge, 60 (13-4-1-42)
***** (65%) Swamp-ironwood *Sp-SuFW*
** Oak, acorns *FW*
* Blackgum, fr. and lf. *FW*
* Greenbrier, lf. and fr. *SpFW*
* Ferns *Su*
* Blueberry, Creeping *FW*
* Holly *FWSp*
+ Red Maple, Soybeans, Pine, Waxmyrtle, Chokeberry, Three-awn

Alabama, 309 (291-4-10-4)
**** Oak *FWSu*
** Greenbrier *FW*
* Pine *W*
* Sumac *W*
* Dogwood *W*
+ Crossvine, Jasmine, Panicgrass, Blueberry, Blackgum, Bayberry

Texas, Edwards Plateau, 103 (47-0-8-48)
***** (52%) Oak, Live *FW*
*** Persimmon, Black lf. and fr. *F*
** Redcedar *W*
** Snakeweed *F*
* Mistletoe *FW*
+ Pricklypear, Grasses, Mesquite, Greenbrier, Doveweed, Sorghum, Wildprivet

South Dakota, Black Hills, 140, all seasons
*** Bearberry *WSpSu*
*** Rose *SuFWSp*
** Aspen, Quaking *SpSu*
* Bluegrass *SpSuFW*
* Snowberry, Western *WSp*
* Pine, Ponderosa *WSp*
* Serviceberry *WSp*
* Wheatgrass *SpSuFW*
+ Creeping Barberry, Bur Oak, Dogwood, Pussytoes, Ceanothus

Montana, 101 (95-5-1-0)
*** Oregon-grape *W*
*** Pine *WSp*
** Spruce *WSp*
** Willow *WSp*
** Fir *W*
** Hemlock *W*
* Bearberry *W*
* Mountainlover *W*
* Douglasfir *W*
* Birch *W*
* Poplar *WSp*
* Alfalfa *WSp*
* Wheatgrass *W*
+ Cedar, Reedgrass, Ceanothus, Serviceberry, Twinflower, Arborvitae, Alder

References: Food Preferences and Requirements of the White-tailed Deer in New York State. *N.Y. State Conserv. Dept. and N.Y. State Col. of Agr. Bul.* 1, 1935. 35 pp.

White-tailed Deer. W. M. Newsom. Charles Scribner's Sons, New York, 1926. 288 pp.

Hunting North American Deer. Arthur H. Carhart. The Macmillan Company, New York, 1947. 232 pp.

The Pennsylvania Deer Problem. *Board of Game Commissioners, Commonwealth of Pennsylvania, Bul.* 12, 1930. 66 pp.

The White-tailed Deer on the Pisgah National Game Preserve, N.C. Frederick J. Ruff. 1939. 249 pp.

Michigan Deer. I. H. Bartlett. Michigan Dept. of Conservation, 1950. 50 pp.

A History of Wisconsin Deer. Ernest Swift. Wisconsin Conservation Dept., 1946. 96 pp.

MULE DEER
Odocoileus hemionus

The mule deer, a larger, heavier relative of the whitetail, with long mule-like ears, is the principal big-game species in the western states. Thousands of sportsmen hunt it every year. Its present range includes the

Pacific coast region, a large part of the Rocky Mountains, and some of the neighboring territory to the east. Mule deer still occur in the Dakotas but were formerly present as far southeastward as Kansas and Oklahoma. The habitat of this black-tailed, white-rumped deer varies markedly from wooded uplands to desert plateaus. In general, however, it prefers open, broken country and generally avoids heavy woodlands. In many places it moves to higher altitudes during the hot weather and returns to the foothills and valleys in the winter.

The mule deer is entirely vegetarian. It browses extensively on trees and shrubs, especially in winter, but it also consumes grasses and other herbaceous plants.

Nebraska, Nebr. Nat. Forest, 53 (53-0-0-0)
* **** Snowberry
* *** Pine, Jack
* *** Sunflower
* ** Rose, Wild
* * Cottonwood
* * Willow
* * Ash
* + Redcedar, Ceanothus, Choke-cherry, Poison-oak

South Dakota, 74 fall and winter
* *** Barberry, Creeping
* *** Bearberry
* ** Snowberry, Western
* ** Ceanothus, Snowbush
* ** Cedar
* * Bluegrass
* * Pussytoes
* * Rose

* * Clover
* + Serviceberry, Ponderosa Pine, Bur Oak, Willow, Twin-flower, Oats, Corn, Lichen

Northern Mt.–Desert, 367 (265-40-31-31)
* *** Serviceberry *SuF*
* *** Sagebrush *WSp*
* ** Oak *SuF*
* ** Fescuegrass *SpSu*
* ** Bluegrass *SpSu*
* ** Bromegrass *SpSu*
* ** Koeleria *SpSu*
* ** Needlegrass *SpSu*
* ** Wheatgrass *SpSu*
* ** Ricegrass *SpSu*
* ** Pine *WSp*
* ** Cherry, Wild *SuF*
* * Barberry *W*
* * Poplar (incl. Aspen) *F*
* * Mountainlover *F*
* * Douglasfir *WSp*
* * Snowberry *F*
* * Ceanothus *W*
* * Rabbitbrush *FW*
* * Bitterbrush *F*
* * Cedar *W*
* + Manzanita, Willow, Alfalfa, Phlox, Russianthistle

Southern Mt.–Desert (Ariz. and N. Mex.), 61 (10-3-25-23)
* *** Cedar *FW*
* *** Oak *SuF*
* *** Mountain-mahogany *WSpSuF*
* *** Cliffrose *F*
* ** Sagebrush *W*
* ** Fir *Su*
* ** Bitterbrush *Su*
* ** Poplar *F*
* ** Silktassel *SpSuF*
* ** Pine *F*
* * Needlegrass *SuF*
* * Gramagrass *SuF*
* * Lupine *Su*
* * Rose, Wild *Su*
* * Fendlera *W*
* * Paintbrush *F*
* + Rabbitbrush, Sotol, Knotweed, Locust, Dwarfmistletoe, Eriogonum, Mistletoe, Apacheplume

Oregon, Malheur Nat. Forest, winter observations

**** Bitterbrush
*** Mountain-mahogany, Curlleaf
*** Juniper, Sierra
** Rabbitbrush
** Sagebrush
** Ceanothus
California, observations in all seasons
**** Ceanothus *FW*
*** Oak *FWSp*
*** Deervetch *SpSu*
** Fescuegrass *SpSuFW*
** Manzanita *FWSp*
** Pine *SuFW*
** Cherry, Wild *F*
* Eriogonum *SuF*
* Knotweed *Su*
* Aspen, Quaking *F*

* Sedge *FWSu*
* Oats, Wild *WSp*
* Bluegrass *Su*
* Bromegrass *WSp*
* Thimbleberry *Su*
* Sagebrush *F*
* Dock, Curly *Su*
* Mountain-mahogany *W*
* Serviceberry *F*
* Elderberry *Su*
* Evening-primrose *Su*
* Dogwood *SuFWSp*
* Bitterbrush *W*
+ Filaree, Burclover, White Fir, Mesquite, Tesota, Currant, Gooseberry, Mustard, Yerbasanta

Reference: A Study of the Life History and Food of Mule Deer in California. Joseph S. Dixon. *Calif. Fish and Game*, Vol. 20, pp., 182–282 and 315–354, 1934.

BLACK-TAILED DEER (COAST DEER)
Odocoileus columbianus

The black-tailed deer is a somewhat smaller relative of the western mule deer. By some it is now regarded as a mule deer subspecies. The name "coast deer" is appropriate since this deer is confined to the long narrow coastal strip of forests extending from Sitka to San Diego. Two native forms are recognized. The Columbian blacktail, present in California, Oregon, and Washington, is the principal one in the United States. The southern blacktail is confined to an area south of San Francisco Bay. A third subspecies, the Sitka blacktail, is present in Alaska.

The blacktails, though of restricted natural range, are prolific—usually bearing twins. They are likely to maintain their numbers if their woodland habitat is not destroyed. Their spring and summer diet includes nearly equivalent amounts of woody browse and herbaceous vegetation.

California, 24 (2-13-9-0)
**** Oak *SpSu*
*** Filaree *Sp*
*** Bromegrass *SpSu*
*** Fescuegrass *SpSu*
*** Oats, Wild *SpSu*
** Manzanita *WSp*
** Ceanothus *SpSu*
** Mountain-mahogany *SpSu*
* Chamise *Su*
* Buckthorn *Sp*
* Buttercup *Sp*
+ Knotweed, Baccharis, Burclover

MOOSE
Alces americana

The moose, the largest of all deer, is a characteristic animal of the North. Its present range in this country is limited to the extreme northern borders, except in the Rockies. In former times it extended down into New York and Pennsylvania.

The typical habitat of the moose is coniferous or mixed woodlands interspersed with lakes, swamps, or streams. Most of the summer feeding of these animals is aquatic. They seek out tender herbaceous growths and are particularly fond of waterlilies and

pondweeds. In winter the feeding is largely on woody plants—especially willows, birch, aspen, and mountain-ash.

Maine to Michigan, observations
 *** Willow *SuW*
  ** Horsetail *WSp*
  ** Sedge *W*
  ** Poplar *W*
  ** Birch *W*
   * Alder *W*
   − Cowparsnip *Su*
   − Bluegrass *Su*
   − Wheatgrass *Su*
   − Maple *Sp*
   − Blackberry *Su*
   − Cherry, Wild *Su*
   − Waterlily *Su*
   − Pondweed *Su*
Michigan, Isle Royale, observations
 *** Aspen
 *** Birch, White
 *** Fir, Balsam
 *** Mountain-ash
  ** Willow
  ** Dogwood, Redosier

   * Maple
   * Yew (Ground Hemlock)
   * Serviceberry
   * Cherry, Fire
   * Waterlily
   * Hazelnut
   + Sumac, Pondweed, Sedge, Alder, Ash
Northern Mt.–Desert, winter observations
  ** Birch
  ** Mountain-ash
  ** Poplar
  ** Grasses
  ** Waterlily
  ** Deervetch
  ** Willow
   * Cherry, Wild
   * Fireweed
   * Maple
   * Alder
   * Dogwood
   * Labrador-tea
   * Fir
   + Pine

Reference: The Moose and its Ecology. N. W. Hosley. *U.S. Fish and Wildlife Service Leaflet* 312, 1949. 51 pp.

Antelope: *Antilocapridae*

PRONGHORN ANTELOPE
Antilocapra americana

The pronghorn is the only species of its genus. There are, however, two subspecies in Mexico.

Pronghorn antelopes prefer flat or rolling open country, particularly in the upland prairies and semiarid plains where sagebrush and grasses abound. They are also found in hilly regions and in the parks of the Rocky Mountains. Sheep and cattle using the western range have pushed the antelope back into limited areas and have usurped

273

the lowland domain that served best for winter survival. The present range of the remaining scattered bands is only about half of the former extent. The former population, comparable to the bison hordes, has been estimated at 20 to 40 million; but by 1908 only 17,000 antelope were left. Under management the population has increased to about 200,000 in 1948, and in several states, where open seasons have been instituted, the antelope is again a game animal. But in much of its range, it is still one of the threatened species needing continued attention.

True to its name, the pronghorn has simple branched or pronged horns. These are hollow and are shed each year. The animals are keensighted, alert, and possessed of inquisitiveness that is often their undoing. When frightened, they expose a white rump patch as they run away. Antelopes are reputed to run faster than any other native animal. In flight from an enemy they make prodigious leaps but will not tackle high obstacles, as deer do. In the North, pronghorns move seasonally to winter and summer ranges which may be several hundred miles apart. In the South they occupy more permanent areas which are limited to a radius of 10 or 15 miles.

Pronghorns, like other ruminants, are not known to take animal food purposely. Many kinds of plants are consumed, but particularly prominent in the diet are the foliage and twigs of woody species. Sagebrush is an outstanding antelope food. Grasses, weeds, and other nonwoody plants are also eaten freely. In very arid regions, succulent plants serve as the only source of water.

Northern Prairies and Mt.–Desert (excl. S. Dak. and S.E. Mont.), 111 (16-5-17-73) plus observations
**** Sagebrush *SuFWSp*
*** Rabbitbrush *SuFWSp*
** Saltbush *SuFW*
* Gramagrass *WSp*
* Wheatgrass *SuFW*
* Cedar *SuF*
* Mountain-mahogany *Su*
* Tansymustard *SuF*
* Pricklypear *SpSuF*
+ Bitterbrush, Phlox, Alfalfa, Russianthistle, Eveningprimrose, Globemallow, Spurge, Snakeweed, Penstemon, Buffalograss

South Dakota, 49 (August to October)
**** Sagebrush
*** Snowberry
** Rabbitbrush
** Alfalfa
* Knotweed
* Rose, Wild
+ Russianthistle, Milkweed, Sweetclover

Southeastern Montana, 24 (mainly fall)
***** (51%) Sagebrush
*** Snakeweed
*** Snowberry
* Wheatgrass
* Gramagrass
* Pricklypear
+ Saltbush, Greasewood, Bromegrass, Locoweed, Knotweed, Thistle, Mallow, Pigweed, Ragweed

New Mexico, 31 (1-0-4-26) plus observations
**** Sagebrush *SuFW*
*** Cedar *FW*
** Buffalograss *F*
** Wheatgrass *F*
** Broomsedge *F*

* Pricklypear *W*
* Phlox *F*
* Saltbush *F*
* Jointfir *F*
+ Pigweed, Gayfeather, Bitterbrush, Russianthistle, Locoweed

References: The Pronghorn Antelope and Its Management. Arthur S. Einarsen. Wildlife Management Institute, 1947. 256 pp.
The Pronghorn Antelope in California. Donald D. McLean. Calif. Fish and Game, 1944. 20 pp.

Bison, Mountain Sheep, Mountain Goat: *Bovidae*

AMERICAN BISON (BUFFALO)
Bison bison

The American bison, or buffalo, has come close to sharing the fate of its cousin the European bison. The latter species has been depleted to such an extent that it now consists only of specimens in zoos and preserves. The American bison was fast approaching that state when last-ditch conservation measures saved the depleted herds. The number of buffalo in colonial days was estimated at between 30 and 75 million, but by 1895 only a pitiful remnant of about 800 had survived. Since then, through Federal, state, and private action, the total numbers in this country and Canada have increased to more than 15,000. Of the present bison population, a considerable proportion of those in Canada belong to the subspecies known as the wood bison. Another subspecies, the eastern bison, formerly present in the eastern states, is now extinct.

With the destruction of the great herds of bison, one of the most characteristic species of wildlife of this country went into retirement. The domestic economy of many Indian tribes in the western plains had been based largely on the buffalo. The food, clothing, and shelter of the aborigines came from this source, and their customs and folklore centered on these animals.

The food of bison, like that of other ruminants, is entirely plant life. The limited data from two different herds indicate that the diet consists largely of grasses.

Oklahoma, Wichita Refuge, observations
*** Gramagrass, Blue *SpSuF*
*** Dropseedgrass, Sand *SpSuF*
** Windmillgrass, Tumble *Su*
** Paspalum *Sp*
* Buffalograss *F*
* Bluestem, Little *F*
Arizona, 7 (7-0-0-0)
***** (71%) Saltbush
** Gramagrass
** Hilaria
* Jointfir

Reference: The American Bison. Martin S. Garretson. N.Y. Zoological Society, 1938. 254 pp.

BIGHORN, MOUNTAIN SHEEP
Ovis canadensis

There are many different kinds of mountain sheep of the genus *Ovis* in the world. Two are native to North America: the bighorn in the Rocky Mountains and Sierra Nevadas, and the Dall sheep in Alaska and Yukon.

The habitat of the bighorn varies considerably within different parts of the range of its six recognized subspecies. Some are found living in semiarctic cold above the timber line on our highest mountains, while others thrive on arid, desert ranges where temperatures are comparatively high.

The bighorn is a prized game animal. Both its horns and flesh are valued by the sportsman. Hunting pressure and competition with livestock have caused this magnificent American species to disappear from many parts of its former native range.

The food of the bighorn is entirely of plant origin. It includes a large proportion of grasses together with other herbaceous plants and some woody browse.

Northern Mt.–Desert, 15 (8-2-3-2)
*** Fescuegrass *FWSp*
** Wheatgrass *WSp*
** Sagebrush *W*
* Needlegrass *Su*
* Ricegrass *W*
* Muhlygrass *W*
* Mountain-mahogany *Su*
* Mountainlover
* Twinflower *Su*
* Sedge *Su*
+ Serviceberry, Rabbitbrush, Barberry, Wild Cherry, Saltbush
Montana, winter observations
** Bluegrass
** Wheatgrass

** Fescuegrass
* Sagebrush, Fringed
* Gooseberry
+ Bearberry, Serviceberry, Maple, Limber Pine, Douglasfir
New Mexico, observations, various seasons
− Selaginella
− Brittlebush, White
− Centuryplant
− Acacia, Catclaw
− Mountain-mahogany
− Giantcactus
− Paloverde, Littleleaf
− Filaree
− Oak, Scrub Live
− Coachwhip
− Pricklypear
− Tesota
− Fendlera
− Silktassel, Wrights
− Cottontop, Arizona
− Sotol, Wheeler
− Globemallow
Nevada, Las Vegas, observations
*** Hilaria
** Pricklypear
** Pine, Piñon, sd.
* Gramagrass
* Needlegrass
California, fall observations
**** Grasses
* Eriogonum
* Saltbush
* Gumweed
* Jointfir
* Sumac
* Buckthorn

Reference: A Wyoming Bighorn-Sheep Study. Ralph F. Honess and Nedward M. Frost. *Wyo. Game and Fish Dept., Bul.* 1, 1942. 126 pp.

MOUNTAIN GOAT
Oreamnos americanus

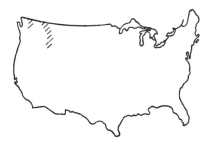

The mountain goat is peculiar to North America, inhabiting the wild rugged slopes and ledges of our highest mountains, from Oregon and Idaho north to Alaska. Its comparatively inaccessible environment helps to explain how the animal has continued to survive in limited numbers within an undiminished range during the past 400 years, at least. The unpalatable flesh and unattractive horns, too small for good trophies are additional reasons why this bearded mountaineer has persisted as well as it has.

In its feeding, the mountain goat is strictly vegetarian. During winter it feeds considerably on woody growths, but in other seasons it subsists largely on grasses and weedy plants.

Montana, Bighorn Range, observations, spring and summer
- Groundsel
- Bromegrass, Mountain
- Mosses
- Ceanothus, Snowbush
- Reedgrass
- Dogwood, Redosier
- Alder, Thinleaf
- Ninebark

Montana, Glacier Nat. Park, 1 (1-0-0-0)
- Hemlock
- Douglasfir
- Fir, Alpine

CHAPTER THIRTEEN

Fish, Amphibians, and Reptiles

BIRDS AND MAMMALS hold the spotlight in this book, partly because they have priority in the usual meaning of "wildlife," and even more because they are extensive users of plants. Fish, amphibians, and reptiles are given a secondary place here since only limited amounts of their food are obtained directly from plants.

Relatively little is known about the identity of plants eaten by those kinds of fish which do include vegetable materials in their diet. Our information on this score may be summed up by stating that they are mainly microscopic aquatics which, unlike land plants, cannot be managed readily by man except in ponds and small lakes. As to the amphibians and reptiles, not only is their use of plants minor and little studied, but these groups of cold-blooded vertebrates are also secondary in importance and interest to man. Consequently, the treatment of these three classes of wildlife will be limited to a concise and necessarily incomplete survey of their constituency, economics, and foods.

Fish

Marine and fresh-water fisheries constitute a tremendous economic and recreational resource well worth trying to maintain. During the past two centuries pollution, siltation, and turbidity from agriculture and industry have greatly reduced fresh-water fish populations. Along our marine seaboards, there have been drastic reductions in the catch of certain species because of marked decreases of their numbers.

The zoologist classifies "fish" into three large groups, only one of which includes the animals we eat on Friday. The lowest group on the family tree includes the lampreys and hagfish—fish that lack jaws and paired fins. They are mainly carnivorous and parasitic on other fish. At this writing, the spread of lampreys into the Great Lakes is raising a serious problem since they feed on our best and largest fresh-water food fishes.

Sharks and rays form the second group of fish. These are characterized by a skeleton of cartilage instead of true bone. They are mainly marine; no fresh-water forms occur in North America. Plant food does not enter into their diet either. Recently sharks have turned out to be an important source of vitamins, and shark fishing has increased enormously.

The bony fish form the principal fish group—the bulk of the 1,700 species of fish in or near the United States mainland. Included are most of the fish we prize as food and game.

If plant life plays any important role in the diet of fish, it is predominantly for the young fry which live directly on marine and fresh-water plankton. Algae, including diatoms and desmids, make up much of this early-stage food. Observers have noted "a remarkable similarity" between the food of young fish belonging to several different families in which the food habits of the adults were widely different. Many kinds of young fish depend on plant food at a critical time of their lives, but they generally wean themselves from it as they mature, feeding subsequently on a diet of smaller fish or other aquatic animal life. The condition is almost the reverse of many birds that feed their young a diet that is almost completely animal food, while the adults feed largely on plant matter. Young fish that do not take algae directly, remove the process only one step since their small invertebrate prey subsist largely on plant material.

Adult marine game fish, like bluefish, weakfish, swordfish, bonita, sea trout, sailfish, tuna, and many others, take no plant food at all. Neither do such commercial fish as flounder, halibut, herring, mackerel, cod, or even the lowly pilchard. The few marine fish which do live on brown algae and other marine plant life are reputed to have ill-flavored flesh. The fresh-water fish that sportsmen prize—trout, pickerel, bass, perch, pike—are all carnivorous. They subsist largely on smaller fish, crustaceans, mollusks, and insects. However, there is a minority that feed on plants to a greater or lesser extent, and a few of these will be mentioned.

Of the lower fish, only the sturgeon makes noticeable use of plant foods, with algae being the principal vegetative ingredient in its diet. Among other plant eaters are the buffalo fish and the suckers. Both feed upon a wide variety of aquatic plants as well as on mollusks, fish, etc. The carp is a large bottom-feeding minnow that takes a good deal of plant food as it grubs along. Though its habits of stirring up the bottom mud make the carp intolerable in waters where other fish are desired, it is of some commercial significance since 15 to 20 million pounds are caught and marketed yearly.

Some other minnows are reported to consume considerable quantities of plants. For example, the roach, or golden shiner, a hardy fish of ponds and slow streams uses up to 90% plant food in its diet. In the common shiner, or dace, a similar fish that is found in nearly all small streams east of the Rockies, about 80% of its food consists of aquatic plants, mainly algae. The chub is reported to eat a "large amount" of algae. Catfish and bullheads also feed extensively on plants, with crustaceans and insects prominent in the remainder of their diet. A study of the stomach contents of 106 bullheads gave evidence of a varied diet in which plant material ran as high as 40%. Bullheads seem to favor plant food only when animal food is scarce. Eels, being bottom feeders, also take some plant material, and killifish are reported making occasional use of seeds of aquatic plants.

The movement to encourage the growing of fish in farm ponds has met with unusual success, especially in the South. In these fish ponds a rapid, luxurious growth of microscopic types of algae is induced by applications of commercial fertilizer in the spring. The algae grow and multiply rapidly till the water is deeply colored by them—usually a greenish-brown. Small invertebrates including the larvae of aquatic insects feed avidly on the algae, creating an immediate and plentiful supply of animal food for the fish stocked in the pond.

Details of management of the fish-pond cycle depend on how the pond is to be stocked. Bass are often desired as the final product, and they will feed on sunfish or any other young fish available. Bluegills, or common sunfish, often act as the intermediary. Bluegills and some perch make consistent but minor use of plant foods. Chara and other algae account for 12% of the bluegill's diet. Otherwise, these fish live largely on insect larvae and aquatic crustaceans which, in turn, feed directly on the algae.

Amphibians

The amphibians of the United States belong in two orders, the salamanders (*Urodela*) in one and the toads and frogs (*Anura*) in the other. As might be expected, our knowledge of their food habits is largely limited to occasional field observations or notes on specimens in captivity. Very few quantitative studies

of amphibian foods have been made. In general, however, it appears that the food of adults is obtained largely from the animal kingdom and consists mainly of small invertebrates.

Most frogs and toads make a decided shift in diet between early stages of growth and maturity. The tadpoles are primarily herbaceous, feeding freely on filamentous green and blue-green algae. They also eat diatoms, desmids, and decaying bits of aquatic plants. To some extent they act as scavengers, taking any dead animal matter they find on the bottom. The intestine of the tadpole is a long, coiled affair, typical of plant eaters. As the tadpole matures and changes into a frog or toad, its change in diet is as dramatic as its change in body form. As an adult it becomes a carnivorous animal, living on insects (such as flies, mosquitoes, beetles, caterpillars, and bugs), worms, snails, and small crustaceans.

Adult bullfrogs occasionally take juniper berries and other small fruits, but this seems exceptional. Stomach analyses of 502 common toads[1] showed 89% animal food—earthworms, snails, grubs, and small adult insects, especially ants. Plant material amounted to 8% of the stomach contents. This consisted of bits of wood, bark, seeds, and conifer needles, all of which seemed to have been taken accidentally as the toads hunted their food.

Young salamanders are reported to be largely carnivorous. Typical species feed on worms, sowbugs, aquatic insects, and small crustaceans. In the few cases wherein plant material has been found in the stomachs of salamanders, it appeared that the occurrence might well have been accidental. One exception seems to be the siren, a large eel-like salamander of the Southeast that lives in swamps and roadside ditches. Reports indicate that it occasionally "filled itself with filamentous algae."

Reptiles

Nearly all members of the four orders of American reptiles (alligators, lizards, snakes, and turtles) are wholly or largely carnivorous. There are a few exceptions, but the use of plants as food by reptiles as a group is minor. On the other hand, plants are important for cover. Thus, saltbush, cactus, and sagebrush provide vital shelter for desert lizards and snakes from the heat of the day and from preying enemies. In general, reptiles have little direct economic value, but it is to be hoped that our broad programs of wildlife conservation will, as a secondary feature, prevent the needless killing of harmless members of this group.

The largest of our reptiles are the alligator and its close but less common relative the crocodile. Both feed on crustaceans, fish, insects, birds, small mammals, or whatever other animal food they can get. Kellogg, reporting on the analysis of 157 stomachs,[2] found alligators taking tubers of *Scirpus*, hickory nuts, and some seeds in their diet—but this use seems minor and perhaps accidental.

Lizards are mainly carnivorous, feeding largely on insects, spiders, earthworms, and other invertebrates. This is true of the skinks, racerunners, alligator lizards, horned toads, and our only poisonous lizard, the Gila monster. A few species do feed on plants, and the chuckwalla, one of our largest and most abundant southwestern lizards, is a plant eater. Its diet includes leaves, flowers, fruits, and any other tender parts of available succulent plants. Young plants are eaten in their entirety. The iguanas, common south of the United States, are plant eaters, too. The small species of iguana which occur in the Southwest take an appreciable amount of plant foods though they fare primarily on grasshoppers and other insects. Stomach analyses of 20 gridiron-tailed lizards showed that berries, leaves, and buds made up to 60% of the stomach contents. In the collared lizard, legu-

[1] *U.S. Biol. Survey Leaflet* 664, 1922.
[2] *U.S. Dept. Agr. Tech. Bul.* 147, 1929.

281

minous pods and leaves varied from 15 to 90 % of the total food taken. There is evidence that with some lizards the use of plant food is seasonal—being confined to spring and summer when tender plant parts are available.

Snakes, the best known of the reptiles, are completely carnivorous in their rather varied diet, which includes earthworms, insects, birds' eggs, fish, amphibians, other snakes, and small mammals. General features of the diet of these reptiles have been established by numerous field observations extending over several decades. More recently, this information has been supplemented by stomach analyses. In one unit of research which included analyses of stomach contents of some 900 snakes taken in the George Washington National Forest in Virginia, Francis M. Uhler reported that any plant food in the diet was wholly accidental.

Turtles make wider use of plants than any other order of American reptiles. Yet, turtles are far from being truly herbivorous. Some turtles take only small amounts of plant food or none at all. But for a good many species, fruits, leaves, tender shoots, or aquatic plants form an important, if not major, part of their diet. The data on the food of turtles are, in large measure, based on field observations backed by a few laboratory studies. These studies have involved some of the more common species—especially those of economic importance.

The mud and musk turtles take water plants and other vegetable matter as part of their food. The yellow mud turtle seems to take more than others. The spotted turtle, in contrast, takes very little. The wood turtle makes considerable use of plants, having been observed feeding on berries, fruits, leaves and tender shoots, and even on mushrooms. Muhlenberg's turtle is an eater of berries and fruits also. Blanding's turtle, when on land, takes fruit including berries of various kinds.

The box turtle is well known, and its food habits have been studied in some detail. Plant material averages about 50% of the diet, with fruits and mushrooms dominant. Blackberries and strawberries in season are preferred foods. The desert turtle and the gopher turtle of the West are also plant eaters, making use of grasses, succulent shoots, flowers, and fruits.

Analyses of 470 snapping turtle stomachs showed that plant food was largely from aquatics—including algae and foliage or stems of waterweed, pondweeds, and waterlilies. This vegetation formed 13 to 59% of the contents of individual stomachs and gave an average of 37% plant food for the whole diet. A sidelight on the feeding of snapping turtles is their frequent depredation upon young and adult waterfowl in some localities. Diamond-backed terrapins, map turtles, spotted turtles, and the hieroglyphic turtle have been observed to use only small amounts of plant food. The soft-shelled turtle does not seem to eat any. In contrast to it, about half of the food taken by the painted turtle is algae and other aquatic plants. The *Pseudemys* group all take considerable plant food, including arrowheads and other aquatic plants.

The great sea turtles do not use much plant food. The green turtle is the only one of the group which uses eelgrass and algae to any extent. This turtle also feeds on shoots of mangrove. The hawksbill turtle is reported as taking "some sea plants" as food, but neither the leatherback nor loggerhead eat plants to any significant extent. Shellfish, crabs, and other crustaceans enter considerably in their diet.

General References: Reptiles of North America. Raymond L. Ditmars. Doubleday & Company, Inc., New York, 1936.
Field Book of Snakes. Karl P. Schmidt and D. Dwight Davis. G. P. Putnam's Sons, New York, 1941.

Turtles of the United States and Canada. Clifford H. Pope. Alfred A. Knopf, Inc., New York, 1939.

Handbook of Lizards. Hobart M. Smith. The William T. Comstock Company, New York, 1946.

Handbook of Frogs and Toads. Anna A. Wright and Albert H. Wright. The William T. Comstock Company, New York, 1942.

Handbook of Salamanders. Sherman C. Bishop. The William T. Comstock Company, New York, 1943.

American Food and Game Fishes. David Starr Jordan and Barton Warren Evermann. Doubleday & Company, Inc., New York, 1908.

Field Book of Fresh-water Fishes of North America North of Mexico. Ray Schrenkeisen. G. P. Putnam's Sons, New York, 1938.

Fishery Resources of the United States. *Senate Document* 51, U.S. Government Printing Office, 1945.

Field Book of Marine Fishes of the Atlantic Coast from Labrador to Texas. Charles M. Breder, Jr. G. P. Putnam's Sons, New York, 1929.

North American Game Fishes. Francesca LaMonte. Doubleday & Company, Inc., 1946.

Marine Game Fishes of the Pacific Coast. Lionel A. Walford. University of California Press, Berkeley, 1937.

PART III

PLANTS USEFUL TO WILDLIFE

T HIS PART OF the book deals with the wildlife plants of the United States. It is concerned with all the genera of plants—herbaceous and woody, wild and cultivated, upland and aquatic—that furnish food to our wildlife in significant amounts.

To serve the diverse interests of foresters, farmers, upland game hunters, water-fowlers, horticulturists, and naturalists, wildlife plants have been classed into four major groups: Woody Plants (Chap. Fourteen); Upland Weeds and Herbs (Chap. Fifteen); Marsh and Aquatic Plants (Chap. Sixteen); and Cultivated Plants (Chap. Seventeen). Within each chapter, the plants are presented in family sequence.

Some overlapping of these four categories is unavoidable, but it does not constitute a serious problem. Holly and maples are common as both wild and cultivated plants, but since the bulk of them are wild, these plants are treated in Chap. Fourteen. Plants such as partridgeberry and wintergreen are not typical woody plants; yet they fit that category better than the herbaceous group.

Intelligent multiple-purpose utilization of land by the amateur or by the technician requires that he know what plants are valuable to what animals. Chapters Fourteen to Seventeen will help to answer this question and so will the final chapter (Eighteen) on Wildlife Plants Ranked According to Their Value.

CHAPTER FOURTEEN

Woody Plants

THE WORD "WILD" is implied as part of the heading Woody Plants. However, a number of plants in this category are also grown for shade or ornamental purposes—maples, elms, oaks, dogwoods, and Virginia creeper, for example. Since these native plants are far more abundant in the wild than in cultivation, it seems appropriate that they be treated here. Cultivated plants are treated in Chap. Seventeen.

Trees, shrubs, and vines form a large, conspicuous, and important part of the American flora throughout all the country except the Prairie region. Besides providing essential cover and nesting habitat for many wildlife species, the fruits, seeds, and foliage of woody plants also furnish a large share of their food. Oaks and pines, particularly, are outstanding sources of wildlife food. Wild cherries, dogwoods, blackberries, hollies, and many others are valuable too.

A few small woody species provide classification problems. Wintergreen, bunchberry, bearberry, and a few other small plants with somewhat woody stems are neither typical woody plants nor true herbs. They are, however, included here as the better alternative.

General References: Manual of the Trees of North America. Charles Sprague Sargent. Houghton Mifflin Company, Boston, 1921. 910 pp.

North American Trees. Nathaniel Lord Britton. Henry Holt and Company, New York, 1908. 894 pp.

Native Woody Plants of the United States. William R. Van Dersal. *U.S. Dept. Agr. Misc. Publ.* 303, 1938. 362 pp.

Pine Family: *Pinaceae*

PINES
Pinus

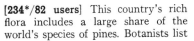

[234*/82 users] This country's rich flora includes a large share of the world's species of pines. Botanists list 28 to 36 species for the United States and a total of 66 to 100 for the world. Many of our pines are abundant in

287

extensive areas of their diverse habitats and are noticeably absent only in some parts of the prairies and deserts. Pines are particularly abundant in the Southeast where young trees, like woody weeds, take over fields that are left fallow for several years.

Pines rank near the very top in importance to wildlife. Their seeds constitute more than 50% of the diet of three birds, the red crossbill, Clarke nutcracker, and white-headed woodpecker—an unusual wildlife record. In addition, there are a number of 4-star and 3-star users of pine seeds, and many birds and mammals feed on these nutritious, oily seeds to a lesser degree. Unfortunately the annual crop of pine seeds varies considerably—some years bring a heavy yield and in others the crop is light.

Pine needles are consumed by some species of grouse and by several browsers. Porcupines and small rodents use the bark and wood as food. Pines are also valuable as cover for wildlife. Young trees with foliage spreading near the ground make good all-year cover for gamebirds, fur bearers, hoofed browsers, and other ground animals. Larger pines are favorite roosting places for robins during migration and also are one of the most common nesting sites for mourning doves. Pine needles are used as nest material by several species of songbirds.

Pines of the country that are especially important to wildlife and man include the following:

NORTHEAST: White (*strobus*), pitch (*rigida*)

SOUTHEAST: Loblolly (*taeda*), longleaf (*palustris*),shortleaf (*echinata*), scrub (*virginiana*), slash (*caribaea*)

MT.–DESERT: Piñon (*cembroides*), limber (*flexilis*)

MT.–DESERT AND PACIFIC: Ponderosa (*ponderosa*), lodgepole (*contorta*)

PACIFIC: Western white (*monticola*), sugar (*lambertiana*), digger (*sabiniana*)

The importance of pines to man is too well known to require elaboration. Not only are they important for lumber, but also as a source of turpentine and pitch. These handsome evergreens are widely used for ornamentals and shade plantings. The seeds of piñon pine, called pine nuts, are sold commercially for human food.

Upland Gamebirds (seeds, needles)
 Dove
** Ground, *Gulf Coast*
* Mourning, *SE*
 Grouse
** Blue, *No.Mt.–Des.;* *Pac.NW
** Franklin, *B.C.*
* Sharp-tailed, *Minn. and Mich.*
**** Spruce, *NW and Canada*
*** Pigeon, Band-tailed, *So.Mt.–Des.;* +*Pac.*
+ Prairie Chicken, Greater, *Wis.*
*** Quail, Bobwhite, *Fla.;* **SE*
*** Turkey, Wild, *Ariz. and N. Mex.;* **SE*

Songbirds (seeds)
 Chickadee
** Black-capped, *NE*
** Carolina, *SE*
** Chestnut-backed, *Pac.*
* Hudsonian, *N*
* Mountain, *Mt.–Des. and Pac.*
* Creeper, Brown, *U.S.*
 Crossbill
***** (66%) Red, *U.S.*
*** White-winged, *NE*
 Finch
+ House, Common, *Calif.*
** Rosy, *Pac.*
+ Flicker, Red-shafted, *Pac.*
+ Goldfinch, *E*
 Grosbeak
*** Evening, *W*
**** Pine, *NE;* **Pac. NW*
 Jay
** California, *Calif.*
** Florida, *Gulf*
**** Piñon, *N.Mex.* (piñon pine)
+ Steller, *Pac.*
**** Woodhouse, *So.Mt.–Des.* (piñon pine)
 Junco
+ Oregon, *Calif.*
+ Slate-colored, *NE*

+ Magpie, American, *Mt.–Des.*
* Meadowlark, *SE*
***** (74%) Nutcracker, Clark, *NW*
Nuthatch
**** Brown-headed, *SE*
**** Pygmy, *Calif.*
**** Red-breasted, *E and Pac.*
** White-breasted, *Pac.; *E and E.Pr.*
+ Sapsucker, Yellow-bellied, *E* (sap)
** Siskin, Pine, *U.S.*
Sparrow
+ English, *Mt.–Des.*
+ Pine-woods, *SE*
* Thrasher, Brown, *SE;* +*NE*
Titmouse
+ Plain, *Calif.*
+ Tufted, *SE*
* Towhee, *SE;* +*NE*
Warbler
*** Hermit, *Calif.*
+ Myrtle, *E*
** Pine, *E*
Woodpecker
** Lewis, *Mt.–Des. and Pac.*
* Red-bellied, *E*
*** Red-cockaded, *Gulf Coast*
***** (71%) White-headed, *Calif.* (piñon pine)
+ Wren, Carolina, *E*
Fur and Game Mammals (seeds, bark, foliage)
** Bear, Black, *W* (piñon pine)
** Beaver, *U.S.*
*** Chickaree, Douglas, *Pac.*
**** Hare, Varying, *N.Y.;* +*Minn. and Wis.*

* Pika, *Pac.NW*
*** Porcupine, *Mt.–Des.; *NE*
Rabbit
+ Cottontail, Eastern, *Conn.*
+ Cottontail, Mearns, *Pa.*
+ Cottontail, New England, *Conn.*
Squirrel
+ Fox, *Mich.*
– Fremont, *Colo.*
**** Gray, *Calif.; *E*
** Red, *W; *E*
Small Mammals (seeds)
Chipmunk
* Lake Superior, *Minn.*
**** Various spp., *Mt.–Des. and Pac.*
*** Northwest, *Pac.NW*
Ground Squirrel
** Antelope, *Mt.–Des. and Calif.*
* Mantled, *W*
** Mouse, White-footed, *W; *E*
+ Rat, Kangaroo, *Calif.*
Hoofed Browsers (foliage, twigs)
Deer
*** Mule, *Nebr.; **No.Mt.–Des.;* +*So.Mt.–Des., Calif., and S.Dak.*
*** White-tailed, *Mont.; **Wis. and Minn.; *Ala., N.C. Mts., and N.Dak.;* +*Pa., N.Y., and N.C.*
** Elk, *No.Mt.–Des.*
+ Moose, *No.Mt.–Des.*
** Sheep, Mountain, *Nev.* (piñon pine); +*Mont.*

Reference: The Identification of the Pines of the United States, Native and Introduced. W. M. Harlow. *N.Y. State Col. of Forestry Bul.* 2a, Vol. IV. 1931. 30 pp.

LARCHES
Larix

[16*/6 users] Three species of larch are native in cool, moist, sometimes boggy situations in the Northeast and in the Pacific Northwest. Locally they are sometimes called tamaracks or hackmatacks. The larches are interesting conifers. Unlike most of their relatives they are not evergreen but lose their clusters of needles in winter.

The record of wildlife use of larches is not impressive. Two gamebirds, the spruce grouse and the blue grouse, consume its needles and buds freely, and the red crossbill feeds on its seeds to a 1-star extent. The wood of larch is of some value, and the trees are planted widely for ornamental purposes.

Upland Gamebirds (leaves, buds)
Grouse
* Blue, *Pac. NW*
*** Spruce, *NW and Canada*
Songbirds (seeds)
* Crossbill, Red, *U.S.*

Fur and Game Mammals (bark, seeds)
− Hare, Varying, *Wis.*
+ Porcupine, Eastern, *NE*
− Squirrel, Richardson Red. *Mont. and Idaho*

SPRUCES
Picea

[**36*/22 users**] Three species of spruce occur in the Northeast and four or five in the Northwest. These northern conifers grow on our higher mountains where the climate is cool and considerable rain falls.

The wildlife value of spruces is confined to northern animals. Grouse, especially the spruce grouse, Franklin grouse, and blue grouse, obtain much of their food from spruce needles which incidentally are four-sided in contrast to firs. The foliage and twigs are also browsed extensively by rabbits and deer in winter. The small, winged seeds of spruce are a valuable food of the white-winged crossbill and are eaten by several other kinds of birds as well as by squirrels and chipmunks.

Besides their use for timber and pulp, spruces are valued as ornamentals, the Colorado blue spruce being especially popular. When planted about residences, spruces provide excellent nesting, roosting, and winter cover for birds.

Upland Gamebirds (needles)
Grouse
* Blue, *No.Mt.–Des. and Pac. NW*
** Franklin, *B.C.*
*** Spruce, *NW and Canada*
Songbirds (seeds)
* Chickadee, Hudsonian, *N*
Crossbill
* Red, *N*
**** White-winged, *NE*
+ Grosbeak, Pine, *NE*
* Nuthatch, Red-breasted, *NE*
+ Siskin, Pine, *W.Va.*
+ Waxwing, Cedar, *W.Va.*
Fur and Game Mammals (bark, seeds, needles)
*** Hare, Varying, *N.Y.; *Maine and Wis.*
** Porcupine, Eastern, *Vt.*
+ Rabbit, Cottontail, Mearns, *Pa.*
Squirrel
* Gray, *NE*
** Red, *NE; *W*
Small Mammals (seeds)
Chipmunk
− Fremont, *Colo.*
+ Lake Superior, *Minn.*
Hoofed Browsers (foliage, twigs)
** Deer, White-tailed, *Mont.; +Wis.*
+ Elk, *No.Mt.–Des.*
+ Sheep, Mountain, *Yellowstone Park and Colo.*

References: Eastern Spruce. H. S. Betts. American woods series. *U.S. Dept. Agr. Forest Service*, 1945. 9 pp.
The Red Spruce, Its Growth and Management. L. S. Murphy. *U.S. Dept. Agr. Bul.* 544, 1917. 100 pp.

HEMLOCKS
Tsuga

[**23*/17 users**] Of the seven to nine species of hemlocks recognized the world over, four species are native to the United States.

food for the pine siskin, the crossbills, chickadees, blue grouse, and several rodents including the red squirrel. Porcupines are fond of New England hemlock and occasionally kill young trees by stripping the bark and wood. Hemlocks are planted as ornamentals, either as shade trees or hedge plants.

These tall, straight-trunked conifers are typical of moist, cool slopes, mainly in the northern latitudes or on the higher mountains. Hemlocks often invade areas where other trees have been cleared away. The dense, low foliage of young plants makes excellent winter cover for ruffed grouse, wild turkey, deer, and other wildlife. Hemlock groves are also favorite nesting places for several kinds of northern birds—the veery, black-throated blue warbler, black-throated green warbler, Blackburnian warbler, and junco. The small, winged seeds are important

Upland Gamebirds (buds, leaves)
   Grouse
  *   Blue, *Pac.NW*
  +   Ruffed, *NE*
Songbirds (seeds)
   Chickadee
  *   Black-capped, *NE*
  +   Hudsonian, *N*
   Crossbill
  *   Red, *U.S.*
  **   White-winged, *NE*
  *** Siskin, Pine, *NE*
Fur and Game Mammals (bark, wood, seeds)
  +   Beaver, *N.Y.*
  **   Chickaree, Douglas, *Pac.*
  +   Hare, Varying, *Wis.*
  *** Porcupine, *NE and Vt.*
  +   Rabbit, Cottontail, Mearns, *Pa.*
  *   Squirrel, Red, *W*
Small Mammals (seeds, leaves)
  +   Mouse, White-footed, *NE*
  +   Rat, Allegheny Wood, *NE*
Hoofed Browsers (foliage, twigs)
  **   Deer, White-tailed, *NE*
  +   Goat, Mountain, *Mont.*

Reference: The Eastern Hemlock (*Tsuga canadensis*, Linn. Carr.). E. H. Frothingham. *U.S. Dept. Agr. Bul.* 152, 1915. 43 pp.

DOUGLASFIR
Pseudotsuga taxifolia

[30*/20 users] There are two species of this genus in the United States (of four in the world), but only the common douglasfir (*P. taxifolia*) is widespread and important. The bigcone douglasfir (*P. macrocarpa*) is confined to mountain slopes in Southern California.

The common douglasfir occurs on moist, well-drained mountain slopes and in valleys throughout the Rockies and in the Pacific Northwest. In the

latter region it becomes a gigantically tall tree, often exceeding 200 feet in height. The one-piece flagpole of the Oregon building at the Panama Pacific International Exposition of 1915 was a douglasfir trunk, 299 feet, 7 inches long.

The small, winged seeds of this conifer are used by western squirrels and other rodents. The foliage and twigs are important to several kinds of

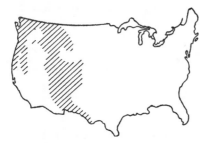

browsers. Douglasfir needles, together with some of the staminate cones, constitute a top-rank winter food of the blue grouse.

Upland Gamebirds (foliage, staminate cones)
**** Grouse, Blue, *No.Mt.–Des.;* ***Pac. NW*
Songbirds (seeds)
+ Crossbill, Red, *U.S.*
+ Siskin, Pine, *W*
Fur and Game Mammals (seeds, wood, foliage)
** Beaver, *W*
Chickaree
** Douglas, *Pac.*
*** Fremont, *Ariz.;* +*Colo.*
** Hare, Varying, *Utah*

Squirrel
** Red, *W*
+ Red, Richardson, *Idaho and Mont.*
+ Red, Wind River Mt., *Utah*
Small Mammals (seeds)
+ Mouse, Red Tree, *Calif.*
+ Rat, Dusky-footed Wood, *Oreg.*
*** Shrew, *Oreg.*
Hoofed Browsers (twigs, foliage)
+ Antelope, *Idaho*
Deer
* Mule, *No.Mt.–Des.*
*** White-tailed, *Mont.;* *Oreg.*
* Elk, *No.Mt.–Des.*
+ Goat, Mountain, *Mont.*
+ Sheep, Mountain, *Mont.*

References: Douglas Fir: a Study of the Pacific Coast and Rocky Mountain Forms. *U.S. Dept. Agr. Forest Service Circ.* 150, 1909. 38 pp.

Growth of Douglas-fir Trees of Known Seed Source. *U.S. Dept Agr. Tech. Bul.* 537, 1936. 40 pp.

Yield of Douglas-fir in the Pacific Northwest. R. E. McArdle. *U.S. Dept. Agr. Tech. Bul.* 201, 1930. 64 pp.

FIRS
Abies

[40*/23 users] This important genus of conifers is represented by at least

nine native species—about a third of the world's total. Seven species occur in the West and two in the East.

Firs prefer moist cool situations in the northern parts of the country or in the higher mountains. Some of the largest and most abundant native species, the silver firs (*A. amarabilis* and *A. alba*), grow in the coastal rain forests of Oregon and Washington. The white fir (*A. concolor*), alpine fir (*A. lasiocarpa*), and grand fir (*A. grandis*) are western species of extensive distribution in the Pacific and Mountain–Desert regions. In the East there are only two species, both of them known as balsam fir (*A. balsamea* and *A. fraseri*). The latter is confined largely to the Appalachians and the former to the northern part of the Northeast and Canada.

The wildlife importance of firs is moderate. The evergreen foliage of young trees is useful to mammals and gamebirds for cover, especially in winter. The blue grouse and sharp-tailed grouse make fir needles a major part of their diet. Browsers, particularly northern deer and moose, resort to fir foliage as a large part of their winter menu. The winged seeds are eaten from the cones by several birds, notably the Hudsonian chickadee, crossbills, and Clarke nutcracker. The seeds are also sought by squirrels and chipmunks. Firs are attractive for plantings about homes and have particular usefulness to birds for roosting and nesting sites.

Upland Gamebirds (leaves)
Grouse
***   Blue, *Pac.NW*
+   Ruffed, *NE*
**   Spruce, *NW and Canada*

Songbirds (seeds mainly)
*   Chickadee, Hudsonian, *N*
     Crossbill
+   Red, *U.S.*
*   White-winged, *NE*
+   Magpie, Yellow-billed, *Calif.*
*   Nutcracker, Clark, *NW*
+   Nuthatch, Pygmy, *W, mainly Calif.*
+   Sapsucker, Yellow-bellied, *E* (sap)

Fur and Game Mammals (seeds, bark, wood)
+   Beaver, *NE*
***   Chickaree, Douglas, *Pac.*
*   Hare, Varying, *NE*
+   Pika, *Pac.*
**   Porcupine, *Vt.; +NE*
*   Squirrel, Red, *U.S.*

Small Mammals (seeds)
*   Chipmunk, Western, *Mt.–Des. and Pac.*
+   Mouse, White-footed, *E*

Hoofed Browsers (foliage, twigs)
Deer
**   Mule, *So.Mt.–Des.; +Calif.*
***   White-tailed, *Wis. and Minn.; **Mont.*
*   Elk, *No.Mt.–Des.*
+   Goat, Mountain, *Mont.*
***   Moose, *Mich.; *No.Mt.–Des.*

References: Balsam Fir. Raphael Zon. *U.S. Dept. Agr. Bul.* 55, 1914. 68 pp.
Balsam Fir; Noble Fir; White Fir. H. S. Betts. American woods series. *U.S. Dept. Agr. Forest Service*, three leaflets, 1945. 8 pp.; 5 pp.; 12 pp.

BALDCYPRESSES
Taxodium

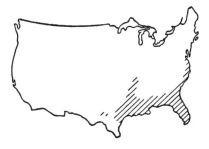

[2*/3 users] Of the three species of *Taxodium* in the world, two are native

in the United States. These are the common baldcypress (*T. distichum*) and the pondcypress (*T. ascendens*). The gigantic Montezuma baldcypress (*T. mucronatum*) occurs in Mexico.

These tall, straight-trunked, deciduous-leafed conifers are swamp inhabitants—primarily in the lowlands of the southeastern coastal plain. They are prized for lumber but have very little value for wildlife. The seeds and leaves are eaten by the Florida crane, and the seeds are also used by ducks.

Waterfowl (seeds)
Ducks
\+   Gadwall, *SE*
\+   Mallard, Common, *SE*

Marshbirds and Shorebirds (leaves and seeds)
**   Crane, Florida, *Fla.*

ARBORVITAE, WHITE CEDAR
Thuja

[6*/8 users] Of the four to six species of *Thuja* in the world, two occur in the United States—eastern arborvitae (*T. occidentalis*) and giant arborvitae (*T. plicata*) of the Pacific Northwest. These evergreen trees grow in swampy bottom lands or stream margins, often forming dense growths.

The winged seeds (in the very small cones) are eaten extensively by the pine siskin in the Northeast, and the foliage and twigs are useful to the white-tailed deer. Value to other wildlife is slight. The trees, however, are important both for their lumber and for ornamental plantings.

Songbirds (seeds)
\+   Redpoll, *NE*
***   Siskin, Pine, *NE*
Fur and Game Mammals (foliage, etc.)
\+   Beaver, *Maine*
\+   Hare, Varying, *Maine and Wis.*
\+   Porcupine, *Mt.–Des.*
\+   Squirrel, Northern Red, *N*
Hoofed Browsers (twigs, foliage)
***   Deer, White-tailed, *Wis. and Minn.;* *Maine; +Mont.*

CEDARS, JUNIPERS
Juniperus

[66*/44 users] Twelve species of cedar or juniper grow in the United States: nine in the West and three in the East. These pungent, evergreen trees are especially plentiful on slopes and ridges in the arid West. Overgrazing in this section is causing them to increase in abundance and extend their domain into places formerly occupied by grasses. In the East, the one widespread, abundant species, the common redcedar (*J. virginiana*), grows in pastures, fence rows, and other open places.

Cedars are important to wildlife throughout the country, except in the Prairies. Their twigs and foliage are eaten extensively by hoofed browsers, but the chief attraction to wildlife is the bluish-black berry-like fruit. The cedar waxwing, living up to its name, is one of the principal users of cedar berries, but numerous other birds and mammals, both large and small, make these fruits an important part of their diet.

In addition to their wildlife food value, cedars provide important pro-

tective and nesting cover. Chipping sparrows, robins, song sparrows, and mockingbirds use these trees as one of their favorite nesting sites. Juncos, myrtle warblers, sparrows of various kinds, and other· birds use the dense foliage as roosting cover. In winter their dense protective shelter is especially valuable. Cedars, particularly the redcedar, have ornamental value, and their wildlife utility makes them especially worth planting. On the other hand, redcedar can be a detriment to apple orchards since it is an alternate host for apple rust.

Upland Gamebirds (fruit)
\+   Pigeon, Band-tailed, *So.Mt.– Des.*

Quail
+ Mountain, *Pac.*
+ Scaled, *SW*
* Turkey, Wild, *Tex.; +Ariz. and N.Mex.*

Songbirds (fruit mainly)
* Bluebird, *E*
+ Catbird, *E*
+ Crossbill, White-winged, *N*
** Finch, Purple, *E*
+ Flicker, Yellow-shafted, *E and E.Pr.*
Grosbeak
*** Evening, *NW*
** Pine, *NE*
** Jay, Piñon, *Mt.–Des.*
* Mockingbird, *SE and Calif.*
+ Nutcracker, Clark, *NW*
* Robin, *NE; +SE*
Sapsucker
+ Red-naped, *So.Pr.* (sap)
* Yellow-bellied, *E* (sap)
** Solitaire, Townsend, *W*
+ Starling, *NE*
* Swallow, Tree, *E*
+ Thrasher, Brown, *NE*
+ Thrush, Hermit, *E*
* Warbler, Myrtle, *E*
**** Waxwing, Cedar, *NE*
Fur and Game Mammals (fruit)
+ Armadillo, *Tex.*

+ Bear, Black, *W.Va.*
+ Beaver, *Mo.* (wood)
** Cat, Ring-tailed, *Tex.*
+ Coyote, *W*
+ Fox, Gray, *Tex.*
+ Opossum, *Okla, and Tex.*
Small Mammals (fruit)
* Chipmunk, Western, *Mt.–Des. and Pac.*
* Ground Squirrel, Antelope, *Mt.– Des. and Calif.*
Mouse
+ Meadow, *Canada*
** Pocket, *W.Pr. and Mt.–Des.*
** White-footed, *W*
Rat
− Kangaroo, Tulare, *Calif.*
* Wood, *S.Pr.*
** Rock Squirrel, *Tex.*
Hoofed Browsers (twigs, foliage)
*** Antelope, *N.Mex.; *No.Pr.*
Deer
*** Mule, *So.Mt.–Des. and Oreg.; **S.Dak.; *No.Mt.–Des.; +Nebr.*
** White-tailed, *Tex.; +Mont. and Mo.*
− Elk, *Mont.*
− Sheep, Mountain, *Colo.*

References: Eastern Red Cedar; Western Red Cedar. H. S. Betts. American wood series. U.S. Dept. Agr. Forest Service, two leaflets, 1945. 4 pp.; 5 pp.
Notes on the Red Cedar. C. Mohr. *U.S. Forest Service Bul.* 31, 1901. 37 pp.

Gnetum Family: *Gnetaceae*

JOINTFIRS
Ephedra

[7*/6 users] Ten or eleven species of jointfir are found in the arid parts of the Southwest, from Wyoming and Texas to Southern California. These minute-leaved, green-twigged semi-desert shrubs or small trees have a limited list of wildlife users, and yet because all plant food is relatively scarce in their range, the plants are of moderate wildlife importance. The seeds (nutlets) are eaten by the mountain quail, and the plant is browsed by deer, bison, and antelope. Early western settlers, Indians, and Mexicans brewed a hot drink known as Mormon tea or Brigham Young tea from the stems of the jointfir.

Upland Gamebirds (seeds)
** Quail, Mountain, *Pac.*
Fur and Game Mammals (bark, foliage)
* Rabbit, Cottontail, *So.Mt.–Des.*

Hoofed Browsers (twigs, foliage)
* Antelope, *N.Mex.*
* Bison, *Okla.*

\+ Deer, Mule, *So.Mt.–Des.*
** Sheep, Mountain, *So.Mt.–Des and Calif.*

Palm Family: *Palmaceae*

PALMETTOS
Sabal

[7*/9 users] There are four or five kinds of palmettos in the United States. Ours are shrubs or, occasionally, tall trees native to bottom-land swamps and sandy areas near the Gulf and South Atlantic coasts. The fruit of the palmetto, ripening in late fall, is relished by robins, the fish crow, and the raccoon.

Songbirds (fruit)
* Crow, Fish, *SE*
\+ Mockingbird, *SE*
*** Robin, *Fla.*
\+ Warbler, Myrtle, *SE*
Woodpecker
\+ Pileated, *SE*
\+ Red-bellied, *SE*
Fur and Game Mammals (fruit)
*** Raccoon, *SE*
– Squirrel, Gray, *E.Tex.*

Smilax Family: *Smilaceae*

GREENBRIERS
Smilax

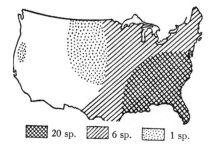

20 sp.   6 sp.   1 sp.

and nutritional value is probably limited largely to the big tough seeds. Nevertheless the berries are eaten extensively by some birds—particularly by the fish crow, ruffed grouse, mockingbird, and catbird. The fish crow's surprisingly high record of use is doubtless influenced by the large numbers of specimens taken in Florida. The plant also rates as one of the most important secondary foods for southern white-tailed deer.

[27*/33 users] We have 21 to 24 kinds of greenbriers—the majority of them in the Southeast. This tropical or subtropical genus totals 210 to 225 species in the world.

Greenbriers are partial to moist lowlands but are also common in upland areas. They are woody, usually thorny, vines. A few southern species are evergreen; the others are deciduous.

Besides providing good protective cover for rabbits and other small wildlife species, greenbriers also are important as a source of winter food. The fleshy covering of the fruit is very thin,

Waterfowl (fruit)
\+ Duck, Wood, *Md.*
Upland Gamebirds (fruit, leaves, buds)
*** Grouse, Ruffed, *Va. Alleghenies; *NE*
\+ Pheasant, Ring-necked, *NE*
\+ Prairie Chicken, Greater, *No. Pr.*
* Turkey, Wild, *SE*
Songbirds (fruit)
\+ Cardinal, *NE*
** Catbird, *SE; *NE*
Crow
\+ Common, *E*
**** Fish, *SE*

+ Flicker, Yellow-shafted, *E and E.Pr.*
** Mockingbird, *SE;* +*NE*
* Robin, *SE;* +*NE and E.Pr.*
Sparrow
+ Fox, *E*
+ White-throated, *NE*
+ Thrasher, Brown, *SE*
Thrush
+ Gray-cheeked, *NE*
* Hermit, *E*
* Olive-backed, *Pr.*; +*NE*
+ Waxwing, Cedar, *NE*
+ Woodpecker, Pileated, *E*
Fur and Game Mammals (fruit, stems)
* Bear, Black, *Va. and W.Va.*

+ Beaver, *Miss.*
+ Opossum, *Mo.*
Rabbit
+ Cottontail, Mearns, *NE*
+ Marsh, Florida, *Fla.*
** Raccoon, *SE;* +*NE and Tex.*
Squirrel
+ Fox, *Ohio*
+ Fox, Western, *Mich.*
+ Gray, *Fla.*
Small Mammals (fruit)
Rat
+ Wood, Attwater, *Tex.*
* Wood, *S.Pr.*
Hoofed Browsers (foliage, stems)
** Deer, White-tailed, *N.C.Mts. and Ala.;* +*Mo. and Tex.*

Walnut Family: *Juglandaceae*

NATIVE WALNUTS
Juglans

[7*/6 users] Of the 12 species of *Juglans* in the world, 6 are native to the United States. Besides the widespread common black walnut (*J. nigra*) which extends through most of the East and part way into the Prairies, there are two species of black walnut in California and two in the Southwest. In addition there is the closely related butternut, or white walnut, in the Northeast.

Doubtless all our native walnuts are useful to wildlife, but only the eastern black walnut has recognized importance. Four species of squirrels eat the nuts.

Songbirds (nuts)
− Woodpecker, Red-bellied, *Ky.*
Fur and Game Mammals (nuts mainly)
+ Beaver, *Miss.* (wood)
Squirrel
** Fox, *Ohio*
** Fox, Western, *Mich.*
* Gray, *E*
* Red, *NE*

References: Black Walnut; Butternut. H. S. Betts. American woods series. U.S. Dept. Agr. Forest Service, two leaflets, 1945. 6 pp.; 4 pp.
Utilization of Black Walnut. W. D. Brush. *U.S. Dept. Agr. Bul.* 909, 1921. 89 pp.
Black Walnut for Timber and Nuts. Wilbur R. Mattoon and C. A. Reed. *U.S. Dept. Agr. Farmers' Bul.* 1392, 1924. 30 pp.

HICKORIES AND PECANS
Carya

[23*/25 users] The hickories are almost exclusively an American group; only 3 of the 14 to 23 recognized species grow outside our borders. Ours are

confined to the East and occur in a variety of lowland and upland situations. The swamp, water, nutmeg, and bitternut hickories as well as the bitter pecan are found on moist bottom lands, while the mockernut, shellbark, pignut, and other hickories are characteristic of well-drained areas.

Hickories grow slowly and may live as long as 250 years. It is reported that the shellbark hickory (*C. ovata*) does not mature until about 80 years of age when it may produce one to two bushels of nuts annually. Squirrels and chipmunks as well as other wildlife relish the nuts and man enjoys them too—especially if they are thin-shelled, as in the pecans. Pecan growing in the South constitutes a major industry from which some wildlife species glean incidental benefit.

Waterfowl (nuts)
  ** Duck, Wood, *SE*
Upland Gamebirds (nuts)
  + Pheasant, Ring-necked, *NE*
  + Quail, Bobwhite, *SE*
  * Turkey, Wild, *SE*

Songbirds (nuts, flowers)
  + Crow, *E*
  * Grosbeak, Rose-breasted, *NE*
  + Jay, Northern Blue, *E*
  + Nuthatch, White-breasted, *E and E.Pr.*
  + Sapsucker, Yellow-bellied, *E* (sap)
  * Woodpecker, Red-bellied, *E*
Fur and Game Mammals (nuts, bark)
  + Bear, Black, *Va. and W.Va.*
  + Fox, Gray, *Va.*
    Rabbit
  +   Cottontail, Eastern, *Conn.*
  +   Cottontail, Mearns, *N.Y.*
  +   Cottontail, New England, *Conn.*
  + Raccoon, *E and Iowa*
    Squirrel
  ***   Fox, *Ohio and Mich.;* **NE*
  ***   Gray, Eastern, *E*
  ***   Red, *E*
Small Mammals (nuts, leaves)
  ** Chipmunk, Eastern, *NE*
    Mouse
  +   Pocket, Prairie, *Okla.*
  +   White-footed, *E and NE*
  + Rat, Attwater Wood, *Tex.*
Hoofed Browsers (foliage, twigs, nuts)
  + Deer, White-tailed, *Tex.*

References: Hickory; Pecan. H. S. Betts. American woods series. U.S. Dept. Agr. Forest Service, two leaflets, 1945. 10 pp.; 9 pp.

Pecan Growing in Florida. G. H. Blackmon. *Fla. Agr. Exp. Sta. Bul.* 191, 1927. 58 pp.

The Commercial Hickories. Anton T. Boisen and J. A. Newlin. *U.S. Dept. Agr. Forest Service Bul.* 80, 1910. 64 pp.

Waxmyrtle Family: *Myricaceae*

WAXMYRTLES, BAYBERRIES
Myrica

[23*/36 users] Seven species of *Myrica* are native to the United States: six in the East and one along the Pacific coast. They are confined largely to

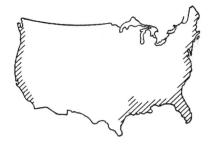

coastal areas, but locally they extend inland quite a few miles. The names bayberry and waxmyrtle are used interchangeably for these evergreen shrubs or small trees.

The waxy-coated fruit and its seed (nutlet) are eaten by many kinds of birds, generally in small quantities. It is a curious fact that along the Atlantic coast the tree swallow consumes many of the berries, though practically all the rest of its food consists of insects. The myrtle warbler lives up to its name by patronizing these plants freely when in the regions where they grow. If pen-raised quail eat large quantities of the fruit, the waxy, substance interferes with digestion and may even prove fatal.

Because of their dense, shiny, evergreen foliage *Myrica* bushes have value as ornamentals. The waxy coating of the fruits has been used since colonial times in making candles and in scenting soaps.

Waterfowl (fruit)
* Duck, Florida, *Fla.*

Marshbirds and Shorebirds (fruit)
+ Dowitcher, Eastern, *E*
Rail
+ King, *SE*
+ Yellow, *E*

Upland Gamebirds (fruit)
+ Grouse, Ruffed, *NE*
+ Quail, Bobwhite, *E*
+ Turkey, Wild, *SE*

Songbirds (fruit)
* Bluebird, *NE*; +*SE*
** Catbird, *SE*; *NE*
Chickadee
+ Black-capped, *NE*
+ Carolina, *SE*
+ Chestnut-backed, *Pac.*
Crow
+ Common, *E*
+ Fish, *E*
+ Flicker, Yellow-shafted, *E*
+ Grackle, Boat-tailed, *SE*
* Meadowlark, *NE*; +*SE*
+ Mockingbird, *SE*
+ Phoebe, *E*
+ Sparrow, Ipswich, *NE*
* Starling, *NE*
**** Swallow, Tree, *Atl. Coast*
+ Tanager, Scarlet, *NE*
* Thrasher, Brown, *SE*
+ Thrush, Hermit, *E*
+ Titmouse, Tufted, *SE*
+ Towhee, *NE*
* Vireo, White-eyed, *E*
Warbler
+ Audubon, *Calif.*
* Myrtle, *E*; +*Calif.*
Woodpecker
* Red-bellied, *E*
+ Red-cockaded, *Gulf Coast*
+ Wren, Carolina, *E*
* Wren-tit, *Calif.*

Fur and Game Mammals (fruit)
+ Fox, Gray, *Tex.*

Hoofed Browsers (twigs, foliage)
+ Deer, White-tailed, *N.C. and Ala.*

SWEETFERN
Comptonia peregrina

[2*/5 users] Sweetfern, as treated here, is the only species of its genus, *Comp-* *tonia.* However, some botanists merge this genus with *Myrica*, the waxmyrtle or bayberry. Sweetfern is a northern shrub extending from Canada down through the Appalachians to North Carolina and westward to Minnesota. It is partial to upland slopes where trees are sparse or absent and often forms solid stands in such places. The wildlife value of this sweet-scented, fern-leafed plant is limited. Deer browse on it in the Alleghenies, and gamebirds and rabbits also make minor use of it.

Upland Gamebirds (buds, catkins, foliage)
+ Grouse, Ruffed, *Pa.*
− Prairie Chicken, *Wis.*
Fur and Game Mammals (foliage, stems)
    Rabbit
+ Cottontail, Eastern, *Conn.*
+ Cottontail, New England, *Conn.*
Hoofed Browsers (foliage, branches)
** Deer, White-tailed, *Maine and Pa.; +Wis., Minn., and N.Y.*

Willow Family: *Salicaceae*
ASPENS AND POPLARS
Populus

 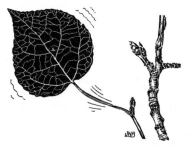

[46*/28 users] Aspens as well as cottonwoods are, strictly speaking, poplars, all belonging to the genus *Populus*. The so-called yellow poplar or tulip poplar (tuliptree) of the Southeast is not a true poplar. Of this group, the aspens and poplars, there are 15 to 19 species in the country and 30 to 40 in the world. The genus is more characteristic of the northern tier of states than of the South. In many northern areas where the native forests have been removed by fire or ax, aspens spring up rapidly and make extensive stands. The cottonwoods (*P. deltoides* and *P. sargenti*) are also widespread and are particularly common on prairie lowlands and near streams and houses in the West.

The two common aspens (quaking aspen, *P. tremuloides*, and large-toothed aspen, *P. grandidentata*) are the most important members of the poplar group

as far as wildlife are concerned. Their resinous buds and catkins are valuable winter and spring food for various kinds of grouse; the tender bark, twigs, and foliage are eaten freely by rabbits and hoofed browsers; and the wood or bark is relished by beavers and porcupines.

Upland Gamebirds (buds, catkins)
    Grouse
+ Blue, *No.Mt.–Des. and Pac. NW*
*** Ruffed, *NE; +Va. Alleghenies*
** Sharp-tailed, *N.Dak.; *Great Lakes Area*
** Prairie Chicken, Greater, *Wis.*
** Quail, Valley, *Nev.* (seeds)
Songbirds (buds)
− Finch, Purple, *E*
+ Towhee, Abert, *Ariz.*
Fur and Game Mammals (bark, foliage, buds)

300

**** Beaver, *W*; ***NE*
**** Hare, Varying, *Wis.*; ****Minn.;*
    ***N.Y.*
 + Mountain Beaver, *Pac.*
 − Muskrat, *Iowa*
 * Porcupine, *NE*; +*Mt.–Des.*
  Rabbit
 +   Cottontail, *Utah*
 +   Cottontail, Eastern, *Conn.*
 +   Cottontail, Mearns, *Pa.*
 +   Cottontail, New England, *Conn.*
 +   Cottontail, Oklahoma, *Okla.*
 −   Swamp, *Okla.*
    Squirrel

 +   Fox, *Ohio*
 +   Red, *N*
Small Mammals (bark)
 +   Mouse, Meadow, *E*
Hoofed Browsers (twigs, foliage)
    Deer
 ** Mule, *So.Mt.–Des.*; *No.Mt.– Des. and Calif.*
 *** White-tailed, *Wis. and Minn.;* ***N.Y. and S.Dak.;* *Mont.;* +*Maine and Pa.*
 * Elk, *No.Mt.–Des.*
 *** Moose, *Mich.*; ***Maine to Mich. and No.Mt.–Des.*
 − Sheep, Mountain, *Colo.*

References: Aspen in the Central Rocky Mountain Region. F. S. Baker. *U.S. Dept. Agr. Bul.* 1291, 1925. 47 pp.
Aspen—Availability, Properties and Utilization. R. P. A. Johnson and J. Kittredge, Jr. *Univ. Minn. Agr. Exp. Sta. Tech. Bul.* 70, 1930. 72 pp.
The Aspens: Their Growth and Management. W. G. Weigle and E. H. Frothingham. *U.S. Dept. Agr. Forest Service Bul.* 93, 1911. 35 pp.

WILLOWS
Salix

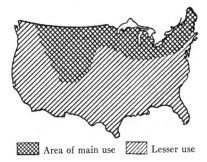

   ▨ Area of main use   ▨ Lesser use

[37*/25 users] There are between 200 and 300 kinds of willows in the world, about one-third of them growing in the United States, mainly in the North. Willows like moist fertile soils of bottom lands, river banks, and lake margins, but some are found in upland rocky places. They vary from large trees (the black willow, *S. nigra*, becomes 100 or more feet high and 2 to 3 feet in diameter) to small, practically herbaceous growths of 6 inches or less height in some alpine or subarctic species.

The principal wildlife usefulness of willows is in the North, not only because the plants are more plentiful there, but also because it is the region where browsing and bud-eating species are more common. The buds and small tender portions of the twigs are staple foods of several species of grouse, particularly the Franklin and sharp-tailed grouse. Ptarmigans, existing north of our territory, subsist in large part on willow buds. Other animals notably rabbits and hoofed browsers, such as elk, moose and deer, eat the twigs, foliage, and bark.

Upland Gamebirds (buds, twigs)
    Grouse
 * Blue, *No.Mt.–Des.*; +*Pac. NW*
 *** Franklin, *B.C.*
 * Ruffed, *NE*
 *** Sharp-tailed, *N.Dak.*; *Great Lakes Area;* +*Utah*
 − Prairie Chicken, Greater, *Wis. and Minn.*
Songbirds (buds)
 ** Grosbeak, Pine, *Pac.*

Fur and Game Mammals (bark, buds, wood)
*** Beaver, *W*; **NE; +*Mo.*
*** Hare, Varying, *Minn.;* **Utah
\+ Muskrat, *NE*
\+ Pika, *Pac.*
Rabbit
\- Cottontail, Mearns, *NE*
\+ Cottontail, New England, *Conn.*
\- Swamp, *Okla.*
Squirrel
\+ Fox, *Ohio and Mich.*
\+ Gray, *E.Tex.*
++ Red, *NE*

Small Mammals (foliage, catkins)
\+ Mouse, Meadow, *E*
Rat
\- Wood, Dusky-footed, *Oreg.*
\- Wood, Portola, *Calif.*
Hoofed Browsers (twigs, foliage)
Deer
* Mule, *Nebr.;* +*S.Dak.* and *No.Mt.–Des.*
** White-tailed, *Pa. and Mont.;* **N.Y., Wis., and Minn.;* +*S*
** Elk, *No.Mt.–Des.*
*** Moose, *Maine to Mich.;* ***No. Mt.–Des.*

Reference: Willows: Their Growth, Use, and Importance. George N. Lamb. *U.S. Dept. Agr. Bul.* 316, 1915. 52 pp.

Birch Family: *Betulaceae*

HORNBEAM
Carpinus caroliniana

[4*/10 users] The hornbeam, or blue beech, is confined to the East where it is one of the more common trees in rich moist soil of bottom lands, swamps, and river margins. The smooth bluish-gray bark distinguishes it from its cousin, the scaly-barked hop-horn-beam. Like the latter, this tree is of secondary importance to wildlife. Its seeds (nutlets) are eaten by several kinds of birds and by squirrels; its

catkins and buds are also used to a limited extent.

Waterfowl (seeds)
\+ Duck, Wood, *SE*
Upland Gamebirds (seeds, buds, catkins)
\+ Grouse, Ruffed, *E*
\+ Pheasant, Ring-necked, *N.Y.*
\+ Quail, Bobwhite, *NE*
Songbirds (seeds)
\+ Warbler, Myrtle, *E*
Fur and Game Mammals (seeds, bark, wood)
* Beaver, *NE*
\+ Rabbit, Mearns Cottontail, *N.Y.*
Squirrel
\+ Fox, *Ohio*
* Gray, Eastern, *E*
Hoofed Browsers (twigs, foliage)
* Deer, White-tailed, *N.Y.*

HOP-HORNBEAM
Ostrya virginiana

[0*/11 users] The American hop-horn-beam, or ironwood (*O. virginiana*), is the only member of the genus which is

widespread and of known use to wild-life. It is confined to the wooded sections of the East and is found mainly

in upland forests. Another species, *O. knowltoni*, is confined to northern Arizona and southern Utah.

Though 11 wildlife users of hop-hornbeam are listed below, there are no stars, and this fact denotes its rather limited value. The seeds (nutlets), enclosed by hop-like bracts, are eaten by several kinds of birds; buds and catkins are also taken by some gamebirds and other animals.

Upland Gamebirds (buds, catkins)
  Grouse
  + Ruffed, *NE*
  + Sharp-tailed, *Mich.*
  + Ptarmigan, *NE*

Songbirds (seeds)
  + Finch, Purple, *E*
  + Grosbeak, Rose-breasted, *NE and No.Pr.*
  + Woodpecker, Downy, *E and E.Pr.*
Fur and Game Mammals (seeds, buds)
  Squirrel
  + Fox, *Ohio and Mich.*
  + Red, *Wis.*
Small Mammals (seeds, buds)
  + Mouse, White-footed, *E*
Hoofed Browsers (twigs, foliage)
  + Deer, White-tailed, *N.Y.*

HAZELNUTS
Corylus

[**15*/23 users**] Three species of hazelnuts are natives of the United States. Two grow in the East and one in the Pacific region.

The low dense growth of these spreading bushes makes them useful for cover and as nesting sites. They occur commonly on pasture slopes, woods margins, and ditch banks. Hazelnuts are regarded as good hedgerow or wood-border plants. Squirrels, chipmunks, and other rodents feed on the nuts; grouse commonly eat the catkins; while rabbits, deer, and moose browse on the plants as a whole. Filberts are cultivated hazelnuts, grown in various parts of Europe and northwestern United States.

Upland Gamebirds (catkins, buds, nuts)
    Grouse
   ***   Ruffed, *Wis.;* **NE
   +   Sharp-tailed, *Great Lakes Area*
   +   Prairie Chicken, Greater, *No.Pr.*
   +   Turkey, Wild, *Pa.*
Songbirds (nuts)
   +   Woodpecker, Red-bellied, *E*
Fur and Game Mammals (nuts, stems, foliage)
   **   Beaver, *NE*
       Chickaree

   +   Douglas, *Pac.*
   *   Redwood, *Calif.*
  ** Hare, Varying, *Minn.*
   +   Rabbit, Mearns Cottontail, *N.Y.*
   +   Raccoon, *NE*
       Squirrel
   *   Fox, *Ohio*
   +   Fox, Western, *Mo. and Iowa*
   *   Red, *W; NE*
Small Mammals (nuts)
       Chipmunk
  ** Gray, Eastern, *NE; Wis.*
   +   Lyster, *Ontario*
   +   Ground Squirrel, Douglas, *Oreg.*
   +   Mouse, White-footed, *Minn.*
   +   Rat, Dusky-footed Wood, *Oreg. and Calif.*
Hoofed Browsers (twigs, foliage)
   +   Deer, White-tailed, *N.Y.*
   *   Moose, *Mich.*

BIRCHES
Betula

[**52*/24 users**] Of the 35 to 40 birches in the north temperate and subarctic parts of the world, 12 to 15 grow in the United States. Our native species are typically northern with the exception of the river birch (*B. nigra*) which is found on river banks and flood plains as far south as Florida and Texas. They prefer moist fertile soils but also grow in gravelly humus among rocks (mountainous or northern species) or silty-loam bottom lands (river birch).

Birches are short-lived. A few northern species are shrubby. Like their near relatives the alders, they bear catkins and small seed cones. Several birches are distinct in appearance because of their shredding or paper-white

bark. The yellow birch (*B. lutea*), black or sweet birch (*B. lenta*), paper birch

304

(*B. papyrifera*), and gray birch (*B. populifolia*) are well-known northern or northeastern species of importance to both man and wildlife. The water birch, or western red birch (*B. fontinalis*), is a shrub or small tree that is widely distributed in the Rockies.

The wildlife importance of birches, though considerable, is confined largely to the North and to northern animals. Prominent among the northern users are the sharp-tailed, spruce, and ruffed grouse (feeding on catkins, buds, and seeds), the redpoll and pine siskin (seeds), and browsing or wood-eating mammals such as the moose, snowshoe or varying hares, porcupine, and beaver. The river birch though common throughout the Southeast has very little recognized value for any wildlife.

Upland Gamebirds (catkins, buds, seeds)
Grouse
** Ruffed, *NE*; **Wis.*
**** Sharp-tailed, *Great Lakes Area*
** Spruce, *NW and Canada*
* Prairie Chicken, Greater, *N.Pr.*
Songbirds (seeds mainly)
* Chickadee, Black-capped, *NE*
+ Finch, Purple, *E* (buds)

*** Redpoll, Common, *N*
+ Sapsucker, Yellow-bellied, *E* (sap)
*** Siskin, Pine, *E*
Sparrow
* Fox, *E*
+ Tree, *NE*
Fur and Game Mammals (various parts)
** Beaver, *NE and W;* +*Mo.* (bark, wood)
** Hare, Varying, *NE*
** Porcupine, *Vt.*; *NE (bark, wood)
Rabbit (bark, twigs, foliage)
* Cottontail, *Conn.*
+ Cottontail, Rocky Mountain, *Utah*
− Squirrel, Red, *Wis.* (seeds, buds)
Small Mammals (seeds)
− Chipmunk, Lake Superior, *Minn.*
− Rat, Allegheny Wood, *E*
Hoofed Browsers (twigs, foliage)
Deer
+ Mule, *NW*
* White-tailed, *N.Y. and Mont.*; +*Wis. and Minn.*
+ Elk, *No.Mt.–Des*
*** Moose, *Mich.*; ***Maine to Mich. and No.Mt.–Des.*

References: Paper Birch in the Northeast. S. T. Dana. *U.S. Dept. Agr. Forest Service Circ.* 163, 1909. 37 pp.
Some Soil and Moisture Relationships of Sweetgum and River Birch in Southern Maryland. F. B. Trenk. *Proc. Iowa. Acad. Sci.*, Vol. 32, pp. 133–142, 1926.

ALDERS
Alnus

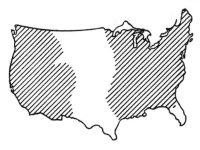

[36*/16 users] About 9 species of alder are found in this country of some 20 to

30 species found the world over. Alders are primarily north temperate in their distribution and are more prominent in our northern latitudes than southward. They occur in moist meadows and are common on stream banks and flood plains.

Though these catkin-bearing plants are mainly shrubs, the red alder (*A. rubra*) of the Pacific Northwest is a tree, generally about 35 to 40 feet high and occasionally up to 90 feet. Alders are closely related to the birches, and a few species are more or less intermediate between these two genera. Birches and alders are similar in their catkins, seed cones, and also in the seeds (nutlets) themselves, which are small, flattish, and margined with either a woody or papery wing.

The wildlife food value of alders is low in proportion to the widespread abundance of the plants. Nevertheless their seeds are important in the diet of redpolls, siskins, and goldfinches. Other parts of the plants are eaten by gamebirds and browsers. Dense copses of alder provide effective wildlife cover from enemies and from unfavorable weather.

Upland Gamebirds (buds, catkins, seeds)
  Grouse
+   Ruffed, *N*
**   Sharp-tailed, *Gt. Lakes Area*

+ Woodcock, *NE*
Songbirds (seeds)
*   Goldfinch, *E*
     Redpoll
***   Common, *N*
***   Hoary, *N*
*   Siskin, Pine, *NW*
Fur and Game Mammals (wood, foliage)
*   Beaver, *NE*; +*Mo.*
*   Hare, Varying, *Minn. and Wis.*
Hoofed Browsers (twigs, foliage)
  Deer
−   Mule, *Minn.*
*   White-tailed, *Wis. and Minn.; +Mont.*
+ Elk, *Wash.*
+ Goat, Mountain, *Mont.*
* Moose, *Maine to Mich., No.Mt.– Des.; +Mich.*
− Sheep, Mountain, *Mont.*

Reference: Red Alder in the Pacific Northwest. H. M. Johnson, E. J. Hanzlik, and W. H. Gibbons. *U.S. Dept. Agr. Bul.* 1437, 1926. 46 pp.

Beech Family: *Fagaceae*

BEECH
Fagus grandifolia

[**38*/31 users**] The American beech is one of four known species. Our single species is confined to eastern woodlands where it occurs on fertile bottom lands and uplands. Ecologists class the beech as a "climax" plant. It prefers cool, shady, moist locations but ranges all the way southward to Florida and Texas.

Full grown, the beech is a large, handsome tree with bright green foliage that turns to a beautiful copper color or golden yellow in the fall. Its smooth, gray bark provides a favorite place for youngsters to carve their initials. Like its close relatives, the oaks and chestnuts, the beech bears its small wind-pollinated flowers in catkins; the fruit is a small triangular nut. Beechnuts are eaten by birds as well as by mammals and are a particularly important food for squirrels and chipmunks. When, as frequently happens, the crop of beech mast is a failure, it works a noticeable hardship on these animals. The beech is popular as an ornamental and shade tree.

Waterfowl (nuts)
* Duck, Wood, *NE*

Upland Gamebirds (nuts, buds)
Grouse
** Ruffed, *Ohio;* +*NE*
* Spruce, *NW and Canada*
+ Pheasant, Ring-necked, *Ohio and N.Y.*
* Turkey, Wild, *SE;* +*Va.*

Songbirds (nuts mainly)
+ Blackbird, Rusty, *NE*
– Chickadee, *Md.*
+ Finch, Purple, *E* (buds)
+ Grackle, *NE*
* Grosbeak, Rose-breasted, *NE*
* Jay, Northern Blue, *E*
+ Nuthatch, White-breasted *E*

+ Sapsucker, Yellow-bellied, *E* (sap)
** Titmouse, Tufted, *E*
Woodpecker
– Downy, *Md.*
– Hairy, *Md.*
+ Red-bellied, *E*

Fur and Game Mammals (nuts mainly)
**** Bear, Black, *Pa.*
+ Beaver, *W.Va.* (wood)
Fox
+ Gray, *E*
+ Red, *E*
*** Porcupine, *Vt.;* *NE* (wood)
+ Raccoon, *NE*
Squirrel
*** Flying, *NE*
*** Fox, *Ohio;* *NE*
** Fox, Western, *Mich.*
** Gray, *E*
** Red, *E*

Small Mammals (nuts)
** Chipmunk, Eastern, *NE*
+ Mouse, White-footed, *E*

Hoofed Browsers (twigs, foliage, nuts)
+ Deer, White-tailed, *N.Y.*

References: American Beech. H. S. Betts. American woods series. U.S. Dept. Agr. Forest Service, 1945. 8 pp.
Uses of Commercial Woods of the United States: Beeches, Birches and Maples. H. Maxwell. *U.S. Dept. Agr. Forest Serv. Bul.* 12, 1913. 56 pp.

CHESTNUT
Castanea dentata

[2*/7 users] Fifty years ago the chestnut ranked as one of the most important wildlife plants of the eastern United States. Today it is not much more than a memory, though in many places the blasted trunks of former chestnut forests still stand as dead relics of the past. The chestnut blight, introduced into this country from Asia about 1904, has practically exterminated this valuable forest tree on which deer, squirrels, the wild turkey, and numerous other wildlife are reported to have fared. The chestnuts which are now available on the market are from foreign stock.

The chinkapin (*Castanea pumila* and several other species), a diminutive

cousin of the chestnut, has been spared the chestnut's fate, but unfortunately its wildlife value is relatively low. The bur-covered nuts of these shrubs are similar to those of chestnut though smaller. They are eaten to the extent of a 1-star rating by chipmunks as well as by fox and red squirrels in the Northeast.

Fur and Game Mammals (nuts)
Rabbit
– Cottontail, Eastern, *Conn.*
– Cottontail, New England, *Conn.*
* Squirrel, Red, *NE*

Small Mammals (nuts)
* Chipmunk, Eastern, *NE*

   — Rat, Allegheny Wood, *E*
   — Squirrel, Western Fox, *Mo.*

Hoofed Browsers (twigs, foliage)
   — Deer, White-tailed, *NE*

Reference: Chestnut. H. S. Betts. American woods series. U.S. Dept. Agr. Forest
Service, 1945. 6 pp.

OAKS
Quercus

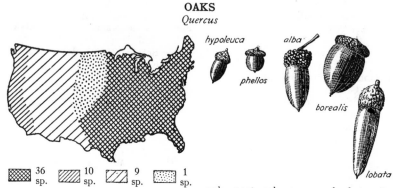

▨ 36 sp.	▨ 10 sp.	▨ 9 sp.	▨ 1 sp.

[263*/96 users] Oak trees are of major importance to both man and wildlife in temperate regions. Two hundred to five hundred species are known, and of these 54 to 85 are natives of the United States. They include some of our largest and most stately trees though a number of species are shrublike. As the range map shows, oaks are widely distributed over the country but are scarce or absent in the northern prairies. They thrive at different altitudes and in many different types of soil.

Acorns rate a position at, or very near, the top of the wildlife food list, not so much because they are a preferred food item but because they constitute a good and abundantly available staple—the staff of life for many wildlife species. The star-studded list and the use ratio of 263 stars over 96 animals is proof of the importance of oaks to wildlife. Their greatest value is in the critical winter season when other foods are scarce. When, as sometimes happens, the acorn crop is a failure, a number of wildlife species may be hard pressed for sustenance.

There is evidence that acorns of the white oak group (the white oak, valley oak, post oak, cow or basket oak, chestnut oak, etc.) are more palatable to wildlife just as they were preferred by the Indians and early settlers. Their palatability appears to be inversely proportionate to the amount of tannin present in them. Black oak acorns are bitter and are used less even though the black oak group produces an annual crop of acorns. The comparatively small acorns of the water oak, willow oak, and pin oak are often available near ponds and streams where they are eaten by ducks—especially by wood ducks and mallards. Quail swallow small acorns such as the above or will peck out the meats of larger ones. Wild turkeys swallow the acorns whole regardless of size; an individual meal of 77 black oak acorns has been recorded and also one of 35 of the giant acorns of the northern red oak. Squirrels and other rodents store the acorns for winter use, and the California woodpecker also indulges in this practice. Deer are fond of the larger acorns and also browse on the foliage and twigs.

In addition to their food value, oaks also provide useful wildlife cover. A few are evergreen. Young trees of some species, such as the widespread white oak, retain their dried, dead leaves through much of the winter. Oak leaves and twigs are used by many birds as nesting material.

Some of the species of oaks of particular importance to wildlife in different regions of the country are:

EAST (rather widespread species): White (*Quercus alba*), black (*velutina*), scarlet (*coccinea*), pin (*palustris*)

NORTHEAST: Northern red (*borealis maxima*), swamp-white (*bicolor*), jack (*ellipsoidalis*), chestnut (*montana*), bur (*macrocarpa*)

SOUTHEAST: Water (*nigra*), willow (*phellos*), live (*virginiana*), southern red (*rubra*), post (*stellata*), black-jack (*marilandica*), swamp-chestnut (*prinus*), laurel (*laurifolia*)

PRAIRIES: Bur (*macrocarpa*)

MT.–DESERT: Gambel (*gambeli*), Emory (*emoryi*), Utah (*utahensis*)

PACIFIC: Valley (*lobata*), canyon live (*chrysolepis*), Oregon white (*garryana*), California black (*kelloggii*), blue (*douglasii*)

Oaks are the most important group of broad-leaf timber trees in the country and constitute a major proportion of our eastern forests. Their hard durable wood has many uses. In addition, oaks are among the best shade trees planted along our city streets and about our homes.

Waterfowl (acorns)
 Duck
 * Mallard, *E*
 + Pintail, *Tex.*
***** (62%) Wood, *Wis.;* ****SE*;
   **NE*
Marshbirds and Shorebirds (acorns)
 + Rail, Clapper, *U.S.*
Upland Gamebirds (acorns, buds)
 * Dove, White-winged, *Ariz.*
 Grouse
 *** Ruffed, *Va.Alleghenies;*
   **Ohio;* +*NE and Pr.*
 + Sharp-tailed, *N.Dak.*
 * Pheasant, Ring-necked, *NE;*
   +*NW*
**** Pigeon, Band-tailed, *So.Mt.–
   Des.;* ****Pac.*
 Prairie Chicken
 * Greater, *No.Pr. and Wis.*

***** (52%) Lesser, *Okla.*
 Quail
** Bobwhite, *SE and Tex.–Okla.;*
   **NE;* +*Pr.*
* California, *Calif.*
*** Mearns, *SW*
** Mountain, *Pac.*
** Valley, *Calif.*
 Turkey
** Merriam, *Ariz. and N.Mex.*
**** Wild, *SE and Pa.;* ****Mo.
   and Tex.;* ***Allegheny Mts.
   and Ariz.–N.Mex.*
Songbirds (acorns)
+ Blackbird, Rusty, *NE*
+ Chickadee, Mountain, *Mt.–Des.
   and Pac.*
 Crow
+ Common, *Pr.*
* Eastern, *E*
 Flicker
** Red-shafted, *Pac.*
+ Yellow-shafted, *E and E.Pr.*
+ Goldfinch, Willow, *Calif.*
*** Grackle, Purple and/or Bronzed,
   SE; ***NE*
+ Grosbeak, Rose-breasted, *NE
   and No.Pr.*
 Jay
**** Blue, *E*
**** Blue, Florida, *Gulf States*
**** California, *Calif.*
**** Florida, *Fla.*
**** Steller, *Pac.*
*** Woodhouse, *So.Mt.–Des.*
**** Lark, California Horned, *Calif.*
+ Meadowlark, *SE*
+ Nutcracker, Clark, *NW*
*** Nuthatch, White-breasted, *E;*
   +*E.Pr. and Pac.*
+ Sapsucker, Yellow-bellied, *E*
   (sap)
+ Starling, *NE*
 Thrasher
*** Brown, *Tex.;* ***SE;* **NE*
* California, *Calif.*
 Titmouse
** Plain, *Calif.*
** Tufted, *E*
*** Thrush, Varied, *Pac.*
 Towhee
** Red-eyed, *NE*
** Spotted, *Pac.*

	Woodpecker	—	Gila, *Ariz.*
****	Ant-eating, *Pac.*, *mainly Calif.*	—	Lyster, *NE*
+	Downy, *E and Pr.*	*	Western, *Mt.–Des and Pac.*
***	Lewis, *Mt.–Des. and Pac.*	***	Gopher, Pocket, *Calif.*
***	Red-bellied, *E*		Ground Squirrel
+	Red-cockaded, *Gulf Coast*	**	Columbian, *No.Mt.–Des. and*
***	Red-headed, *E*		*Pac.*
+	Wren, Carolina, *E*	***	Beechey, *Calif.*

Fur and Game Mammals (acorns, bark, wood)

****	Bear, Black, *Va.*, *W.Va.*, and *Pa.*	+	Douglas, *Oreg.*
+	Beaver, *Mo.*	*	Mantled, *W*
+	Cat, Ring-tailed, *Tex.*		Mouse
	Fox	+	Meadow, *E*
+	Gray, *S*	**	White-footed, *E*; **W*
+	Red, *NE*		Rat
+	Hare, Varying, *Minn.*		Kangaroo, *Calif.*
+	Muskrat, *NE*	**	Wood, *So.Pr.*
*	Opossum, *Okla. and Tex.;* +*E*	—	Wood, Allegheny, *NE*
	Rabbit	—	Wood, Attwater, *NE*
*	Cottontail, Eastern, *Mich.;* +*Iowa*	—	Wood, Dusky-footed, *Pac.*
+	Cottontail, Mearns, *Conn.*	—	Wood, Large-eared, *Calif.*
*	Cottontail, New England, *NE*	—	Wood, Portola, *Calif.*
****	Raccoon, *NE* and *E.Tex.;* ***SE; ***Pac.*	***	Rock Squirrel, *Tex.*

Hoofed Browsers (twigs, foliage, acorns)

	Squirrel		Deer
**	Flying, *NE*	****	Black-tailed, *Calif.*
***	Fox, *E*	***	Mule, *So.Mt.–Des. and Calif.;* ***No.Mt.–Des.;* +*S.Dak.*
****	Fox, Western, *Mich.*	*****	(52%) White-tailed, *Tex.;* *****Mo. and Ala.;* ****N.C. Mts.;* ***Maine;* **N.Y.*, *Pa.*, and *N.C. Coast;* +*Wis.*, *Minn.*, and *S.Dak.*
****	Gray, *E*		
****	Gray, Western, *Calif.*		
**	Red, *E*	+	Elk, *No. Mt.–Des.*

Small Mammals (acorns)

	Chipmunk	****	Peccary, *Tex. and Ariz.*
**	Eastern, *NE*	+	Sheep, Mountain, *N.Mex.*

References: Oaks. H. S. Betts. American woods series. U.S. Dept. Agr. Forest Service, 1945. 16 pp.

White Oak in the Southern Appalachians. W. B. Greeley and W. W. Ashe. *U.S. Dept. Agr. Forest Serv. Circ.* 105, 1907. 27 pp.

Elm Family: *Ulmaceae*

ELMS
Ulmus

[17*/20 users] Our six or seven native species of elm are primarily eastern trees. The American elm (*U. americana*) is the outstanding species in distribution, abundance, and impor- tance to man and animals. It and the rock elm are large trees, commonly 100 feet high. Elms grow in a wide variety of sites varying from moist bottom lands and stream margins to

relatively dry uplands. The winged, slippery, cedar and red elms are small or medium-sized trees.

The wildlife value of elms is low as compared with oaks, maples, and dogwoods. Nevertheless the seeds and buds are used considerably by songbirds and gamebirds as well as by squirrels. The seeds of cedar elm and red elm ripen in the fall, but in other native species they mature early in the spring long before most seeds are available. The wildlife utility of the Chinese elm, introduced widely into the West, is not known yet. Birds often nest in the thick elm foliage, the American elm being a favorite nesting site for the Baltimore oriole.

Waterfowl (seeds)
+ ** Duck, Wood, *N.Y.*

Upland Gamebirds (seeds, buds)
+ Grouse, Sharp-tailed, *Mich.*
+ Pheasant, Ring-necked, *Wis.*

+ Prairie Chicken, *Wis.*
** Turkey, Wild, *Tex.*

Songbirds (seeds, buds)
+ Chickadee, Carolina, *SE*
*** Finch, Purple, *E*
+ Goldfinch, Eastern, *E*
* Grosbeak, Rose-breasted, *NE and No.Pr.*
+ Sapsucker, Yellow-bellied, *Md.* (sap)
Sparrow
* Clay-colored, *E.Pr.*
+ English, *E and Pr.*
+ Warbler, Myrtle, *E*

Fur and Game Mammals (buds, seeds, wood)
+ Beaver, *Mo.*
+ Muskrat, *Ohio*
* Rabbit, Cottontail, *Pr.*; +*Iowa*
Squirrel
* Fox, *Mich.*
+ Gray, *E*
** Red, *NE*

Hoofed Browsers (twigs, foliage)
+ Deer, White-tailed, *N.Y.*

References: Elm. H. S. Betts. American woods series. U.S. Dept. Agr. Forest Service, 1945. 10 pp.

Utilization of Elms. W. D. Brush. *U.S. Dept. Agr. Bul.* 683, 1918. 43 pp.

HACKBERRIES
Celtis

[54*/48 users] Eight of the world's 50 to 75 species of hackberries are native to the United States. These trees (occasionally shrubby) occur over a large proportion of the country in habitats ranging from swampy flood plains to limestone hills. Their greatest importance to wildlife is in the West.

Hackberry fruits (drupes) are popular with many winter birds and especially with the cedar waxwing, yellow-bellied sapsucker, mockingbird, and robin. Flocks of cedar waxwings visit the trees in late fall or winter as long as fruit remains. The local name sugarberry gives recognition to the palatability of the fruit. The thin, fleshy pulp covers a large hard, chalky-walled stone containing the seed.

Hackberries are used commonly for

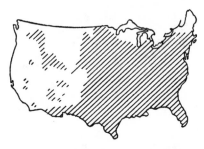

shade and ornament in the Middle West. These trees are susceptible to the witches-broom causing a profusion of twigs near the ends of branches. This characteristic does not seriously impair their horticultural value, nor does it destroy their importance to birds.

Upland Gamebirds (fruit)
+ Dove, White-winged, *Tex. and Ariz.*
* Pigeon, Band-tailed, *So.Mt.– Des.*
Quail
+ Bobwhite, *Tex.*
+ Gambel, *Ariz.*
* Scaled, Chestnut-bellied, *Tex.*
* Turkey, Wild, *Tex. and Mo.*

Songbirds (fruit)
* Bluebird, Eastern, *SE*
* Cardinal, *Pr.*
+ Catbird, *SE*
Crow
+ Common, *Pr.*
* Fish, *E*
* Flicker, Yellow-shafted, *E and E.Pr.*
* Grosbeak, Evening, *NW*
* Magpie, American, *Mt.–Des.*
*** Mockingbird, *Tex.;* *SE
+ Oriole, Bullock, *SW*
+ Phoebe, *E*
+ Raven, White-necked, *SW*
*** Robin, *E.Pr.;* ***Mt.–Des.;* **SE;* +*NE*
Sapsucker (sap)
** Red-naped, *Tex. and Okla.*

**** Yellow-bellied, *So.Pr.;* +*E*
+ Solitaire, Townsend, *W*
* Sparrow, Fox, *W*
+ Starling, European, *NE*
Thrasher
** Brown, *Tex.;* +*SE*
+ Curve-billed, *SW*
Thrush
+ Hermit, *E*
*** Olive-backed, *Pr.*
+ Titmouse, Tufted, *SE*
+ Towhee, *SE*
* Waxwing, Cedar, *NE*
*** Woodpecker, Golden-fronted, *Tex.*

Fur and Game Mammals (fruit)
+ Beaver, *Tex.* (wood)
* Cat, Ring-tailed, *Tex.*
* Fox, Gray, *SW*
* Opossum, *Tex. and Okla.;* +*Mo.*
+ Raccoon, *NE*
Skunk
+ Hog-nosed, *Tex.*
+ Striped, *Tex.*
Squirrel
* Flying, *NE*
+ Fox, *Ohio.*
+ Fox, Western, *Mich.*

Small Mammals (fruit)
Rat
+ Wood, Attwater, *Tex.*
+ Wood, White-throated, *Ariz.*

Hoofed Browsers (twigs, foliage)
Deer
** Mule, *Utah*
* White-tailed, *S*

References: The Southern hardwoods—Hackberry. *Southern Lumberman*, Vol. 162 (2038), p. 31, 1941.
Hackberry. H. S. Betts. American woods series. U.S. Dept. Agr. Forest Service, 1945. 6 pp.

Mulberry Family: *Moraceae*

MULBERRIES
Morus

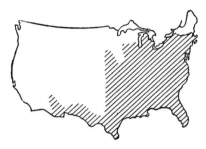

[**35*/38 users**] Eight to twelve species of mulberries are widely distributed over the north temperate regions. Two species are native to this country, and two others have been introduced. Of our native species, the Texas mulberry (*M. microphylla*) grows as a small tree or shrub in the arid Southwest from Texas to Arizona while the red mulberry (*M. rubra*) is widely distributed in moist places of eastern woodlands. The white mulberry (*M. alba*), native of Asia, but naturalized widely in the United States, is the tree on which silkworms feed, and until recently it was indirectly the world's principal source of silk. Black mulberry (*M. nigra*), also Asiatic, is relatively rare in this country and therefore of no importance to wildlife.

Mulberry fruits ripen in early summer and at this season are one of the most popular foods of songbirds. A tree or two near one's home is sure to attract songsters. The birds do not even wait until the mulberries are ripe before they start eating them. The seeds (akenes), the part more readily recognized in stomach analyses, may be as nutritious as the fleshy part of the fruit. The trees are subject to a deformity known as witches-broom.

Upland Gamebirds (fruit)
* * Pigeon, Band-tailed, *So.Mt.– Des.*

Songbirds (fruit)
* * Cardinal, *E and Pr.*
* * Catbird, *W;* +*E*
* Crow
* * Common, *E;* +*Pr.*
* ** Fish, *E*
* + Flycatcher, Crested, *E*
* + Grackle, Purple, *E*
* + Grosbeak, Rose-breasted, *E and Pr.*
* + Jay, Northern Blue, *E*
* + Kingbird, *E*
* * Mockingbird, *SE*
* Oriole
* * Baltimore, *NE*
* + Bullock, *Calif.*
* ** Orchard, *E.Pr.;* **NE;* +*SE*
* * Phainopepla, *Calif. and Ariz.*
* + Robin, *E and Pr.*
* + Sparrow, English, *E*
* * Starling, *NE*
* Tanager
* + Scarlet, *NE*
* + Summer, *S*
* * Western, *Pac.*
* * Thrasher, Brown, *Pr.;* +*E*
* Thrush
* + Russet-backed, *Calif.*
* * Wood, *NE*
* + Titmouse, Tufted, *E*
* * Waxwing, Cedar, *NE*
* Woodpecker
* * Red-bellied, *E*
* * Red-headed, *E and Pr.*

313

Fur and Game Mammals (fruit)
+ Armadillo, *Tex.*
− Fox, Red, *Iowa*
* Opossum, *Mo.*; +*SE, Okla.-Tex.*
* Raccoon, *Tex.*; −*Iowa*
Skunk
− Eastern, *Mich.*

+ Hog-nosed, *Tex.*
* Spotted, *Iowa*
Squirrel
* Fox, *Ohio;* +*NE*
− Fox, Western, *Mo.*
* Gray, Western, *Calif.*
* Gray, Eastern, *E*

OSAGE-ORANGE
Maclura pomifera

[0*/3 users] The osage-orange, a thorny tree of rich bottom lands in the Osage Indian country, was widely used as a hedge plant. Hedge-apple is another common name for it. There is very little to qualify the osage-orange as a wildlife food plant, though it does have usefulness for cover. Squirrels and bobwhite feed on the seeds of the oranges occasionally. The present trend is to plant living fences of multiflora rose instead of osage-orange hedges.

Upland Gamebirds (seeds)
+ Quail, Bobwhite, *E*
Fur and Game Mammals (seeds)
Squirrel
− Fox, *Ohio*
+ Fox, Western, *Mich.*

Mistletoe Family: *Loranthaceae*
MISTLETOES
Phoradendron and Arceuthobium

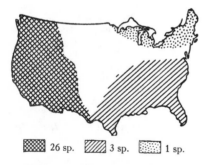

26 sp. 3 sp. 1 sp.

[12*/17 users] Those who know mistletoe only as a Christmas ornament may be surprised to learn that there are 22 kinds of them native in the United States. The American species fall into two genera: American mistletoes (*Phoradendron*) and dwarfmistletoes (*Arceuthobium*). The former are parasitic on broad-leaved trees; the latter, on conifers. The common southeastern mistletoe (*P. flavescens*) is gathered and sold as a Christmas decoration. Most of the other species, especially the dwarfmistletoes, occur in the Mountain–Desert and Pacific regions.

Mistletoe berries are generally available to wildlife in the late fall and winter. They are relished by cedar waxwings, the phainopepla, and bluebirds as well as by other species. The feeding of birds on mistletoe fruit is doubtless essential to the spread of these plants.

Upland Gamebirds (fruit)
+ Grouse, Blue, *E.Wash.*
+ Pigeon, Band-tailed, *So.Mt.-Des.*
Quail
+ Gambel, *SW*
− Mountain, *Calif.*
Songbirds (fruit)
Bluebird
* Chestnut-backed, *W*
+ Eastern, *E*
* Western, *Calif.*
+ Crow, *W*
** Phainopepla, *Calif. and Ariz.*
+ Raven, *Mt.–Des. and Pac.*
+ Robin, *Mt.–Des. and Pac.*

+ Thrasher, California, *Calif.*
+ Thrush, Hermit, *Pac.*
** Waxwing, Cedar, *SE and Pac.*
Fur and Game Mammals (fruit)
* Cat, Ring-tailed, *Tex.*

Hoofed Browsers (branches, foliage, fruit)
Deer
+ Mule, *So.Mt.–Des.*
* White-tailed, *Tex.*

Goosefoot Family: *Chenopodiaceae*

SALTBUSHES
Atriplex

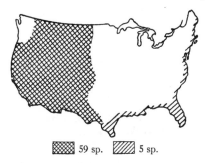

▨ 59 sp. ▨ 5 sp.

[29*/22 users] Most of the 60 species of saltbush in the United States are grayish or light-colored shrubs, characteristic of moderately alkaline soils of the Far West. Frequently these plants are associated with sagebrush. A few species also occur along the seacoasts.

Saltbush, also called shadscale, is of fair importance to western wildlife. The seeds (borne in bracts) are used by several kinds of birds and small mammals. The twigs and scurfy foliage are eaten by antelopes, rabbits, and other browsers. In addition, their cover value in relatively open country is an asset to wildlife of deserts and plains.

Waterfowl (seeds, leaves, stems)
+ Goose, Canada, *Utah and Pac.*
Upland Gamebirds (seeds)
+ Quail, Gambel, *SW*
Songbirds (seeds)
+ Lark, Horned, *W, excl. Calif.*
Sparrow
** Ipswich, *NE*

** Seaside, *Atl. and Gulf Coasts*
+ Sharp-tailed, *Atl. Coast*
Fur and Game Mammals (leaves, stems)
** Jack Rabbit, Black-tailed, *Utah*
Small Mammals (seeds, leaves)
Gopher
+ Pocket, Brown, *Mont.*
+ Pocket, Western, *Mont.*
+ Ground Squirrel, Antelope, *Mt.– Des. and Calif.*
* Mouse, Pocket, *W.Pr. and Mt.– Des.; +Calif.*
Prairie Dog
* Black-tailed, *W.Pr.*
**** White-tailed, *Wyo.–Mont.*
Rat
* Kangaroo, *Calif.*
+ Kangaroo, Giant, *Calif.*
* Kangaroo, Ord, *W*
− Kangaroo, Tulare, *Calif.*
Hoofed Browsers (twigs, foliage)
** Antelope, *No.Pr. and Mt.–Des.; *N.Mex.; +SE Mont.*
***** (71%) Bison, *Ariz.*
+ Deer, Mule, *Utah*
* Sheep, Mountain, *Calif.; +No. Mt.–Des.*

Reference: Saltbushes and Their Allies in the United States. G. L. Bidwell and E. O. Wooten. *U.S. Dept. Agr. Bul.* 1345, 1925. 40 pp.

Magnolia Family: *Magnoliaceae*

MAGNOLIAS
Magnolia

[0*/7 users] This genus of 21 to 35 species is represented by 8 or 9 native trees in the United States. Our native magnolias are confined to the East. The southern magnolia (*M. grandiflora*), also known as bullbay, is a beautiful glossy-leaved evergreen widely grown as a shade tree in the warmer parts of the country. The other swamp-inhabiting magnolia, the sweetbay or swampbay (*M. virginiana*), is a common, widespread species. Several Asiatic species of magnolias are also planted as ornamentals.

The wildlife use of magnolias is low, though the berry-like seeds are eaten by several species of birds and small mammals. Several birds use the leaves of the sweetbay in nest building.

Songbirds (seeds)
+ Sapsucker, Yellow-bellied, *E* (sap)
+ Towhee, *SE*
+ Vireo, Red-eyed, *E*
+ Woodpecker, Red-cockaded, *Gulf Coast*

Fur and Game Mammals (seeds)
− Squirrel, Gray, *Fla.*

Small Mammals (seeds)
+ Mouse, White-footed, *E*

Hoofed Browsers (leaves, twigs)
+ Deer, White-tailed, *E*

Reference: Magnolia. H. S. Betts. American woods series. U.S. Dept. Agr. Forest Service, 1945. 6 pp.

TULIPTREE
Liriodendron tulipifera

[7*/14 users] There are two species of *Liriodendron*, one in the eastern United States, and one in Asia. The tuliptree (called poplar, yellow poplar, or tulip-poplar in the South) grows best on moist but well-drained soil, on either bottom lands or slopes.

These stately trees with their large, beautiful flowers and unique squarish leaves are of only moderate significance to wildlife. The seeds (winged samaras) occur in cone-like clusters that ripen in the fall. They are eaten by several species of birds and squirrels—the purple finch and cardinal being the principal users. Some of the tuliptree seeds persist in the cones through the winter and are of special value for this reason.

Songbirds (seeds mainly)
+ Blackbird, Redwing, *Md.*
* Cardinal, *NE*
− Chickadee, Carolina, *Md.*
** Finch, Purple, *E*
+ Goldfinch, *E*
− Hummingbird, Ruby-throated, *Md.* (nectar)
+ Sapsucker, Yellow-bellied, *E* (sap)

Fur and Game Mammals (seeds, wood)
− Beaver, *Va.*

Squirrel
+ Fox, *Ohio*
+ Gray, *E*
* Red, *E*

Small Mammals (seeds)
    * Mouse, White-footed, *E*
Hoofed Browsers (twigs, foliage)
    — Deer, White-tailed, *Va.*

Reference: Yellow-poplar—Characteristics, Growth, and Management. E. F. McCarthy. *U.S. Dept. Agr. Tech. Bul.* 356, 1933. 58 pp.

Barberry Family: *Berberidaceae*

BARBERRIES
Berberis

[8*/11 users] There are about 15 species of barberry in the United States. As treated here the genus *Berberis* includes the Oregon-grape and other species that some botanists segregate with other genera.

Barberries ordinarily grow in upland situations, generally in well-drained loam. They are shrubs, many of them spiny, with small yellow flowers, yellow wood, and small berries ranging in color from red to blue.

Their principal value to wildlife is in the West where hoofed browsers, especially deer, eat the plants freely. The fleshy fruits (berries) are eaten by birds only to a limited degree. The relatively low rank of barberries may be partly due to the fact that much of the common barberry of the East has been eradicated because of its role as a host for one phase of the wheat rust. The bright-colored fruits of the common hedge plant, Japanese barberry (*B. thunbergii*), are available to birds throughout the winter, but they do not seem to be relished. Birds make use of them only in critical periods when other foods are scarce or absent.

Upland Gamebirds (fruit)
    + Grouse, Ruffed, *New England*
    * Pheasant, Ring-necked, *N.Y.*
Songbirds (fruit)
    — Mockingbird, *Md.*
    + Waxwing, Cedar, *NE*
Fur and Game Mammals (bark, leaves, twigs)
    + Cat, Ring-tailed, *Tex.*
    + Hare, Varying, *Utah*
    + Rabbit, Rocky Mountain Cottontail, *Utah* (Oregon-grape)
Hoofed Browsers (twigs, foliage)
    Deer
    *** Mule, *S.Dak.;* **No.Mt.–Des.*
    *** White-tailed, *Mont.* (Oregon-grape); +*S.Dak.*
    * Elk, *No.Mt.–Des.*
    + Sheep, Mountain, *No.Mt.–Des.*

Laurel Family: *Lauraceae*

SASSAFRAS
Sassafras albidum

[8*/23 users] There is just one species of sassafras in the United States and one or two others in Asia. Ours is a small or medium-sized tree, confined to the East and found most commonly in the Southeast. It grows along fence rows and roads, in abandoned fields, and in other open or semiopen places. The dark bluish fruits of sassafras ripening in the fall are eaten by various birds—but the quantities taken are too limited to rate the plant as an important wildlife food source. It is interesting to note that the kingbird, crested flycatcher, and phoebe, all members of the flycatcher family and all subsisting primarily on insects, eat sassafras fruits.

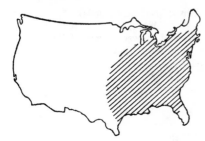 

Upland Gamebirds (fruit)
+ Quail, Bobwhite, *E*
+ Turkey, Wild, *Pa.*

Songbirds (fruit)
* Catbird, *E*
− Flicker, *Pa.*
* Flycatcher, Crested, *E*
* Kingbird, *E*
+ Mockingbird, *SE*
+ Phoebe, Eastern, *E*
+ Sapsucker, *E*
+ Thrasher, Brown, *NE*
  Thrush
+ Gray-cheeked, *NE*
+ Hermit, *E*

+ Olive-backed, *NE*
− Towhee, *Pa.*
  Vireo
+ Red-eyed, *E*
+ White-eyed, *E*
* Woodpecker, Pileated, *E*
+ Warbler, Yellowthroat, *Md.*

Fur and Game Mammals (fruit, bark, wood)
+ Bear, Black, *Pa.*
− Beaver, *Miss.*
+ Rabbit, Mearns Cottontail, *Mich.*
+ Squirrel, Fox, *Iowa*

Hoofed Browsers (twigs, foliage)
+ Deer, White-tailed, *N.Y.*

SPICEBUSHES
Lindera

[3*/12 users] Two species of spicebush are native to the United States, the common spicebush (*L. aestivale*) in the Northeast and the southern, or downy, spicebush (*L. melissaefolia*) in the Southeast. These aromatic-leaved shrubs are typical undergrowths in moist bottom lands or flood-plain forests. Their reddish fruits, containing a single large seed, are relished by thrushes, particularly by the wood thrush and veery, but are eaten only sparingly by other birds.

Upland Gamebirds (fruit)
+ Pheasant, Ring-necked, *NE*
+ Quail, Bobwhite, *NE*

Songbirds (fruit)
+ Catbird, *NE*
+ Flycatcher, Crested, *E*
+ Kingbird, Eastern, *E*
+ Robin, *NE*
  Thrush
+ Gray-cheeked, *NE*
+ Hermit, *E*
* Veery, *NE*
** Wood, *NE*
+ Vireo, Red-eyed, *E*

Gooseberry Family: *Grossulariaceae*

GOOSEBERRIES AND CURRANTS
Grossularia, Ribes

[31*/32 users] This complex of 100 to 150 species has 70 to 80 or more repre- sentatives in the United States. Botan- ists disagree in their treatment of the group: some recognizing the two genera listed above, some only one, *Ribes*, and still others four distinct genera.

Gooseberries and currants are largely western, though a number of them are present in the East too. The different species grow under varied conditions, but they are typical of moist, open places, often by streams or springs. The whitestem gooseberry (*G. inermis*), wax currant (*R. cereum*), western black currant (*R. petiolare*), sticky currant (*R. viscosissimum*), and golden currant (*R. aureum*) are prominent among the more widespread western species. Gooseberries and currants are alternate hosts of the white pine blister rust, and in recent decades the number of these plants has been reduced considerably by special campaigns of eradication within white pine areas. Though their fruits still have considerable value for songbirds, chipmunks, ground squirrels, and other animals, the wildlife importance of the group was probably greater in former days.

Waterbirds (fruit)
+ Gull, Ring-billed, *U.S.*
Upland Gamebirds (fruit, foliage)
Grouse
* Blue, *No.Mt.–Des.; +Pac. NW*
+ Sharp-tailed, *N.Dak.*
Songbirds (fruit)
* Catbird, *W*; *+NE*
* Jay, Woodhouse, *So.Mt.–Des.*
* Magpie, American, *Mt.–Des.*

* Robin, *Mt.–Des.*
* Solitaire, Townsend, *W*
Thrasher
+ Brown, *Pr.*
+ Sage, *W*
+ Towhee, Spotted, *Pac.*
* Waxwing, Cedar, *Pac.*
* Woodpecker, Lewis, *Mt.–Des. and Pac.*
Fur and Game Mammals (fruit, foliage)
+ Coyote, *Calif.*
+ Fox, Red, *Iowa*
+ Mountain Beaver, *Pac.*
* Raccoon, *Iowa*
+ Skunk, Eastern, *N.Y. and Mich.*
+ Squirrel, Red, *NE*
Small Mammals (fruit)
Chipmunk
** Least, *W.Pr. and Mt.–Des.*
+ Long-eared, *Calif.*
* Various spp., *Mt.–Des. and Pac.*
Ground Squirrel
** Harris, *Ariz.*
** Mantled, *W*
Mouse
+ Deer, *Wis.*
+ Meadow, *Wis.*
+ White-footed, *NE*
Rat
+ Wood, Dusky-footed, *Oreg.*
+ Wood, Portola, *Calif.*
Hoofed Browsers (twigs, foliage)
+ Deer, Mule, *Calif.*
+ Elk, *Colo.*
* Sheep, Mountain, *Mont.*

Reference: Currants and Gooseberries, Their Culture and Relation to White-pine Blister Rust. *U.S. Dept. Agr. Bul.* 1398, 1944. 36 pp.

Witch-hazel Family : *Hamamelidaceae*

SWEETGUM
Liquidambar styraciflua

[11*/13 users] Besides our native sweetgum there is one species in South America and two others in Asia. This star-leaved, straight-trunked tree is common in the Coastal Plain and Piedmont sections of the Southeast. It often forms nearly pure forest stands on bottomlands or in other moist areas.

Despite the abundance of sweetgum within its natural range, this plant is used only to a small extent by wildlife. Birds, particularly goldfinches and purple finches, eat the winged seeds, picking them out of the horny, ball-like fruit heads. Squirrels and chipmunks feed on the seeds. Sweetgum is

+ Quail, Bobwhite, *SE*
Songbirds (seeds)
+ Chickadee, Carolina, *Md.*
* Finch, Purple, *E*
** Goldfinch, Eastern, *E*
+ Junco, *NE*
− Sapsucker, Yellow-bellied, *Md.* (sap)
+ Sparrow, White-throated, *Md.*
+ Towhee, *SE*
+ Wren, Carolina, *E*
Fur and Game Mammals (seeds, wood)
*** Beaver, *SE* (wood)
* Squirrel, Gray, *E*
Small Mammals (seeds)
+ Chipmunk, Eastern, *NE*

planted widely as a shade and ornamental tree.

Waterfowl (seeds)
+ Duck, Mallard, *SE*
Upland Gamebirds (seeds)

Reference: Some Soil and Moisture Relationships of Sweetgum and River Birch in Southern Maryland. F. B. Trenk. *Proc. Iowa Acad. Sci.*, Vol. 32, pp. 133–142, 1926.

WITCH-HAZEL
Hamamelis virginiana

[5*/6 users] The common witch-hazel of the eastern United States is split by some botanists into three species, but here it is treated as one. This winter-flowering, woodland shrub or small tree is found commonly along stream margins or on moist slopes.

The woody seeds, available from fall into winter, are eaten by ruffed grouse and by squirrels, but the wildlife value of witch-hazel is generally rather low.

Upland Gamebirds (seeds)
** Grouse, Ruffed, *Ohio; *Pa.*
+ Turkey, Wild, *E*
Fur and Game Mammals (bark, foliage, seeds)
− Beaver, *W.Va.*
+ Rabbit, Mearns Cottontail, *N.Y.*
* Squirrel, Fox, *Ohio*
Hoofed Browsers (twigs, foliage)
** Deer, White-tailed, *N.Y.*

Sycamore Family: *Platanaceae*

SYCAMORES
Platanus

[2*/4 users] Three of the six or seven species of sycamores are native to the United States. One is widespread in the East, and two are southwestern. All are water-loving trees, occurring characteristically along stream margins and lake sides but are also planted commonly as shade trees.

Sycamores are typical of the American scene in many parts of the country. Their beauty of form, foliage, and mottled bark is admired by all. Unfortunately their value does not include any appreciable importance to wildlife. The pendant seed balls are utilized by only a few wildlife species: the purple finch being the only bird using the seeds to a starred extent.

Songbirds (seeds)
* Finch, Purple, *E*
+ Goldfinch, *E*

Fur and Game Mammal (seeds, wood)
+ Beaver, *Mo.*
+ Squirrel, Fox, *Ohio*

Rose Family: *Rosaceae*

HAWTHORNS
Crataegus

■■■ Region of main use ▨▨ Lesser use

[22*/29 users] Hawthorns are so difficult to classify that botanists disagree whether the number of species listed for the United States should be about 100 or should range as high as 1,200. For the world the number of recognized species runs from 150 to 1,500. The majority of our hawthorns occur in the Northeast, mainly in clearings and open hillside pastures.

The thorniness, dense branching, and heavy foliage of these shrubs or small trees makes them favorite nesting sites for many birds. The small apple-like fruits are not used by wildlife to nearly so great an extent as might be anticipated. Fox sparrows and cedar waxwings are the principal songbird users.

The several species of hawthorns used in ornamental plantings do not seem to be utilized by wildlife any more than the wild species.

Waterfowl (fruit)
+ Duck, Wood, *SE*

Upland Gamebirds (fruit, buds)
    Grouse
+   Blue, *Idaho and Wash.*
*   Ruffed, *NE and Ohio*
*   Sharp-tailed, *N.Dak.;* +*Minn.*
+ Pheasant, Ring-necked, *E*
+ Pigeon, Band-tailed, *Pac.*
+ Turkey, Wild, *SE*

Songbirds (fruit)
+ Grosbeak, Pine, *NE*
+ Magpie, American, *Mt.–Des.*
+ Robin, *E*
+ Solitaire, Townsend, *W*
*** Sparrow, Fox, *E*
*** Waxwing, Cedar, *W*
* Woodpecker, Lewis, *Mt.–Des. and Pac.*

Fur and Game Mammals (fruit, wood)
** Bear, Black, *Minn.*
+ Beaver, *Wash.*
+ Coyote, *W*
+ Fox, Gray, *NE*
+ Rabbit, Cottontail, *Iowa*
* Raccoon, *Tex.;* +*E*
+ Skunk, Illinois, *Iowa*
    Squirrel
+   Fox, *Ohio*
+   Fox, Western, *Mo.*
+   Gray, *E*

Small Mammals (fruit)
+ Ground Squirrel, Douglas, *Oreg.*
+ Mouse, Pine, *NE*
+ Rat, Dusky-footed Wood, *Oreg.*

Hoofed Browsers (foliage, twigs, fruit)
    Deer
+   Mule, *N.Y.*
+   White-tailed, *NE*

MOUNTAIN-ASHES
Sorbus

[16*/14 users] Our four to seven species of mountain-ash are northern plants. They prefer cool, moist habitats along borders of swamps or on woody hillsides in our northern or mountainous states and in Canada.

These trees or shrubs are admirable for ornamental planting in the cooler parts of the country. Their foliage and bright reddish fruits are not only attractive to look at but also are useful to wildlife. Birds, especially grosbeaks, cedar waxwings, and various species of grouse, are regular feeders on mountain-ash berries. The fact that the fruit persists on the trees through the winter makes them especially valuable to wildlife.

Upland Gamebirds (fruit, buds)
  Grouse
    *   Blue,   *No.Mt.–Des.;*   +*Pac. NW*
    +   Ruffed, *NE*
  ***   Sharp-tailed, *Great Lakes Area*
Songbirds (fruit)
    +   Catbird, *W*
  Grosbeak
    *   Evening, *NE*
    **   Pine, *NE*
  Thrush
    +   Olive-backed, *NE*
    +   Veery, *NE*
    *   Waxwing, Cedar, *NE*
Fur and Game Mammals (fruit)
    *   Chickaree, Douglas, *Pac.*
    *   Marten, *No.Mt.–Des.*
Small Mammals (fruit)
    *   Ground Squirrel, Douglas, *Pac.*
    −   Rat, Allegheny Wood, *Allegheny Mts.*
Hoofed Browsers (foliage, twigs)
  ***   Moose, *Mich.;* ***No.Mt.–Des.*

CHOKEBERRIES
Aronia

[4*/11 users] Our three species of chokeberry are confined to the eastern United States. They are found in swamps and wet woods or in moist situations along roadsides and fence rows, from Maine and the Great Lakes to Florida and Louisiana.

The firm, dark, berry-like fruits appear to be of minor importance to wildlife though they are widely available and persist on the shrubs through much of the winter.

Upland Gamebirds (fruit, buds)
  Grouse
    +   Ruffed, *NE*
    *   Sharp-tailed, *Great Lakes Area*
Songbirds (fruit)
    +   Chickadee, Black-capped, *NE*
    +   Meadowlark, *SE*
    *   Waxwing, Cedar, *NE*
Fur and Game Mammals (fruit, foliage)
    **   Bear, Black, *Va. and W.Va.*
    +   Fox, Red, *Mass.*
    +   Rabbit, New England Cottontail, *Conn,*

+ Squirrel, Western Fox, *Mich.*
Small Mammals (fruit)
+ Mouse, White-footed, *Minn.*

Hoofed Browsers (twigs, foliage)
+ Deer, White-tailed, *N.C. and Pa.*

CHRISTMASBERRY
Photinia arbutifolia

The records of use of the bright red fruits of Christmasberry are not impressive. However, the wildlife value, such as it is, adds to the usefulness of this ornamental evergreen tree or shrub.

Upland Gamebirds (fruits)
+ Pigeon, Band-tailed, *Calif.*
Songbirds (fruits mainly)
+ Sapsucker, Northern Redbreasted, *Calif.* (sap)
+ Thrasher, California, *Calif.*
* Wren-tit, *Calif.*
Small Mammals (fruit)
Rat
− Wood, Large-eared, *Calif.*
− Wood, Portola, *Calif.*

[1*/6 users] Christmasberry—also known as toyon—is limited entirely to California and Lower California. It is the only member of its genus in this country though there are about 30 other species of *Photinia* elsewhere.

SERVICEBERRIES
Amelanchier

[46*/58 users] The serviceberries are primarily North American trees and shrubs. Four or five species are native in the East and 15 to 20 in the West. They grow in a variety of habitats ranging from swamps to dry, rocky hillsides. Only three of our species attain the stature of trees. Various common names such as serviceberry, Juneberry, shadblow, and shadbush are used locally. The latter two names are supposed to originate from the fact that the plants bloom when the shad are running. The downy service-berry (*A. canadensis*), an eastern tree, is one of the most widespread and abundant species. Its juicy, sweet fruits are sought by thrushes and many other songbirds and they are an important wildlife food during the early summer period (June and July). Squirrels, chipmunks, and even bears relish serviceberry fruits. Hoofed browsers, particularly the mule deer, feed on the foliage and twigs of western species such as the common serviceberry (*A. alnifolia*).

The dainty, white, long-petaled flowers of serviceberries are among the first spring blooms of our native woody plants. Because of its horticultural merits combined with wildlife utility the downy serviceberry is worthy of extensive planting as an ornamental.

Upland Gamebirds (fruit, buds)
 Grouse
 + Blue, *Pac.NW*
 + Ruffed, *Me.*
 + Sharp-tailed, *N.Dak.*
 + Pheasant, Ring-necked, *N.Y. and Utah*
Songbirds (fruit)
 + Bluebird, Eastern, *NE*
 + Cardinal, *NE*
 * Catbird, *NE*; +*W*
 + Chickadee, Black-capped, *NE*
 ** Crow, *Mt.–Des.*; +*E and Pr.*
 + Flicker, Yellow-shafted, *E and E.Pr.*
 Grosbeak
 * Evening, *NW*
 + Rose-breasted, *NE*
 Jay
 + Blue, *E*
 + Woodhouse, *Ariz.*
 * Magpie, American, *Mt.–Des.*
 + Mockingbird, *U.S.*
 * Oriole, Baltimore, *NE*
 * Robin, *Mt.–Des.*; +*NE and Pac.*
 + Solitaire, Townsend, *W*
 Tanager
 + Scarlet, *NE*
 * Western, *Pac.*
 Thrasher
 + Brown, *NE*
 * Sage, *W*
 Thrush
 * Hermit, *E*

 *** Olive-backed, *Pr.*
 * Russet-backed, *NE and Pr.*
 * Veery, *NE*
 + Wood, *NE*
 + Titmouse, Tufted, *NE*
 Towhee
 * Green-tailed, *Mt.–Des.*
 + Red-eyed, *NE*
 * Waxwing, Cedar, *NE*
 Woodpecker
 + Downy, *E and E.Pr.*
 + Hairy, *E and E.Pr.*
 * Lewis, *Mt.–Des.*
Fur and Game Mammals (fruit, bark, twigs)
 * Bear, Black, *W*
 ** Beaver, *NE*
 + Fox, Red, *NE*
 * Hare, Varying, *Utah*
 ** Marmot, *W.Pr.*
 + Skunk, Eastern, *Mich.*
 Squirrel
 − Flying, Eastern, *NE*
 * Fox, Western, *Mich.*
 ** Red, *E.*
Small Mammals (fruit)
 ** Chipmunk, Northwest, *Mt.– Des. and Pac.NW*
 Ground Squirrel
 + Douglas, *NE*
 + Mantled, *W*
 Mouse
 − Red-backed, *E*
 − White-footed, *E*
 − Rat, Dusky-footed Wood, *Oreg.*
Hoofed Browsers (twigs, foliage)
 Deer
 *** Mule, *No.Mt.–Des.*; *Calif.*; +*S.Dak.*
 * White-tailed, *S.Dak.*; +*Pa., N.Y., and Mont.*
 + Elk, *No.Mt.–Des.*
 * Moose, *Mich.*
 + Sheep, Mountain, *No.Mt.–Des. and Mont.*

BLACKBERRIES
Rubus

[118*/97 users] Blackberries and their kin are a tangle in more ways than one. The number of species in the world has been estimated from about 200 to 400, and the number in the United States ranges, according to different botanists, from about 50 to 390 (Bailey). The genus *Rubus* includes several main

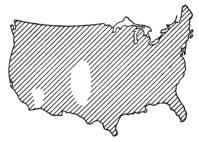

subdivisions among which are the true blackberries, the raspberries, dewberries, thimbleberries, and cloudberries. In this book, especially in tables of data, the name "blackberry" is ordinarily used to designate the whole group—not merely the true blackberries.

Most of the common species thrive in relatively open, moist places. In the Southeast, this habitat preference frequently puts them into direct competition with Japanese honeysuckle. Other species, however, such as the swamp blackberry (*R. hispidus*) of the East or the thimbleberries (*R. parviflorus* and *R. odoratus*), cloudberry (*R. chamaemorus*), and salmonberry (*R. spectabilis*) of the North and Northwest are typical woodland inhabitants and prefer shade. Wild raspberries as well as dewberries and blackberries are common along roadsides, field borders, fence rows, and in abandoned fields.

Blackberries (the whole group) rank at the very top of summer foods for wildlife. Even the dried or drying berries are eaten to some extent late into the fall or winter, but the principal use is while the fruit is juicy. Probably the berries taste as palatable to wildlife as they do to us. The other important factor in the extensive use of this genus is its widespread availability in most parts of the country. Birds are particularly prominent among the long list of wildlife users. Indeed the list could have been built up to considerably more than 97 if the many bird records of slight use were included. Locally, blackberries are important to some gamebirds such as grouse, ring-

necked pheasant, prairie chicken, bobwhite quail, and others. Among the songbirds, principal users include such common species as the catbird, cardinal, yellow-breasted chat, pine grosbeak, robin, orchard oriole, summer tanager, brown thrasher, thrushes, and towhees. Blackberry fruits are also popular with raccoons, chipmunks, and squirrels as well as with some other rodents. In addition, the leaves and stems of the plants are eaten extensively by deer and rabbits.

Besides their great value as a food source, the various species of this group have much value as effective cover for wildlife. Often the thorny brambles make impenetrable thickets where birds, rabbits and other animals can find comparative security. In winter, cottontails feed on the stems of these plants while also obtaining protective cover from them. Blackberry patches are a common site for the nests of small birds.

Upland Gamebirds (fruit)
   Grouse
     *   Dusky, *Pac.NW* (thimbleberry)
  ***   Franklin, *B.C.* (thimbleberry)
   **   Ruffed, *Wis.;* *NE
    *   Sharp-tailed, *Great Lakes Area*
  *** Pheasant, Ring-necked, *N.Y.*
    *   Pigeon, Band-tailed, *Pac.* (thimbleberry)
     Prairie Chicken
   **   Attwater, *Tex.*

***   Greater, *Ill.;* **Wis.*
*   Quail, Bobwhite, *NE*; +*SE*
*   Turkey, Wild, *Allegheny Mts.;*
      +*E*
*   Woodcock, *Maine;* +*E*
Songbirds (fruit)
     Blackbird
+   Redwing, *SE*
+   Rusty, *NE*
     Bluebird
+   Eastern, *NE*
+   Western, *Calif.*
−   Bunting, Indigo, *E*
**   Cardinal, *SE*; +*NE and Pr.*
*** Catbird, *E*; **W
     Chat
*   Long-tailed, *Pac.* (thimble-
      berry)
***   Yellow-breasted, *E*
+ Chickadee, Chestnut-backed,
      Pac. (thimbleberry)
     Crow
+   Common, *E*
**   Fish, *E*
+ Flicker, Yellow-shafted, *E and*
     E.Pr.
+ Flycatcher, Crested, *E*
* Grackle, Purple, *E and Pr.*
     Grosbeak
*   Black-headed, *Calif.*
+   Evening, *NE*
*** Pine, *NE*
*   Rose-breasted, *NE and No.Pr.*
     Jay
*   Blue, *E*
**   California, *Calif.*
*   Steller, *Pac., mainly Calif.*
+ Kingbird, *E*
* Mockingbird, *SE*; +*SW and*
     Calif.
* Mynah, Crested, *B.C.*
     Oriole
*   Baltimore, *NE*
*   Bullock, *Calif.*
**   Orchard, *SE*; +*NE and E.Pr.*
+ Phoebe, *E*
** Robin, *SE*; **NE and Pac.;*
     +*E.Pr.*
     Sparrow
**   Fox, *E*; *W
*   Henslow, *NE*
+   Song, *Pac.*

*   White-crowned, *Mt.–Des. and*
     Pac.
+   White-throated, *NE*
     Tanager
*   Scarlet, *NE*
***   Summer, *SE*
*   Western, *Pac.*
     Thrasher
**   Brown, *E*; +*Pr.*
*   California, *Calif.*
+   Sage, *NW*
     Thrush
+   Gray-cheeked, *NE*
+   Hermit, *Pac.*
+   Olive-backed, *NE*
*   Russet-backed, *Calif.*
**   Varied, *Pac.*
*   Veery, *NE*
*   Wood, *NE*
* Titmouse, Tufted, *E*
     Towhee
+   Brown, *Calif.*
**   Red-eyed, *SE*; *NE
**   Spotted, *Pac.*
     Vireo
+   Red-eyed, *E*
+   White-eyed, *SE*
* Waxwing, Cedar, *NE and W*
+ Woodpecker, Red-headed, *E*
* Wren-tit, *Calif.*
Fur and Game Mammals (fruit, stems)
+ Armadillo, *Tex.*
+ Bear, Black, *NE*
     Fox
+   Gray, *SE*
+   Red, *E*
− Hare, Varying, *Wis.*
** Marmot, *W.Pr. and Mt.–Des.*
* Mountain Beaver, *Pac.*
+ Opossum, *Mo.*
** Rabbit, Cottontail, *Conn. and*
     Mich.; +*Iowa*
* Raccoon, *Iowa;* +*E.Tex.*
     Skunk
+   Eastern, *E*
*   Florida, *SE*
     Squirrel
*   Fox, *NE*; +*Ohio and Mich.*
+   Gray, *E*
+   Red, *NE*
Small Mammals (fruit)
     Chipmunk
*   Eastern, *NE*

*** Least, *Minn.;* + *Mt.–Des. and Pac.*
 * Ground Squirrel, Douglas, *Oreg.*
 Mouse
 — Meadow, *Wis.*
 — Red-backed, *U.S.*
 — White-footed, *NE*
 — Rat, Portola Wood, *Calif.*
Hoofed Browsers (stems, foliage)

Deer
 — Black-tailed, Columbian, *Oreg.*
 * Mule, *Calif.* (thimbleberry)
** White-tailed, *Maine;* + *Pa. and N.Y.*
 — Elk, *NW*
 + Moose, *Maine–Mich.*
 + Sheep, Mountain, *Colo.*

Reference: Species Batorum. L. H. Bailey. *Gentes Herbarum*, Vol. V, fasc. 1 to 10, 1941–1945. 918 pp.

MOUNTAIN-MAHOGANIES
Cercocarpus

[13*/6 users] Mountain-mahogany is a North American genus of 19 to 21 species of which 14 to 17 are listed for the United States. These deciduous, small-leafed shrubs occur mainly in dry, mountainous areas of the West. Their wildlife value consists primarily in use as browse by deer, antelope, and other hoofed browsers.

Upland Gamebirds (seeds, leaves)
 + Grouse, Blue, *Pac. NW*
Hoofed Browsers (twigs, foliage)
 * Antelope, *No.Pr. and Mt.–Des.*
 Deer
** Black-tailed, *Calif.*
*** Mule, *So.Mt.–Des. and Oreg.;* *Calif.*
 * Elk, *No.Mt.–Des.*
 * Sheep, Mountain, *No.Mt.–Des.;* +*N.Mex.*

CHAMISE
Adenostoma fasciculata

[5*/4 users] This thicket-forming shrub is abundant locally in the dry California coast range mountains. Chamise constitutes a major part of the brushy chaparral in that area. Its dense growth provides effective cover for some species of wildlife, but the food utility of its seeds (akenes) and foliage is low.

Songbirds (seeds)
** Goldfinch, Lawrence, *Mt.–Des. and Pac.*
Small Mammals (foliage, flower clusters)
 — Rat, Large-eared Wood, *Calif.*
Hoofed Browsers (twigs, foliage)
 Deer
 * Black-tailed, *Calif.*
 — Mule, *Calif.*

BITTERBRUSHES
Purshia

[15*/9 users] There are two species of bitterbrush in the world—both of them confined to arid slopes and valleys of the Mountain–Desert region. One, antelope bitterbrush (*P. tridentata*), is common and widespread in the Rocky

327

Mountains and adjoining regions. It is important to wildlife. The other species, desert bitterbrush (*P. glandulosa*), is limited to desert areas in southern California.

Bitterbrush is a tough and widely branched shrub with small three-pronged leaves, attractive pale yellow flowers, and spindle-shaped, large seeds (akenes). The latter are important food items for western chipmunks and are also eaten by the pocket mouse and mantled ground squirrel. The principal

wildlife value of bitterbrush, however, is for browsing animals—particularly for the mule deer. In this use there is some degree of competition with western livestock since bitterbrush is palatable to and used by domestic range animals.

Fur and Game Mammals (foliage, twigs)
   Rabbit
    −   Cottontail, Black Hills, *Utah*
    +   Cottontail, *Utah*
Small Mammals (seeds, foliage)
   Chipmunk
   ***   Least, *W.Pr. and Mt.–Des.*
   *   Northwest, *Pac.NW*
   * Ground Squirrel, Mantled, *W*
Hoofed Browsers (twigs, foliage)
   + Antelope, *No.Pr. and Mt.–Des.*
   **** Deer, Mule, *Oreg.;* **So.Mt.–Des.; *No.Mt.–Des.; +Calif.*
   + Elk, *No.Mt.–Des.*

WILD ROSES
Rosa

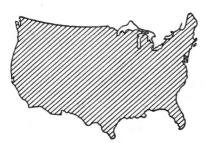 

[**15*/24 users**] Probably 35 or more species of wild roses occur in the United States. They are partial to meadows, open woods, stream margins, fence rows, roadsides, and woods borders. In favorable localities wild roses form thickets.

Many of us, at one time or another, have nibbled on the colorful wild rose hips, and wildlife species do the same. Besides the fleshy exterior of the fruits, wildlife eat the numerous bony seeds (akenes) inside. The hips remaining on the shrubs through the winter and into

the following year are available as food (probably not the choicest) when other preferable sources of nourishment are covered with snow. For this reason wild roses are important to upland game-birds in the northern (particularly the northwestern) parts of the country. The fruits and other parts of the plants are eaten by mammals and especially by hoofed browsers. Thickets of wild roses are excellent nesting and protective cover for gamebirds and songbirds. Multiflora rose (*R. multiflora*) is an especially valuable plant for hedges and living fences.

Upland Gamebirds (fruit, buds)
Grouse
+ Blue, *No.Mt.–Des.*
+ Ruffed, *Va.Alleghenies and Wis.*
**** Sharp-tailed, *No.Dak. and Nebr.; *Great Lakes Area; +Utah*
+ Pheasant, Ring-necked, *NW*
*** Prairie Chicken, Greater, *No.Pr.; +Ill.*
+ Quail, Bobwhite, *E.Pr.*
Songbirds (fruit)
+ Solitaire, Townsend, *NW*
* Thrush, Olive-backed, *Pr.*
+ Vireo, Philadelphia, *NE*
Fur and Game Mammals (fruit, stems, foliage)

+ Bear, Black, *NE*
+ Beaver, *N.Dak.*
Rabbit
+ Cottontail, *Mich.*
− Cottontail, Audubon, *Calif.*
+ Cottontail, Mearns, *N.Y. and Wis.*
+ Skunk, Eastern, *N.Y.*
+ Squirrel, Red, *NE*
Small Mammals (fruit)
+ Mouse, White-footed, *NE*
Rat
− Wood, *Pac.*
− Wood, Dusky-footed, *Oreg.*
Hoofed Browsers (twigs, foliage)
* Antelope, *S.Dak.*
Deer
** Mule, *Nebr.*
*** White-tailed, *S.Dak.; +E*
+ Elk, *Mont.*
+ Sheep, Mountain, *Colo.*

References: The Distribution of North American Rose Species. Thomas M. Little. *Amer. Rose Ann.*, pp. 37–49, 1942.
Living Fences. Durward L. Allen. *Sports Afield*, pp. 46–48 and 118–121, September, 1948.

WILD CHERRIES
Prunus

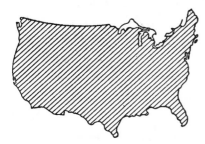

[**104*/81 users**] There are about 14 native species of wild cherries widely distributed in the country. The different species occur in a variety of habitats including moist bottom lands, hill slopes, and semiarid situations. They range in size from shrubs to large trees; the wild black cherry (*P. serotina*) often growing 50 to 60 feet tall and occasionally reaching 100 feet.

Wild cherries are among our most important wildlife food plants. Outstanding in importance are the wide-spread wild black cherry, mentioned above, the choke cherry (*P. virginiana*), (including both its western and eastern forms), the bitter cherry (*P. emarginata*) of the West, and the pin cherry

(*P. pennsylvanica*) of the Northeast. Important gamebirds and common songbirds eat the fruits as they ripen in the summer and fall—or sometimes before they are ripe. It is a common sight to see robins and starlings, flying back and forth to wild cherry trees, load themselves with the fruits and then, perching in nearby trees, regurgitate the pits. Sometimes as many as two or three dozen birds will make a nearly continuous flow of aerial traffic into a single cherry tree or group of trees—often with a dozen or more feeding actively at the same time.

In addition to their use by birds, the fruits of the wild cherries are also relished by fur and game mammals and by small mammals. Often these animals feed on the cherries which have fallen to the ground after the birds have taken their harvest on the trees. Hoofed browsers and rabbits feed extensively on the twigs, foliage, and bark of wild cherries.

Upland Gamebirds (fruit, buds)
Grouse
* Blue, *No.Mt.–Des.*
** Ruffed, *Wis.; *NE*
*** Sharp-tailed, *N.Dak. and Utah; *Great Lakes Area* (pin cherry)
* Pheasant, Ring-necked, *NE; +NW*
* Prairie Chicken, Greater, *Ill.*
+ Quail, Bobwhite, *E*
+ Turkey, Wild, *E*
Songbirds (fruit)
+ Bluebird, Eastern, *NE*
+ Cardinal, *SE*
* Catbird, *U.S.*
* Crow, *E*
* Flicker, Yellow-shafted, *E and E.Pr.*
+ Flycatcher, Crested, *E*
+ Grackle, Purple, *NE*
Grosbeak
*** Evening, *N*
** Rose-breasted, *NE and No.Pr.*
Jay
+ Blue, *E*
+ California, *Calif.*

+ Steller, *Pac.*
* Kingbird, *E*
* Magpie, *Mt.–Des*
+ Mockingbird, *SE and Tex.*
* Mynah, Crested, *B.C.*
+ Oriole, Baltimore, *NE*
* Phainopepla, *Calif. and Ariz.*
*** Robin, *NE and No.Pr.*
* Sapsucker, Yellow-breasted, *E*
+ Solitaire, Townsend, *W* (bitter cherry)
+ Sparrow, White-throated, *NE*
** Starling, *NE*
Tanager
+ Scarlet, *NE*
+ Summer, *SE*
** Thrasher, Brown, *NE*
Thrush
* Gray-cheeked, *NE*
+ Hermit, *E*
*** Olive-backed, *Calif.; **NE*
* Varied, *Pac.*
+ Veery, *NE*
* Wood, *NE*
+ Towhee, *NE*
Vireo
+ Red-eyed, *U.S.*
+ Warbling, *U.S.*
*** Waxwing, Cedar, *NE*
Woodpecker
+ Hairy, *E and Pr.*
** Pileated, *Oreg.* (choke cherry)
* Red-bellied, *E*
* Red-headed, *E and Pr.*
Fur and Game Mammals (fruit, bark, wood)
**** Bear, Black, *Pa.; *W*
− Beaver, *E and No.Pr.*
Fox
* Gray, *SE; +NE*
* Red, *E; +Mass.*
+ Hare, Varying, *Minn.*
+ Opossum, *SE*
Rabbit
* Cottontail, Eastern, *Conn.*
* Cottontail, Mearns, *Mich.*
+ Cottontail, New England, *NE*
** Cottontail, Rocky Mountain, *Utah*
* Raccoon, *Pac.; +Iowa*
Skunk
+ Eastern, *NE*
+ Spotted, Prairie, *Iowa*

Squirrel
+ Fox, *Ohio*
* Fox, Western, *Mich.*
+ Gray, *E*
* Red, *E*
Small Mammals (fruit)
Chipmunk
* Eastern, *NE*
** Least, *W.Pr. and Mt.–Des.*
− Lyster, *N.H.*
* Various spp., *Mt.–Des. and*
  Pac.
Mouse
− Deer, *Wis.*
− Meadow, *Wis.*

− Pocket, Prairie, *Okla.*
* White-footed, LeConte, *E*
− White-footed, Northern, *NE*
Rat
− Wood, Allegheny, *E*
− Wood, Large-eared, *Calif.*
Hoofed Browsers (twigs, foliage)
Deer
** Mule, *No.Mt.–Des. and Calif.*
* White-tailed, *N.Y.*; +*E*
+ Elk, *No.Mt.–Des.*
* Moose, *Mich. and No.Mt.–Des.;*
  +*Maine to Mich.*
+ Sheep, Mountain, *No.Mt.–Des.*

Reference: Native American Species of *Prunus*. W. F. Wright. *U.S. Dept. Agr. Bul.* 179, 1915. 75 pp.

WILD PLUMS
Prunus

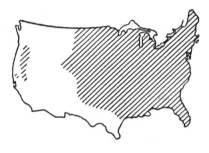

[1*/4 users] Wild plums belong with the wild cherries botanically, but their differences in growth, fruit, and wild-life use set them apart. About 16 species of plums are present in various parts of the country, but their fruits are not used so much by wildlife as might be anticipated. Foxes are the chief customers. Plum thickets often furnish valuable protective shelter.

Songbirds (fruit)
+ Grosbeak, Black-headed, *Calif.*
Fur and Game Mammals (fruit)
+ Cat, Ring-tailed, *Tex.*
Fox
* Gray, *SE*; +*NE*
+ Red, *E*

Mimosa Family: *Mimosaceae*

ACACIAS
Acacia

[7*/7 users] Of the 300 to 550 acacias in the world (according to different botanists) only 10 to 20 are native to the United States. There are, however, numerous introduced ornamental and shade species in California and Florida. These fine-leaved (bipinnate), pod-bearing shrubs or trees, both native and exotic, are confined largely to the warm, subtropical, arid parts of the Southwest.

The native acacias are of moderate food and cover value within their restricted range. The seeds are eaten extensively by gamebirds, especially by the chestnut-bellied scaled quail and by the western white-winged dove. The cultivated, introduced species are not known to be valuable to wildlife.

Upland Gamebirds (seeds)
Dove

331

+ Mourning, *Mt.–Des.*
+ White-winged, Eastern, *Tex.*
** White-winged, Western, *Ariz.*
    Quail
+ Gambel, *SW* (mescat acacia)
**** Scaled, Chestnut-bellied, *Tex.*, (catclaw acacia)

Small Mammals (seeds)
  * Rat, White-throated Wood, *Ariz.*
Hoofed Browsers (twigs, foliage, and fruit)
+ Sheep, Bighorn, *N.Mex.*

Reference: Legumes for Erosion Control and Wildlife. Edward H. Graham. *U.S. Dept. Agr. Misc. Pub.* 412, 1941. 153 pp.

MESQUITES
Prosopis

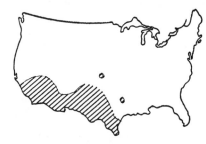

[52*/24 users] Three or four species of mesquite are recognized in the United States of the 15 to 30 in the world. Ours inhabit arid parts of the Southwest.

These lacey-leaved, spiny shrubs or small trees are essential to a number of wildlife species in the southwestern deserts and plains. The seeds, borne in tough pods, ripen in the summer or fall and are eaten extensively by jack rabbits, Gambel quail, and various native rodents as well as by domestic livestock. The foliage is consumed by many kinds of wild animals and also by cattle and goats. Since mesquite is one of the few trees present in the arid areas, its shade though sparse is welcome to wildlife species. Birds frequently nest in its branches.

Upland Gamebirds (seeds)
+ Dove, Western White-winged, *Ariz.*
    Quail
+ Bobwhite, *So.Tex.*
*** Gambel, *SW*
* Scaled, Arizona, *SW*

+ Scaled, Chestnut-bellied, *Tex.*
Songbirds (seeds)
+ Raven, American, *Mt.–Des. and Pac.*
Fur and Game Mammals (seeds, leaves, bark)
+ Cat, Ring-tailed, *Tex.*
+ Coyote, *W*
+ Fox, Gray, *Tex.*
    Jack Rabbit
**** Antelope, *Ariz.*
**** California, *Ariz. and N.Mex.*
**** Rabbit, Cottontail, *Ariz.*
**** Skunk, Northern Hooded, *Ariz.*
* Wolf, Texan Red, *SW*
Small Mammals (seeds, leaves)
* Chipmunk, Western, *Pac.NW*
** Ground Squirrel, Harris, *Ariz.*
*** Mouse, Pocket, *W.Pr. and Mt.–Des.*
    Rat
* Kangaroo, Banner-tailed, *Ariz.*
* Kangaroo, Merriam, *SW*
** Kangaroo, various spp., *So. Pr. and Mt.–Des.*
+ Wood, *So.Pr.*
**** Wood, White-throated, *Ariz.*

| Hoofed Browsers (foliage, twigs) | + | Mule, *Calif.* |
| Deer | + | White-tailed, *Tex.* |

Reference: The Conquering Mesquite. J. Frank Dobie. *Nat. Hist.*, Vol. 51, pp. 208–217, 1943.

Senna Family: *Caesalpiniaceae*

PALOVERDES
Cercidium

[7*/4 users] This is an American genus of which three to five species occur along our southern border in Arizona and California. These shrubs or small trees with showy, yellow flowers are common in river canyons and watercourses of desert regions. Paloverde seeds are used by several kinds of rodents in summer and fall. The plants are a source of honey, and their wood is sometimes used for fuel.

Small Mammals (seeds)
Ground Squirrel
* Antelope, *Mt.–Des and Calif.*
** Harris, *Ariz.*
* Rat, Merriam Kangaroo, *SW*
Hoofed Browsers (twigs, foliage)
+ Sheep, Mountain, *N.Mex.*

Pea Family: *Fabaceae*

BLACK LOCUST
Robinia pseudoacacia

Original range ▨ Extended range ▨

[1*/4 users] The black locust is native to open mountain slopes in the East but is now naturalized through much of the country in many kinds of habitats. It tolerates poor soil, grows rapidly, and develops an extensive root system. For these reasons it is well suited to help control soil erosion in gullies and ravines. It is also planted for ornament and has value for lumber. Bees make good honey from its fragrant white flowers.

Despite its widespread distribution the black locust rates low as a wildlife plant. Its seeds are consumed to a limited extent by quail, other gamebirds, and also by squirrels, but the small extent of wildlife use stands out in contrast with its widespread availability.

Upland Gamebirds (seeds)
Quail
+ Bobwhite, *E*
* Valley, *Nev.*
Small Mammals (seeds)
+ Squirrel, Western Fox, *Mich.*
Hoofed Browsers (foliage)
+ Deer, Mule, *So.Mt.–Des.*

Caltrop Family: *Zygophyllaceae*

CREOSOTE
Larrea tridentata

[8*/4 users] This small, resinous, desert shrub (sometimes recognized as two distinct species) is a native of hot, dry wastelands from Southern California

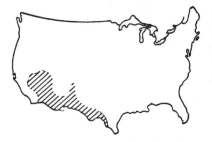

and southern Nevada to western Texas. Creosote grows where other woody plants are scarce, and consequently its shelter and shade as well as its seeds are of value to several kinds of southwestern wildlife. Rodents, especially, make good use of the seeds.

Small Mammals (seeds)
- Ground Squirrel, El Paso, *Tex.*
** Mouse, Pocket, *W.Pr. and Mt.–Des.*
Rat
* Kangaroo, Merriam, *SW*
* Kangaroo, various spp., *Pr. and Mt.–Des.*

Crowberry Family: *Empetraceae*

CROWBERRY
Empetrum nigrum

[8*/6 users] Crowberry is a low, evergreen subarctic shrub that enters the United States only along our northern borders. If the British Columbia data for Franklin grouse were excluded from the listing below, the records of use would be particularly weak. Farther north, in Canada and Alaska, crowberry is probably an important wildlife plant. The dark, berry-like fruits remain on the twigs the year round.

Waterbirds (berries)
- Gull, Herring, *N.*
Upland Gamebirds (berries)
*** Grouse, Franklin, *B.C.*
Songbirds (berries)
* Bunting, Snow, *N.*
* Grosbeak, Pine, *NE*
- Sparrow, Tree, *NE*
Fur and Game Mammals (foliage, fruit)
- Pika, *Pac.*

Cashew Family: *Anacardiaceae*

SUMACS
Rhus

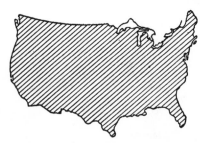 

[46*/50 users] There are about 15 species of sumac in the United States aside from the poison-ivy, poison-oak, poison-sumac, and laurel-sumac which are also classed in the genus *Rhus* by many botanists but here are treated separately. Three of the most common ones in the East, dwarfsumac (*R. copallina*), smooth sumac (*R. glabra*), and staghorn sumac (*R. typhina*), are generally small trees; the other species are largely shrubs. Ordinarily, sumacs grow in moist, sunny, open places—in pastures, along fence rows, stream borders, and roads. They die when shaded out by other trees and are short-lived at best.

Sumacs do not provide choice or preferred food for wildlife, yet they are an important winter sustenance for many species in the East and Prairie regions. The bright red clusters of fuzzy fruits ripening in the fall remain on the plants far into the winter and are widely available when other more desirable foods are scarce. It has been found that the fruits are a good source of provitamin A. When a 50% diet of sumac seeds in combination with other high-caloric feedstuffs was supplied to captive bobwhite quails, the birds thrived and gained weight. Several of our most important gamebirds rely on sumac as a winter food and so do some of the songbirds which winter in the North. Sometimes, in especially severe weather, gamebirds will remain near a copse of sumacs until the supply of fruit is exhausted. In addition, rabbits and hoofed browsers feed on the bark and on the twigs and fruit of these plants.

Upland Gamebirds (fruit)
** Grouse, Ruffed, *Ohio;* *NE and No.Pr.;* +Wis.
  * Pheasant, Ring-necked, *N.Y.*: +NE
  * Pigeon, Band-tailed, *So.Mt.–Des.*
    Prairie Chicken
  + Greater, *No.Pr.*
  * Lesser, *Okla.* (dwarfsumac)
    Quail
  * Bobwhite, *NE, Tex.,* and *Okla.;* +SE and E.Pr.
  * Mountain, *Pac.*
** Turkey, Wild, *Tex.;* +E

Songbirds (fruit)
  * Bluebirds, *E*
  * Cardinal, *NE*
  * Catbird, *NE*
  * Chat, Long-tailed, *Pac.*
    Crow
  * Common, *Pr.*
  + Fish, *E*
  + Finch, Purple, *Ky.*
    Flicker
  + Red-shafted, *Pac.*
  + Yellow-shafted, *E and E.Pr.*
  + Grosbeak, Evening, *NW*
    Jay
  + California, *Calif.*
  + Woodhouse, *So.Mt.–Des.*
  + Junco, Slate-colored, *Md.*
  + Magpie, American, *Mt.–Des.* (skunkbush)
  * Mockingbird, *SE;* +Tex. and *Calif.*
  * Phoebe, *E*
** Robin, *NE;* +E.Pr., *NE,* and *Mt.–Des.;* +SE
  + Solitaire, Townsend, *W*
** Starling, *NE*
  + Tanager, Scarlet, *NE*
  * Thrasher, Brown, *SE;* +NE and *Tex.*
    Thrush
  * Hermit, *NE*
  + Olive-backed, *NE*
  + Varied, *Pac.*
  + Veery, *NE*
    Vireo
  + Red-eyed, *E*
  + Warbling, *NE*
  + Warbler, Pine, *E*
  + Woodpecker, Golden-fronted, *Tex.* (skunkbush)
  + Wren, Cactus, *Calif. and Ariz.*

Fur and Game Mammals (bark, fruit)
  * Hare, Varying, *Minn.*
    Rabbit
*** Cottontail, *Iowa;* +Conn.
**** Cottontail, Mearns, *Mich.*
** Cottontail, New England, *NE*

Small Mammals (fruit)
  * Chipmunk, Western, *Mt.–Des.* and *Pac.*
  + Rat, Wood, *SE*

Hoofed Browsers (twigs, foliage)
    Deer
  + Mule, *Utah*
** White-tailed, *N.Y.;* *Me., Mo., and Ala.*
  + Moose, *Mich.*
  * Sheep, Mountain, *Calif.*

Reference: A Monographic Study of *Rhus* and Its Immediate Allies. Fred Alexander Barkeley. *Mo. Bot. Garden Ann.*, Vol. 24, 1937. 234 pp.

LAUREL-SUMAC
Malosma laurina

[3*/8 users] Laurel-sumac is the only species in the genus *Malosma*. However, some botanists place it in *Rhus* along with other sumacs. The range of laurel-sumac is limited to Southern and Lower California—in valleys near the coast. The small whitish fruits of this glossy-leaved evergreen shrub or small tree are eaten by a number of songbirds.

Songbirds (fruit)
+ Mockingbird, *Calif.*
* Thrasher, California, *Calif.*
+ Thrush, Hermit, *Calif.*
  Towhee
+   Brown, *Calif.*
+   Spotted, *Calif.*
* Warbler, Audubon, *Calif.*
* Wren-tit, *Calif.*

Small Mammals (leaves, flowers)
− Rat, Large-eared Wood, *Calif.*

POISON-IVY AND POISON-OAK
Toxicodendron

[66*/61 users] We have, in the United States, three species of poisonous shrubs to which the names poison-oak or poison-ivy are applied. Common poison-ivy (*T. radicans*) has the widest range, extending through the East to the Rocky Mountains. It frequently assumes the form of a vine, climbing up tree trunks and on fences. Some botanists split this widespread species into two, one eastern and the other western. There are also two bushy species: the hairy-leafed poison-oak of the Southeast (*T. quercifolium*) and the Pacific poison-oak (*T. diversilobum*). These poisonous plants are closely allied to the sumacs, and some botanists class the two groups together.

All three species of poison-ivy or poison-oak as well as the closely related but less abundant poison-sumac seem to be equally popular with wildlife. It is interesting to note that flickers and other members of the woodpecker group that are fond of ants, despite their formic acid, are also partial to the fruits of these poisonous plants. Poison-ivy and poison-oak fruits are consumed by many kinds of birds—primarily in winter when other foods are scarce. These common plants are a nuisance to man because of the serious skin irritations they cause, but they have some compensation in their considerable wildlife value.

Upland Gamebirds (seeds)
* Grouse, Sharp-tailed, *Minn. and Nebr.*
+ Pheasant, Ring-necked, *NE*
  Quail

* Bobwhite, *NE and Pr.*
* California, *Calif.*
* Turkey, Wild, *SE;* +*NE*

Songbirds (seeds)
+ Bluebird, *E*
+ Bush-tit, *Calif.*
** Catbird, *SE*
   Chickadee
* Black-capped, *NE*
* Carolina, *SE*
* Chestnut-backed, *Pac.*
* Mountain, *Mt.–Des. and Pac.*
+ Crow, *E and Pr.*
+ Finch, Purple, *E*
   Flicker
** Red-shafted, *Pac.*
*** Yellow-shafted, *E and E.Pr.*
   Junco
+ Oregon, *Calif.*
+ Slate-colored, *NE*
** Kinglet, Ruby-crowned, *Calif.*
   Magpie
+ American, *Mt.–Des.*
+ Yellow-billed, *Calif.*
* Mockingbird, *Calif.;* +*Tex.*
+ Phoebe, *E*
   Sapsucker
** Red-breasted, *Pac.*
** Yellow-bellied, *So.Pr.*
+ Solitaire, Townsend, *W*
   Sparrow
* Fox, *W;* +*E*
* Golden-crowned, *Calif.*
+ White-crowned, *Pac.*
* White-throated, *NE*
* Starling, *NE*
   Thrasher
+ Brown, *E and Tex.*
** California, *Calif.*

   Thrush
** Hermit, *Pac.*
** Russet-backed, *Calif.*
+ Varied, *Pac.*
   Titmouse
+ Plain, *Calif.*
+ Tufted, *E*
* Towhee, Spotted, *Pac.*
   Vireo
+ Warbling, *Pac.*
+ White-eyed, *E*
   Warbler
* Audubon, *Calif.*
+ Cape May, *Md.*
* Myrtle, *E and Calif.*
+ Waxwing, Cedar, *NE*
   Woodpecker
** Downy, *E and Pr.*
* Hairy, *E and Pr.*
+ Lewis, *Mt.–Des. and Pac.*
** Nuttall, *Calif.*
+ Pileated, *E*
* Red-bellied, *E*
+ Red-cockaded, *Gulf Coast*
   Wren
+ Cactus, *Calif. and Ariz.*
+ Carolina, *E*
*** Wren-tit, *Pac.*

Fur and Game Mammals (leaves, stems, seeds)
+ Bear, Black, *Pa.*
− Muskrat, *Md.*
+ Rabbit, Mearns Cottontail, *N.Y.*

Small Mammals (seeds, leaves)
*** Mouse, Pocket, *Calif.*
− Rat, Wood, *Calif.*

Hoofed Browsers (foliage, twigs)
+ Deer, Mule, *Nebr.*

References: A Monographic Study of Rhus and Its Immediate Allies. Fred Alexander Barkley. *Mo. Bot. Garden Ann.*, Vol.'24, 1937. 234 pp.

Poison-ivy, Poison-oak and Poison-sumac, Identification, Precautions, Eradications. Donald M. Crooks and Leonard W. Kephart. *U.S. Dept. Agr. Farmers Bul.* 1972, 1946. 30 pp.

Holly Family: *Aquifoliaceae*

HOLLIES
Ilex

[25*/36 users] We have 14 or 15 native hollies—only a small fraction of the 175 to 200 species now recognized. Our species are confined to the East and occur characteristically in moist woods. Most of us have a mental picture of

holly based entirely on the evergreen American holly (*I. opaca*) used for Christmas decorations. It may be surprising for some to learn that about half of our kinds of holly are shrubs instead of trees and only about half are evergreen. Clusters of reddish fruits are typical of all species.

Its bright colored fruits and attractive foliage makes the American holly one of the most useful plants for the dual purpose of ornament and attracting birds. Many songbirds, particularly the thrushes, mockingbird, robin, catbird, bluebird, and thrasher, use the fruit extensively. The evergreen species are of additional value to wildlife because of the all-year protective shelter they offer. In using the American holly for ornamental purposes, it is considered essential to plant both male and female trees to ensure a crop of fruit.

Waterfowl (fruit)
    Duck
+   Black, *SE*
+   Florida, *Fla.*
Upland Gamebirds (fruit)
+   Dove, Mourning, *SE*
+   Grouse, Ruffed, *NE*
+   Quail, Bobwhite, *SE*
*   Turkey, Wild, *SE*
Songbirds (fruit)
** Bluebird, *SE*; +*NE*
** Catbird, *SE*; +*NE*
+   Flicker, Yellow-shafted, *E and E.Pr.*

+ Jay, Florida Blue, *Gulf States*
** Mockingbird, *E*; +*Tex.*
+ Phoebe, *E*
** Robin, *Fla.*; *SE*
   Sapsucker
*   Red-naped, *So.Pr.* (sap)
**   Yellow-bellied, *So.Pr.*; +*E* (sap)
+ Sparrow, White-throated, *NE*
   Thrush
+   Gray-cheeked, *NE*
**   Hermit, *E*
*   Olive-backed, *Pr.*
+   Wood, *NE*
** Thrasher, Brown, *Tex.*; *SE*
+ Towhee, *E*
+ Vireo, White-eyed, *E*
+ Waxwing, Cedar, *NE*
* Woodpecker, Pileated, *E*
Fur and Game Mammals (fruit)
+ Armadillo, *Tex.*
+ Bear, Black, *Va. and W.Va.*
* Raccoon, *Tex.*; +*E*
+ Skunk, Striped, *Tex.*
   Squirrel
+   Fox, *Tex.*
+   Fox, Western, *Mo.*
+   Gray, *Tex.*
Small Mammals (fruit)
+ Mouse, White-footed, *E*
+ Rat, Attwater Wood, *Tex.*
Hoofed Browsers (foliage, twigs)
* Deer, White-tailed, *Pa. and N.C.*

References: Growing Christmas Holly on the Farm. Perkins Coville. *U.S. Dept. Agr. Farmers' Bul.* 1693, 1940. 22 pp.
Vegetative Propagation of Holly. W. Zimmerman and A. E. Hitchcock. *Am. Jour. Botany*, Vol. 16, pp. 556–570, 1929.

Bittersweet Family: *Celastraceae*

BITTERSWEET
Celastrus scandens

The decorative value of the plant's colorful dry fruits has caused people, driving through the countryside, to help themselves to bunches of bittersweet branches. As a consequence, this attractive shrub has become scarce in many places where it was formerly plentiful.

[1*/9 users] There is only one *Celastrus* in the United States though 30 to 50 species are recognized in the tropical and subtropical parts of the world. Our one species, bittersweet, is a rambling vine confined to the eastern half of the country. It occurs along fence rows, by streams, and in woodlands. The bright-colored fruit capsules produce large seeds that are eaten by several species of birds. The utility of bittersweet to wildlife, however, is very limited.

Upland Gamebirds (seeds, buds)
* Grouse, Ruffed, *No.Cent.States and Ohio*
+ Pheasant, Ring-necked, *Pa.*
+ Quail, Bobwhite, *Mo.*
+ Turkey, Wild, *Pa.*
Songbirds (seeds)
+ Bluebird, Eastern, *NE*
+ Robin, *NE and E.Pr.*
Fur and Game Mammals (seeds, leaves)
+ Rabbit, Cottontail, *Conn. and N.Y.*
Squirrel
+ Fox, *Ohio*
+ Fox, Western, *Mo.*

Maple Family: *Aceraceae*

MAPLES (INCLUDING BOXELDER)
Acer

[61*/33 users] Of the world's 60 to 150 kinds of maples, only 12 to 19 are listed for the United States. Our species are widely distributed over the more humid parts of the country. They prefer moist locations but are frequently found on hills and slopes. Two of the most common, widespread eastern species, the red maple (*A. rubrum*) and silver maple (*A. saccharinum*), are typical of bottom lands or river margins. The sugar maple (*A. saccharum*) and mountain maple (*A. spicatum*) are characteristic of the cooler parts of the Northeast. In the Far West the Rocky Mountain maple (*A. glabrum*), bigleaf maple (*A. macrophyllum*), and vine maple (*A. circinatum*) are the common species. The only conspicuous member of the maple group in the prairies and in other semiarid regions is the boxelder (*A. negundo*). It is planted extensively as a shade tree in the West.

Maple seeds ripen in the spring, summer, or fall, depending on the particular species. They, as well as the buds and flowers, provide food for many kinds of birds and other animals. Squirrels eat the seeds, frequently storing them in caches after removing the hull and wing. Chipmunks do the same. Birds use the leaves and seed stalks commonly in nest building. Young red maples, three to six feet high, are favorite nesting sites of the prairie warbler.

Maples, both native and introduced, are used extensively as shade trees. The brilliant fall coloring of some of the species adds to their ornamental value.

Upland Gamebirds (buds, twigs, seeds)
Grouse
* Ruffed, *Maine;* +*NE*
** Sharp-tailed, *Utah*
* Quail, Bobwhite, *Fla.*
+ Prairie Chicken, *Wis.*
+ Turkey, Wild, *NE*

Songbirds (seeds, buds, flowers)
+ Chickadee, Carolina, *SE* (red maple)
* Finch, Purple, *E*
+ Goldfinch, *E*
Grosbeak
**** Evening, *NE;* *NW*
** Pine, *NE*
* Rose-breasted, *NE*
* Nuthatch, Red-breasted, *E*
+ Sapsucker, Yellow-bellied, *E* (sap)

Fur and Game Mammals (seeds, flowers, bark, twigs)
+ Bear, Black, *Pa.*
* Beaver, *NE;* +*Mo.*
* Hare, Varying, *Utah;* +*Minn.*
**** Porcupine, *Vt.;* *NE*
* Rabbit, Cottontail, *Conn.*
+ Raccoon, *E.Pr.*
Squirrel
* Flying, *NE*
** Fox, *Mich.;* +*Ohio*
** Gray, *E*
** Red, *E*

Small Mammals (seeds)
** Chipmunk, Eastern, *NE*
Mouse
+ Meadow, *E*
* White-footed, *E;* +*W*
** Rat, Dusky-footed Wood, *Oreg.*

Hoofed Browsers (twigs, foliage)
Deer
** Mule, *Utah*
**** White-tailed, *N.Y.;* **Maine and N.C.Mts.;* *Wis. and Minn.*
* Elk, *No.Mt.–Des.*
** Moose, *Mich. and No.Mt.–Des.;* +*Maine*
+ Sheep, Mountain, *Mont.*

References: Maple. H. S. Betts. American woods series. U.S. Dept. Agr. Forest Service, 1945. 12 pp.
The Maples. J. S. Illick. *Amer. Forestry,* Vol. 28 (357), pp. 12–19, 1932.

Buckthorn Family: *Rhamnaceae*]

[CONDALIAS
Condalia

[7*/10 users] This genus of woody plants inhabits dry slopes and plains of the arid Southwest, from Texas to Southern California. Our six native condalias are shrubs or small trees, generally spiny and with dark, per-

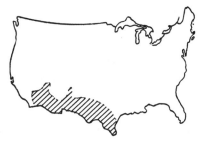

sistent, berry-like fruits that ripen in summer. Bluewood condalia (*C. obovata*) and lotewood condalia (*C. obtusifolia*) are two of the more widespread, important species.

Upland Gamebirds (fruit)
　* Dove, Western, White-winged, *Ariz.*
　+ Pigeon, Band-tailed, *Pac.*
Songbirds (fruit)
　* Mockingbird, *SW, mainly Tex.*
　+ Oriole, Bullock, *SW*
　+ Phainopepla, *Ariz.*
　− Raven, White-necked, *Tex.*
　* Thrasher, Curve-billed, *SW*
　+ Woodpecker, Golden-fronted, *Tex.*
Fur and Game Mammals (fruit)
　+ Cat, Ring-tailed, *Tex.*
　+ Fox, Gray, *SW*

BUCKTHORNS
Rhamnus

[24*/25 users] Of the 60 to 100 buckthorns in the world, about 10 to 15 species occur in this country. They are present in most parts of the United States except for the western prairies and some areas in the Mountain–Desert region. Despite this wide distribution it is largely in the West and particularly in the Pacific region that the genus is important to wildlife. Apparently this is due to the relative abundance of certain species in the area, such as California buckthorn (*R. californica*), cascara buckthorn (*R. purshiana*), alder buckthorn (*R. alnifolia*), and hollyleaf buckthorn (*R. crocea*). In the East, Carolina buckthorn (*R. caroliniana*) is probably the most common representative, but it is nowhere abundant compared with other wildlife plants.

The small, black, fleshy fruits ripening in the fall are attractive to wildlife. In Oregon, the pileated woodpecker feeds on the fruits to a 3-star extent. Elsewhere in the West it is an important food for the mockingbird, catbird, crested mynah, phainopepla, thrushes, and others. Several mammals of the East and the West eat buckthorn fruits to a limited extent. Deer and bighorn sheep browse on the plants in California. The hollyleaf buckthorn is

evergreen and for this reason probably has special cover value.

Upland Gamebirds (fruit)
　* Pigeon, Band-tailed, *Pac.* (cascara buckthorn)
Songbirds (fruit)
　** Catbird, *W*
　** Mockingbird, *Calif.*
　** Mynah, Crested, *B.C.*
　** Phainopepla, *Calif. and Ariz.*
　+ Robin, *Pac.*
　* Sapsucker, Northern Red-breasted, *Pac.*
　　Thrasher
　* 　Brown, *Pr.*
　* 　California, *Calif.*
　　Thrush
　+ 　Hermit, *Pac.*
　** 　Russet-backed, *Calif.*
　+ 　Varied, *Pac.*
　*** Woodpecker, Pileated, *Oreg.*
Fur and Game Mammals (fruits, stems, foliage)
　+ Bear, Black, *NE*
　+ Cat, Ring-tailed, *Tex.*
　− Hare, Varying, *NE and No.Pr.*
　+ Rabbit, Cottontail, *Mich.*
　* Raccoon, *Pac.*
Small Mammals (fruit)
　　Ground Squirrel
　− 　Beechey, *Calif.*

341

+   Douglas, *Oreg.*
    Rat
−   Wood, Dusky-footed, *Oreg.*
−   Wood, Portola, *Calif.*

Hoofed Browsers (twigs, foliage)
    Deer
*   Black-tailed, *Calif.*
+   Mule, *Pac.*
*   Sheep, Bighorn, *Calif.*

Reference: Propagation of the Cascara Tree, a Conservation Measure. *Dept. Agr. British Columbia Bul.* 108, 1941. 9 pp.

CEANOTHUS
Ceanothus

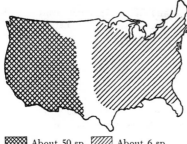

▨ About 50 sp. ▨ About 6 sp.

[20*/18 users] Shrubs of the genus *Ceanothus* have their main home base in the western United States. Of the 55 species in the world, 4 occur in the East and 40 in the West—the greatest number being in California and neighboring states. They are partial to dry or well-drained upland soils and are especially plentiful in burned or cleared areas—often being the dominant growth in such places.

It is unfortunate that there is no widely accepted common name for this important genus. The names bluebrush, mountain-lilac, and California-lilac have been applied to some western species which have colorful masses of minute flowers. Snowbrush is the name widely used for the valuable browse species *C. velutinus* and New Jersey-tea for the common, eastern *C. americanus.* None of these names, however, apply to the group as a whole. So the scientific name ceanothus is used here for want of something better, though it is particularly unsatisfactory if one wishes to use the plural.

The principal wildlife use of ceanothus, aside from cover, is browse for western mammals—especially for deer, elk, and rabbits. Chipmunks and other rodents as well as quail (including, occasionally, the bobwhite) make some use of the small hard seeds.

Upland Gamebirds (seeds)
    Quail
+   Mountain, *Pac.*
+   Valley, *Calif.*

Fur and Game Mammals (stems, foliage)
−   Hare, Varying, *Utah*
*   Mountain Beaver, *Pac.*
+   Porcupine, Yellow-haired, *Mt.– Des.*
    Rabbit
**   Cottontail, *Calif.*
+   Cottontail, Mearns, *Pa.*

Small Mammals (flowers, foliage, seeds)
*   Chipmunk, *Mt.–Des. and Pac.NW*
+   Ground Squirrel, *Calif.*
    Rat
+   Wood Large-eared, *Calif.*
+   Wood Portola, *Calif.*

Hoofed Browsers (twigs, foliage)
    Deer
**   Black-tailed, *Calif.*
****   Mule, *Calif.*; ***S.Dak. and Oreg.*; +*Nebr.*
*   White-tailed, *Pa.*; +*S.Dak. and Mont.*
    Elk
**   American, *No.Mt.–Des.*
**   Roosevelt, *Calif.*
+   Goat, Mountain, *Mont.*
−   Sheep, Mountain, *Mont.*

Reference: Ceanothus. Maunsell Van Rensselaer. Santa Barbara Botanic Garden, 1942. 308 pp.

Grape Family: *Vitaceae*

GRAPES
Vitis

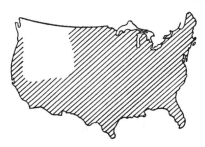

[94*/75 users] Half or more of the grapes in the world are native to the United States; 24 to 30 species occur widely distributed throughout this country.

Grapevines like moist, fertile soils and are commonly found along stream banks, fence rows, and near margins of woods. They need sunlight and will reach far to get it, sometimes harming plants over which they climb.

Wild grapes are vigorous plants with few serious pests except for the Japanese beetle which has a strong partiality for its leaves. The different grape species vary in details of their broad leaves, in the size and quantity of their fruit, and in other characteristics, but all have value to wildlife. The fruit is a favorite food of gamebirds, many songbirds, and some fur bearers. Even the old, dried clusters are sought in winter. The yield of wild grapes varies greatly from year to year; sometimes the crop is a total failure. Unfortunately cultivated grapes are just as acceptable to wildlife as the native wild ones, and local damage to vineyards is frequent. Most of the grapes that are eaten by wildlife in California are from cultivated plants.

In the summer the dense foliage provides good escape and shelter cover as well as nesting sites for songbirds. In addition, the bark of grapevines is often used in nest building.

Waterfowl (fruit)
* * Duck, Wood, *NE*

Upland Gamebirds (fruit)
* + Dove, Western White-winged, *Ariz.*
* *** Grouse, Ruffed, *Va.Alleghenies;* **Ohio;* *NE*
* ** Pheasant, Ring-necked, *N.Y.;* *NE*
* * Pigeon, Band-tailed, *So.Mt.– Des.*
* + Prairie Chicken, Attwater, *Tex.*
* * Quail, Bobwhite, *NE;* +*E.Pr.*
* *** Turkey, Wild, *Allegheny Mts.;* **Va.;* *Mo.;* +*SE*

Songbirds (fruit)
* + Blackbird, Rusty, *NE*
  Bluebird
* + Eastern, *NE*
* * Mountain, *W, mainly Mt.– Des.*
* ** Western, *Calif.*
* *** Cardinal, *NE;* +*SE*
* * Catbird, *NE;* +*SE*
  Crow
* + Common, *E*
* + Fish, *E*
* + Finch, Purple, *E*
  Flicker
* * Red-shafted, *Pac.*
* + Yellow-shafted, *E and E.Pr.*
* + Flycatcher, Crested, *E*
  Grackle
* + Boat-tailed, *SE*
* + Purple, *NE*

Jay
+   Blue, *E*
*   Blue, Florida, *Gulf Coast*
+   Junco, *Md.*
    Kingbird
**   Cassin, *SW*
+   Eastern, *E*
*   Magpie, Yellow-billed, *Calif.*
****   Mockingbird, *Calif.; *SE; +NE*
+   Mynah, Crested, *B.C.*
   Oriole
+   Baltimore, *NE*
+   Bullock, *SW*
+   Orchard, *E*
***   Phainopepla, *Calif.*
***   Robin, *E.Pr. and Pac.; *E*
+   Sapsucker, Yellow-bellied, *E*
     (sap)
    Sparrow
+   English, *U.S.*
***   Fox, *W; +E*
+   White-throated, *NE*
+   Starling, *NE*
    Tanager
+   Scarlet, *NE*
.+   Summer, *SE*
    Thrasher
*   Brown, *SE; +NE, Tex., and Pr.*
*   California, *Calif.*
*   Sage, *W*
    Thrush
*   Gray-cheeked, *NE*
*   Hermit, *E; +Pac.*
*   Olive-backed, *NE*
+   Russet-backed, *Calif.*

+   Varied, *Pac.*
*   Wood, *NE*
+   Titmouse, Tufted, *NE*
+   Towhee, Red-eyed, *E*
   Vireo
+   Philadelphia, *NE*
*   Warbling, *E.Pr.*
   Warbler
+   Audubon, *Calif.*
+   Pine, *E*
***   Waxwing, Cedar, *Pac.; *NE; +SE and W*
   Woodpecker
**   Pileated, *E*
**   Red-bellied, *E*
+   Red-headed, *E*
*   Wren-tit, *Pac.*

Fur and Game Mammals (fruit)
**   Bear, Black, *NE*
+   Cat, Ring-tailed, *Tex.*
+   Coyote, *W*
   Fox
+   Gray, *E*
+   Red, *Mass. and Iowa*
*   Opossum, *E; +Mo.*
+   Rabbit, Cottontail, *Mich.* (various parts)
**   Raccoon, *SE, and E.Tex.; *NE; +Pac, and Iowa*
   Skunk
*   California, *Calif.*
**   Eastern, *NE*
*   Spotted, Prairie, *Iowa*
*   Squirrel, Fox, *NE*

Hoofed Browsers (foliage, stems)
+   Deer, White-tailed, *E*

References: The Species of Grapes Peculiar to North America. Liberty H. Bailey. *Gentes Herbarum*, Vol. 3, pp. 149–244, 1943.
Grapes for Different Regions. *U.S. Dept. Agr. Bul.* 1936, 1943. 38 pp.

VIRGINIA-CREEPERS
Parthenocissus

[26*/30 users] There are two or three species of this genus in the United States. All are vines and are close relatives of the grape. Like wild grapes, the Virginia-creeper also favors moist, sunny clearings, fence rows, roadsides, and stream banks. Though this five-leafleted climber occurs far west of the Mississippi River its principal home is in the East, where it is one of the commonest vines of the countryside. Frequently it may be found growing with poison-ivy with which it is sometimes confused. The latter may be distinguished by its three leaflets and whitish fruits.

The grape-like clusters of Virginia-creeper fruits are important fall and winter food for wildlife. The berries ripen in the fall but many of them cling

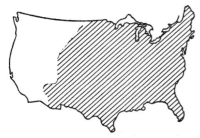 

onto the vines until late winter, or until eaten by birds. Among the principal users of its fruit are such well-known songbirds as the mockingbird, robin, bluebird, brown thrasher, and various thrushes. Virginia-creeper growing as a wall cover or climbing over fences, trellises, or on tree trunks is not only ornamental but also attractive to songbirds. The leaves turn brilliant scarlet in the fall.

Songbirds (fruit)
　　Bluebird
　* 　Eastern, *SE*
　− 　Mountain, *N.Mex.*
　+ Catbird, *E*
　+ Chickadee, Black-capped, *NE*
　+ Crow, *E*
　* Flicker, Yellow-shafted　*E and E.Pr.*
　* Flycatcher, Crested, *E*
　** Mockingbird, *SE*; **Tex.*
　+ Nuthatch, White-breasted, *E and E.Pr.*
　* Robin, *NE*; +*SE and E.Pr.*

　　Sapsucker
　* 　Red-naped, *So.Pr.*
　** 　Yellow-breasted, *E.Pr.; *E*
　* Sparrow, Fox, *E*
　+ Starling, *NE*
　+ Swallow, Tree, *E*
　* Thrasher, Brown, *SE*
　　Thrush
　+ 　Hermit, *E*
　* 　Olive-backed, *NE*
　+ 　Veery, *NE*
　* 　Wood, *NE*
　+ Titmouse, Tufted, *SE*
　　Vireo
　* 　Red-eyed, *E*
　+ 　White-eyed, *SE*
　　Woodpecker
　+ 　Downy, *E and E.Pr.*
　+ 　Hairy, *E and E.Pr.*
　* 　Pileated, *E*
　* 　Red-bellied, *E*

Fur and Game Mammals (fruit, foliage)
　+ Fox, Red, *NE*
　+ Rabbit, Mearns Cottontail, *N.Y.*
　+ Skunk, Eastern, *N.Y.*

Basswood Family: *Tiliaceae*

BASSWOODS
Tilia

[**7*/10 users**] Botanists disagree in their interpretations of this genus. Native species of *Tilia* are listed as 3 to 15 and the total for the world as 12 to 50 species depending on which authority you prefer. The famous limes or lindens of Europe belong to this genus. Our native species are generally called basswoods. These heart-leafed trees with small, fragrant flowers are confined to the East, growing on well-drained bottom lands, along streams and lakes, or on moist, fertile slopes.

Basswood is of relatively minor importance to wildlife. Squirrels and chipmunks eat the seeds (nutlets), and rabbits and hoofed browsers feed on other parts of the plant. The seeds are of practically no use to birds.

Upland Gamebirds (seeds)
+ Quail, Bobwhite, *NE*
Fur and Game Mammals (seeds, bark)
** Rabbit, Cottontail, *Iowa*

* Porcupine, *NE*
  Squirrel
* Fox, Western, *Mich.*
+ Gray, *Va.*
− Red, Northern, *N.Dak.*
Small Mammals (seeds)
** Chipmunk, Eastern, *NE*
+ Ground Squirrel, Franklin, *No.Pr.*
− Mouse, White-footed, *NE*
Hoofed Browsers (twigs, foliage)
* Deer, White-tailed, *N.Y.*

Reference: Utilization of Basswood. W. D. Brush. *U.S. Dept. Agr. Bul.* 1007, 1922. 64 pp.

Cactus Family: *Cactaceae*

GIANTCACTUS
Cereus giganteus

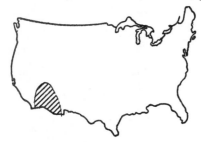

[5*/4 users] There are 200 or more species of *Cereus* in the world, but this particular one, giantcactus, is so unique that it has been classed by some botanists in another genus, *Carnegia*. It is found on rocky dry slopes and flats in the southern deserts of Arizona and California. This giant of all native cacti sometimes attains a height of 60 feet or more. Its cylindrical, fluted or ribbed trunk, covered with spines, extends upward as a simple column or, more commonly, produces one to several candelabra-like branches.

Besides the use of its seeds by several species of desert wildlife, these tree-like plants also serve as homes for several kinds of birds in a region where real trees are absent or very scarce. The gila woodpecker and the Mearns gilded flicker peck nest holes into the trunk and branches, generally at heights of 10 to 20 feet from the ground. Such holes are also used by the elf owl, the ferruginous pygmy owl, the ash-throated flycatcher, the Arizona crested flycatcher, the cactus wren, and other species. Probably some of these species of wildlife could not continue to survive in the absence of this slow-growing, easily destroyed desert plant.

Upland Gamebirds (seeds)
** Dove, Western White-winged, *Ariz.*
Songbirds (seeds)
* Sapsucker, Northern Red-breasted, *Pac., mainly Calif.*
Small Mammals (simple seeds)
** Rat, White-throated Wood, *Ariz.*
Hoofed Browsers (veg. parts)
+ Sheep, Mountain, *N.Mex.*

PRICKLYPEARS
Opuntia

[62*/44 users] There are, according to some botanists, as many as 100 species of pricklypear cactus in the United States. Most of ours are natives of the southwestern desert areas where they are outstandingly important wildlife

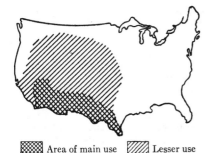 

 Area of main use Lesser use

food plants. The fruits, seeds, and stems of these thorny succulents are eaten by at least 44 kinds of animals to an appreciable extent. Rodents are particularly partial to the seeds which constitute two-thirds of the food of the Harris ground squirrel in Arizona and are consumed by many other species. Deer and other browsers eat the spiny fruits and slabs (stems) without apparent injury from the thorns.

Sometimes when forage becomes scarce, cattle are fed cactus slabs after they have been ground up like ensilage or after they have had some of the thorns burnt off with a blowtorch. Pricklypear inclines to invade and spread in overstocked grazing ranges.

Upland Gamebirds (seeds, fruits)
  Dove
  + White-winged, Eastern, *Tex.*
  + White-winged, Western, *Ariz.*
  Quail
  + Gambel, *SW*
  * Mearns, *SW*
  * Scaled, Arizona, *SW*
  * Scaled, Chestnut-bellied, *Tex.*
  + Turkey, Wild, *SW*
Songbirds (seeds, fruit)
  * Raven, White-necked, *SW, mainly Tex.*
  ** Thrasher, Curve-billed, *SW*
  ** Woodpecker, Golden-fronted, *Tex.*
  * Wren, Cactus, *Calif. and Ariz.*
  + Wren-tit, *Pac.*
Fur and Game Mammals (fruit, stems)
  + Cat, Ring-tailed, *Tex.*
  + Coyote, *W*

  + Fox, Gray, *SW*
  Jack Rabbit
  * Antelope, *Ariz.*
  * California, *Ariz. and N.Mex.*
  — Colorado Desert, *Utah*
  *** Rabbit, Cottontail, *Ariz.*
  Skunk
  * Hog-nosed, *Tex.*
  * Striped, *Tex.*
  + Wolf, Texan Red, *SW*
Small Mammals (seeds, fruit)
  ** Chipmunk, Western, various spp., *Mt.–Des. and Pac.*
  Gopher
  + Pocket, Brown, *Mont.*
  + Pocket, Western, *Mont.*
  Ground Squirrel
  *** Antelope, *Mt.–Des. and Calif.*
  ***** (65%) Harris, *Ariz.*
  * Thirteen-lined, *Pr.*
  Mouse
  — Desert, Western, *Ariz.*
  * Pocket, various spp., *W.Pr. and Mt.–Des.*
  Prairie Dog
  * Black-tailed, *W.Pr.*
  * White-tailed, *Mont. and Wyo.*
  Rat
  + Kangaroo, Merriam, *SW*
  * Kangaroo, Ord, *W*
  + Kangaroo, various spp., *Pr. and Mt.–Des.*
  * Wood, *Calif.*
  — Wood, Large-eared, *Calif.*
  **** Wood, White-throated, *Ariz.*
  ** Rock Squirrel, *Tex.; *Calif.*
Hoofed Browsers (veg.parts, fruit)
  * Antelope, *No.Pr. and Mt.–Des.; +SE Mont. and N.Mex.*
  + Deer, White-tailed, *Tex.*
  * Peccary, *Tex. and Ariz.*
  ** Sheep, Mountain, *Nev.; +N. Mex.*

Reference: Spreading of *Opuntia* in Overgrazed Pastures in Kansas. John H. Schaffner. *Ecology*, Vol. 19, pp. 348–350, 1938.

Elaeagnus Family: *Elaeagnaceae*

RUSSIANOLIVE
Elaeagnus angustifolia

[17*/6 users] The Russianolive, a native of Europe and western Asia, is now established widely in the West, particularly in the Northwest. This small tree or shrub tolerates some alkalinity and has proved itself hardy to droughts. The Soil Conservation Service regards it as a good plant for soil cover in western areas. Its fleshy, silvery-yellowish fruit clings to the plants through most of the winter and is an important food for the cedar waxwing, robin, and evening grosbeak.

The silverberry (*E. argentea*) is a related native species. It is a northern shrub which has some importance to wildlife, but the records of its use are scant.

Upland Gamebirds (fruit)
    – Pheasant, Ring-necked, *Minn.*
    + Quail, Gambel, *SW*
Songbirds (fruit)
    ** Grosbeak, Evening, *NW*
    ** Robin, *Mt.–Des.; *E.Pr.*
    *** Waxwing, Cedar, *W*
Hoofed Browsers (twigs, foliage)
    – Elk, *Mont.*

BUFFALOBERRIES
Shepherdia

[15*/7 users] The three kinds of buffaloberries native to the United States are the only ones in the world. One or more of them occurs in practically all parts of the country except the Southeast. Though these thorny, silvery-leafed, fleshy-berried shrubs are widespread, they are not abundant enough in any region to be valuable to wildlife. The records of use listed in the table below are all western—apparently their value to eastern wildlife is negligible.

Upland Gamebirds (fruit)
    * Quail, Valley, *Nev.*
Songbirds (fruit)
    ** Catbird, *W*
    + Thrasher, Brown, *Pr.*
Fur and Game Mammals (fruit)
    * Bear, Black, *W*
Small Mammals (fruit)
    Chipmunk
    *   Northwest, *Pac.NW*
    *   Least, *Pr. and Mt.–Des.*
    * Ground Squirrel, *No.Mt.–Des. and Pac.*

Aralia Family: *Araliaceae*

ARALIAS
Aralia

[0*/7 users] There are about half a dozen aralias in the United States and 30 to 40 in the world. Ours are shrubs or small trees, some armed with sharp spines. Though the genus is represented to some extent in the Far West, aralias are more conspicuous in fertile, moist woodlands of the eastern United States. The very spiny hercules club or devil's walkingstick (*A. spinosa*) is a common species; so is the well-known wild sarsaparilla (*A. nudicaulis*).

The small fleshy fruits and their seeds are eaten by thrushes and by other birds as well as by a few mammals. The aggregate wildlife value of these plants is low.

Upland Gamebirds (fruit)
+ Pigeon, Band-tailed, *So.Mt.– Des.*

Songbirds (fruit)
+ Sparrow, White-throated, *NE*

Thrush
+ Olive-backed, *NE*
+ Wood, *NE*

Fur and Game Mammals (fruit)
+ Fox, Red, *E*
+ Skunk, Eastern, *NE*

Small Mammals (fruit)
+ Chipmunk, Eastern, *NE*

Dogwood Family: *Cornaceae*

BLACKGUM
Nyssa sylvatica

[26*/33 users] Of the eight recognized species of *Nyssa*, six occur in the United States. Only one, the blackgum, is important to wildlife. Locally it is called sourgum or tupelogum. The narrow-leafed form, common in southern swamps, is recognized as a distinct species (*N. biflora*) by some botanists, but here it is treated as simply a variety (*N. sylvatica biflora*).

Blackgum is confined to eastern woodlands. The typical northern form is found in uplands as well as in lowlands, but the southern variety is almost exclusively a tree of swamps and wet bottom lands.

Probably blackgum is more valuable to wildlife than is indicated in the following table. For most songbirds the big, heavy-walled pits are too large to be swallowed; so only the flesh of the fruit is consumed. Since flesh and skin of fruits are difficult to identify, it is conceivable that considerable blackgum material may have remained undetermined in some analyses. The wood duck, wild turkey, robin, pileated woodpecker, mockingbird, brown thrasher, thrushes, flicker, and starling are prominent among its users. Black bears and foxes also relish the fruits, while white-tailed deer and beaver feed on other parts of the plant. Probably the value of the fruit to wildlife would be greater if it remained longer on the trees. Normally it drops on the ground in the fall, not long after ripening. The tree is a good honey plant and is excellent for shade or ornamental plantings. Its glossy leaves turn brilliant scarlet in the fall.

Waterfowl (fruit)
* Duck, Wood, *SE*

Upland Gamebirds (fruit, buds)
+ Grouse, Ruffed, *NE*
+ Quail, Bobwhite, *E*
* Turkey, Wild, *SE*; +*NE*

Songbirds (fruit)
+ Bluebird, *E*
+ Crow, *E*
+ Finch, Purple, *E*
* Flicker, Yellow-shafted, *E and E.Pr.*
* Mockingbird, *SE*
*** Robin, *Fla.*; **NE; +*SE*
+ Sapsucker, Yellow-bellied, *E* (sap)

* Starling, *NE*
+ Tanager, Scarlet, *NE*
* Thrasher, Brown, *NE*; +*SE*
  Thrush
*   Gray-cheeked, *NE*
+   Hermit, *E*
+   Olive-backed, *NE*
*   Wood, *NE*
+ Titmouse, Tufted, *Md.*
+ Vireo, Red-eyed, *E*
+ Waxwing, Cedar, *NE*
  Woodpecker
+   Hairy, *E*
**   Pileated, *E*

+   Red-bellied, *E*

Fur and Game Mammals (fruit mainly)
** Bear, Black, *W.Va. and Va.*
− Beaver, *Miss. and Tex.* (wood)
+ Fox, Gray, *Tex.*
+ Opossum, *SE*
+ Raccoon, *Md.*
  Squirrel
+   Fox, *NE*
*   Fox, Western, *Ohio*
*   Gray, *E*

Hoofed Browsers (twigs, foliage)
* Deer, White-tailed, *N.C. and Mo.*; +*Ala.*

Reference: Tupelo. H. S. Betts. American woods series. U.S. Dept. Agr. Forest Service, 1945. 8 pp.

DOGWOODS
Cornus

Panicled Dogwood

[84*/64 users] There are about 50 dogwoods (sometimes called cornels) in the world and about 17 in the United States. All are shrubs except the flowering and Pacific dogwoods which often attain the stature of small trees. The different species vary in their habitat requirements, but most dogwoods prefer fertile, moist soil in open woods or along streams, roadsides, or fence rows. They occur naturally in hedgerows and are excellent for this purpose.

The dogwood genus covers much of the country from East to West, but its representatives are more plentiful and more important to wildlife in the Northeast than elsewhere. Prominent species in the Northeast and East are the beautiful and valuable flowering dogwood (*C. florida*), the pale dogwood (*C. obliqua*), gray dogwood (*C. racemosa*), and pagoda dogwood (*C. alternifolia*). Roughleaf dogwood (*C. asperi-*

folia) though extending into the East, particularly the Southeast, is a principal representative in the prairies. Red-osier dogwood (*C. stolonifera*) has the widest range of any and occurs all the way across the northern half of the country. Important western species are western dogwood (*C. occidentalis*), Pacific dogwood (*C. nuttallii*) which is the western counterpart of the flowering dogwood, and California dogwood (*C. californica*). The unique bunchberry (*C. canadensis*), which barely deserves inclusion among woody plants, has been segregated on page 352.

Fruits and browse of dogwood are readily identified in stomach analyses. The nutlet is unique in its two-celled characteristic, and the foliage of the

350

genus *Cornus* has distinctive two-way whitish hairs flattened to the surface and attached at the middle rather than at an end. The fleshy fruits of dogwoods are very valuable to wildlife, particularly in the Northeast. They ripen in late summer, and besides being available through the fall, some of the berry-like drupes may persist on the plants into the winter months. For plantings intended both to beautify the landscape and to attract birds, flowering dogwood is one of the very best.

Flowering Dogwood

Waterfowl (fruit)
*** Duck, Wood, *N.Y.*; +*NE*
Upland Gamebirds (fruit, buds)
    Grouse
  ** Ruffed, *Ohio;* **Wis.;* +*NE*
  + Spruce, *NW and Canada*
  + Pheasant, Ring-necked, *E*
  ** Pigeon, Band-tailed, *Pac.*
  * Prairie Chicken, Greater, *Ill.;* +*No.Pr. and Wis.*
  * Quail, Bobwhite, *SE*; +*NE*
  ** Turkey, Wild, *E*
Songbirds (fruit)
  * Bluebird, *E*
  ** Cardinal, *NE*; **Pr.*; +*SE*
  * Catbird, *NE*; +*SE and W*
  * Chat, Long-tailed, *Pac.*
  * Crow, *Pr.*; +*E.Mt.–Des. and Pac.*
  * Finch, Purple, *E*
  * Flicker, Yellow-shafted, *E and E.Pr.*
  + Flycatcher, Crested, *E*
    Grosbeak
  **** Evening, *NE*; *******NW*
  ** Pine, *Pac.;* *NE
  * Kingbird, *E*
  + Magpie, American, *Mt.–Des.*
  + Mockingbird, *SE*
  ** Mynah, Crested, *B.C.*
  + Oriole, Bullock, *SW*
  ** Robin, *NE*; *SE; +*E.Pr. and Mt.–Des.*
  * Sapsucker, Yellow-bellied, *E*
  + Starling, European, *NE*
  + Swallow, Tree, *E*
  + Tanager, Scarlet, *NE*
  * Thrasher, Brown, *NE and Pr.;* +*SE*

    Thrush
  ** Gray-cheeked, *NE*
  * Hermit, *NE*; +*Pac.*
  * Olive-backed, *NE*
  * Russet-backed, *Calif.*
  ** Wood, *NE*
    Vireo
  * Red-eyed, *E*
  * Warbling, *NE, Pr., and Pac.*
  * Warbler, Pine, *E*
  ** Waxwing, Cedar, *NE*; +*W*
    Woodpecker
  * Downy, *E and E.Pr.*
  + Hairy, *E*
  * Lewis, *Mt.–Des. and Pac.*
  + Pileated, *E*
  + Red-bellied, *E*
Fur and Game Mammals (fruit, wood, foliage)
  + Bear, Black, *W*
  + Beaver, *N.Dak.*
  + Mountain Beaver, *Pac.*
  ** Rabbit, Cottontail, *Mich.;* **Conn., Iowa*
  + Raccoon, *NE*
  − Skunk, Eastern, *NE*
    Squirrel
  * Fox, *Ohio*
  * Fox, Western, *Mo.*
  * Gray, *E*
Small Mammals (fruit)
  * Chipmunk, Eastern, *NE*; *Minn.*
  + Mouse, White-footed, *E*
  + Rat, Allegheny Wood, *E*
Hoofed Browsers (twigs, foliage)
    Deer
  + Black-tailed, *Oreg.*
  * Mule, *Calif.*

* White-tailed, *Wis. and Minn.*, *N.Y.*, *N.C.Mts.*, and *Ala.*; +*S.Dak.*	* Elk, *Idaho and Mont.* + Goat, Mountain, *Mont.* ** Moose, *Mich.*; *No.Mt.–Des.*

References: Flowering Dogwood. H. S. Betts. American wood series. U.S. Dept. Agr. Forest Service, 1945. 4 pp.
Utilization of Dogwood and Persimmon. J. B. Cuno. *U.S. Dept. Agr. Bul.* 1436, 1926. 43 pp.

BUNCHBERRY
Cornus canadensis

[8*/6 users] Bunchberry is so distinct from the other dogwoods that there is considerable argument for classifying it, as some botanists do, in a separate genus. It is the smallest of the dogwoods—a tiny, unbranched, woodland shrub rarely over a foot high, with whorled leaves and clusters of bright red berries. Colonies of bunchberry are generally found only in cool damp localities in the northern part of the United States.

Upland Gamebirds (fruit, buds)
 Grouse
* Franklin, *B.C.*
+ Sharp-tailed, *Great Lakes Area*
Songbirds (fruit)
+ Sparrow, Ipswich, *NE*
** Thrush, Veery, *NE*
 Vireo
* Philadelphia, *NE*
** Warbling, *NE and Mt.–Des.*

Heath Family: *Ericaceae*

RHODODENDRONS
Rhododendron

[4*/5 users] There are 8 to 10 native rhododendrons growing mainly in cool, mountainous sections of the East and Far West. The azaleas which many botanists also class in the genus *Rhododendron* are excluded in this treatment —partly because they have even less wildlife value.

Rhododendrons often occur in dense growths that provide good all-year cover for wildlife, but their value as a food source is quite limited. The browsing of foliage by deer is the principal food use recorded. The attractive ever-green foliage and beautiful flowers of these shrubs make them desirable for horticultural purposes.

Upland Gamebirds (buds)
+ Grouse, Ruffed, *NE*
Fur and Game Mammals (twigs)
* Mountain Beaver, *Pac.*
Small Mammals (leaves)
+ Mouse, White-footed, *E*
− Rat, Allegheny Wood, *NE*
Hoofed Browsers (foliage, twigs)
*** Deer, White-tailed, *N.C.Mts.*; +*NE*

MOUNTAINLAUREL
Kalmia latifolia

[4*/3 users] The North American genus *Kalmia* has six or seven species, four of which occur in the United States. Only the one species, mountainlaurel (*K. latifolia*), is of appreciable wildlife importance. This attractive, evergreen shrub is more abundant in the Alleghenies than elsewhere. Here ruffed grouse and deer feed extensively on the foliage, buds, and twigs. The plants

352

are fully as important for winter cover in deciduous woods as they are for food.

Mountainlaurel has the reputation of being poisonous to livestock and man, but wildlife seems to be generally immune to its toxic properties. The evergreen foliage and beautiful light pink flowers make this shrub valuable for ornamental purposes.

Upland Gamebirds (leaves, buds)
   * Grouse, Ruffed, *Va.Alleghenies and Pa.*

Fur and Game Mammals (capsules, leaves)
   + Bear, Black, *W.Va. and Va. Mts.*

Hoofed Browsers (foliage, twigs)
   ** Deer, White-tailed, *N.C.Mts.; *Pa.; +Wis and Minn.*

WINTERGREEN
Gaultheria procumbens

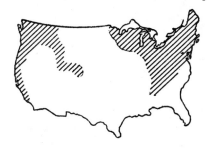

[3*/6 users] Wintergreen, locally called checkerberry or teaberry, is common in woodlands of the Northeast. It is a trailing plant with erect branches that are generally less than six inches high— a midget relative of salal of the Pacific region.

On the whole the wildlife utility of wintergreen is comparatively low. The

bright red berries, usually two or three together and persisting on the plants from fall until the following spring, are eaten to only a limited extent by gamebirds and mammals. The foliage is taken as food by ruffed grouse and by the white-tailed deer. The leaves are also taken by man for an aromatic extract, oil of wintergreen.

Upland Gamebirds (fruit, buds, leaves)
   * Grouse, Ruffed, *Va.Alleghenies; +NE*
   + Turkey, Wild, *Pa.*

Fur and Game Mammals (fruit)
   + Bear, Black, *Va.Alleghenies*

Small Mammals (fruit)
   − Mouse, White-footed, *NE*

Hoofed Browsers (plants)
   ** Deer, White-tailed, *Pa., Wis., and Minn.; +E*

SALAL
Gaultheria shallon

[7*/8 users] This tall, coarse shrub is so distinct from its relative, wintergreen, in appearance, range, and wildlife use that the two are treated separately. Salal is confined to the Pacific coast from Alaska to central California. Its fruits are eaten by several kinds of birds, including three important game-birds. The plants are also browsed by deer. The glossy evergreen foliage is sold by florists.

Upland Gamebirds (fruit, buds, leaves)
Grouse
+   Blue, *Pac.NW*
*   Spruce, *NW and Canada*
* Pigeon, Band-tailed, *Pac.NW*

Songbirds (fruit)
+ Wren-tit, *Calif.*
Fur and Game Mammals (fruit)
* Chickaree, Douglas, *Pac.*
Hoofed Browsers (plants)
Deer
**   Black-tailed, *Oreg.*
−   Black-tailed, Columbian, *Oreg.*
− Elk, Roosevelt, *No.Calif.*

PACIFIC MADRONE
Arbutus menziesii

[5*/6 users] Pacific madrone is a handsome, glossy-leaved, reddish-barked tree of the Coast Ranges and Sierra Nevada from British Columbia to Southern California. It grows typically on high, well-drained slopes but occasionally is found in valleys. Two restricted and less-known relatives are in the Southwest, one in southern Arizona and New Mexico and the other in Texas. The numerous reddish berries of the Pacific madrone ripen in September and are an important food of the band-tailed pigeon, the long-tailed chat, and the varied thrush.

Upland Gamebirds (fruit)
* Pigeon, Band-tailed, *Pac.*
Songbirds (fruit)
** Chat, Long-tailed, *Pac.*
** Thrush, Varied, *Pac.*
Small Mammals (fruit)
− Rat, Portola Wood, *Calif.*
Hoofed Browsers (twigs, foliage)
Deer
−   Black-tailed, *Calif.*
−   Mule, *Calif.*

BEARBERRY
Arctostaphylos uva-ursi

[18*/8 users] Because of its distinctive form (prostrate) and small size, and also because of its wide distribution in northern latitudes, we have treated this species separately from the manzanitas though they also belong to the genus *Arctostaphylos*.

Bearberry is plentiful in Canada, Alaska, and in northern parts of other continents. It is present in the United States only along our northern boundary or on high mountains, generally in sandy or gravelly loam in partial shade.

The clusters of pink or red berries are eaten by gamebirds, especially by northern species of grouse. The trailing shrub with its leathery, evergreen foliage is browsed extensively by deer. Bearberry is probably more important to wildlife north of our Canadian boundary than it is in this country.

Upland Gamebirds (fruit)
Grouse
**   Blue, *Pac.NW; *No.Mt.–Des.*
+   Franklin, *B.C.*
**   Spruce, *NW and Canada*
* Pigeon, Band-tailed, *So.Mt– Des.*
Songbirds (fruit)
* Thrasher, California, *Calif.*
Hoofed Browsers (leaves, twigs)
Deer
***   Mule, *S.Dak.*
***   White-tailed, *S.Dak.; *Mont.*
+ Sheep, Mountain, *Mont.*

MANZANITAS
Arctostaphylos

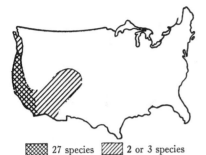

27 species ▨ 2 or 3 species

[36*/19 users] Thirty-six of the nearly 50 manzanitas are native to the United States. The others are largely Mexican. Our species are concentrated in the Pacific coast states, especially on slopes of mountains and hills in California. They constitute a large part of the so-called chaparral growth of the Pacific uplands.

These spreading, evergreen, red-barked shrubs provide useful food and cover to Pacific wildlife. The dense evergreen foliage gives excellent protective shelter, and the small fruits are relished by gamebirds, songbirds, and small mammals. Deer browse on the plants extensively.

Upland Gamebirds (fruit)
  * Grouse, Sooty, *NW*

Songbirds (fruit)
  ** Grosbeak, Evening, *NW*
  + Jay, California, *Calif.*
  + Mockingbird, *Calif.*
  *** Sparrow, Fox, *W*
Fur and Game Mammals (fruit)
  + Raccoon, *Pac.*
  Skunk
  * California, *Calif.*
  *** Hooded, Northern, *Ariz.*
Small Mammals (fruit)
  ** Chipmunk, Western, *Mt.–Des. and Pac.*
  Ground Squirrel
  + California, *Calif.*
  + Mantled, *W*
  * Rat, Merriam Kangaroo, *SW*
  ** Rock Squirrel, *Calif.*
Hoofed Browsers (leaves, twigs)
  Deer
  ** Black-tailed, *Calif.*
  ** Mule, *Calif.*
  — White-tailed, *No.Mt.–Des.*

HUCKLEBERRIES
Gaylussacia

[1*/14 users] There are 5 species of huckleberry in the United States, 40

to 50 in the world. Our species are confined to the East where they occur as undergrowth in woods or clearings—often in dense stands.

Huckleberries resemble blueberries, to which they are closely related, the fruits of the former being more seedy.

Upland Gamebirds (fruit)
  + Grouse, Ruffed, *NE*
  + Quail, Bobwhite, *E*
  + Turkey, Wild, *E*

Songbirds (fruit)
+ Catbird, *SE*
+ Crossbill, White-winged, *NE*
+ Grosbeak, Pine, *NE*
+ Jay, Florida, *Fla.*
+ Oriole, Orchard, *SE*
+ Tanager, Scarlet, *NE*
+ Towhee, Red-eyed, *NE*

Fur and Game Mammals (fruit)
+ Fox, Gray, *Pa.*
   Squirrel
+   Fox, *Ohio*
−   Fox, Western, *Mo.*

Hoofed Browsers (twigs, foliage)
* Deer, White-tailed, *Maine*

BLUEBERRIES
Vaccinium

[**57*/53 users**] The blueberry genus, *Vaccinium*, is centered mainly in the Northern Hemisphere. Its aggregate species number 120 to 150, about 25 to 35 of which are native to the United States. As treated here the genus embraces not only the true blueberries but also the deerberries, cranberries, farkleberry, and bilberry, each of which is classed by some botanists in a separate genus. For present purposes, blueberry is used as a key name for all vacciniums except the cranberries—just as blackberry is used to designate the *Rubus* group. Locally the name huckleberry is used for some species, but this name is more commonly applied to the related genus *Gaylussacia*.

Blueberries are widespread over the country but are particularly plentiful in the eastern Coastal Plain and Alle-ghenies. Like many other members of the heath family they prefer acid soil. They are found most commonly in relatively open woods or in clearings. Some species spread subterraneanly and form continuous thickets. Outstanding in abundance in the East are the highbush blueberry (*V. corymbosum*), lowbush blueberry (*V. angustifolium*), and blueridge blueberry (*V. pallidum*). In the Far West the dwarf blueberry (*V. cespitosum*), box blueberry (*V. ovatum*), and big whortleberry (*V. membranceum*) are prominent representatives of the group.

Blueberries are important to American wildlife. This fact is generally indicated by the ratio of **57*/53** users. The fruits are the chief attraction—probably for the same juicy, sweet tastiness that appeals to us. For several

species of grouse, blueberries are among the most important summer and early fall foods. They are also important to the scarlet tanager, bluebird, thrushes, and other songbirds as well as to the black bear, chipmunk, white-footed mouse, and other mammals. Deer and rabbits browse freely on the plants. Because of their food value to wildlife and their dense shrubby growth, some of the taller species of blueberries are worthy of inclusion in hedgerows.

Waterbirds (fruit)
* Gull, Herring, *U.S.*

Marshbirds and Shorebirds (fruit)
   Crane
*   Florida, *Fla.*
+   Sandhill, *W*

Upland Gamebirds (fruit, leaves)
   Grouse
**   Blue, *No.Mt.–Des. and Pac. NW*
***   Franklin, *B.C.*
**   Ruffed, *Maine;* *Va.Alleghenies and Pa.;* +*NE*
***   Spruce, *NW and Canada*
+   Pigeon, Band-tailed, *Pac.*
+   Turkey, Wild, *E*

Songbirds (fruit)
** Bluebird, *SE*
* Catbird, *E;* +*W*
* Chat, Yellow-breasted, *E*
+ Chickadee, Black-capped, *NE*
+ Crow, Fish, *E*
+ Flicker, Yellow-shafted, *E*
+ Flycatcher, Crested, *E*
   Jay
+   Blue, Florida, *Fla.*
+   Blue, Northern, *E*
+   Florida, *Fla.*
+ Kingbird, *E*
   Oriole
+   Baltimore, *NE*
*   Orchard, *E*

+ Phoebe, *E*
* Robin, *Pr.;* +*E*
   Sparrow
*   Pine-woods, *SE*
+   Tree, *NE*
+   White-throated, *NE*
*** Tanager, Scarlet, *NE*
* Thrasher, Brown, *E*
   Thrush
*   Gray-cheeked, *NE*
+   Hermit, *E and Pac.*
*   Veery, *NE*
+   Wood, *NE*
* Titmouse, Tufted, *SE;* +*NE*
* Towhee, Red-eyed, *NE*

Fur and Game Mammals (fruit, twigs, foliage)
**** Bear, Black, *Minn.;* ***Va. and W.Va.*
   Fox
+   Gray, *SE*
+   Red, *E*
+ Opossum, *SE*
+ Pika, *Pac.*
* Rabbit, Cottontail, *Conn.*
+ Raccoon, *Pac.*
   Skunk
*   Eastern, *NE*
+   Spotted, Allegheny, *NE*
+   Squirrel, Fox, *NE and Mich.*

Small Mammals (fruit)
*** Chipmunk, Least, *Minn.*
+ Ground Squirrel, Mantled, *W*
   Mouse
–   Red-backed, *NE*
**   White-footed, *E*

Hoofed Browsers (branches, foliage, fruit)
   Deer
–   Mule, *Oreg.*
–   Black-tailed, Columbian, *Oreg.*
**   White-tailed, *Maine;* *N.C.;* +*N.Y. and Ala.*
+ Elk, *No.Mt.–Des.*

CRANBERRIES
Vaccinium (Oxycoccus)

[5*/2 users] Cranberries are raised commercially in only a few localities— Massachusetts, New Jersey, Wisconsin, and Oregon. This fact may help to explain their limited use by wildlife. Three species occur along the northern borders of the country, and in Maine wild cranberries are fairly plentiful.

Marshbirds and Shorebirds (fruit)
  * Godwit, Hudsonian, *N*

Upland Gamebirds (fruit)
  * Grouse, Sharp-tailed, *Lake States Area*

Ebony Family : *Ebenaceae*

PERSIMMONS
Diospyros

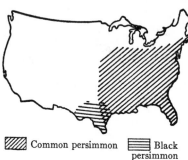

▨ Common persimmon   ☰ Black persimmon

[**28*/19 users**] There are only two native persimmons in the United States, the common persimmon (*D. virginiana*) and the Texas or black persimmon (*D. texana*). In the warmer parts of the world, however, 160 to 200 kinds have been described.

The common persimmon is particularly abundant in the southeastern states where it is found along roadsides, fence rows, ditch banks, field borders, and in sandy bottom lands. Frequently persimmon and sassafras share dominance in abandoned, weedy fields until pines come in and overshadow them.

Both of our persimmons are valuable to wildlife, though the Texas species is comparatively restricted in range. The fleshy fruit, ripening in the fall and often hanging on the trees far into winter, is an important food for foxes, raccoons, opossums, skunks, and ringtailed cats as well as for birds. It is probably a more important food for birds than stomach analyses have indicated since the fleshy pulp cannot always be identified in laboratory studies. In Texas, persimmon is an important browse plant for deer.

Upland Gamebirds (fruit)
  + Turkey, Wild, *Allegheny Mts. and Va.*
Songbirds (fruit)
  * Catbird, *E*
  − Mockingbird, *Md.*
  * Robin, *SE*
  − Sapsucker, Yellow-breasted, *Md.*
  + Warbler, Myrtle, *E*
  * Waxwing, Cedar, *E*
Fur and Game Mammals (fruit)
  ** Cat, Ring-tailed, *Tex.*
    Fox
  *   Gray, *S*; +*NE*
  ***   Red, *Ala.*; +*E*
  * Opossum, *SE*; +*Tex.*
  *** Raccoon, *E.Tex.*; **E*
    Skunk
  +   Florida, *SE*
  **   Hog-nosed, *Tex.*
  *   Spotted, Allegheny, *E*
  + Wolf, Texan Red, *SW*
Small Mammals (fruit)
    Mouse
  +   Pine, *NE*
  −   Pocket, Prairie, *Okla.*
Hoofed Browsers (twigs, foliage, fruit)
  *** Deer, White-tailed, *Tex.*; +*SE*

References: The Place of the Native Persimmon in Nature, in Relation to Other Plant Communities and to Certain Economic Insects. C. O. Eddy. *Ohio Jour. Sci.*, Vol. 27, pp. 189–199, 1927.
The Native Persimmon. W. F. Fletcher. *U.S. Dept. Agr. Bul.* 685, 1942. 22 pp.

Olive Family: *Oleaceae*

ASHES
Fraxinus

[12*/20 users] Of the 30 to 60 species of this genus, 18 to 21 are native to the United States. The white ash (*F. americana*) and red ash (*F. pennsylvanica*) are the most widespread and important species in the East. The green ash (*pennsylvanica* var. *lanceolata*) is prominent in the prairies.

Ashes are typical inhabitants of such moist places as river margins, river bottom lands, and wet slopes. All are trees, commonly 40 to 100 feet high and characterized by compound leaves, catkins, winged seeds, opposite branching, and large leaf scars.

These trees, though numerous and widespread, are only of moderate importance to wildlife. The winged seeds (samaras) are eaten by a number of birds and mammals. Rodents and sometimes wild turkeys shuck off the wing and eat only the seed inside. Ash trees are planted extensively for shade.

Waterfowl (seeds)
  * Duck, Wood, *SE*; +*NE*
Upland Gamebirds (seeds)
  * Quail, Bobwhite, *NE*; +*SE and Pr.*
  + Turkey, Wild, *E*
Songbirds (seeds largely)
  + Cardinal, *NE*
  * Finch, Purple, *E*
  Grosbeak
  + Evening, *N*
  * Pine, *NE*; +*Pac.*
  + Waxwing, Cedar, *NE*
  + Sapsucker, Yellow-bellied, *E* (sap)
Fur and Game Mammals (seeds, wood)
  + Bear, Black, *Pa.*
  ** Beaver, *SE*; *NE
  + Chickaree, Douglas, *Pac.*
  * Porcupine, *Vt.*; +*NE*
  + Rat, Dusky-footed Wood, *Oreg.*
  * Squirrel, Western Fox, *Mich.*
Small Mammals (seeds)
  + Mouse, White-footed, *E*
Hoofed Browsers (twigs, foliage)
  Deer
  * Mule, *Nebr.*
  * White-tailed, *N.Y.*
  + Moose, *Mich.*

References: Ash. H. S. Betts. American wood series. U.S. Dept. Agr. Forest Service, 1945. 12 pp.
The Ashes; Their Characteristics and Management. W. D. Sterrett. *U.S. Dept. Agr. Bul.* 299, 1915. 88 pp.

WILDPRIVETS
Forestiera

[4*/5 users] There are about 15 species of wildprivet in the two American continents. Of these, 7 or 8 are found in the southern part of the United States.

These small-leaved shrubs or trees grow in moist to fairly dry habitats. They frequently form thickets on low ground or along stream courses. Only in a limited area west of the Mississippi River from Missouri to Texas are they plentiful enough to be of significant value to wildlife. Wildprivet is recognized as a very important food for the chestnut-bellied scaled quail in southern Texas.

Waterfowl (fruit)
    Duck
+   Mallard, *La.*
+   Wood, *La.*

Upland Gamebirds (fruit)
**** Quail, Chestnut-bellied Scaled, *Tex.*
Songbirds (fruit)
+   Robin, *N.Mex.*
Hoofed Browsers (twigs, foliage)
+   Deer, White-tailed, *Tex.*

Vervain Family: *Verbenaceae*

BEAUTYBERRY
Callicarpa americana

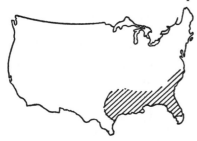

[5*/10 users] Though there are 40 to 45 species of *Callicarpa* in the world, only one species is native in this country. Beautyberry is confined to the Southeast. It grows typically in woodland openings or along sunny woods margins—thriving in fertile loams but maintaining itself in various kinds of soils.

The clusters of small, bright-violet berry-like fruits in the leaf axils are sought by some of our best known birds, notably the robin, mockingbird, catbird, and brown thrasher. This, combined with the ornamental value of its fruit and foliage, makes beautyberry worth planting about southern homes.

Upland Gamebirds (fruit)
+   Quail, Bobwhite, *SE*
Songbirds (fruit)
*   Catbird, *SE*
*   Mockingbird, *SE*
** Robin, *Fla.;* +*SE*
*   Thrasher, Brown, *SE;* +*Tex.*
+   Towhee, *SE*
Fur and Game Mammals (fruit)
+   Armadillo, *Tex.*
+   Raccoon, *Tex.*
Small Mammals (leaves)
+   Rat, Attwater Wood, *Tex.*
Hoofed Browsers (twigs, foliage)
+   Deer, White-tailed, *Tex.*

Potato Family: *Solanaceae*

LYCIUMS
Lycium

[5*/4 users] This is a large genus of 75 to 100 species of which 17 grow in the United States. These shrubby (some spiny) plants inhabit sandy or clay soil, often in alkali areas of the Southwest and along the Gulf and Atlantic coasts. The reddish-colored berries are eaten by a few kinds of wildlife.

Waterfowl (fruit)
* Goose, Canada, *Gulf Coast*

Upland Gamebirds (fruit)
* Dove, Western White-winged, *Ariz.*
+ Quail, Gambel, *SW*
Small Mammals (fruit)
* Rat, Ord Kangaroo, *W*

Madder Family: *Rubiaceae*

BUTTONBUSH
Cephalanthus occidentalis

[3*/11 users] Our native buttonbush is one of six to eight species of *Cephalanthus* in the world. It is widely distributed in swamps and other wet places in the East and also in California and Arizona. Except for the fact that it is a woody plant, buttonbush might well have been included in the Marsh and Aquatic Plant category. The characteristic wetness of this shrub's habitat is reflected in the fact that waterfowl are the principal users of its seeds (nutlets or akenes). In the lower part of the Mississippi basin, ducks feed extensively on the seeds. But in general, use of buttonbush by wildlife is slight in proportion to its abundance, and in many places the plant deserves to be regarded as a woody weed. Because of its attractive foliage and

flowers, buttonbush is planted as an ornamental occasionally.

Waterfowl (seeds)
   Ducks
+ Florida, *Fla.*
+ Gadwall, *SE*
* Mallard, Common, *SE*; +*NE*
+ Ring-necked, *SE*
+ Teal, Blue-winged, *SE*
+ Teal, Green-winged, *SE*
+ Wood, *SE*
Marshbirds and Shorebirds (seeds)
+ Rail, Virginia, *E*
Fur and Game Mammals (wood)
+ Beaver, *Miss.*
Hoofed Browsers (twigs, foliage)
+ Antelope, *Okla.*
* Deer, White-tailed, *Pa. and Tex.*

PARTRIDGEBERRY
Mitchella repens

[0*/7 users] We have a single species of partridgeberry in the United States. One other grows in Japan. Ours is a small trailing shrub with pairs of white

flowers joined below, somewhat like Siamese twins. The partridgeberry, also known as checkerberry and twinberry, grows in moist eastern woodlands. Its bright red fruit ripening in the fall and persisting through the winter is eaten by gamebirds and some mammals but does not appear to be of real importance to any form of wildlife.

Upland Gamebirds (fruit)
+ Grouse, Ruffed, *NE*
+ Quail, Bobwhite, *NE*
+ Turkey, Wild, *SE*

361

Fur and Game Mammals (fruit)
+ Fox, Red, *N.Y. and New England*

+ Skunk, Eastern, *N.Y.*
Small Mammals (fruit)
— Mouse, White-footed, *E*

Honeysuckle Family: *Caprifoliaceae*

ELDERBERRIES
Sambucus

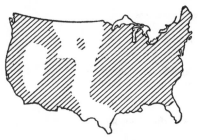

[51*/79 users] Though there are about a dozen species of elderberry in different parts of the United States (about 20 to 42 in the world), only two are abundant and outstandingly important to wildlife—American elderberry (*S. canadensis*) and blue elderberry (*S. cerulea*). Two western species, blue elderberry and Pacific red-elderberry (*S. callicarpa*), and one Gulf coast species, Florida elderberry (*S. simpsonii*), attain the stature of trees but the remainder are shrubs. All are characterized by pithy twigs, compound leaves, and clusters of blue, purplish, or red berries about the size of BB shot. They are found mainly in moist, fertile soil and so are scarce or absent in some arid parts of the West.

The American elderberry (or American elder) is well known in the East—along roadsides, near streams, on ditch banks, and in other moist places. Its showy flat-topped clusters of small white flowers are followed by dark fruits which are popular for wine, pies, and jellies.

This species and the blue elderberry are especially important sources of summer food for many kinds of songbirds. Though the fruit, even when mature, is none too palatable to man, robins and catbirds consume the berries

eagerly before they are fully ripe. Gamebirds, squirrels and other rodents, and several kinds of browsers also feed on the fruit or foliage of elderberries.

Upland Gamebirds (fruit)
Grouse
+   Ruffed, *Maine;* +*Wis.*
+   Sooty, *Pac.NW*
 *   Pheasant, Ring-necked, *NE*
** Pigeon, Band-tailed, *Pac.*
Songbirds (fruit)
+   Blackbird, Rusty, *NE*
    Bluebird
 *   Eastern, *SE;* +*NE*
+   Mountain, *W mainly Mt.–Des.*
 *   Western, *Calif.*
+   Bunting, Indigo, *E*
+   Cardinal, *E*
 *   Catbird, *E*
 *   Chat, Yellow-breasted, *E*
+   Finch, Common House, *Calif.*
 *   Flicker, Red-shafted, *Pac.*
+   Flycatcher, Ash-throated, *Calif.*
    Grosbeak
**   Black-headed, *Calif.*
**   Rose-breasted, *NE and No.Pr.*
    Jay
+   California, *Calif.*
**   Steller, *Pac.*
    Kingbird
 *   Arkansas, *W mainly Calif.*

* Cassin, *SW*
+ Eastern, *E*
+ Kinglet, Ruby-crowned, *Calif.*
+ Magpie, American, *Mt.–Des.*
* Mockingbird, *SE*; +*Calif.*
** Mynah, Crested, *B.C.*
Nuthatch
+ Red-breasted, *Pac.*
+ White-breasted, *E and E.Pr.*
Oriole
+ Bullock, *SW and Calif.*
+ Hooded, Arizona, *Ariz. and Calif.*
**** Phainopepla, *Calif. and Ariz.*
+ Phoebe, *E*
+ Robin, *NE*
+ Sapsucker, Yellow-bellied, *E* (sap)
Sparrow
+ Song, *Pac.*
+ Swamp, *NE*
+ White-crowned, *NE and Pac.*
+ White-throated, *NE*
* Starling, *NE*
Tanager
+ Scarlet, *NE*
* Western, *Pac.*
+ Titmouse, Tufted, *NE*
Thrasher
** Brown, *SE*; **NE*
* California, *Calif.*
Thrush
+ Gray-cheeked, *NE*
+ Hermit, *E*
* Olive-backed, *NE*
** Russet-backed, *Calif.*
* Veery, *NE*
+ Wood, *NE*
Towhee

* Brown, *Calif.*
+ Spotted, *Pac.*
Vireo
+ Red-eyed, *E*
+ Warbling, *Mt.–Des. and Pac.*
+ White-eyed, *SE*
+ Warbler, Audubon, *Calif.*
+ Waxwing, Cedar, *NE*
Woodpecker
+ Ant-eating, *Pac.*
** Lewis, *Mt.–Des. and Pac.*
* Nuttall, *Calif.*
*** Pileated, *Oregon*
+ Red-bellied, *E*
+ Red-headed, *E*
+ Wren, Cactus, *Calif. and Ariz.*
* Wren-tit, *Calif.*

Fur and Game Mammals (fruit, bark)
* Rabbit, Mearns Cottontail, *Pa.*; +*Iowa*
Squirrel
+ Fox, Western, *Mich.*
+ Red, *NE*
+ Woodchuck, *Pa.*

Small Mammals (fruit)
+ Chipmunk, Lyster, *NE*
* Ground Squirrel, Beechey, *Calif.*
+ Mouse, White-footed, *NE*
Rat
+ Wood, Large-eared, *Calif.*
* Wood, Portola, *Calif.*

Hoofed Browsers (twigs, foliage)
Deer
+ Black-tailed, Columbian, *Oreg.*
* Mule, *Calif.*
+ White-tailed, *E*
* Elk, *Idaho and Mont.*
+ Moose, *Mont.*

VIBURNUMS
Viburnum

[8*/25 users] About 15 to 20 species of viburnum occur in the United States, most of them growing in moist, shaded woodlands of the East.

These opposite-leafed shrubs or small trees produce clusters of small drupes which ripen in the late summer or fall and are eaten by many kinds of wildlife. The quantitative use of viburnums by animals is, however, small, only the

ruffed grouse, brown thrasher, cedar waxwing, red squirrel, and white-tailed deer having records as high as 1 star in the areas studied. The blackhaw (*V. prunifolium*), possumhaw (*V. nudum*), arrowwood (*V. dentatum*), nannyberry (*V. lentago*), and mapleleaf viburnum (*V. acerifolium*) are the most common and useful species.

Viburnums, both native and exotic,

363

are planted as ornamentals about homes because of their attractive flowers and foliage. Their usefulness to wildlife for food and cover is an added asset.

Upland Gamebirds (fruit)
- Grouse
  - * Ruffed, *Va.Alleghenies;* +*NE*
  - + Sharp-tailed, *Great Lakes Area*
- + Pheasant, Ring-necked, *NE*
- + Turkey, Wild, *E*

Songbirds (fruit)
- + Cardinal, *E*
- + Flycatcher, Crested, *E*
- + Robin, *E*
- + Starling, *NE*
- * Thrasher, Brown, *Tex.*
- Thrush
  - + Gray-cheeked, *NE*
  - + Hermit, *E*
- + Olive-backed, *NE*
- * Waxwing, Cedar, *NE*
- + Woodpecker, Pileated, *E*

Fur and Game Mammals (fruit, wood)
- − Bear, Black, *Pa.*
- − Beaver, *N.Dak.*
- + Fox, Red, *N.Y.*
- + Rabbit, Cottontail, *NE*
- + Skunk, Eastern, *NE*
- Squirrel
  - + Fox, *E*
  - + Gray, *E*
  - * Red, *W*

Small Mammals (fruit)
- * Chipmunk, Eastern, *NE*
- − Mouse, White-footed, *NE*

Hoofed Browsers (twigs, foliage)
- * Deer, White-tailed, *N.Y.:* +*Maine*

Reference: The American Cranberrybush. The Domestication of *Viburnum americanum*—A New Fruit for the Northern United States. George M. Darrow. *Jour. Heredity*, Vol. 15, pp. 243–253, 1924.

SNOWBERRIES
Symphoricarpos

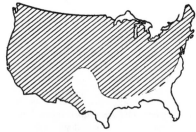

[**32*/27 users**] There are about 14 snowberries altogether: 10 in the western United States, 2 in the East, 1 in

Mexico, and 1 in China. But not all have the snow-white berries that give this genus its name. One common species, coralberry (*S. orbiculatus*), has purplish-red fruits.

These shrubs grow in varied habitats but are partial to well-drained slopes. They frequently form thickets in pastures. Some species are found along drainage ditches, streams, or near springs.

Snowberries are an important wildlife food in the western states. The fruits ripen in the fall and frequently remain available on the bushes for half a year or more. They are especially valuable as food for the sharp-tailed and Franklin grouse, pine grosbeak, robin, and varied thrush. The foliage and twigs are eaten extensively by deer and antelope. Snowberry is also useful as nesting cover and protective shelter for gamebirds, rabbits, and other animals.

Upland Gamebirds (fruit, buds)
    Grouse
    **   Franklin, *B.C.*
    +   Ruffed, *Minn. and Idaho*
    *** Sharp-tailed, *Minn.;* *W. Nebr.;* +*N.Dak.*
    * Pheasant, Ring-necked, *Mont.;* +*NW*
    + Prairie Chicken, Greater, *N.Pr.*
    + Quail, Bobwhite, *E.Pr.*
Songbirds (fruit)
    − Finch, Purple, *Ky.*
    Grosbeak
    *   Evening, *NW*
    **** Pine, *Pac.*

+ Hummingbird, *Md.*
+ Magpie, American, *Mt.–Des.*
** Robin, *SE*
    Thrush
+   Hermit, *Pac.*
+   Russet-backed, *Calif.*
** Varied, *Pac.*
+ Towhee, Spotted, *Pac.*
+ Vireo, Warbling, *Pac.*
+ Wren-tit, *Pac.*
Fur and Game Mammals (bark, fruit, foliage)
+ Bear, Black, *N*
− Beaver, *N.Dak.*
* Hare, Varying, *Utah*
Small Mammals (fruit, foliage)
− Rat, Wood, *Pac.*
Hoofed Browsers (twigs, foliage)
*** Antelope, *S.Dak.;* +*S.E.Mont.*
    Deer
**** Mule, *Nebr.;* **S.Dak.;* *Mt.– Des.*
*** White-tailed, *Mo.;* *S.Dak.;* +*E*
+ Elk, *No.Mt.–Des.*

JAPANESE HONEYSUCKLE
Lonicera japonica

[**4*/14 users**] Though there are about 24 kinds of native honeysuckles in the United States (100 to 160 in the world), the introduced Asiatic species, Japanese honeysuckle, is the only one having considerable importance to wildlife —mainly because of its abundance.

This aggressive vine ranges through much of the East but is especially prevalent in the Southeast where it prefers relatively open, moist situations on roadside embankments, clearings, and fence rows. It carpets the ground climbing over and stifling other plants—including species of value to wildlife such as blackberries, dogwoods, and the like. Its disorderly growth and the difficulty of eradication has made this vine a decided pest in some localities.

In its favor are the advantageous features of good cover and food for birds and rabbits, especially during critical winter weather, excellent soil binding on embankments, and the fragrance and beauty of its flowers.

Other species of honeysuckle in the country—most of them bushes rather than vines—have little importance to wildlife. Occasional use of the fruits of some western species has been recorded. The exotic Tatarian honeysuckle (*L. tatarica*) is planted commonly in wildlife hedges or borders.

Upland Gamebirds (fruit)
 + Quail, Bobwhite, *SE*
 + Turkey, Wild, *Va.*
Songbirds (fruit)
 + Bluebird, *NE*
 * Finch, Purple, *E*
 + Goldfinch, Eastern, *E*
 * Grosbeak, Pine, *Pac.*
 + Junco, *NE*
 + Robin, *Fla.*
 + Sparrow, White-throated, *NE*
 + Thrush, Hermit, *E*
Fur and Game Mammals (foliage, fruit)
 − Rabbit, Audubon Cottontail, *Calif.*
 Rat
 − Wood, Large-eared, *Calif.*
 − Wood, Portola, *Calif.*
Hoofed Browsers (branches, foliage)
 * Deer, White-tailed, *SE*

Reference: Japanese Honeysuckle in Wildlife Management. C. O. Handley. *Jour. Wildlife Mgt.*, Vol. 9 (4), pp. 261–264, 1945.

Daisy Family: *Compositae*

SAGEBRUSH
Artemisia

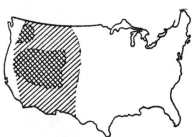

▨ Area of main use ▨ Lesser use

[40*/22 users] Nearly 300 species of sagebrush grow the world over, and about 65 of them are found in the United States. The best known of these and probably most abundant is big sagebrush (*A. tridentata*). Fringed sagebrush (*A. frigida*) and cudweed (*A. gnaphalodes*) are also abundant and widespread.

These fragrant, grayish-green shrubs are largely inhabitants of the West and Southwest. They are the dominant vegetation in many parts of the western range and desert regions, occurring abundantly on the arid and semiarid plains, covering fertile hills, and extending up the lower mountain slopes. Big sagebrush and some other related species tolerate moderately alkaline soil and thus are able to grow where few other plants can compete for existence.

Sagebrush furnishes essential cover for many of the smaller desert animals. Its foliage and flower clusters constitute most of the diet of the sage grouse, and these parts together with the twigs bearing them are the primary source of food for antelope and mule deer.

Range cattle also make good use of sagebrush as forage. Where wood is scarce, the trunks of big sagebrush are often used for fuel. The sage used in seasoning is not obtained from these plants but from members of the mint family.

Upland Gamebirds (foliage, flowers, seeds)
Grouse
***** (71%) Sage, *N.Mt.–Des.*
* Sharp-tailed, *Utah*
Fur and Game Mammals (foliage, stems)
Jack Rabbit
+ Black-tailed, *Utah*
** California, *Utah*
+ White-tailed, *Utah*
+ Rabbit

+ Cottontail, Rocky Mountain, *Utah*
+ Pygmy, *Utah*
Small Mammals (foliage, seeds)
* Chipmunk, *W.Pr. and Mt.–Des.*
Gopher
* Pocket, *Mont.*
* Pocket, Western, *Mont.*
** Ground Squirrel, *Pac. and Great Basin*
Mouse
+ Meadow, *Manitoba*
+ Meadow, Sagebrush, *Calif. and Nev.*
+ Pocket, *W.Pr. and Mt.–Des.*
Prairie Dog
* Black-tailed, *W.Pr.*
** White-tailed, *Wyo.–Mont.*
Rat
* Kangaroo, *Mt.–Des. and Pr.*
+ Wood, White-throated, *Ariz.*
Hoofed Browsers (foliage, twigs)
***** (51%) Antelope, *S.E.Mont.; ****Pr., Mt.–Des.*
*** Deer, Mule, *No.Mt.–Des.; **So. Mt.–Des., and Oreg.; *Calif.*
* Elk, *No.Mt.–Des.*
** Sheep, Mountain, *No.Mt.–Des.; *Mont.*

CHAPTER FIFTEEN

Upland Weeds
and Herbs

T HE PLANTS TREATED in this chapter can best be defined in a negative way: they are *not* woody, *not* cultivated, and *not* aquatic. Included are most of our common herbaceous inhabitants of open fields, roadsides, and woodlands—weeds, flowers, grasses, and the like.

The whole group could be subdivided into two major categories on the basis of whether or not the plants live more than one year. In perennial herbs the aerial stems die back in winter, but the underground parts (roots, rootstocks, corms, bulbs, and the like) survive and renew growth in the following season. Among such perennials are the well-known goldenrods, thistles, field daisies, beggarweeds, pokeweed, and many of the common grasses.

In contrast to the perennial herbs, annuals depend entirely on their large crops of seeds for survival from year to year. As a consequence, these transitory plants are on the whole more valuable to seed-eating wildlife than are perennials. Usually annual plants are pioneers that thrive in broken soil or in open places, where vegetative competition is low. Ordinarily, however, perennial species crowd them out within two or three years unless plowing or other factors intervene. This fact is important in managing areas for the benefit of upland game-birds or ground-feeding songbirds.

Annual, farmland weeds such as ragweed, bristlegrass, crabgrass, Russian-thistle, and filaree constitute an extremely important group of plants for our many kinds of ground-feeding birds and small mammals. The wildlife value of these weeds is a partial compensation for their nuisance to man. Woodland herbs like springbeauty, dutchman's-breeches, anemone, self-heal, and other nonweedy plants have limited local importance to birds and mammals. In general, they, like other common wildflowers that are attractive to man, are not particularly attractive to wildlife. Grasses are an especially important segment of Upland Weeds and Herbs—important both to man and wildlife. Their seeds are valuable to birds and small mammals, their leaves and stems are used by rabbits, deer, and other herbivores, and in addition the plants provide protective cover to many small and medium-sized animals.

General References: Weeds. Walter Conrad Muenscher. The Macmillan Company, New York, 1935. 577 pp.

Range Plant Handbook. W. A. Dayton and others. U.S. Forest Service, 1937. 546 pp.

Manual of the Grasses of the United States. A. S. Hitchcock. *U.S. Dept. Agr. Misc. Pub.* 200, 1935. 1040 pp.

Grass, The Yearbook of Agriculture, 1948. Alfred Stefferud, editor. U.S. Department of Agriculture Yearbook, 1948. 892 pp.

MOSSES

[4*/4 users] Though mosses are represented by hundreds of native species and are plentiful in moist, wooded sections of the country, they have very little value for wildlife. Besides the limited usefulness of mosses as food for a few species of birds and mammals, these small, delicate plants are used by some birds in nest building.

Waterfowl (plants)
* Swan, Trumpeter, *Mont. and B.C.* (aquatic mosses)

Upland Gamebirds (spore capsules)
* Grouse, Spruce, *NW and Canada*

Small Mammals (spore capsules and other parts)
+ Mouse, Lemming, *NE and No. Pr.*

Hoofed Browsers (plants)
+ Goat, Mountain, *Mont.*

FERNS

[4*/5 users] Ferns, like mosses, are widespread and locally abundant, especially in moist woodlands. Yet despite this availability, wildlife use them only to a minor extent. The minute size of fern spores eliminates them from significance as food. Their leaves are eaten by several wildlife species. In the Northeast, the evergreen Christmasfern (*Polystichum acrostichoides*) has considerable value in seasons when other green plants are scarce. The same is true of the small, partly evergreen grapefern (*Botrychium*).

Upland Gamebirds (fronds)
   Grouse
* Ruffed, *Ohio*, *Va.Alleghenies, and Pa.*
+ Spruce, *NW and Canada* (woodfern and Christmas-fern)
+ Turkey, Wild, *E* (grapefern)

Fur and Game Mammals (fronds)
** Hare, Varying, *Minn.*

Hoofed Browsers (fronds)
* Deer, White-tailed, *Pa.*, *Wis.*, *Minn., and N.C.*

Grass Family: *Poaceae*

BROMEGRASSES
Bromus

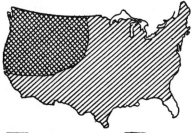

▨ Region of main use   ▨ Lesser use

[36*/37 users] Thirty-six bromegrasses, or bromes, are recorded in the United States—about half the total number in the world. The genus is best represented in the Far West—on the open

ranges. Here mountain (*B. carinatus*), smooth (*B. inermis*), nodding (*B. anomalus*), and downy bromegrass (*B. tectorum*) are among the more prevalent species.

A few species of bromegrasses are annuals and are known as chess or cheat. Among these is the very common and widespread grainfield weed, common chess (*B. secalinus*). Rescue bromegrass (*B. catharticus*) is frequent in coastal regions and in the South. It is used considerably by wildlife.

The good-sized seeds of bromegrass are eaten by a number of kinds of birds and rodents. The leaves or other parts of the plants are consumed by hoofed

369

browsers, especially while the plants are young.

Waterfowl (young plants)
  ** Goose, Canada, *Pac.; *Mt.–Des.*
Upland Gamebirds (seeds)
  + Grouse, Ruffed, *Ohio*
  ** Partridge, Hungarian, *NW*
  + Pheasant, Ring-necked, *Wash.*
  Quail
    * California, *Calif.*
    ** Mountain, *Pac.*
  + Turkey, Wild, *Ariz. and N.Mex.*
Songbirds (seeds)
  + Bunting, Snow, *NW*
  + Lark, California Horned, *Calif.*
  Sparrow
    * Golden-crowned, *Calif.*
    * Lark, Western, *Mt.–Des.*
    * Savannah, *Calif.*
    + Song, *Pac.*
    + Vesper, *Mt.–Des.*
    + White-crowned, *Pac.*
    * Towhee, Brown, *Calif.*
Fur and Game Mammals (plants)
  Rabbit
    – Cottontail, Audubon, *Calif.*
    – Cottontail, Black Hills, *Utah*

Small Mammals (seeds)
  Chipmunk
    * Least, *W.Pr. and Mt.–Des.*
    ** Northwest, *Pac.NW*
    * Western, *Mt.–Des. and Pac.*
  *** Gopher, Pocket, *Calif.*
  Ground Squirrel
    * Beechey, *Calif.*
    – Townsend, *Wash.*
  Mouse
    * Grasshopper, *No.Pr.*
    – Harvest, Long-tailed, *Calif.*
    * Pocket, *Pr. and Mt.–Des.*
  Prairie Dog
    * Black-tailed, *W.Pr.*
    + White-tailed, *Mont. and Wyo.*
  **** Rat, Kangaroo, *Calif.*
Hoofed Browsers (plants)
  + Antelope, *S.E.Mont.*
  Deer
    ** Mule, *No.Mt.–Des.; *Calif.*
    – White-tailed, *Tex.*
    * Elk, *No.Mt.–Des.*
    + Goat, Mountain, *Mont.*
    – Moose, Yellowstone Park, *Mont.*
    – Sheep, Mountain, *Mont. and Idaho*

FESCUEGRASSES
Festuca

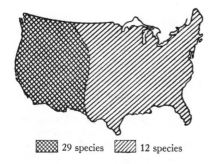

29 species   12 species

[26*/23 users] Thirty-four species of fescuegrass are present in different parts of the country. These close relatives of bromegrass (like smaller editions) are particularly plentiful on well-drained slopes along the Pacific coast and Mountain–Desert regions. It is here that their wildlife value is great-

est. Sixweeks fescuegrass (*F. octoflora*) is a widely distributed, small, annual species. Its seeds are eaten commonly by birds, but other species are also used extensively.

Upland Gamebirds (seeds)
  * Turkey, Wild, *Ariz. and N.Mex.*
Songbirds (seeds)
  + Bunting, Snow, *NE*
  Finch
    + Rosy, *Pac.*
    + Rosy, Brown-capped, *So.Mt.–Des.*
  + Lark, California Horned, *Calif.*
  Sparrow
    *** Golden-crowned, *Calif.*
    + White-crowned, *Pac.*
    * Towhee, Brown, *Calif.*
Fur and Game Mammals (seeds, foliage)
  + Rabbit, Cottontail, *Calif.*

Small Mammals (seeds, foliage)
  * Gopher, Pocket, *Calif.*
  \+ Ground Squirrel, Beechey, *Calif.*
  Mouse
  \+ Harvest, Long-tailed, *Calif.*
  * Pocket, *W.Pr. and Mt.–Des.*
  \+ Pika, *Pac.*
  Prairie Dog
  * Black-tailed, *W.Pr.*
  \+ White-tailed, *Mont. and Wyo.*
  Rat
  ** Kangaroo, *Calif.*

  \+ Kangaroo, Banner-tailed,
  Ariz. and N.Mex.
  ** Kangaroo, Merriam, *SW*
Hoofed Browsers (plants)
  ** Deer, Mule, *No.Mt.–Des. and Calif.*
  * Elk, *No.Mt.–Des.*
  * Moose, *Idaho*
  *** Sheep, Mountain, *No.Mt.–Des.;*
  ***Mont.*

BLUEGRASSES
Poa

▨ Region of main use ▨ Lesser use

[27*/30 users] Bluegrass generally brings to mind the famous Kentucky bluegrass (*P. pratensis*). Actually, there are about 75 species of bluegrass in the United States of a total of about 200 in the world. Kentucky bluegrass is widely distributed throughout the country except in arid regions but is partial to limestone soils and therefore is especially characteristic of Kentucky. It is one of our most common lawn plants. Annual bluegrass (*P. annua*) is another common, widespread species and, like Kentucky bluegrass, also has much value for wildlife—especially for seed-eating birds. Some species of bluegrass grow in moist soils while others prefer drier upland localities. Sods of this grass develop most readily in fairly moist open areas, and once established they resist invasion by other plants, including trees.

Bluegrass seeds are eaten by several kinds of songbirds and rodents, and the leaves are grazed by rabbits and big game.

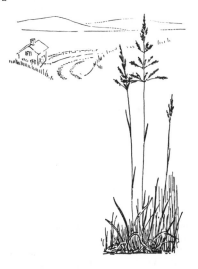

Waterfowl (blades)
  **** Coot, *Wis.*
Upland Gamebirds (seeds)
  \+ Dove, Mourning, *Ala.*
  \+ Pheasant, Ring-necked, *N*
  \+ Prairie Chicken, *Wis.*
  Quail
  \+ California, *Calif.*
  \+ Mountain, *Pac.*
  * Valley, *Calif.*
  * Turkey, Wild, *Alleghenies*
Songbirds (seeds)
  * Bunting, Lazuli, *Pac.*
  \+ Junco, Oregon, *Calif.*
  Sparrow
  \+ Chipping, *Mt.–Des. and Calif.*
  \+ English, *E*

* Field, *Pr.*
* Savannah, *Calif.*
** Vesper, *Mt.–Des.*
* White-crowned, *Pac.*
* Towhee, Brown, *Calif.*

Fur and Game Mammals (plants, seed-heads)
— Muskrat, *Pa. and Iowa*
Rabbit
— Cottontail, Audubon, *Calif.*
— Cottontail, Eastern, *NE*
** Cottontail, New England, *Conn.*
— Cottontail, Mearns, *Iowa*

Small Mammals (plants, seedheads)
* Ground Squirrel, Richardson, *No.Pr.*
Mouse
+ Meadow, *E*
+ Sage, *Oreg.*
Prairie Dog
* Black-tailed, *W.Pr.*
* White-tailed, *Wyo. and Mont.*

Hoofed Browsers (plants)
** Deer, Mule, *No.Mt.–Des.; *S.Dak. and Calif.*
+ Moose, *Maine to Mich.*
** Sheep, Mountain, *Mont.*

References: The History of Kentucky Bluegrass and White Clover in the United States. Lyman Carrier and Katherine S. Bort. *Jour. Amer. Soc. Agron.*, Vol. 8, pp. 256–266, 1916.
Annual Bluegrass and Its Requirements for Growth. H. B. Sprague and G. W. Burton. *N.J. Agr. Exp. Sta. Bul.* 630, 1937. 24 pp.

ORCHARDGRASS
Dactylis glomerata

[0*/3 users] Orchardgrass is a familiar weed of orchards, fields, and roadsides in many parts of the country. There is only the one native species. Its seeds are eaten sparingly by birds.

Songbirds (seeds)
+ Lark, Horned, *E*
+ Sparrow, Chipping, *E*

Hoofed Browsers (plants)
+ Deer, White-tailed, *E*

WHEATGRASSES
Agropyron

[21*/16 users] Twenty-five or more species of *Agropyron* (about half of the number in the world) grow in the United States. They are found in fields, on roadsides, and in open waste lands, both in the East and West. In the West, wheatgrass is a very important range plant. Among the most important range species are bluestem (*A. smithii*), slender (*A. pauciflorum*), and crested wheatgrass (*A. cristata*). The common quackgrass (*A. repens*) also has some forage value in the West, but it is a pernicious weed in other parts of the country. The principal value of these grasses to wildlife is in their use as forage.

Upland Gamebirds (seeds)
+ Grouse, Sharp-tailed, *Minn.*
+ Pheasant, Ring-necked, *N.Y.*

Songbirds (seeds)
* Bunting, Eastern Snow, *No. U.S.*

Fur and Game Mammals (plants)
— Jack Rabbit, White-tailed, *Utah*
  Rabbit
— Cottontail, Mearns, *Iowa*
— Cottontail, Sacramento Valley, *Calif.*

Small Mammals (plants, seeds)
  Prairie Dog
** Black-tailed, *W.Pr.*
** Gunnison, *SW*

** White-tailed, *Wyo.–Mont.*
— Ground Squirrel, Townsend, *Wis.*

Hoofed Browsers (plants)
** Antelope, *N.Mex.;* *No.Pr., *Mt.–Des.,* and *S.E.Mont.*
  Deer
** Mule, *No.Mt.–Des.*
* White-tailed, *S.Dak.;* + *Mont.*
* Elk, *No.Rocky Mt.*
+ Moose, *Maine to Mich.*
** Sheep, Mountain, *No.Mt.–Des.*

Reference: Quackgrass. L. W. Kephart. *U.S. Dept. Agr. Farmers Bul.* 1307, 1931. 29 pp.

WILDBARLEYS
Hordeum

[7*/10 users] Our five or more species of wildbarley are widely distributed. Foxtail barley (*H. jubatum*) also known as squirreltail is probably the most familiar. It occurs in the East but is much more abundant in the West. Its fluffy, waving heads are conspicuous in grain fields, pastures, along roadsides, and in low moist places like the margins of receding lakes. The long awns of this species are sometimes injurious to livestock. Little barley (*H. pusillum*) and meadow barley (*H. nodosum*) may not be quite so conspicuous as foxtail, but they seem to have as much value to wildlife. The seeds, and to some extent the leaves, are taken by waterfowl and by rodents.

Waterfowl (seeds, leaves)
+ Duck, Gadwall, *W*
  Goose
** Canada, *Pac.;* *Utah
* Snow, *W*

Small Mammals (seeds, leaves)
+ Gopher, Pocket, *Calif.*
— Ground Squirrel, Beechey, *Calif.*
  Mouse
— Pocket, Pacific, *Calif.*
— Pocket, Prairie, *Okla.*
* Prairie Dog, Black-tailed, *W.Pr.*
  Rat
+ Kangaroo, Merriam, *SW*
+ Kangaroo, various spp , *Calif.*

RYEGRASSES
Lolium

[6*/9 users] Three species of ryegrass are rather widespread in the United States, but the use of these grasses by wildlife is negligible except in California where the seeds are eaten by several kinds of birds and by the pocket mouse. Italian ryegrass (*L. multiflorum*) is planted near impoundments in some regions for the use of geese.

Waterfowl (seeds)
  Duck
— Mallard, *Oreg.*

— Pintail, *Oreg.*
Upland Gamebirds (seeds)
  Quail
* California, *Calif.*
+ Valley, *Calif.*
Songbirds (seeds)
  Sparrow
* Golden-crowned, *Calif.*
* Savannah, *Calif.*
+ White-crowned, *Pac.*
** Towhee, Brown, *Calif.*
Small Mammals (seeds)
* Mouse, Pocket, *Calif.*

BEACHGRASSES
Ammophila

[5*/3 users] There are two species of beachgrass in the country: American beachgrass (*A. breviligulata*) in the East and European beachgrass (*A. arenaria*) on the Pacific coast. They are tall plants of sandy beaches along the North Atlantic and Pacific coasts, as well as some of the Great Lakes. Besides being valuable as food for the Ipswich sparrow and the snow bunting,

American beachgrass provides cover for various kinds of wildlife and is valuable as a soil binder to help hold coastal dunes and beach sand.

Upland Gamebirds (seeds)
 — Pheasant, Ring-necked, *Wash.*
Songbirds (seeds)
 * Bunting, Snow, *NE*
 **** Sparrow, Ipswich, *NE*

DROPSEEDGRASSES
Sporobolus

[25*/18 users] There are about 30 species of dropseedgrass widely distributed over the United States. They are particularly plentiful and important in the Prairie region but are also well represented in open areas in the East and in low places in western deserts and plains.

The seeds of dropseedgrasses are important to ground-feeding birds. Sand dropseedgrass (*S. cryptandrus*) is outstanding in extent of use, but the seeds of other species have also appeared commonly in stomach examinations.

Upland Gamebirds (seeds)
 * Turkey, Wild, *Tex., Ariz., and N.Mex.*
Songbirds (seeds)
 Bunting
 + Lark, *Pr.*
 * Snow, *NE*

 + Grosbeak, Blue, *SW*
 *** Junco, *Pr.*; **NE*
 + Lark, Horned, *E and W*
 Longspur
 *** Chestnut-collared, *W.Pr.*
 + Lapland, *NE and No.Pr.*
 **** Smith, *Ill.*
 Sparrow
 + Brewer, *W*
 ** Field, *Pr.*; +NE*
 * Savannah, *So.Pr.*
 * Tree, *NE and Pr.*
 * White-crowned, *E.Pr. and Mt.–Des.*
Small Mammals (seeds)
 * Prairie Dog, Gunnison, *N.Mex., Ariz., and Colo.*
 + Rat, Kangaroo, *Pr. and Mt.–Des.*
Hoofed Browsers (plants)
 *** Bison, *Okla.*
 + Deer, White-tailed, *Tex.*

RICEGRASSES
Oryzopsis

[5*/8 users] A dozen species of ricegrass are present in the United States, but only in the West are these hardseeded grasses plentiful and significant for wildlife. Indian ricegrass (*O. hymenoides*) is by far the most common species. It is grazed on extensively by mule deer.

Upland Gamebirds (seeds)
 + Dove, Mourning, *Mt.–Des.*
 + Quail, Valley, *Nev.*
Songbirds (seeds)
 + Towhee, Green-tailed, *Mt.–Des.*
Small Mammals (seeds)
 * Chipmunk, Least, *W.Pr. and Mt.–Des.*
 — Rat, Dusky-footed Wood, *Oreg.*

Hoofed Browsers (plants)
Deer
** Mule, *No.Mt.–Des.*

+ White-tailed, *Wis.*
* Sheep, Mountain, *No.Mt.–Des.*

NEEDLEGRASSES
Stipa

[**18*/14 users**] This western genus of 32 species is especially plentiful in the Southwest. Only two are present in the East. Needlegrasses are plants of plains, prairies, and other dry, well-drained areas. They have some value as range plants for western livestock.

The long, hard, sharp-pointed seeds of needlegrass are an important food for songbirds and rodents. The plants are also consumed by hoofed browsers.

Songbirds (seeds)
Bunting
** Lark, *Pr.*
** Lazuli, *Pac.*
Longspur
** Chestnut-collared, *W.Pr.*
** McCown, *Pr.*

** Smith, *Pr.*
+ Sparrow, Chipping, *Mt.–Des. and Pac.*
Small Mammals (seeds)
Chipmunk
* Northwest, *Pac.NW*
+ Western, *Mt.–Des. and Pac.*
Ground Squirrel
* Mantled, *No.Pr.*
* Thirteen-lined, *Pr.*
+ Mouse, Grasshopper, *No.Pr.*
Hoofed Browsers (plants)
Deer
** Mule, *No.Mt.–Des.; *So.Mt.–Des.*
+ White-tailed, *Tex.*
* Elk, *No.Mt.–Des.*
** Sheep, Mountain, *No.Mt.–Des.*

THREE-AWNS
Aristida

[**4*/9 users**] Approximately 40 species of three-awn are widely distributed throughout the country. Except for restricted localities, these grasses are ordinarily not abundant enough to be important for either wildlife or livestock. Some species are known as povertygrass, and the tendency to thrive in poor soil characterizes the group. Their long-awned, sharp-pointed, hard seeds are used by only a few kinds of wildlife.

Songbirds (seeds)
+ Junco, *NE*

* Longspur, Chestnut-collared, *W. Pr.*
+ Sparrow, Pine-woods, *SE*
Fur and Game Mammals (plants)
Jack Rabbit
+ Antelope, *Ariz.*
+ California, *Ariz. and N.Mex.*
Small Mammals (seedheads, plants)
+ Mouse, White-footed, *W*
+ Prairie Dog, Gunnison, *SW*
*** Rat, Large Kangaroo, *Ariz.*
Hoofed Browsers (plants)
— Deer, White-tailed, *Tex.*

BERMUDAGRASS
Cynodon dactylon

[**3*/5 users**] Bermudagrass, though present in some northern states, is chiefly a southern plant. In the Gulf states it is an important pasture grass which is sometimes cut for hay. Its seeds and other parts are of minor value to wildlife.

Waterfowl (plants)
** Goose, Canada, *Gulf Coast*
Marshbirds and Shorebirds (seeds)
+ Gallinule, Purple, *SE*
Fur and Game Mammals (plants, seeds)
— Rabbit, Audubon Cottontail, *Calif.*

Small Mammals (plants)
  * Gopher, Pocket, *Calif.*

Hoofed Browsers (plants)
  — Deer, White-tailed, *Tex. and Ark.*

Reference: Eradication of Bermuda Grass, *U.S. Dept. Agr. Farmers Bul.* 945, 1924. 8 pp.

GRAMAGRASSES
Bouteloua

▨ 21 spp.　▨ 4 spp.　▨ 1 spp.

[30*/20 users] This North American genus includes nearly 20 species that grow in dry, open areas of the United States. In the Southwest, gramagrasses are important range plants, forming much of the thin grass cover of the plains and mesas and ascending to elevations of 7,500 feet. The flag-like, loose flower clusters are distinctive. Among the more important species for both livestock and wildlife are blue (*B. gracilis*), black (*B. eriopoda*), six-weeks (*B. barbata*), and hairy gramagrass (*B. hirsuta*).

Upland Gamebirds (seeds)
  * Turkey, Wild, *Ariz. and N.Mex.*
Songbirds (seeds)
  ** Finch, Brown-capped Rosy, *So. Mt.–Des.*
  Longspur
  * Chestnut-collared, *W.Pr.*
  ** McCown, *Pr.*
  * Sparrow, Brewer, *W*
Fur and Game Mammals (plants)
  Jack Rabbit
  *** Antelope, *Ariz.*
  ** Gray-sided, *Ariz. and N.Mex.*
Small Mammals (seedheads, plants)
  + Mouse, Prairie Pocket, *Pr.*

Prairie Dog
  * Black-tailed, *W.Pr.*
  * Gunnison, *N.Mex., Ariz., and Colo.*
Rat
  * Kangaroo, *SW*
  *** Kangaroo, Banner-tailed *Ariz.*
Hoofed Browsers (plants)
  * Antelope, *No.Pr. and Mt.–Des.;* +*S.E.Mont.*
  *** Bison, *Okla.;* **Ariz.*
  Deer
  * Mule, *So.Mt.–Des.*
  + White-tailed, *Tex.*
  + Elk, *No.Mt.–Des.*
  * Sheep, Mountain, *Nev.;* +*Colo.*

Reference: How to Keep and Increase Black Grama on Southwest Ranges. *U.S. Dept. Agr. Leaflet* 180, 1939. 9 pp.

BUFFALOGRASS
Buchloe dactyloides

[8*/5 users] Buffalograss stands alone as the only species of its genus. Its range is confined to central North America where it is most abundant in the western prairie area from western Nebraska south to west-central Texas —all former buffalo territory.

The principal value of this low, perennial grass is for hoofed browsers, but its large seed, enclosed in a hard bur, is eaten by the McCown longspur and probably has some value for other avian species.

Waterfowl (young plants)
* Goose, Snow, *W*

Songbirds (seeds)
** Longspur, McCown, *Pr.*

Hoofed Browsers (plants)
** Antelope, *N.Mex.;* +*No.Pr. and Mt.–Des.*
* Bison, *Okla.*
+ Deer, White-tailed, *Tex.*

CANARYGRASSES
Phalaris

[4*/6 users] Of the nine species of canarygrass in this country, only those in the Far West have demonstrated more than slight food value for wildlife. Reed canarygrass (*P. arundinacea*) is a common marsh or marsh-meadow plant. Other species grow in fields or waste areas. The well-known canarygrass seed imported for cagebirds is obtained from the exotic species (*P. canariensis*).

Upland Gamebirds (seeds)
+ Pheasant, Ring-necked, *NE and Pr.*
+ Quail, Bobwhite, *Tex.*

Songbirds (seeds)
* Bunting, Lazuli, *Pac.*
* Pipit, American, *Pac.*
* Sparrow, Savannah, *Calif.*
* Towhee, Abert, *Ariz.*

Reference: Reed Canary Grass. *U.S. Dept. Agr. Farmers' Bul.* 1602, 1938. 12 pp.

CRABGRASSES
Digitaria

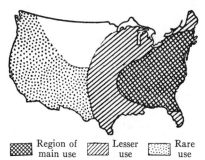

Region of main use / Lesser use / Rare use

[58*/22 users] The crabgrasses, so-called because of their creeping habit, number about 15 species in the United States and total approximately 60 in the tropical and temperate regions of the world. They are abundant in the East and particularly the Southeast.

377

The common species are annuals that thrive as pioneers in recently disturbed soil. Like other annuals they produce many seeds. This is the reason why crabgrass has such value to wildlife and is such a nuisance to farmers and gardeners. Because the plants appear in early summer, crabgrass is called Junegrass in some localities.

Three widespread and abundant species of crabgrass are outstanding in usefulness to songbirds and upland gamebirds. These are the hairy (*D. sanguinalis*), smooth (*D. ischaemum*), and slender crabgrass (*D. filiformis*). A number of our most familiar ground-feeding songbirds obtain a considerable part of their food from crabgrasses.

Upland Gamebirds (seeds)
    Dove
  +   Ground, *Gulf Coast*
  ** Mourning, *SE*; *NE
  +   Quail, Bobwhite, *E*

*** Turkey, Wild, *Mo.*; **Alleghenies; +*Pa.*
Songbirds (seeds)
  *   Cowbird, *NE*; +*SE*
  ** Junco, Slate-colored, *NE*; **Pr.*
  *   Lark, Horned, *E*; +*W*
    Longspur
  *** Lapland, *NE and No.Pr.*
  +   Smith, *Ill.*
  *   Pipit, American, *E*
    Sparrow
  *** Chipping, *E*
  ** Clay-colored, *E.Pr.*
  ** English, *E*; +*Pr.*
  *** Field, *E*; ***Pr.*
  ** Lincoln, *NE*
  *   Pine-woods, *SE*
  *** Savannah, *NE*
  *   Song, *NE*
  *   Swamp, *NE*
  *** Tree, *NE*; ***E.Pr.*
  *   White-crowned, *NE*
Fur and Game Mammals (plants)
  ** Rabbit, Cottontail, *NE*

PASPALUMS
Paspalum

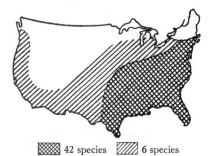

▨ 42 species   ▨ 6 species

[18*/19 users] The genus *Paspalum* resembles its close relative *Panicum* in being a large group (42 species in this country, about 250 in the world) and in having its center of abundance in the warmer regions. Our paspalums are most plentiful in the Southeast, both in numbers of species and in abundance of plants. Fringeleaf paspalum (*P. ciliatifolium*) and field paspalum (*P. laeve*) are especially abundant, widespread species in the East.

Bull paspalum (*P. boscianum*) is a common species along ditches, roadsides, and other moist places in the Southeast.

The nearly hemispheric seeds of paspalums are eaten by upland gamebirds and by other birds. Fringeleaf, field, and bull paspalums are the species used most extensively.

Waterfowl (seeds, plants)
    Duck
  *   Mottled, *Gulf Coast*
  +   Teal, Green-winged, *SE*
  +   Goose, Canada, *Tex.*
Marshbirds and Shorebirds (seeds)
  ** Gallinule, Purple, *SE*
  ** Rail, Sora, *SE*
Upland Gamebirds (seeds)
    Dove
  *** Ground, *Gulf Coast*
  *   Mourning, *SE*; +*Pr.*
  *   Quail, Bobwhite, *SE*; +*NE*
  ** Turkey, Wild, *Mo.*; +*E*
Songbirds (seeds)
  *   Blackbird, Redwing, *La.*; +*E*

* Cowbird, *E*
+ Junco, *NE*
+ Pyrrhuloxia, *Tex.*
  Sparrow
*   Pine-woods, *SE*
+   Vesper, *E*
* Towhee, *SE*

Fur and Game Mammals (plants)
+ Rabbit, Eastern Cottontail, *E*
Hoofed Browsers (plants)
** Bison, *Okla.*
+ Deer, White-tailed, *Tex.*

Reference: The North American Species of *Paspalum*. Agnes Chase. *Smithsonian Inst., U.S. Nat. Museum*, Vol. 28, Part 1, 1929. 310 pp.

PANICGRASSES
Panicum

▨ 150 species ⫽ 33 species

[**108*/67 users**] One hundred and sixty species of *Panicum*—about one-third of the total in the world—grow in the United States. The center of abundance of our species is in the Southeast, though some panicgrasses are encountered in all parts of the country. The plants are mainly inhabitants of fields and upland waste places, but a few, such as maidencane (*P. hemitomon*) and switchgrass (*P. virgatum*), occur in moist, low areas. Panicgrasses are rather diverse in form and height, varying from a few inches tall to several feet. All have a single, somewhat ovoid, glossy-coated seed at the end of each branchlet. The name of the genus is presumably derived from its more or less diffuse panicle or flower cluster.

The common witchgrass (*P. capillare*) is one of the most widespread and abundant of panicgrasses. Fall panicgrass (*P. dichotomiflorum*) and the minute-seeded *P. agrostoides* are two other species abundant in the East and, to some extent, in the Prairies. Panicgrasses are plentiful enough, par-

ticularly in the Southeast, to be of considerable forage value for livestock.

The genus, because of its abundance and wide distribution, is one of the country's most important sources of food for ground-feeding songbirds and gamebirds.

Waterfowl (seeds, young foliage)
  Duck
*   Baldpate, *SE*
***   Florida, *Fla.*
+   Gadwall, *SE*
*   Teal, Blue-winged, *SE*
***   Teal, Green-winged, *SE*
  Goose
+   Blue, *Gulf Coast*
+   Canada, *Tex.*
*   Snow, *Gulf Coast*
**   White-fronted, *La.*
Marshbirds and Shorebirds (seeds)
+ Gallinule, Purple, *SE*
+ Rail, Sora, *E*
+ Sandpiper, Pectoral, *SE*
* Snipe, Wilson, *SE*
Upland Gamebirds (seeds)
  Dove
**   Ground, *Gulf Coast*
*   Mourning, *SE and Pr.*
+   White-winged, Eastern, *Tex.*
+ Pheasant, Ring-necked, *NE*

** Quail, Bobwhite, *Tex.–Okla.;*
Pr.; +*E*
** Turkey, Wild, *Mo.;* +*E*
+ Woodcock, *E*

Songbirds (seeds)
*** Blackbird, Redwing, *SE;* **Pr.;*
+*NE*
* Bobolink, *SE;* +*NE*
Bunting
+ Lark, *Pr.*
* Painted, *Tex.*
+ Snow, *NE*
* Cardinal, *SE;* +*Pr.*
*** Cowbird, *SE;* +*W*
+ Creeper, Brown, *U.S.*
+ Dickcissel, *Pr.*
** Grosbeak, Blue, *E*
* Junco, *NE and Pr.*
+ Lark, Horned, *E and W*
Longspur
* Chestnut-collared, *Pr.*
* Lapland, *NE and Nö.Pr.*
*** Smith, *Ill.*
+ Meadowlark, *SE*
Pipit
+ American, *E*
+ Sprague, *Pr.*
** Pyrrhuloxia, *Tex.*
Sparrow
* Botteri, *Tex.*
* Chipping, *E, Mt.–Des. and Pac.*

*** Clay-colored, *E.Pr.*
+ English, *E*
** Field, *NE and Pr.*
** Grasshopper, *W;* +*NE*
+ Harris, *Pr.*
+ Henslow, *NE*
+ Ipswich, *NE*
*** Lark, Western, *Pr.;* *Mt.–Des.*
*** Lincoln, *NE and E.Pr.*
*** Pine-woods, *SE*
**** Savannah, *So.Pr.;* **NE and W*
+ Sharp-tailed, *Atl. Coast*
** Song, *NE;* +*Pac.*
** Swamp, *NE*
*** Tree, *NE;* *E.Pr.*
* Vesper, *E and Mt.–Des.*
** White-crowned, *NE;* *E.Pr.*
* White-throated, *NE*
** Towhee, *SE*
+ Warbler, Pine, *E*

Fur and Game Mammals (foliage, plants)
Jack Rabbit
+ Antelope, *Ariz.*
+ California, *Ariz. and N.Mex.*
** Muskrat, *La. and Md.*
* Rabbit, Cottontail, *Conn.*

Hoofed Browsers (plants)
+ Antelope, *Okla.*
+ Deer, White-tailed, *Ala.*

Reference: The North American Species of *Panicum.* A. S. Hitchcock and Agnes Chase. *Smithsonian Inst., U.S. Nat. Museum,* Vol. 15, 1910. 390 pp.

BRISTLEGRASSES
Setaria

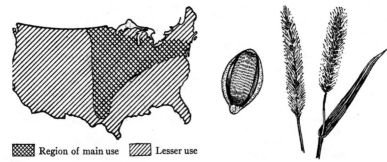

▨ Region of main use ▨ Lesser use

[226*/77 users] Thirteen kinds of bristlegrass are listed for the United States and about 65 for the world. Most of our species are native, but the most widespread and abundant ones are introduced weeds brought from Europe or elsewhere.

Two bristlegrasses (also known as pigeongrass and foxtailgrass) are outstanding in abundance and in importance to wildlife: yellow bristlegrass (*S. lutescens*) and green bristlegrass (*S. viridis*). They occur in grain, corn, and clover fields and in many other open places where the ground has been broken. These two are annuals, but nearly half of the other species are perennials. One southwestern annual bristlegrass (*S. grisebachii*) is of considerable value to quail and other ground-feeding birds.

These bristly-headed grasses top all other weeds in the country in food value to wildlife. This is indicated in the national listing of plants ranked according to value on page 476. This importance is due largely to their abundance and wide distribution, but the fairly large size of their many seeds is doubtless another telling factor. Besides being popular with upland gamebirds and some rodents, bristlegrasses are extremely valuable to ground-feeding songbirds. In addition to the 5-star (70%) listing for the painted bunting in Texas, there are numerous 4- or 3-star records for other songbirds.

A cultivated species, (*S. italica*), with varieties known as golden millet, German millet, Hungarian millet, etc., is used commonly in cagebird feed mixtures.

Waterfowl (seeds)
    Duck
+   Pintail, *W*
**   Blue-winged Teal, *W*; +*NE*
*   Green-winged Teal, *NE*
Marshbirds and Shorebirds (seeds)
    Rail
+   King, *NE*
*   Yellow, *E*
+   Sandpiper, Pectoral, *U.S.*
+   Snipe, Wilson, *U.S.*
Upland Gamebirds (seeds)

    Dove
**   Ground, *Gulf Coast*
*** Mourning, *E and Pr.;* **Mt.– Des.;* +*Pac.*
*   White-winged, Eastern, *Tex.*
+   Grouse, Sharp-tailed, *N.Dak.*
    Partridge
−   Chukar, *Mo.*
*** Hungarian, *NE*; **NW
*   Pheasant, Ring-necked, *NW*; +*NE*
*   Prairie Chicken, Greater, *No. Pr.*
    Quail
*** Bobwhite, *Pr.*; **NE; +*SE*
+   Gambel, *SW*
*   Valley, *Nev.*
*   Turkey, Wild, *Alleghenies;* +*E*
+   Woodcock, *E*
Songbirds (seeds)
    Blackbird,
+   Brewer, *W*
**** Redwing, *Pr.*; ***E; +*La. and Calif.*
**   Rusty, *NE*
*** Yellow-headed, *W*
*** Bobolink, *NE*; **W; +*SE*
    Bunting
−   Indigo, *E*
***** (70%) Painted, *Tex.*
*** Snow, *NE*
*** Cardinal, *SE*; **Pr.*; +*NE*
**** Cowbird, *W*; ***E
+   Crossbill, White-winged, *NE*
**** Dickcissel, *Pr.*
    Grackle
+   Boat-tailed, *SE*
+   Purple, *E and Pr.*
*** Grosbeak, Blue, *E and SW;* *NW
*** Junco, *Pr.*; **NE
**** Lark, Horned, *E*; ***W
    Longspur
*   Chestnut-collared, *W.Pr.*
**** Lapland, *Pr.*
*   McCown, *Pr.*
*** Smith, *Pr.*
*** Meadowlark, *W*; **SE and E.Pr.;* +*NE*
*   Pipit, American, *SE*
**** Pyrrhuloxia, *Tex.*
    Sparrow
**   Chipping, *E*; *W

****	Clay-colored, *E.Pr.*	*	Red-eyed, *NE*
*	English, *E and Pr.*	+	Thrasher, Curve-billed, *SW*
***	Field, *NE and Pr.*		**Fur and Game Mammals (foliage,**
*	Fox, *E*		**seeds)**
****	Grasshopper, *W excl. Calif.;*		Jack Rabbit
	****NE*	*	Antelope, *Ariz.*
**	Harris, *E.Pr.*	+	California, *Ariz. and N.Mex.*
*	Henslow, *NE*	+	Muskrat, *La.*
***	Lark, *Pr.*		Rabbit
***	Lincoln, *Pr.;* **NE*	+	Cottontail, Eastern, *Conn.*
*	Pine-woods, *SE*	+	Cottontail, Mearns, *Iowa*
***	Savannah, *NE;* **So.Pr.*		**Small Mammals (seeds)**
*	Seaside, *Atl. and Gulf Coasts*	**	Ground Squirrel, Thirteen-lined,
***	Song, *NE*		*Pr.*
+	Swamp, *NE*		Mouse
****	Tree, *E.Pr.;* ****NE*	+	Grasshopper, *No.Pr.*
***	Vesper, *E*	*	Pocket, *Pr. and Mt.–Des.*
***	White-crowned, *NE;* **Pr.*		Rat
*	White-throated, *NE*	+	Kangaroo, Ord, *W*
	Towhee	+	Kangaroo, various spp., *Mt.–*
**	Abert, *Ariz.*		*Des. and Pr.*

Reference: The Bristlegrass (*Setaria* spp.) in California. Margaret K. Bellue. *Calif. Dept. Agr. Bul.* Vol. 27, pp. 210–214, 1938.

SANDBURS
Cenchrus

[2*/2 users] Seven species of sandburs are found along our coasts and in other sandy areas. Their seeds, enclosed in prickly burs, are eaten by a few birds—notably the pyrrhuloxia, but the value of the plants to wildlife is slight.

Songbirds (seeds)
** Pyrrhuloxia, *Tex.*
Hoofed Browsers (plants)
− Deer, White-tailed, *Tex.*

BROOMSEDGE AND BLUESTEM
Andropogon

[8*/12 users] This genus is represented by about 150 species of which 32 or more occur in the United States. The group is complicated by the use of different common names in different sections. The name broomsedge is applied to *A. virginicus*, the most common species in the East, and it is also used for some of the other eastern species. Species that range westward, and which once constituted much of the prairie vegetation, are called bluestem and beardgrass. Little or prairie bluestem (*A. scoparius*) and cane bluestem (*A. barbinodis*) are important examples. Western species have also

been called bunchgrasses—a name that has been used for various perennial grasses with a bunchy habit of growth. The principal wildlife use of these tall, slender-stemmed grasses is by songbirds and hoofed browsers. In the East, broomsedge sometimes is of special value to small birds when, during winter snows, seeds of other plants are not readily available. In winter, field sparrows or juncos are often seen perched on the stalks, plucking off the feathery parts and eating the seeds.

The cover value of broomsedge, though considerable, is often reduced by its tendency to become too dense for some of the more desirable wildlife species.

Upland Gamebirds (seeds)
+ Prairie Chicken, *Tex.*

+ Turkey, Wild, *Tex.*
Songbirds (seeds)
* Finch, Rosy, *Pac.*
+ Junco, *NE*
Sparrow
+ Chipping, *E*
** Field, *NE*
* Tree, *NE*
Small Mammals (seeds, leaves)
Mouse
− Meadow, *E*
− Pocket, *Okla.*
Hoofed Browsers (plants)
** Antelope, *N.Mex.*
* Bison, *Okla.*
* Deer, White-tailed, *SE*

Sedge Family: *Cyperaceae*

SEDGES
Carex

[86*/67 users] Species of *Carex* in this country number about 500—nearly half of the world's total. They occur in all regions, but the great majority grow in moist soils of meadows, marshes, bogs, and near ditches and roadsides. A few species thrive in relatively dry places. Sedges also grow at high altitudes, and they constitute a large part of the vegetation in northern regions. Species of *Carex* along with various grasses make up much of the wild meadow hay cut by middlewestern and western farmers in sloughs and along the borders of ponds or lakes.

Because of their wide availability in both lowland and upland situations the triangular or lens-shaped seeds of sedges (akenes enclosed in a special envelope) are eaten by many kinds of wildlife. The plants are not abundant enough near the water margins of pond, lakes, and streams to make their seeds of major importance to waterfowl, but ducks eat them frequently in small to fair amounts. Sedges are also of value to rails, grouse, and to seed-eating songbirds such as the swamp sparrow, tree sparrow, Lincoln sparrow, snow bunting, larkspurs, and redpoll. Carex seeds, along with in-

sects, are the most regular items in the diet of ruffed grouse chicks in the Northeast. In addition to providing food for many wildlife species, sedges are also valuable for cover. Frequently they provide nesting cover for ducks, and their tufted growths furnish concealment to other animals.

Waterfowl (seeds)
+ Coot, *NE*
Duck
+ Baldpate, *NE*
* Black, *NE*
+ Canvasback, *W*

383

+ Goldeneye, American, *NE and W*
* Mallard, *W and Wis.*
+ Pintail, *NE*
+ Redhead, *NE and W*
* Ring-necked, *W;* +*NE*
+ Ruddy, *W*
+ Scaup, Lesser, *NE and W*
* Shoveller, *W;* +*SE*
* Teal, Blue-winged, *NE;* +*W*
** Teal, Cinnamon, *Mt.–Des. and Pac.*
** Teal, Green-winged, *NE;* *W*
* Wood, *NE*

Marshbirds and Shorebirds (seeds)
+ Dowitcher, Long-billed, *W*
Rail
+ Clapper, *U.S.*
*** Sora, *N*
+ Virginia, *E*
** Yellow, *E*
Sandpiper
+ Semipalmated, *Atl.Coast*
+ Stilt, *U.S.*
+ White-rumped, *E*
* Snipe, Wilson, *W;* +*SE*

Upland Gamebirds (seeds)
Grouse
* Blue, *Pac.NW;* +*No.Mt.–Des.*
** Ruffed, young, *NE*
+ Sharp-tailed, *Great Lakes Area*
* Spruce, *NW and Canada*
+ Pheasant, Ring-necked, *N.Y.*
* Prairie Chicken, Greater, *Wis.*
+ Turkey, Wild, *E*
+ Woodcock, *E*

Songbirds (seeds)
Bunting
+ Painted, *Tex.*
*** Snow, *NW;* *NE*
* Cardinal, *E;* +*Pr.*
Finch
+ House, Common, *Calif.*

* Rosy, *Pac.*
+ Junco, Slate-colored, *NE and Pr.*
* Lark, Horned, *E and W*
Longspur
+ Chestnut-collared, *W.Pr.*
** Lapland, *NE and No.Pr.*
+ McCown, *Pr.*
+ Smith, *Ill.*
Redpoll
+ Common, *No.U.S. and Canada*
** Hoary, *Mich. and Canada*
Sparrow
+ Grasshopper, *W*
** Lincoln, *NE and Calif.*
* Savannah, *So.Pr.*
* Song, *NE*
*** Swamp, *NE*
** Tree, *E*
* Towhee, Red-eyed, *NE*

Fur and Game Mammals (seeds, leaves)
+ Bear, Black, *Va.*
+ Jack Rabbit, White-tailed, *Utah*
+ Pika, *Pac.*
+ Porcupine, Yellow-haired, *Mt.–Des.*
Squirrel
+ Gray, Eastern, *E*
+ Fox, *Ohio*

Small Mammals (seeds, leaves, roots)
Chipmunk
** Least, *W.Pr.;* *Mt.–Des.*
+ Northwest, *Pac.NW*
+ Mole, Common, *E*

Hoofed Browsers (plants)
Deer
* Mule, *Calif.*
* White-tailed, *N.C.Mts.*
* Elk, *No.Mt.–Des.*
** Moose, *Maine to Mich.*
* Sheep, Mountain, *No.Mt.–Des.*

Arum Family: *Araceae*

SKUNKCABBAGE
Symplocarpus foetidus

[1*/4 users] Skunkcabbage, a single American species, is common in northeastern swamps and boggy places. The large seeds of this ill-scented plant are eaten by several gamebirds including the ring-necked pheasant.

Waterfowl (seeds)
+ Duck, Wood, *NE*
Upland Gamebirds (seeds)

+ Grouse, Ruffed, *NE*
* Pheasant, Ring-necked, *NE*
+ Quail, Bobwhite, *NE*

JACK-IN-THE-PULPIT
Arisaema

[1*/3 users] There are several species of jack-in-the-pulpit in rich eastern woodlands. Both the bright red fruit and the leaves are eaten by wildlife to a limited extent.

Upland Gamebirds (fruit, leaves)
* Pheasant, Ring-necked, *NE*
+ Turkey, Wild, *SE*
Songbirds (fruit)
+ Thrush, Wood, *NE*

Dayflower Family : *Commelinaceae*

DAYFLOWERS
Commelina

[2*/5 users] There are about 10 species of dayflower in the country—confined to the East and the Southwest. They are partial to moist places and to sandy soil. The blue color of dayflowers is so attractive that the plants are used as ornamentals.

Upland Gamebirds (seeds)
* Dove, Mourning, *Ala.*
* Quail, Bobwhite, *Okla.*; +*SE*
Songbirds (seeds)
+ Blackbird, Redwing, *La.*
+ Cardinal, *Miss.*
Hoofed Browsers (plants)
− Deer, White-tailed, *Tex.*

Lily Family : *Liliaceae*

SOLOMONPLUMES
Smilacina

[0*/7 users] Five species of these attractive white-flowered, red- or green-berried plants are present in woodlands of the United States. The berries have minor value for a few kinds of wildlife. Berries of the closely related solomon-seal (*Polygonatum*) are also used to a limited extent.

Upland Gamebirds (fruit)
+ Grouse, Ruffed, *NE*

+ Pigeon, Band-tailed, *So.Mt.-Des.*
Songbirds (fruit)
Thrush
+ Gray-cheeked, *NE*
+ Olive-backed, *NE*
+ Veery, *NE*
Small Mammals (fruit)
+ Mouse, White-footed, *NE*
+ Rat, Wood, *Pac.*

BEADRUBY
Maianthemum

[1*/5 users] Beadruby, also known as wild lily-of-the-valley or Canada mayflower, is represented by two species, one in the Northeast and the other in the Pacific Northwest. Both are low, woodland herbs, with bright red berries that are eaten to a limited extent by wildlife.

Upland Gamebirds (fruit)
+ Grouse, Ruffed, *NE*

Fur and Game Mammals (plants)
  * Hare, Varying, *Minn.*

Small Mammals (fruit)
  — Chipmunk, Lyster, *Ont.*
  — Mouse, White-footed, *Minn.*

Buckwheat Family: *Polygonaceae*

ERIOGONUMS
Eriogonum

158   73   1 or 2 spp.

[**17***/**21 users**] This North American group of plants includes more than 200 species. About 175 are found in the United States—all in the West. Eriogonums grow in dry, well-drained soil and are found from desert lowlands up into high altitudes of the western mountains. They are variable in size and appearance, but most of them are characterized by a widely branched umbrella-like cluster of minute flowers. The seeds and other parts of eriogonums are moderately important as food for wildlife. Among the more widely distributed and used species are *E. umbellatum, E. cernuum, E. alatum,* and *E. nudum.*

Upland Gamebirds (foliage)
  ** Grouse, Blue, *No.Mt.–Des.;*
    **Pac.NW*

  + Quail, Mearns, *SW*
  * Turkey, Wild, *Ariz. and N.Mex.*
Songbirds (seeds)
  + Bobolink, *W*
  + Finch, Common House, *Calif.*
  + Junco, Oregon, *Calif.*
  + Lark, California Horned, *Calif.*
  * Redpoll, *N*
  *** Sparrow, Bell, *Calif.*
    Towhee
  +   Brown, *Calif.*
  +   Spotted, *Pac.*
Fur and Game Mammals (plants)
  * Jack Rabbit, California, *Ariz. and N.Mex.*
Small Mammals (flower heads, leaves)
  * Ground Squirrel, California, *Calif.*
  * Prairie Dog, Gunnison, *N.Mex., Ariz., and Colo.*
    Rat
  +   Kangaroo, Banner-tailed, *Ariz.*
  +   Kangaroo, Tulare, *Calif.*
  +   Wood, Large-eared, *Calif.*
  +   Wood, White-throated, *Ariz.*
  * Rock Squirrel, *Calif.*
Hoofed Browsers (plants)
  + Deer, Mule, *So.Mt.–Des.*
  * Sheep, Mountain, *Idaho and Calif.*

SHEEPSORREL AND DOCKS
Rumex

[**21***/**35 users**] The genus *Rumex*, including sheepsorrel and the various docks (but not burdock), includes about 140 species of which 30 are widely distributed in this country. They are plants of moist places.

  Sheepsorrel, or sourgrass (*R. aceto-* sella), is by far the most important member of this group in so far as wildlife is concerned. It is one of the most abundant weeds in the whole country, though this fact may be obscured because the low rosettes of arrow-shaped leaves and slender flower stems are so

386

inconspicuous. Sheepsorrel has long been regarded as an indicator of acid soil.

Both the seeds and leaves of sheepsorrel are eaten by wildlife. The small triangular seeds are such a common item in the diet of ground-feeding birds that the record of their use is a long one. People occasionally gather the foliage for greens.

Other species of *Rumex*, generally called dock, grow along roadsides, in swamps, marshes, and other low or wet places. Golden dock (*R. persicarioides*) and curly dock (*R. crispa*) are the most common and widespread. The seeds of the former are eaten occasionally by western ducks.

Waterfowl (seeds)
* * Teal, Cinnamon, *Mt.–Des. and Pac.*
* \+ Goose, Canada, *Utah*

Marshbirds and Shorebirds (seeds)
* \+ Rail, Sora, *W*

Upland Gamebirds (leaves, seeds)
* Grouse
* \+   Blue, *Pac.NW*
* *   Ruffed, *Va.Alleghenies and Pa.; +NE*
* \+ Pheasant, Ring-necked, *NE*
* \+ Prairie Chicken, Greater, *No. Pr.*
* \+ Quail, Bobwhite, *E*
* \+ Turkey, Wild, *E*
* \+ Woodcock, *NE*

Songbirds (seeds)
* * Blackbird, Redwing, *NE*
* \+ Bobolink, *NE*
* \+ Cowbird, *NE*
* \+ Junco, Oregon, *Calif.*

* \+ Lark, Horned, *E*
* \+ Pipit, American, *Pac.*
* ** Redpoll, Hoary, *No.U.S.*
* Sparrow
* \+   Field, *NE*
* \+   Fox, *E*
* **   Grasshopper, Eastern, *NE*
* \+   Henslow, *NE*
* *   Rufous-crowned, *Calif.*
* *   Savannah, *Calif.*
* *   Song, *NE*; +*Calif.*
* *   Swamp, *NE*
* *   Tree, *NE*
* \+   Vesper, *E*
* *   White-crowned, *NE*
* \+ Towhee, Spotted, *Pac.*

Fur and Game Mammals (leaves, plants)
* ** Rabbit, Cottontail, *Conn.*

Small Mammals (seeds, leaves)
* * Ground Squirrel, Mantled, *W*
* Mouse
* \+   Meadow, *E*
* \+   Pine, *NE*
* \+   White-footed, *E*
* \+ Rat, Banner-tailed Kangaroo, *Ariz.*

Hoofed Browsers (plants)
* * Deer, Mule, *Calif.*

Reference : Red Sorrel and Its Control (*Rumex acetosella*). F. J. Pipal. *Ind. Agr. Exp. Sta. Bul.* 1947, 1916. 28 pp.

KNOTWEEDS
Polygonum

[86*/61 users] The name knotweed is used here as a sort of key name for all the upland species of *Polygonum*. This group includes not only the true knotweeds but also the black bindweeds or cornbinds, false buckwheats, and tear-

thumbs. The smartweeds, which some botanists place in a separate genus, *Persicaria*, are treated under Marsh and Aquatic Plants.

The 30 or so species which make up this diverse group occur in practically every part of the United States. The habitat of different species varies considerably. Some of the true knotweeds, like *P. aviculare*, and *P. erectum*, grow in the hard-packed ground of roadways and yards. Black bindweeds, especially *P. convolvulus*, thrive in grain fields and cultivated areas in the Prairies and the East. False buckwheats are eastern plants found along fences and field borders. The viny tearthumbs are partial to moist places, either in the open or in partial shade. They too are confined largely to the East.

The large seeds of black bindweeds and false buckwheats are of special value to upland gamebirds. The true knotweeds are important for ground-feeding songbirds. Smartweed seeds are eaten by songbirds also.

Upland Gamebirds (seeds)
** Dove, Mourning, *Pr.*; *NE and Mt.–Des.*; +*Pac.*
* Grouse, Sharp-tailed, *Gr.Lakes Area*; +*N.Dak.*
** Partridge, Hungarian, *NW*; *NE*
* Pheasant, Ring-necked, *NW*
*** Prairie Chicken, Greater, *No.Pr.*
Quail
* Bobwhite, *Pr.*
+ Mountain, *Pac.*
+ Woodcock, *E*
Songbirds (seeds)
Blackbird
+ Brewer, *W*
* Redwing, *Pr. and Calif.*; +*Mt.–Des.*
* Redwing, Tricolored, *Calif.*
+ Yellow-headed, *W*
* Bobolink, *W*
Bunting
+ Lark, *Pr.*
* Snow, *NE*; +*NW*
* Cowbird, *NE*; +*W*
Finch
** House, Common, *Calif.*
+ Rosy, *Pac.*
**** Rosy, Brown-capped, *So.Mt.– Des.*
+ Goldfinch, Lawrence, *Mt.–Des. and Pac.*

pennsylvanicum   *punctatum*   *persicaria*

dumetorum   *aviculare*

Junco
* Oregon, *Calif.*
* Slate-colored, *Pr.*
** Lark, Horned, *Pr. and Mt.– Des.*; +*Calif.*
Longspur
+ Lapland, *No.Pr.*
*** McCown, *Pr.*
+ Pipit, American, *Pac.*
* Redpoll, Common, *NW*
Sparrow
* English, *E*; +*W*
** Fox, *W*
* Golden-crowned, *Calif.*
*** Grasshopper, Western, *Calif.*
** Harris, *Pr.*
** Lark, Western, *Calif.*
* Lincoln, *Calif.*
*** Savannah, *Calif.*; +*Pr.*
** Song, *Pac.*
* Tree, *Pr.*
* Vesper, *Mt.–Des.*
*** White-crowned, *Mt.–Des.*; +*Pr. and Pac.*
Fur and Game Mammals (plants)
+ Porcupine, Western, *Mt.–Des.*
Small Mammals (seeds)
Chipmunk
** Least, *Minn.*
+ Western, various spp., *Mt.– Des. and Pac.*
Ground Squirrel
** Mantled, *W*
* Richardson, *No.Pr.*
** Thirteen-lined, *Pr.*
Mouse
+ Pocket, *W*
* White-footed, *E*; +*W*
+ Prairie Dog, Black-tailed, *W.Pr.*

Hoofed Browsers (plants)
* * Antelope, *S.Dak.;* +*SE Mont.*

Deer
+ Black-tailed, *Calif.*
* * Mule, *Calif.;* +*So.Mt.–Des.*

Goosefoot Family : *Chenopodiaceae*

GOOSEFOOT
Chenopodium

[61*/40 users] Of the 60 or more species in the genus *Chenopodium*, about 20 occur in the United States. Our goosefoots, both native and introduced, are present in practically all parts of the country. These common weeds, covered with a white, floury coating, are particularly conspicuous in rich soil of gardens, near barns or fields, and along roadsides. Probably the most widespread and abundant is lambsquarters goosefoot (*C. album*), but mapleleaf (*C. hybridum*) and wormseed goosefoot (*C. ambrosioides*) are also used by wildlife in many parts of the country.

Goosefoot seeds are relished by many kinds of songbirds, and the persistence of some seeds on the plants, late in the year, makes these weeds particularly valuable to wildlife. Nearly 75,000 seeds have been counted on a single plant of lambsquarters and about 175,000 on red goosefoot (*C. rubrum*).

Upland Gamebirds (seeds)
+ Dove, Mourning, *Pr. and Mt.– Des.*
+ Grouse, Sharp-tailed, *Minn.*
+ Partridge, Hungarian, *N.Dak.*
+ Pheasant, Ring-necked, *NE and Wash.*
  Quail
+ Bobwhite, *Pr.*
* * Valley, *Nev.*

Songbirds (seeds)
  Bunting
+ Lark, *W.Pr.*
* ** Snow, *NE;* +*NW*
+ Finch, Brown-capped Rosy, *So. Mt.–Des.*
* * Goldfinch, *E*

Junco
* * Oregon, *Mt.–Des. and Pac.*
* ** Slate-colored, *Pr.;* *E
Lark
* ** Horned, *W;* *E
+ Horned, California, *Calif.*
Longspur
+ Chestnut-collared, *W.Pr.*
+ Lapland, *NE and No.Pr.*
* ** McCown, *Pr.*
+ Pyrrhuloxia, *Tex.*
* *** Redpoll, Common, *N*
Sparrow
+ Brewer, *W*
+ Chipping, *E*
* ** Clay-colored, *E.Pr.*
+ English, *E*
+ Field, *NE and Pr.*
* * Harris, *E.Pr.*
* * Lincoln, *NE, Pr. and Calif.*
* * Savannah, *So.Pr.;* +*Calif.*
* * Song, *NE;* +*Pac.*
+ Swamp, *NE*
* * Tree, *NE and E.Pr.*
* * Vesper, *Mt.–Des.;* +*E*
* *** White-crowned, *Mt.–Des.;* ***E.Pr.;* **Pac.;* +*NE*

Small Mammals (seeds)
* * Chipmunk, Least, *W.Pr. and Mt.–Des.*
Gopher
* * Pocket, Brown, *Mont.*
+ Pocket, Western, *Mont.*
* ** Ground Squirrel, Richardson, *N.Pr.*
Rat
* * Kangaroo, Merriam, *SW*
* * Kangaroo, various spp., *Mt.– Des. and Pr.*

Hoofed Browsers (plants)
* * Deer, White-tailed, *Ohio*

RUSSIANTHISTLE
Salsola kali

[39*/23 users] Russianthistle, also known as tumbleweed or saltwort, is an abundant, important weed. It was introduced accidentally with flax seed

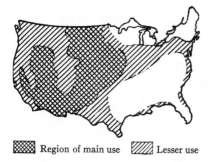

▨ Region of main use ▨ Lesser use

in South Dakota in 1886 and since then has become plentiful in the Prairies and Southwest. This spiny, red-lined plant occurs in cultivated fields, along roadsides, and in waste places where the soil has been broken. During drought years when forage is short, farmers have cut the Russianthistle before its spines have hardened and then raked it into large stacks for feeding to livestock. In these emergencies it has been a help to agriculture, compensating in a small measure for its usual nuisance as a weed.

The spirally coiled, snail-like seeds of Russianthistle are of good size and provide food for birds and rodents. In addition, hoofed browsers feed on the young plants.

Upland Gamebirds (seeds)
* Pheasant, Ring-necked, *NW*; +*Mont.*
Quail
** Gambel, *SW*
* Valley, *Nev.*
Songbirds (seeds)
− Bunting, Lazuli, *Okla.*
* Goldfinch, Lawrence, *Mt.–Des. and Pac.*
+ Lark, Horned, *W*
+ Redpoll, Common, *N*
* Sparrow, White-crowned, *Mt.– Des.*
Small Mammals (seeds, foliage, stems)
Gopher
* Pocket, Brown, *Mont.*
+ Pocket, Western, *Mont.*
Ground Squirrel
* Antelope, *Mt.–Des. and Calif.*
* Thirteen-lined, *Pr.*
Mouse
* Grasshopper, *W*
* Pocket, *W.Pr. and Mt.–Des.*
* White-footed, *W*
Prairie Dog
** Black-tailed, *W.Pr.*
*** Gunnison, *SW*
*** White-tailed, *Mont. and Wyo.*
* Rat, Merriam Kangaroo, *SW*
Hoofed Browsers (plants)
+ Antelope, *No.Pr., Mt.–Des.*
+ Deer, Mule, *So.Mt.–Des.*
+ Elk, *Colo.*

Pigweed Family: *Amaranthaceae*

PIGWEEDS
Amaranthus

[114*/55 users] About half of the 60-odd species of pigweed occur in the United States. They are found throughout the country in gardens, cultivated fields, and waste places—generally in fair to good soil. Pigweeds are common in rich soil near barns and pigpens. Possibly that is how they got their name.

All our species are coarse, annual weeds, yet some exotic forms are attractive garden plants, with bright reddish foliage. These are called ama-

ranths and include varieties such as Josephs-coat, moltenfire, and others.

Pigweeds produce a tremendous number of small, shiny, circular seeds. A total of 129,000 was counted on a single plant. Some seeds persist in the densely clustered spikes and remain available for use by songbirds into the winter (and possibly spring) when other foods are scarce. These despised common weeds are one of the most important foods of many of our best loved songbirds. In addition, they are of

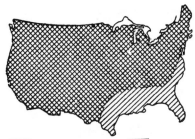

Region of main use [////] Lesser use
considerable value for upland gamebirds and other wildlife species.

Waterfowl (seeds)
+ Teal, Green-winged, *NE and W*
Upland Gamebirds (seeds)
Dove
* Ground, *Gulf Coast*
*** Mourning, *Pr.*; **Mt.–Des.*;
Pac.; +*NE*
+ Pheasant, Ring-necked, *NE*
Quail
+ Bobwhite, *Pa.*
* California, *Calif.*
* Scaled, Arizona, *SW*
+ Valley, *Nev.*
Songbirds (seeds)
Bunting
* Lark, *Pr.*
+ Lazuli, *Okla.*
+ Painted, *Tex.*
*** Snow, *NE*; *NW
Finch
** House, Common, *Calif.*
* Rosy, Brown-capped, *So.Mt.–
Des.*
Goldfinch
** Green-backed, *Calif.*
**** Lawrence, *Mt.–Des and Pac.*
+ Grosbeak, Rose-breasted, *NE*
Junco
** Oregon, *Calif.*
** Slate-colored, *Pr.*; *NE
Lark
** Horned, *W*; *E
* Horned, California, *Calif.*
Longspur
* Chestnut-collared, *Pr.*
** Lapland, *NE and No.Pr.*
+ McCown, *Pr.*
+ Pipit. American, *SE and Pac.*
Redpoll

** Common, *N*
** Hoary, *Mich. and Canada*
Sparrow
* Brewer, *W*
** Chipping, *Mt.–Des. and Pac.*;
+*E*
*** Clay-colored, *E.Pr.*
+ Field, *NE*
* Fox, *W*
* Golden-crowned, *Calif.*
* Grasshopper, *Calif.*
+ Lark, Eastern, *Pr.*
+ Lark, Western, *Mt.–Des. and
Calif.*
**** Lincoln, *Calif.*; *NE
+ Rufous-crowned, *Calif.*
*** Savannah, *Calif.*; **Pr.*;
+*NE*
*** Song, *Pac.*; *NE
** Tree, *E.Pr.*; *NE
** Vesper, *Mt.–Des.*; *E
*** White-crowned, *Mt.–Des. and
Pac.*; **E.Pr.*; *NE
+ White-throated, *NE*
Towhee
+ Abert, *Ariz.*
* Brown, *Calif.*
* Green-tailed, *Mt.–Des.*
Fur and Game Mammals (plants)
+ Rabbit, Mearns Cottontail, *Pa.*
Small Mammals (seeds)
** Mouse, Pocket, *W.Pr. and Mt.–
Des.*

Rat
+ Kangaroo, Large, *Ariz.*
*** Kangaroo, Merriam, *SW*
* Kangaroo, Ord, *W*

Hoofed Browsers (plants)
+ Antelope, *N.Mex. and S.E.Mont.*
+ Deer, Mule, *Mt.–Des.*

Pokeweed Family: *Phytolaccaceae*

POKEWEED
Phytolacca americana

[**12*/28 users**] The common pokeweed known as pokeberry, poke, scoke, redweed, and pigeonberry is the only well-known species in this country. It is one of the most common large weeds (4 to 12 feet tall), growing in garbage dumps, near old sheds, along woodsides, and elsewhere in rich moist soil. The dark purple berries and large, shiny black seeds are popular with songbirds in the fall and are an important source of food for the mourning dove. Birds have been reported becoming intoxicated from eating pokeweed berries.

Upland Gamebirds (fruit)
** Dove, Mourning, *NE*; *SE*
Songbirds (fruit)
* Bluebird, *SE*; +*NE*
+ Cardinal, *E*
* Catbird, *E*
+ Chat, Yellow-breasted, *E*
+ Crow, Fish, *E*
+ Flycatcher, Crested, *E*
+ Grosbeak, Rose-breasted, *NE and Pr.*

+ Kingbird, *E*
** Mockingbird, *SE*; +*Tex.*
+ Phoebe, *E*
+ Robin, *NE*
+ Sapsucker, Yellow-bellied, *E*
+ Starling, *NE*
+ Thrasher, Brown, *SE*
Thrush
+ Gray-cheeked, *NE*
+ Hermit, *E*
+ Olive-backed, *NE*
* Veery, *NE*
+ Vireo, Warbling, *NE*
* Waxwing, Cedar, *NE*
Woodpecker
* Golden-fronted, *Tex.*
+ Hairy, *E and Pr.*
Fur and Game Mammals (fruit)
Fox
+ Gray, *NE*
+ Red, *Pa.*
+ Opossum, *NE, Okla.–Tex., and Mo.*
* Raccoon, *NE*; +*E.Tex.*
Small Mammals (fruit)
— Mouse, White-footed, *NE*

Four-O'Clock Family: *Nyctaginaceae*

SPIDERLINGS
Boerhaavia

[**8*/6 users**] There are about a dozen species of spiderlings in the Southwest —mainly in arid sandy or stony soils. The seeds of these widely branched, weed-like plants are of considerable value to a few species of desert wildlife.

Upland Gamebirds (seeds)
** Quail, Gambel, *SW*
Fur and Game Mammals (plants)
   Jack Rabbit
* Antelope, *Ariz.*

* Gray-sided, *Ariz. and N.Mex.*
Small Mammals (seeds)
   Rat
* Kangaroo, *SW*
+ Kangaroo, Banner-tailed, *Ariz.*
+ Wood, White-throated, *Ariz.*

Purslane Family : *Portulacaceae*

REDMAIDS
Calandrinia caulescens

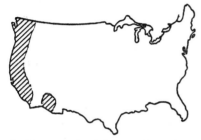

[21*/23 users] This low, semisucculent, bright-flowered herb is one of four species in the Pacific and adjoining Mountain–Desert region. The rose or magenta flowers of this spring-blooming annual color acres of cultivated ground in some localities. The other three species are not nearly as plentiful. Redmaids, sometimes called kisses, rates with filaree, minerslettuce, and burclover as one of the most abundant spring herbs in California. Its medium-small, black, shiny seeds are an important food for some songbirds as well as for the mourning dove and for rodents.

Upland Gamebirds (seeds)
** Dove, Mourning, *Pac.*

   Quail
+ California, *Calif.*
+ Valley, *Calif.*
Songbirds (seeds)
* Blackbird, Redwing, *Calif.*
+ Finch, Rosy, *Pac.*
* Goldfinch, Lawrence, *Mt.–Des. and Pac.*
+ Grosbeak, Black-headed, *Calif.*
** Junco, Oregon, *Calif.*
**** Lark, California Horned, *Calif.*
+ Nuthatch, White-breasted, *Pac.*
** Pipit, American, *Pac.*
   Sparrow
+ Chipping, *Mt.–Des. and Pac.*
*** Lark, Western, *Calif.*
* Savannah, *Calif.*
+ Song, *Pac.*
+ White-crowned, *Pac.*
   Towhee
+ Brown, *Calif.*
* Green-tailed, *Mt.–Des.*
− Spotted, *Pac.*
Small Mammals (seeds, plants)
* Ground Squirrel, California, *Calif.*
+ Rat, Tulare Kangaroo, *Calif.*
** Rock Squirrel, *Calif.*

MINERSLETTUCE
Montia perfoliata

[15*/21 users] Minerslettuce is one of the most abundant springtime weeds in orchards, vineyards, and lowland pastures of the Pacific region. It extends as far eastward as western North Dakota, but its main abundance and importance is in California and neigh- boring states. There are 14 other species of *Montia* in the West, but minerslettuce is the only one of consequence as a wildlife food. These succulent herbs are said to have earned the name minerslettuce when used as salad plants by the early pioneers. They have con-

Region of main use  Lesser use

siderable value for livestock. The black, shiny seeds are an important source of food for western songbirds.

Upland Gamebirds (seeds)
+ Dove, Mourning, *Pac.*
  Quail
+   California, *Calif.*
+   Mountain, *Calif.*
+   Valley, *Calif.*
Songbirds (seeds)
** Bunting, Lazuli, *Pac.*
+ Finch, Common House, *Calif.*
+ Goldfinch, Green-backed, *Calif.*
* Grosbeak, Pine, *Pac.*
** Junco, Oregon, *Calif.*

* Lark, California Horned, *Calif.*
* Siskin, Pine, *Pac.*
  Sparrow
+   Chipping, *Mt.–Des. and Pac.*
** Rufous-crowned, *Calif.*
*   Savannah, *Calif.*
*   Song, *Calif.*
+   Vesper, *Mt.–Des.*
*   White-crowned, *Calif.*
  Towhee
*   Brown, *Calif.*
*   Green-tailed, *Mt.–Des.*
*   Spotted, *Pac.*
Small Mammals (leaves, seeds)
+ Rat, Kangaroo, *Calif.*

PURSLANES
Portulaca

[18*/13 users] About a dozen representatives of the genus *Portulaca* are found in this country. Common purslane (*P. oleracea*), a native of Europe, occurs in gardens, fields, and waste places in all regions. It is the only representative of this group of semisucculent plants in the northern half of the United States. The other species are mainly in the Southwest. The gay-colored, familiar garden portulacas (*P. grandiflora*) are natives of South America.

The small seeds of purslanes are relished by birds and rodents. Though the plants do not become large, their seed production is tremendous. Fifty-two thousand, three hundred seeds have been counted on a single common purslane plant.

Upland Gamebirds (seeds)
+ Dove, Ground, *Gulf Coast*
Songbirds (seeds)
** Bunting, Lark, *Pr.*
* Lark, Horned, *W*
+ Longspur, Lapland, *NE and No. Pr.*
  Sparrow
*   Botteri, *Tex.*
*   Brewer, *W*
+   Chipping, *E*
+   Vesper, *E*
Fur and Game Mammals (plants)
  Jack Rabbit
*   Antelope, *Ariz.*
+   California, *Ariz. and N.Mex.*
Small Mammals (seeds, capsules, plants)

Rat
* Kangaroo, Merriam, *SW*
* Kangaroo, Ord, *W*

* Kangaroo, various spp., *Pr.
and Mt.–Des.*

Pink Family: *Caryophyllaceae*

CHICKWEED
Stellaria media

[**25***/**36 users**] Botanists disagree about this genus—not only as to the name, *Stellaria* or *Alsine*, but also as to the number of species. According to the inclusive concept there are about 75 species—about one-third of them in the United States. Only the one species, common chickweed (*S. media*), is of importance to wildlife. It occurs in moist soil throughout the country and, for that matter, practically throughout the world. The plants, though annuals, start growing in the fall, survive the rigors of winter, even in the North, begin flowering in late winter, and complete their seed production and life cycle in the spring.

Common chickweed is a low, reclining plant that is high in value to birds. Its numerous, minute seeds, in papery capsules, and its tender leaves are relished by gamebirds and songbirds. A complete list of the birds that use chickweed as food would be a very long one.

Upland Gamebirds (seeds)
    Dove
    * Ground, *Gulf Coast*
    * Mourning, *SE and Pac.*
    Quail
    + Bobwhite, *E*
    + California, *Calif.*
    + Gambel, *Calif.*

Songbirds (seeds)
    + Blackbird, Brewer, *Calif.*
    + Bunting, Lazuli, *Pac.*
    Finch
    * House, Common, *Calif.*
    *** Rosy, Brown-capped, *So.Mt.–Des.*
    Goldfinch
    + Common, *E*
    * Lawrence, *Calif.*
    *** Junco, Oregon, *Pac.*

Lark
+ Horned, *W*
+ Horned, California, *Calif.*
* Pipit, American, *Pac.*
+ Siskin, Pine, *W*
Sparrow
+ Belding, *Calif.*
* Chipping, *W*; +*E*
+ English, *U.S.*
+ Fox, *W*
* Gambel, *Pac.*
* Golden-crowned, *Calif.*
+ Lark, Western, *Calif.*
* Lincoln, *Calif.*; +*NE*
* Rufous-crowned, *Calif.*
* Savannah, *NE, So.Pr., and Calif.*
* Song, *Pac., mainly Calif.*
+ Tree, *NE*
* White-crowned, *NE*; +*Pac.*
+ White-throated, *NE*
Towhee
* Brown, *Calif.*
+ Red-eyed, *NE*
Fur and Game Mammals (plants)
    Rabbit
    + Cottontail, Audubon, *Calif.*
    + Cottontail, Eastern, *Conn.*
Hoofed Browsers (plants)
    − Sheep, Mountain, *Colo.*

Buttercup Family: *Ranunculaceae*

BANEBERRIES
Actaea

[0*/2 users] Three species of baneberry occur in the United States—two in the East and one in the Pacific region. The berries of these woodland plants are somewhat poisonous to man.

Upland Gamebirds (fruit)
+ Grouse, Ruffed, *Pa.*
Small Mammals (fruit)
− Mouse, White-footed, *E*

BUTTERCUPS
Ranunculus

[4*/21 users] Of about 300 species of buttercups that are found in the cool, temperate regions of the world, nearly 40 are widely distributed over the United States. Buttercups generally prefer moist meadows and marshes. A few are fully aquatic. One of the most abundant buttercups in meadows and lawns in the East is the attractive introduced species *R. bulbosus.*

Though the seeds (akenes) are eaten by several kinds of birds and rodents, the amounts eaten are generally small.

Waterfowl (seeds, plants)
* Duck, Wood, *SE*
Marshbirds and Shorebirds (seeds)
+ Rail, Sora, *W*
Upland Gamebirds (seeds, foliage)
+ Grouse, Ruffed, *NE*
+ Pheasant, Ring-necked, *N*
Quail
+ California, *Calif.*
+ Valley, *Calif.*
* Turkey, Wild, *Alleghenies and Mo.*
Songbirds (seeds)
* Bunting, Snow, *NE*
+ Redpoll, Hoary, *NE*
+ Sparrow, Golden-crowned, *Calif.*
Fur and Game Mammals (plants, seeds)

+ Muskrat, *NE*
+ Rabbit, Cottontail, *NE*
− Skunk, Eastern, *N.Y.*
Squirrel
+ Fox, *E.Tex.*
+ Gray, *E.Tex.*
Small Mammals (seeds)
+ Chipmunk, Eastern, *NE*
− Ground Squirrel, Beechey, *Calif.*
Mouse
+ Lemming, *NE and No.Pr.*
+ Meadow, *E*
+ Pine, *NE*
Hoofed Browsers (plants)
* Deer, Black-tailed, *Calif.*

Poppy Family: *Papaveraceae*

CALIFORNIA-POPPY
Eschscholtzia californica

[2*/4 users] The California-poppy is abundant locally along the Pacific coast and in some western parts of the Mountain–Desert region. Here, the

 Main range ░░░ Local occurrence

lacey-leaved plants cover extensive areas with masses of beautiful golden

blooms. However, the wildlife value of the California-poppy is very limited— a principal user being the mourning dove.

Upland Gamebirds (seeds)
** Dove, Mourning, *Calif.*
Songbirds (seeds)
+ Meadowlark, Western, *Pac.*
Small Mammals (seeds)
− Ground Squirrel, Beechey, *Calif.*
− Rat, Banner-tailed Kangaroo, *Ariz.*

PRICKLYPOPPIES
Argemone

[1*/2 users] Half a dozen or more species of these large-flowered prickly weeds occur in the West and Southwest. It is somewhat surprising that their numerous spherical seeds are eaten so seldom by birds.

Upland Gamebirds (seeds)
* Dove, White-winged, Western, *Ariz.*
Songbirds (seeds)
+ Grosbeak, Pine, *Mt.–Des.*

Mustard Family: *Brassicaceae*

PEPPERGRASSES
Lepidium

[4*/7 users] Nearly 25 species of peppergrass, or pepperweed, are well distributed throughout the United States. Though these common weeds of back yards and open areas are widespread and locally abundant, their use by wildlife is slight and is confined largely to the West. The small seeds, two to a pod, are eaten by birds and rodents.

Waterfowl (plants)
* Goose, Canada, *Utah*

Songbirds (seeds)
* Finch, Rosy, *Pac.*
+ Goldfinch, Lawrence, *Mt.–Des. and Pac.*
Small Mammals (pods, leaves)
Rat
+ Kangaroo, Banner-tailed, *Ariz.*
** Kangaroo, Giant, *Calif.*
− Kangaroo, Tulare, *Calif.*
Hoofed Browsers (plants)
+ Deer, White-tailed, *Tex.*

Reference: Perennial Peppergrass. E. A. Helgeson. *N. Dak. Agr. Col. Exp. Sta. Bul.* 292, pp. 13–24, 1940.

MUSTARDS
Brassica

[6*/10 users] The genus *Brassica* is represented by five species widely distributed over the United States. Only in the Pacific region, and particularly in California, are mustards abundant and important. In season, California lowlands and slopes are yellow with the flowers of these prolific weeds.

The oily seeds of these plants, often

397

fed to cagebirds, are relished by game-birds and songbirds.

Upland Gamebirds (seeds)
** Dove, Mourning, *Pac.*
* Pheasant, Ring-necked, *Wash.*
− Woodcock, *NE*
Songbirds (seeds)
*** Finch, Common House, *Calif.*
+ Lark, California Horned, *Calif.*

+ Nuthatch, Pygmy, *Calif.*
Fur and Game Mammals (plants)
+ Rabbit, Cottontail, *Conn.*
Small Mammals (seeds)
+ Ground Squirrel, Townsend, *Wash.*
− Mouse, Pocket, *Pac.*
Hoofed Browsers (plants)
+ Deer, Mule, *Calif.*

WINTERCRESS
Barbarea

[1*/2 users] The yellow, mustard-like flowers of wintercress are a common sight in eastern fields, meadows, road-sides, and gardens. Three species occur in the East and one in the Northwest.

Upland Gamebirds (seeds)
+ Dove, Mourning, *NE*
Songbirds (seeds)
* Grosbeak, Pine, *NE*

TANSYMUSTARD
Descurainia (sophia)

[13*/7 users] This genus of cut-leaved, yellow-flowered plants has about 10 representatives in the West—mainly in the Mountain–Desert and Pacific regions. Tansymustards grow in fields, roadsides, near ditches, and in other open areas where there is a medium amount of moisture. Their small seeds are eaten, sometimes pods and all, by western quail, and the plants are utilized by other wildlife.

Waterfowl (plants)
+ Goose, Canada, *Pac.*
Upland Gamebirds (seed, pods)
Quail
** Gambel, *SW*
** Scaled, Arizona, *SW*
+ Valley, *Nev.*
Small Mammals (plants)
Prairie Dog
+ Black-tailed, *W.Pr.*
+ White-tailed, *Mont. and Wyo.*
Hoofed Browsers (plants)
* Antelope, *No.Pr. and Mt.–Des.*

Caper Family: *Capparidaceae*

BEEPLANTS
Cleome

[4*/3 users] About half a dozen species of beeplants grow in the United States, but only in the West are these attrac-tive-flowered plants abundant enough to have even limited value for wildlife.

Upland Gamebirds (seeds)
+ Dove, Mourning, *Mt.–Des.*
− Pheasant, Ring-necked, *Utah*
Small Mammals (seeds)
** Mouse, Pocket, *W.Pr. and Mt.–Des.*

Rose Family: *Rosaceae*

STRAWBERRIES (Wild and Cultivated)
Fragaria

[6*/31 users] Strawberries are raised throughout most of the United States.

Also they grow wild practically every-where except in arid regions. Some of

the common wild strawberries are simply naturalized escapes from cultivation. Four species are listed.

It would be difficult to say with certainty whether the consumption of strawberries by wildlife involves wild plants more than garden strawberries, but it seems probable that the widely distributed wild plants predominate in wildlife use. For this reason strawberries are listed under Upland Weeds and Herbs. Upland gamebirds feed on the tender leaves of wild strawberries as well as on the fruit.

The eating of garden strawberries by birds or other wildlife involves definite damage, though often the extent of loss is negligible when the total crop is considered. Though not listed in the tabulation below, the robin is recognized as a problem where strawberries are raised.

Upland Gamebirds (leaves, fruit)
Grouse
+   Blue, *No.Mt.–Des. and Pac. NW*
*   Ruffed, *NE*
*   Pheasant, Ring-necked, *N.Y.*
+   Prairie Chicken, Greater, *Wis.*
+   Quail, Valley, *Calif.*
Songbirds (fruit)
+   Crow, *E*
+   Catbird, *W*
+   Finch, Brown-capped Rosy, *So. Mt.–Des.*

+   Grosbeak, Pine, *Pac.*
Sparrow
+   Swamp, *NE*
+   White-throated, *NE*
+   Thrasher, Brown, *NE and Pr.*
+   Towhee, *NE*
+   Veery, *NE*
**   Waxwing, Cedar, *Pac.*
Fur and Game Mammals (fruit, leaves)
*   Hare, Varying, *Minn.*
+   Opossum, *NE*
Rabbit
−   Cottontail, Eastern, *Conn.*
*   Cottontail, New England, *New England*
−   Skunk, Eastern, *N.Y.*
Squirrel
−   Fox, Western, *Mich.*
−   Red, *NE*
Small Mammals (fruit, leaves)
Chipmunk
+   Eastern, *NE*
−   Lyster, *N.H.*
+   Ground Squirrel, Franklin, *No. Pr.*
Mouse
+   Meadow, *E*
−   White-footed, *E*
−   Rat, Portola Wood, *Calif.*
Hoofed Browsers (plants)
Deer
+   Mule, *Utah*
+   White-tailed, *E*

CINQUEFOILS
Potentilla

9*/10 users] About 100 species of cinquefoils are found in the United States. Though common to abundant in many places, their wildlife value is

399

relatively low. The usefulness of the cinquefoils is confined largely to the West.

Upland Gamebirds (seeds, foliage)
+ Grouse, Ruffed, *Maine*
+ Woodcock, *E*
Songbirds (seeds)
+ Bunting, Snow, *NW*
* Finch, Rosy, *Pac.*

Fur and Game Mammals (foliage)
+ Rabbit, Cottontail, *E*
Small Mammals (seeds, foliage)
** Chipmunk, Least, *W.Pr. and Mt.–Des.*
Ground Squirrel
* Richardson, *No.Pr.*
* Mantled, *W*
Hoofed Browsers (plants)
− Sheep, Mountain, *Mt.–Des.*

Senna Family: *Caesalpiniaceae*

PARTRIDGEPEAS
Chamaecrista

Region of main use   Lesser use

[**4*/4 users**] This yellow-flowered, fern-leaved genus of plants is largely tropical. The 20 or so species of *Chamaecrista* found in this country are mainly in the South. Partridgepeas are upland plants of fields, roadsides, and waste places. The two most common and most important species in the Southeast are showy partridgepea (*C. fasciculata*) and sensitive partridgepea (*C. procumbens*). *C. leptadenia* is a principal species in the Southwest.

The hard, flattish, pitted seeds of partridgepeas are a valuable food for the bobwhite quail in the Southeast, but beyond this, the wildlife importance of the plants is limited.

Upland Gamebirds (seeds)
Prairie Chicken
* Greater, *Ill.*
+ Lesser, *Okla.*
** Quail, Bobwhite, *SE*; +*NE*
Small Mammals (seeds)
* Rat, Banner-tailed Kangaroo, *Ariz.*
Hoofed Browsers (plants)
+ Deer, White-tailed, *Ala.*

Reference: Useful Partridge Peas. Allen M. Pearson. Alabama Conservation, 1943. 4 pp.

Pea Family: *Fabaceae*

LUPINES
Lupinus

[**19*/13 users**] The lupines, called bluebonnets in Texas, are primarily an American genus. Nearly 200 species are present in this country—mostly in the West. They grow in habitats ranging from arid plains and deserts to

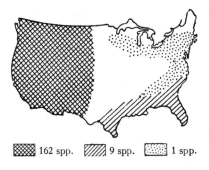

▩ 162 spp. ▨ 9 spp. ▥ 1 spp.

moist stream margins. Some lupines are poisonous to livestock. Others, because of their ornamental value, are used in horticulture. The hard smooth seeds of these beautiful, finger-leafed plants are valuable to several species of western upland gamebirds.

Upland Gamebirds (seeds)
 Quail
 ** California, *Calif.*
 ** Gambel, *SW*
 *** Mountain, *Pac.*
 ** Scaled, Chestnut-bellied, *Tex.*
 * Valley, *Calif.*
 + Turkey, Wild, *Ariz. and N.Mex.*
Songbirds (seeds)
 + Nutcracker, Clark, *NW*
Fur and Game Mammals (plants)
 + Mountain Beaver, *Pac.*
Small Mammals (seeds)
 − Chipmunk, Gila, *Ariz.*
 * Ground Squirrel, California, *Calif.*
 Rat
 * Kangaroo, Merriam, *SW Ariz.*
 + Kangaroo, various spp., *Calif.*
 ** Rock Squirrel, *Calif.*
Hoofed Browsers (plants)
 * Deer, Mule, *So.Mt.–Des.*

Reference: Lupines, New Legumes for the South. *U.S. Dept. Agr. Farmers' Bul* 1946, 1943. 10 pp.

BURCLOVERS
Medicago

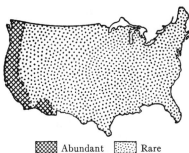

▩ Abundant ▥ Rare

[14*/9 users] There are 40 or 50 species of burclovers or medicks in the world, all native to the Mediterranean region. Four species are now well established in this country, and still others are being introduced for trial as forage plants. Burclovers are abundant only on the Pacific coast, and here they are of major value to some kinds of wildlife. The outstanding species is the California, or toothed, burclover (*M. hispida*). Spotted burclover (*M. arabica*) is becoming increasingly plentiful in California and may eventually rival California burclover in usefulness to wildlife. Burclover along with filaree and minerslettuce makes a lush growth in West coast orchards and fields during the late winter and spring. During these seasons its herbage is used extensively by California quail.

Upland Gamebirds (leaves, pods)
 + Pheasant, Ring-necked, *NW*
 Quail
 ** California, *Calif.*
 *** Valley, *Nev.*

Songbirds (seeds)
   * Grosbeak, Blue, *SW*
Small Mammals (pods)
   + Ground Squirrel, Beechey, *Calif.*
   *** Rat, Santa Cruz Kangaroo, *Calif.*

   *** Rock Squirrel, *Calif.*
Hoofed Browsers (plants)
   Deer
   + Black-tailed, *Calif.*
   + Mule, *Calif.*

Reference: Bur-clover Cultivation and Utilization. *U.S. Dept. Agr. Farmers' Bul.* 1741, 1942. 12 pp.

SWEETCLOVERS
Melilotus

[7*/14 users] Sweetclover occurs throughout most of tne country but is more abundant in the West. Of our three species, one white-flowered and two yellow, the former is generally the more common. It (*M. alba*) is grown in some sections as a forage crop and is esteemed as a valuable honey plant. White sweetclover is particularly common along California roadsides, but it and its yellow-flowered relatives are plentiful near highways, along ditches, and in waste places in other parts of the country. The seeds are of moderate value to some upland gamebirds.

Upland Gamebirds (seeds)
   *** Grouse, Sharp-tailed, *Nebr.*
   ** Partridge, Hungarian, *Minn.*
   + Pheasant, Ring-necked, *NW*
   + Prairie Chicken, Greater, *Minn. and Wis.*
   Quail
   +   Gambel, *SW*
   **   Valley, *Nev.*
Fur and Game Mammals (foliage, stems)
   − Muskrat, *Iowa*
   Rabbit
   − Cottontail, Eastern, *Ohio*
   − Cottontail, Oklahoma, *Okla.*

   − Swamp, *Okla.*
Small Mammals (seed pods, leaves)
   − Ground Squirrel, Beechey, *Calif.*
Hoofed Browsers (plants)
   + Antelope, *S.Dak.*
   Deer
   + Mule, *S.Dak.*
   + White-tailed, *Mo.*

References: Sweetclover in Corn Belt Farming. M. A. Crosby and L. W. Kephart. *U.S. Dept. Agr. Farmers' Bul.* 1653, 1939. 24 pp.
Sweet Clover. *U.S. Dept. Agr. Leaflet* 23, 1939. 8 pp.

CLOVERS
Trifolium

[49*/40 users] A majority of the 75 or more species of true clover (*Trifolium*) in the United States are found in the Pacific and Mountain–Desert regions. Among the native western species of importance to wildlife are tomcat

402

clover (*T. tridentatum*), clammy clover
(*T. obtusiflorum*), and foothill clover
(*T. ciliolatum*).

In the East there are 20 or more
species of clover, but only two or three
are of real consequence to wildlife.
The most important of these are red
clover (*T. pratense*), white or dutch
clover (*T. repens*), and alsike clover
(*T. hybridum*). All three of these introduced forage plants have become
common in fields, meadows, roadsides,
and other moist places. White clover,
in addition, is commonly grown in
lawns. The small, yellow-flowered hop
clover (*T. procumbens*), rabbitfoot
clover (*T. arvense*), and other species
are locally plentiful in the East, but
their value to wildlife is slight.

Wild animals, like domestic livestock, relish the foliage of clovers. The
small, hard seeds of western clovers
are important to quail, but other upland gamebirds limit their use of
clovers almost entirely to the foliage.
Small quantities of clover seeds have
been taken by many birds other than
those listed.

**Marshbirds and Shorebirds (foliage,
seeds)**
+ Sandpiper, Pectoral, *U.S.*
Upland Gamebirds (foliage, seeds)
Grouse
* Blue, *Pac.NW*
*** Ruffed, *Wis.*; **NE
* Sage, *No.Mt.–Des.*
*** Sharp-tailed, *Great Lakes Area
and W.Nebr.*
* Partridge, Hungarian, *NW*
+ Pheasant, Ring-necked, *N*
*** Prairie Chicken, Greater, *Wis.;
No.Pr.
Quail
* Bobwhite, *So.Tex.*
* California, *Calif.*
*** Mountain, *Pac.*
* Scaled, Chestnut-bellied, *Tex.*
*** Valley, *Calif.*
* Turkey, Wild, *Mo.*; +*E*

Songbirds (seeds)
+ Lark, Horned, *E*
+ Pipit, *Pac.*
+ Longspur, Smith, *Ill.*
+ Nuthatch, Pygmy, *Calif.*
Sparrow
+ Lincoln, *Calif.*
+ Sharp-tailed, *Atl. Coast*
**Fur and Game Mammals (foliage,
plants)**
− Beaver, *N.Y.*
* Hare, Varying, *Minn.*; −*Wis.*
*** Marmot, *NW*
− Muskrat, *Ohio and Iowa*
+ Porcupine, *Mt.–Des.*
Rabbit
** Cottontail, *Conn. and Ohio;
+Calif.*
− Cottontail, Mearns, *Iowa*
+ Raccoon, *Iowa*
* Skunk, Eastern, *N.Y.*
*** Woodchuck, *NE*
Small Mammals (pods, foliage)
+ Gopher, Pocket, *NE and No.Pr.*
Ground Squirrel
+ Douglas, *Oreg.*
** Thirteen-lined, *Pr.*
Mouse
+ Lemming, *NE and No.Pr.*
− Meadow, *E*
+ Pine, *NE*
Hoofed Browsers (plants)
Deer
* Mule, *S.Dak.*
+ White-tailed, *E*
− Sheep, Mountain, *Colo.*

References: Red Clover Culture. *U.S. Dept. Agr. Farmers' Bul.* 1339, 1926. 30 pp.
White Clover. *U.S. Dept. Agr. Leaflet* 119, 1936. 8 pp.

Crimson Clover. *U.S. Dept. Agr. Leaflet* 160, 1938. 8 pp.
Ladino White Clover for the Northeastern States. *U.S. Dept. Agr. Farmers' Bul.* 1910, 1942. 10 pp.

DEERVETCHES
Lotus

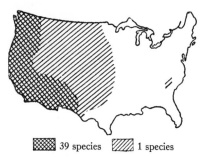

Deervetch seeds, various species

☒☒☒ 39 species ▨▨ 1 species

[27*/15 users] The deervetches are almost exclusively western, with about 40 species growing in the Pacific and Mountain–Desert regions. These small clover-like plants grow in open waste places varying from arid to moist. In some areas they are abundant locally and have forage value for livestock. Among the more common and important species are Spanishclover (*L. americanus*), coast (*L. formosissimus*), foothill (*L. humistratus*), and Chilean deervetch (*L. subpinnatus*). As with the clovers, both the seeds and foliage are relished by wildlife. The seeds are particularly important to western species of quail and to small rodents.

Upland Gamebirds (seeds)
+ Dove, Mourning, *Pac.*
+ Pheasant, Ring-necked, *S.Dak.*
　Quail
* 　California, *Calif.*
*** 　Gambel, *SW*
* 　Mountain, *Pac.*
* 　Scaled, Arizona, *SW*
*** 　Valley, *Calif.*
Fur and Game Mammals (plants)
** Rabbit, Cottontail, *Calif.*
Small Mammals (seeds, foliage)
*** Mouse, Pocket, *Calif.; *W.Pr. and Mt.–Des.*
　Rat
* 　Kangaroo, Banner-tailed, *Ariz.*
+ 　Kangaroo, Ord, *W*
+ 　Kangaroo, Tulare, *Calif.*
* Rock Squirrel, *Calif.*
Hoofed Browsers (plants)
*** Deer, Mule, *Calif.*
** Moose, *No.Mt.–Des.*

LOCOWEEDS
Astragalus

[9*/10 users] This very large genus of at least 1,000 species includes some 200 in the United States—the great majority of them in the West. Many are poisonous to livestock and cause serious losses in dry seasons when good forage plants are scarce. The locoweeds, including poisonvetches and milkvetches, produce pods of hard seeds which are eaten by western gamebirds and rodents. Big game feed on these plants to a limited extent but whether

or not locoweeds are poisonous to such wildlife is not known.

Upland Gamebirds (seeds)
　Quail
+ 　California, *Calif.*
+ 　Gambel, *SW*
+ 　Scaled, Chestnut-bellied, *Tex.*
+ Turkey, Wild, *Tex.*
Fur and Game Mammals (pods, seeds)
** Marmot, *W.Pr. and Mt.–Des.*

Small Mammals (seeds)
Mouse
+   Harvest, California, *Calif.*
** Pocket, *W.Pr. and Mt.–Des.*
*   Rat, Banner-tailed Kangaroo,
    Ariz.

Hoofed Browsers (plants)
+ Antelope, *N.Mex. and S.E. Mont.*
− Sheep, Mountain, *Yellowstone Nat. Park*

BEGGARWEEDS
Desmodium

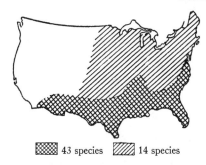

[████] 43 species   [▨▨] 14 species

[2*/4 users] There are more than 50 species of beggarweeds in the United States—most of them in the Southeast. After a late summer ramble through old fields many of us have had the chore of picking their flat seeds from our clothing. Though common in fields, along fence rows, and in open woods in the East, beggarweeds have only limited value for wildlife. The bobwhite quail is the only species known to feed on them to any extent.

Upland Gamebirds (seeds)
** Quail, Bobwhite, *SE*; +*Tex. and Okla.*
+ Turkey, Wild, *Mo.*
Small Mammals (seeds)
− Mouse, White-footed, *Minn.*
Hoofed Browsers (plants)
+ Deer, White-tailed, *E*

LESPEDEZAS
Lespedeza

[9*/7 users] Our lespedezas, both native and introduced, are confined to the East and the eastern part of the Prairies. There are about 15 native species, most of them with upright wand-like stems. In addition we have several introduced lespedezas, and still others, new to this country, are being tested by the Department of Agriculture. Two widespread introduced species, common lespedeza (*L. striata*) and Korean lespedeza (*L. stipulacea*), are the only annual ones that have real importance to wildlife. Common lespedeza is particularly plentiful in the Southeast, while the Korean species is more prevalent farther north. Sericea lespedeza (*L. cuneata*), a perennial shrubby species from the orient, has been planted extensively in southeastern field borders during the past decade. Shrub lespedeza (*L. bicolor*), another recent introduction, has given promise of being valuable to bobwhite quail, both for food and cover. The native species of lespedeza are common and yet nowhere abundant.

Ordinarily we think of lespedezas as plants of considerable importance to wildlife; so it may be surprising to find that the genus has a use ratio of only 9*/7 users. The explanation, in part, is found in the data below. The plants have real importance to only one wildlife species though a very important one, the bobwhite quail. The use of lespedezas by songbirds is slight.

Upland Gamebirds (seeds)
+   Dove, Mourning, *SE*
+   Grouse, Ruffed, *Pa. and Ohio*
−   Partridge, Chukar, *Mo.*
**** Quail, Bobwhite, *SE*; +*NE*
*   Turkey, Wild, *Va. and Mo.*

Songbirds (seeds)
+ Junco, *NE*

Hoofed Browsers (plants)
*** Deer, White-tailed, *Mo.*

References: The Annual Lespedezas as Forage and Soil Conserving Crops. A. J. Pieters. *U.S. Dept. Agr. Circ.* 536, 1939. 53 pp.
Growth and Distribution of Japan Clover in Ohio. M. V. Bailey. *Jour. Amer. Soc. Agron.*, Vol. 20, pp. 118–122, 1928.

VETCHES
Vicia

[1*/13 users] Vetches, both native and naturalized, total about 25 species in the United States. Though they are widely distributed, these attractive blue or purple flowered, viny herbs are most common in the East. Both the seeds and foliage are eaten to a limited extent by birds and rodents.

Upland Gamebirds (seeds, leaves)
+ Dove, Mourning, *SE*
    Grouse
*   Blue, *No.Mt.–Des.*
+   Ruffed, *NE and Ohio*
+   Sharp-tailed, *Great Lakes Area*

+ Pheasant, Ring-necked, *Pac. NW*
+ Prairie Chicken, Greater, *N.Dak.*
    Quail
+   Bobwhite, *SE*
+   Scaled, Arizona, *SW*
+ Turkey, Wild, *Alleghenies*
Songbirds (seeds)
+ Sparrow, Song, *NE*
Small Mammals (seeds, plants)
+ Ground Squirrel, Douglas, *Oreg.*
+ Moles, *Oreg.*
+ Rat, Wood, *Calif.*

Reference: Vetch Culture and Uses. *U.S. Dept. Agr. Farmers' Bul.* 1740, 1934. 22 pp.

HOGPEANUTS
Amphicarpa (Falcata)

[3*/5 users] This twining woodland vine is represented by two species in the East. One peculiarity of the plant is the fact that some of its pods become subterranean, as in the peanut. Quail eat both the aerial and subterranean seeds of hogpeanuts, but the vines are locally abundant at best and so are of limited significance to wildlife.

Upland Gamebirds (seeds, leaves)
+ Grouse, Ruffed, *NE*
+ Pheasant, Ring-necked, *Mich.*
* Quail, Bobwhite, *NE*; +*SE*
Small Mammals (seeds)
    Mouse
+   Meadow, *N.Dak.*
*   White-footed, *E*

BEANS
Phaseolus

[4*/4 users] There are about a dozen species of native wild beans (*Phaseolus*) in the South. These close relatives of our cultivated beans are plentiful enough locally to be of some small value to gamebirds.

Upland Gamebirds (seeds)
    Quail
+   Bobwhite, *SE*
*   Gambel, *SW*
*   Scaled, Chestnut-bellied, *Tex.*
Songbirds (seeds)
+ Jay, Piñon, *Mt.–Des.*

Geranium Family: *Geraniaceae*

WILD GERANIUMS
Geranium

[4*/9 users] There are 30 or more species of wild geranium or cranesbill in the United States—about 20 in the West and 10 in the East. They are more closely related to filaree, or heronbill (*Erodium*), than to the common potted geraniums which belong to another genus, *Pelargonium*. Some, such as the common wild cranesbill (*Geranium maculatum*) of the East, are woodland species while others grow in open places. Carolina geranium (*G. carolinianum*) is the only common open-field species in the East, but the numerous western ones are mainly residents of open areas. The seeds of wild geraniums are eaten by birds and rodents.

Upland Gamebirds (seeds)
  * Dove, Mourning, *SE*; +*NE*
  + Quail, Bobwhite, *SE*

Songbirds (seeds)
  + Towhee, Brown, *Calif.*
Small Mammals (seeds)
  Chipmunk
  * Lake Superior, *Minn.*
  * Northwest, *Pac.NW*
  * Least, *Minn.*
Hoofed Browsers (plants)
  Deer
  + Mule, *Utah*
  + White-tailed, *N.C.*
  + Moose, Shiras, *Yellowstone Park*

FILAREES
Erodium

Abundant—5 sp.
Common—2 sp.   Rare—1 sp.

[84*/50 users] This Mediterranean genus is abundant in California and neighboring states but is sparingly represented by a single species in the rest of the country. Of the five species in the Far West, the most important are common (*E. cicutarium*), musk (*E. moschatum*), and big filaree (*E. botrys*).

Filaree, also, known as heronbill,

makes a lush growth in Pacific coast orchards and fields during winter and early spring. It also occurs on slopes and mesas in the western parts of the Mountain–Desert region. This dainty-flowered annual is a valued forage for livestock and has major importance for western wildlife. The awl-shaped hard seeds are eaten by many kinds of birds, and the foliage is relished by various browsers.

Upland Gamebirds (seeds, foliage)
+ Dove, Mourning, *Mt.–Des. and Pac.*
  Quail
*** California, *Calif.*
* Gambel, *SW*
* Mountain, *Pac.*
* Scaled, Arizona, *SW*
*** Valley, *Calif.*
* Turkey, Wild, *Ariz. and N.Mex.*

Songbirds (seeds)
  Blackbird
* Brewer, *Calif.*
+ Redwing, *Calif.*
* Redwing, Tricolored, *Calif.*
+ Bunting, Lazuli, *Pac.*
**** Finch, Common House, *Calif.*
  Goldfinch
+ Green-backed, *Calif.*
*** Willow, *Calif.*
* Grosbeak, Black-headed, *Calif.*
* Junco, Oregon, *Calif.*
** Lark, California Horned, *Calif.*
+ Meadowlark, Western, *Pac.*
**** Siskin, Pine, *W*
  Sparrow
* Bell, *Calif.*
*** Chipping, *SW*
+ English, *Mt.–Des.*
+ Golden-crowned, *Calif.*
* Large-billed, *Calif.*
+ Lark, Western, *Mt.–Des. and Pac.*
** Rufous-crowned, *Calif.*
+ Savannah, *Calif.*
+ Song, *Pac.*
+ White-crowned, *Pac.*
+ Thrush, Varied, *Pac.*
  Towhee
* Brown, *Calif.*
+ Green-tailed, *Mt.–Des.*
+ Spotted, *Calif.*
+ Waxwing, Cedar, *Pac.*
+ Wren, Cactus, *Calif. and Ariz.*

Fur and Game Mammals (plants)
+ Jack Rabbit, California, *Calif.*
+ Rabbit, Audubon Cottontail, *Calif.*

Small Mammals (seeds, foliage, plants)
*** Gopher, Pocket, *Calif.*
  Ground Squirrel,
**** Beechey, *Calif.*
** Columbian, *No.Mt.–Des. and Pac.*
**** Nelson, *Calif.*
*** Mouse, Pocket, *Calif.*
  Rat
+ Kangaroo, Banner-tailed, *Ariz.*
**** Kangaroo, Giant, *Calif.*
* Kangaroo, Merriam, *SW*
+ Kangaroo, Tulare, *Calif.*
*** Rock Squirrel, *Calif.*

Hoofed Browsers (plants)
  Deer
*** Black-tailed, *Calif.*
+ Mule, *Calif.*
+ Sheep, Bighorn, *N.Mex.*

Reference: Alfileria (Filaree) Seed. W. A. Dayton. *Rhodora*, Vol. 39 (463), 1937. 3 pp.

Woodsorrel Family: *Oxalidaceae*

WOODSORRELS
Oxalis

[11*/16 users] The genus *Oxalis* has about 20 species in the United States. Some are attractive woodland plants, but more are common weeds of moist open or semiopen areas. The most abundant of these acid-tasting plants is common yellow woodsorrel (*O. stricta*). Violet woodsorrel (*O. violacea*) and two or three other species have subterranean bulbs which are of some value to wildlife. The succulent, three-leaflet leaves and minute seeds are also eaten.

Upland Gamebirds (seeds, leaves, bulbs)
  Dove
+ Ground, *Gulf Coast*
+ Mourning, *E and Pr.*
+ Grouse, Ruffed, *NE*

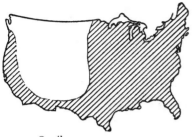

Quail
+   Bobwhite, *E*
**   Mearns, *SW*
Songbirds (seeds)
+   Bunting, Painted, *Tex.*
    Junco
+   Oregon, *Calif.*
*   Slate-colored, *NE*
+   Lark, Horned, *E and W*
    Sparrow
+   Field, *NE*

+   Grasshopper, Eastern, *NE*
*   Grasshopper, Western, *W*
*   Savannah, *So.Pr.; +NE*
+   Tree, *E.Pr.*
Fur and Game Mammals (leaves)
−   Rabbit, Cottontail, *Conn.*
Hoofed Browsers (plants)
+   Deer, White-tailed, *Tex.*

Spurge Family: *Euphorbiaceae*

DOVEWEEDS
Croton

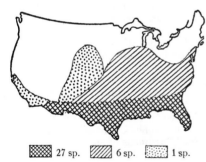

▨ 27 sp. ▥ 6 sp. ⬚ 1 sp.

doves. Among the most important species are common (*C. glandulosus*), one-seed (*C. monanthogynus*), woolly (*C. capitatus*), and Texas doveweed (*C. texensis*).

[35*/21 users] Of the 700 odd species of *Croton*, about 30 are present in this country—mainly in the South. These weedy plants occur in fields, pastures, on railroad embankments, and in other open places.

The large, oily seeds of doveweeds are useful to upland gamebirds and songbirds in the South. The plants earn their common name by being of especial value to three kinds of native

Upland Gamebirds (seeds)
    Dove
***   Ground, *Gulf Coast*
***   Mourning, *So.Pr. and So.Mt.−Des.; *SE; +NE*
**** White-winged, Eastern, *Tex.*
**   White-winged, Western, *Ariz.*
*   Prairie Chicken, Atwater, *Tex.*
    Quail
**   Bobwhite, *Tex.–Okla.; +SE and E.Pr.*
+   Scaled, Arizona, *SW*

409

* Scaled, Chestnut-bellied, *Tex.*
+ Turkey, Wild, *Tex. and Mo.*
Songbirds (seeds)
** Blackbird, Redwing, *SE*
* Cardinal, *Pr.*
** Cowbird, *SE*
    Pipit
* American, *S*
** Sprague, *Pr.*
*** Pyrrhuloxia, *Tex.*

    Sparrow
* Lark, Western, *Pr.*
+ Pine-woods, *SE*
+ White-crowned, *Pr.*
Small Mammals (seeds)
    Mouse
+ Pocket, Pacific, *Calif.*
+ Pocket, Prairie, *Pr.*
Hoofed Browsers (plants)
+ Deer, White-tailed, *Tex.*

TURKEYMULLEIN
Eremocarpus setigerus

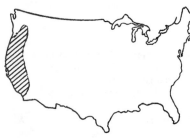

[31*/20 users] Turkeymullein is closely related to the doveweeds (*Croton*) and was at one time classed with that genus. This low hairy herb is confined to California and adjoining areas. It makes up for its restricted distribution by abundance—particularly in fields and pastures of the California central valley.

Within its limited distribution, turkeymullein is an important wildlife food plant. Its medium-large oily seeds are relished by gamebirds, songbirds, and rodents. The leaves of this plant were formerly crushed and thrown into streams by the California Indians to poison or stupefy fish.

Upland Gamebirds (seeds)
**** Dove, Mourning, *Pac.*
    Quail
** California, *Calif.*

* Mountain, *Pac.*
*** Valley, *Calif.*
Songbirds (seeds)
*** Finch, Common House, *Calif.*
* Goldfinch, Green-backed, *Calif.*
+ Lark, Horned, *Calif.*
    Sparrow
**** Bell, *Calif.*
* Golden-crowned, *Calif.*
+ Lark, Western, *Calif.*
*** Savannah, *Calif.*
+ Towhee, Brown, *Calif.*
+ Wren-tit, *Pac.*
Fur and Game Mammals (plants)
+ Rabbit, Cottontail, *Calif.*
Small Mammals (seeds, plants)
    Ground Squirrel
− Beechey, *Calif.*
** Columbian, *No.Mt.–Des. and Pac.*
+ Mantled, *W*
**** Nelson, *Calif.*
+ Rat, Kangaroo, *Calif.*
** Rock Squirrel, Colorado, *Calif.*

SPURGES
Euphorbia

[14*/15 users] As treated here, the genus *Euphorbia* includes the ground-spurges (*Chamaesyce*) and several other groups that some botanists recognize

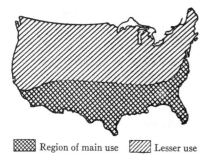

 Region of main use Lesser use

as distinct genera. There are about 75 spurges widely distributed in the United States. About two-thirds are the spreading or low-growing ground-spurges. The South and particularly the Southeast has more than its proportionate share of these milky-juiced, small-flowered plants. The flowering (*E. corollata*) and spotted spurges (*E. maculata*) are outstanding in abundance. The seeds of spurges, regularly borne three in a capsule, are popular

with several upland gamebirds and with the pipit.

Upland Gamebirds (seeds)
    Dove
  *   Ground, *Gulf Coast*
  ** Mourning, *So.Pr.;* +*E* and *Mt.–Des.*
  ** Prairie Chicken, Greater, *Ill.*
    Quail
  +   Bobwhite, *SE*
  ** Gambel, *SW*
  +   Mearns, *SW*
  +   Scaled, Chestnut-bellied, *Tex.*

Songbirds (seeds)
  + Bunting, Painted, *Tex.*
  + Lark, Horned, *E*
 *** Pipit, American, *SE*
  + Sparrow, Chipping, *E*

Small Mammals (seeds, plants)
    Rat
  *   Kangaroo, Merriam, *SW*
  −   Kangaroo, Tulare, *Calif.*

Hoofed Browsers (plants)
  + Antelope, *No.Pr. and Mt.–Des.*
  + Sheep, Mountain, *N.Mex.*

Reference: Leafy Spurge, Life History and Habits. Herbert C. Hanson and Velva E. Rudd. *N. Dak. Agr. Exp. Sta. Bul.* 266, 1933. 24 pp.

Jewelweed Family: *Balsaminaceae*

JEWELWEEDS
Impatiens

Snap!

[**4***/**7 users**] Three species of jewelweed occur in the Northwest and two in the East. Only the eastern species are of known value to wildlife. Jewelweeds, also called snapweeds or touch-me-nots, like shade and are generally found in moist soil near springs, streams, or swamps, and on seasonally flooded

411

areas. The large seeds are eaten by several kinds of birds. The nectar from jewelweeds' tubular flowers is a favorite of hummingbirds.

Upland Gamebirds (seeds)
+ Grouse, Ruffed, *NE*
+ Pheasant, Ring-necked, *NE*

+ Prairie Chicken, Greater, *Wis.*
+ Quail, Bobwhite, *E*
Songbirds (nectar)
** Hummingbird, Ruby-throated, *E*
Fur and Game Mammals (plants)
− Hare, Varying, *Wis.*
Small Mammals (seeds)
+ Mouse, White-footed, *E*

Violet Family: *Violaceae*

VIOLETS
Viola

[2*/9 users] Of the nearly 250 violets in the world, about 85 occur in the United States. Species of violets are found in practically every section of the country, but their greatest abundance is in the East. The seeds of violets are eaten by several upland gamebirds, and the tuberous roots are relished by the wild turkey.

Upland Gamebirds (seeds)
Dove
+ Ground, *Gulf Coast*
+ Mourning, *NE*

+ Grouse, Ruffed, *NE*
Quail
+ Bobwhite, *SE*
* Valley, *Nev.*
+ Turkey, Wild, *E*
Songbirds (seeds)
* Junco, *NE*
Fur and Game Mammals (foliage, plants)
+ Rabbit, Cottontail, *Conn.*
Small Mammals (seeds)
Mouse
+ Pine, *NE*
+ White-footed, *E*

Evening Primrose Family: *Onagraceae*

FIREWEEDS
Epilobium (Chamaenerion)

[6*/5 users] We have two species of fireweed in most of the northern wooded sections of the country: the common (*C. angustifolium*) and alpine fireweed (*C. latifolium*). The former has much the wider range of the two. These beautiful, tall, lavender-flowered plants spring up as a temporary covering in unsightly areas produced by forest fires or lumbering operations. They are valuable honey plants, and beekeepers have been known to follow logging camps to take advantage of them. It is probable that fireweed is

used by western hoofed browsers to a greater extent than indicated in the listing below.

Small Mammals (seeds)
Chipmunk
** Northwest, *Pac.NW*
+ Various spp., *Mt.–Des. and Pac.*
* Pika, *Pac.*
Hoofed Browsers (plants)
+ Deer, Columbian Black-tailed, *Oreg.*
* Moose, *No.Mt.–Des.*

Parsley Family: *Umbelliferae*

WILDCARROT
Daucus carota

[1*/5 users] The common wildcarrot, also known as Queen-Anne's-lace, is one of the most abundant eastern weeds but is of only slight value to wildlife.

The prickle-covered seeds of wildcarrot are eaten to only a small extent in view of their great abundance. A smaller, less abundant species, *D. pusillus*, occurs in the West.

Upland Gamebirds (seeds)
+ Grouse, Ruffed, *NE*

+ Pheasant, Ring-necked, *NE*
Small Mammals (seeds, roots)
* Mole, Townsend, *Wash. and Oreg.*
+ Mouse, Pine, *NE*
+ Rat, Cotton, *SE*

Morning-glory Family: *Convolvulaceae*

MORNING-GLORIES
Ipomoea

[5*/9 users] Most of the 50-odd species of morning-glory in the United States are in the South (including the Southwest). The large funnel-shaped flowers are attractive, but the plants have little value for wildlife. The large, angled seeds are occasionally eaten by upland gamebirds. The related genus *Evolvulus* has some usefulness for quail in the Southwest.

Upland Gamebirds (seeds)
+ Pheasant, Ring-necked, *N.Y.*

Quail
+ Bobwhite, *Pa.*
+ Gambel, *SW*
+ Mearns, *SW*
* Scaled, Arizona, *SW*
Fur and Game Mammals (leaves)
− Rabbit, Audubon Cottontail, *Calif.*
Small Mammals (roots)
Mouse
− Meadow, Least, *Manitoba*
* Pocket, *W.Pr. and Mt.–Des.*
+ Prairie Dog, Gunnison, *SW*

Phlox Family: *Polemoniaceae*

GILIAS
Gilia

[4*/9 users] This North American genus includes about 120 species of which nearly 100 grow in the United States—mainly in the West. The seeds of these attractively flowered plants are used by a few species of upland gamebirds and rodents.

Upland Gamebirds (seeds)
Grouse
+ Blue, *No.Mt.–Des.*
+ Sage, *No.Des.*

Quail
+ California, *Calif.*
+ Gambel, *SW*
+ Mountain, *Pac.*
* Valley, *Calif.*
Small Mammals (seeds, flowers, plants)
Ground Squirrel
* Columbian, *No.Mt.–Des. and Pac.*
* Mantled, *Calif.*
Hoofed Browsers (plants)
+ Sheep, Nelson Mountain, *Nev.*

Borage Family: *Boraginaceae*

FIDDLENECKS
Amsinckia

[11*/14 users] This American genus includes 15 species, all of them present in the Pacific and Mountain-Desert regions. Fiddlenecks are among the most

413

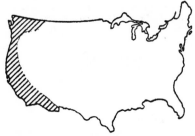

common weedy plants of open slopes and fields of the Pacific states. The limited consumption of the hard, ridged seeds (nutlets) does not seem to be entirely proportionate to the abundance of the plants. Fireweed fiddleneck (*A. intermedia*), Douglas fiddleneck (*A. douglasiana*), and devilslettuce (*A. tessalata*) are among the most common species that have been recorded as used by wildlife.

Upland Gamebirds (seeds)
*** Dove, Mourning, *Pac.*
  + Partridge, Hungarian, *NW*
Quail
  + California, *Calif.*
  + Mountain, *Pac.*
  + Plumed, *Pac.*
  + Valley, *Calif.*
Songbirds (seeds)
*** Goldfinch, Lawrence, *Mt.–Des. and Pac.*
Lark
  + Horned, *Calif.*
  + Meadow, *Pac.*
Towhee
 ** Abert, *Ariz.*
  + Brown, *Calif.*
  + Wren, Cactus, *Calif. and Ariz.*
Small Mammals (seeds)
  + Gopher, Pocket, *Calif.*
  + Ground Squirrel, Beechey, *Calif.*

Vervain Family: *Verbenaceae*

VERVAINS
Verbena

[4*/10 users] Vervains, or verbenas, include about 25 species. Blue (*V. hastata*), woolly (*V. stricta*), and white vervain (*V. urticaefolia*) are slender erect plants. Some southern species resemble the garden verbena in being semiprostrate and spreading. Vervains are locally abundant but have only slight value for wildlife. Their oblong seeds (nutlets) are eaten by several kinds of birds—generally in small amounts.

Marshbirds and Shorebirds (seeds)
  + Sandpiper, Stilt, *W*
Songbirds (seeds)
  * Bunting, Lark, *Pr.*
  * Cardinal, *NE*
  + Junco, *NE and Pr.*

Sparrow
  + Field, *Pr.*
  + Song, *NE*
 ** Swamp, *NE*
  + Tree, *NE*
  + White-crowned, *NE*
Fur and Game Mammals (plants)
  − Rabbit, Cottontail, *NE*

Potato Family: *Solanaceae*

GROUNDCHERRIES
Physalis

[1*/11 users] Groundcherries are present in all sections of the country: in fields, waste places, and on the open range. The characteristic berry, enclosed in a large yellowish, bladder-like covering is relished by gamebirds as well as by fur and game mammals, but the total extent of its use by wildlife is minor.

Upland Gamebirds (fruit)
+ Grouse, Sharp-tailed, *Minn. and Nebr.*
+ Pheasant, Ring-necked, *NW*
+ Quail, Bobwhite, *E*
+ Turkey, Wild, *E*

Fur and Game Mammals (fruit)
+ Cat, Ring-tailed, *Tex.*
+ Opossum, *Mo.*
Skunk
+ Eastern, *N.Y.*
+ Spotted, Prairie, *Iowa*
* Striped, *Iowa*
Small Mammals (fruit)
Mouse
+ Pine, *NE*
+ White-footed, *W*

NIGHTSHADES
Solanum

Region of main use · Lesser use

[17*/45 users] Of 1,000 or more species of nightshade (mainly in the tropics) only about 30 kinds are found in this country. In the main, they are partial to moist localities, though several species are common in well-drained soil of the open prairies. In the Northeast, only two species, black (*S. nigrum*) and the red-berried bitter nightshade (*S. dulcamara*), are common enough to be of value to wildlife. The yellow berries of Carolina horse-nettle (*S. carolinense*), a prickly, persistent weed, widespread throughout the Southeast, are eaten by both birds and mammals. Of the 15 to 20 species occurring in the Southwest, silverleaf nightshade (*S. elaeagnifolium*) is one of the more common and useful.

It is not surprising that wildlife appreciates nightshade fruits since they are closely related to tomatoes and eggplants. A complete listing of all nightshade users would be a long one.

Waterfowl (fruit)
* Duck, Wood, *N.Y.*
Marshbirds and Shorebirds (fruit)
+ Rail, Sora, *NE*
Upland Gamebirds (fruit)
+ Dove, Eastern White-winged, *Tex.*
+ Grouse, Ruffed, *Wis.*
+ Pheasant, Ring-necked, *NE*
Quail
+ Bobwhite, *S*
+ Scaled, Arizona, *SW*
+ Turkey, Wild, *E*
Songbirds (fruit)
+ Cardinal, *NE*
+ Catbird, *NE*
+ Chat, Long-tailed, *Pac.*
+ Goldfinch, Green-backed, *Calif.*
+ Magpie, American, *Mt.–Des.*
+ Meadowlark, Eastern, *E.Pr.*
+ Mockingbird, *Calif.*
+ Oriole, Hooded, *Calif. and Ariz.*
+ Phainopepla, *Calif. and Ariz.*
Sparrow
+ Fox, *W*
* Golden-crowned, *Calif.*
** Large-billed, *Calif.*
* Song, *Pac.*
+ Swamp, *NE*
* White-crowned, *Pac.*
Thrasher
+ California, *Calif.*
+ Curve-billed, *Tex. and Ariz.*
Thrush
+ Gray-cheeked, *NE*
+ Hermit, *Pac.*

415

+ Russet-backed, *Calif.*
+ Varied, *Pac.*
  Towhee
* Brown, *Calif.*
+ Spotted, *Pac.*

Fur and Game Mammals (fruit)
+ Raccoon, *Pac. and Iowa*
  Skunk
** California, *Calif.*
+ Eastern, *NE*
+ Illinois, *Ill.*
− Spotted, Prairie, *Iowa*

Small Mammals (fruit, leaves)
+ Gopher, Pocket, *Pr.*
− Moles, *Oreg.*
* Mouse, Pocket, *Calif.; +W.Pr. and Mt.–Des.*
  Prairie Dog
+ Black-tailed, *W.Pr.*
** Gunnison, *SW*
+ Rat, Banner-tailed Kangaroo, *Ariz.*
* Rock Squirrel, *Calif.*

Figwort Family: *Scrophulariaceae*

PENSTEMONS
Penstemon

[12*/5 users] *Penstemon* is a North American genus of perhaps 250 or more species. Most of them are found in the western part of the country; only about a dozen grow in the East. The eastern species are not particularly attractive, but many of the western ones are so beautiful that they are used in cultivation and are popular with rock gardeners. In the West, penstemons occur at varying altitudes in diverse soil conditions—generally where it is moderately moist. In Colorado and adjoining states they form beautiful showy masses along railroad embankments.

Penstemons, like many other wild flowers attractive to man, are low in attractiveness to wildlife. The small irregular seeds are eaten primarily by western rodents.

Songbirds (seeds)
+ Finch, Rosy, *Pac.*

Small Mammals (seeds, foliage)
*** Ground Squirrel, Mantled, *W*
   Rat
* Kangaroo, Merriam, *SW*
+ Kangaroo, various spp., *Pr. and Mt.–Des.*

Hoofed Browsers (foliage, stems)
+ Antelope, *No.Pr. and Mt.–Des.*

PAINTBRUSHES
Castilleja

[1*/2 users] This colorful well-known plant of the western plains is a most attractive representative of our native wildflowers. Unfortunately, however, the 35 species of paintbrush have only slight value for wildlife.

Songbirds (nectar)
− Hummingbird, Broad-tailed, *Ariz. and N.Mex.*

Hoofed Browsers (plants)
* Deer, Mule, *So.Mt.–Des.*

Plantain Family: *Plantaginaceae*

PLANTAINS
Plantago

[17*/19 users] Nearly 20 kinds of plantains are present in this country. Woolly Indianwheat (*P. purshii*) of the West and bottlebrush Indianwheat (*P. aristata*) of the East and Prairies are locally abundant on poor dry soil. Buckhorn

(*P. lanceolata*) and rippleseed plantain (*P. major*) are widespread weeds and lawn pests.

Though the cardinal and grasshopper sparrow are the only songbird users listed below, the seeds of these plants are eaten to a slight extent by many birds. Buckhorn plantain seeds are often fed to cage birds. Plantain leaves are a favorite food of rabbits, and rodents eat the seeds freely.

Upland Gamebirds (leaves)
+ Grouse, Ruffed, *Va. and Ohio*
Songbirds (seeds)
+ Cardinal, *SE*
+ Sparrow, Grasshopper, *NE*
Fur and Game Mammals (leaves, capsules)
    Rabbit
**   Cottontail, Eastern, *Conn.*
**   Cottontail, Mearns, *Pa.*
*   Cottontail, New England, *New England*
    Squirrel
+ Fox, *Tex.*
+ Gray, *Tex.*
Small Mammals (capsules, plants)
    Ground Squirrel

—   Townsend, *Wash.*
*   Various spp., *Pr.*
*   Mouse, Pocket, various spp., *W.Pr. and Mt.–Des.*
    Prairie Dog
+ Black-tailed, *W.Pr.*
+ Gunnison, *SW*
    Rat
+ Kangaroo, Banner-tailed, *Ariz.*
+ Kangaroo, Giant, *Calif.*
*   Kangaroo, Large, *Ariz.*
**   Kangaroo, Merriam, *SW*
*   Kangaroo, various spp., *Pr. and Mt.–Des.*
Hoofed Browsers (plants)
+ Deer, White-tailed, *E*

Madder Family: *Rubiaceae*

BUTTONWEED
Diodia teres

[**4*/4 users**] Buttonweed, also known as rough buttonweed or poorjoe, occurs widely through the East. It is one of the most abundant weeds on poor, sandy soil in the Southeast. The hard-coated, seed-like fruits are eaten to a limited extent by upland gamebirds. Bobwhite quail feed occasionally on buttonweed, but the quantities consumed are too small to constitute an appreciable part in the diet. The value of this plant is negligible in proportion to its abundance.

Upland Gamebirds (seeds)
    Prairie Chicken
*   Attwater, *Tex.*
*** Greater, *Ill.*
+ Turkey, Wild, *S*
Hoofed Browsers (plants)
— Deer, White-tailed, *Tex.*

Daisy Family: *Compositae*

SNAKEWEEDS
Gutierrezia

[**14*/9 users**] Snakeweed, also known as broomweed or matchweed, is a west- ern genus represented in this country by about 10 species. These densely branched, semishrubby plants inhabit dry, stony soil on the plains and adjoining uplands. Broom snakeweed (*G. sarothrae*) is the most abundant species and is widely distributed. The plants are more plentiful southward and are, in the main, of greater importance in the Southwest than elsewhere. The seeds of these tiny-flowered weeds are eaten extensively by the scaled quail and by kangaroo rats. Snakeweeds are browsed by rabbits, antelopes, and deer.

Upland Gamebirds (seeds)
 Quail
 — Bobwhite, *So.Tex.*

** Scaled, Arizona, *SW*
Fur and Game Mammals (foliage, plants)
*** Jack Rabbit, White-tailed, *Utah*
 + Rabbit, Cottontail, *Utah*
Small Mammals (seeds)
 Rat
 * Kangaroo, Banner-tailed, *Ariz.*
 * Kangaroo, Merriam, *Ariz. and N.Mex.*
 — Kangaroo, Tulare, *Calif.*
Hoofed Browsers (plants)
*** Antelope, *S.E.Mont.;* +*No.Pr. and Mt.–Des.*
** Deer, White-tailed, *Tex.*

GOLDENRODS
Solidago

[6*/20 users] Goldenrods (about 125 species) are present in all sections of the country. They are more plentiful in the East than elsewhere and are particularly abundant in the Northeast. The wildlife utility of these fall-blooming weeds is very low in proportion to their abundance and availability. Records of their use are limited mainly to the East.

Upland Gamebirds (leaves)
 Grouse
 + Ruffed, *NE*
 + Sharp-tailed, *Great Lakes Area*
 + Spruce, *N*
** Prairie Chicken, Greater, *Ill.*
Songbirds (seeds)
 Goldfinch
 * Common, *E*
 + Green-backed, *N.Mex. and Ariz.*
 + Junco, *NE*
 + Siskin, Pine, *Md.*
 Sparrow
 + Swamp, *NE*
 + Tree, *NE*
Fur and Game Mammals (foliage, plants)

 + Beaver, *Iowa*
 + Porcupine, *Mt.–Des.*
 Rabbit
 + Cottontail, Eastern, *NE*
 + Cottontail, Mearns, *NE*
 * Cottontail, New England, *Conn.*
 + Swamp, *Okla.*
Small Mammals (seed heads, foliage)
 Mouse
 + Meadow, *E*
 + Pine, *NE*
 * Rat, Wood, *S.Pr.*
Hoofed Browsers (plants)
 + Deer, White-tailed, *Pa.*

RABBITBRUSH
Chrysothamnus

[14*/12 users] Rabbitbrush is strictly a North American genus. About 70

species occur on the plains and arid foothills of the West—often in sterile

soil and sometimes in mildly alkaline areas. These dense, shrubby, narrow-leaved, goldenrod-like plants, covered in the summer and fall with masses of small yellow flowers, are so abundant that they constitute one of the most characteristic features of our western vegetation. Douglas (*C. viscidiflorus*) and small rabbitbrush (*C. stenophyllus*) are two of the more important species. Besides furnishing useful cover in otherwise open areas, their seed heads

and foliage are consumed by wildlife —especially by rabbits and hoofed browsers.

Songbirds (seeds)
- Finch, Common House, *N.Mex.*
- Siskin, Pine, *N.Mex.*

Fur and Game Mammals (foliage, twigs)
    Jack Rabbit
-    Black-tailed, *Utah*
**   California, *Utah*
***   White-tailed, *Utah*
- Rabbit, Pygmy, *Utah*

Small Mammals (seed heads)
- Ground Squirrel, various spp., *Pr.*
- Mouse, Pacific Pocket, *Calif.*

Hoofed Browsers (twigs, foliage)
*** Antelope, *No.Pr. and Mt.–Des.*
** Deer, Mule, *Oreg.*; **No.Mt.–Des.*; +*So.Mt.–Des.*
+ Elk, *No.Mt.–Des.*
+ Sheep, Mountain, *No.Mt.–Des.*

ASTERS
Aster

[1*/12 users] The common wild asters are a complex group of about 250 or more species. Of this number more than half are found in the United States. This fall-flowering genus is represented all over the country but is most conspicuous in the East—in old fields and along roadsides. Some species are found in open woods. A number of asters are so attractive that they are used as garden flowers. The common, large, double-flowered garden asters, however, belong to quite a different genus, *Callistephus*. Though abundant in many places, asters have relatively little importance to wildlife. Besides the animals listed below, there are records of occasional or slight use by a number of other species.

Upland Gamebirds (leaves, seeds)
+ Grouse, Ruffed, *Va.Alleghenies*
+ Turkey, Wild, *Va.*

Songbirds (seeds)
+ Sparrow, Tree, *NE*

Fur and Game Mammals (leaves)
    Rabbit
+   Cottontail, *Conn., Pa., and Okla.*
+   Swamp, *Okla.*

Small Mammals (seeds, leaves)
+ Chipmunk, Lake Superior, *Minn.*
+ Mouse, White-footed, *Minn.*

Hoofed Browsers (plants)
+ Antelope, *Okla.*
    Deer
+   Mule, *Utah*
*   White-tailed, *NE*
+ Moose, *Mont.*

PUSSYTOES
Antennaria

[6*/9 users] These inconspicuous gray-ish-green plants are plentiful enough to be of some minor use to a few species of wildlife. Pussytoes, also known as everlasting, grow in well-drained soil in eastern woods or open places in the West. Their seeds are too minute to be significant as wildlife food, but several kinds of birds and mammals relish the tender rosettes of leaves.

Upland Gamebirds (leaves, seed heads)
    Grouse
    *   Blue, *No.Mt.–Des.*
    *   Ruffed, *Va.Alleghenies*

    +   Sage, *No.Mt.–Des.*
    + Quail, Bobwhite, *Nebr.*
Fur and Game Mammals (plants)
    ** Hare, Varying, *Minn.*
    — Rabbit, New England Cottontail, *Conn.*
Small Mammals (plants)
    + Gopher, Brown Pocket, *Mont.*
Hoofed Browsers (plants)
    Deer
    *   Mule, *S.Dak.*
    *   White-tailed, *Mo.;* +*S.Dak.*

RAGWEEDS
Ambrosia

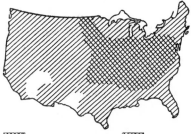

▨ Region of main use   ▨ Lesser use

[164*/71 users] About 15 species of ragweed are known. Six or more of them are found in this country, but of these only two are of major consequence to wildlife. They are common (*A. artemisiifolia*) and western ragweed (*A. psilostachya*). The blood ragweed (*A. aptera*) is also of some importance as a wildlife food in the Southwest, but the giant ragweed (*A. trifida*) of the East is of little value. Its seeds are large and have a tough coat which is the probable reason why birds use it so little.

These weeds are found in cultivated and fallow fields, along roadsides, and in city lots. They are pioneer invaders of broken soil, and in many parts of the country the mere disking of the ground opens the way for a good crop of ragweeds. They occur regularly with grain crops and commonly take over the fields as soon as the grain is harvested. Being annuals, ragweeds are generally replaced in two to four years by perennial plants such as the goldenrod, aster, or broomsedge if the land is allowed to remain fallow.

Few people have a good word to say for these unattractive abundant weeds unless they happen to know about their wildlife value. A glance at the list below will show how important they are for gamebirds, including the bobwhite quail, and for many of our best-loved songbirds such as the goldfinch, song sparrow, white-throated sparrow, and junco or snowbird. The seeds are rich in oil, and the seed production per plant is enormous. Some of the seeds persist on the plants into the winter and remain available for use when, in the North, other foods are covered by snow. Consequently ragweeds are one of the most valuable winter foods for all ground-feeding birds.

Waterfowl (seeds)
    * Teal, Blue-winged, *W*

Marshbirds and Shorebirds (seeds)
Rail
+ King, *NE*
+ Yellow, *E*
+ Snipe, Wilson, *E*
Upland Gamebirds (seeds)
Dove
* Ground, *Gulf*
** Mourning, *E*; +*Pr.*
+ Grouse, Sharp-tailed, *Minn. and N.Dak.*
Partridge
+ Chukar, *Mo.*
*** Hungarian, *NE*
** Pheasant, Ring-necked. *NE*; *NW
Prairie Chicken
** Greater, *Ill.*
** Attwater, *Tex.*
Quail
**** Bobwhite, *NE and Pr.;* **SE
+ Gambel, *Ariz.*
** Turkey, Wild, *Ariz. and Nev.*; +*E*
+ Woodcock, *E*
Songbirds (seeds)
Blackbird
*** Redwing, *NE*; ***Pr. and SE;* +*Mt.-Des. and La.*
* Rusty, *NE*
* Yellow-headed, *W*
+ Bobolink, *NE*
Bunting
+ Indigo, *NE*
+ Lazuli, *Okla.*
*** Snow, *NE*
+ Cardinal, *E*
Crossbill
+ Red, *U.S.*
* White-winged, *NE*
* Finch, Purple, *E*
*** Goldfinch, Eastern, *E*
* Grackle, Purple, *NE*
* Grosbeak, Pine, *NE*
*** Junco, Slate-colored, *NE and Pr.*
*** Lark, Horned, *E*; *W

Longspur
* Lapland, *NE and No.Pr.*
+ McCown, *Pr.*
+ Smith, *Ill.*
+ Meadowlark, Eastern, *NE*
Pipit
+ American, *NE*
+ Sprague, *Pr.*
**** Redpoll, Common, *N*
+ Robin, *NE*
Sparrow
+ Chipping, *E*
* English, *E*; +*Pr.*
+ Field, *NE*
*** Fox, *U.S.*
** Grasshopper, *W*
**** Harris, *E.Pr.*
*** Henslow, *NE*
* Large-billed, *Calif.*
*** Lark, Eastern, *Pr.*
*** Lincoln, *NE*; **E.Pr.*
** Savannah, *NE*; **S.Pr.*
*** Song, *NE*
+ Swamp, *NE*
* Tree, *NE and E.Pr.*
*** Vesper, Eastern, *E*
***** (52%) White-crowned, *Pr.*; *NE
**** White-throated, *NE*
+ Starling, *N*
+ Titmouse, Tufted, *NE*
*** Towhee, Red-eyed, *NE*
+ Waxwing, Cedar, *NE*
Fur and Game Mammals (foliage, plants)
+ Rabbit, Cottontail, *Conn.*
Small Mammals (seeds)
** Chipmunk, Least, *W.Pr. and Mt.-Des.*
Ground Squirrel
** Columbian, *No.Mt.-Des.*
*** Thirteen-lined, *Pr.*
+ Mouse, Meadow, *E*
* Rat, Kangaroo, *W*
Hoofed Browsers (plants)
+ Antelope, *S.E.Mont.*
+ Deer, White-tailed, *E*

SUNFLOWERS
Helianthus

[**73***/60 users] About 60 species of sun-flowers, nearly two-thirds of all the sunflowers in the world, grow in the United States. They occur throughout

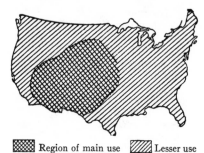

▨ Region of main use ▨ Lesser use

the country in a wide variety of habitats. Some are woodland plants, but the majority like sunny, open places. Sunflowers are most abundant in the West, particularly in the Prairies. Annual species such as the common (*H. annuus*) and prairie sunflowers (*H. petiolaris*) grow in cultivated fields as well as along roadsides and in waste places where the sod has been broken. The Jerusalem-artichoke sunflower (*H. tuberosus*) prefers moist soil along fence rows or near ditches and streams.

The large, nutritious seeds of sunflowers are eaten by gamebirds, songbirds, and rodents. These attractive weedy plants are of outstanding value to wildlife in the Prairies and other parts of the West.

Marshbirds and Shorebirds (seeds)
+ Snipe, Wilson, *W*
Upland Gamebirds (seeds)
    Dove
**   Mourning, *Pr. and Mt.–Des.; *Pac.*
***   White-winged, Eastern, *Tex.*
+   White-winged, Western, *Ariz.*
    Grouse
**   Sharp-tailed, Columbian, *Utah*
***   Sharp-tailed, Prairie, *Utah*
−   Partridge, Hungarian, *N.Dak.*
*   Pheasant, Ring-necked, *NW; +Mont.*
    Quail
**   Bobwhite, *Pr.*
+   Gambel, *SW*
**   Mearns, *SW*
*   Scaled, Arizona, *SW*

Songbirds (seeds)
    Blackbird
+   Brewer, *Calif.*
*   Redwing, *Mt.–Des.; +Pr.*
*   Yellow-headed, *W*
+ Bobolink, *W*
− Bunting, Lazuli, *Okla.*
+ Chickadee, Black-capped, *NE*
+ Cowbird, *W*
* Crossbill, White-winged, *NE*
* Crow, *Pr.; +Pac.*
− Finch, House, *N.Mex.*
    Goldfinch
*   Eastern, *E*
+   Green-backed, *Calif.*
*** Willow, *Calif.*
+ Grackle, Purple, *Pr.*
* Lark, Horned, *W*
    Longspur
**   Chestnut-collared, *Pr.*
*** McCown, *Pr.*
* Meadowlark, *W. and E.Pr.; +SE*
+ Nuthatch, White-breasted, *E*
+ Pyrrhuloxia, *Tex.*
+ Raven, White-necked, *SW, mainly Tex.*
    Sparrow
*** English, *Mt.–Des.; +Pr.*
+   Grasshopper, *W*
+   Harris, *Pr.*
*   Lark, Eastern, *Pr.*
*   Lincoln, *E.Pr.*
*   Savannah, *Pr.*
+   Tree, *E.Pr.*
*   Vesper, *So.Mt.–Des.*
*** White-crowned, *Mt.–Des.; **E.Pr.*
+ Titmouse, Tufted, *NE*
Fur and Game Mammals (stems, foliage)
− Muskrat, *Ohio*
Small Mammals (seeds)
* Chipmunk, Least, *W.Pr. and Mt.–Des.*
+ Gopher, Eastern Pocket, *NE and No.Pr.*
    Ground Squirrel
*   Richardson, *No.Pr.*
**   Thirteen-lined, *Pr.*
    Mouse
+   Lemming, *NE and No.Pr.*
+   Meadow, *Pa. and N.Dak.*

+ Meadow, various spp., *E*
* Pocket, *W.Pr. and Mt.–Des.*
+ White-footed, *W*
+ Prairie Dog, Black-tailed, *W.Pr.*
* Rat, Kangaroo, various spp.,
    Pr. and Mt.–Des.

Hoofed Browsers (plants)
+ Antelope, *S.Dak.*
Deer
*** Mule, *Nebr.*
+ White-tailed, *Mo. and Wis.*
– Moose, Shiras, *Yellowstone Park*

GOLDEN CROWNBEARD
Verbesina encelioides

[8*/4 users] There are several crown-beards in the country, but the only one of recognized value to wildlife is the wide-ranging western species, golden crownbeard. It is a common weed of roadsides and other waste places, from Kansas and Texas to Montana and California. The seeds of this sunflower-like plant are of moderate value to some birds and rodents.

Upland Gamebirds (seeds)
Quail
+ Bobwhite, *So.Tex.*
* Gambel, *SW*
Songbirds (seeds)
** Towhee, Abert, *Ariz.*
Small Mammals (seeds)
* Rat, Ord Kangaroo, *W*

BEGGARTICKS
Bidens

[1*/7 users] About 25 species of *Bidens* grow in the East. These golden-flow-ered, moist-ground plants have various common names such as Spanish-needles, beggarlice, beggarticks, and pitchforks. The stick-tight character-istic of the barbed seeds (akenes) as well as the similarity in names are likely to cause confusion with the unre-lated beggarweeds (*Desmodium*). The seeds of beggarticks are of minor value to wildlife.

Waterfowl (seeds)
* Duck, Wood, *SE*
Upland Gamebirds (seeds)
+ Pheasant, Ring-necked, *NE*
+ Quail, Bobwhite, *Okla.*
Songbirds (seeds)
+ Finch, Purple, *E*
+ Redpoll, Common, *NE*
+ Sparrow, Swamp, *NE*
Fur and Game Mammals (foliage)
+ Rabbit, Cottontail, *Conn.*

TARWEEDS
Madia and Hemizonia

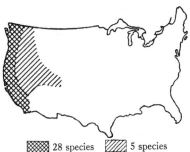

[▨] 28 species [▧] 5 species

[29*/27 users] Tarweeds belong to the two closely related western genera *Madia* and *Hemizonia*. There are about 10 species of the former and 18 of the

423

latter. Both genera are particularly abundant in California—in fields and orchards, on dry hillslopes, and in the valleys. Anyone who has worked among these plants is familiar with their sticky, pungent leaves and stems. Except for this disagreeable secretion, some of the tarweeds are attractive wildflowers.

The common tarweed (*Madia elegans*) is one of the most abundant of the group and is particularly handsome. The so-called spikeweed (*Hemizonia pungens*) is another very common species. The dark seeds (akenes) of tarweeds are used as food by many birds and also by rodents.

Upland Gamebirds (seeds)
- * Dove, Mourning, *Pac.*
- ** Partridge, Hungarian, *NW*
  Quail
- \+ California, *Calif.*
- \+ Mountain, *Pac.*
- * Valley, *Calif.*

Songbirds (seeds)
  Blackbird
- \+ Brewer, *Calif.*

- \+ Redwing, *Calif.*
- * Finch, Common House, Calif
  Goldfinch
- * Green-backed, *Calif.*
- * Willow, *Calif.*
- \+ Junco, Oregon, *Calif.*
- * Lark, California Horned, *Calif.*
- \+ Meadowlark, Western, *Pac.*
- ** Pipit, American, *Pac.*
  Sparrow
- \+ Fox, *W*
- * Golden-crowned, *Calif.*
- * Lark, Western, *Calif.*
- * Savannah, *Calif.*
- \+ Song, *Pac.*
- * White-crowned, *Pac.*
  Towhee
- * Brown, *Calif.*
- \+ Spotted, *Pac.*

Fur and Game Mammals (plants)
- \+ Rabbit, Cottontail, *Calif.*

Small Mammals (seeds, plants)
- ** Chipmunk, Northwest, *Pac.NW*
  Ground Squirrel
- ** Columbian, *No.Mt.–Des. and Pac.*
- ** Douglas, *Oreg.*
- ** Various spp., *Calif.*

MAYWEED
Anthemis cotula

[2*/7 users] Mayweed, also known as dogfennel or camomile, is a small, pungent, daisy-flowered plant common in yards, fields, waste places, and along roadsides all over the United States. In California, where it is especially abundant, its seeds are eaten by several kinds of birds.

Songbirds (seeds)
- \+ Goldfinch, Green-backed, *Calif.*
- \+ Junco, Oregon, *Calif.*
  Sparrow
- \+ Golden-crowned, *Calif.*
- * Lincoln, *Calif.*
- \+ Savannah, *Calif.*
- * White-crowned, *Calif.*
- \+ Towhee, Brown, *Calif.*

YARROWS
Achillea

[1*/5 users] Yarrow or milfoil is one of our most familiar weeds. Common yarrow (*A. millefolium*) abounds in the East and is also present locally in parts of the West. Western yarrow (*A. lanulosa*) is the principal representative on western range lands. Its finely divided, sage-scented leaves are eaten to a small extent by a few wildlife species.

Upland Gamebirds (leaves)
  Grouse
- \+ Ruffed, *NE*
- \+ Sharp-tailed, *Utah*

Fur and Game Mammals (leaves)
- * Rabbit, Cottontail, *Mich.*

Small Mammals (leaves)
- \+ Mouse, Pine, *NE*

Hoofed Browsers (plants)
- \− Sheep, Mountain, *Colo.*

STAR-THISTLES
Centaurea

[**24*/18 users**] There are about a dozen species of *Centaurea* in the United States. All except one, the American star-thistle (*C. americana*), are introduced. Only two species are important to wildlife. These are Napa or Malta (*C. melitensis*) and yellow star-thistle (*C. solstitialis*). The Napa star-thistle is the more plentiful of the two and is used more by wildlife. Both of these yellow-flowered, prickly plants are common in the Pacific region—especially in California grainfields. Elsewhere they are widely but sparsely distributed. The hard, bristle-topped seeds (akenes) are popular with birds, including the mourning dove and California quail, and are especially important for western goldfinches.

Upland Gamebirds (seeds)
** Dove, Mourning, *Pac.*
* Quail, California, *Calif.*

Songbirds (seeds)
* Finch, Common House, *Calif.*
  Goldfinch
***** (54%) Green-backed, *Calif.*
** Lawrence, *Mt.–Des. and Pac.*
*** Willow, *Calif.*
+ Junco, Oregon, *Calif.*
* Siskin, Pine, *W*
  Sparrow,
+ Lincoln, *Calif.*
* Golden-crowned, *Calif.*
* Song, *Pac.*
* White-crowned, *Pac.*
  Titmouse
+ Plain, *Calif.*
+ Tufted, *Calif.*
  Towhee
* Brown, *Calif.*
* Spotted, *Pac.*

Small Mammals (seeds)
— Ground Squirrel, Beechey, *Calif.*
— Mouse, Pacific Pocket, *Calif.*

DANDELIONS
Taraxacum

▨ Region of main use ▨ Lesser use

[**23*/33 users**] The well-known dandelion of lawns, meadows, pastures, roadsides, and other open, moist places consists of three or more species in the United States and about 25 in the world. The most widespread species and, in the East, by far the most abundant is the common dandelion (*T. officinale*). Its deep tap root, the numerous plume-borne seeds (akenes), and the flattish rosette of leaves that often escape the lawnmower all help to explain why this plant is so plentiful and persistent.

Despite their great abundance in the East, dandelions have their principal value to wildlife in the West. Dandelion foliage, relished as greens by man, is palatable to wildlife, and the parachute-like seeds, so frequently eaten by the goldfinch and English sparrow, are also popular with other birds and with rodents.

Upland Gamebirds (foliage, seed heads)
  Grouse
+ Blue, *No.Mt.–Des.*
+ Ruffed, *NE*
** Sage, *No.Des.*
*** Sharp-tailed, *W.Nebr.; *Great Lakes Area; +N.Dak. and Utah*
* Partridge, Hungarian, *NE*

425

* Pheasant, Ring-necked, *NW*
+ Prairie Chicken, Greater, *No.Pr.*
  Quail
+   Bobwhite, *NE*
+   Valley, *Nev.*
+ Turkey, Wild, *Ariz. and N.Mex.*
Songbirds (seeds)
  Blackbird
+   Brewer, *W*
+   Yellow-headed, *W*
*   Goldfinch, *E*
−   Siskin, Pine, *N.Mex.*
  Sparrow
+   Brewer, *W*
+   Chipping, *E*
+   English, *E*
+   Sharp-tailed, *Atl.Coast*
+   Vesper, *Mt.–Des.*
+ Towhee, Green-tailed, *Mt.–Des.*
Fur and Game Mammals (foliage, plants)

* Hare, Varying, *Minn.*
+ Porcupine, Western, *Mt.–Des.*
+ Rabbit, Cottontail, *NE*
Small Mammals (seeds, foliage, plants)
  Chipmunk
*   Least, *W.Pr. and Mt.–Des.*
*   Northwest, *Pac.NW*
  Gopher
*****   (67%) Pocket, *Utah*
+   Pocket, Western, *Mont.*
* Ground Squirrel, Richardson, *No.Pr.*
+ Mouse, Pine, *NE*
*** Prairie Dog, Gunnison, *N.Mex., Ariz., and Colo.*
Hoofed Browsers (plants)
  Deer
+   Mule, *Utah*
+   White-tailed, *N.Y.*

WILDLETTUCE
Lactuca

[0*/5 users] Wildlettuce is a common garden, roadside, and field weed. About a dozen species of these tall milky-juiced plants grow widely distributed over the United States. Prickly wildlettuce (*L. scariola*), chicory wildlettuce (*L. pulchella*), and Canada wildlettuce (*L. canadensis*) are the most common. The seeds of wildlettuce are occasionally eaten by wildlife.

Upland Gamebirds (seeds)
+ Pheasant, Ring-necked, *Utah and Mont.*
Songbirds (seeds)
+ Goldfinch, *E*
Small Mammals (foliage, stems)
+ Prairie Dog, White-tailed, *Mont. and Wyo.*
Hoofed Browsers (plants)
+ Antelope, *Idaho*
+ Deer, White-tailed, *E*

HAWKWEEDS
Hieracium

0*/6 users] There are nearly 50 kinds of hawkweeds widely distributed in this country. These yellow- or orange-flowered, daisy-like plants grow in woodlands, clearings, pastures, and along waysides. Their hairy, basal leaves are eaten by several wildlife species.

Upland Gamebirds (leaves, seeds)

  Grouse
+   Blue, *No.Mt.–Des.*
+   Ruffed, *NE*
+ Turkey, Wild, *Pa.*
Fur and Game Mammals (leaves, plants)
+ Rabbit, Mearns Cottontail, *Pa.*
Hoofed Browsers (plants)
+ Deer, White-tailed, *N.Y.*
+ Sheep, Mountain, *Idaho*

426

CHAPTER SIXTEEN

Marsh and Aquatic Plants

T HE PLANTS INVOLVED in this category are all herbaceous—no trees or shrubs—though conceivably a few woody species like buttonbush and baldcypress could have been included. The group, as treated here, ranges from submerged or emergent aquatic plants to species growing in marshy or wet soils. Sedges and other moist-land or meadow plants are classed as upland plants in the previous chapter on Upland Weeds and Herbs. In a few cases, the distinctions between these groups are not clear cut.

The wet-land habitat generally supports both a flora and fauna distinct from upland areas. Marsh and aquatic plants are the mainstay of one of our most important wildlife groups: waterfowl. In addition, plants of this environment are of great value to marshbirds and shorebirds, to some fur and game mammals such as the muskrat, raccoon, and otter, and to songbirds such as the redwing, yellow-headed blackbird, swamp sparrow, and marsh wren.

Marsh and aquatic vegetation is more widely distributed than many people realize. There are extensive marsh areas in the plains and prairies and even in the desert regions. Generally, the more arid the region, the more important are the marsh and aquatic habitats in it. Brackish marshes along both the Atlantic and Gulf coasts are particularly extensive and valuable to wildlife.

General References: A Manual of Aquatic Plants. Norman C. Fassett. McGraw-Hill Book Company, Inc., New York, 1940. 382 pp.

Aquatic Plants of the United States. Walter Conrad Muenscher. Comstock Publishing Company, Inc., Ithaca, 1944. 374 pp.

Food of Game Ducks in the United States and Canada. A. C. Martin and F. M. Uhler. *U.S. Dept. Agr. Tech. Bul.* 634, 1939. 156 pp.

Wildfowl Food Plants. W. L. McAtee. Collegiate Press, Inc., Ames, Iowa, 1939. 141 pp.

ALGAE

[109*/27 users] These primitive plants, including thousands of species, and varying from microscopic unicellular organisms to the gigantic kelps growing 100 or more feet long, are primarily submerged aquatics. They inhabit both fresh and saline waters. Some species grow on moist wood, stone, or soil.

Roughly, the algae can be divided into three principal types: the microscopic one-celled or few-celled forms; secondly, the thread-like forms; and finally, the coarser ones including the kelps, seaweeds, and rockweeds. The minute types of algae, often consisting of one or two cells, make up a large proportion of the plankton of the oceans. As such they are the main support of the small aquatic animal life which in turn serves as the principal food for fish, waterfowl, and other marine wildlife.

The thread-like or filamentous algae are especially common in stagnant, inland waters and are also plentiful in coastal areas. They are the plants which make up the common greenish scum, often called frog spit, on ponds, lakes, and streams. These algae are eaten by ducks in considerable quantity, though one suspects that the animal life resident in the meshes of the algal mass are as much a food inducement as the alga itself.

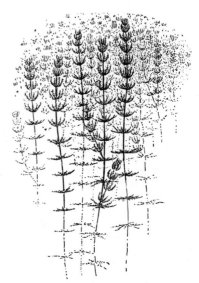

The muskgrasses (primarily *Chara*) are usually grouped with the algae. In coarseness they are somewhat intermediate between the thread-like forms and the seaweed-kelp group. Muskgrasses are among the top-ranking foods of ducks. They account for more than half (63) of the 109 stars credited to all algae. Ducks appear particularly fond of the plants when they bear multitudes of the microscopic spore-like oögonia. More than 300,000 of these minute reproductive structures have been found in the stomach of a single duck. The 50 or more American species of *Chara* are widely distributed through the country—in fresh-water lakes, coastal bays, reservoirs, and ponds or tanks in the cow country. These lime-coated algae grow at depths varying from a few inches to 30 or more feet, in fresh, alkaline, or moderately brackish water. Their characteristic musky odor makes them a nuisance in city reservoirs, and the plants are reported to flavor the flesh of waterfowl that feed on them. In fish-hatchery ponds the rapid growth of muskgrasses necessitates periodic draining to remove the excessive mass of vegetation. *Nitella* and *Tolypella* are less abundant genera related to *Chara*. It is assumed that these also may have some usefulness to waterfowl.

The rockweeds, seaweeds, and kelps are not of great importance to wildlife except for forms such as the sea-let-tuce. The latter is one of the principal foods for brant on the North Atlantic coast.

Algae—Exclusive of Muskgrasses:
Waterfowl (plants)

Brant
***** (76%) American, *No.Atl. Coast* (1932 to 1941)
 + Black, *Pac.Coast*
 ** Coot, *NE and W; +SE*
 Duck
 ** Baldpate, *W; *NE; +SE*
 ** Black, *SE; +NE*
 + Bufflehead, *NE*
 * Canvasback, *SE*
 *** Gadwall, *W; **SE*
 + Goldeneye, Barrow, *NW*
 * Mallard, *W*
 * Pintail, *NE; +W*
 * Redhead, *W; +SE*
 + Ring-necked, *SE and W*
 + Scoter, American, *Atl. and Pac.Coasts*
 + Scoter, Surf, *Atl. and Pac. Coasts*
 * Shoveller, *SE; +W*
 * Teal, Blue-winged, *SE; +NE*

Marshbirds and Shorebirds (plants)
 + Avocet, *W*
 * Rail, Sora, *SE; +W*

Muskgrasses:
Waterfowl (plants)
*** Coot, *SE and W;* **NE
    Duck
**   Baldpate, NE; *SE; +W
+   Black, *NE*
+   Bufflehead, *W*
+   Canvasback, *SE*
+   Goldeneye, American, *NE*
*   Mallard, *W;* +*NE*
**   Pintail, *SE*
*** Redhead, *W;* +*E*
*** Ring-necked, *W;* +*E*
*   Ruddy, *E;* +*W*

**   Scaup, Greater, *SE and W;*
    +*NE*
*   Scaup, Lesser, *SE and W*
+   Scoter, American, *Atl. and*
    Pac.Coasts
+   Shoveller, *SE*
*   Teal, Blue-winged, *W;* +*E*
**   Teal, Green-winged, *NE;* *W;
    +*SE*
*   Wood, *SE*
+   Swan, Whistling, *E*
Marshbirds and Shorebirds (plants)
+   Sandpiper, Semipalmated, *Atl.*
    Coast

Fern Allies

HORSETAILS
Equisetum

[18*/6 users] Our dozen or more species of horsetails are relics of a tremendous and varied group of plants that were prominent in the primeval flora of the coal ages, long before man came on the scene. The American horsetails (also called scouring rushes or bottlebrushes) grow in widespread, diverse habitats varying from aquatic or moist soil to well-drained sites such as on highway or railroad embankments. They are more plentiful in the northern states.

Horsetails, like their relatives the ferns, produce microscopic spores and no seeds.

Waterfowl (rootstocks, stems)
    Goose
**   Blue, *Pr.*
*   Snow, *U.S.*
*** Swan, Whistling, *W;* +*E*
Fur and Game Mammals (plants)
+   Bear, Black, *W*
+   Muskrat, *NE*
Hoofed Browsers (plants)
**   Moose, *Maine to Mich.*

Cattail Family: *Typhaceae*

CATTAILS
Typha

[17*/17 users] Everyone is familiar with the tall, strap-leaved plants with sausage-like heads so conspicuous in wet places throughout the country. For that matter they are common through the tropical and temperate regions of the world. In the United States, cattails (also known as flags) are particularly abundant in the Northeast, but they are also plentiful elsewhere, especially in the fresher parts of cóastal marshlands. There are four species in this country.

The masses of minute seeds, thousands of them in one head, are borne among downy hairs that blow about when the heads are mature. These multitudes of tiny, wind-carried seeds are too small and too hairy to be attractive to birds. A few exceptional instances have been noted in teal captured near Lake Picacho, Arizona, and Salton Sea, California—they contained thousands of cattail seeds.

Cattail rootstocks are much more valuable as food for wildlife than are the seeds. Geese and muskrats use the starchy underground stems a great deal. For this reason cattails are one of the best plants for muskrat marshes.

Additional value in these marsh plants is the shelter and nesting cover they provide. Long-billed marsh wrens, red-wings, and yellow-headed blackbirds nest regularly in cattail marshes.

For ducks, cattails have relatively little value. They furnish cover, it is true, but they also take the place of more useful plants that would furnish both food and cover. Consequently, cattails are regarded as undesirable weeds in places intended primarily for ducks. It has been found that mowing cattails after the heads are well formed but not mature and then following up with another mowing about a month later, when new growth is two or three feet high, will kill at least 75% of the plants.

Waterfowl (rootstocks, seeds)
　　* Teal, Green-winged, *W*
　　　Goose
　**** 　Blue, *Pr.*; **Gulf Coast*
　+ 　Canada, *Mt.–Des.*
　** 　Snow, *Gulf Coast*
　** 　Tule, *Calif.*
Marshbirds and Shorebirds (seeds)
　+ Sandpiper, Semipalmated, *Atl.*
　　Coast
Fur and Game Mammals (rootstocks, culms, leaves)
　**** Muskrat, *NE*; **La. and Iowa*

Reference: Taxonomy and Distribution of N. American Cat-tails. Neil Hotch-kiss and Herbert L. Dozier. *Am. Midland Naturalist* Vol. 41(1), 237–254. 1949.

Burreed Family: *Sparganiaceae*

BURREEDS
Sparganium

[27*/19 users] Eight or ten species of burreeds occur in the northern half of the United States. They are more plentiful in the North, and it is here that they have their principal importance for wildlife. Some species grow immersed in streams and lakes with their strap-like leaves extending to the surface. Others like the important and widespread giant burreed (*S. eury-carpum*) occur more commonly along water margins. Burreeds do not develop extensive beds like some other marsh plants but tend to produce local colonies, generally near the water margin.

The bur-like heads of seeds (akenes)—often several burry balls in a series—identify the plants readily. The seeds of burreeds are eaten commonly by waterfowl and marshbirds. Muskrats use the entire plant. The somewhat spongy leaves are slightly triangular instead of perfectly flat.

Waterfowl (seeds)
+   Coot, *NE and W*
    Duck
*   Baldpate, *NE*
*   Black, *NE*
+   Bufflehead, *NE*
*   Canvasback, *W*
*** Mallard, *Minn.; *Pac.; +E and W*
+   Redhead, *NE*
*   Ring-necked, *W; +NE*
*   Scaup, Greater, *NE*

+   Teal, Blue-winged, *E*
+   Teal, Cinnamon, *Mt.–Des. and Pac.*
** Wood, *NE*
*** Swan, Whistling, *W*

Marshbirds and Shorebirds (seeds)
+   Crane, Little Brown, *W*
    Rail
+   King, *NE*
+   Sora, *NE*
+   Virginia, *W*
+   Snipe, Wilson, *U.S.*

Fur and Game Mammals (stems, foliage)
*** Muskrat, *Md.; **NE*

Pondweed Family: *Potamogetonaceae*

EELGRASS
Zostera marina

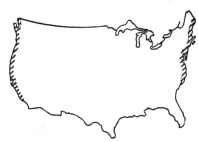

[**19*/15 users**] Eelgrass, a tape-leaf marine plant of brackish coastal estuaries, became the center of much popular interest following its phenomenal demise along much of the eastern seaboard in the early 1930's. Recently it has made a good comeback in many of the localities where it abounded formerly and may again become as plentiful as it was prior to 1932. The broader leafed west coast relative, usually considered a variety of the eastern species, was not damaged by the eelgrass malady and retained its abundance in bays along the Pacific coast.

These plants belong to the same family as the pondweeds and widgeongrass. The latter is often associated with eelgrass in the same brackish, coastal habitats. Doubtless the indirect

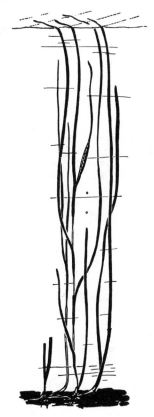

431

benefit of eelgrass to marine fisheries is very considerable, but the greatest evident value is to waterfowl. Brant, since time immemorial, have relied on the stems and leaves of eelgrass as their staple food. When, after 1932, great eastern beds of this plant disappeared, the American brant had a difficult time adjusting itself to a new diet. Many of the birds became emaciated and perished. Ducks also feed on the leaves and seed-producing portions of the plant.

Waterfowl (seeds, leaves, rootstocks)
Brant
***** (88%) American, *No.Atl. Coast before 1932; ** No.Atl. Coast after 1932*
*** Black, *Pac.Coast*

Duck
** Baldpate, *Pac.Coast;* +*No. Atl.Coast*
* Black, *No.Atl.Coast*
+ Goldeneye, American, *No. Atl. Coast*
+ Mallard, *No.Atl.Coast*
+ Pintail, *Pac.Coast*
* Scaup, Greater, *No.Atl.Coast*
+ Scaup, Lesser, *No.Atl.Coast*
* Scoter, American, *Atl. and Pac.Coasts*
* Scoter, Surf, *Atl. and Pac. Coasts*
* Scoter, White-winged, *Atl. and Pac.Coasts*
Goose
+ Canada, *Atl.Coast*
+ Emperor, *Oreg.*
Marshbirds and Shorebirds (seeds)
+ Knot, American, *No.Atl.Coast*

PONDWEEDS
Potamogeton

[286*/40 users] The United States has a good share (half or more) of the 65 or more species of this largest and most important group of seed-bearing aquatics. Pondweeds circle the temperate parts of the globe, and though some of them are present in practically all parts of this country, the great majority of American species are in the northern states. The Northeast is particularly rich in pondweeds—both in point of number of species and in abundance of the plants. They are the dominant vegetation in the thousands of lakes and ponds in the Great Lakes region and eastward into New England. In other regions, these aquatics are also important though the wealth of species is less.

Most of the pondweeds are fresh-water species, but a few thrive in moderate salinity or alkalinity. They grow in ponds, lakes, streams, and bays at various depths, depending largely on the clarity and constancy of the water. Some are large with coarse leaves and have little value to wildlife except for their seeds (drupelets). Many

others are relatively delicate with moderate-sized or small leaves and with practically all parts of the plant edible for waterfowl.

Sago pondweed (*P. pectinatus*) is the outstanding species in this outstanding genus. It occurs throughout the country, grows well in either fresh or moderately brackish water, and is by far the most valuable pondweed for wildlife. In many of the mildly alkaline lakes of the West, sago pondweed is particularly conspicuous, owing to the absence or scarcity of other species that require fresh water. The importance of this narrow-leafed aquatic depends only partly on its widespread availability. Other factors in its extensive use are the abundance of its large seeds, its palatable tubers (unusual among pondweeds), and the edibility of all other parts of the plant: stems, leaves, and rootstocks.

A listing of all the useful pondweeds would exclude only a very few species that are largely sterile or too rare or local to be significant. Practically all of them have value. In general, the

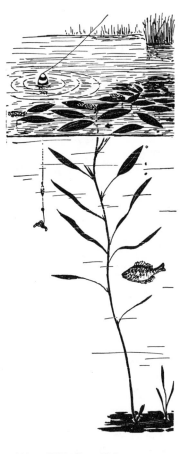

▨ Region of main use (about 40 sp.)

▨ Lesser use (about 20 sp.)

extent of wildlife importance of the various species is proportionate to their availability, the size and abundance of their seeds, and the tenderness of their leaves and stems.

Waterfowl (seeds, plants)

**** Coot, *W;* ***NE; **SE

Duck

***   Baldpate, *N and W;* **SE

***   Black, *E*

**   Bufflehead, *W;* *NE

***** (53%) Canvasback, *W;* ***E

***   Gadwall, *W;* *SE

***   Goldeneye, American, *W;* **NE

*   Goldeneye, Barrow, *NW*

****   Mallard, *Minn.;* ***NE and *W;* **SE

***   Pintail, *NE and W;* *SE

****   Redhead, *NE and W;* ***SE

****   Ring-necked, *NE;* ***W; *SE

***   Ruddy, *U.S.*

***   Scaup, Greater, *NE and W;* *SE

***   Scaup, Lesser, *NE;* **W; *SE

+   Scoter, Surf, *Atl. and Pac. Coasts*

+   Scoter, White-winged, *Atl. and Pac. Coasts*

***   Shoveller, *W;* **SE

**   Teal, Blue-winged, *NE;* *W; +SE

***   Teal, Cinnamon, *Mt.–Des. and Pac.*

***   Teal, Green-winged, *W;* *E

***   Wood, *NE*

Swan

***** (60%) Trumpeter, *Mont.; B.C.*

***   Whistling, *U.S.*

**** Goose, Canada, *Pac.;* ***Utah

Marshbirds and Shorebirds (seeds)

*** Avocet, *W*

Dowitcher

*   Eastern, *E*

**   Long-billed, *W*

**** Godwit, *W*

+ Knot, American, *E*

Rail

+   King, *E*

+   Sora, *SE and W*

+   Virginia, *NE and W*

Sandpiper

+   Pectoral, *U.S.*

+   Stilt, *U.S.*

+ Snipe, Wilson, *E*

Fur and Game Mammals (plants)
   * Muskrat, *NE*

Hoofed Browsers (plants)
   + Moose, *Maine to Mich.*

References: The Linear-leaved North American Species of *Potamogeton.* M. L. Fernald. *Amer. Acad. Arts and Sci. Mem.,* Vol. XVII, Part K, 1932. 184 pp. The Broad-leaved Species of *Potamogeton* of North America. E. C. Ogden. *Rhodora,* Vol. 45, 1943. 214 pp.

WIDGEONGRASS
Ruppia maritima

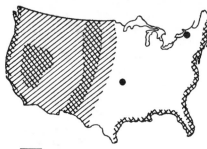

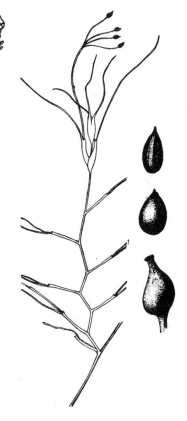

▨ Region of greatest abundance
▨ Less abundant

[104*/33 users] Widgeongrass like its relative sago pondweed rates as one of the most valuable species of submerged aquatics in the whole country. Its partiality to alkaline or saline areas is indicated by the range map. Frequently it is found in association with sago pondweed, both in coastal areas and in brackish inland waters. Unlike sago pondweed, however, widgeongrass rarely occurs in fresh-water bodies. Sometimes it is a little difficult to distinguish the young growth of sago pondweed from widgeongrass. The latter inclines to be distinct in its zigzag rootstocks and in the very short rounded stipules.

One reason for the great value of widgeongrass is the fact that it thrives in an alkaline environment unfavorable to most plants. In addition to this, practically all parts of the plant are edible and are consumed by waterfowl: the seeds, branches, leaves, and rootstocks. Its importance is indicated by the 3-star rating for eight species of waterfowl—from a tenth to a quar-

ter of their total food in the regions specified.

Waterfowl (seeds, plants)
   *** Brant, American, *Atl.Coast*
   *** Coot, *SE;* **W*
       Duck
   ***   Baldpate, *U.S.*
   **   Black, *SE;* **NE*

* Bufflehead, *W*
* Canvasback, *W*; +*SE*
*** Gadwall, *SE*; ***W*
+ Goldeneye, A m e r i c a n, *NE and W*
+ Goldeneye, Barrow, *NW*
* Mallard, *SE*; +*NE and W*
+ Mottled, *Gulf Coast*
** Pintail, *SE*; *W
*** Redhead, *SE*; *W; +*NE*
* Ring-necked, *W*; +*SE*
** Ruddy, *W*; *E
*** Scaup, Greater, *SE*; *W
*** Scaup, Lesser, *SE*; ***W*; +*NE*
+ Scoter, American, *Atl. and Pac.Coasts*
+ Scoter, Surf, *Atl. and Pac. Coasts*
* Shoveller, *SE*; +*W*

** Teal, Blue-winged, *SE and W*; *NE
* Teal, Cinnamon, *Mt.–Des. and Pac.*
* Teal, Green-winged, *W*; +*E*
*** Goose, Canada, *Atl.Coast*; ***Utah

Marshbirds and Shorebirds (seeds, foliage)
Dowitcher
+ Eastern, *E*
+ Long-billed, *W*
+ Gallinule, Purple, *SE*
* Knot, American, *E*
+ Rail, King, *SE*
Sandpiper
+ Pectoral, *U.S.*
+ Semipalmated, *Atl.Coast*
+ Stilt, *E*
* White-rumped, *E*

HORNED-PONDWEED
Zannichellia palustris

[28*/12 users] This relative of the true pondweeds (*Potamogeton*) has cosmopolitan distribution through the world's temperate and tropical regions. Horned-pondweed thrives in both fresh and moderately brackish water of lakes, streams, coastal ponds, and shallow marine estuaries. It is surprisingly abundant in the carp-infested Snake River in Idaho.

The vegetative parts of horned-pondweed and its horn-like seeds (nutlets), produced throughout the summer and early fall, are relished by ducks. This plant is not so abundant as some of the true pondweeds but, in proportion to its availability, it appears to be a choice duck food.

Waterfowl (seeds, plants)
Duck
* Baldpate, *SE*
*** Gadwall, *W*
+ Goldeneye, Barrow, *NW*
** Mallard, *W*; +*SE*
+ Pintail, *SE and W*
* Redhead, *W*; +*SE*
+ Ruddy, *W*
** Scaup, Lesser, *SE*
+ Shoveller, *SE and W*
** Teal, Cinnamon, *Mt.–Des. and Pac.*
* Teal, Green-winged, *W*; +*NE*
Marshbirds and Shorebirds (seeds)
+ Dowitcher, Long-billed, *W*

Naiad Family: *Najadaceae*

NAIADS
Najas

[38*/19 users] Of the half dozen or more species of *Najas* in the United States only two are noteworthy: northern naiad, or bushy pondweed (*N. flexilis*), and southern naiad (*N. guadal-* *upensis*). The former is abundant in the Northeast, often associated with true pondweeds and wildcelery, while the other, as its name implies, is primarily a plant of the South. A third species, spiny naiad (*N. marina*), is of limited local significance in Florida and in the few other localities where it occurs. The genus ranges into the West, but it is uncommon and unimportant there. In the main, naiads are fresh-water plants, but they tolerate mild brackishness—especially southern naiad.

These delicate, small-leaved members of the pondweed family are among the choicest\ of native eastern duck foods. Practically all parts of the plant are eaten: the stems, leaves, and numerous small seeds (nutlets), borne in the leaf axils.

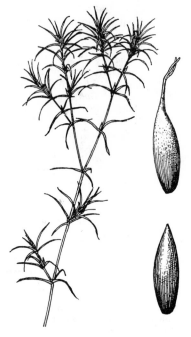

Waterfowl (branches, leaves, seeds)
*** Coot, *NE*; **SE*; +*W*
    Duck
  ***   Baldpate, *Wis.*; **E*
   **   Black, *SE*; *NE*
   **   Bufflehead, *NE*
    +   Canvasback, *E*
   **   Gadwall, *SE*; +*W*
    *   Mallard, *E*
   **   Mottled, *Gulf Coast*
    *   Pintail, *NE*; +*SE*
    *   Redhead, *E*
    *   Ring-necked, *NE*; +*SE*
    *   Ruddy, *E*
   **   Scaup, Greater, *NE*; *SE*
 ****   Scaup, Lesser, *Wis.*; **NE*
    +   Shoveller, *NE*

   **   Teal, Blue-winged, *NE*
    *   Teal, Green-winged, *NE*
    *   Goose, Canada, *Gulf Coast;* +*Atl.Coast*

Marshbirds and Shorebirds (seeds, leaves)
  +   Rail, King, *SE*

Water Plantain Family: *Alismaceae*

ARROWHEADS
Sagittaria

[25*/19 users] There are about 20 or more species of *Sagittaria* widely distributed in wet, nonsaline places throughout the country. Not all of them are arrow-leafed as their name implies. Some species have linear or lanceolate leaf blades.

A few species of tuber-forming arrowheads, called duckpotato or wapato, are of considerable value to wildlife. Prominent among these are the two common species *S. cuneata* and *S. latifolia*. They are widely distributed

though both have their principal abundance in the East. The tubers of the latter species are often too large and too deeply buried to be useful to ducks. Unless the plants are growing in water or very soft mud, the tubers may not be available to waterfowl. Another duckpotato (*S. heterophylla*) has some value in the Northeast, and the delta duckpotato (*S. platyphylla*) is important in Gulf and South Atlantic marshes. The small, flattish seeds of arrowheads are eaten by ducks, but the tubers are most valuable to wildlife.

The nutritious tubers of duckpotato arrowheads were used as food by the settlers as well as by the Indians in the early days.

Waterfowl (seeds, tubers)
    Duck
   *   Black, *NE*
 *** Canvasback, *SE*: +*NE*
 **   Gadwall, *SE*
 +   Mottled, *Gulf Coast*
 *   Mallard, *SE*: +*NE*
 *   Pintail, *SE*
 *   Ring-necked, *SE*
 +   Ruddy, *E*
 *   Scaup, Greater, *W*
 *   Scaup, Lesser, *NE*; +*SE*
 +   Teal, Blue-winged, *NE*
 *   Wood, *NE*
 + Goose, Canada, *Mt.–Des.*
    Swan
 **   Trumpeter, *Mont. and B.C.*
 **   Whistling, *E*

Marshbirds and Shorebirds (seeds)
 *   Rail, King, *NE*

Fur and Game Mammals (tubers, plants)
 ** Muskrat, *Md.*; *NE*
 *   Porcupine, *NE*

Frogbit Family: *Hydrocharitaceae*

WATERWEED
Anacharis (Elodea)

[1*/5 users] This tender, rapidly growing aquatic is common in northern waters. Only rarely does it produce seeds—its reproduction being almost entirely by vegetative means. Probably the lack of seeds is the main reason that it has a low rating as a duck food. Waterweed's vigorous growth often fills pools and ponds causing it to be recognized as an aquatic weed in many localities.

Waterfowl (leafy stems)
 *   Coot, *NE*
    Duck
 +   Bufflehead, *W*
 +   Canvasback, *W*
 +   Goldeneye, American, *NE*
 +   Redhead, *W*

WILDCELERY
Vallisneria spiralis

[31*/16 users] Wildcelery is one of the most familiar and valuable duck foods in the Northeast. This tape-leafed fresh-water aquatic grows in lakes, ponds, and slow streams and is particularly partial to sandy or silty bottoms. It tolerates only very mild salinity in coastal waters and in this regard differs from another long-leafed aquatic, eelgrass, which is confined to brackish bays and estuaries. Locally, wildcelery is also known by the name eelgrass. It has a broader leafed, less valuable relative (regarded as either

437

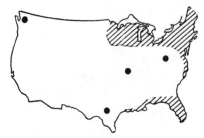

a variety or a distinct species) along the Gulf coast.

All parts of wildcelery plants are relished by waterfowl. Diving ducks are partial to the growing tips of the rootstocks, while other species consume the seeds and leaves. Frequently shoalwater ducks, especially teal, can be seen waiting for and feeding on fragments of wildcelery that float to the surface when diving species uproot submerged parts of the plants. True to its scientific name, the canvasback (*Aythya valisineria*) makes extensive use of *Vallisneria*.

Waterfowl (foliage, seeds, rootstocks)
* Coot, *NE*
  Duck
* Baldpate, *NE*; +*SE*
* Black, *NE*; +*SE*
* Bufflehead, *NE*
**** Canvasback, *NE*
* Goldeneye, American, *NE*
** Mallard, *NE*
+ Pintail, *NE*
*** Redhead, *NE*
* Ring-necked, *NE*

** Ruddy, *NE*
** Scaup, Greater, *NE*; *SE*
*** Scaup, Lesser, *NE*; *SE*
+ Teal, Green-winged, *NE*
* Wood, *NE*
*** Swan, Whistling, *E*

Grass Family: *Poaceae*

SALTGRASSES
Distichlis

[28*/11 users] All the four known species of saltgrass are American. Only two are important to wildlife: coastal (*D. spicata*) and desert saltgrass (*D. stricta*). They are confined to salty areas (alkaline or brackish) and for this reason are conspicuous only in the West and in seaboard marshes. In coastal areas they often occur in a zonal association with cordgrass. The creeping rootstocks of saltgrass produce dense sods and correspondingly dense (though low) marsh growths. The latter provide nesting cover for various waterfowl, notably the shoveller and cinnamon teal.

Goose

Region of greatest abundance

Less abundant

***   Canada, *Utah;* ***Gulf Coast;* +*Atl. and Pac.Coasts*

*   Snow, *U.S.*

Waterfowl (seed heads, young plants, rootstocks)

   Duck

\+   Black, *SE*

\+   Redhead, *W*

**   Shoveller, *W;* +*SE*

*   Teal, Blue-winged, *W*

**   Teal, Cinnamon, *Mt.–Des. and Pac.*

Marshbirds and Shorebirds (seeds)

\+   Dowitcher, Long-billed, *W*

\+   Rail, Sora, *W*

Small Mammals (seeds)

**   Ground Squirrel, Antelope, *Mt.– Des. and Calif.*

Hoofed Browsers (plants)

−   Deer, White-tailed, *Tex.*

CORDGRASSES
Spartina

[46*/15 users] Cordgrasses form a major part of the vegetation of our brackish coastal marshes. Six species are present along the coasts, and two others are found inland. The two most abundant and important species are the medium-tall, tidewater plant, salt-marsh cordgrass (*S. alterniflora*), and the smaller, finer saltmeadow cord-grass (*S. patens*). The latter grows on slightly higher ground exposed only to the higher tides. These two, growing in adjoining zones, are the dominant marsh plants of the Atlantic and Gulf coasts. They are often accompanied by the tall but less abundant big cordgrass (*S. cynosuroides*) which grows along canals and on the edges of sloughs and ponds. Two other species are restricted to the Gulf coast and still another to the scant marshlands of the Pacific coast. The two inland species are of little consequence to wildlife.

Cordgrass seeds are eaten by several kinds of ducks but are important only to the black duck. They are eaten by marshbirds too and are very important to two songbirds: the seaside and sharp-tailed sparrows. A very significant gamebird value of these grasses is the use of their rootstocks by geese. The rootstocks of both saltmarsh and saltmeadow cordgrass form a large proportion of the food of geese wintering along our coasts. Muskrats also feed on the underground parts of the plants. Cordgrass also provides a protective cover that benefits many species besides those which feed on it.

Waterfowl (rootstocks, seeds)
+ Brant, American, *Atl.Coast*
  Duck
** Black, *NE;* *SE
+ Mallard, *SE*
+ Teal, Green-winged, *NE*

Goose
** Blue, *Gulf Coast*
**** Canada, *Atl.Coast;* ***Gulf Coast*
*** Snow, *Atl.Coast;* **Gulf Coast*
Marshbirds and Shorebirds (seeds)
  Rail
* Clapper, *U.S.*
* Sora, *SE*
* Virginia, *SE*
Songbirds (seeds)
  Sparrow
*** Seaside, *Atl. and Gulf Coasts*
**** Sharp-tailed, *Atl.Coast*
Fur and Game Mammals (rootstocks, plants)
* Muskrat, *La.*
Hoofed Browsers (plants)
+ Deer, White-tailed, *Tex.*

RICE CUTGRASS
Leersia oryzoides

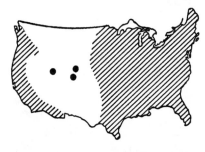

[**17***/**14 users**] Rice cutgrass (not related to giant cutgrass or sawgrass) is widely distributed in the United States but has its chief abundance along margins of eastern fresh-water lakes and streams. The light green growth of this grass forms a zone of variable width in rich, fine soil near, or partly within, the water's edge. The finely saw-toothed edges of the leaves, in combination with the rice-like grain, give the plant its name. Four other species of *Leersia* are present in this country, but they are not plentiful enough to be important for wildlife.

The seeds of rice cutgrass are eaten by ducks, swamp and tree sparrows, and by the sora rail. Ducks also pull up the rootstocks and eat them in quantity.

Waterfowl (seeds, rootstocks)
  Duck
** Baldpate, *NE*
** Black, *Wis.*
** Mallard, *Wis.;* *NE
+ Pintail, *NE*
* Ring-necked, *NE*
+ Scaup, Lesser, *NE*
* Teal, Blue-winged, *NE*
* Teal, Green-winged, *NE*
**** Various spp., 3,200 individuals, *Ill.*
+ Wood, *SE*
Marshbirds and Shorebirds (seeds)
* Rail, Sora, *NE*

440

Songbirds (seeds)
   Sparrow
  *   Swamp, *NE*

   *   Tree, *NE*
Fur and Game Mammals (plants)
  ** Muskrat, *Md.*; +*La.*

WILDRICE
Zizania aquatica

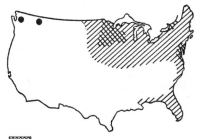

▨ Region of greatest abundance
▨ General range

[54*/23 users] Wildrice, in its two native varieties, is present in many parts of the East from the Canadian border to the Gulf of Mexico. However, its stands are relatively local and insignificant south of the coastal portion of the Carolinas. This famous duck food grows in greatest abundance in the northern tier of states from Maine to the eastern margin of the Prairies and in fresh-water marshes along the Atlantic coast. Wildrice thrives in shallow water where bottoms are mucky or silty and is partial to water areas in which there is enough circulation to prevent stagnation.

The rod-like seeds of this tall, plume-topped grass are a favorite food of ducks, rails, blackbirds, and the bobolink. Wildrice rates as a top duck food in the Northeast. The plant has been introduced successfully in a few localities outside its normal range, but unless the prerequisites of deep, soft mud and slowly circulating water are present, there is little likelihood of satisfactory growths, year after year.

Waterfowl (seeds)
  *** Coot, *NE*

   Duck
  *   Baldpate, *NE*
  ** Black, *NE* ;**SE*
  *   Bufflehead, *NE*
  ** Canvasback, *NE*
 **** Mallard, *Minn.*; ****NE*;
     +*SE*
  ** Pintail, *NE*
 *** Redhead, *NE*
  ** Ring-necked, *NE*
  + Scaup, Greater, *NE*
  ** Scaup, Lesser, *NE*
 *** Teal, Blue-winged, *Wis.*;
     **NE*; +*SE*
  ** Teal, Green-winged, *NE*;
     +*SE*
 *** Wood, *NE*
  * Goose, Snow, *E*
Marshbirds and Shorebirds (seeds)
   Rail
 *** Sora, *NE*
  ** Virginia, *NE*
Songbirds (seeds)
   Blackbird
  ** Redwing, *NE*
  ** Rusty, *NE*
 *** Bobolink, *NE*
  * Crow, Fish, *E*
   Sparrow
  ** Sharp-tailed, *Atl.Coast*
  + Song, *NE*

References: The Salt Water Limits of Wild Rice. Carl S. Scofield. *U.S. Dept. Agr. Bul.* 72, 1905. 5 pp.

Wild Rice. Charles E. Chambliss. *U.S. Dept. Agr. Circ.* 229, 1922. 13 pp.
The Botany and History of Wild Rice. Charles E. Chambliss. *Smithsonian Inst. Pub.* 3622, 1941. 14 pp.

WILDMILLETS
Echinochloa

▓▓ Region of greatest abundance

▨▨ General range

[49*/29 users] Wildmillet, also known as barnyard grass and watergrass, is a cosmopolitan species found throughout the country in a variety of habitats. It grows in upland areas as well as in low, wet places, but its greatest abundance is near water—especially on mud flats from which water has receded early in the growing season.

Common wildmillet (*E. crusgalli*) is the widespread species found nearly everywhere in the country. It is represented by several varieties including the introduced one *E. frumentacea*, known locally as Japanese millet. Junglerice (*E. colonum*) is common in parts of the Gulf region—especially in rice fields. Walter wildmillet (*E. walteri*) is confined to the East and has its greatest abundance in Gulf coast marshes and near the Great Lakes.

The smooth, moderately large seeds of these grasses are important food for ducks and are also used by other birds. All three species have wildlife value. A practice advocated in waterfowl management is the seeding of wildmillet and smartweed onto moist mud flats over which water can be brought in the fall.

Waterfowl (seeds)
    Duck
     * Baldpate, *NE and W*

* Black, *Wis.*
* Gadwall, *W*
+ Goldeneye, American, *W*
** Mallard, *E;* *W*
+ Mottled, *Gulf Coast*
** Pintail, *NE and W;* *SE*
* Redhead, *W*
* Ring-necked, *W;* +*NE*
+ Scaup, Greater, *W*
* Shoveller, *SE*
+ Teal, Blue-winged, *E*
** Teal, Green-winged, *NE and W;* *SE*
** Goose, White-fronted, *Calif.*
Marshbirds and Shorebirds (seeds)
  * Gallinule, Purple, *SE*
  * Rail, Sora, *NE and W*
  + Snipe, Wilson, *U.S.*
Upland Gamebirds (seeds)
  + Dove, Mourning, *E*
  + Pheasant, Ring-necked, *Pa.*
  + Quail, Valley, *Nev.*
Songbirds (seeds)
    Blackbird
  +   Redwing, *SE and Calif.*
  *   Redwing, Tricolored, *Calif.*
  + Cowbird, *SE*
  + Longspur, Smith, *Ill.*
    Sparrow
  +   English, *E*
  +   Lincoln, *NE*
  *   Savannah, *NE*
Fur and Game Mammals (foliage, plants)
  − Muskrat, *Iowa*
  + Rabbit, New England Cottontail, *Conn.*

Sedge Family: *Cyperaceae*

CHUFA AND ALLIES
Cyperus

▓▓▓ Region of greatest use of chufa
▒▒▒ General range of chufa

[**23*/23 users**] Of a total of about 600 species in the genus *Cyperus*, there are nearly 90 representatives in the United States. This large group of moist soil plants has no well-established common name, though sweetrush, galingale, and flatsedge are sometimes used. The name chufa is properly applied to a single important species, *C. esculentus*.

The wildlife value of chufa, also known as nutgrass, nutrush, or ground almond, is probably much greater than that of all other species of *Cyperus* combined. Both the edible tubers of chufa and its seeds are sought by waterfowl, upland gamebirds, and songbirds. Most of the records in the listing below are based on this particular species. Chufa is often abundant in mud flats that are covered by water in the late fall or winter season. In such places the plant's nutritious tubers are readily available to ducks. It also occurs as a vigorous, unwelcome weed in many fields and gardens—particularly in sandy soil or light loam. In such places, upland gamebirds and rodents like to dig for the tubers.

Common, widespread kinds of *Cyperus* include *C. strigosus*, *C. erythrorhizos*, *C. ferax*, *C. ovularis*, and *C. compressus*. The seeds of these species are eaten frequently by a number of birds.

Waterfowl (seeds, tubers)
+ Coot, *S and W*
   Duck
*   Florida, *Fla.*
*   Mallard, *SE*; +*W*
+   Pintail, *SE*
+   Ring-necked, *SE*
+   Ruddy, *W*
*   Teal, Blue-winged, *SE*; +*W*
+   Teal, Cinnamon, *Mt.–Des. and Pac.*
** Teal, Green-winged, *NE*; *SE and W

Upland Gamebirds (seeds, tubers)
   Dove
** Ground, *Gulf Coast*
+   White-winged, *Ariz.*
**** Quail, Mearns, *SW*
* Turkey, Wild, *SE*
− Woodcock, *NE*

Songbirds (tubers, seeds)
+ Blackbird, Redwing, *La.*
+ Bobolink, *SE*
* Crow, *Pac.*; +*E*
* Grackle, Boat-tailed, *SE*
+ Lark, California Horned, *Calif.*
* Sparrow, Tree, *NE*
* Thrasher, Curve-billed, *SW*

443

Fur and Game Mammals (tubers)
— Squirrel, Western Fox, *Mo.*

Small Mammals (tubers)
+ Rat, Ord Kangaroo, *W*

BULRUSHES
Scirpus

[206*/52 users] The 40 or more species of bulrush present in the United States form one of the most conspicuous plant groups in American marshlands. These representatives of the sedge family range considerably in size. Some are less than one foot high and hardly deserve the group name bulrush (implying large rush). On the other hand, tall species may reach a height of seven feet. Bulrushes vary in form and appearance; some have cylindrical or whip-like stems (round-stemmed group), some are triangular-stemmed and bare of leaves (threesquares), while still others have angular stems and conspicuous leaves or bracts (leafy bulrushes). The most important species in the three groups are:

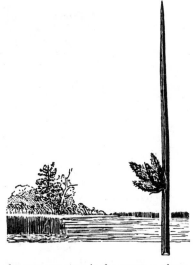

ROUND-STEMMED BUL-RUSHES. Hardstem (*acutus*), mainly northern and western; softstem (*validus*), widespread; slender (*heterochaetus*), northern; southern (*californicus*), southern

THREESQUARES. Common (*americanus*), widespread; Olney (*olneyi*), coastal and southwestern; Torrey (*torreyi*), northeastern; swamp (*etuberculatus*), southeastern

LEAFY BULRUSHES: Alkali (*paludosus*), western; saltmarsh (*robustus*), coastal in East; river (*fluviatilis*), northern

The hard-coated seeds (akenes) of bulrushes are one of the more important and most commonly used foods of ducks and of certain marshbirds and shorebirds. The stems and underground parts are eaten by muskrats and geese. Furthermore, bulrushes furnish important nesting cover for waterfowl as well as for marsh wrens and blackbirds and give concealing protection to muskrats, otters, raccoons, and other animals.

An outstandingly important species,

the country over, is the common threesquare (*S. americanus*). Ordinarily, it does not grow in extensive stands like some of the others, but it frequently forms fringes along the edge of ponds, lakes, and streams. These locations tend to make the plant's seeds readily available to ducks. Its close relative, Olney threesquare, has little value for ducks but is one of the favorite foods of coastal muskrats.

Hardstem bulrush is the most common and valuable marsh plant of inland areas of the West, particularly in the Northwest. It tolerates some alkalinity but not so much as the alkali bulrush, another western species of considerable value. Saltmarsh bulrush is a useful food for ducks, geese, and muskrats along the Atlantic and Gulf coasts. Softstem and slender bulrushes and other species have value in their respective regions.

Waterfowl (seeds mainly)
*** Coot, *NE and W;* +*SE*

Duck
** Baldpate, *E; *W*
** Black, *NE; *SE*
+ Bufflehead, *NE and W*
*** Canvasback, *SE; +NE*
*** Gadwall, *SE; *W*
+ Goldeneye, American, *W*
*** Mallard, Common, *W; **SE; *Wis.; +NE*
**** Mottled, *Gulf Coast*
*** Pintail, *NE and W; **SE*
*** Redhead, *W; **NE; +SE*
* Ring-necked, *U.S.*
*** Ruddy, *W; **E*
* Scaup, Greater, *W; +E*
** Scaup, Lesser, *W; *NE; +SE*
*** Shoveller, *SE; **W*
*** Teal, Blue-winged, *W; **E*
*** Teal, Cinnamon, *Mt.–Des. and Pac.*
*** Teal, Green-winged, *U.S.*
Goose
**** Blue, *Gulf Coast* (stems)
*** Canada, *Pac.; **Gulf Coast and Utah; +Atl. Coast* (stems)
*** Snow, *W; **Gulf Coast* (stems)
** Tule, *Calif.* (stems)
Swan
* Trumpeter, *Mont. and B.C.* (seeds and stems)
+ Whistling, *E* (seeds and stems)
Marshbirds and Shorebirds (seeds, rootstocks)
+ Avocet, *W*
*** Crane, Florida, *Fla.*

Dowitcher
+ Eastern, *E*
* Long-billed, *W*
Godwit
*** Hudsonian, *N*
+ Marbled, *W*
+ Knot, American, *E*
Rail
+ Clapper, *U.S.*
+ King, *SE*
*** Sora, *W; **NE*
* Virginia, *NE and W; +SE*
+ Yellow, *E*
Sandpiper
+ Pectoral, *U.S.*
* Semipalmated, *Atl.Coast*
+ Stilt, *U.S.*
* Snipe, Wilson, *U.S.*
Upland Gamebirds (seeds)
+ Pheasant, Ring-necked, *Utah*
* Quail, Mearns, *N.Mex. and Ariz.*
Songbirds (seeds)
+ Blackbird, Tricolored Redwing, *Calif.*
+ Bunting, Snow, *NE*
+ Crossbill, Red, *No.U.S.*
+ Longspur, Smith, *Ill.*
Sparrow
+ Botteri, *Tex.*
+ Song, *NE*
Fur and Game Mammals (rootstocks, aerial stems)
*** Muskrat, *NE and La.*
Small Mammals (seeds)
+ Mouse, Meadow, *E*

SPIKERUSHES
Eleocharis

[66*/29 users] Spikerushes are a varied group of essentially leafless, sedge-family plants varying in size from midgets, one or two inches high, to others that are two or three feet tall. There are about 45 species in the country— some being present near the margins of most of our aquatic areas. Like the bulrushes, their stems vary from cylindrical to triangular. But unlike typical bulrushes, spikerush stems are capped by a single compact spike.

The cluster of tubercle-topped seeds (akenes) in the spike is the principal attraction of these plants to wildlife. Spikerushes are moderately valuable to ducks, but only about half a dozen species contribute appreciably to this importance. Common spikerush (*E. palustris*), now construed as a complex of several species by many botanists, is one of our most familiar, widespread examples. Its slender, cylindrical stems are about a foot high. Dwarf spikerush (*E. parvula*), a minute, stocky species, is particularly sought by ducks. Wher-

445

ever the plants occur—mainly in the alkaline West and along the coasts—ducks very commonly eat the underground tubers as well as the seeds. The slender spikerush (*E. acicularis*) forms plush-like mats of growth along water margins in many parts of the country; yet its minute spikes and seeds are eaten only sparingly. Squarestem spikerush (*E. quadrangulata*) is a valuable, medium-tall species that is abundant locally along the Atlantic and Gulf coasts and in the Mississippi Valley. In the South also, jointed (*E. interstincta*) and Gulf coast spikerushes (*E. cellulosa* and *E. equisetoides*) are common enough to be useful to waterfowl. A fairly common but apparently worthless southern species is the generally sterile submerged spikerush (*E. prolifera*).

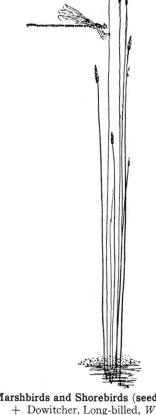

Waterfowl (seeds, culms, tubers)
- * Coot, *SE*; +*NE and W*
- Duck
  - ** Baldpate, *W*; +*SE*
  - ** Black, *SE*; +*NE*
  - + Florida, *Fla.*
  - + Gadwall, *SE*
  - ** Mallard, *SE*; *W
  - *** Mottled, *Gulf Coast*
  - * Pintail, *NE and W;* +*SE*
  - + Redhead, *U.S.*
  - ** Ring-necked, *SE*
  - + Scaup, Lesser, *W*
  - ** Shoveller, *W*; *SE
  - * Teal, Blue-winged, *U.S.*
  - * Teal, Cinnamon, *Mt.–Des. and Pac.*
  - ** Teal, Green-winged, *W*; *E
- Goose
  - ** Blue, *Gulf Coast*
  - *** Canada, *Atl.Coast*
  - ** Snow, *Gulf Coast*
- ** Swan, Whistling, *E*

Marshbirds and Shorebirds (seeds)
- + Dowitcher, Long-billed, *W*
- * Gallinule, Purple, *SE*
- Rail
  - * King, *SE*
  - * Sora, *NE*; +*SE*
  - * Virginia, *NE*; +*SE*
  - + Yellow, *E*
- + Sandpiper, Stilt, *W*
- + Snipe, Wilson, *SE*

Fur and Game Mammals (plant)
- + Rabbit, Cottontail, *Calif.*
- + Muskrat, *NE*

SAWGRASS
Cladium jamaicensis

[4*/14 users] Sawgrass is a semitropical saw-edged member of the sedge family. In Louisiana, Florida, and other southern coastal areas it produces extensive stands of tall, dense growth through which even trappers and hunters hesi-

tate to penetrate. Two other species of *Cladium* occur in the country—one in the Northeast and the other in Southern California—but neither of them are significant to wildlife.

Seeds (akenes) of sawgrass are used commonly by southern ducks, but generally in small quantities. The plant is far from being a choice duck food. Locally it provides sanctuary to waterfowl by serving as a barrier to hunters.

Waterfowl (seeds)
    Duck
  +   Florida, *Fla.*
  +   Gadwall, *SE*
  +   Mallard, *SE*
  *   Mottled, *Gulf Coast*
  +   Pintail, *SE*
  +   Redhead, *SE*

  *   Shoveller, *SE*
  *   Teal, Blue-winged, *SE*
  +   Teal, Green-winged, *SE*
  +   Wood, *SE*
  *   Goose, White-fronted, *La.*
Marshbirds and Shorebirds (seeds)
  + Gallinule, Purple, *SE*
  + Snipe, Wilson, *SE*
Fur and Game Mammals (stems)
  + Muskrat, *La.*

Arum Family: *Araceae*

ARROW-ARUM
Peltandra virginica

[3*/2 users] Two species of arrow-arum are recognized, one in the Northeast and the other in the Southeast. The northern one has given evidence of some value to wildlife. These broad-leaved marsh plants have large berries which are relished by the wood duck and are occasionally eaten by other birds.

Waterfowl (seeds)
  *** Duck, Wood, *N.Y.*; **NE*
Marshbirds and Shorebirds (seeds)
  + Rail, King, *NE*

Duckweed Family: *Lemnaceae*

DUCKWEEDS
Lemna, Spirodela, Wolffia, Wolffiella

[30*/16 users] In late summer millions of these midgets of the plant world form green coverings over the water surface in swamps, sheltered ponds,

and other quiet waters throughout the United States. Common duckweed (*Lemna minor*), not much larger than a pinhead, is by far the most widespread and abundant, but there are about five other species of *Lemna* in the country—some of them quite local. Star duckweed (*L. trisulca*), a species that is generally suspended in the water (rather than floating on the surface), is encountered in many places in the northern states.

There are three other duckweed or duckweed-like genera, all of lesser abundance and importance. Big duckweed (*Spirodela polyrhiza*), a rather coarse species with purplish-tinged lower side, is frequently associated with common duckweed. Sometimes one finds mixtures of these two, together with the tiny, almost granular appearing ducksmeal (*Wolffia*)—the smallest of all flowering plants. *Wolffiella floridana*, a semitransparent, tongue-like duckweed, is confined largely to coastal sections of the Southeast.

All four of these duckweed genera (*Lemna, Spirodela, Wolffia,* and *Wolffiella*) are used as food by wildlife and have been recorded from duck stomachs. However, about nine-tenths of this use consists in feeding on common duckweed. When waterfowl eat this salad-like fare, they doubtless obtain considerable numbers of minute animal organisms associated with it. The prin-cipal use of duckweeds is in summer and early fall—before the arrival of frost.

Waterfowl (plants)
**** Coot, *SE*; **NE*; +*W*
    Duck
****   Baldpate, *Wis.*; +*NE*
+   Black, *NE*
+   Bufflehead, *NE*
**   Mallard, *SE*; +*NE*
*   Mottled, *Gulf Coast*
*   Redhead, *SE*
**   Ring-necked, *SE*
*   Shoveller, *SE*; +*W*
***   Teal, Blue-winged, *NE*; +*SE*
+   Teal, Cinnamon, *Mt.–Des. and Pac.*
**   Teal, Green-winged, *SE*; +*W*
**   Wood, *SE*; **NE*
Marshbirds and Shorebirds (plants)
** Gallinule, Purple, *SE*
* Rail, Sora, *SE*; +*NE*

Pickerelweed Family: *Pontederiaceae*

PICKERELWEED
Pontederia cordata

[2*/4 users] The bright blue spires of flowers and heart- or lance-shaped leaves of pickerelweed are a common sight along marshy, mucky margins of shallow ponds and sluggish streams throughout the East. The narrow-leafed form of the Southeast is sometimes classed as a distinct species. Despite its prevalence, the value of pickerelweed to wildlife is low.

Waterfowl (seeds)
    Duck
+   Black, *NE*
**   Mottled, *Gulf Coast*
+   Wood, *NE*
Fur and Game Mammals (seeds)
+ Muskrat, *NE*

Buckwheat Family: *Polygonaceae*

SMARTWEEDS .
Polygonum

[128*/66 users] Only the 15 to 20 amphibious species of *Polygonum*—the ones known as smartweed—are included here. The rest of the genus is definitely upland and is treated on page 387 under the name "knotweed." Smartweeds are widely distributed in fresh-water areas of the country. One species is strictly aquatic, but the remainder thrive in moist alluvial soils along water margins and also in fertile cultivated fields that become water-soaked in late winter and spring. In some places—particularly in the northern states—smartweeds form extensive marshes. Locally, they may cover one to several acres and occasionally much larger areas.

The really important species of smartweed can be counted on one's hand. Ladysthumb (*P. persicaria*), bigseed smartweed (*P. pennsylvanicum*), and dotted smartweed (*P. punctatum*) are widespread species that are common to abundant in moist places. Nodding (*P. lapathifolium*) and marsh smartweed (*P. muhlenbergii*) produce extensive marsh growths in the northern half of the country. Species of more localized value are water smartweed (*P. amphibium*), common on western lakes, swamp smartweed (*P. hydropiperoides*), a small triangular-seeded species plentiful in the Southeastern Coastal Plain, and Puerto Rico smartweed (*P. portoricense*) of the Gulf region and Coastal Plain.

Any aquatic area bordered by extensive growths of smartweed is likely to be popular with ducks. In places where the water level recedes in summer, leaving exposed mud flats, these plants can thrive and produce a harvest of seeds for waterfowl. Rivaling the importance of smartweeds for waterfowl is their value to many of our most common and best-loved songbirds.

Waterfowl (seeds)
+ Coot, *NE*
  Duck
+ Baldpate, *NE and W*
*** Black, *Wis.*; **SE; *NE
+ Bufflehead, *NE*
+ Canvasback, *W*
*** Florida, *Fla.*
+ Gadwall, *W*
+ Goldeneye, American, *NE and W*
**** Mallard, *Wis.*; ***NE; **SE; *Pac.*; +W
+ Mottled, *Gulf Coast*
*** Pintail, *NE*
* Redhead, *NE and W*
** Ring-necked, *NE*; *W
+ Ruddy, *U.S.*
* Scaup, Greater, *W*
* Scaup, Lesser, *SE and W*; +NE
+ Shoveller, *SE and W*
*** Teal, Blue-winged, *SE and W*; *NE
* Teal, Cinnamon, *Mt.–Des. and Pac.*
** Teal, Green-winged, *W*
** Wood, *NE*; +SE
** Goose, Canada, *Utah*
** Swan, Whistling, *E*
Marshbirds and Shorebirds (seeds)
+ Dowitcher, Eastern, *E*
+ Godwit, Hudsonian, *N*
  Rail
+ Clapper, *U.S.*
+ King, *E*
* Sora, *U.S.*
+ Virginia, *E*
** Yellow, *E*
  Sandpiper
+ Pectoral, *U.S.*
+ Stilt, *W*
* Snipe, Wilson, *NE*; +SE and W
Upland Gamebirds (seeds)
− Partridge, Chukar, *Mo.*
+ Prairie Chicken, *Ill.*
*** Quail, Bobwhite, *NE*

Songbirds (seeds)
- ** Blackbird, Redwing, *NE*; **SE*
- * Bobolink, *E*
- *** Cardinal, *NE*; **Pr.*; +*SE*
- + Cowbird, *NE*
- * Grosbeak, Rose-breasted, *NE and Pr.*
- * Junco, Slate-colored, *E*
- * Lark, Horned, *E*
- + Meadowlark, *NE*
- + Pipit, *NE*
- *** Redpoll, Common, *NE*
- Sparrow
  - + Chipping, *E*
  - **** Fox, *E*
  - * Grasshopper, Eastern, *NE*
  - + Henslow, *NE*
  - + Lark, *Pr.*

- * Savannah, *NE*; +*Pr.*
- * Seaside, *Atl. and Gulf Coasts*
- *** Song, *NE*
- *** Swamp, *NE*
- + Tree, *NE*
- ** Vesper, *E*
- ** White-crowned, *NE*
- *** White-throated, *NE*
- ** Towhee, Brown, *NE*; **SE*

Fur and Game Mammals (plants, seeds)
- − Muskrat, *Iowa*
- + Raccoon, *Iowa*
- − Squirrel, Fox, *Ohio*

Small Mammals (seeds)
- ** Chipmunk, Western, *Mt.–Des. and Pac.*

Goosefoot Family: *Chenopodiaceae*

GLASSWORTS
Salicornia

[10*/5 users] These succulent, somewhat glassy members of the goosefoot family include at least four species in saline areas of the United States. Glassworts are typical of muddy, brackish tidal flats of coastal marshlands or alkaline mud flats bordering western lakes. They grow in salty environments, taste salty, and are sometimes called saltworts.

Geese feed on the slightly fleshy branches of glasswort. In the fall ducks, particularly the pintail, eat the seed-containing stem tips when they turn reddish with maturity.

Waterfowl (stems, seeds, leaves)
- Duck
  - + Gadwall, *W*
  - ** Pintail, *SE*
  - + Scaup, Greater, *SE*
- Goose
  - *** Canada, *Utah;* **Gulf Coast; +Atl.Coast*
  - * Snow, *W*

Pigweed Family: *Amaranthaceae*

WATERHEMPS
Acnida

[3*/2 users] At least half a dozen species of *Acnida* are present in the United States—mainly in the East or Southeast. These tall, weedy, moist-soil members of the pigweed family produce large numbers of seeds (as much as two quarts per plant) and are of local value to ducks. Tall waterhemp (*A. altissima*) has wide range throughout the East, and its minute seeds have been used by ducks in several places. Tidemarsh waterhemp (*A. cannabina*) is of local importance along the Atlantic coast. Its relatively large seeds (about one-eighth inch across) have been eaten in large quantities by the black ducks both in New Jersey and Connecticut.

Waterfowl (seeds)
Duck
+ Black, *NE*
*** Teal, Green-winged, *Wis.*

Waterlily Family: *Nymphaeaceae*

WATERSHIELD
Brasenia schreberi

[**7*/6 users**] Watershield, a small-leaved, small-flowered member of the waterlily group is a comparatively uncommon aquatic, but it is by no means rare. It occurs locally throughout much of the East—particularly in limestone areas. The hard spherical seeds are eaten freely by ducks. If watershield were less locally distributed, it would probably rate as a valuable duck food. It has been transplanted with success into a number of ponds along the South Atlantic coast.

Waterfowl (seeds)
Duck
+ Mallard, *E*
+ Pintail, *E*
+ Redhead, *SE*
*** Ring-necked, *SE and Wis.*
+ Scaup, Lesser, *S*
* Wood, *NE*

WATERLILIES
Nymphaea (formerly *Castalia*)

[**27*/17 users**] At least eight species of waterlily have been listed in the United States. Their distribution is restricted largely to eastern ponds and lakes. Two of these attractive aquatics are far more common than all the others. They are American waterlily (*N. odorata*), common in acid waters near the seaboard, and magnolia waterlily (*N. tuberosa*) which occurs in limey areas farther inland. The seeds of these two species and of others are eaten frequently by ducks, but only in the Gulf region are they important as a duck food.

Banana waterlily (*N. flava*) has

demonstrated much value for ducks in the relatively few areas where it is available. This yellow-flowered species grows locally along the Gulf coast and has been transplanted– because of its wildlife value—to ponds along the South Atlantic coast and elsewhere. Its rootstocks, banana-like tubers, and seeds have been eaten extensively by the canvasback and by several other species of ducks.

The moose makes waterlily pads a principal item of its diet. Beaver, muskrat, and porcupine feed on various parts of the plants.

Waterfowl (seeds, rootstocks)
  Duck
   *** Canvasback, *SE*
   + Florida, *Fla.*

  + Mottled, *Gulf Coast*
  + Pintail, *SE*
  ** Redhead, *SE*
  * Ring-necked, *SE*
  + Scaup, Greater, *NE*
  * Scaup, Lesser, *SE*; +*NE*
  * Shoveller, *SE*
  * Teal, Blue-winged, *SE*
  ** Wood, *SE*; +*NE*

Marshbirds and Shorebirds (stems, roots, seeds)
  ** Crane, Florida, *Fla.*
  + Gallinule, *SE*

Fur and Game Mammals (plants)
  ** Beaver, *NE and W*
  * Muskrat, *Md.*
  * Porcupine, *E*

Hoofed Browsers (foliage, plants)
  ** Moose, *No.Mt.–Des.*; *Mich.*; +*Maine*

COWLILIES
Nuphar

[10*/8 users] The familiar, yellow-flowered cowlily, or pondlily, that grows in ponds and shallow lakes and on the borders of sluggish streams includes about five species in the United States. Spatterdock cowlily (*N. advena*) is common in the East, Rocky Mountain cowlily (*N. polysepalum*) is the only representative in the West, and arrow cowlily (*N. sagittifolium*)—often called bonnets—is an interesting long-leafed species restricted to the Southeast.

These large-leafed aquatics are tolerant of muddy, fluctuating water—conditions that commonly prevent the growth of more desirable plants. Despite their abundance, cowlilies have low wildlife value. Their seeds are eaten by ducks to a limited extent, but the plants cannot be classed as good duck foods. In some localities they compete successfully with valuable plants.

Waterfowl (seeds)
  Duck
   * Florida, *Fla.*
   * Mallard, *Pac.*
   *** Ring-necked, *Wis.*; +*W*
   * Wood, *NE*

Marshbirds and Shorebirds (seeds)
  + Crane, Florida, *Fla.*
  + Rail, Virginia, *E*

Fur and Game Mammals (plants)
  ** Beaver, *NE*
  ** Porcupine, Eastern, *NE*

Coontail Family: *Ceratophyllaceae*

COONTAIL
Ceratophyllum demersum

[10*/12 users] One of the most common and widely distributed of our sub-merged aquatics is coontail. Besides being common in nature, it is popular in fish bowls or aquariums. This aggressive, fine-leaved water plant is peculiar in not having or needing roots. Its lower end may be anchored in the mud, or the whole plant may be unattached. The length of individual plants varies greatly, depending on whether or not breaks have occurred in the branching stem. Small broken-off pieces can function as new plants. In the fall some of the tips become coarse and rather bunchy. These eventually sink to the bottom serving as winter buds to tide the plant over until the next growing season. Seeds (akenes) also are produced, sometimes abundantly and sometimes scant or absent.

Under favorable conditions coontail can practically fill a pond with a dense matting of its vegetation. It is tolerant of fluctuating water levels and moderate turbidity and under these conditions finds little competition from other plants. Because of this adaptability it is plentiful in mucky-bottomed sloughs, ponds, and lakes of the Mississippi Valley.

The seeds and leaves are eaten by ducks, but the quantities taken are hardly in proportion to the abundance and widespread availability of the plant. It does not seem to be a choice food. A good growth of coontail is preferable to no aquatics at all, but there is also the probability that in many places it competes with, and crowds out, more desirable plants.

Waterfowl (plants, seeds)
* *   Coot, *NE*; *W*
*   Duck
* \+   Baldpate, *SE*
* \+   Bufflehead, *NE*
* \+   Canvasback, *U.S.*
* **   Gadwall, *SE*
* *   Mallard, *SE*; *+NE and W*
* *   Redhead, *NE*; *+SE*
* **   Ring-necked, *SE*; **NE*; *+W*
* \+   Ruddy, *U.S.*
* *   Scaup, Greater, *NE*; *+SE*
* \+   Scaup, Lesser, *U.S.*

Marshbirds and Shorebirds (seeds)
* \+   Sandpiper, Stilt, *W*

Watermilfoil Family: *Haloragidaceae*

WATERMILFOILS
Myriophyllum

[13*/14 users] About 10 species of watermilfoils grow in quiet ponds, swamps, and shallow bays of lakes in different parts of the country. These cut-leafed, rather coarse, submerged aquatics become abundant in some localities but in general they are not so plentiful as pondweeds and other valuable duck foods. The woody seeds (nutlets) of *M. spicatum* are eaten to a considerable extent in prairie lakes of the Dakotas and adjoining states. Other common species are *M. verticillatum* in the Northeast and *M. heterophyllum* in the Southeast. Though seeds of watermilfoil are often found in duck stomachs, their quantity is generally small. At best, the plants are low-grade duck foods—near the border line of being aquatic weeds.

453

Waterfowl (seeds, foliage)
    Duck
  *   Baldpate, *W*
  +   Bufflehead, *W*
  *   Canvasback, *W*; +*NE*
  *   Mallard, *Pac.;* +*W*
  +   Pintail, *W*
  +   Ruddy, *W*
  *   Scaup, Lesser, *W*; +*NE*
  *   Shoveller, *W*

+   Teal, Blue-winged, *NE*
+   Teal, Cinnamon, *Mt.–Des. and Pac.*
+   Teal, Green-winged, *SE*
Marshbirds and Shorebirds (seeds)
+   Dowitcher, *E*
  Sandpiper
+   Pectoral, *U.S.*
+   Stilt, *E*

CHAPTER SEVENTEEN

Cultivated Plants

G RAIN AND FORAGE FIELDS, fruit orchards, gardens, and vineyards are extremely important sources of wildlife food. And wherever cultivated crops are raised, weeds are likely to accompany them. Nowadays the majority of our wildlife species obtain part or all of their livelihood on farm land. This is a highly significant fact in wildlife management.

With both man and wildlife obtaining food from the same environment, it is inevitable that conflict occurs. A considerable proportion of the economic toll can be controlled by local measures. Ordinarily, the period of danger to crops, particularly to fruits, is brief, often limited to a couple of critical weeks. During this short interval, frightening devices may give adequate protection from wildlife damage. If deterrents prove ineffective and damage is considerable, shooting of the marauders may be the only practical recourse. But first there should be approval from Federal and state authorities in the region concerned since many species are protected by law.

Damage to grain crops can usually be lessened if the farmer employs harvesting practices which will avoid prolonged exposure of ripe crops to hungry wildlife. Leaving shocked grain in the field unnecessarily for extended periods and also the practice of hogging corn are dinner invitations to nearby wildlife.

On the other hand, field studies have shown that a considerable proportion of the grain and fruit eaten by wildlife represents no economic loss. The kernels of wheat garnered by gamebirds, songbirds, or small mammals from stubble fields are no deprivation to the farmer. Similarly, the pecking of fallen fruits by birds or their consumption by foxes, raccoons, or opossums usually does not involve any toll of significance.

In addition to cultivated plants of grain fields, orchards, gardens, and vineyards, another category is included in this chapter: ornamental and shade plants. This group consists primarily of trees and shrubs. Unfortunately, knowledge on the wildlife use of these plants is rather limited because the great majority of bird and mammal specimens obtained for food-habits analysis were collected in rural areas, away from ornamental plantings. Much more information on the wildlife value of ornamental and shade plants is needed. Sometimes we assume that certain plants such as the Japanese barberry are valuable to wildlife simply because their fruits look attractive to us. Home owners and landscapers, interested in attracting birds as well as beautifying their grounds, could make good use of more complete knowledge on this subject.

General References: The Standard Cyclopedia of Horticulture. L. H. Bailey. The Macmillan Company, New York, 1933. 3 volumes.

Manual of Cultivated Plants. L. H. Bailey. The Macmillan Company, New York, 1949. 1116 pp.

Manual of the Cultivated Trees and Shrubs. Alfred Rehder. The Macmillan Company, New York, 1927. 930 pp.

Ecological Crop Geography. Karl H. W. Klages. The Macmillan Company, New York, 1942. 615 pp.

Grass Family: *Poaceae*

WHEAT
Triticum

▨ Region of greatest production

▨ Lesser production

[260*/94 users] Wheat has the distinction of standing near the head of the parade in point of star rating. Its 260 stars is topped only by pondweed's 286 stars and corn's 265. On the basis of this rough index, wheat is one of the most valuable wildlife plants in the whole country. The source of man's "staff of life" is also the mainstay for wild creatures.

Wheat is grown practically everywhere in the United States, but its main production is in the northern half or two-thirds of the country. The arid and often alkali areas of the Southwest are not well suited for wheat raising, and in the Southeast cotton and tobacco crowd out most cereals except for corn. In the East only one common species (*T. aestivum*) is grown. In the West a number of different species are raised, and there both spring and winter wheat are common.

In some localities white-winged doves, English sparrows, or flocks of other birds sometimes do appreciable damage to shocked or standing wheat. In the main, however, the very extensive use of wheat by wildlife represents the salvaging of otherwise wasted kernels. Not only is wheat available to wildlife practically everywhere in the country—and in most regions it is available abundantly—but it is also an all-year food. Some kernels of wheat, either on the ground or on dried plants near the margin of fields, are eaten in winter and spring. If the farmer wishes to aid upland gamebirds and other wildlife, with negligible costs to himself, he can do so by leaving a narrow strip of unharvested wheat adjoining suitable cover.

Another wildlife value of wheat, in addition to the usefulness indicated by its total of 260 stars, is its fostering of another important wildlife crop, ragweed. Wheatfields serve as an ideal nursery for common ragweed. Generally the best crops of this weed develop and mature in the stubble of the cut grain.

Waterbirds (seeds, young plants)
+ Duck, Mallard, *Pac.*
  Goose
**   Canada, *Utah and Pac.*
***   Snow, *W*
***   Tule, *Calif.*
**   White-fronted, *Okla.*
* Gull, Franklin, *U.S.*
Marshbirds and Shorebirds (seeds)
  Crane
***   Brown, Little, *W*

**** Sandhill, *W*
\+ Rail, King, *NE*
Upland Gamebirds (seeds)
Dove
\+ Ground, *Gulf Coast*
**** Mourning, *Mt.–Des.;* ***NE;*
**Pr. and Pac.; *SE*
*** White-winged, Western, *Ariz.*
**** Grouse, Sharp-tailed, *Utah;*
Great Lakes Area
**** Partridge, Hungarian, *NW;*
***NE*
** Pheasant, Ring-necked, *NW and*
*N.Y.; *NE*
** Pigeon, Band-tailed, *So.Mt.–*
Des. and Pac.
Prairie Chicken
** Greater, *No.Pr.*
** Lesser, *Okla.*
Quail
** Bobwhite, *NE;* ***Pr.*; +*SE*
** Mountain, *Pac.*
* Scaled, Arizona, *SW*
*** Valley, *Nev.*
* Turkey, Wild, *Alleghenies;*
+*Tex.*
Songbirds (seeds)
Blackbird
* Brewer, *W*
*** Redwing, *Mt.–Des.;* **Calif.;*
**E and Pr.*
* Rusty, *NE*
* Yellow-headed, *W*
\+ Bobolink, *NE and W*
Bunting
– Indigo, *E*
***** (53%) Snow, *NW;* ***NE*
** Cowbird, *SE;* ***NE*
Crow
*** Common, *W;* ***E*
** Fish, *E*
\+ Dickcissel, *Pr.*
** Finch, Rosy, *Pac.*
** Grackle, Purple, *NE;* +*Pr.*
Grosbeak
\+ Black-headed, *Calif.*
**** Blue, *E;* ***SW*
* Rose-breasted, *NE and No.*
Pr.
Jay
\+ Blue, *E*
\+ Florida, *Fla.*
** Piñon, *Mt.–Des.*

* Steller, *Pac.*
** Woodhouse, *So.Mt.–Des.*
Junco
* Slate-colored, *Pr.*
\+ Oregon, *Calif.*
Lark
* Horned, *W;* +*E*
** Horned, California, *Calif.*
Longspur
*** Chestnut-collared, *W.Pr.*
** Lapland, *NE and No.Pr.*
*** McCown, *Pr.*
** Smith, *No.Ill.*
Magpie
** American, *Mt.–Des.*
** Yellow-billed, *Calif.*
** Meadowlark, *Pac.;* ***NE and*
Pr.; +*SE*
* Nutcracker, Clark, *W*
Nuthatch
\+ Red-breasted, *E*
* White-breasted, *Pac.;* +*E and*
E.Pr.
\+ Oriole, Bullock, *SW*
** Pipit, *Pac.;* ***SE*
\+ Robin, *Mt.–Des. and Pac.*
Sparrow
***** (62%) English, *Mt.–Des.;*
****Pac.;* ***E and Pr.*
\+ Field, *Pr.*
* Golden-crowned, *Calif.*
\+ Harris, *Pr.*
*** Lark, *Mt.–Des.;* **Calif.;* **Pr.*
\+ Savannah, *NE and Pr.*
\+ Song, *Pac., mainly Calif.*
* Vesper, *Mt.–Des.*
\+ White-crowned, *Pr.*
Thrasher
– Bendire, *Ariz.*
\+ California, *Calif.*
** Curve-billed, *SW*
\+ Thrush, Varied, *Pac.*
Towhee
\+ Abert, *Ariz.*
* Spotted, *Pac.*
Fur and Game Mammals (seeds, young
foliage)
*** Rabbit, Cottontail, *Ohio*
Skunk
** Eastern, *NE*
\+ Spotted Prairie, *Iowa*
Squirrel
** Fox, *NE*

+ Fox, Western, *Mich.*
Small Mammals (seeds, young plants)
Chipmunk
* Eastern, *NE*
*** Least, *W.Pr. and Mt.–Des.*
+ Gopher, Pocket, *NE and No.Pr.*
Ground Squirrel
*** Douglas, *Oreg.*
** Richardson, *No.Pr.*
* Thirteen-lined, *Pr.*
Mole
+ Common, *E*

− Western, *Oreg.*
Mouse
** Grasshopper, *No.Pr.; *W*
+ Meadow, *E*
* Prairie Dog, White-tailed, *Mont. and Wyo.*
** Rock Squirrel, *Calif.*
Hoofed Browsers (plants)
Deer
+ Mule, *S.Dak.*
+ White-tailed, *E and S.Dak.*

Reference: Classification of Wheat Varieties Grown in the United States in 1939. J. Allen Clark and B. B. Bayles. *U.S. Dept. Agr. Tech. Bul.* 795, 1942. 146 pp.

RYE
Secale cereale

[3*/6 users] Rye, as compared with the other cereals, is raised too sparsely in this country to be significant for wildlife. Where planted as a soil binder on roadsides and similar areas, it is probably just as useful for wildlife as on the relatively few and far-between farms where it is raised as a crop.

Upland Gamebirds (seeds)
+ Pheasant, Ring-necked, *NE*
− Prairie Chicken, Greater, *Wis.*
* Quail, Bobwhite, *Va.; +SE*
Songbirds (seeds)
* Blackbird, Brewer, *Calif.*
Fur and Game Mammals (plants)
+ Rabbit, Cottontail, *Ohio*
Hoofed Browsers (plants)
* Deer, White-tailed, *Ohio*

BARLEY
Hordeum vulgare

▨ Region of greatest production
▨ Secondary production

[76*/50 users] A very large proportion of the recorded use of barley by wildlife occurs in California, where this cereal ranks as one of the leading grain crops. More barley is grown in the northern prairies, but in this region it is over-

shadowed by the even greater production of wheat, oats, and corn.

Much of the utilization of barley by wildlife represents gleaning after the harvest has been completed. Instances of economic damage are, on the whole, more the exception than the rule, though in some localities waterfowl, blackbirds, and white-winged doves are perennial problems in barley fields. Geese like to feed on the foliage of the young plants and, if the flocks are large, may do serious damage, both by uprooting plants and by puddling the ground.

Waterfowl (seeds, young plants)
Duck
+ Baldpate, *W*
*** Black, *Wis.*
** Mallard, *Pac.*

* Pintail, *W*
+ Teal, Green-winged, *W*
Goose
*** Canada, *Pac.*
* Ross, *Calif.*
*** Tule, *Calif.*
* White-fronted, *Calif.*
Upland Gamebirds (seeds)
Dove
* Mourning, *Mt.–Des.*
**** White-winged, Western, *Ariz.*
* Grouse, Sharp-tailed, *Minn.*
*** Partridge, Hungarian, *NW*; +*NE*
*** Pheasant, Ring-necked, *Mont.*; **NW; **N.Y.*
+ Pigeon, Band-tailed, *Pac.*
+ Prairie Chicken, Greater, *No.Pr.*
Quail
** California, *Calif.*
* Mountain, *Pac.*
** Valley, *Nev.*
+ Turkey, Wild, *Pa.*, *Ariz.*, *and N.Mex.*
Songbirds (seeds)
Blackbird
* Brewer, *Calif.*
** Redwing, *Calif.*
** Redwing, Tricolored, *Calif.*
+ Yellow-headed, *W*
+ Bobolink, *NE*

** Bunting, Snow, *NW*
*** Crow, *Pac.*; +*Pr.*
Jay
+ Piñon, *Mt.–Des.*
+ Steller, *Pac.*
** Junco, Oregon, *Pac.*
* Magpie, Yellow-billed, *Calif.*
Sparrow
* English, *Pac.*; +*Mt.–Des.*
+ Fox, *E and W*
+ Golden-crowned, *Calif.*
** Large-billed, *Calif.*
*** Lincoln, *Calif.*
* Savannah, *Calif.*
* Thrasher, Curve-billed, *SW*
Towhee
* Abert, *Ariz.*
** Brown, *Calif.*
+ Spotted, *Pac.*
Fur and Game Mammals (seeds)
+ Raccoon, *Pac.*
Small Mammals (seeds)
*** Ground Squirrel, Nelson, *Calif.*
Mouse
+ Grasshopper, *No.Pr.*
+ Meadow, *E*
* Pocket, *W.Pr. and Mt.–Des.*
+ Rat, Merriam Kangaroo, *SW*
*** Rock Squirrel, *Calif.*
Hoofed Browsers (seed heads)
− Elk, Roosevelt, *No.Calif.*

OATS, CULTIVATED AND WILD
Avena

▨ Region of greatest production
▨ Secondary production

[208*/91 users] Except for the Pacific region, and to a lesser extent the Mountain–Desert, the cultivated species of oats (*A. sativa*) is the only one that is

459

of use to wildlife. Therefore "oats" as recorded for the East and Midwest invariably means the cultivated form.

In the Pacific states, however, wild oats (*A. fatua* and *A. barbata*) are very common weeds of roadsides and agricultural land. Their seeds are used freely by wildlife and when partially digested are difficult to distinguish from cultivated oats. For this reason the many stomach records of "oats" in western birds have made it impossible, in some cases, to be sure whether it was the wild or cultivated oats that was used. Consequently the two are lumped together in the data presentation below. If records of use of wild oats could have been segregated satisfactorily, the plants would have been treated in the weed category.

Cultivated oats probably deserves credit for at least three-fourths of the 208 stars totaled for oats. And of this, it appears that most of the use by wildlife represents gleanings rather than crop damage. The hard, adherent coat over the grain greatly reduces the value of oats for animals that do not hull the seeds. The fibers of the hull are durable and resist digestion.

Though this cereal is still raised abundantly, it is not so important a farm crop as in the horse-and-buggy days. Production has remained about the same since 1910 while other grains have increased steadily. Its wildlife utilization has dropped proportionately too.

Waterbirds (seeds, young plants)
* Duck, Mallard, *Pac.*; +*W*
  Goose
* Canada, *Pac.*
***** (83%) Ross, *Calif.*
+ Gull, Franklin, *U.S.*
Marshbirds and Shorebirds (seeds)
* Crane, Sandhill, *W*
Upland Gamebirds (seeds)
  Dove
* Mourning, *SE*
+ White-winged, Western, *Ariz.*
* Grouse, Sharp-tailed, *Great Lakes Area*; +*N.Dak.*

  Partridge
— Chukar, *Mo.*
*** Hungarian, *NW*; +*NE*
** Pheasant, Ring-necked, *Mont.*; *N
** Pigeon, Band-tailed, *Pac.*
**** Prairie Chicken, Greater, *Wis.*; ***No.Pr.
  Quail
* California, *Calif.*
* Scaled, Arizona, *SW*
** Turkey, Wild, *Tex.*; *SE; +*Ariz. and N.Mex.*

Songbirds (seeds)
  Blackbird
**** Brewer, *Calif.*; **W
**** Redwing, *Calif.*; ***Pr.; **NE and Pr.; *Mt.–Des.
** Rusty, *NE*
*** Yellow-headed, *W*
*** Bobolink, *W*; **NE; *SE
  Bunting
— Indigo, *E*
+ Lark, *Pr.*
*** Lazuli, *Pac.*
** Snow, *NE*; *NW
* Cardinal, *NE*; +*SE and Pr.*
*** Cowbird, *NE*; **SE and W
  Crow
*** Common, *Pac.*; **Mt.–Des.; *E and Pr.
+ Fish, *E*
* Dickcissel, *Pr.*
*** Finch, Rosy, *Pac.*
+ Goldfinch, Green-backed, *Calif.*
  Grackle
+ Boat-tailed, *SE*
** Bronzed, *Pr.*
** Purple, *NE*
  Grosbeak
* Black-headed, *Calif.*
** Blue, *No.Pr.*
+ Rose-breasted, *NE and No. Pr.*
  Jay
* California, *Calif.*
+ Piñon, *Mt.–Des.*
* Steller, *Pac.Coast, mainly Calif.*
*** Junco, Oregon, *Calif.*
**** Lark, Horned, *Calif.*; *E and W
** Magpie, Yellow-billed, *Calif.*

Meadowlark
* Eastern, *E.Pr.;* +*E and W*
*** Western, *Pac.*
* Nutcracker, Clark, *W*
+ Nuthatch, White-breasted, *E, E.Pr., and Pac.*
+ Oriole, Bullock, *SW*
+ Pipit, American, *Pac.*
+ Robin, *E.Pr.*
Sparrow
**** Bell, *Calif.*
* Chipping, *E, Mt.–Des.,* and *Pac.*
**** English, *Pac.;* ****E and Pr.;* **Mt.–Des.*
* Field, *NE*
** Golden-crowned, *Calif.*
*** Grasshopper, *Calif.;* ***NE*
* Harris, *Pr.*
*** Large-billed, *Calif.*
+ Lark, *Pr.*
*** Lark, Western, *Calif.;* *Mt.–Des.*
*** Rufous-crowned, *Calif.*
** Savannah, *Calif.*
* Song, *NE and Pac.*
* Tree, *Pr.*
** Vesper, *Mt.–Des.;* *E*
*** White-crowned, *NE;* **E.Pr., Mt.–Des., and Pac.*
* White-throated, *NE*

+ Titmouse, Plain, *Calif.*
Towhee
+ Abert, *Ariz.*
*** Brown, *Calif.*
+ Red-eyed, *NE*
* Spotted, *Pac.*

Fur and Game Mammals (seeds)
+ Opossum, *NE*
* Rabbit, Cottontail, *Ohio*
+ Raccoon, *Ohio*
Skunk
+ Illinois, *E.Pr.*
+ Spotted, Prairie, *Iowa*
+ Striped, *Iowa*
+ Squirrel, Fox, *Mich.*

Small Mammals (seeds, young leaves)
Ground Squirrel
+ Beechey, *Calif.*
+ Douglas, *Oreg.*
Mole
+ Townsend, *Oreg.*
− Western, *Wash. and Oreg.*
Mouse
− Harvest, Long-tailed, *Calif.*
+ Meadow, *E*
* Pocket, *Calif.*
** Rat, Kangaroo, *Calif.*

Hoofed Browsers (plants)
Deer
* Mule, *Calif.;* +*S.Dak.*
+ White-tailed, *Pr.*

TIMOTHY
Phleum pratense

▓ Region of greatest production
▨ Lesser production

[16*/25 users] In the broad agricultural belt from New York State to Iowa, timothy or timothy combined with clover is the principal hay crop.

Timothy hay is raised in many other parts of the country, but not so abundantly. Wherever this grass is raised as a farm crop it is useful as escape cover—not only in hay fields but also along fence rows and roads. Probably songbirds feed on the seeds of roadside and fence-row timothy at least as much as on the hayfield plants.

Alpine timothy (*P. alpinum*), a wild native species, occurs in the mountains of the West, but its usefulness to wildlife seems to be very limited.

Upland Gamebirds (seeds)
+ Quail, Bobwhite, *E*
Songbirds (seeds)
+ Blackbird, Redwing, *NE*
+ Bobolink, *W*
+ Bunting, Snow, *NW*
* Cowbird, *W*
* Finch, Rosy, *Pac.*
+ Goldfinch, *E*
* Junco, Slate-colored, *NE*

+ Lark, Horned, *W*
* Longspur, Smith, *Ill.*
Redpoll
* Common, *N*
** Hoary, *NE*
Sparrow
+ Brewer, *W*
* Chipping, *E*
+ English, *E*
+ Field, *NE*
+ Fox, *E*
+ Harris, *E.Pr.*
* Song, *NE*
+ Swamp, *NE*
* Tree, *E.Pr.*
+ Vesper, *E*
Small Mammals (seeds)
− Chipmunk, Lake Superior, *Minn.*
Hoofed Browsers (plants)
− Deer, White-tailed, *Ohio and Wis.*
− Moose, *Mont.*

RICE
Oryza sativa

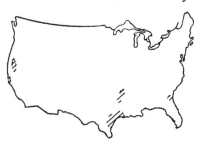

[38*/20 users] There are at present three limited areas in the United States in which rice production is an important industry: the Gulf coastal sections of Louisiana and Texas, eastern Arkansas, and the Sacramento Valley of California. In former times considerable rice was also raised in the coastal part of the Carolinas and in Georgia, and some is still produced in this area.

Rice kernels are not only nutritious and palatable to wildlife, but they are also available in an ideal environment for use by certain species of waterfowl,

marshbirds and shorebirds, and some of the blackbird group. A considerable share of the eating of rice by waterfowl represents gleaning, but if ducks arrive early enough or if the harvest is not removed in time—and sometimes the weather prevents this—much local destruction to the crop can occur. Where blackbirds become abundant in rice fields, control measures must be taken to prevent serious losses.

Waterfowl (seeds, seed heads)
* Coot, *Calif.*
Duck
** Mallard, *SE*
** Mottled, *Gulf Coast*
* Pintail, *SE*; +*Calif.*
+ Ring-necked, *SE*
* Teal, Blue-winged, *SE*
+ Teal, Green-winged, *SE*
Goose
* Snow, *Gulf*
*** White-fronted, *Calif.*
Marshbirds and Shorebirds (seeds)
*** Crane, Sandhill, *Tex.*

*** Gallinule, Purple, *SE*
    Rail
+   King, *SE*
**   Sora, *SE*
Upland Gamebirds (seeds)
  * Quail, Bobwhite, *E.Ark. and S.*
    Tex.
+ Turkey, Wild, *S.C.*

Songbirds (seeds)
.   Blackbird
****   Redwing, *La.;* ***SE and Calif.*
****   Redwing, Tricolored, *Calif.*
***   Bobolink, *SE*
    Grackle
***   Boat-tailed, *SE*
+   Purple, *SE*

References: Rice: Its Cultivation, Production and Distribution. Amory Austin. *U.S. Dept. Agr. Misc. Series Report* 6, 1893. 89 pp.
How to Grow Rice in the Sacramento Valley. Jenkins W. Jones. *U.S. Dept. Agr. Farmers' Bul.* 1240, 1931. 34 pp.
Rice Culture in the Southern States. Jenkins W. Jones and J. Mitchell Jenkins. *U.S. Dept. Agr. Farmers' Bul.* 1808, 1938. 28 pp.

SORGHUM (MILO, KAFFIR, ETC.)
Sorghum vulgare

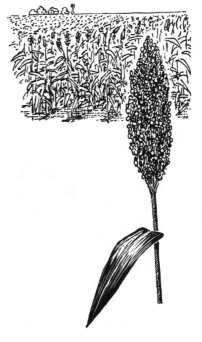

[70*/34 users] Only during the past century has sorghum, a native of Africa, become an important agricultural crop in the United States. The principal area of production in this country is, as indicated on the map, in the prairie region. The many common varieties raised in the United States all belong to the one species, *S. vulgare.* Sorghum is closely related to corn and is like it nutritionally. The smaller size of sorghum kernels is of definite advantage to several species of wildlife.

In recent years mallards have been attracted, in increasingly large numbers, to the Panhandle section of Texas and other sorghum-growing areas. Considerable damage has resulted locally. Reduction of losses from this source will require cooperation from the farmer.

Waterfowl (seeds)
  Duck
**   Mallard, *SW;* +*Pac.*

+   Teal, Cinnamon, *Mt.–Des. and Pac.*
+   Teal, Green-winged, *W*
Marshbirds and Shorebirds (seeds)
**** Crane, Little Brown, *SW*
Upland Gamebirds (seeds)
  Dove
  * Ground, *Gulf Coast*

463

CULTIVATED PLANTS

+ Mourning, *U.S.*
** White-winged, Eastern, *Tex.*
** White-winged, Western, *Ariz.*
*** Partridge, Chukar, *Mo.*
+ Pheasant, Ring-necked, *Mont. and No.Pr.*
Prairie Chicken
+ Greater, *No.Pr.*
+ Lesser, *Okla.*
Quail
*** Bobwhite, *Tex., Okla.; *Pr.; +SE*
** Scaled, Arizona, *SW*
+ Scaled, Chestnut-bellied, *Tex.*
*** Turkey, Wild, *Tex.; +E*
Songbirds (seeds)
Blackbird
* Redwing, *SE*
* Yellow-headed, *W*
** Bunting, Lark, *Pr.*
+ Cowbird, *SE*

** Crow, *Pr.*
* Grackle, Purple, *S*
+ Jay, Piñon, *Mt.–Des.*
+ Lark, Horned, *E and W*
+ Meadowlark, *S, E.Pr., and W*
+ Nuthatch, White-breasted, *E and E.Pr.*
+ Oriole, Bullock, *Calif.*
* Pyrrhuloxia, *Tex.*
**** Raven, White-necked, *SW, mainly Tex.*
Sparrow
*** English, *Pr.; **E; *Pac.*
* Lark, *Pr.*
+ White-crowned, *Pac.*
+ Thrasher, California, *Calif.*
Small Mammals (seeds)
*** Rat, Ord Kangaroo, *W*
Hoofed Browsers (plants)
+ Deer, White-tailed, *Tex.*

Reference: Growing and Feeding Grain Sorghums. J. H. Martin and others. *U.S. Dept. Agr. Farmers' Bul.* 1764, 1936. 46 pp.

CORN
Zea mays

Region of greatest production
Main corn-producing region

[**265***/100 users] Corn, with its 265 stars, is one of the leading wildlife foods of this country. The greatest use of this distinctive American cereal occurs where the production is greatest, namely, in the East and the Prairies.

A considerable proportion of the wildlife species that use corn do so in ways that are not in conflict with man's interests. Many of the kernels eaten by birds and mammals are picked up after the harvest or while fields of standing ripe corn are being hogged. On the other hand, crows, meadowlarks, and pheasants may become locally troublesome by pulling up seedling

464

corn, raccoons occasionally take a heavy toll on some fields (with a marked preference for sweet corn), and flocks of blackbirds sometimes feed on ears in the milk stage.

Yellow corn has a comparatively high vitamin A content and is one of the most valuable winter foods for upland gamebirds. In the North it is a common conservation practice to leave some corn on the stalks for wildlife to use when snow makes other foods scarce.

Waterfowl (seeds)
Duck
* Black, *NE*; +*SE*
* Mallard, *NE and W*; +*SE*
* Pintail, *SE*; +*NE*
Marshbirds and Shorebirds (seeds)
Crane
**** Little Brown, *W*
*** Sandhill, *W*
− Gallinule, Purple, *SE*
Upland Gamebirds (seeds)
Dove
+ Ground, *Gulf Coast*
*** Mourning, *E and Pr.*
** White-winged, Eastern, *Tex.*
+ White-winged, Western, *Ariz.*
* Grouse, Sharp-tailed, *Great Lakes Area and N.Dak.*
Partridge
− Chukar, *Mo.*
*** Hungarian, *NE and No.Pr.*
**** Pheasant, Ring-necked, *NE*; **Mont.; *NW*
Prairie Chicken
* Attwater, *Tex.*
*** Greater, *No.Pr.*
Quail
**** Bobwhite, *NE and Pr.*; *SE*
+ California, *Calif.*
+ Gambel, *SW*
+ Mearns, *SW*
** Valley, *Nev.*
** Turkey, Wild, *Va.*; *Alleghenies; +*E*
Songbirds (seeds)
Blackbird
*** Brewer, *W*; *Calif.*
*** Redwing, *SE and Pr.*; **NE*
** Redwing, Tricolored, *Calif.*

*** Rusty, *NE*
*** Yellow-headed, *W*
** Cardinal, *E and Pr.*
** Cowbird, *NE*; *SE and W*
+ Chickadee, Black-capped, *NE*
* Creeper, Brown, *U.S.*
Crow
**** Common, *E*
*** Fish, *Pr. and Pac.*
+ Dickcissel, *Pr.*
Flicker
* Red-shafted, *Pac.*
+ Yellow-shafted, *E and E.Pr.*
Grackle,
**** Boat-tailed, *SE*
***** (55%) Purple, *Pr.*; ****E*
Grosbeak
**** Blue, *No.Pr.*; **SW*
* Rose-breasted, *NE and No. Pr.*
Jay
*** Blue, *E*
* Blue, Florida, *Gulf States*
** California, *Calif.*
* Piñon, *Mt.–Des.*
+ Steller, *Pac., mainly Calif.*
+ Woodhouse, *So.Mt.–Des.*
+ Junco, *NE*
* Lark, Horned, *U.S.*
+ Magpie, American, *Mt.–Des.*
*** Meadowlark, *E.Pr.*; **E*; *W*; +*Pac.* (incl. seedlings)
+ Nutcracker, Clark, *NW*
Nuthatch
+ Red-breasted, *E*
** White-breasted, *E*
+ Oriole, Baltimore, *NE*
+ Pipit, American, *SE*
Raven
* American, *Mt.–Des. and Pac.*
** White-necked, *SW, mainly Tex.*
** Robin, *SE*; +*NE and E.Pr.*
Sparrow
**** English, *E and Pr.*; **Pac.*; +*Mt.–Des.*
+ Fox, *E*
* Golden-crowned, *Pr.*
** Harris, *E.Pr.*
+ Lark, *Pr.*
** Lincoln, *Pr.*
+ Song, *NE*
+ Tree, *NE and Pr.*

465

+   White-crowned, *E.Pr.*
*   White-throated, *NE*
+   Starling, *NE*
    Thrasher
*   Brown, *E and Pr.*
+   Curve-billed, *SW*
*   Titmouse, Tufted, *NE;* +*SE*
    Towhee
+   Brown, *Calif.*
**   Red-eyed, *NE;* *SE
    Woodpecker
*   Ant-eating, *Pac.*
+   Downy, *E and Pr.*
+   Hairy, *E and Pr.*
+   Lewis, *Mt.–Des. and Pac.*
**   Red-bellied, *E*
*   Red-cockaded, *Gulf Coast*
**   Red-headed, *E and Pr.*

Fur and Game Mammals (seeds, stems, foliage)
+   Beaver, *Mo.*
    Fox
+   Gray, *E*
*   Red, *Ala.;* +*E*

*   Muskrat, *NE;* +*Iowa*
**   Opossum, *Mo.;* +*E*
+   Rabbit, Cottontail, *NE and No. Pr.*
****   Raccoon, *NE and Iowa;* *SE
−   Skunk, Prairie Spotted, *Iowa*
    Squirrel
***   Fox, *NE and Ohio*
***   Fox, Western, *Mich.*

Small Mammals (seeds)
*   Chipmunk, Eastern, *NE*
+   Gopher, Pocket, *NE and No.Pr.*
−   Ground Squirrel, Piute, *Nev.*
*   Moles, *E.Wash. and Oreg.*
    Mouse
+   Meadow, *E*
*   White-footed, *E and W*

Hoofed Browsers (plants)
    Deer
+   Mule, *S.Dak.*
*   White-tailed, *Mo. and N.C. Mts.*
−   Elk, Roosevelt, *Calif.*

Reference: Corn Culture. Frederick D. Richey. *U.S. Dept. Agr. Farmers' Bul.* 1714, 1933. 26 pp.

Walnut Family: *Juglandaceae*

ENGLISH WALNUT
Juglans regia

[4*/4 users] Large groves of English walnuts (also known as Persian walnuts) are common in Southern and central California. Only in this area of the country are these nuts raised extensively. In addition to the strong-billed birds listed below as principal users of English walnuts, jays are also known to peck through the shells and eat the meats. Damage by crows and jays is reported to be serious in some localities.

Songbirds (nuts)
***   Crow, Western, *Pac.*
+   Flicker, Red-shafted, *Pac.*
+   Titmouse, Plain, *Calif.*
*   Woodpecker, Ant-eating, *Calif.*

Mulberry Family: *Moraceae*

FIG
Ficus carica

[15*/17 users] Most of the fig-raising industry is concentrated in Southern California, and it is here that birds make the greatest use of this fruit. Figs are grown on a smaller scale in the South—near the Gulf coast in Louisiana and Texas.

The consumption of figs by birds is a definite though often small loss to the commercial grower since the fruit is usually attacked while still on the tree. Even a few pecks are sufficient to ruin a fig for commercial use.

Songbirds (fruit)
+ Bluebird, Western, *Calif.*
+ Crow, Fish, *SE*
** Finch, Common House, *Calif.*
* Grackle, Boat-tailed, *SE*
*** Grosbeak, Black-headed, *Calif.*
* Magpie, Yellow-billed, *Calif.*
*** Mockingbird, *Calif.*
Oriole
* Bullock, *Calif.*

* Hooded, Arizona, *Calif. and Ariz.*
+ Robin, *Pac.*
+ Sapsucker, Northern Red-breasted, *Pac.*
+ Thrush, Russet-backed, *Calif.*
+ Towhee, Spotted, *Pac.*
Warbler
* Audubon, *Calif.*
* Myrtle, *Calif.*
Fur and Game Mammals (fruit)
+ Coyote, *Calif.*
+ Raccoon, *Calif.*

Reference: Fig Growing in the South Atlantic and Gulf States. H. P. Gould. *U.S. Dept. Agr. Bul.* 1031, 1935. 34 pp.

Buckwheat Family: *Polygonaceae*

BUCKWHEAT
Fagopyrum esculentum

[6*/12 users] Wildlife use of the large, triangular seeds of buckwheat is rather limited, as might be expected from the sparse availability of this crop plant. Buckwheat is raised widely in the Northern states, but it is grown only here and there in relatively small fields. Reports on damage to this crop by wildlife are negligible. In some areas buckwheat has been planted as a food for pheasants and other upland gamebirds.

Upland Gamebirds (seeds)
** Dove, Mourning, *NE*
− Grouse, Sharp-tailed, *Wis.*
* Partridge, Hungarian, *NE;* +*NW*
* Pheasant, Ring-necked, *NE*
+ Prairie Chicken, Greater, *Pr.*
+ Quail, Bobwhite, *Pa.*
+ Turkey, Wild, *Va.Mts. and Pa.*

Songbirds (seeds)
* Crow, *E*
Fur and Game Mammals (seeds)
+ Squirrel, Western Fox, *Mich.*
Small Mammals (seeds)
− Mouse, Prairie Pocket, *Okla.*
Hoofed Browsers (plants)
− Deer, White-tailed, *Va. and Wis.*

Reference: Experiments with Buckwheat. J. W. White, F. J. Holben, and A. C. Richer. *State Col. Pa. Agr. Expt. Sta. Bul.* 403, 1941. 62 pp.

Rose Family: *Rosaceae*

FIRETHORNS
Pyracantha

In California, firethorns are among the most widely used ornamentals.

These beautiful, exotic bushes are also grown elsewhere in the country, particularly in the South, but nowhere are they as plentiful as on the West coast. There are several species but a particularly attractive and common one is *P. coccinea*. The catbird, mockingbird, and purple finch are known to relish firethorn fruits. The related shrubs known as *Cotoneaster* are also recognized as being attractive to birds.

PEAR
Pyrus communis

[5*/12 users] Probably the main reason that pears, as compared to apples, are low in extent of wildlife use is the fact that they are much less plentiful. Damage to this cultivated crop includes not only injury to ripened fruit but also spring disbudding by some birds.

Upland Gamebirds (buds, fruit)
   * Grouse, Ruffed, *Pa.*
Songbirds (fruit, seeds, buds, blossoms)
  ** Finch, Purple, *E*
  + Oriole, Baltimore, *NE*

   Sparrow
  + English, *NE*
  + Fox, *E*
Fur and Game Mammals (fruit, bark)
  + Coyote, *W*
   Fox
  + Gray, *NE*
  + Red, *E*
  + Muskrat, *NE*
   Rabbit
  + Cottontail, Eastern, *Conn.*
  + Cottontail, New England, *Conn.*
  + Squirrel, Gray, *Va.*

APPLE
Malus pumila

[46*/51 users] Apples are grown throughout the United States, but as indicated on the accompanying map, their principal production is in the Northeast and the Far West. Naturally, the greatest use to wildlife is in these two regions.

Wildlife use of apples is usually not regarded as a damage problem. Often the old fallen fruits on the ground or diseased ones left on the tree are eaten by birds or mammals. Run-down, abandoned orchards are especially popular with deer and ruffed grouse. On the other hand, destructive pecking of marketable fruit also occurs, and some local damage to bark or to sapling trees is caused by rabbits and mice.

The mockingbird is not listed among the principal users of apple, but one of the surest ways to make these songsters happy near your home is to place chunks of the fruit within easy access.

Upland Gamebirds (fruit, seeds, and buds)
   * Grouse, Ruffed, *NE*
  ** Pheasant, Ring-necked, *N.Y.*

+ Prairie Chicken, Greater, *Wis.*
+ Quail, Bobwhite, *E*
Songbirds (fruit and seeds)
* Chickadee, Chestnut-backed, *Pac.*
+ Crow, *Pac.*
Finch
+ House, Common, *Calif.*
** Purple, *E*
* Flicker, Red-shafted, *Pac.*
+ Grackle, *NE*
+ Jay, Blue, *Md.*
+ Magpie, American, *Mt.–Des.*
+ Mynah, Crested, *B.C.*
Oriole
+ Baltimore, *NE*
+ Orchard, *NE*
* Robin, *Pac.; +NE and E.Pr.*
+ Sapsucker, Yellow-bellied, *E*
* Starling, *NE*
* Thrush, Varied, *Pac.*
Titmouse
+ Plain, *Calif.*
* Tufted, *NE*
+ Towhee, Red-eyed, *NE*
*** Waxwing, Cedar, *W; +E*
Woodpecker
+ Downy, *E and E.Pr.*
+ Hairy, *E and E.Pr.*
** Lewis, *Mt.–Des.*
+ Red-bellied, *Md.*
+ Red-headed, *E*
Fur and Game Mammals (fruit, bark)

** Bear, Black, *E*
+ Coyote, *W*
Fox
* Gray, *NE; +SE*
*** Red, *Mass.; +E*
** Marmot, *W.Pr. and Mt.–Des.*
+ Opossum, *NE*
* Porcupine, *Vt.*
Rabbit
** Cottontail, *Iowa; *Mich.; +Conn.*
+ Cottontail, Mearns, *E and Pr.*
* Raccoon, *N.Y. and Miss.*
Skunk
+ Eastern, *E*
+ Spotted, Prairie, *Iowa*
Squirrel
+ Fox, *Ohio*
+ Fox, Western, *Mo.*
+ Gray, *Va.*
* Red, *W*
Small Mammals (fruit, bark)
+ Ground Squirrel, Douglas, *Oreg.*
Mouse
+ Deer, *Wis.*
+ Meadow, *E*
+ Pine, *NE*
Rat
+ Wood, Allegheny, *E*
+ Wood, Dusky-footed, *Oreg.*
Hoofed Browsers (twigs, foliage)
* Deer, White-tailed, *N.Y., N.C. Mts.; +Pa.*

CHERRIES
Prunus (part)

[56*/34 users] Two species of cultivated cherries are common in the United States: the sweet (*P. avium*) and sour cherry (*P. cerasus*). There are numerous varieties of both species.

Almost everywhere that cherries are raised, either commercially or for home consumption, there is recurrent damage by songbirds. In some orchards the destruction has been as high as three-fourths of the whole crop. Apparently the liking of birds for this tasty fruit is as natural and great as our own.

Upland Gamebirds (fruit, buds)
*** Pigeon, Band-tailed, *So.Mt.– Des. and Pac.*
Songbirds (fruit)
* Blackbird, Brewer, *Calif.*
** Catbird, *NE*

+ Crow, *Mt.–Des.*
　Finch
　*　House, Common, *Calif.*
　**　Purple, *E*
+ Grackle, *NE*
** Grosbeak, Black-headed, *Calif.*
　Jay
***　California, *Calif.*
+　Woodhouse, *So.Mt.–Des.*
　*　Steller, *Pac.*
+ Magpie, *Mt.–Des.*
　Oriole
+　Baltimore, *NE*
　*　Bullock, *Calif.*
+ Phoebe, *E*
*** Robin, *NE;* ***E.Pr. and Pac.;*
　*SE
+ Sapsucker, Northern Red-
　breasted, *Pac.* (sap)
+ Sparrow, English, *U.S.*
** Starling, *NE*

　Tanager
+　Scarlet, *NE*
***　Western, *Pac.*
** Thrasher, Brown, *Pr.;* +*SE*
　Thrush
**　Russet-backed, *Calif.*
+　Veery, *NE*
　* Titmouse, Plain, *Calif.*
　Vireo
+　Red-eyed, *E*
+　Warbling, *NE*
**** Waxwing, Cedar, *W. excl.Pac.;*
　****Pac.*
　Woodpecker
+　Hairy, *E and E.Pr.*
**　Lewis, *Mt.–Des. and Pac.*
　*　Red-bellied, *E*

Fur and Game Mammals (fruit, foliage)
+ Armadillo, *Tex.*
+ Fox, Red, *Ala.*
+ Squirrel, Eastern Gray, *E*

PRUNES
Prunus domestica

[6*/8 users] The prune industry of this country is confined almost exclusively to California and Oregon, with the major center of production in the Santa Clara Valley of California. Damage to the fruit by wildlife is generally negligi-ble. Orchards bordered by woods are likely to have some of the fallen fruits partially eaten, but ordinarily the toll by birds is not much, if any, greater than that taken by the prune pickers. Disbudding by house finches may become serious locally.

Songbirds (fruit)
** Finch, Common House, *Calif.*
+ Flicker, Red-shafted, *Pac.*
+ Grosbeak, Black-headed, *Calif.*
　* Jay, California, *Calif.*
** Robin, *Pac.*
+ Thrasher, *Calif.*
　Thrush
+　Russet-backed, *Calif.*
　* Varied, *Pac.*

ALMONDS
Prunus amygdalus

[2*/1 user] Practically all the commercial production of almonds in the United States is confined to California where several kinds of wildlife use the nut-like fruits as a choice food item. Almonds rank as a 2-star food for the California woodpecker. For other species known to feed on the fruits, buds, or roots of almond trees, accurate data on extent of use is lacking. Gophers, ground squirrels, crows, bluejays, blackbirds, house finches, sapsuckers, and magpies are said to be enemies of almond orchards.[1]

[1] Almond Culture in California. Milo N. Wood. *Calif. Extension Service Circ.* 103, p. 73, 1947.

Pea Family: *Fabaceae*

ALFALFA
Medicago sativa

[31*/25 users] Alfalfa, though raised in practically all sections of the country, is a particularly important crop of the arid or semiarid West. This bluish-flowered legume develops a deep penetrating root system except where irrigation makes this unnecessary.

Green fields of alfalfa are particularly attractive to wildlife where other fresh growth is scarce or lacking. Both the foliage and seed pods are relished by several groups of birds and mammals. Ordinarily, its use by wildlife does not involve extensive crop damage.

Waterfowl (foliage and other parts)
    Duck
**   Baldpate, *W*
+   Mallard, *Pac.*
Marshbirds and Shorebirds (foliage and other parts)
*   Crane, Little Brown, *W*
Upland Gamebirds (foliage and seeds)
    Grouse
*   Sage, *No.Mt.–Des.*
**   Sharp-tailed, *Utah*
*   Partridge, Hungarian, *NW*
+   Pheasant, Ring-necked, *Mont.*

    Quail
+   Bobwhite, *NE*
**   Gambel, *SW*
**   Valley, *Nev.*
Songbirds (seeds)
*   Grosbeak, Blue, *SW*
Fur and Game Mammals (foliage and other parts)
**   Jack Rabbit, *Ariz. and N.Mex.*
*   Marmot, *W.Pr. and Mt.–Des.*
+   Muskrat, *Iowa*
    Rabbit
**   Cottontail, Eastern, *Ohio*
+   Cottontail, Mearns, *NE*
+   Raccoon, *Pac.*
Small Mammals (seeds and foliage)
+   Gopher, Pocket, *NE and No.Pr.*
+   Ground Squirrel, Piute, *Nev.*
    Mouse
+   Meadow, *E*
+   White-footed, Leconte, *E*
+   White-footed, Northern, *E*
+   Prairie Dog, Gunnison, *N.Mex., Ariz., and Colo.*
Hoofed Browsers (plants)
**   Antelope, *So.Dak.;* + *No.Pr. and Mt.–Des.*
    Deer
+   Mule, *No.Mt.–Des.*
*   White-tailed, *Mont.*

PEANUT
Arachis hypogaea

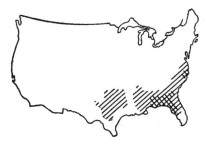

[7*/20 users] It is only natural that a food as nutritious and wholesome as peanuts should be eaten by birds and mammals, even though they have to dig the seeds up from underground and extract them from coarse protective shells. Rarely does wildlife use of this crop constitute serious economic damage.

Upland Gamebirds (seeds)
+   Dove, Mourning, *SE*
+   Quail, Bobwhite, *SE*
+   Turkey, Wild, *Va.*
Songbirds (seeds)
–   Flicker, Northern, *N.C.*
*   Raven, White-necked, *SW, mainly Tex.*

Fur and Game Mammals (seeds)
    Fox
*   Gray, *SE*; +*SW*
+   Red, *E*

*** Skunk, Florida, *SE*
Small Mammals (seeds)
+ Mole, Common, *E*
+ Rat, Cotton, *SE*

Reference: Peanut Growing. W. R. and J. H. Beattie. *U.S. Dept. Agr. Bul.* 1656, 1938. 28 pp.

SOYBEAN
Glycine max

[4*/11 users] Soybeans, though a common farm crop in the East, have a rather low star rating of wildlife use. Songbirds, as a group, do not seem to be interested in soybean seeds. Recent observations in Maryland indicated that mourning doves were obtaining a very large share of their winter food in soybean fields—the old plants providing suitable cover while feeding.

Marshbirds and Shorebirds (seeds)
+ Rail, Clapper, *SE*
Upland Gamebirds (seeds)
+ Dove, Mourning, *E*

– Grouse, Sharp-tailed, *Wis.*
+ Partridge, Chukar, *Mo.*
+ Pheasant, Ring-necked, *NE*
* Prairie Chicken, Greater, *Wis.*
* Quail, Bobwhite, *SE*
Songbirds (seeds)
– Sparrow, Song, *Md.*
Fur and Game Mammals (foliage, plants)
** Rabbit, Eastern Cottontail, *Ohio*
+ Squirrel, Fox, *Ohio*
Hoofed Browsers (plants)
– Deer, White-tailed, *Va., N.C., and Wis.*

Reference: Soybeans: Culture and Varieties. W. J. Morse and J. L. Carter. *U.S. Dept. Agr. Farmers' Bul.* 1520, 1939. 39 pp.

COWPEAS
Vigna sinensis

[4*/4 users] The cowpea though raised abundantly in the South is recognized as an important food for only two wildlife species, the bobwhite quail and mourning dove. These popular gamebirds do practically all their feeding on seeds of this plant after the crop is harvested.

Upland Gamebirds (seeds)
** Dove, Mourning, *SE*
** Quail, Bobwhite, *SE*
Songbirds (seeds)
+ Crow, *E*
Hoofed Browsers (plants)
+ Deer, White-tailed, *N.C.*

GARDEN PEA
Pisum sativum

[3*/6 users] The garden pea, whether raised on a small scale in gardens or in extensive field plantings, is eaten to only a limited extent by a few wildlife species. Ordinarily this use does not cause damage except locally in the West where large flocks of band-tailed pigeons sometimes feed in unharvested fields.

Upland Gamebirds (seeds)
* Pigeon, Band-tailed, *Pac.*
Songbirds (seeds)
* Grosbeak, Rose-breasted, *NE and Pr.*
+ Oriole, Baltimore, *NE*
Small Mammals (seeds, plants)
+ Ground Squirrel, Douglas, *Oreg.*
  Mole
+   Coast, *Oreg.*
+   Townsend, *Oreg.*

Chinaberry Family: *Meliaceae*

CHINABERRY
Melia azedarach

[2*/3 users] The large-stoned fruit of the chinaberry, an excellent Asiatic shade tree, common in the South, is eaten to a limited extent by some of our best-known songbirds—robins in particular. The fruit contains a narcotic capable of causing paralysis.

Songbirds (fruit)
+ Catbird, *SE*
+ Mockingbird, *SE*
** Robin, *SE*

Cashew Family: *Anacardiaceae*

CALIFORNIA PEPPERTREE
Schinus molle

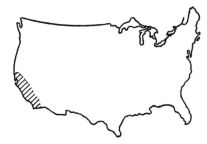

[17*/11 users] This beautiful, lacy-leaved, pink-berried South American tree is so common and well-established on lawns and along streets in the southern two-thirds of California that it is called the California peppertree. An unfavorable feature of this tree is the fact that it harbors the black scale, a menace to citrus orchards. Except for this drawback—which is likely to be serious only in the vicinity of citrus groves—the California peppertree is a very valuable addition to our flora since it is attractive to wildlife as well as to man.

Songbirds (fruit)
+ Bluebird, Western, *Calif.*
+ Flicker, Red-shafted, *Calif.*
*** Mockingbird, *Calif.*
* Phainopepla, *Calif. and Ariz.*
*** Robin, *Calif.*

** Sapsucker, Northern Red-breasted, *Calif.* (sap)
Thrush
** Hermit, *Calif.*
* Russet-backed, *Calif.*
+ Varied, *Calif.*
+ Warbler, Audubon, *Calif.*
**** Waxwing, Cedar, *Calif.*

Olive Family: *Oleaceae*

PRIVETS
Ligustrum

[2*/4 users] Privet hedges are extremely common in the East—and especially in the Southeast—and yet stomach examinations have given very little evidence that the fruits of this plant are of value to wildlife. It is not unusual to see the fruits of both the common (*L. vulgare*) and Ibota privet (*L. ibota*) remain on the plants far into winter, untouched by birds.

Upland Gamebirds (fruit)
+ Quail, Bobwhite, *SE*
Songbirds (fruit)
+ Bluebird, *Md.*
+ Sparrow, Tree, *Md.*
** Waxwing, Cedar, *SE*; +*NE*

Melon Family: *Cucurbitaceae*

MELONS
Citrullus and *Cucumis*

[4*/7 users] The seeds, and to a more limited extent the flesh, of watermelons, cantaloupes, and other melons are enjoyed by birds. Because of this, melon seeds are often used as a food item at winter feeding stations for songbirds. Ravens and crows cause considerable damage to both commercial and home melon patches. Even a few pecks into the fruit are likely to make it unmarketable. Mammals too, particularly skunks and raccoons, are known to feed on melons.

Upland Gamebirds (seeds)
    Dove
+ White-winged, Eastern, *Tex.*
* White-winged, Western, *Ariz.*
+ Quail, Bobwhite, *Ala.*
Songbirds (flesh, seeds)
+ Crow, *Pr.*
    Raven
+ American, *Mt.–Des. and Pac.*
* White-necked, *SW*
Fur and Game Mammals (flesh)
+ Skunk, Striped, *Iowa*

CHAPTER EIGHTEEN

Wildlife Plants Ranked According to Their Value

F OOD-HABITS DATA on more than 300 species of birds and mammals have made it possible to determine approximately the extent to which about 250 different genera of plants have been used by wildlife. This food-use information, though far from perfect, can aid in planning wildlife habitat developments on farms, forests, marshlands, grazing ranges, wildlife refuges, and residential areas. To this end, two listings are presented below. The first is nationwide and includes only those plants which total 25 stars or more by the star-user basis described on page 40. The second, much longer listing makes available more detailed indication of the extent to which particular kinds of plants in different regions have been utilized by each of seven wildlife categories.

In addition to statistical limitations previously acknowledged, there may be possible fallibility in the star-user ratings in one other regard: the fact that extent of use of a plant for food is not always an accurate gauge of its value in wildlife management. In some seasons or places, certain plants have been utilized considerably not so much because they are excellent, good, or even fair food sources but because better ones were not readily available. However, such instances are probably somewhat exceptional and, until knowledge advances much further, actual use of foods will remain the principal criterion of value to wildlife.

National Listing by Plant Groups

(Including only plants totaling 25 or more stars)

WOODY PLANTS

Oak................263*/96	Birch...............52*/25	Alder...............36*/16
Pine..............234*/82	Mesquite..........52*/24	Mulberry...........35*/38
Blackberry........118*/97	Elderberry........51*/79	Snowberry..........32*/27
Wild Cherry.......104*/81	Serviceberry......46*/58	Gooseberry.........31*/32
Dogwood...........75*/64	Sumac..............46*/50	Douglasfir.........30*/20
Grape.............69*/75	Aspen..............46*/28	Saltbush...........29*/22
Poison-ivy........66*/61	Fir................40*/23	Persimmon..........28*/19
Cedar.............66*/44	Sagebrush.........40*/22	Greenbrier.........27*/33
Pricklypear.......62*/44	Beech.............38*/31	Blackgum...........26*/33
Maple.............61*/33	Willow............37*/25	Virginia-creeper.....26*/30
Blueberry.........57*/63	Spruce............36*/22	Holly..............25*/36
Hackberry.........54*/48	Manzanita.........36*/19	

WILDLIFE PLANTS RANKED ACCORDING TO THEIR VALUE

UPLAND WEEDS AND HERBS

Bristlegrass.......226*/77	Sunflower.........73*/60	Gramagrass........30*/20
Ragweed.........164*/71	Goosefoot........61*/40	Tarweed...........29*/27
Pigweed..........114*/55	Crabgrass.........58*/22	Bluegrass..........27*/30
Panicgrass........108*/67	Clover............49*/40	Deervetch.........27*/15
Oats.............98*/53	Russianthistle......39*/23	Fescuegrass........26*/22
Sedge............86*/67	Bromegrass.......36*/37	Chickweed.........25*/36
Knotweed.........86*/61	Doveweed........35*/21	Dropseedgrass......25*/18
Filaree............84*/50	Turkeymullein.....31*/20	

MARSH AND AQUATIC PLANTS

Pondweed........286*/40	Wildrice..........54*/23	Duckweed.........30*/16
Bulrush..........206*/52	Wildmillet........48*/29	Horned-pondweed...28*/12
Smartweed.......128*/66	Cordgrass.........46*/15	Saltgrass...........28*/11
Widgeongrass.....104*/33	Algae.............43*/19	Waterlily..........27*/23
Spikerush..........66*/29	Naiad.............38*/19	Burreed............27*/19
Muskgrass.........66*/20	Wildcelery........31*/10	Arrowhead.........25*/26

CULTIVATED PLANTS

Corn.............265*/190	Sorghum..........70*/34	Rice...............38*/20
Wheat............260*/94	Cherry...........56*/33	Alfalfa.............31*/25
Oats.............110*/91	Apple............46*/51	Grape.............25*/16
Barley............76*/50		

Regional Listing of Wildlife Plants

Northeast Region

	Water-birds	Marsh-Shore-birds	Upland Game-birds	Song-birds	Fur & Game Mamm.	Small Mamm.	Brows-ers
WOODY PLANTS							
Oak (71*/43)	7*/3	0*/1	11*/5	25*/17	21*/14	4*/2	3*/1
Blackberry (50*/56)	—	—	13*/5	27*/34	4*/10	4*/5	2*/2
Wild Cherry (44*/56)	—	—	4*/5	27*/29	9*/13	2*/7	2*/2
Pine (43*/33)	—	—	1*/2	30*/18	8*/10	2*/2	2*/1
Dogwood (42*/47)	3*/2	—	6*/5	25*/28	4*/6	1*/4	3*/2
Grape (37*/53)	1*/1	—	15*/5	14*/37	7*/8	0*/2	—
Maple (36*/27)	—	—	2*/4	13*/7	12*/11	3*/3	6*/2
Beech (34*/31)	1*/1	—	2*/3	8*/12	21*/12	2*/2	0*/1
Blueberry (29*/37)	1*/2	—	3*/2	9*/21	9*/7	5*/3	2*/2
Birch (27*/22)	—	—	6*/3	8*/7	9*/8	0*/2	4*/2
Sumac (23*/28)	—	—	4*/3	10*/19	7*/4	—	2*/2
Aspen (23*/17)	—	—	5*/3	0*/1	12*/10	0*/1	6*/2
Spruce (20*/16)	—	—	—	11*/8	9*/6	0*/1	0*/1
Hickory (17*/19)	—	—	0*/1	6*/6	9*/9	2*/3	—
Fir (16*/13)	—	—	0*/1	6*/4	4*/5	0*/1	6*/2
Alder (14*/11)	—	—	2*/3	7*/3	3*/3	—	2*/2
Poison-ivy (13*/28)	—	—	2*/4	11*/21	0*/3	—	—
Blackgum (13*/27)	0*/1	—	0*/3	9*/18	4*/5	—	—
Mulberry (13*/25)	—	—	—	11*/21	2*/4	—	—
Elm (13*/15)	2*/1	—	0*/3	8*/6	3*/4	—	0*/1
Cedar (13*/8)	—	—	—	13*/7	0*/1	—	—
Serviceberry (12*/39)	—	—	0*/2	6*/25	5*/6	0*/4	1*/2
Hazelnut (12*/16)	—	—	3*/3	0*/1	6*/6	2*/4	1*/2

WILDLIFE PLANTS RANKED ACCORDING TO THEIR VALUE

Northeast Region (cont.)

	Water-birds	Marsh-Shore-birds	Upland Game-birds	Song-birds	Fur & Game Mamm.	Small Mamm.	Brows-ers
WOODY PLANTS (cont.)							
Willow (12*/13)	—	—	2*/3	—	5*/7	0*/1	5*/2
Hemlock (12*/13)	—	—	0*/1	7*/5	3*/4	0*/2	2*/1
Greenbrier (11*/23)	0*/1	—	4*/3	6*/14	1*/5	—	—
Ash (11*/18)	0*/1	—	1*/2	6*/6	3*/5	0*/2	1*/2
Elderberry (10*/36)	—	—	1*/2	8*/28	1*/3	0*/2	0*/1
Virginia-creeper (10*/22)	—	—	—	10*/19	0*/3	—	—
Tuliptree (10*/14)	—	—	—	7*/7	1*/4	1*/2	1*/1
Mountain-ash (10*/9)	—	—	3*/2	4*/5	—	0*/1	3*/1
Holly (6*/20)	—	—	0*/1	5*/14	0*/2	0*/2	1*/1
Hawthorn (6*/15)	—	—	1*/3	3*/3	2*/6	0*/1	0*/2
Black Walnut (6*/4)	—	—	—	—	6*/4	—	—
UPLAND WEEDS AND HERBS							
Ragweed (67*/49)	—	3*/3	11*/6	53*/37	0*/1	0*/1	0*/1
Bristlegrass (62*/40)	1*/1	0*/4	9*/6	52*/29	—	—	—
Sedge (32*/43)	6*/13	5*/7	2*/5	16*/12	0*/3	0*/1	3*/2
Crabgrass (32*/20)	—	—	3*/4	27*/15	2*/1	—	—
Panicgrass (28*/32)	—	0*/1	0*/4	25*/25	3*/2	—	—
Pigweed (16*/21)	—	—	0*/3	16*/16	0*/1	—	0*/1
Clover (15*/21)	—	0*/1	8*/5	0*/3	7*/7	0*/4	0*/1
Sheepsorrel (12*/23)	—	—	1*/5	9*/14	2*/1	0*/3	—
Goosefoot (12*/18)	—	—	0*/2	11*/15	—	1*/1	—
Dropseedgrass (8*/7)	—	—	—	8*/7	—	—	—
Bluegrass (7*/9)	4*/1	—	1*/2	0*/1	2*/3	0*/1	0*/1
Pokeweed (6*/25)	—	—	2*/1	3*/19	1*/4	0*/1	—
Dandelion (5*/14)	—	—	3*/5	1*/4	1*/3	0*/1	0*/1
Plantain (5*/6)	—	—	0*/1	0*/1	5*/3	—	0*/1
MARSH AND AQUATIC PLANTS							
Smartweed (59*/50)	18*/16	4*/9	3*/2	34*/22	0*/1	—	—
Pondweed (59*/32)	55*/23	4*/9	—	—	—	—	—
Wildrice (48*/25)	32*/16	5*/2	1*/1	10*/6	—	—	—
Bulrush (37*/36)	26*/17	8*/12	—	0*/4	3*/2	0*/1	—
Wildcelery (26*/17)	26*/16	0*/1	—	—	—	—	—
Naiad (21*/17)	21*/17	—	—	—	—	—	—
Cordgrass (17*/8)	9*/5	1*/1	—	7*/2	—	—	—
Widgeongrass (16*/22)	14*/15	2*/7	—	—	—	—	—
Cutgrass (13*/13)	8*/9	1*/1	—	2*/1	2*/2	—	—
Spikerush (12*/14)	8*/8	4*/5	—	—	0*/1	—	—
Eelgrass (12*/12)	12*/11	0*/1	—	—	—	—	—
Burreed (11*/13)	8*/9	0*/3	—	—	3*/1	—	—
Wildmillet (10*/16)	8*/7	1*/2	0*/2	1*/4	0*/1	—	—
Duckweed (10*/9)	10*/7	0*/2	—	—	—	—	—
Algae (9*/10)	9*/9	0*/1	—	—	—	—	—
Arrowhead (7*/6)	4*/4	3*/2	—	—	—	—	—
Muskgrass (6*/16)	6*/14	0*/2	—	—	—	—	—
Arrow-arum (5*/2)	5*/1	0*/1	—	—	—	—	—

WILDLIFE PLANTS RANKED ACCORDING TO THEIR VALUE

Northeast Region (concl.)

	Water-birds	Marsh-Shore-birds	Upland Game-birds	Song-birds	Fur & Game Mamm.	Small Mamm.	Brows-ers
CULTIVATED PLANTS							
Corn (73*/52)	2*/1	—	17*/7	40*/30	11*/9	2*/4	1*/1
Wheat (42*/37)	1*/1	0*/1	11*/6	22*/20	7*/4	1*/4	0*/1
Oats (36*/33)	0*/1	—	6*/3	29*/23	1*/5	0*/1	—
Apple (17*/33)	—	—	3*/3	4*/13	9*/11	0*/4	1*/2
Cult. Cherry (10*/15)	—	—	—	10*/14	0*/1	—	—
Timothy (8*/9)	—	—	—	7*/7	—	1*/1	0*/1
Barley (5*/5)	3*/1	2*/3	—	0*/1	—	—	—

Southeast Region

	Water-birds	Marsh-Shore-birds	Upland Game-birds	Song-birds	Fur & Game Mamm.	Small Mamm.	Brows-ers
WOODY PLANTS							
Oak (62*/37)	4*/2	0*/1	6*/4	33*/17	12*/10	2*/2	5*/1
Pine (47*/29)	—	—	7*/4	34*/20	4*/3	1*/1	1*/1
Blackberry (28*/33)	—	—	0*/3	27*/24	1*/5	0*/1	—
Wild Cherry (17*/30)	—	—	2*/3	11*/16	3*/8	1*/2	0*/1
Greenbrier (16*/17)	0*/1	—	1*/1	10*/10	2*/4	—	3*/1
Grape (14*/32)	—	—	0*/1	.11*/27	3*/3	—	0*/1
Blueberry (14*/25)	—	3*/2	0*/1	8*/17	0*/3	2*/1	1*/1
Hickory (14*/12)	2*/1	—	1*/2	5*/5	6*/2	0*/2	—
Blackgum (13*/21)	2*/1	—	1*/2	7*/14	2*/3	—	1*/1
Holly (12*/22)	0*/2	—	1*/3	11*/14	0*/1	0*/2	—
Poison-ivy (12*/20)	—	—	1*/1	11*/19	—	—	—
Beech (12*/14)	—	—	1*/2	7*/6	4*/5	0*/1	—
Maple (12*/10)	—	—	1*/1	6*/5	4*/2	1*/2	—
Virginia-creeper (11*/20)	—	—	—	11*/20	—	—	—
Persimmon (11*/15)	—	—	0*/1	3*/4	8*/9	—	0*/1
Waxmyrtle (10*/27)	1*/4	—	0*/2	9*/19	—	—	0*/2
Dogwood (9*/23)	—	—	0*/2	8*/17	1*/1	0*/2	0*/1
Mulberry (8*/20)	—	—	—	7*/18	1*/2	—	—
Tuliptree (8*/11)	—	—	—	6*/5	1*/3	1*/2	0*/1
Ash (8*/8)	1*/1	—	0*/2	5*/2	2*/1	0*/2	—
Palmetto (7*/9)	—	—	—	4*/6	3*/3	—	—
Sweetgum (7*/6)	—	—	—	3*/4	4*/2	—	—
Elderberry (6*/17)	—	—	—	6*/16	—	—	0*/1
Cedar (6*/10)	—	—	—	6*/10	—	—	—
Hackberry (5*/13)	—	—	—	4*/12	—	—	1*/1
Swamp-ironwood (5*/1)	—	—	—	—	—	—	5*/1
UPLAND WEEDS AND HERBS							
Panicgrass (39*/39)	11*/9	1*/4	3*/6	22*/18	2*/1	—	0*/1
Bristlegrass (32*/30)	—	0*/3	6*/6	26*/20	0*/1	—	—
Ragweed (22*/21)	—	0*/2	5*/6	17*/11	—	0*/1	0*/1
Paspalum (13*/15)	0*/2	4*/2	5*/4	4*/6	—	—	0*/1
Crabgrass (13*/11)	—	—	2*/4	11*/7	—	—	—
Doveweed (9*/9)	—	—	4*/3	5*/5	—	0*/1	—
Sedge (7*/18)	0*/1	2*/7	0*/2	4*/4	0*/2	0*/1	1*/1
Pokeweed (6*/17)	—	—	1*/1	5*/14	0*/2	—	—
Lespedeza (5*/2)	—	—	5*/2	—	—	—	—

WILDLIFE PLANTS RANKED ACCORDING TO THEIR VALUE

Southeast Region (concl.)

	Water-birds	Marsh-Shore-birds	Upland Game-birds	Song-birds	Fur & Game Mamm.	Small Mamm.	Brows-ers
MARSH AND AQUATIC PLANTS							
Bulrush (44*/35)	35*/21	6*/11	—	—	3*/2	0*/1	—
Pondweed (35*/29)	31*/18	4*/11	—	—	—	—	—
Widgeongrass (33*/28)	31*/20	2*/8	—	—	—	—	—
Cordgrass (29*/16)	15*/8	3*/3	—	10*/3	1*/1	—	0*/1
Smartweed (28*/31)	13*/10	3*/10	—	12*/11	—	—	—
Spikerush (25*/24)	22*/17	3*/7	—	—	—	—	—
Duckweed (18*/12)	15*/9	3*/3	—	—	—	—	—
Naiad (17*/15)	17*/14	0*/1	—	—	—	—	—
Waterlily (14*/13)	11*/10	2*/2	—	—	1*/1	—	—
Muskgrass (13*/17)	13*/15	0*/2	—	—	—	—	—
Chufa (12*/14)	4*/6	0*/1	7*/3	1*/4	—	—	—
Arrowhead (11*/10)	9*/9	2*/1	—	—	—	—	—
Algae (8*/13)	7*/11	1*/2	—	—	—	—	—
Cattail (7*/4)	5*/2	0*/1	—	—	2*/1	—	—
Wildmillet (6*/12)	5*/6	1*/2	0*/1	0*/3	—	—	—
Coontail (6*/10)	6*/10	—	—	—	—	—	—
Wildrice (6*/5)	3*/3	—	—	3*/2	—	—	—
Saltgrass (5*/5)	5*/5	—	—	—	—	—	—
Wildcelery (5*/5)	5*/5	—	—	—	—	—	—
CULTIVATED PLANTS							
Corn (50*/40)	1*/3	4*/1	1*/3	41*/27	2*/4	1*/2	—
Rice (28*/18)	7*/7	8*/4	1*/2	12*/5	—	—	—
Wheat (17*/22)	1*/1	1*/1	1*/3	14*/14	—	0*/2	0*/1
Oats (12*/16)	0*/1	—	2*/2	10*/12	—	0*/1	—
Apple (5*/14)	—	—	—	2*/6	3*/6	0*/2	—

Prairie Region

	Water-birds	Marsh-Shore-birds	Upland Game-birds	Song-birds	Fur & Game Mamm.	Small Mamm.	Brows-ers
WOODY PLANTS							
Oak (35*/28)	0*/1	0*/1	11*/6	3*/8	5*/5	7*/5	9*/2
Hackberry (29*/25)	—	—	2*/4	25*/14	2*/6	0*/1	—
Pricklypear (16*/20)	—	—	1*/2	6*/3	2*/3	5*/9	2*/3
Wild Rose (14*/8)	—	—	7*/3	1*/1	0*/1	—	6*/3
Wild Cherry (13*/18)	—	—	3*/1	8*/11	0*/4	2*/2	—
Cedar (13*/15)	—	—	1*/1	0*/2	2*/5	5*/3	5*/4
Grape (13*/15)	—	—	1*/3	9*/6	3*/6	—	—
Sagebrush (13*/10)	—	—	—	—	—	6*/8	7*/2
Snowberry (12*/9)	—	—	2*/5	—	0*/1	—	10*/3
Sumac (11*/13)	—	—	5*/5	2*/6	3*/1	—	1*/1
Poison-ivy (10*/12)	—	—	2*/2	8*/9	—	—	0*/1
Persimmon (10*/7)	—	—	—	—	7*/5	0*/1	3*/1
Mulberry (8*/18)	—	—	—	5*/9	3*/9	—	—
Dogwood (8*/13)	—	—	0*/1	6*/7	2*/3	0*/1	0*/1
Serviceberry (8*/13)	—	—	0*/1	5*/7	2*/1	—	1*/4
Saltbush (8*/8)	—	—	—	—	—	6*/6	2*/2
Holly (7*/17)	0*/2	—	1*/3	6*/6	0*/5	0*/1	—
Blackberry (7*/15)	—	—	2*/1	2*/7	3*/6	0*/1	—
Pine (7*/4)	—	—	2*/1	5*/2	0*/1	—	—
Mesquite (6*/8)	—	—	0*/2	—	0*/2	6*/3	0*/1

WILDLIFE PLANTS RANKED ACCORDING TO THEIR VALUE

Prairie Region (concl.)

	Water-birds	Marsh-Shore-birds	Upland Game-birds	Song-birds	Fur & Game Mamm.	Small Mamm.	Brows-ers
WOODY PLANTS (cont.)							
Alder (6*/5)	—	—	0*/1	6*/1	0*/1	—	0*/2
Barberry (6*/4)	—	—	—	—	0*/1	—	6*/3
Bearberry (6*/2)	—	—	—	—	—	—	6*/2
Virginia-creeper (5*/9)	—	—	—	5*/9	—	—	—
Rabbitbrush (5*/3)	—	—	—	—	—	0*/1	5*/2
UPLAND WEEDS AND HERBS							
Bristlegrass (60*/41)	—	0*/2	11*/6	47*/30	0*/1	2*/2	—
Ragweed (39*/21)	1*/1	—	8*/5	25*/11	—	5*/3	0*/1
Sunflower (32*/42)	—	—	11*/7	12*/21	—	6*/10	3*/4
Panicgrass (31*/27)	0*/1	—	6*/4	25*/22	—	—	—
Knotweed (25*/23)	—	—	10*/6	10*/12	—	5*/5	—
Pigweed (25*/21)	—	—	3*/1	16*/16	—	6*/3	0*/1
Doveweed (19*/15)	—	—	11*/5	8*/8	0*/1	0*/1	—
Goosefoot (18*/26)	—	—	0*/3	12*/17	—	6*/6	—
Russianthistle (14*/12)	—	—	—	14*/11	—	—	0*/1
Crabgrass (13*/8)	—	—	3*/1	10*/7	—	—	—
Dropseedgrass (12*/13)	—	—	1*/1	11*/10	—	0*/1	0*/1
Clover (10*/13)	—	0*/1	7*/5	—	0*/3	2*/3	1*/1
Needlegrass (10*/8)	—	—	—	8*/4	—	2*/3	0*/1
Sedge (9*/13)	—	0*/2	—	7*/10	—	2*/.1	—
Fescuegrass (9*/9)	—	—	—	5*/5	—	2*/3	2*/1
Gramagrass (8*/8)	—	—	—	3*/2	—	1*/2	4*/4
MARSH AND AQUATIC PLANTS							
Pondweed (62*/26)	50*/18	12*/8	—	—	—	—	—
Bulrush (35*/27)	29*/16	6*/10	—	0*/1	—	—	—
Widgeongrass (17*/18)	17*/16	0*/2	—	—	—	—	—
Muskgrass (16*/11)	16*/11	—	—	—	—	—	—
Smartweed (14*/26)	9*/13	1*/5	0*/1	2*/4	0*/2	2*/1	—
Wildmillet (10*/12)	9*/10	1*/2	—	—	—	—	—
Spikerush (9*/11)	9*/9	0*/2	—	—	—	—	—
Algae (9*/7)	9*/5	0*/2	—	—	—	—	—
Burreed (8*/7)	5*/4	3*/3	—	—	—	—	—
Horsetail (8*/4)	5*/3	3*/1	—	—	—	—	—
Horned-pondweed (7*/8)	7*/7	0*/1	—	—	—	—	—
Watermilfoil (5*/9)	5*/8	0*/1	—	—	—	—	—
Burreed (5*/8)	5*/5	0*/3	—	—	—	—	—
Cattail (5*/2)	5*/2	—	—	—	—	—	—
CULTIVATED PLANTS							
Corn (80*/48)	1*/1	7*/1	19*/8	45*/29	6*/6	1*/1	1*/2
Wheat (52*/41)	6*/2	7*/2	7*/5	23*/23	0*/1	9*/6	0*/2
Oats (34*/35)	0*/2	1*/1	8*/4	25*/24	0*/2	—	0*/2
Sorghum (23*/16)	—	—	7*/6	16*/9	—	0*/1	—
Apple (8*/11)	—	—	—	3*/4	5*/7	—	—
Alfalfa (7*/6)	2*/1	1*/1	—	—	1*/2	—	3*/2
Barley (5*/10)	1*/3	—	3*/2	0*/3	—	1*/2	—

WILDLIFE PLANTS RANKED ACCORDING TO THEIR VALUE

Mountain-Desert Region

	Water-birds	Marsh-Shore-birds	Upland Game-birds	Song-birds	Fur & Game Mamm.	Small Mamm.	Brows-ers
WOODY PLANTS							
Pine (65*/30)	—	—	9*/4	24*/12	11*/5	9*/5	12*/4
Sagebrush (38*/16)	—	—	6*/2	—	1*/1	21*/9	10*/4
Mesquite (35*/19)	—	—	4*/2	5*/3	13*/7	13*/6	0*/1
Pricklypear (32*/32)	—	—	2*/5	4*/3	5*/8	17*/12	4*/4
Oak (31*/21)	—	0*/1	12*/6	6*/4	1*/2	5*/4	7*/4
Cedar (21*/19)	—	—	1*/4	7*/5	0*/2	6*/4	7*/4
Manzanita (18*/12)	—	—	4*/3	6*/3	3*/1	4*/3	1*/2
Douglasfir (17*/14)	—	—	4*/1	0*/2	6*/6	3*/1	4*/4
Wild Cherry (16*/16)	—	—	4*/3	3*/6	3*/2	3*/2	3*/3
Serviceberry (15*/20)	—	—	0*/1	8*/11	2*/3	2*/2	3*/3
Gooseberry (15*/15)	—	0*/1	1*/1	6*/7	—	7*/4	1*/2
Aspen (14*/12)	—	—	3*/3	0*/1	4*/4	—	7*/4
Hackberry (13*/16)	—	—	1*/2	7*/9	2*/2	0*/1	3*/2
Saltbush (12*/11)	0*/1	—	0*/1	0*/1	2*/1	2*/3	8*/4
Fir (12*/11)	—	—	2*/1	2*/4	1*/1	1*/1	6*/4
Willow (10*/8)	—	—	1*/2	—	5*/3	—	4*/3
Birch (10*/8)	—	—	2*/2	3*/1	2*/2	—	3*/3
Blackberry (9*/13)	—	—	2*/1	5*/6	2*/2	0*/2	0*/2
Rabbitbrush (9*/11)	—	—	—	0*/2	5*/4	—	4*/5
Maple (9*/8)	—	—	2*/1	1*/1	1*/1	0*/1	5*/4
Spruce (8*/9	—	—	5*/3	2*/2	1*/1	0*/1	0*/2
Bitterbrush (7*/8)	—	—	—	—	0*/2	4*/2	3*/4
Alder (7*/5)	—	—	0*/1	7*/2	—	—	0*/2
Creosote (7*/5)	—	—	—	—	—	7*/5	—
Elaeagnus (7*/4)	—	—	0*/1	7*/3	—	—	—
Blueberry (6*/6)	1*/1	0*/1	5*/2	0*/1	—	0*/1	—
Buffaloberry (6*/5)	—	—	1*/1	2*/1	1*/1	2*/2	—
Grape (5*/8)	—	—	1*/2	4*/4	0*/2	—	—
Barberry (5*/6)	—	—	—	—	0*/2	—	5*/4
UPLAND WEEDS AND HERBS							
Bristlegrass (43*/26)	2*/2	0*/2	5*/5	34*/12	1*/2	1*/3	—
Pigweed (29*/23)	—	—	3*/3	20*/13	—	6*/5	0*/2
Sunflower (27*/22)	—	0*/1	13*/5	11*/12	—	3*/4	—
Ragweed (22*/18)	1*/1	—	4*/2	12*/9	—	5*/5	0*/1
Sedge (20*/27)	6*/11	4*/5	1*/2	4*/3	0*/2	3*/2	2*/2
Knotweed (20*/23)	—	—	4*/3	14*/14	0*/1	2*/4	0*/1
Gramagrass (19*/12)	—	—	1*/1	3*/2	5*/2	5*/3	5*/4
Russianthistle (18*/22)	—	—	4*/4	2*/5	—	12*/10	0*/3
Dandelion (15*/17)	—	—	6*/4	0*/6	0*/1	9*/5	0*/1
Filaree (13*/13)	—	—	3*/3	7*/6	—	3*/3	0*/1
Goosefoot (13*/12)	—	—	1*/1	9*/8	—	3*/3	—
Wheatgrass (12*/6)	—	—	—	—	—	4*/2	8*/4
Fescuegrass (11*/8)	—	—	1*/1	0*/1	—	3*/2	7*/4
Snakeweed (10*/7)	—	—	2*/1	—	3*/2	2*/2	3*/2
Bromegrass (9*/15)	1*/1	—	2*/2	0*/2	0*/1	3*/4	3*/5
Deervetch (8*/6)	—	—	4*/2	—	—	2*/3	2*/1
Locoweed (7*/6)	—	—	0*/1	—	2*/1	5*/2	0*/2
Eriogonum (6*/10)	—	—	3*/3	1*/2	1*/1	1*/3	0*/1

481

WILDLIFE PLANTS RANKED ACCORDING TO THEIR VALUE

Mountain-Desert Region (concl.)

	Water-birds	Marsh-Shore-birds	Upland Game-birds	Song-birds	Fur & Game Mamm.	Small Mamm.	Browsers
UPLAND WEEDS AND HERBS (cont.)							
Purslane (6*/7)	—	—	—	2*/2	1*/2	3*/3	—
Bluegrass (6*/6)	—	—	0*/1	2*/2	—	1*/1	3*/2
Needlegrass (6*/6)	—	—	—	0*/1	—	0*/1	6*/4
Doveweed (6*/5)	—	—	5*/4	1*/1	—	—	—
Tarweeds (6*/4)	—	—	2*/1	0*/1	—	4*/2	—
Clover (5*/6)	—	—	2*/3	—	3*/2	—	0*/1
Plantain (5*/6)	—	—	—	—	—	5*/6	—
Spiderling (5*/5)	—	—	2*/1	—	2*/1	1*/3	—
Fiddleneck (5*/4)	—	—	0*/1	5*/3	—	—	—
Crownbeard (5*/4)	—	—	1*/1	2*/1	—	2*/2	—
Hilaria (5*/2)	—	—	—	—	—	0*/1	5*/1
MARSH AND AQUATIC PLANTS							
Pondweed (71*/29)	55*/21	16*/8	—	—	—	—	—
Bulrush (47*/32)	38*/19	8*/10	1*/2	0*/1	—	—	—
Widgeongrass (20*/21)	20*/19	0*/2	—	—	—	—	—
Muskgrass (16*/11)	16*/11	—	—	—	—	—	—
Smartweed (15*/25)	12*/15	1*/6	—	—	—	2*/4	—
Saltgrass (11*/10)	9*/6	0*/2	—	—	—	2*/1	0*/1
Spikerush (10*/12)	10*/10	0*/2	—	—	—	—	—
Wildmillet (10*/12)	9*/9	1*/2	0*/1	—	—	—	—
Horned-pondweed (10*/10)	10*/9	0*/1	—	—	—	—	—
Algae (9*/9)	9*/7	0*/2	—	—	—	—	—
Watermilfoil (5*/10)	5*/9	0*/1	—	—	—	—	—
Burreed (5*/8)	5*/5	0*/3	—	—	—	—	—
CULTIVATED PLANTS							
Wheat (75*/37)	6*/3	7*/3	23*/9	34*/19	—	5*/3	—
Oats (28*/26) (partly wild)	0*/2	1*/1	5*/5	22*/18	—	—	—
Corn (28*/24)	1*/1	7*/2	3*/5	16*/14	—	1*/2	—
Sorghum (26*/16)	2*/2	4*/1	10*/4	7*/7	3*/1	0*/1	—
Barley (18*/18)	1*/3	—	12*/6	4*/7	—	1*/2	—
Alfalfa (15*/12)	2*/1	1*/1	8*/5	1*/1	3*/1	0*/2	0*/1
Cult. Cherry (10*/7)	—	—	3*/1	7*/6	—	—	—
Apple (8*/7)	—	—	—	5*/3	3*/2	0*/2	—

Pacific Region

	Water-birds	Marsh-Shore-birds	Upland Game-birds	Song-birds	Fur & Game Mamm.	Small Mamm.	Browsers
WOODY PLANTS							
Pine (72*/39)	—	—	5*/4	40*/22	12*/5	15*/7	0*/1
Oak (64*/37)	—	0*/1	11*/6	29*/14	6*/3	11*/11	7*/2
Elderberry (29*/38)	—	—	2*/2	24*/31	—	2*/3	1*/2
Poison-oak (29*/29)	—	—	1*/1	25*/26	—	3*/2	—
Blackberry (24*/34)	—	—	1*/2	20*/24	1*/1	1*/4	1*/3
Manzanita (18*/14)	—	—	2*/1	5*/4	1*/2	6*/5	4*/2
Buckthorn (17*/20)	—	—	1*/1	13*/11	1*/1	0*/4	2*/3

Pacific Region (cont.)

	Water-birds	Marsh-Shore-birds	Upland Game birds	Song-birds	Fur & Game Mamm.	Small Mamm.	Browsers
WOODY PLANTS (cont.)							
Wild Cherry (14*/18)	—	—	0*/1	9*/12	2*/2	1*/2	2*/1
Pricklypear (14*/18)	—	—	2*/4	3*/3	1*/4	8*/7	—
Ceanothus (14*/12)	—	—	0*/2	—	3*/2	1*/4	10*/4
Cedar (13*/13)	—	—	0*/2	6*/5	0*/1	4*/4	3*/1
Douglasfir (13*/10)	—	—	3*/1	0*/2	4*/2	5*/4	1*/1
Fir (12*/12)	—	—	5*/2	2*/5	1*/2	4*/2	0*/1
Dogwood (11*/18)	—	—	2*/2	8*/12	0*/2	—	1*/2
Mesquite (11*/8)	—	—	4*/2	0*/1	5*/2	2*/2	0*/1
Serviceberry (9*/9)	—	—	0*/1	3*/4	1*/1	4*/2	1*/1
Spruce (8*/8)	—	—	5*/5	2*/2	1*/1	—	—
Willow (8*/5)	—	—	0*/1	—	8*/2	0*/2	—
Gooseberry (7*/16)	—	0*/1	0*/1	4*/6	0*/2	3*/5	0*/1
Snowberry (7*/11)	—	—	0*/1	7*/8	0*/1	0*/1	—
Bitterbrush (7*/5)	—	—	—	—	—	3*/3	4*/2
Alder (7*/5)	—	—	0*/1	7*/3	—	—	0*/1
Birch (7*/3)	—	—	2*/1	3*/1	2*/1	—	—
Sagebrush (7*/3)	—	—	—	—	—	5*/2	2*/1
Mistletoe (6*/11)	—	—	0*/3	6*/8	—	—	—
Blueberry (6*/11)	—	1*/2	5*/2	0*/2	0*/2	0*/1	0*/2
Aspen (6*/6)	—	—	1*/2	—	4*/3	—	1*/1
Mountain-mahogany (6*/4)	—	—	0*/1	—	—	—	6*/3
Salal (5*/8)	—	—	2*/3	0*/1	—	1*/1	2*/3
Madrone (5*/6)	—	—	1*/1	4*/2	—	0*/1	0*/2
Buffaloberry (5*/4)	—	—	—	2*/1	1*/1	2*/2	—
UPLAND WEEDS AND HERBS							
Wild Oats (98*/55)	7*/4	1*/2	8*/5	78*/36	—	3*/7	1*/1
Filaree (61*/45)	—	—	9*/6	25*/26	0*/2	24*/9	3*/2
Pigweed (44*/27)	—	—	3*/3	37*/21	—	4*/2	0*/1
Bristlegrass (29*/22)	2*/3	0*/2	3*/4	24*/12	—	0*/1	—
Turkeymullein (29*/19)	—	—	9*/4	12*/8	0*/1	8*/6	—
Knotweeds (27*/33)	—	—	3*/4	21*/23	—	2*/4	1*/2
Tarweeds (23*/27)	—	—	4*/5	11*/17	0*/1	8*/4	—
Redmaids (22*/23)	—	—	5*/5	14*/15	—	3*/3	—
Bromegrass (21*/22)	2*/1	—	5*/4	3*/7	0*/1	10*/8	1*/1
Star-thistle (20*/18)	—	—	3*/2	17*/14	—	0*/2	—
Sedge (18*/25)	4*/7	4*/5	0*/2	7*/7	0*/1	2*/2	1*/1
Deervetch (18*/11)	—	—	9*/5	—	2*/1	4*/4	3*/1
Chickweed (15*/26)	—	—	1*/3	14*/22	0*/1	—	—
Minerslettuce (14*/18)	—	—	0*/4	14*/13	—	0*/1	—
Ragweed (14*/11)	1*/1	—	2*/1	10*/8	—	1*/1	—
Nightshade (12*/22)	—	—	0*/2	6*/16	2*/1	4*/3	—
Fescuegrass (12*/14)	—	—	—	5*/6	0*/1	5*/6	2*/1
Clover (12*/13)	—	0*/1	9*/5	0*/3	3*/2	0*/2	—
Sunflower (11*/16)	—	0*/1	5*/4	6*/10	—	0*/1	—
Lupine (11*/9)	—	—	8*/4	0*/1	0*/1	3*/3	—
Eriogonum (10*/16)	—	—	1*/2	5*/8	1*/1	2*/4	1*/1

WILDLIFE PLANTS RANKED ACCORDING TO THEIR VALUE

Pacific Region (concl.)

	Water-birds	Marsh-Shore-birds	Upland Game-birds	Song-birds	Fur & Game Mamm.	Small Mamm.	Brows-ers
UPLAND WEEDS AND HERBS (cont.)							
Goosefoot (10*/12)	—	—	0*/1	9*/10	—	1*/1	—
Burclover (9*/8)	—	—	2*/2	1*/1	—	6*/3	0*/2
Russianthistle (8*/10)	—	—	0*/3	1*/2	—	7*/5	—
Bluegrass (6*/13)	—	—	1*/4	4*/6	0*/1	0*/1	1*/1
Fiddleneck (6*/13)	—	—	3*/6	3*/5	—	0*/2	—
MARSH AND AQUATIC PLANTS							
Pondweed (59*/31)	47*/23	12*/8	—	—	—	—	—
Bulrush (42*/31)	36*/19	6*/10	—	0*/2	—	—	—
Widgeongrass (18*/22)	18*/20	0*/2	—	—	—	—	—
Muskgrass (15*/12)	15*/12	—	—	—	—	—	—
Smartweed (12*/22)	11*/15	1*/6	—	—	—	0*/1	—
Wildmillet (12*/14)	10*/10	1*/2	—	—	1*/2	—	—
Spikerush (10*/13)	10*/10	0*/2	—	—	—	0*/1	—
Eelgrass (9*/8)	9*/8	—	—	—	—	—	—
Algae (8*/13)	8*/11	0*/2	—	—	—	—	—
Horned-pondweed (7*/10)	7*/9	0*/1	—	—	—	—	—
Saltgrass (7*/9)	5*/6	0*/2	—	—	—	2*/1	—
Watermilfoil (6*/11)	6*/10	0*/1	—	—	—	—	—
Burreed (6*/9)	6*/6	0*/3	—	—	—	—	—
Horsetail (6*/3)	3*/2	3*/1	—	—	—	—	—
CULTIVATED PLANTS							
Wheat (74*/42)	9*/3	7*/3	13*/5	39*/27	—	6*/4	—
Barley (48*/36)	11*/8	—	8*/5	23*/18	0*/1	6*/3	0*/1
Corn (35*/29)	1*/1	7*/2	1*/1	24*/22	—	2*/2	0*/1
Cult. Cherry (25*/22)	—	—	—	25*/20	0*/2	—	—
Grape (25*/16)	—	—	—	25*/14	0*/2	—	—
Sorghum (15*/20)	2*/3	4*/1	3*/3	3*/12	3*/1	—	—
Calif. Peppertree (15*/11)	—	—	—	15*/11	—	—	—
Fig (13*/15)	—	—	—	13*/13	0*/2	—	—
Rice (10*/5)	4*/3	—	—	6*/2	—	—	—
Apple (8*/11)	—	—	—	7*/8	1*/1	0*/2	—
Alfalfa (7*/7)	2*/2	1*/1	3*/2	1*/1	0*/1	—	—

Index

Common and scientific names (the latter italicized) of animals and plants are included in this index. Though some common names have been cross-indexed, most designations consisting of two or more words have been entered solely under the final one. Bell sparrow, for example, is listed only under "Sparrows."

Names mentioned casually in the text have generally been excluded. However, numerous plants listed in tables of data but not discussed because of their minor importance are indexed, accompanied by their scientific name for at least the genus. Except for these minor-plant entries, Latin names of plants have been omitted when they nearly duplicate the common name, as in magnolias (*Magnolia*), roses (*Rosa*), or violets (*Viola*).

INDEX

INDEX

INDEX

J

Jack-in-the-pulpit, 385
Jack rabbits, 239
Jasmine (*Gelsemium*), 270
Jays, 130
  Blue, 131
  Piñon, 137
  Scrub, 132
  Steller, 131
Jewelweeds, 411
Jointfirs, 295
Jojoba (*Simmondsia*), 113
Juglans, 297
  regia, 466
Jujube (*Zizyphus*), 113
Juncos, 199
  Oregon (*Junco oreganus*), 200
  Slate-colored (*Junco hyemalis*), 200
Junipers, 294
  Sierra (*Juniperus occidentalis*), 272

K

Kaffir, 463
Kalmia latifolia, 352
Kangaroo rats, 257
Killdeer, 85
Kingbirds, 126–127
  Arkansas, 127
  Cassin, 127
  Eastern, 126
Kingfishers, 118
Kinglets, 156
  Ruby-crowned, 157
Kites, 215
Knot, American, 87
Knotweeds, 387
Koeleria (*Koeleria*), 268, 271

L

Labrador-tea (*Ledum*), 269, 273
Lactuca, 426
Larches, 289
Larix, 289
Lark, Horned, 129
  (*See also* Meadowlarks)
Larrea tridentata, 333
Larus, 76–77
  argentatus, 76
  delawarensis, 76
  pipixcan, 77
Laurel (Mountainlaurel), 352
Laurel-sumac, 336
Leafcup (*Polymnia*), 188
Leaf-flower (*Phyllanthus*), 199
Leatherleaf (*Chamaedaphne*), 269

Leersia oryzoides, 440
Lemming, 263
Lemna, 447
Lepidium, 397
Lepus, 238–240
  alleni, 240
  americanus, 238
  californicus, 240
  townsendii, 239
Lespedezas, 405
Leucosticte, 186–187
  australis, 186
  tephrocotis, 186
Leucothoe (*Leucothoe*), 270
Lewisia (*Lewisia*), 186
Lichens, 6, 271
Ligustrum, 474
Limnodromus griseus, 88
Limosa, 89–90
  fedoa, 89
  haemastica, 90
Limpkin, 81
Lindera, 318
Lippia (*Lippia*), 133
Liquidambar styraciflua, 319
Liriodendron tulipifera, 316
Lizardtail (*Saururus*), 66
Locoweeds, 404
Locust, Black, 333
Lolium, 373
Longspurs, 209
  Chestnut-collared, 210
  Lapland, 209
  McCown, 209
  Smith, 210
Lonicera japonica, 365
Loons, 47
Loosestrife (*Lysimachia*), 247
Lophortyx, 103–105
  californica, 103
  gambelii, 104
Lotus, 404
Lovegrass (*Eragrostis*), 187, 194, 259
Loxia, 190
  curvirostra, 190
  leucoptera, 190
Lupines, 400
Lyciums, 360
Lynx, 228

M

Maclura pomifera, 314
Madia, 423
Madrone, Pacific, 254
Magnolias, 316
Magpies, 133
  Common, 133

INDEX

INDEX

INDEX

A CATALOG OF SELECTED
DOVER BOOKS
IN ALL FIELDS OF INTEREST

A CATALOG OF SELECTED DOVER
BOOKS IN ALL FIELDS OF INTEREST

DRAWINGS OF REMBRANDT, edited by Seymour Slive. Updated Lippmann, Hofstede de Groot edition, with definitive scholarly apparatus. All portraits, biblical sketches, landscapes, nudes. Oriental figures, classical studies, together with selection of work by followers. 550 illustrations. Total of 630pp. 9⅛ × 12¼.
21485-0, 21486-9 Pa., Two-vol. set $25.00

GHOST AND HORROR STORIES OF AMBROSE BIERCE, Ambrose Bierce. 24 tales vividly imagined, strangely prophetic, and decades ahead of their time in technical skill: "The Damned Thing," "An Inhabitant of Carcosa," "The Eyes of the Panther," "Moxon's Master," and 20 more. 199pp. 5⅜ × 8½. 20767-6 Pa. $3.95

ETHICAL WRITINGS OF MAIMONIDES, Maimonides. Most significant ethical works of great medieval sage, newly translated for utmost precision, readability. Laws Concerning Character Traits, Eight Chapters, more. 192pp. 5⅜ × 8½.
24522-5 Pa. $4.50

THE EXPLORATION OF THE COLORADO RIVER AND ITS CANYONS, J. W. Powell. Full text of Powell's 1,000-mile expedition down the fabled Colorado in 1869. Superb account of terrain, geology, vegetation, Indians, famine, mutiny, treacherous rapids, mighty canyons, during exploration of last unknown part of continental U.S. 400pp. 5⅜ × 8½. 20094-9 Pa. $6.95

HISTORY OF PHILOSOPHY, Julián Marías. Clearest one-volume history on the market. Every major philosopher and dozens of others, to Existentialism and later. 505pp. 5⅜ × 8½. 21739-6 Pa. $8.50

ALL ABOUT LIGHTNING, Martin A. Uman. Highly readable non-technical survey of nature and causes of lightning, thunderstorms, ball lightning, St. Elmo's Fire, much more. Illustrated. 192pp. 5⅜ × 8½. 25237-X Pa. $5.95

SAILING ALONE AROUND THE WORLD, Captain Joshua Slocum. First man to sail around the world, alone, in small boat. One of great feats of seamanship told in delightful manner. 67 illustrations. 294pp. 5⅜ × 8½. 20326-3 Pa. $4.95

LETTERS AND NOTES ON THE MANNERS, CUSTOMS AND CONDITIONS OF THE NORTH AMERICAN INDIANS, George Catlin. Classic account of life among Plains Indians: ceremonies, hunt, warfare, etc. 312 plates. 572pp. of text. 6⅛ × 9¼. 22118-0, 22119-9 Pa. Two-vol. set $15.90

ALASKA: The Harriman Expedition, 1899, John Burroughs, John Muir, et al. Informative, engrossing accounts of two-month, 9,000-mile expedition. Native peoples, wildlife, forests, geography, salmon industry, glaciers, more. Profusely illustrated. 240 black-and-white line drawings. 124 black-and-white photographs. 3 maps. Index. 576pp. 5⅜ × 8½. 25109-8 Pa. $11.95

THE BOOK OF BEASTS: Being a Translation from a Latin Bestiary of the Twelfth Century, T. H. White. Wonderful catalog real and fanciful beasts: manticore, griffin, phoenix, amphivius, jaculus, many more. White's witty erudite commentary on scientific, historical aspects. Fascinating glimpse of medieval mind. Illustrated. 296pp. 5⅜ × 8¼. (Available in U.S. only) 24609-4 Pa. $5.95

FRANK LLOYD WRIGHT: ARCHITECTURE AND NATURE With 160 Illustrations, Donald Hoffmann. Profusely illustrated study of influence of nature—especially prairie—on Wright's designs for Fallingwater, Robie House, Guggenheim Museum, other masterpieces. 96pp. 9¼ × 10¾. 25098-9 Pa. $7.95

FRANK LLOYD WRIGHT'S FALLINGWATER, Donald Hoffmann. Wright's famous waterfall house: planning and construction of organic idea. History of site, owners, Wright's personal involvement. Photographs of various stages of building. Preface by Edgar Kaufmann, Jr. 100 illustrations. 112pp. 9¼ × 10.
23671-4 Pa. $7.95

YEARS WITH FRANK LLOYD WRIGHT: Apprentice to Genius, Edgar Tafel. Insightful memoir by a former apprentice presents a revealing portrait of Wright the man, the inspired teacher, the greatest American architect. 372 black-and-white illustrations. Preface. Index. vi + 228pp. 8¼ × 11. 24801-1 Pa. $9.95

THE STORY OF KING ARTHUR AND HIS KNIGHTS, Howard Pyle. Enchanting version of King Arthur fable has delighted generations with imaginative narratives of exciting adventures and unforgettable illustrations by the author. 41 illustrations. xviii + 313pp. 6⅛ × 9¼. 21445-1 Pa. $6.50

THE GODS OF THE EGYPTIANS, E. A. Wallis Budge. Thorough coverage of numerous gods of ancient Egypt by foremost Egyptologist. Information on evolution of cults, rites and gods; the cult of Osiris; the Book of the Dead and its rites; the sacred animals and birds; Heaven and Hell; and more. 956pp. 6⅛ × 9¼.
22055-9, 22056-7 Pa., Two-vol. set $20.00

A THEOLOGICO-POLITICAL TREATISE, Benedict Spinoza. Also contains unfinished *Political Treatise*. Great classic on religious liberty, theory of government on common consent. R. Elwes translation. Total of 421pp. 5⅜ × 8½.
20249-6 Pa. $6.95

INCIDENTS OF TRAVEL IN CENTRAL AMERICA, CHIAPAS, AND YU-CATAN, John L. Stephens. Almost single-handed discovery of Maya culture; exploration of ruined cities, monuments, temples; customs of Indians. 115 drawings. 892pp. 5⅜ × 8½. 22404-X, 22405-8 Pa., Two-vol. set $15.90

LOS CAPRICHOS, Francisco Goya. 80 plates of wild, grotesque monsters and caricatures. Prado manuscript included. 183pp. 6⅛ × 9⅜. 22384-1 Pa. $4.95

AUTOBIOGRAPHY: The Story of My Experiments with Truth, Mohandas K. Gandhi. Not hagiography, but Gandhi in his own words. Boyhood, legal studies, purification, the growth of the Satyagraha (nonviolent protest) movement. Critical, inspiring work of the man who freed India. 480pp. 5⅜ × 8½. (Available in U.S. only)
24593-4 Pa. $6.95

ILLUSTRATED DICTIONARY OF HISTORIC ARCHITECTURE, edited by Cyril M. Harris. Extraordinary compendium of clear, concise definitions for over 5,000 important architectural terms complemented by over 2,000 line drawings. Covers full spectrum of architecture from ancient ruins to 20th-century Modernism. Preface. 592pp. 7½ × 9⅜. 24444-X Pa. $14.95

THE NIGHT BEFORE CHRISTMAS, Clement Moore. Full text, and woodcuts from original 1848 book. Also critical, historical material. 19 illustrations. 40pp. 4⅝ × 6. 22797-9 Pa. $2.25

THE LESSON OF JAPANESE ARCHITECTURE: 165 Photographs, Jiro Harada. Memorable gallery of 165 photographs taken in the 1930's of exquisite Japanese homes of the well-to-do and historic buildings. 13 line diagrams. 192pp. 8⅜ × 11¼. 24778-3 Pa. $8.95

THE AUTOBIOGRAPHY OF CHARLES DARWIN AND SELECTED LETTERS, edited by Francis Darwin. The fascinating life of eccentric genius composed of an intimate memoir by Darwin (intended for his children); commentary by his son, Francis; hundreds of fragments from notebooks, journals, papers; and letters to and from Lyell, Hooker, Huxley, Wallace and Henslow. xi + 365pp. 5⅜ × 8. 20479-0 Pa. $6.95

WONDERS OF THE SKY: Observing Rainbows, Comets, Eclipses, the Stars and Other Phenomena, Fred Schaaf. Charming, easy-to-read poetic guide to all manner of celestial events visible to the naked eye. Mock suns, glories, Belt of Venus, more. Illustrated. 299pp. 5¼ × 8¼. 24402-4 Pa. $7.95

BURNHAM'S CELESTIAL HANDBOOK, Robert Burnham, Jr. Thorough guide to the stars beyond our solar system. Exhaustive treatment. Alphabetical by constellation: Andromeda to Cetus in Vol. 1; Chamaeleon to Orion in Vol. 2; and Pavo to Vulpecula in Vol. 3. Hundreds of illustrations. Index in Vol. 3. 2,000pp. 6⅛ × 9¼. 23567-X, 23568-8, 23673-0 Pa., Three-vol. set $38.85

STAR NAMES: Their Lore and Meaning, Richard Hinckley Allen. Fascinating history of names various cultures have given to constellations and literary and folkloristic uses that have been made of stars. Indexes to subjects. Arabic and Greek names. Biblical references. Bibliography. 563pp. 5⅜ × 8½. 21079-0 Pa. $7.95

THIRTY YEARS THAT SHOOK PHYSICS: The Story of Quantum Theory, George Gamow. Lucid, accessible introduction to influential theory of energy and matter. Careful explanations of Dirac's anti-particles, Bohr's model of the atom, much more. 12 plates. Numerous drawings. 240pp. 5⅜ × 8½. 24895-X Pa. $4.95

CHINESE DOMESTIC FURNITURE IN PHOTOGRAPHS AND MEASURED DRAWINGS, Gustav Ecke. A rare volume, now affordably priced for antique collectors, furniture buffs and art historians. Detailed review of styles ranging from early Shang to late Ming. Unabridged republication. 161 black-and-white drawings, photos. Total of 224pp. 8⅜ × 11¼. (Available in U.S. only) 25171-3 Pa. $12.95

VINCENT VAN GOGH: A Biography, Julius Meier-Graefe. Dynamic, penetrating study of artist's life, relationship with brother, Theo, painting techniques, travels, more. Readable, engrossing. 160pp. 5⅜ × 8½. (Available in U.S. only) 25253-1 Pa. $3.95

HOW TO WRITE, Gertrude Stein. Gertrude Stein claimed anyone could understand her unconventional writing—here are clues to help. Fascinating improvisations, language experiments, explanations illuminate Stein's craft and the art of writing. Total of 414pp. 4⅜ × 6⅜. 23144-5 Pa. $5.95

ADVENTURES AT SEA IN THE GREAT AGE OF SAIL: Five Firsthand Narratives, edited by Elliot Snow. Rare true accounts of exploration, whaling, shipwreck, fierce natives, trade, shipboard life, more. 33 illustrations. Introduction. 353pp. 5⅜ × 8½. 25177-2 Pa. $7.95

THE HERBAL OR GENERAL HISTORY OF PLANTS, John Gerard. Classic descriptions of about 2,850 plants—with over 2,700 illustrations—includes Latin and English names, physical descriptions, varieties, time and place of growth, more. 2,706 illustrations. xlv + 1,678pp. 8½ × 12¼. 23147-X Cloth. $75.00

DOROTHY AND THE WIZARD IN OZ, L. Frank Baum. Dorothy and the Wizard visit the center of the Earth, where people are vegetables, glass houses grow and Oz characters reappear. Classic sequel to *Wizard of Oz*. 256pp. 5⅜ × 8. 24714-7 Pa. $4.95

SONGS OF EXPERIENCE: Facsimile Reproduction with 26 Plates in Full Color, William Blake. This facsimile of Blake's original "Illuminated Book" reproduces 26 full-color plates from a rare 1826 edition. Includes "The Tyger," "London," "Holy Thursday," and other immortal poems. 26 color plates. Printed text of poems. 48pp. 5¼ × 7. 24636-1 Pa. $3.50

SONGS OF INNOCENCE, William Blake. The first and most popular of Blake's famous "Illuminated Books," in a facsimile edition reproducing all 31 brightly colored plates. Additional printed text of each poem. 64pp. 5¼ × 7. 22764-2 Pa. $3.50

PRECIOUS STONES, Max Bauer. Classic, thorough study of diamonds, rubies, emeralds, garnets, etc.: physical character, occurrence, properties, use, similar topics. 20 plates, 8 in color. 94 figures. 659pp. 6⅛ × 9¼. 21910-0, 21911-9 Pa., Two-vol. set $15.90

ENCYCLOPEDIA OF VICTORIAN NEEDLEWORK, S. F. A. Caulfeild and Blanche Saward. Full, precise descriptions of stitches, techniques for dozens of needlecrafts—most exhaustive reference of its kind. Over 800 figures. Total of 679pp. 8⅛ × 11. Two volumes. Vol. 1 22800-2 Pa. $11.95
Vol. 2 22801-0 Pa. $11.95

THE MARVELOUS LAND OF OZ, L. Frank Baum. Second Oz book, the Scarecrow and Tin Woodman are back with hero named Tip, Oz magic. 136 illustrations. 287pp. 5⅜ × 8½. 20692-0 Pa. $5.95

WILD FOWL DECOYS, Joel Barber. Basic book on the subject, by foremost authority and collector. Reveals history of decoy making and rigging, place in American culture, different kinds of decoys, how to make them, and how to use them. 140 plates. 156pp. 7⅞ × 10¾. 20011-6 Pa. $8.95

HISTORY OF LACE, Mrs. Bury Palliser. Definitive, profusely illustrated chronicle of lace from earliest times to late 19th century. Laces of Italy, Greece, England, France, Belgium, etc. Landmark of needlework scholarship. 266 illustrations. 672pp. 6⅛ × 9¼. 24742-2 Pa. $14.95

ILLUSTRATED GUIDE TO SHAKER FURNITURE, Robert Meader. All furniture and appurtenances, with much on unknown local styles. 235 photos. 146pp. 9 × 12. 22819-3 Pa. $7.95

WHALE SHIPS AND WHALING: A Pictorial Survey, George Francis Dow. Over 200 vintage engravings, drawings, photographs of barks, brigs, cutters, other vessels. Also harpoons, lances, whaling guns, many other artifacts. Comprehensive text by foremost authority. 207 black-and-white illustrations. 288pp. 6 × 9. 24808-9 Pa. $8.95

THE BERTRAMS, Anthony Trollope. Powerful portrayal of blind self-will and thwarted ambition includes one of Trollope's most heartrending love stories. 497pp. 5⅜ × 8½. 25119-5 Pa. $8.95

ADVENTURES WITH A HAND LENS, Richard Headstrom. Clearly written guide to observing and studying flowers and grasses, fish scales, moth and insect wings, egg cases, buds, feathers, seeds, leaf scars, moss, molds, ferns, common crystals, etc.—all with an ordinary, inexpensive magnifying glass. 209 exact line drawings aid in your discoveries. 220pp. 5⅜ × 8¼. 23330-8 Pa. $3.95

RODIN ON ART AND ARTISTS, Auguste Rodin. Great sculptor's candid, wide-ranging comments on meaning of art; great artists; relation of sculpture to poetry, painting, music; philosophy of life, more. 76 superb black-and-white illustrations of Rodin's sculpture, drawings and prints. 119pp. 8⅜ × 11¼. 24487-3 Pa. $6.95

FIFTY CLASSIC FRENCH FILMS, 1912–1982: A Pictorial Record, Anthony Slide. Memorable stills from Grand Illusion, Beauty and the Beast, Hiroshima, Mon Amour, many more. Credits, plot synopses, reviews, etc. 160pp. 8¼ × 11. 25256-6 Pa. $11.95

THE PRINCIPLES OF PSYCHOLOGY, William James. Famous long course complete, unabridged. Stream of thought, time perception, memory, experimental methods; great work decades ahead of its time. 94 figures. 1,391pp. 5⅜ × 8½. 20381-6, 20382-4 Pa., Two-vol. set $19.90

BODIES IN A BOOKSHOP, R. T. Campbell. Challenging mystery of blackmail and murder with ingenious plot and superbly drawn characters. In the best tradition of British suspense fiction. 192pp. 5⅜ × 8½. 24720-1 Pa. $3.95

CALLAS: PORTRAIT OF A PRIMA DONNA, George Jellinek. Renowned commentator on the musical scene chronicles incredible career and life of the most controversial, fascinating, influential operatic personality of our time. 64 black-and-white photographs. 416pp. 5⅜ × 8¼. 25047-4 Pa. $7.95

GEOMETRY, RELATIVITY AND THE FOURTH DIMENSION, Rudolph Rucker. Exposition of fourth dimension, concepts of relativity as Flatland characters continue adventures. Popular, easily followed yet accurate, profound. 141 illustrations. 133pp. 5⅜ × 8½. 23400-2 Pa. $3.95

HOUSEHOLD STORIES BY THE BROTHERS GRIMM, with pictures by Walter Crane. 53 classic stories—Rumpelstiltskin, Rapunzel, Hansel and Gretel, the Fisherman and his Wife, Snow White, Tom Thumb, Sleeping Beauty, Cinderella, and so much more—lavishly illustrated with original 19th century drawings. 114 illustrations. x + 269pp. 5⅜ × 8½. 21080-4 Pa. $4.50

SUNDIALS, Albert Waugh. Far and away the best, most thorough coverage of ideas, mathematics concerned, types, construction, adjusting anywhere. Over 100 illustrations. 230pp. 5⅜ × 8½. 22947-5 Pa. $4.50

PICTURE HISTORY OF THE NORMANDIE: With 190 Illustrations, Frank O. Braynard. Full story of legendary French ocean liner: Art Deco interiors, design innovations, furnishings, celebrities, maiden voyage, tragic fire, much more. Extensive text. 144pp. 8⅜ × 11¾. 25257-4 Pa. $9.95

THE FIRST AMERICAN COOKBOOK: A Facsimile of "American Cookery," 1796, Amelia Simmons. Facsimile of the first American-written cookbook published in the United States contains authentic recipes for colonial favorites—pumpkin pudding, winter squash pudding, spruce beer, Indian slapjacks, and more. Introductory Essay and Glossary of colonial cooking terms. 80pp. 5⅜ × 8½. 24710-4 Pa. $3.50

101 PUZZLES IN THOUGHT AND LOGIC, C. R. Wylie, Jr. Solve murders and robberies, find out which fishermen are liars, how a blind man could possibly identify a color—purely by your own reasoning! 107pp. 5⅜ × 8½. 20367-0 Pa. $2.50

THE BOOK OF WORLD-FAMOUS MUSIC—CLASSICAL, POPULAR AND FOLK, James J. Fuld. Revised and enlarged republication of landmark work in musico-bibliography. Full information about nearly 1,000 songs and compositions including first lines of music and lyrics. New supplement. Index. 800pp. 5⅜ × 8¼. 24857-7 Pa. $14.95

ANTHROPOLOGY AND MODERN LIFE, Franz Boas. Great anthropologist's classic treatise on race and culture. Introduction by Ruth Bunzel. Only inexpensive paperback edition. 255pp. 5⅜ × 8½. 25245-0 Pa. $5.95

THE TALE OF PETER RABBIT, Beatrix Potter. The inimitable Peter's terrifying adventure in Mr. McGregor's garden, with all 27 wonderful, full-color Potter illustrations. 55pp. 4¼ × 5½. (Available in U.S. only) 22827-4 Pa. $1.75

THREE PROPHETIC SCIENCE FICTION NOVELS, H. G. Wells. *When the Sleeper Wakes, A Story of the Days to Come* and *The Time Machine* (full version). 335pp. 5⅜ × 8½. (Available in U.S. only) 20605-X Pa. $5.95

APICIUS COOKERY AND DINING IN IMPERIAL ROME, edited and translated by Joseph Dommers Vehling. Oldest known cookbook in existence offers readers a clear picture of what foods Romans ate, how they prepared them, etc. 49 illustrations. 301pp. 6⅛ × 9¼. 23563-7 Pa. $6.50

SHAKESPEARE LEXICON AND QUOTATION DICTIONARY, Alexander Schmidt. Full definitions, locations, shades of meaning of every word in plays and poems. More than 50,000 exact quotations. 1,485pp. 6½ × 9¼. 22726-X, 22727-8 Pa., Two-vol. set $27.90

THE WORLD'S GREAT SPEECHES, edited by Lewis Copeland and Lawrence W. Lamm. Vast collection of 278 speeches from Greeks to 1970. Powerful and effective models; unique look at history. 842pp. 5⅜ × 8½. 20468-5 Pa. $11.95

THE BLUE FAIRY BOOK, Andrew Lang. The first, most famous collection, with many familiar tales: Little Red Riding Hood, Aladdin and the Wonderful Lamp, Puss in Boots, Sleeping Beauty, Hansel and Gretel, Rumpelstiltskin; 37 in all. 138 illustrations. 390pp. 5⅜ × 8½. 21437-0 Pa. $5.95

THE STORY OF THE CHAMPIONS OF THE ROUND TABLE, Howard Pyle. Sir Launcelot, Sir Tristram and Sir Percival in spirited adventures of love and triumph retold in Pyle's inimitable style. 50 drawings, 31 full-page. xviii + 329pp. 6½ × 9¼. 21883-X Pa. $6.95

AUDUBON AND HIS JOURNALS, Maria Audubon. Unmatched two-volume portrait of the great artist, naturalist and author contains his journals, an excellent biography by his granddaughter, expert annotations by the noted ornithologist, Dr. Elliott Coues, and 37 superb illustrations. Total of 1,200pp. 5⅜ × 8.

Vol. I 25143-8 Pa. $8.95
Vol. II 25144-6 Pa. $8.95

GREAT DINOSAUR HUNTERS AND THEIR DISCOVERIES, Edwin H. Colbert. Fascinating, lavishly illustrated chronicle of dinosaur research, 1820's to 1960. Achievements of Cope, Marsh, Brown, Buckland, Mantell, Huxley, many others. 384pp. 5¼ × 8¼. 24701-5 Pa. $6.95

THE TASTEMAKERS, Russell Lynes. Informal, illustrated social history of American taste 1850's-1950's. First popularized categories Highbrow, Lowbrow, Middlebrow. 129 illustrations. New (1979) afterword. 384pp. 6 × 9.
23993-4 Pa. $6.95

DOUBLE CROSS PURPOSES, Ronald A. Knox. A treasure hunt in the Scottish Highlands, an old map, unidentified corpse, surprise discoveries keep reader guessing in this cleverly intricate tale of financial skullduggery. 2 black-and-white maps. 320pp. 5⅜ × 8½. (Available in U.S. only) 25032-6 Pa. $5.95

AUTHENTIC VICTORIAN DECORATION AND ORNAMENTATION IN FULL COLOR: 46 Plates from "Studies in Design," Christopher Dresser. Superb full-color lithographs reproduced from rare original portfolio of a major Victorian designer. 48pp. 9¼ × 12¼. 25083-0 Pa. $7.95

PRIMITIVE ART, Franz Boas. Remains the best text ever prepared on subject, thoroughly discussing Indian, African, Asian, Australian, and, especially, Northern American primitive art. Over 950 illustrations show ceramics, masks, totem poles, weapons, textiles, paintings, much more. 376pp. 5⅜ × 8. 20025-6 Pa. $6.95

SIDELIGHTS ON RELATIVITY, Albert Einstein. Unabridged republication of two lectures delivered by the great physicist in 1920-21. *Ether and Relativity* and *Geometry and Experience*. Elegant ideas in non-mathematical form, accessible to intelligent layman. vi + 56pp. 5⅜ × 8½. 24511-X Pa. $2.95

THE WIT AND HUMOR OF OSCAR WILDE, edited by Alvin Redman. More than 1,000 ripostes, paradoxes, wisecracks: Work is the curse of the drinking classes, I can resist everything except temptation, etc. 258pp. 5⅜ × 8½. 20602-5 Pa. $4.50

ADVENTURES WITH A MICROSCOPE, Richard Headstrom. 59 adventures with clothing fibers, protozoa, ferns and lichens, roots and leaves, much more. 142 illustrations. 232pp. 5⅜ × 8½. 23471-1 Pa. $3.95

PLANTS OF THE BIBLE, Harold N. Moldenke and Alma L. Moldenke. Standard reference to all 230 plants mentioned in Scriptures. Latin name, biblical reference, uses, modern identity, much more. Unsurpassed encyclopedic resource for scholars, botanists, nature lovers, students of Bible. Bibliography. Indexes. 123 black-and-white illustrations. 384pp. 6 × 9. 25069-5 Pa. $8.95

FAMOUS AMERICAN WOMEN: A Biographical Dictionary from Colonial Times to the Present, Robert McHenry, ed. From Pocahontas to Rosa Parks, 1,035 distinguished American women documented in separate biographical entries. Accurate, up-to-date data, numerous categories, spans 400 years. Indices. 493pp. 6½ × 9¼. 24523-3 Pa. $9.95

THE FABULOUS INTERIORS OF THE GREAT OCEAN LINERS IN HISTORIC PHOTOGRAPHS, William H. Miller, Jr. Some 200 superb photographs capture exquisite interiors of world's great "floating palaces"—1890's to 1980's: *Titanic, Ile de France, Queen Elizabeth, United States, Europa,* more. Approx. 200 black-and-white photographs. Captions. Text. Introduction. 160pp. 8⅜ × 11¾. 24756-2 Pa. $9.95

THE GREAT LUXURY LINERS, 1927–1954: A Photographic Record, William H. Miller, Jr. Nostalgic tribute to heyday of ocean liners. 186 photos of Ile de France, Normandie, Leviathan, Queen Elizabeth, United States, many others. Interior and exterior views. Introduction. Captions. 160pp. 9 × 12. 24056-8 Pa. $9.95

A NATURAL HISTORY OF THE DUCKS, John Charles Phillips. Great landmark of ornithology offers complete detailed coverage of nearly 200 species and subspecies of ducks: gadwall, sheldrake, merganser, pintail, many more. 74 full-color plates, 102 black-and-white. Bibliography. Total of 1,920pp. 8⅜ × 11¼. 25141-1, 25142-X Cloth. Two-vol. set $100.00

THE SEAWEED HANDBOOK: An Illustrated Guide to Seaweeds from North Carolina to Canada, Thomas F. Lee. Concise reference covers 78 species. Scientific and common names, habitat, distribution, more. Finding keys for easy identification. 224pp. 5⅜ × 8½. 25215-9 Pa. $5.95

THE TEN BOOKS OF ARCHITECTURE: The 1755 Leoni Edition, Leon Battista Alberti. Rare classic helped introduce the glories of ancient architecture to the Renaissance. 68 black-and-white plates. 336pp. 8⅜ × 11¼. 25239-6 Pa. $14.95

MISS MACKENZIE, Anthony Trollope. Minor masterpieces by Victorian master unmasks many truths about life in 19th-century England. First inexpensive edition in years. 392pp. 5⅜ × 8½. 25201-9 Pa. $7.95

THE RIME OF THE ANCIENT MARINER, Gustave Doré, Samuel Taylor Coleridge. Dramatic engravings considered by many to be his greatest work. The terrifying space of the open sea, the storms and whirlpools of an unknown ocean, the ice of Antarctica, more—all rendered in a powerful, chilling manner. Full text. 38 plates. 77pp. 9¼ × 12. 22305-1 Pa. $4.95

THE EXPEDITIONS OF ZEBULON MONTGOMERY PIKE, Zebulon Montgomery Pike. Fascinating first-hand accounts (1805–6) of exploration of Mississippi River, Indian wars, capture by Spanish dragoons, much more. 1,088pp. 5⅜ × 8½. 25254-X, 25255-8 Pa. Two-vol. set $23.90

A CONCISE HISTORY OF PHOTOGRAPHY: Third Revised Edition, Helmut Gernsheim. Best one-volume history—camera obscura, photochemistry, daguerreotypes, evolution of cameras, film, more. Also artistic aspects—landscape, portraits, fine art, etc. 281 black-and-white photographs. 26 in color. 176pp. 8⅜ × 11¼. 25128-4 Pa. $12.95

THE DORÉ BIBLE ILLUSTRATIONS, Gustave Doré. 241 detailed plates from the Bible: the Creation scenes, Adam and Eve, Flood, Babylon, battle sequences, life of Jesus, etc. Each plate is accompanied by the verses from the King James version of the Bible. 241pp. 9 × 12. 23004-X Pa. $8.95

HUGGER-MUGGER IN THE LOUVRE, Elliot Paul. Second Homer Evans mystery-comedy. Theft at the Louvre involves sleuth in hilarious, madcap caper. "A knockout."—Books. 336pp. 5⅜ × 8½. 25185-3 Pa. $5.95

FLATLAND, E. A. Abbott. Intriguing and enormously popular science-fiction classic explores the complexities of trying to survive as a two-dimensional being in a three-dimensional world. Amusingly illustrated by the author. 16 illustrations. 103pp. 5⅜ × 8½. 20001-9 Pa. $2.25

THE HISTORY OF THE LEWIS AND CLARK EXPEDITION, Meriwether Lewis and William Clark, edited by Elliott Coues. Classic edition of Lewis and Clark's day-by-day journals that later became the basis for U.S. claims to Oregon and the West. Accurate and invaluable geographical, botanical, biological, meteorological and anthropological material. Total of 1,508pp. 5⅜ × 8½.
21268-8, 21269-6, 21270-X Pa. Three-vol. set $25.50

LANGUAGE, TRUTH AND LOGIC, Alfred J. Ayer. Famous, clear introduction to Vienna, Cambridge schools of Logical Positivism. Role of philosophy, elimination of metaphysics, nature of analysis, etc. 160pp. 5⅜ × 8½. (Available in U.S. and Canada only) 20010-8 Pa. $2.95

MATHEMATICS FOR THE NONMATHEMATICIAN, Morris Kline. Detailed, college-level treatment of mathematics in cultural and historical context, with numerous exercises. For liberal arts students. Preface. Recommended Reading Lists. Tables. Index. Numerous black-and-white figures. xvi + 641pp. 5⅜ × 8½.
24823-2 Pa. $11.95

28 SCIENCE FICTION STORIES, H. G. Wells. Novels, *Star Begotten* and *Men Like Gods,* plus 26 short stories: "Empire of the Ants," "A Story of the Stone Age," "The Stolen Bacillus," "In the Abyss," etc. 915pp. 5⅜ × 8½. (Available in U.S. only)
20265-8 Cloth. $10.95

HANDBOOK OF PICTORIAL SYMBOLS, Rudolph Modley. 3,250 signs and symbols, many systems in full; official or heavy commercial use. Arranged by subject. Most in Pictorial Archive series. 143pp. 8⅛ × 11. 23357-X Pa. $5.95

INCIDENTS OF TRAVEL IN YUCATAN, John L. Stephens. Classic (1843) exploration of jungles of Yucatan, looking for evidences of Maya civilization. Travel adventures, Mexican and Indian culture, etc. Total of 669pp. 5⅜ × 8½.
20926-1, 20927-X Pa., Two-vol. set $9.90

DEGAS: An Intimate Portrait, Ambroise Vollard. Charming, anecdotal memoir by famous art dealer of one of the greatest 19th-century French painters. 14 black-and-white illustrations. Introduction by Harold L. Van Doren. 96pp. 5⅜ × 8½.
25131-4 Pa. $3.95

PERSONAL NARRATIVE OF A PILGRIMAGE TO ALMANDINAH AND MECCAH, Richard Burton. Great travel classic by remarkably colorful personality. Burton, disguised as a Moroccan, visited sacred shrines of Islam, narrowly escaping death. 47 illustrations. 959pp. 5⅜ × 8½. 21217-3, 21218-1 Pa., Two-vol. set $19.90

PHRASE AND WORD ORIGINS, A. H. Holt. Entertaining, reliable, modern study of more than 1,200 colorful words, phrases, origins and histories. Much unexpected information. 254pp. 5⅜ × 8½. 20758-7 Pa. $4.95

THE RED THUMB MARK, R. Austin Freeman. In this first Dr. Thorndyke case, the great scientific detective draws fascinating conclusions from the nature of a single fingerprint. Exciting story, authentic science. 320pp. 5⅜ × 8½. (Available in U.S. only) 25210-8 Pa. $5.95

AN EGYPTIAN HIEROGLYPHIC DICTIONARY, E. A. Wallis Budge. Monumental work containing about 25,000 words or terms that occur in texts ranging from 3000 B.C. to 600 A.D. Each entry consists of a transliteration of the word, the word in hieroglyphs, and the meaning in English. 1,314pp. 6⅜ × 10.
23615-3, 23616-1 Pa., Two-vol. set $27.90

THE COMPLEAT STRATEGYST: Being a Primer on the Theory of Games of Strategy, J. D. Williams. Highly entertaining classic describes, with many illustrated examples, how to select best strategies in conflict situations. Prefaces. Appendices. xvi + 268pp. 5⅜ × 8½. 25101-2 Pa. $5.95

THE ROAD TO OZ, L. Frank Baum. Dorothy meets the Shaggy Man, little Button-Bright and the Rainbow's beautiful daughter in this delightful trip to the magical Land of Oz. 272pp. 5⅜ × 8. 25208-6 Pa. $4.95

POINT AND LINE TO PLANE, Wassily Kandinsky. Seminal exposition of role of point, line, other elements in non-objective painting. Essential to understanding 20th-century art. 127 illustrations. 192pp. 6½ × 9¼. 23808-3 Pa. $4.50

LADY ANNA, Anthony Trollope. Moving chronicle of Countess Lovel's bitter struggle to win for herself and daughter Anna their rightful rank and fortune—perhaps at cost of sanity itself. 384pp. 5⅜ × 8½. 24669-8 Pa. $6.95

EGYPTIAN MAGIC, E. A. Wallis Budge. Sums up all that is known about magic in Ancient Egypt: the role of magic in controlling the gods, powerful amulets that warded off evil spirits, scarabs of immortality, use of wax images, formulas and spells, the secret name, much more. 253pp. 5⅜ × 8½. 22681-6 Pa. $4.00

THE DANCE OF SIVA, Ananda Coomaraswamy. Preeminent authority unfolds the vast metaphysic of India: the revelation of her art, conception of the universe, social organization, etc. 27 reproductions of art masterpieces. 192pp. 5⅜ × 8½.
24817-8 Pa. $5.95

CHRISTMAS CUSTOMS AND TRADITIONS, Clement A. Miles. Origin, evolution, significance of religious, secular practices. Caroling, gifts, yule logs, much more. Full, scholarly yet fascinating; non-sectarian. 400pp. 5⅜ × 8½.
23354-5 Pa. $6.50

THE HUMAN FIGURE IN MOTION, Eadweard Muybridge. More than 4,500 stopped-action photos, in action series, showing undraped men, women, children jumping, lying down, throwing, sitting, wrestling, carrying, etc. 390pp. 7⅞ × 10⅝.
20204-6 Cloth. $21.95

THE MAN WHO WAS THURSDAY, Gilbert Keith Chesterton. Witty, fast-paced novel about a club of anarchists in turn-of-the-century London. Brilliant social, religious, philosophical speculations. 128pp. 5⅜ × 8½.
25121-7 Pa. $3.95

A CEZANNE SKETCHBOOK: Figures, Portraits, Landscapes and Still Lifes, Paul Cezanne. Great artist experiments with tonal effects, light, mass, other qualities in over 100 drawings. A revealing view of developing master painter, precursor of Cubism. 102 black-and-white illustrations. 144pp. 8¾ × 6⅜.
24790-2 Pa. $5.95

AN ENCYCLOPEDIA OF BATTLES: Accounts of Over 1,560 Battles from 1479 B.C. to the Present, David Eggenberger. Presents essential details of every major battle in recorded history, from the first battle of Megiddo in 1479 B.C. to Grenada in 1984. List of Battle Maps. New Appendix covering the years 1967–1984. Index. 99 illustrations. 544pp. 6½ × 9¼.
24913-1 Pa. $14.95

AN ETYMOLOGICAL DICTIONARY OF MODERN ENGLISH, Ernest Weekley. Richest, fullest work, by foremost British lexicographer. Detailed word histories. Inexhaustible. Total of 856pp. 6½ × 9¼.
21873-2, 21874-0 Pa., Two-vol. set $17.00

WEBSTER'S AMERICAN MILITARY BIOGRAPHIES, edited by Robert McHenry. Over 1,000 figures who shaped 3 centuries of American military history. Detailed biographies of Nathan Hale, Douglas MacArthur, Mary Hallaren, others. Chronologies of engagements, more. Introduction. Addenda. 1,033 entries in alphabetical order. xi + 548pp. 6½ × 9¼. (Available in U.S. only)
24758-9 Pa. $11.95

LIFE IN ANCIENT EGYPT, Adolf Erman. Detailed older account, with much not in more recent books: domestic life, religion, magic, medicine, commerce, and whatever else needed for complete picture. Many illustrations. 597pp. 5⅜ × 8½.
22632-8 Pa. $8.50

HISTORIC COSTUME IN PICTURES, Braun & Schneider. Over 1,450 costumed figures shown, covering a wide variety of peoples: kings, emperors, nobles, priests, servants, soldiers, scholars, townsfolk, peasants, merchants, courtiers, cavaliers, and more. 256pp. 8⅜ × 11¼.
23150-X Pa. $7.95

THE NOTEBOOKS OF LEONARDO DA VINCI, edited by J. P. Richter. Extracts from manuscripts reveal great genius; on painting, sculpture, anatomy, sciences, geography, etc. Both Italian and English. 186 ms. pages reproduced, plus 500 additional drawings, including studies for *Last Supper, Sforza* monument, etc. 860pp. 7⅞ × 10¾. (Available in U.S. only) 22572-0, 22573-9 Pa., Two-vol. set $25.90

CATALOG OF DOVER BOOKS

THE ART NOUVEAU STYLE BOOK OF ALPHONSE MUCHA: All 72 Plates from "Documents Decoratifs" in Original Color, Alphonse Mucha. Rare copyright-free design portfolio by high priest of Art Nouveau. Jewelry, wallpaper, stained glass, furniture, figure studies, plant and animal motifs, etc. Only complete one-volume edition. 80pp. 9⅜ × 12¼. 24044-4 Pa. $8.95

ANIMALS: 1,419 COPYRIGHT-FREE ILLUSTRATIONS OF MAMMALS, BIRDS, FISH, INSECTS, ETC., edited by Jim Harter. Clear wood engravings present, in extremely lifelike poses, over 1,000 species of animals. One of the most extensive pictorial sourcebooks of its kind. Captions. Index. 284pp. 9 × 12. 23766-4 Pa. $9.95

OBELISTS FLY HIGH, C. Daly King. Masterpiece of American detective fiction, long out of print, involves murder on a 1935 transcontinental flight—"a very thrilling story"—NY Times. Unabridged and unaltered republication of the edition published by William Collins Sons & Co. Ltd., London, 1935. 288pp. 5⅜ × 8½. (Available in U.S. only) 25036-9 Pa. $4.95

VICTORIAN AND EDWARDIAN FASHION: A Photographic Survey, Alison Gernsheim. First fashion history completely illustrated by contemporary photographs. Full text plus 235 photos, 1840–1914, in which many celebrities appear. 240pp. 6½ × 9¼. 24205-6 Pa. $6.00

THE ART OF THE FRENCH ILLUSTRATED BOOK, 1700–1914, Gordon N. Ray. Over 630 superb book illustrations by Fragonard, Delacroix, Daumier, Doré, Grandville, Manet, Mucha, Steinlen, Toulouse-Lautrec and many others. Preface. Introduction. 633 halftones. Indices of artists, authors & titles, binders and provenances. Appendices. Bibliography. 608pp. 8⅜ × 11¼. 25086-5 Pa. $24.95

THE WONDERFUL WIZARD OF OZ, L. Frank Baum. Facsimile in full color of America's finest children's classic. 143 illustrations by W. W. Denslow. 267pp. 5⅜ × 8½. 20691-2 Pa. $5.95

FRONTIERS OF MODERN PHYSICS: New Perspectives on Cosmology, Relativity, Black Holes and Extraterrestrial Intelligence, Tony Rothman, et al. For the intelligent layman. Subjects include: cosmological models of the universe; black holes; the neutrino; the search for extraterrestrial intelligence. Introduction. 46 black-and-white illustrations. 192pp. 5⅜ × 8½. 24587-X Pa. $6.95

THE FRIENDLY STARS, Martha Evans Martin & Donald Howard Menzel. Classic text marshals the stars together in an engaging, non-technical survey, presenting them as sources of beauty in night sky. 23 illustrations. Foreword. 2 star charts. Index. 147pp. 5⅜ × 8½. 21099-5 Pa. $3.50

FADS AND FALLACIES IN THE NAME OF SCIENCE, Martin Gardner. Fair, witty appraisal of cranks, quacks, and quackeries of science and pseudoscience: hollow earth, Velikovsky, orgone energy, Dianetics, flying saucers, Bridey Murphy, food and medical fads, etc. Revised, expanded In the Name of Science. "A very able and even-tempered presentation."—The New Yorker. 363pp. 5⅜ × 8. 20394-8 Pa. $6.50

ANCIENT EGYPT: ITS CULTURE AND HISTORY, J. E Manchip White. From pre-dynastics through Ptolemies: society, history, political structure, religion, daily life, literature, cultural heritage. 48 plates. 217pp. 5⅜ × 8½. 22548-8 Pa. $4.95

SIR HARRY HOTSPUR OF HUMBLETHWAITE, Anthony Trollope. Incisive, unconventional psychological study of a conflict between a wealthy baronet, his idealistic daughter, and their scapegrace cousin. The 1870 novel in its first inexpensive edition in years. 250pp. 5⅜ × 8½. 24953-0 Pa. $5.95

LASERS AND HOLOGRAPHY, Winston E. Kock. Sound introduction to burgeoning field, expanded (1981) for second edition. Wave patterns, coherence, lasers, diffraction, zone plates, properties of holograms, recent advances. 84 illustrations. 160pp. 5⅜ × 8¼. (Except in United Kingdom) 24041-X Pa. $3.50

INTRODUCTION TO ARTIFICIAL INTELLIGENCE: SECOND, EN-LARGED EDITION, Philip C. Jackson, Jr. Comprehensive survey of artificial intelligence—the study of how machines (computers) can be made to act intelligently. Includes introductory and advanced material. Extensive notes updating the main text. 132 black-and-white illustrations. 512pp. 5⅜ × 8½. 24864-X Pa. $8.95

HISTORY OF INDIAN AND INDONESIAN ART, Ananda K. Coomaraswamy. Over 400 illustrations illuminate classic study of Indian art from earliest Harappa finds to early 20th century. Provides philosophical, religious and social insights. 304pp. 6⅛ × 9⅜. 25005-9 Pa. $8.95

THE GOLEM, Gustav Meyrink. Most famous supernatural novel in modern European literature, set in Ghetto of Old Prague around 1890. Compelling story of mystical experiences, strange transformations, profound terror. 13 black-and-white illustrations. 224pp. 5⅜ × 8½. (Available in U.S. only) 25025-3 Pa. $5.95

ARMADALE, Wilkie Collins. Third great mystery novel by the author of *The Woman in White* and *The Moonstone*. Original magazine version with 40 illustrations. 597pp. 5⅜ × 8½. 23429-0 Pa. $9.95

PICTORIAL ENCYCLOPEDIA OF HISTORIC ARCHITECTURAL PLANS, DETAILS AND ELEMENTS: With 1,880 Line Drawings of Arches, Domes, Doorways, Facades, Gables, Windows, etc., John Theodore Haneman. Sourcebook of inspiration for architects, designers, others. Bibliography. Captions. 141pp. 9 × 12. 24605-1 Pa. $6.95

BENCHLEY LOST AND FOUND, Robert Benchley. Finest humor from early 30's, about pet peeves, child psychologists, post office and others. Mostly unavailable elsewhere. 73 illustrations by Peter Arno and others. 183pp. 5⅜ × 8½. 22410-4 Pa. $3.95

ERTÉ GRAPHICS, Erté. Collection of striking color graphics: *Seasons, Alphabet, Numerals, Aces* and *Precious Stones*. 50 plates, including 4 on covers. 48pp. 9⅜ × 12¼. 23580-7 Pa. $6.95

THE JOURNAL OF HENRY D. THOREAU, edited by Bradford Torrey, F. H. Allen. Complete reprinting of 14 volumes, 1837-61, over two million words; the sourcebooks for *Walden*, etc. Definitive. All original sketches, plus 75 photographs. 1,804pp. 8½ × 12¼. 20312-3, 20313-1 Cloth., Two-vol. set $80.00

CASTLES: THEIR CONSTRUCTION AND HISTORY, Sidney Toy. Traces castle development from ancient roots. Nearly 200 photographs and drawings illustrate moats, keeps, baileys, many other features. Caernarvon, Dover Castles, Hadrian's Wall, Tower of London, dozens more. 256pp. 5⅜ × 8¼. 24898-4 Pa. $5.95

AMERICAN CLIPPER SHIPS: 1833–1858, Octavius T. Howe & Frederick C. Matthews. Fully-illustrated, encyclopedic review of 352 clipper ships from the period of America's greatest maritime supremacy. Introduction. 109 halftones. 5 black-and-white line illustrations. Index. Total of 928pp. 5⅜ × 8½.
25115-2, 25116-0 Pa., Two-vol. set $17.90

TOWARDS A NEW ARCHITECTURE, Le Corbusier. Pioneering manifesto by great architect, near legendary founder of "International School." Technical and aesthetic theories, views on industry, economics, relation of form to function, "mass-production spirit," much more. Profusely illustrated. Unabridged translation of 13th French edition. Introduction by Frederick Etchells. 320pp. 6⅛ × 9¼. (Available in U.S. only)
25023-7 Pa. $8.95

THE BOOK OF KELLS, edited by Blanche Cirker. Inexpensive collection of 32 full-color, full-page plates from the greatest illuminated manuscript of the Middle Ages, painstakingly reproduced from rare facsimile edition. Publisher's Note. Captions. 32pp. 9⅜ × 12¼.
24345-1 Pa. $4.95

BEST SCIENCE FICTION STORIES OF H. G. WELLS, H. G. Wells. Full novel *The Invisible Man*, plus 17 short stories: "The Crystal Egg," "Aepyornis Island," "The Strange Orchid," etc. 303pp. 5⅜ × 8½. (Available in U.S. only)
21531-8 Pa. $4.95

AMERICAN SAILING SHIPS: Their Plans and History, Charles G. Davis. Photos, construction details of schooners, frigates, clippers, other sailcraft of 18th to early 20th centuries—plus entertaining discourse on design, rigging, nautical lore, much more. 137 black-and-white illustrations. 240pp. 6⅛ × 9¼.
24658-2 Pa. $5.95

ENTERTAINING MATHEMATICAL PUZZLES, Martin Gardner. Selection of author's favorite conundrums involving arithmetic, money, speed, etc., with lively commentary. Complete solutions. 112pp. 5⅜ × 8½.
25211-6 Pa. $2.95

THE WILL TO BELIEVE, HUMAN IMMORTALITY, William James. Two books bound together. Effect of irrational on logical, and arguments for human immortality. 402pp. 5⅜ × 8½.
20291-7 Pa. $7.50

THE HAUNTED MONASTERY and THE CHINESE MAZE MURDERS, Robert Van Gulik. 2 full novels by Van Gulik continue adventures of Judge Dee and his companions. An evil Taoist monastery, seemingly supernatural events; overgrown topiary maze that hides strange crimes. Set in 7th-century China. 27 illustrations. 328pp. 5⅜ × 8½.
23502-5 Pa. $5.95

CELEBRATED CASES OF JUDGE DEE (DEE GOONG AN), translated by Robert Van Gulik. Authentic 18th-century Chinese detective novel; Dee and associates solve three interlocked cases. Led to Van Gulik's own stories with same characters. Extensive introduction. 9 illustrations. 237pp. 5⅜ × 8½.
23337-5 Pa. $4.95

Prices subject to change without notice.

Available at your book dealer or write for free catalog to Dept. GI, Dover Publications, Inc., 31 East 2nd St., Mineola, N.Y. 11501. Dover publishes more than 175 books each year on science, elementary and advanced mathematics, biology, music, art, literary history, social sciences and other areas.